1958

G
Music and Western man

P9-ASK-624

3 0301 00024194 9

1954   may be kept

MUSIC AND WESTERN MAN

MUSIC

AND WESTERN MAN

Edited by Peter Garvie

*The Canadian Broadcasting
Corporation Series*

PHILOSOPHICAL LIBRARY

LIBRARY
College of St. Francis
JOLIET, ILL.

Published 1958 by Philosophical Library Inc.
15 East 40th Street · New York · N.Y.
All rights reserved
Printed in Great Britain for Philosophical Library
by
The Aldine Press · Letchworth · Herts

780.4
G244

PREFACE

MUSIC is both something heard and something lived, and the two cannot be dissociated. Hearing a piece of music may seem a simple experience; the sounds are received by the ear and made meaningful by the mind. Certainly the immediacy, the excitement, the sense of a direct communication between composer and listener are valuable, and without them music would probably cease to be an experience —something that we live—and become only a subject for study. But when we say we are listening to Beethoven we are only expressing a part of the truth. We are using a metaphor that simplifies a complex experience. For the variables of the musical experience are infinite; the more we know of them, the better we know the masterpiece itself, and the more it will mean to us.

There is, theoretically at least, an ideal relationship between the listener and the music, almost an identification. Yet to attain this a listener would have to know everything there is to know, first, about the work itself, and then about the work in relation to the composer who wrote it, the society of which he was a part, and the whole history of music of which the work is a part. And that is only one side of the equation. There is also the listener's background; in time and place, the kind of person he is and the beliefs he holds, his general attitude to music, and all the occasions on which he has heard this particular work before.

Nevertheless, we do not despair of music or of ourselves. Perhaps we conceive the truth of a particular work (the truth or reality of it for each listener) as at the centre of a maze, and we know we will never reach the centre; yet we still go on. It is one way in which we distinguish a masterpiece from a commonplace; a masterpiece is inexhaustible and continues to reveal aspects of itself, however familiar it is to us; a commonplace work of art has no reserves of meaning, and we know all about it all too quickly. We look into great works and always see something new; we look at ordinary works and see through them.

Most of our exploration of a great work is by listening to it,

4-24-58 Published $7.74

28479

but a valuable part, the part that gives the work its context, is
founded upon commentary. The less familiar the work the less
we are likely to know of its context. If we know how and why and
for whom a work was composed we can at least approach it from
the right direction. We turn for counsel to those who have
special knowledge or special gifts of understanding, and the ability
to communicate their understanding to us; and we apply all that
we can learn from them to illuminate the music and enrich our
experience of it. Expert commentary can re-create the context
for us, though it should never be regarded as in any sense replacing
the music. The purpose of commentary is to enable the music
to speak for itself to a mind that is prepared to receive it.

This defines too the purpose of *Music and Western Man*—the
book and the series of broadcasts from which it is drawn. A
chief responsibility of a national radio system like the Canadian
Broadcasting Corporation is to attend to the needs of music lovers,
and they are a surprisingly high percentage of the total radio
audience. This responsibility cannot be discharged simply by
offering the standard concert and recital repertoire; that is, the
more familiar part of a mere two centuries' music. We have
more than twenty centuries of western music as our legacy, and in
a country like Canada, with its small centres of population in a
great area, the organization that can best reveal this legacy is the
national radio system. Isolated performances of earlier music
can do little but indicate that these works exist. Commentary
is needed at the initial stage, for the works must be given a context.
Accordingly, in 1955 the Canadian Broadcasting Corporation
organized a series of fifty one-hour programmes to be broadcast
weekly. Each programme would consist of commentary and
recorded musical illustrations, and each programme would be
repeated the following day. Later in the week music of the
period under discussion would be broadcast as a supplement to
the lectures.

A committee of four drew up the outline for the series. This
outline went through many drafts, and while it is by no means the
only way in which such a series could be organized, it seemed to
my colleagues and myself the best way. The contributors were
then chosen, and in each case an expert knowledge of the subject
was the first requirement. A glance at the list of contributors
will show their quality. As a rule each contributor recorded his

talk wherever he was and sent it to Vancouver, and he also chose
his music examples. For this book some abridgment of the
scripts has been necessary, but any changes have been approved
by the contributors. The music examples have been retained in
the text so that the references to records are adjacent to the discussion of that particular piece of music. So the record collector
can, as it were, *play* through the book as well as read it. At the
end of the book a short list of books for further reading and a list
of other relevant records has been added.

It was decided to give the broadcasts permanent form for a
number of reasons. A great many listeners tuned in to the repeat
of each broadcast and wrote to ask for copies of the scripts and
for information about records heard. A number of universities,
too, expressed great interest in the series. The tributes of listeners
were reinforced by the judges at the Institute for Education by
Radio-Television at Ohio University, who conferred a first award
upon the series. Most important, *Music and Western Man* seems
to have fulfilled a need; a need for a history of music that would
be scholarly and not academic, lucid in style, and accessible to
every inquisitive listener without condescension towards him.

When we first study the role of music in earlier societies we
may be startled, for we tend to regard our contemporary musical
life as the norm. We discover, for instance, that western man
lived for centuries without finding contemporary music a 'problem';
indeed, contemporary music until recently meant more to him than
the music of the past. We discover that concerts and concert
audiences, as we know them, are rather late developments, and it
is only recently that passive listeners have so outnumbered performers. The decline of the amateur and his influence and the
growth of other media for the dissemination of music—notably
broadcasting and records—have radically altered, or soon will
alter, music's part in our lives, both for good and for ill. The
constant and indiscriminate availability of music of all sorts may
have an effect upon our ears like that of billboards upon our eyes,
and the passivity of our experience of music may make our relations with it much less direct—to the detriment of music and
ourselves. On the other hand, twentieth-century scholarship
and the mass media have provided every interested person with a
long view of music that was not to be had before. We may
hope that exploration within that perspective, and the fact that

the works of music themselves do not change as do our circumstances, but offer the same challenge and promise the same reward, will maintain a resilience of mind in our society to ensure the continuing significance of music and the arts in general. If we ignore the legacy and decline the effort of exploration, music may become just a soothing routine, like hot baths. We perhaps lack the talent and training to participate in music directly as composers or performers, but we can at least apply ourselves as *active* listeners to the study of the unfamiliar and the not easily apprehended; a study that will reveal to us as much about the familiar as about the new.

Each of us brings his special knowledge and interests to such a study, and it is perhaps surprising to find how relevant and useful they can be. The historian will discover how peoples expressed themselves in music at different periods, and the influence of the structure of society upon music, and vice versa. Not the least fascinating aspect is the coincidence of historical events and the appearance of works of art, literature, and music. So we find that Machaut composed his great *Mass of Notre Dame* in Chaucer's lifetime, and that both lived through the Black Death: that Leonardo da Vinci was almost the exact contemporary of Josquin des Prés, and that their lifetimes took in the discovery of America, the end of the Wars of the Roses, Sir Thomas More's *Utopia*, and the first days of the German Reformation; that the first operas were contemporary with the later plays of Shakespeare; that Hogarth and Pope were contemporaries of Bach and Handel; and that Wordsworth and Beethoven were born in the same year.

If we have not been aware of such coincidences in time, it is doubtless because the history of man and the history of the various arts are quite separate in our minds, and because the close of one period and the transition to a new one in political history does not often correspond exactly to a similar stage in the evolution of music. Indeed, the more one studies the history of music, the less one relies upon specific dates to mark the beginning or end of a style or period. Tangible things can be ascribed to a particular year—a work is composed or published, a decree is issued by prince or prelate that affects music—but the main current flows over our marked segments of time and only gradually discloses its direction. There are so many factors in any change, and they are complicated by national distinctions and the presence of both conservatives and adventurers in any generation of composers. For example, scholars detect the beginnings of the baroque style in the music of Giovanni Gabrieli at Venice, and Gabrieli, who lived in the latter part of the sixteenth century and early part of the seventeenth, is accounted a Renaissance composer. He died in 1613, and yet sixty years later in the early music of Purcell we see the survival of the string style of Renaissance England.

The student of architecture, like the historian, will find many points at which his interests are involved in this account of music; the influence of acoustics upon the single line of Gregorian Chant or upon the splendid music of Gabrieli and other composers associated with St Mark's in Venice. The student of literature may trace the relations of music and poetry from the troubadours to the present time; the student of theatre may be absorbed by the growth and development of opera. Those whose interests are theological may find a new illumination of their subject in the many different approaches to liturgical texts by composers at different periods. Those interested in painting and sculpture can trace parallels of style between what was drawn, painted, and carved and what was sung or played at various moments of history.

Less important than special interests, however, is the interest that all readers will presumably share in music and in western man. This book aims to provide a history of music in western civilization and to explore western civilization through one of its aspects, music. It is always as well, when we speak of western civilization, to know its constituents; our values derive from individual masterpieces, not from abstract categories. So perhaps the most valuable part of this account is that it directs our attention to certain works of music and illuminates them so that we may experience them directly for ourselves. The tradition will cease to be a succession of trends and periods and names and will become instead a range of masterpieces and near-masterpieces which we have heard and come to know and understand. It will become a living reality, and thus the more valuable, because it will have a variety of individual meanings and emphasis for each of us. The tradition lives in individual experience: the music must matter enough in our own lives. This book is offered as a means to that end.

PETER GARVIE.

Vancouver, October 1955.

THE CONTRIBUTORS

Wilfrid Mellers

English musicologist and composer. Staff tutor in music to the extra-mural department of Birmingham University. His compositions include three operas: *The Tragicall History of Christopher Marlowe*, *The Trial of the Jewelled Peacock*, and *The Shepherd's Daughter*. He has written many articles for periodicals, and his books include *François Couperin and the French Classical Tradition*, *Music and Society*, and *Studies in Contemporary Music*.

Egon Wellesz

Austrian composer and musicologist. He studied with Schönberg and lectured on music history in Vienna before the First World War. As a musicologist he has specialized in baroque opera and Byzantine music. He settled in Oxford in 1939 and is now University Reader in Byzantine Music. His long list of compositions includes six operas, two symphonies, seven string quartets, choral works, and ballets. His books include studies of Byzantine music and a collection of essays on opera.

Alec Robertson

English scholar and critic. He has made a special study of plain-song and published a standard book on the subject. He is music editor of the *Gramophone*, has contributed to a number of journals and to *Grove's Dictionary*, and is well known in Great Britain as a lecturer and broadcaster. In 1945 he was elected a Fellow of the Royal Academy of Music.

Denis Stevens

English scholar and critic. Studied music and musicology at Oxford University. Later joined the B.B.C. Music Division, where he produced many hundreds of pre-classical music programmes and talks. His lecture tours have taken him through Europe and America, and in 1955–6 he was Visiting Professor of Music at Cornell University and Columbia University. His publications include *The Mulliner Book*, *Thomas Tallis: Complete Keyboard Works*, *Altenglische Orgelmusik*, *Tudor Church Music*, and *Thomas Tomkins*.

Willi Apel

German-born musicologist, now resident in the United States. Studied mathematics and the piano and gave recitals in Germany. Taught at various American colleges and is now Professor of Musicology at Indiana University. His publications include *The Notation of Polyphonic Music, 900–1600*.

Paul Henry Lang

American musicologist, born in Hungary. He was educated in Budapest, Paris, and at Cornell. Since 1933 Professor of Musicology at Columbia University. President of the International Musicological Society. Editor of the *Musical Quarterly*. Music critic of the *New York Herald Tribune*. His publications include the monumental *Music in Western Civilization*.

Gustave Reese

American musicologist. Professor in the Graduate School of Arts and Science at New York University. Director of Concert and Opera Publications of Carl Fischer Inc. He was one of the founders and is a past president of the American Musicological Society, and is a member of the Committee on Musicology of the American Council of Learned Societies. His publications include the comprehensive *Music in the Middle Ages* and *Music in the Renaissance*.

J. A. Westrup

English musicologist. He was editor of the *Monthly Musical Record* and has been a music critic. Later Professor of Music at Birmingham University and currently Professor of Music at Oxford. He has been active in the production of unfamiliar operas there. General editor of the *New Oxford History of Music*. His publications include books on Purcell and Handel.

A. K. Holland

Music critic of the *Liverpool Daily Post*. He has lectured widely, chiefly on English music. Author of books on Purcell and the songs of Delius.

H. Wiley Hitchcock

American scholar. Studied in France with Nadia Boulanger and recently spent a year in Italy for studies in the history of the oratorio. His particular field of interest is French and Italian baroque music. He is Professor of Music at the University of Michigan.

Arthur Hutchings

English scholar. Professor of Music at Durham University. His books include studies of Schubert, Delius, and the piano concertos of Mozart.

Anthony Lewis

English musicologist and conductor. Studied with Nadia Boulanger and later served on the music staff of the B.B.C. He is general editor of *Musica Britannica* and has edited and conducted much early music. Barber and Peyton Professor of Music in the University of Birmingham.

Lionel Salter

English pianist, harpsichordist, conductor, and critic. Music critic of the *Gramophone*. Well known as a radio speaker and has often conducted for the B.B.C. and abroad. Now Director of Music Productions for the B.B.C.'s Television Service.

Karl Geiringer

Austrian musicologist. He studied in Vienna and Berlin. Now Professor of History and Theory of Music at Boston University. His publications include books on the Bach family, Haydn, Brahms, and musical instruments.

Alfred Frankenstein

American music critic. Studied at University of Chicago and at Yale. Instructor in music, University of Chicago. Music and art critic, *San Francisco Chronicle*, since 1934. Has lectured on American music and art at a number of universities. Guggenheim Fellow, 1947–8. His publications include *After the Hunt*, a monograph on William Harnett and other American still-life painters.

William Mann

English music critic. Studied at Cambridge and with Matyas Seiber and Ilona Kabos. Assistant music critic of *The Times* since 1948. He is associate editor of *Opera* and has contributed to a variety of books. He is currently engaged on a study of Richard Strauss.

Andrew Porter

English music critic. Organ scholar at University College, Oxford. Music critic of the *Financial Times* and associate editor of *Opera*. Contributes to the *Gramophone* and other periodicals and broadcasts for the B.B.C.

Aaron Copland

American composer. Studied with Nadia Boulanger. His compositions have included scores for films and ballets and a wide variety of other works. He is himself an accomplished pianist. He has written articles on aspects of contemporary music and his books include *Our New Music* and *Music and Imagination*.

Peter Garvie

Born in London and educated at Repton and Clare College, Cambridge. Now makes his home in Vancouver, B.C., where he is a producer with the Canadian Broadcasting Corporation. He has produced concerts, recitals, dramas, and talks programmes and inaugurated the C.B.C.'s weekly programme of commentary on music, *Music Diary*, which has now been on the air almost four years. He was in charge of planning and producing the series, *Music and Western Man*, which in 1956 received a first award from the Institute for Education by Radio-Television at Ohio State University.

In addition, the C.B.C. has included a selection of his poems and a short story on its programme of new writing and has produced his two radio plays, *The Flight of Janus* and *The Summer School*. He has also contributed articles to the *Canadian Music Journal*.

A NOTE ON BOOKS AND RECORDS

FOUR recorded anthologies were used in the broadcasts:

(i) THE HISTORY OF MUSIC IN SOUND.
   RCA VICTOR (10 LP records) or HMV (78 r.p.m.).

(ii) MASTERPIECES OF MUSIC BEFORE 1750.
   HAYDN SOCIETY (3 LP records)
These are recordings of the fifty musical illustrations in the book of the same title.

(iii) ARCHIVE SERIES.
   DEUTSCHE GRAMMOPHON GESELLSCHAFT: released by DECCA in North America. (Still in progress.)

(iv) ANTHOLOGIE SONORE.
Many of the records have been transferred to LP in North America.

The recorded musical illustrations used in each broadcast are identified in the body of each chapter. The appendices contain a list of recommended books and additional records for study in connection with each chapter; these lists have been prepared by the editor in consultation with the contributors. They are not meant to be exhaustive, but simply to be suggestive. Those who wish to explore further can best do so through the comprehensive bibliographies in some of the books cited and through the current record catalogues.

The records listed are there because of the music they contain. No attempt has been made to evaluate each record on the basis of performance and quality of recording. But it should be remembered that each record used as an example in the broadcasts was chosen by the contributor, and where alternative records are listed the one mentioned first is the contributor's choice.

Not all the records used in the broadcasts were easy to obtain, but they have all been listed since they illustrate points made by the contributor. In order to extend the range of usefulness of both the records used as illustrations in the broadcasts and of those given in the appendices, an effort has been made to quote both the

North American and the English catalogue numbers. Where there is no equivalent on the English market of a record from an American source, an alternative has been suggested where available. In the texts of the broadcasts the references are usually to the American numbers, and where the same record is also available in England, its English number is quoted in brackets.

Where a record is not available to the English public an alternative recorded version of the music in question is, where possible, quoted. In such cases the alternative is clearly marked as such. It has not been found possible always to find an equivalent or an alternative; but even here the reader need not despair, because American and continental records can often be found in the stocks of specialist British dealers, or in the private advertisement columns of such magazines as the *Gramophone*.

In the case of the appendices, much the same system has been adopted. Unless otherwise stated, the first listing is by the American number, and its English equivalent, if there is one, follows in brackets. Where no English equivalent is available a particular effort has been made to list an alternative; but in this case it is not necessarily indicated as such. It is thus safe to say that all numbers quoted in brackets refer throughout to the English numbers; and in the case of labels like DECCA and COLUMBIA, which have different meanings in North America and Great Britain, the difference is always marked, when the number is not enclosed in brackets, by the prefix ENGLISH. In some cases the North American and English numbers are identical: VOX is a case in point. Where this is so availability on the English market is indicated by (E) following the number. In the case of OISEAU-LYRE the numbers are also identical; but here availability on one continent implies a similar availability on the other, so no distinction is required. In a few cases also, records available in England have been marked for deletion. These are always quoted when they are equivalents of the American first choice, and even if an alternative is included; but where possible they have been marked with an asterisk. Naturally, the task of finding a suitable alternative is more difficult in the case of the older, and much less extensively recorded, music. But the progressive growth of the DGG Archive Series has been most helpful here, and where possible the latest additions have been incorporated.

There is really no satisfactory way to indicate degrees of

accessibility to the record buyer.   It is broadly true that 78 r.p.m. disks are becoming progressively harder to obtain, and much material on them has not yet been transferred to LP.   Accordingly, the appendices are restricted (with only a few exceptions) to LP records that are obtainable in North America and/or Great Britain. In spite of the gaps in the repertoire (to which attention is drawn) the reader should have no difficulty in collecting his own recorded anthology.

In addition to the books dealing with specific subjects, periods, or composers indicated in the appendices, the following general works are to be recommended:

WILFRID MELLERS: *Music and Society.*

PAUL HENRY LANG: *Music in Western Civilization.*

CARL PARRISH AND JOHN F. OHL: *Masterpieces of Music before 1750.*

SIR DONALD TOVEY: *Musical Articles* (from the *Encyclopaedia Britannica*).

DAVISON AND APEL: *Historical Anthology of Music* (Harvard).

Grove's Dictionary of Music and Musicians, 5th Edition, ED.
SHAWE-TAYLOR AND SACKVILLE WEST: *The Record Guide and Supplement.*

ACKNOWLEDGMENTS

My first thanks must go to the contributors whose enthusiasm, helpfulness, and courtesy have made my work so agreeable. They have had to contend with the special demands of broadcasting and the editing of their broadcast scripts for publication—not to speak of the complications arising from the thousands of miles between them and Vancouver.

I also owe a special debt to Mr Leonard Wilson and Mr Lawrence Cluderay, who not only served on the planning committee, but have throughout a period of two years given generously of their time and trouble. They have been available to comment and advise at all times during the broadcasting of the series and during the preparation of the manuscript.

My thanks must also go to Mr Robert Harlow, Director of Radio for the Canadian Broadcasting Corporation in British Columbia, who encouraged the project from first to last; and to Dr Robert Turner, also of the C.B.C., for his help on the planning committee.

Miss Maxine de Felice and Miss Margaret Fielder of the C.B.C.'s London and New York offices respectively did the work of recording the contributions. Miss Wendy Livett of the C.B.C. in Vancouver typed the manuscript and in addition attended to all the correspondence. They, and many other members of the C.B.C. staff, have done a great deal to make this book possible.

For permission to include copyright material acknowledgments and thanks are made to the following:

The Clarendon Press, Oxford, for an extract from *The Legacy of the Middle Ages*; the Columbia University Press for an extract from *A Short History of Opera* by Donald Grout; J. M. Dent & Sons Ltd for an extract from *Mozart* by Eric Blom; the Oxford University Press Inc. for an extract from *Mozart* by Alfred Einstein; Routledge & Kegan Paul Ltd for an extract from *Some Musicians of Former Days* by Romain Rolland; Simon & Schuster Inc. for an extract from *Chronicle of My Life* by Igor Stravinsky.

XX ACKNOWLEDGMENTS

It would be impossible to thank everyone by name for their help in a great variety of ways, but they will probably recognize their contributions in the text; certainly the editor has been constantly reminded of their part as he has prepared this book. Finally, acknowledgment must be made of the many letters from radio listeners to the broadcast series; their comments encouraged us all.

CONTENTS

I

Wilfrid Mellers

MUSIC AND SOCIETY

WHEN I first started to write music I composed because, as they say, I had to. I wanted to create something, and the medium in which I happened to be able to create most effectively proved to be sound. I found —and I gather that my experience is not unique—that it is only after one has grown into a better or at least a more efficient composer that one begins to face up to the central problem. As one begins to discover what one wants to say and how to say it in sound—the two discoveries being at bottom identical—one comes to see that in the process of composition something other is involved than one's own personality. A language implies someone willing to understand it, someone at the other end of the telegraphic system. Music is willy-nilly a social and perhaps a religious act; and this remains true even though the telegraphic system may, in our day, have got a bit tangled. And so at the beginning of this large-scale survey of the growth of Europe's music, I want to discuss the relationship between a musical idiom and the human experience which it embodies. We are concerned not only with what music is, but with what it is for.

However different the musical techniques of different ages may be, they will have in common certain features which derive from the physical nature of sound. Music exists in time, not space; and it involves the alternation of varying degrees of tension between aural vibrations. (High degrees of tension we call dissonances, relatively low degrees of tension we call consonances.) One might perhaps say that the forms of music are the means whereby men have organized in terms of time the aural relations between tension and relaxation. It is, however, obvious that the ways in which composers have used these basic resources of sound have varied greatly from generation to generation: and that they

have varied according to men's preconceptions about music's
significance and purpose.   Let us consider, from this point of view,
a few pieces of music chosen from widely separated periods of
European history.

First, a typical example of medieval music, a plain-song melody.

Gregorian Chant. (See Chapter 3 for a selection of recorded
examples).

The first thing we shall notice about this chant—bearing in
mind that music is an alternation of tension and relaxation moving
in time—is that it is written in a single unaccompanied line.
There is thus no harmony to provide any conflict between tones
sounded simultaneously.   But more than that, the melody itself
avoids any intervals which could *imply* harmonic stress; it moves
mainly by step, or by very smooth intervals which involve the
minimum of tension.   Its modality is derived from the phrases
the human voice naturally sings.   Then again, the rhythm is
free, non-metrical, and the cadential phrases usually fall by a
whole tone, never rise by a semitone, which would give an impression of finality.   All this means that the music conveys
almost no sense of time, or of conflict and drama.   This is just
what the composers were after, for they were trying to create not
a music that expressed their own passions, but rather a music
that helped one to lose the self in the contemplation of God.
Even when a thirteenth-century composer such as Pérotin put
several lines together in an organum or motet he regarded the
additional parts as extensions and embellishments of the original
melody.   The melody remained fluid and the harmony avoided
any acute tensions.   The music still suggests a dissolution of the
self into eternity.   Order was imposed on the concourse of parts
by almost mathematically conceived rhythmic patterns which
embodied in sound what seemed to be the immutable laws of the
cosmos.

Pérotin: *Organum triplum.* ANTHOLOGIE SONORE AS 1 (AS 65, 78
r.p.m.).

Now let us jump more than two hundred years to the *Agnus Dei*
of Byrd's five-part Mass.

Byrd: *Mass for five voices.* LONDON LL 888 (DECCA LXT 2919).

In this music each vocal part preserves its independence, and the
'form' of the piece appears to be the growth of melody, fugally

imitated in all the parts. If you examine each of the vocal lines separately, it seems to be similar to the unterrestrial serenity of plain-song. The intervals are smooth and vocal, the rhythm non-metrical, the movement unaggressive. Yet not only are the lines modified by a desire for sensuous richness of harmony; but the traditional partiality for independent part-writing is now itself a means of creating some of the most remarkable harmonic effects. Thus, while the music preserves the old-style liturgical polyphony, it uses the technique in a new way. The composer has to think simultaneously of the purely melodic beauty of his lines: and of the emotional possibilities of tension and relaxation between the chords that these lines create. The music is at once liturgical and an expression of the humanist spirit. It acquires a much more 'personal' quality than the Pérotin example—what one might almost call a Shakespearian tragic pathos.

Plain-song and Pérotin's polyphony are 'monistic' acts of praise to God. In Byrd's polyphony each individual part has, while preserving its melodic freedom, to think of the harmonic rights of the others: polyphony has become, as it were, a communal act. We can see this in the changing conception of rhythm. Each part, individually considered, remains freely vocal in rhythm; but the behaviour of the parts when they are sung together depends on the implicit existence of a 'strong' and a 'weak' beat on which the dissonances are prepared and resolved. Dance metre has come to complement vocal rhythm as a basic principle of construction.

When we move on more than another hundred years to our next example we find that dance metre now reigns supreme. In the aria *He shall feed His flock* from Handel's *Messiah* the tonality is unambiguously our modern major and minor, and the clauses are grouped in symmetrical periods dominated by *siciliano* dance rhythm, rounded off by clearly defined cadences.

Handel: *Messiah: He shall feed His flock.*

Here, instead of the continuously evolving texture of polyphony, we have a structure which depends on the architectural grouping of phrases, involving simple changes of key. The balanced repetition of the clauses resembles the symmetrical, terrace-like structure of eighteenth-century gardens and buildings. The lucid system of tonality and the imposition of dance patterns canalizes harmonic passion: just as classical civilization wishes to impose a rigid, state-dominated order on the perversities of individual beings.

Handel's conception of order is harmonic rather than melodic, but it is still based on creative unity; his movements have usually only one theme and a consistent figuration.   When we turn to the sonata epoch, and especially to Beethoven, we find a radically different principle of construction.   Consider the last movement of Beethoven's Seventh Symphony.   Here there is no unified song-melody.   There are striking thematic motives in dynamic-ally obsessive rhythms; and the structure of the music is a dramatic conflict between heterogeneous motives and contradictory keys, on which Beethoven imposes order by the sheer force of his will.

Beethoven: *Symphony No. 7 in A* (Finale).

We have heard this music so often, perhaps, that we can no longer fully experience these savagely abrupt modulations, these sudden pauses and silences, the sheer physical impact of the orchestration, with its fanatically barking horns.   Yet if we can listen afresh we shall find this one of the most terrifying pieces of music ever written, far more scarifying, after a hundred and forty years, than Stravinsky's *Rite of Spring* after forty.   If it is 'joyful,' it can only be the blood-curdling joy of battle: for it is a revolutionary piece which hammers out a new world.   Its order is dualistic, whereas that of Handel—or Byrd or plain-song—is monistic.

For our last example let us take the Prelude to Act I of Wagner's *Tristan und Isolde*.

Wagner: *Tristan und Isolde* (Prelude).

We shall immediately notice that the explosive metres of Beethoven have disappeared; instead, we have a continuous surge of sound.   Moreover, whereas the orchestration of the classical age had aimed at the clearest definition of the main melody, in Wagner's orchestration melodic definition is intentionally submerged in the rich flood of harmony.   Soon we shall notice a further point: this continuous surge of sound negates the structural principle—the exposition, development, and recapitulation—which had characterized the classical sonata up to Beethoven's last works, and negates also the key-system on which that form depended.   Expressive thematic fragments take the place of developed melodies, and the logic of the music tends to become equated with the succession of harmonic tensions, corresponding to different degrees of nervous sensation.

The music's overwhelming intensity derives from the fact that Wagner concentrates on the dissonant harmony at the expense of its resolution; note how it is always the dissonant chord that falls on the strong beat. Moreover, the effect of the passage as a whole depends on the way in which the brief yearning phrase, underlined by its dissonance, is repeated at progressively rising intervals. This building up of tension, followed by only a partial resolution, is used repeatedly by Wagner, and just such a combination of passionate yearning with frustration is the essential theme of his adaptation of the Tristan story, between which and his own life there is a more than usually direct connection. In effect Wagner is saying 'My feelings *are* life; there is nothing except them and death.' This is the triumph of subjectivity; Wagner has created a myth and a world out of his own passion. Music and the opera are now not so much an expression of the values and beliefs of a civilization as a projection of the individual's ego. The deification of the ego could hardly go further than the Wagner cult at Bayreuth, where a temple is built in which to perform the master's creations—instead of the music being composed to serve the needs of the temple, as was Byrd's to serve God or Handel's to serve the State. Wagner thus effects a curious inversion of the religious attitude to music.

I have tried to show, however elliptically, that basic changes in musical technique are not fortuitous. In plain-chant we have a purely melodic, almost conflictless unity whereby the composer strives not to express himself, but to become unified with God. In Byrd's polyphony we have an equilibrium between this ritualistic approach and the demands of personal feeling. In Handel we have personal feeling codified in the interests not of God, but of the God-King or the State. In middle-period Beethoven we have a ferocious conflict to establish a new, revolutionary order: to re-create the past through the assertion of the Will. In Wagner's *Tristan* we have the final subjection of the past, of God and of Society, to the individual's nerves and senses.

But I hope I have also made it clear that no work of art can be 'explained' by reference to its historical connotations. On the contrary, a work of art is itself historical evidence—of a much more inward nature than the documents with which historians

usually have to deal.   It is true that we cannot fully understand
Beethoven without understanding the impulses behind the
French Revolution.   It is equally true that we cannot fully understand the French Revolution without some insight into Beethoven's
music.   We can see in his music those elements which are conditioned by his time (for they could not be otherwise) and yet are
beyond the topical and local.   Beethoven is a part of history.   He
is also the human spirit making history.

This is fairly obvious in the case of an artist who, like Beethoven,
was in conflict with, and wished to change, the world he lived in.
It is equally, if less obviously, true of artists who lived in more
stable and homogeneous societies.   In the sixteenth century there
was a common European idiom which we now know as 'Palestrina
style.'   It was music's common denominator for certain basic
assumptions of the Catholic Church and of Renaissance man.
Yet it matters to us because it was the framework within which men
such as Byrd, Lassus, Victoria, and Palestrina himself expressed
very different attitudes to those assumptions.   Handel's basic
idiom was so universally accepted that he could lift into his own
works large sections of other people's music without anyone
noticing, or caring if they did notice.   Yet what we remember
of eighteenth-century baroque is the revivifying experience of
truly creative minds.   We respond to the profound equilibrium
between acceptance and protest, civilization and revolution, lyricism and drama in the music of Haydn and Mozart: while we have
forgotten the innumerable symphonic hacks who exploited the
small change of rococo style as an easy way of passing the time—
and making money.   Most of all, perhaps, we see Bach's crucial
position in European history in relation to his independence of
time.   Firmly rooted in what was then present, he philosophically
and even technically harked back to a medieval past, while looking
forward not merely to nineteenth-century romanticism, but still
more to the twentieth century.

So in talking of Music and Society, we should not think we have
said anything worth saying in pointing out that there are connections between what has happened in music and what has happened
in the external world.   That is, or should be, a truism.   We
should, however, in listening to the music which great and less
than great men have created at different times in our past, learn
to experience that music as the deepest kind of evidence as to the

ways men have thought, felt, and acted. In order to do this, we need an historical sense only because—or in so far as—the past is relevant to the present. In these programmes we want to give some indication of the significance which this 'past' music had when it was still present: and still more to differentiate between those elements of the past which have lost, and those which preserve, a meaning. We want to see, or rather to hear, music as human experience: for if it is not that, it is a game, no more and no less important than ping-pong.

2

Egon Wellesz

THE CLASSICAL HERITAGE: GREECE AND BYZANTIUM

THE music of western civilization owes its origin to two sources. It has its roots in Hebrew music, in the psalms, in the odes and spiritual songs which early Christianity took over into its services; and in the thought-world of the Greek philosophers which inspired the Fathers of the Church when they stated what kind of music was suitable for the Christian.

There is a fundamental difference between Greek and modern music, namely, the purely melodic structure of Greek music. Harmony (in the modern meaning of the term) was unknown to the Greeks, though they knew occasional concords of higher and lower notes, and also the accompaniment of a melody by an instrument in the higher octave. Music of a purely melodic character demands a different way of listening than that to which we are accustomed (namely, concentration on the flow of the melody, on the characteristic features of the mode). It calls for appreciation of the subtle use of intervals, consisting sometimes of fractions of tones, unheard of in the later music of Europe.

Greek music was both vocal and instrumental. 'Voice and Verse,' however, were not separated in its great epoch. *Mousike* meant music as well as poetry. Chants were partly sung by soloists, partly by a choir in unison, or in octaves, but regularly accompanied by an instrument. Accompanying a song meant either adding a tone from time to time, or playing a variation to the chant. This kind of ornamented playing, by which occasional concords were produced, was called heterophony.

The Greeks had also independent instrumental music, but in Classical times instruments were used singly. Only in the Hellenistic period groups of instruments were introduced. The two main ones were the *kithara*, a stringed instrument, on which

8

sound was produced by plucking the chords, and the *aulos*, a kind of oboe. All sources indicate how much contemporaries admired the skill and even virtuosity exhibited in playing both.

For the Greek, music was a supreme art, aimed at harmonizing body and soul. It had the power of healing by producing a purification of the body, and also of influencing the soul by improving the character. This view is based on the Pythagorean assumption, accepted by Plato, of the existence of a link between the harmony ruling the movements of the universe and the harmony ordering the human soul. The motions of the cosmos were believed to occur according to the same mathematical ratios which produced the musical intervals.

The doctrine of the ethical character of music permeates Greek philosophy as well as Greek musical theory. In the first book of the *Enneads* Plotinus speaks of a path of initiation, enabling the musician whose soul, according to Plato's *Phaedrus*, has kept 'a recollection of those things which it formerly saw when journeying with the Divine,' to rise to the rank of a philosopher, whose soul has a clear vision of 'Absolute Beauty.'

What has come down to us of this music? There are a number of fragments on papyrus but all of them so mutilated that it is hardly possible to reconstruct the music. There are, above all, the two *Hymns to Apollo* carved on marble, from the Treasury of the Athenians at Delphi; the first, dating from about 138 B.C., is the longest piece of Greek music which has come down to us almost undamaged; the second, from about 128 B.C., is only a short fragment, but is also in good condition. Chiselled in stone also is the *Epitaph of Seikilos* for his wife, dating probably from the first century B.C.; it is the only piece of music we possess intact.

From the beginning of the Christian era we possess three hymns, ascribed to Mesomedes, which figure as show-pieces in every history of music. But serious doubts have recently been raised as to their authenticity; they may be of Byzantine origin.

Let us therefore take as examples to illustrate Greek melodies those transmitted on stone which are unquestionably authentic and fairly complete pieces of music. We take first the *Hymn to Apollo* sung at a festival at Delphi in 138 B.C. It is, in fact, a glorification of Delphi, the seat of the Oracle, and of the beauty of Attica.

First Delphi Hymn. HMV DB 21485 (78 r.p.m.).

B

The second hymn starts likewise with an appeal to the muses to honour Apollo and extols the beauty of Greece. Of this song only the beginning is preserved:

'Come to this slope of Parnassus, which loves the dance, seen from afar with its twin peaks, and lead my song, Muses of Pieria, who dwell on the snow-swept rocks of Helicon; and honour with song and dance the golden-haired god of Pytho, Phoebus. . . .'

Second Delphi Hymn. HMV DB 21485 (78 r.p.m.).

Finally, there is the short *Epitaph of Seikilos* which was found near Smyrna in Asia Minor. It dates from the first century of our era. It may have been a popular song which Seikilos ordered to be chiselled on the tombstone:

As long as you live, shine forth and do not grieve at all.
Life is short, and time claims its tribute in the end.

Epitaph of Seikilos. HMV DA 2006 (78 r.p.m.).

The *Epitaph of Seikilos* dates from a time when Greece was already a province of the Roman Empire, which in the following centuries expanded in all directions. Constantine the Great began in 324 to rebuild the small city of Byzantium, made it the capital of the Eastern Empire and called it 'New Rome.' Soon after his death the city was called the 'City of Constantine,' Constantinopolis. Constantinople was from the beginning a Christian town. The language of the administration was Latin, that of the people Greek. But the Byzantine Church took over the liturgy of Jerusalem and Antioch and with it the chant of the Syrian churches, which was, in the main, the traditional chant of the Jewish Synagogue. Following the model of the Jewish liturgy, the morning and evening services kept their prominent place in the Eastern Church and were adorned by a great number of chants, hymns, and songs which varied from day to day.

Mass was celebrated frequently, but not daily, and the chants of the Mass had not that variety which one is used to in the western medieval Church. We know nothing about Byzantine Chant in the early days of the Byzantine Empire. The first hymns with musical signs which have come down to us are in manuscript dating from the ninth, or possibly the eighth century.

These signs are, like the tenth-century western musical signs, a kind of *aide-memoire* for the conductor of the choir, or the *precentor* who sings the solos. This early stage of musical signs cannot be called a notation from which one can know the exact pitch. It is only at the end of the twelfth century that the Byzantine musicians develop a system of notation which not only gives the exact pitch, but also all the nuances of expression and the exact rhythmical value of the notes. Indeed, Byzantine musical notation is an admirable instrument for preserving in writing the intention of the composer; it is a much more elaborate system than anything that one finds in the West, and comparable only to our present notation which surrounds the notes with expression marks and other signs.

Byzantine civilization, whose decay lasted more than a thousand years (330–1453), was, in fact, the most brilliant civilization of the Middle Ages. The position is the same for Byzantine Chant, which has only begun to be deciphered during the last twenty-five years. The more we know of it, the more we are impressed by its greatness and beauty.

One may ask how it is possible to trace the authenticity of these melodies back to the early days of the empire? We must remember that from the sixth to the eighth century the greater part of Italy belonged to the Byzantine Empire, and large parts of the population of southern Italy spoke Greek. Thus it happened that Greek chants were introduced into the Roman churches, sung first in Greek, and afterwards to the same melody in Latin. The Roman Church preserved these chants like holy relics in the liturgy of the great feasts. Thus we find in Beneventan manuscripts of the eleventh century—to quote one example only—a bilingual melody, *Ote to stavro—O quando in cruce*, which was sung on Good Friday during the Adoration of the Cross. The melody of the Latin text is of a simple type which speaks for its antiquity. But listen to the melody as it occurs in thirteenth-century manuscripts written in Byzantine monasteries at Constantinople and Mt Athos. One would hardly recognize this richly ornamented melody, yet the two are as alike as the theme of a Beethoven adagio and one of its variations:

(i) *O quando in cruce*; (ii) *Ote to stavro*. HISTORY OF MUSIC IN SOUND, VOL. II. VICTOR LM 6015 (HMV HMS 10, 78 r.p.m.).

Byzantine manuscripts of the eighth century show that the melody of *Ote to stavro* was as simple as that which survives in the Beneventan manuscripts, and that in later manuscripts more and more embellished versions are found.

By extending the investigation to other melodies we come to the following conclusion:

As we have said, Gregorian Chant retains *unchanged* some melodies taken from the old treasury of Byzantine Chant; they are no longer alive, but preserved like relics. Eastern Chant is alive. The work of the composer consists in treating the old treasury of hymn-melodies as an echo of the Divine beauty, as an echo of the chants of the angels. These tunes cannot be replaced by free compositions as happens in the West, but they can be embellished, and the Byzantine composers make use of this privilege by extending the ornamentation until the core of the melodies can hardly be recognized any longer.

We get a completely different picture when we turn from these liturgical chants to the hymn-tune of the so-called *canons*. The canon is a poetical form consisting of nine odes. Each of these nine odes consists of a number of strophes, sung to the melody of the first stanza, the model-stanza.

Canon writing began at the end of the seventh century, and the first great writers in this new *genre* were Andrew of Crete and John Damascene. They lived at the beginning of the great struggle between State and Church which shattered the foundations of the Byzantine Empire; the struggle between Image-worshippers and Image-breakers. The Image-worshippers saw in the pictures and statues of Our Lord, the Virgin, and the Saints earthly representations which deserved veneration; the Image-breakers, or Iconoclasts, basing their belief on the Old Testament's command that no image of God should be made, condemned the adoration of images as idolatry. The struggle lasted for nearly a century, and since the Emperor and the army were on the side of the Image-breakers, it began with the destruction of nearly all statues, images, and books containing pictures of the saints, and led to the destruction of many monasteries, the confiscation of monastic property, and the expulsion of monks and nuns. Defying torture and death, the monks, however, created in these very days of persecution innumerable hymns which, after the victory of Image-worship, were generally introduced into the eastern liturgy.

The melodies of these hymns are from the beginning of the syllabic type, and remained virtually syllabic down to the end of the Empire. This simplicity was necessary because in the canon, consisting of a hundred and more stanzas, every word had to be heard and understood by the congregation. Only at the cadences, occasionally, a few melismas occur.

Let us take as an example the first stanza of the famous *Resurrection Canon* by John Damascene, sung on Easter Day. It runs in J. M. Neale's verse-translation as follows:

'Tis the day of Resurrection: Earth tell it about abroad!
The Passover of Gladness! the Passover of God!
From death to life eternal—From earth unto the sky,
Our Christ has brought us over—With hymns of victory.

Anastaseos Imera. HISTORY OF MUSIC IN SOUND, VOL. II. VICTOR LM 6015 (HMV HMS 10, 78 r.p.m.).

The Greek version of *Glory to God in the Highest* is again a melody of the embellished type, though not as richly ornamented as the Good Friday chant.

Doxa. HISTORY OF MUSIC IN SOUND, VOL. II. VICTOR LM 6015 (HMV HMS 10, 78 r.p.m.).

Byzantine Chant in the great days of the Eastern Church cannot have sounded very differently from Gregorian Chant, a fact which can be proved by an anedote told by a monk of St Gall.

Charlemagne, king of the Franconian realm, received an embassy from Byzantium at his residence at Aix-la-Chapelle. Hidden behind a curtain, he heard Byzantine monks of the retinue of the ambassador celebrating their Service. Charlemagne was so overcome by the beauty of their chants that he ordered his Franconian singers to write down the music without pausing for eating or drinking.

If the music had sounded strange to his ears—I mean, fundamentally different from plain-song to which he was used—Charlemagne would hardly have forced his choristers to write down the music and to make a Latin translation of the words.

APPENDIX

BOOKS

CURT SACHS: *The Rise of Music in the Ancient World.*

EGON WELLESZ: *A History of Byzantine Music and Hymnography.*

H. J. T. TILLYARD: *Byzantine Music and Hymnography.*

3

Alec Robertson

GREGORIAN CHANT

GREGORIAN Chant takes its name, of course, from Gregory I, Pope and saint, who reigned from 590 to 604.[1] Gregory and his advisers codified and reformed a body of chant already existing but which was not the exclusive work of the Western Church. It included, as we shall see, many eastern elements; and one cannot too often stress that the East was the centre of gravity of the early Christian world. The faith itself, its first theology, ritual, music, monasticism, devotion to the Cross, and to the Mother of God, all arose in the East. Gregorian Chant, strictly speaking, is therefore the music proper to the Roman Church, and remains its only official music. Roman sobriety and sense were applied to many pre-existing bodies of chant, and Rome added its distinctive and very important contributions. These, of course, extend beyond Gregory's reign, but I shall be dealing in the main with the golden age of the composition of Gregorian Chant; that is, with the fifth to the eighth centuries, the ages prior to the Western Church's adoption of harmony.

Plain-song is music: but its principles differ, in many ways, from those of figured music. It has melody, but no harmony—organ accompaniment is a concession to human weakness—and its single and supple melodic line has great rhythmic freedom, being in no way constrained by time signatures or bar lines: its rhythm may be called that of fine musical oratory. In its restrained way plain-song covers a wide range of emotion without using any strong dynamic contrasts: and the principal accents of the Latin

[1] There is no agreement amongst scholars as to precisely what part Gregory took in development and consolidation of the chant, but it is certain that other Popes before, and half a century after him, contributed to the work.

14

words, far from being treated intensively, are more often than not treated lightly, being put on to high notes that throw them into melodic relief and cause them to shine down on the rest of the word—or phrase—in which they come.

The ends, or cadences, of the phrases are characteristically soft and so are the notes at the top of phrases of climax.[1] This gives an ethereal sound to the music, which seems often to float in the upper air. The compass of the melodies is small, rarely exceeding an octave, and sudden leaps up or down are exceptional. The music has what we call a modal flavour. This is due to the fact that our major and minor scale system was then unknown. There were eight ecclesiastical scales, or modes, derived from Greek scales, each one beginning, in modern parlance, on each white note of the piano and continuing upwards on the white notes only. There was no chromaticism such as the Greeks had, except that B could become B flat to give a softening effect. And so these eight modes have a variety of arrangement of their tones and semitones unknown to our typical major-minor system, which simply transposes the same arrangement of tones and semitones into different keys.

There is a certain correspondence between plain-song and the quiet, simple lines and curves of the columns and arches of the nave of a fifth-century Romanesque basilica: but there is no correspondence between Gothic architecture and plain-song. Gothic architecture is a mass in motion, rather than at rest—its intricate lines and decoration accord rather with the polyphonic music of the period in which it arose. It may also be said here that just as a church is not a beautiful arrangement of stone and glass merely intended to awaken aesthetic admiration but is a building disposed for prayer and praise, so plain-song (or indeed any truly liturgical music) is not merely a pleasing and beautiful arrangement of tones and semitones but music also disposed for prayer and praise.

The earliest church music naturally had to build upon the past, and that meant above all Jewish Bible song. No direct trace of this exists, though age-old traditions are preserved by the more remote Jewish communities. Perhaps, in this connection, we tend to forget that up to A.D. 60, at least, the adherents of the new

[1] I speak here of the method followed, and very generally adopted, by the Benedictine monks of the Solesmes Congregation.

faith continued to worship in synagogue and temple. With a measure of poetic licence we could indeed say that the birth of Christian music took place under the shadow of the synagogue, just as the central rite of the Christian faith was instituted at a Jewish Upper Room meeting.

Now the Fathers of the Church, from the first, wanted music to elevate the whole man towards God, and that ideal ran like a golden thread through plain-song. They wanted church music to be different from that heard in the world and they were especially concerned to do battle against the vicious influence of the contemporary theatre: and it *was* a battle.

The Christians in the West ceased to be a persecuted sect by the fourth century, even before Constantine the Great's Edict of Milan. When able to practise their faith openly they received a considerable influx of the rich and learned. Large basilicas were built and it was now possible to begin the shaping of the Liturgy and its music, for the Church went forth singing into the world. Great quantities of melodies were eventually collected for liturgical purposes in the Roman, Milanese, Frankish, and Celtic rites, as well as in the East, which had so strongly influenced the earliest church music of the West. The large churches required that priests addressing their congregations should raise their voices for important pronouncements. This is the simplest kind of plain-song—the inflected monotone used for prayers and Bible readings. A priest with some musical sensibility would be likely to improvise simple embellishments, and by these indicate punctuation. An example is the priest intoning the Epistle for Easter Sunday.

Easter Sunday Mass: Epistle.   DGG APM 14017.

A practice originated in Syrian monasteries and churches (and elsewhere) in the fourth century of the singing of successive verses of the psalms by alternating choruses of men and women and children. This singing was called antiphonal from the Greek word *antiphonia*, which means the octave in Greek theory, and may have been so used, because there was a difference of an octave in pitch between the two choruses. Later, a short sentence was added and repeated as a refrain after each verse, or pair of verses, giving rise eventually to that kind of psalm singing we call antiphonal to-day. The early practice is shown in this example:

the canticle *Nunc Dimittis*. The words of the last verse, 'Lumen ad revelationem, gentium,' etc. (To be a light to lighten the Gentiles), are used for the antiphonal refrain before, during, and after the canticle.

Lumen ad revelationem. HISTORY OF MUSIC IN SOUND, VOL. II. VICTOR LM 6015 (HMV HMS 11, 78 r.p.m.).

There were two other kinds of psalmody, both of them a legacy from the synagogue, one called Direct and the other Responsorial. In the first of these, which came also to be called 'Tract,' a whole psalm was sung as a solo. The Tract in the Roman Missal, sung at penitential seasons, is a developed example of this kind of solo psalmody. In the second kind, Responsorial Psalmody, the cantor, as in the Tract, again sang the whole psalm as a solo, but the people responded with a refrain between the verses. Antiphonal and responsorial singing are therefore closely allied.

Antioch and Constantinople were the first centres of another and very popular kind of music making in church—the singing of hymns. St Ambrose, the great Bishop of Milan, was the father of western hymnody, but the music of his hymns has unfortunately not survived. It is thought, from their enormous popularity, that it was of a folksong-like character. The Roman Church for a long time looked on these hymns with some suspicion which she eventually overcame. Her composers imitated the Ambrosian verse metre, tunefulness, and simplicity, and *Te lucis ante terminum* (Before the ending of the day) from the Office of Compline is a familiar example of the Ambrosian type of hymn.

Hymn: *Te lucis ante terminum.* LONDON LLA 14 (DECCA LXT 2708).

By the time St Gregory and his advisers began to undertake the reform of the Roman Chant, it had developed (along with the Liturgy) into the various forms of chants of the Mass we have to-day. These were gathered together into a book called the *Antiphonale Missarum*—Antiphonal of Masses—later known as the *Graduale Romanum*—Roman Gradual.

The Proper of the Mass is so called because it comprises all that material proper to the season or feast being celebrated. First of all the *Introit*. As its name implies—the entering in—it is a processional chant and is of the antiphonal type. It came into the Roman Mass during the fifth century. The Introit for the

*B

third Sunday after Easter, *Jubilate Deo* (Shout with joy to God), has a threefold alleluia at the end of the antiphon.

Introit: *Jubilate Deo*. London LLA 14 (Decca LXT 2706).

St Gregory's reform worked towards shortening and simplifying the chants.   It had been customary for psalms to be sung between readings from the Old Testament and the New Testament, with the people responding with a short interjection.   But in Gregory's day these psalms were sung as solos and had become so elaborate that they needed virtuoso singers.   These were the gradual psalms—the *gradus* was the step up to the little pulpit from which the gradual was sung, and the music is some of the most difficult and elaborate in Gregorian Chant.   One has to remember that it was sung while there was no action at the altar, and everyone was prepared to listen to the singer using his art (though not always!) for the glory of God.   The gradual responsory for the Epiphany tells the story of the Wise Men: *Omnes de Saba venient*.   The verse 'Surge et illuminare' is particularly fine—the melody rises in great arches of tone at 'illuminare' and 'Gloria Domini.'   And you will notice how at the words 'Saba' and 'surge' the accented syllables have only two or three notes, the unaccented ones a whole shower of notes.   In this way the accented syllables throw their light over the whole word.   *Haec Dies* for Easter Sunday is another splendid gradual.   It sings of Christ's resurrection with ardent spiritual rapture—it is one of the finest pieces of Gregorian Chant in the whole repertoire.

Graduals: (i) *Omnes de Saba venient*; (ii) *Haec Dies*.   London LLA 14 (Decca LXT 2706).

After the gradual comes the alleluia, in which the final vowel of the word is vocalized and was known as the *jubilus*.   St Augustine has a famous passage in one of his Commentaries on the *jubilus* which he rightly calls, 'a song of joy without words.'   Often the music at the end of the verse recapitulates all or part of the alleluia before the latter is sung again.   Our last example was the Easter Gradual; here is its complementary alleluia with the verse *Pascha nostrum* which speaks of Christ sacrificing Himself for us.   On the accented syllable of the word 'Immolatus' there is a wonderful high-pitched phrase of joy.   The alleluia, in this particular case, is not repeated.

Alleluia: *Pascha nostrum*.   DGG APM 14017.

The offertory, like the introit, was originally a processional chant, sung as the people came up to make their offerings. It had an antiphon—later much ornamented by the singer—and a psalm. The psalm has now vanished, leaving only the antiphon. The first offertory I have chosen is *Super flumina Babylonis*, a poignant picture of the exiled Jews weeping by the waters of Babylon as they remember Jerusalem. The rising and falling phrases are most expressive.

The second example of the offertory, *Tollite portas* (Lift up your gates, O ye princes), is a joyful piece of welcome to the King of Glory, with a last phrase like a trumpet fanfare.

Offertory: (i) *Super flumina Babylonis*; (ii) *Tollite portas*. LONDON LLA 14 (DECCA LXT 2707).

The Communion chants are also processional as they were sung as the faithful came up to the altar to communicate. They are antiphonal, like the offertory. The psalm verses are no longer sung, and, as in the offertory, only the antiphon, usually a simple melody, remains. There is, however, one exception to this in the Mass for the Dead. In this beautiful chant *Lux aeterna luceat eis Domine*, there is a verse 'Requiem aeternam dona eis Domine,' with the second half of the antiphon repeated after it.

Communion: (i) *Lux aeterna*. DGG APM 14002; (ii) *Pater si non potest*. LONDON LLA 14 (DECCA LXT 2707).

The invariable part of the Mass is called the Ordinary. It consists of *Kyrie, Gloria, Credo, Sanctus*, and *Agnus Dei*; and it is this part, just because it is invariable, that composers have set to music over and over again and still do. Nearly all chants of the Ordinary were composed after the sixth century and so post-date St Gregory. Many of these chants, though by no means all, are too difficult for congregational use. At the same time there is a folksong-like melodiousness and simplicity in some of them, and because no one recognized the existence of folk music or bothered to write it down, we shall never know how much secular music of the time has found its way into them. The chants we have are dated, most of them, from the tenth to the sixteenth century, but the simplest, litany-like chants are undoubtedly much earlier and would have been known to Gregory. Here is the *Kyrie* from one of these, a Mass for days on which there is no feast. It is only in

the last *Kyrie* of all that a little elaboration comes in, revealing
the hand of the singer-composer.

Kyrie XVII.   ENGLISH DECCA LX 3118.

Kyrie eleison had long been a pagan invocation to the Sun God
when the Eastern Christians took it over. St Gregory speaks of
adding *Christe eleison* to it and repeating each petition a number
of times, the people answering the clergy.   The number of times
was settled in the eighth century at three *Kyries*—three *Christes*—
three *Kyries*.   So a composer could write a contrasted section
of music for the *Christes* and return to the music of the first three
Kyries for the final ones—or he could provide new music all
through.

Let us consider a plain-song setting of a complete Ordinary of
the Mass, omitting only the *Credo*.   I have chosen one of the most
beautiful, No. XI, for Sundays throughout the year.   The first
Kyries in this Mass end with a little up and down phrase (on
eleison) that the composer liked so much that he brought it into
the *Christes* as well—here we have the principle of the motto theme.
The last *Kyrie* is slightly elaborated but ends of course with the
same motto theme.

The *Gloria*, with no repetition of words and a fairly long text,
has, as a rule, simpler music so that it may move more quickly—
mostly it follows the rule of one syllable, one note.   Here too, to
give unity, we find the opening phrase of the *Gloria* is used seven
times in its course.

Next comes the *Sanctus*.   Notice how the *Hosanna* phrases
seem to suggest the obeisance of the people at our Lord's triumphal
entry into Jerusalem.

The music of the *Agnus Dei*, the last section of the Ordinary, is
beautifully contrived, in this setting, to rise higher in pitch with
each of the two repetitions of the words—and here again we have
a device that composers in later years were to use extensively to
heighten emotional appeal.

Mass XI: *Kyrie, Gloria, Sanctus, Agnus Dei.*   LONDON LLA 14
(DECCA LX 3119).

The Divine Office, as we know it to-day, is the great work of
St Benedict, the father of western monasticism.   He called it
Opus Dei (God's work) and directed his monks to devote themselves
to it before all else.   It has an interesting history.

The celebration of the Lord's Supper, the Eucharist, originally held in the evening, was moved to dawn during the times of persecution, and then to the early morning. In a famous letter to the Emperor Trajan, Pliny the Younger described how 'on certain days the Christians get together before sunrise and sing songs to Christ as if he were God.' These vigils, as they were called, were at first limited to Sundays, or rather Saturday night, with the Eucharist celebrated at daybreak on Sunday. Later on the meetings started at dusk when lamps were lit. The psalms and prayers then sung and said are the oldest form of Vespers. Psalm singing was the chief occupation of all at the vigils. We can picture the scene from a report of the conversation of the pilgrims dating from the fifth century—'One of them is astonished by the magnificence and splendour of the ceremonies, another by the vast crowds which they have attracted, a third by the large concourse of bishops. One praises the eloquence of the preachers, another the beauty of the psalmody, another the endurance of the public during the long night office, another the fervour in prayer of the assistants. One recalls the dust, another the stifling heat ... the cries and disputes, the disorder of people getting into each other's way and refusing to give place, each eager to be the first to participate.'[1]

Benedictine communities were established in Rome in the sixth century, civilizing north-western Europe. Not all of the monasteries were true to their high ideals, but Europe owes them an incalculable debt. A by no means uncritical Protestant historian observes that the monks first taught western Europe to work methodically.

The centre of the monks' lives was the singing of the *Opus Dei* from the night office of Mattins through the day offices of Lauds, Prime, Terce, Sext, None, and Vespers to Compline, the 'ending of the day.' In the scriptoria, during the day, some monks and lay assistants would be copying out manuscripts and illuminating them, others would be adapting and composing chants. It required great skill to take the melody of an existing chant and set it to new words, for almost certainly you had to lengthen it or shorten it. There are antiphon 'types' used for over fifty different texts in this way. Sometimes the monks used

[1] *The Legacy of the Middle Ages*, edited by G. C. Crump and E. F. Jacob (Oxford University Press).

a mosaic technique, taking this little group of notes and that one
and piecing them together. A snatch of popular song, drifting
up from the pilgrims in the courtyard, might go into a bit of chant,
or the flight of a bird might suggest a sequence of notes.

Antiphonal psalmody predominates in the Divine Office. The
texts of the antiphons are concerned, of course, with the feasts
and seasons of the year. They are both preludes and points of
meditation, but they also had the practical purpose of setting the
pitch and mode of the psalm to follow. The antiphon is so
devised as to fit without jar on to the psalm tone following and to
join on to the end of it when the psalm was done and the antiphon
repeated.

Monotony in the long procession of psalms in the night office
was avoided by ringing changes on the eight psalm tones, most of
which have also a number of alternate endings. Good chanting
goes rhythmically back and forth between the two sides of the
choir—like the gentle breaking of waves on the seashore.
Here is a typical antiphon and psalm—*Ave Maria*, an antiphon
for one of the feasts of Our Lady—and a short psalm
of praise, *Laudate Dominum omnes gentes* (Praise the Lord all ye
people).

Ave Maria. LONDON LLA 14 (DECCA LXT 2705).

Besides antiphons and psalms each of the canonical hours contains a hymn, and these hymns are among the most tuneful
examples of the chant. The verses are metrical but the chant
avoids any squareness of treatment. There is a distinctly popular
flavour about such hymns as the familiar *Veni Creator Spiritus*.

Veni Creator Spiritus. LONDON LLA 14 (DECCA LXT 2708).

Ave Maris Stella (Hail Star of the Sea) is one of the loveliest of
the Marian hymns. Notice the high melody note on the accented
syllable of *Stella* which shines down over the whole phrase and
hymn.

Hymn: *Ave Maris Stella*. LONDON LLA 14 (DECCA LXT 2708).

The short responsories of the Divine Office are interesting in
point of form, for here we have the idea of the rondo prefigured.
In the example chosen, *Verbum Caro factum est—Alleluia* (an
Easter one), the choir repeat the cantors' words, the cantors
continue, the choir repeat the Alleluias, the cantors sing *Gloria*

Patris, the choir repeat *Verbum Caro*, etc., ending with the Alleluias: and so it is a little rondo in being.

Short Responsory: *Verbum Caro factum est.* LONDON LLA 14 (DECCA LXT 2705).

The long responsories are of a different type, and we will take as our example *O vos omnes* (O, all ye who pass by, see if there be any grief like unto My grief). Half of the first section is repeated after the verse, or middle part of the responsory. Notice how the chant underlines the words 'Attendite et videte,' as if calling us to halt before the Cross and meditate on Christ's redeeming love for us.

Quem vidistis pastores is a joyful responsory. It comes from the Mattins of the Nativity and is a dialogue between some village people and the shepherds. 'What did you see, shepherds?' 'We saw one who was born and a choir of angels praising God.'

Both these responsories are, in the restrained way of Gregorian Chant, dramatic pictures—comparable to the early paintings of the scenes they represent.

Responsories: (i) *O vos omnes*; (ii) *Quem vidistis pastores*. LONDON LLA 14 (DECCA LXT 2708).

At the end of Compline, when the whole monastic family is gathered together before retiring, there is sung one of the three antiphons of Our Lady, of which *Salve Regina* (Hail Holy Queen) is certainly the best known and loved. It has two chants, one simple and one solemn. The solemn (and older) one is especially beautiful and it again emphasizes the complete harmony of word and tone in Gregorian Chant. Notice especially the closing phrases 'O clemens, o pia, o dulcis Virgo Maria,' which are full of the greatest tenderness.

Antiphon: *Salve Regina.* LONDON LLA 14 (DECCA LXT 2705).

The Sequence, the last chant we have to consider, came into being in the first half of the ninth century and thereafter expanded enormously. It grew partly out of a practical consideration. Singers found it hard to remember the long vocalization of the alleluias, and accordingly words were set to them. So began the Sequence—something that follows on, or a succession of notes. Soon sections of the alleluias, given words in this way, became detached from the parent chants as independent compositions. It was a new impetus to invention. *Victimae Paschali*, the Easter

Sequence, has a folksong-like syllabic melody, and is a dramatic dialogue. Mary is asked, after the opening sentences, what she saw at the tomb and she describes the empty tomb, the napkin and linen clothes, and the angels. She hails the risen Christ. It was from such dialogues that the liturgical drama was to come, the birth-place of our modern theatre.

Sequence: *Victimae Paschali laudeo.* LONDON LLA 14 (DECCA LXT 2706).

What impact, it may be asked, did Gregorian Chant make upon the ordinary men and women of the early Middle Ages? They must have picked up and sung or parodied the more popular kind of melodies, but there is all too little evidence as to what part they played in singing at Mass, or what Gregorian Chant meant to them. Much of it was over their heads and trained choirs took over much that was their rightful part. The church was, nevertheless, their concert hall, their library, and their art gallery, and the people must often have been uplifted by what they dimly understood.

In the ninth century the West was able to breathe more freely after the barbarian invasions that had threatened Christianity, and with the Carolingian Renaissance came Charles the Great's determination to develop a Christian culture in an ecclesiastical state with himself as a sort of lay-Pope. It was he, not the reigning Pope, who secured the triumph (in some ways regrettable) of Gregorian Chant over the Gallican and Mozarabic Chants of France and Spain, and it was he who did much to bring about liturgical order with its centre at Rome. But the Popes were determined to be masters in their own home, and after a long struggle became so.

The society of the Middle Ages was not sweetly submissive any more than it was barbarous and ignorant. Its many varieties of religious experience were part of the social structure. Christianity was an inseparable element in men's lives, even if many of them only conformed outwardly, and the Church, whatever scandal some of her ministers gave, was the Ark of Salvation, the teacher of the people. Whatever the failings of the Church of the Middle Ages may have been we can see in its splendid churches, stained glass, illuminated service books, statues, its incomparable architecture, and glorious music a noble expression of the highest ideals of the service and contemplation of God, which called these things forth in unparalleled quantity and richness. And we can be sure that there were in the mass of people thousands of unknown folk, lay and religious, whose lives, inspired by all that is signified by the word Church, were no less beautiful in the sight of God.

APPENDIX

BOOKS

ALEC ROBERTSON: *Sacred Music; The Interpretation of Gregorian Chant.*
WILLI APEL: *Gregorian Chant* (in preparation).
J. S. VAN WAESBERGHE: *Gregorian Chant.*

RECORDS

Most of the examples cited in the chapter were drawn from London LLA 14 (Decca LXT 2704–8). This may be supplemented by the four records London LSA 17 (Decca LX 3118–21) devoted to the Ordinary of the Mass.

Easter Sunday Mass. DECCA ARC 3001 (DGG APM 14017). LONDON LL 1408 (DECCA LXT 5171).
Christmas Vespers. DECCA 7546 (DGG AP 13005).
Good Friday Liturgy. DGG APM 14034.
First Mass for the Dead. DGG APM 14002.
Easter and Christmas Music. ANGEL 35116 (COLUMBIA 33 CX 1193).
Mass of the Day. ENGLISH DECCA LXT 5251.
Solemnis Palmarum Processio. DGG AP 13041.
Ascension and Assumption. ENGLISH DECCA LXT 5227.

28479

LIBRARY
College of St. Francis
JOLIET, ILL.

4

Denis Stevens

THE TROUBADOURS

A<small>N</small> <small>AIR</small> of mystery pervades the lives of the troubadours, inevitably, for they lived eight or nine hundred years ago, and the passage of time has not always been kind to the rare and precious documents that could tell us about the career and character of each man. It is nevertheless possible to judge their achievements by what has survived of their music, for more than two hundred troubadour melodies have been preserved for us in various manuscripts; some elegantly written and beautifully illuminated, and others very obviously the work of some hasty scribe. Before coming to the melodies, it may be well to see whether the troubadours were alone in their intensive cultivation of song and their strange and subtle code of manners.

The art of the troubadours seems to have grown up in the south of France where the language, in the Middle Ages, was known as Provençal, or *langue d'oc*. '*Oc*' was Provençal for 'yes,' and this type of ending can be seen in countless place names in the troubadour country. In the northern part of France the word for 'yes' was pronounced 'ouil,' almost as it is to-day. So the two main language groups were known as the *langue d'ouil* and the *langue d'oc*. The troubadours were followed by another great generation of poets and singers in the north, and these men, the trouvères, used the French language, which had formed the basis of their life and education. The trouvères were to prove even more prolific; about fourteen hundred of their songs have come down to us.

When we inquire what the motive was behind this new, fine, and sensitive musical culture, we find that the French have a phrase for it: *cherchez la femme*. Indeed, the worship of womankind was in very many instances the idea and the emotion which the troubadour needed in order to create his song. But his adoration had to be a distant worship, a discreet declaration of love, both of these

26

inseparable from a vow of purity, without which the troubadour
would be no more than an impostor, a common *jongleur* or juggler.
Not that a jongleur was for ever debarred from becoming a troubadour and knight—we have the example of Raimbaut de Vaqueiras,
who began life as a minstrel, but was eventually knighted. He
fell in love with the prince's sister, but lacked discretion in the
manner of his courtship, with the result that malicious tongues
began to wag. The Lady Beatrice made it plain that she no longer
loved him, and for a long time he was utterly inconsolable. Then
suddenly she turned and spoke to him, begging him to compose a
song for her. Raimbaut did so at once, taking as his tune one of
the *estampies*, or dance tunes, heard earlier in the evening at court.
The song is *Kalenda Maya*: 'On the first of May, neither leaf of
beech, nor song of bird, nor flower of sword lily pleases me, lady
noble and gay, until I receive a speedy messenger from your fair
self.'

Raimbaut de Vaqueiras: *Kalenda Maya*. Decca ARC 3002 (alt.
Vox PL 8110).

Everybody joins in that song. The phrases are thrown briskly
and gaily from one group of singers to the leader, and from the
leader back to the group again. That principle of responding to
a lead was one of the fundamental features of medieval music in
all its aspects. It may well have come originally from the Church
—from responsorial plain-song—and the troubadours often took
their melodies from Gregorian Chant. They adapted them
slightly, but everyone was bound to recognize the contour of the
melody. By no means all of the melodies came from a plain-song
source; some may have been composed by the troubadour himself,
and others have an almost popular lilt which suggests that they
belonged originally to the vast repertory of folk-song.

For melodies of the composed type we can do no better than
turn to the troubadour, Bernart de Ventadour (*c.* 1145–95). He
was the son of a humble servant, but was given both education
and encouragement by his master, Count Ebles, himself the son
of a poet. When the time came for him to leave his native
country of Limousin, he wrote a moving and eloquent song, telling
of his love for the Countess of Ventadour and of his need to depart.
Legend has it that Bernart, like Raimbaut, was indiscreet in his
love. Whatever the reason for his leaving, he must have missed
the colourful and fertile valleys of Corrèze. Bernart was inspired

by the birds as well as by the scenery around him, as in his song
about the lark.

Bernart de Ventadour: *Can vei la lauzeta*. HISTORY OF MUSIC IN
SOUND, VOL. II.   VICTOR LM 6015 (HMV HMS 14, 78 r.p.m.).

Can vei la lauzeta, like the majority of love-songs by the
troubadours and trouvères, was for one voice without accompaniment.   But we may ask whether an instrument was ever used to
accompany the songs, and if so, did it simply double the melody, or
play an introduction and tail-piece?   Did it add harmonies in
the modern sense of the word?   These questions are important,
because they are bound up with modern interpretation of the
songs, and also with the lives and customs of the troubadours
themselves.

The medieval jongleur was a combination of minstrel and juggler.   There are often pictures of them in the manuscripts that
contain troubadour songs, and they are seen playing instruments
like the medieval fiddle or lute, juggling with swords, and even
walking the tightrope.   The function of the jongleurs was to
amuse the audience at courts and castles, acting as a foil to the
serious matter of the evening—the troubadour songs themselves
—and thus a troubadour and a jongleur often formed what we
should nowadays call a 'double act.'   The jongleur was capable
of playing an instrumental accompaniment to his master's songs,
and although not written down, there is no reason to doubt that
these accompaniments once existed, if only in the fertile brain
of the jongleur.   The accompaniments were probably very simple,
making much use of drone basses such as one hears from a bagpipe.
It is almost certainly wrong to think of troubadour songs as bare
melodies, and some editors are imaginative enough to invent
accompaniments.   An example is *Lancan vei la folha*, also by
Bernart de Ventadour.   'When I see the leaves falling from the
tree, whoever may grieve or sorrow, I find it much to my taste.
Do not think that I want to see either flower or leaf, for she scorns
me, she who is the one I most desire.'

Bernart de Ventadour: *Lancan vei la folha*.   Vox PL 8110.

In 1155 Bernart paid a visit to England because his patroness,
Eleanor of Acquitaine, had recently settled there as the queen of
the newly crowned Henry II.   Although many English noblemen
must have listened entranced to Bernart's wonderful store of songs,

there was no apparent desire on the part of the English for a type of art-song similar to Bernart's.

The few secular songs that have come down to us from the twelfth and thirteenth centuries in England bear little relation to the troubadour and trouvère repertoire. The language spoken at the English court was Norman-French; thus rather than foster a local variant of troubadour art, it was easier and more satisfactory to send for one of the troubadours in person. One of the best known of the few English songs that survived is *Worldes blis*, which is sad, even bitter in its sentiments: 'the world's joy lasts no time at all.'

Worldes blis. HISTORY OF MUSIC IN SOUND, VOL. II. VICTOR LM 6015 (HMV HMS 15, 78 r.p.m.).

Bernart did not stay long in England. Eleanor followed him on the long road to Acquitaine, for her relations with Henry II grew steadily worse. Soon she was at Poitiers, holding her fantastic courts of love, where artificial problems were set for lovers, and palms were awarded for excellence in *l'amour courtois*. Troubadours flocked to her court, and some would sing of their brethren absent on the crusades, with no news to tell of their fortunes or whereabouts—as in *Chanterai por mon coraige* by Guiot de Dijon.

Guiot de Dijon: *Chanterai por mon coraige.* HISTORY OF MUSIC IN SOUND, VOL II. VICTOR LM 6015 (HMV HMS 14, 78 r.p.m.).

There were cheerful moments too, when *ballades* and *rondeaux* were sung and played, and the drums were beaten and the flutes piped merrily. There is the rondeau *Tuit cil qui sunt enamourat* or the ballade *A l'entrada del tens clar*: 'When the fine weather comes to bring back joy again and to annoy the jealous, I wish to show the Queen, for she is so much in love. Away, away, jealous ones, leave us to dance among ourselves.'

(i) *Tuit cil qui sunt enamourat.* HISTORY OF MUSIC IN SOUND, VOL. II. VICTOR LM 6015 (HMV HMS 14, 78 r.p.m.).
(ii) *A l'entrada del tens clar.* DECCA ARC 3002.

The rhythm tells us that those songs were meant for dancing, probably a round-dance with a small group of singers and instrumentalists at one side. Dancing was as popular in the Middle Ages as it is to-day, and its influence on troubadour art was very great indeed. I have already mentioned that Raimbaut de Vaqueiras based a song on an *estampie*. We may take two further examples of dance music. The first has no text and no special title, but it reminds us of the dance-songs, nevertheless, because there is a refrain which returns at the end of every phrase. The second example is probably English in origin. Right at the end the single line of melody bursts forth into three-part harmony, as if the minstrels had been saving up their *tour de force*.

(i) *La Quarte Estampie Reale*; (ii) *Estampie: 'Spielmannstanz.'* Vox PL 8110.

We must always remember that the tradition of medieval minstrelsy did not exclude participation by men of more exalted rank. Gifted musicians would often take part and would not lose caste by doing so. Some troubadours were noblemen, some were members of a rich family of merchants, others came from a poor family of townsfolk.

In Spain and Italy we find the same diversity of background. By far the largest collection of Spanish songs was made by King Alfonso X of Castile and Léon, and although music was only a small part of his learning, he deserved the nickname of *Alfonoso el Sabio*—Alfonso the Wise. In these Spanish songs love of womankind has already been further sublimated, for it is the Virgin Mary who is praised beyond all measure. The songs are written in a language that is half Spanish, half Portuguese, but the melodies often have a definite Spanish flavour about them.

(i) *Como peden*; (ii) *Quen â Virgen*. HISTORY OF MUSIC IN SOUND, VOL. II. VICTOR LM 6015 (HMV HMS 15, 78 r.p.m.).

Italy had its troubadour imitators too, though none of their music has come down to us. The spirit of the music survives, however, in the *Laudi Spirituali*, or spiritual hymns sung on pilgrimages throughout Italy during the thirteenth century.

O divina Virgo. HISTORY OF MUSIC IN SOUND, VOL. II. VICTOR LM 6015 (HMV HMS 15, 78 r.p.m.).

In conclusion, I should mention the field of drama. In the late thirteenth century a dramatic pastoral called *Le Jeu de Robin et de Marion* was played before the court of Charles d'Anjou at Naples. The author was Adam de la Halle, whose charming tale of shepherds and shepherdesses is matched by equally charming music.

Adam de la Halle: *Le Jeu de Robin et de Marion*. DECCA ARC 3002 (DGG APM 14018).

(APPENDIX: *See* page 72.)

5

Denis Stevens

THE TROUVÈRES AND THE MINNESINGERS

THE trouvères largely followed the ideals of the troubadours, the texts of their songs being in the Norman-French which is close to the French language spoken to-day. It is difficult for us to understand fully the nature and implications of courtly love—*l'amour courtois*—for the popular love-songs of to-day are not exactly brimming over with courteous restraint in their adulation of the fair sex. Seven centuries ago the singer was bound by a strict code of conduct, and often strove to compose his songs and poems in such a way that their true meaning should be apparent only to the lady concerned. Others might hear the song, but would not understand its true import—or so the theory went. There are certain instances of a seeming lack of impersonality; Bernart de Ventadour begins a song with these words: 'Do not be surprised if I sing better than any other troubadour.' He was not lacking modesty, however; what he wished to convey was that his love and admiration for his lady gave him the power to sing better than anyone else.

It was tacitly assumed that a troubadour or trouvère in love was entirely given up to the fascination of his loved one, and this cult of adoration was marked by a certain mysticism and a certain nobility of sentiment. In order to win the favour of his lady, the singer had to honour her by long service and devotion, and in accepting this devotion the lady became the sovereign ruler of her lover's heart and mind. Yet the singer had no right to ask any reward at first for his service: he was, as it were, entirely at her mercy; and although he might express his sorrow and regret at her seeming lack of interest, he had no right to reproach her. The lady herself was bound to be a paragon of all the virtues. But there were always malicious gossips, and the singer often refers to their wicked attempts to damage the reputation of his lady.

Some of the trouvères became so famous that their names were
celebrated by great poets who lived many years after them. An
example is Gace Brulé, who lived in the twelfth century, for his
name was honoured two centuries later by Dante Alighieri in
De Vulgaris Eloquentia. In Gace Brulé's song *Je ne puis pas si
loing fuir* ('I cannot flee so far') words and music go hand in hand
to describe the lover's sadness; try as he may, he cannot forget
his lady.

Gace Brulé: *Je ne puis pas si loing fuir*. HISTORY OF MUSIC IN SOUND,
VOL. II. VICTOR LM 6015 (HMV HMS 14, 78 r.p.m.).

Many singers tried to forget by going off to the crusades. The
First Crusade (1096–9) was almost contemporary with the first
great phase of troubadour art; three more crusades took place
before the first decade of the thirteenth century, and these saw the
greatest period in the art of the trouvères. In Europe it was the
time when some of the most magnificent of our medieval cathedrals
and abbeys were built. Masons and carvers, artists in coloured
glass and coloured stone-work were working together to create
such unparalleled examples of Gothic art as the cathedrals of
Canterbury, Chartres, Mainz, Notre-Dame de Paris, Lincoln,
Chichester, and Rheims. With cathedrals being put up, and
pagans being put down, there was an opportunity for everyone to
rejoice; and that is why so much of the work of the trouvères—
in spite of their wonderful love-songs—is full of joy. The form
of the *rondeau* is still used, with the alternation between soloist
and chorus, and we may take an example by Guillaume d'Amiens;
Prenes-y garde. A young swain is making amorous advances to
an attractive brunette who is trying to keep her mind on the cows
she is supposed to be looking after. The chorus chimes in after
every verse: 'Keep a look-out! Is anyone watching? If anyone's watching us, give me a shout!'

Guillaume d'Amiens: *Prenes-y garde*. DECCA ARC 3002 (DGG
APM 14018).

The songs of Guillaume d'Amiens are to be found in manuscripts in the Bibliothèque Nationale, Paris, and the Vatican
Library, Rome. For centuries the songs remained there, unknown and unsung. Medieval songs are found in twenty or more
manuscripts scattered throughout the great libraries of Europe,
in France, Italy, Spain, and Germany; and there are many more
manuscripts which contain just the texts of the songs. Some of

the manuscripts are beautifully written and illuminated, ornamented by pictures of the troubadours themselves or their jongleurs, and undoubtedly they were commissioned by some rich
nobleman who wished to have the choicest songs of the time
enshrined in a vellum manuscript of impeccable workmanship.
There are other manuscripts, less sumptuously written, though
the texts and music may be quite as accurate. The impression
they give is that they must have been used by a minstrel as his
day-to-day material.

Each of these manuscript sources has its own character, its own
particular repertoire of songs. Sometimes it looks as if each one
has its own kind of notation because the musical notes of the
Middle Ages assumed many different forms. Most of these
apparent differences are due to the personal handwriting of the
scribes, but we must remember that musical notation was under-
going great changes during the twelfth and thirteenth centuries.
The tendency was to make notation more and more precise so
that no loopholes existed in the matter of rhythm and tempo.
The actual pitch of the notes—to show this is comparatively
straightforward—had been settled for many years.

It is essential to realize that the gradual stabilization of rhythmic
signs was not an unmixed blessing. In the old days troubadour
songs could be performed in a free manner, with no restrictions
about tempo, rhythm, or bar-lines as we know them. When the
trouvères were at the height of their achievement the situation
was very different; their songs can be, and usually are, transcribed
in what is called modal rhythm. This makes use of different
note-patterns within a rhythmical framework of triple-time:
once the mode has been decided upon, there can be little or no
departure from it within the song itself. We may take as an
example the gently undulating rhythm of *Quand je voi yver
retorner*, attributed to Colin Muset.

Colin Muset: *Quand je voi yver retorner*. HISTORY OF MUSIC IN
SOUND, VOL. II. VICTOR LM 6015 (HMV HMS 14, 78 r.p.m.).

The continually repeated phrases at the beginning of this song
make it sound almost as though it were based on a folk-song.
The text too, with its enumeration of staple foods and delicacies
of the table, has an almost goliardic feeling—as though written
by one of the wandering scholars. For although the heyday of
the medieval Latin lyric was long past, there were still scholars to

wander from the newly founded University of Paris to outlying centres of learning, like Padua, Salamanca, and Oxford. Many other scholars besides Peter Abélard must have been musical as well as learned; indeed music was one of the seven liberal arts then taught at all the great universities. The tuition was purely theoretical, but students, then as now, sought to improve their learning by indulging in some practical musical activity.

We may now return to the trouvère ideal, that mystic love which characterized their finest utterances in poetry and in music, and take as an example a song by a trouvère who was also a king: Thibaut IV of Champagne, who was crowned King of Navarre in 1234. Thus we see that the art of song was known to, and practised by, not only the highest rank of the nobility, but even by kings and princes. The melodic contour of Thibaut's *Tuit mi desir* is almost modern in its feeling and tonality; there is more than a hint of what we should call the key of F major. The song is divided into two almost equal halves, and the first half is sung twice in order to accommodate the second pair of verses.

Thibaut IV: *Tuit mi desir*. HISTORY OF MUSIC IN SOUND, VOL. II.
    VICTOR LM 6015 (HMV HMS 14, 78 r.p.m.).

Even more famous as a trouvère than Thibaut of Navarre was Richard the Lion Heart. The story of his imprisonment in France, and his rescue by his servant Blondel, is a picturesque one, though its authenticity has never been proved. But there is no doubt whatever about Richard's skill as a poet and a singer. His mother, Eleanor of Acquitaine, saw to it that Richard learnt music from the finest of the singers at her courts in France and England. When he grew up he liked to take an active part in the music of the royal chapel, and it is said that he used to help in training the choristers. As an absolutely fearless warrior, Richard was renowned above all his contemporaries, but his daring could lead him into difficulties. At one time during the Third Crusade the bad feeling among factions on both the French and English sides rose to such a pitch that Hugh of Burgundy caused a scurrilous song to be sung up and down the army encampments. Richard replied in kind, and was probably well regarded for doing so. The homeward journey, however, took him across the kingdom of Duke Leopold of Austria, whose standard he had caused to be torn down and besmirched. Leopold

had Richard captured and held for ransom.   During his imprisonment Richard wrote his famous song *Ja nun hons pris*, which has,
unfortunately, not yet been recorded.

In Germany medieval song was practised by the minnesingers,
or singers of love. They were aristocratic singers, unlike the
troubadours and trouvères, who were often of humble origin, and
they flourished from the middle of the twelfth century until the
end of the fifteenth, to be followed by the mastersingers.   The
music of the mastersingers was not by any means as good, however,
and it is only in the songs of the minnesingers that we find that
freedom from the binding rules of composition which makes for
freshness, charm, and beauty.   Only one complete song by the
earliest important minnesinger has come down to us: *Nu alerst
leb'ich* by Walther von der Vogelweide, a song about the Crusade
of 1228.   'Now at last my life begins for me, since my sinful eyes
behold the Holy Land, the very soil which men hold in honour.
My prayer is answered: I have come to the land where God in
human form set foot.'

Walter von der Vogelweide: *Nu alerst leb'ich*.   Vox PL 8110 (E).

We may take as our next two examples two songs that praise
the beauties of nature.   The first, by a slightly younger contemporary of Vogelweide, Neithart von Reuenthal, is called
May Song. 'May has lifted up many hearts.   He has shown full
well what his sweet joy can do, when he clothes the blackthorn
in white blossoms.' The accompaniment added there by the
editor is for the psaltery; in the second example, *So schon wir den
Anger nie gesahen* (Never has the green meadow seemed so lovely)
the accompaniment is for viols.

(i) Neithart von Reuenthal: *May Song*; (ii) Anon: *So schon wir den
Anger nie gesahen*.   Vox PL 8110 (E).

One of the outstanding minnesingers of the late thirteenth
century was Heinrich von Meissen.   He was in fact the last of
the old school, and after his death the cult of minnesingers tended
more and more to pass into the domain of city guilds and societies.
He was known to his contemporaries as *Frauenlob* ('Praise of
Ladies'), yet he was not always concerned with courtly love: his
songs in praise of the Virgin Mary are equally typical of his art.

Heinrich von Meissen: *Ey ich sach in dem trone*.   HISTORY OF MUSIC
IN SOUND, VOL. II.   VICTOR LM 6015 (HMV HMS 15, 78 r.p.m.).

Our final example takes our survey up to the fifteenth century. It is again a May song, but with an important difference in the texture; the composer, Oswald von Wolkenstein, has composed his own accompaniment, which is played on the harp. The song is actually an adaptation of a French melody of the fourteenth century; a very tasteful arrangement which preserves all the bird-calls—dove, lark, thrush, nightingale, and cuckoo. The song is an early example of word-painting in music as well as a charming composition in itself.

Oswald von Wolkenstein: *Der May*.   Vox PL 8110 (E).

(APPENDIX: *See* page 72.)

6

Willi Apel

THE BIRTH OF POLYPHONY

DIFFERENT though the song of an Indian warrior, a hymn to Apollo, and an Alleluia from the Roman liturgy may be from one another, they have one trait in common: they consist of nothing but a single melody without harmonies or other additional elements. Such music is called monophonic, this being the Greek term for 'one voice.' Compare with this a symphony by Beethoven, a nocturne by Chopin, a chorus by Mendelssohn, or a fugue of Bach and you have an entirely different type of music. It may be said to consist of many simultaneous parts, if we interpret the term 'part' to denote any additional element, whether produced by the human voice or on an instrument, whether consisting of chords as in a nocturne by Chopin or of individual lines as in a fugue by Bach. This, then, is called polyphonic music. Although polyphony of a more or less primitive kind occurs in many parts of the world, it was only in western Europe that its possibilities were systematically explored in a thousand years' evolution which, we may safely predict, will continue as long as our civilization exists.

We should remember that it is only in the last fifty years that musicologists have traced back this marvellous development to its earlier phases and its very inception. Within my own memory most music lovers believed that nothing worth knowing or hearing had been written before Haydn. In the first or second decade of this century the general public became aware of Bach, and he now occupies Haydn's place as the 'father of music.' Some music lovers have a vague notion about a sort of grandfather called Palestrina, and if you open one of the popular books on music you may learn that there was something called Gregorian Chant, created about a thousand years before Palestrina.

These thousand years are a plain vacuum, a long, long period of 'crude beginnings.' The books will tell you that something *did* happen during this period, but it is so strange that you can hardly believe it. In the ninth century people made a first crude attempt at performing polyphonic music by singing constantly in fifths. About one hundred and fifty years ago, when this fact was discovered, the verdict was, 'horrible!—impossible!' There was then a rule forbidding successive, or as they are usually called, parallel fifths, and people were shocked to learn that these faulty progressions had once formed the very basis of music. One of the foremost historians of the day, Kiesewetter, actually wrote that such music could not have existed 'because parallel fifths are morally impossible.' Gradually a few more examples of medieval polyphony came to light, but they were full of dissonances no less disagreeable to the ear and no less impossible to the mind than the parallel fifths. In 1841 Kiesewetter published a book in which he reproduced three compositions from the thirteenth century with the inscription, 'Very crude counterpoint.'

About 1920 there emerged for the first time a sufficiently complete picture of the entire development of music during the Middle Ages. It appeared under favourable circumstances. The Middle Ages were no longer looked upon as a period of darkness, ignorance, and barbarism. Not a few of the best minds regarded it as a period of the highest spiritual significance. The musical situation also proved remarkably favourable. There had been a Debussy who scattered handfuls of parallel fifths over each page, and there was a Stravinsky who threw arm-loads of dissonances at his listeners. Some of the leading composers, particularly Hindemith, discovered in medieval music a congeniality of basic tendencies and a remarkable similarity of technical methods.

We may turn now to the birth of polyphony. The place is somewhere in the northern part of the Frankish Empire under the successors of Charlemagne; the time is perhaps about 850; and the crown witness is a monk who recorded the memorable event in a book called *Musica enchiriadis* (*Handbook of Music*). The identity of this monk has not been definitely established, although Hucbald seems at present the most likely candidate. Not only did the author of the *Musica enchiriadis* leave the earliest information about polyphonic music, he also treated his subject with much greater clarity and inner conviction than was done during the subsequent two hundred years. Important additional information is found in the closely related *Scholia Enchiriadis* (*Commentary on the Handbook*), which is a dialogue between master and disciple. Both sources include a considerable number of musical illustrations.

What is this early polyphony? It is not free composition in the proper sense of the word. A pre-existing melody is taken from Gregorian Chant, and to this is added another melody. This principle of creating polyphonic music out of plain-song remained valid for three and more centuries, the pre-existing melody being known as a *cantus firmus*, or 'fixed song.' The earliest method of changing a monophonic melody into a polyphonic piece was to have another singer duplicate the melody at the lower fifth or at the lower fourth. Yet other singers could participate by duplicating either of these parts at the octave, resulting in a sort of three-part or even four-part polyphony. Since all the voices move constantly in parallel motion, this type is known as *parallel organum—organum* being the generic term for polyphonic music of the ninth through the twelfth century. This method can be illustrated by taking a commonly employed *cantus firmus* (for example, *Benedicamus Domino*) and hearing it first as a plain-song, then as an organum of the fourth, of the fifth, and as a composite organum with both parts in octave doubling.

Benedicamus Domino (four versions). This was especially recorded for the series by the *Collegium Musicum* of Indiana University.

Nowadays we find the austerity and starkness of such music impressive rather than forbidding—or 'crude' and 'morally impossible.' Another example, actually from the *Musica enchiriadis*, is based on the plain-song: *Sit gloria Domini in saecula: laetabitur Dominus in operibus suis* (May the glory of the Lord abide for ever: the Lord shall rejoice in his works).

Sit gloria Domini. HISTORY OF MUSIC IN SOUND, VOL. II. VICTOR LM 6015 (HMV HMS 16, 78 r.p.m.).

Naturally, parallel organum was too elementary a method to satisfy musicians for very long, and modifications towards greater independence of the voice-parts were bound to follow. Nevertheless, it was used for many centuries because of its very simplicity which made it easily applicable to any chant as an improvised embellishment. When Pope John XXII in 1332 interdicted the use of polyphony in church—polyphony had by then become extremely refined—he made an exception in favour of parallel organum.

The first step away from the rigid parallelism is made in the *Musica enchiriadis* itself. The author describes a modified manner of singing in which the singers of the two parts start and end in unison, using parallel motion for the middle portion of each phrase. This may be called converging organum and is illustrated in the *Musica enchiriadis* by *Rex Coeli*.

Rex Coeli. MASTERPIECES OF MUSIC BEFORE 1750, VOL. I. HAYDN SOCIETY HSL 2071.

The parallel motion here is in fourths, not in fifths. In fact, an organum of the fourth, modified by converging motion, and occasionally interspersed with a fifth or a third, seems to have been the prevailing type of polyphonic music in the tenth and early eleventh centuries. It was not until the second half of the eleventh century that free organum emerged. This is characterized by the gradual abandonment of parallel motion, and by the introduction of various intervals—now an octave, now a fifth, now a fourth, a third, another fifth, etc. Consequently, the parts often move in contrary motion; the added voice moves upwards when the *cantus firmus* moves down, and vice versa. In the old organum the *cantus firmus* was always on top and the additional part was below it. In the free organum the parts frequently cross, so that the Gregorian melody is now above, now below the other part.

There exist a number of treatises in which this novel style is described. One by an unknown author, *Ad organum faciendum* (*How to Make Organum*), is exclusively devoted to polyphonic music, and the author declares it to be much superior to a plain melody. Another author is Johannes Cotto (*c.* 1100), who may have been an Englishman and is therefore often referred to as John Cotton. He recommends careful attention to the variety of motion.

There also exist a number of musical sources, and though most of the compositions cannot be read clearly, five or six pieces can be quite reliably transcribed. Particularly interesting are those in a manuscript from Chartres in northern France. These are not short didactic pieces, but actual compositions of some extension. They indicate the beginning of a later development in which polyphonic composition was applied primarily to the responsorial chants, i.e. the gradual and alleluia. The term 'organum' underwent a certain change of meaning in this connection and came to refer to compositions based on a few special types of chant instead of to a general method of polyphonic treatment. The alleluias from the Chartres manuscript also illustrate an important principle that remained valid throughout the further development of organum: to provide polyphonic treatment only for the soloist sections of the chant, while the choral sections were sung in plain-song. So such a composition consists of an alternation of polyphony and plain-song.

Alleluia Angelus Domini. HISTORY OF MUSIC IN SOUND, VOL. II. VICTOR LM 6015 (HMV HMS 16, 78 r.p.m.).

By far the most extensive source of eleventh-century organa is the manuscript preserved at Corpus Christi College, Cambridge, and known as the *Winchester Troper.* It contains a repertoire of more than one hundred and sixty organal parts. More than one-third of this repertoire of eleventh-century polyphony are alleluias, and the responsories are equally numerous, while graduals are entirely absent. A hundred years later, in the school of Notre-Dame, the graduals occupy an equally important place with the alleluias and the responsories.

The twelfth century is a period of flowering and fulfilment after a long interval of relative stagnation. The feeling of dread that attended the arrival of the year 1000 did not quickly pass, and throughout the eleventh century there prevailed a mood of anxiety. A new enthusiasm for life and activity is only felt at the end of this century and finds its first expression in the First Crusade of 1094. It came to full efflorescence in the twelfth century, which saw the rise of the Gothic cathedrals, the founding of the first universities, the revival of classical Latinity, and the love poetry of the troubadours and trouvères.

Polyphonic music in the twelfth century progresses much more rapidly, and for the first time a centre of activity, or school of music, appears at the monastery of St Martial at Limoges in southern France. From the tenth century on St Martial had contributed monophonic additions to Gregorian Chant, and in the early part of the twelfth century we find the first evidence of polyphonic music there. The novel style that developed at St Martial is called *melismatic organum.* In the earlier types of organum the additional part provided just one note to each note of the *cantus firmus.* We now find a tendency to treat the additional part in a more extended and exuberant fashion, with groups of notes, or shorter or longer melismas, against a single note of the Gregorian

c

melody.   While the note-against-note principle still prevails in the
St Martial organa, it is often interrupted by a melisma.   Whenever
it occurs, it means that the singer of the *cantus firmus* part will have
to sustain his note until the other singer has arrived at the end of
the group of notes.   If melismas of ten or twenty notes occur in
succession, the single tones of the *cantus firmus* will be drawn out
into a series of long sustained notes.   So the term 'tenor' was
introduced.   It derived from the Latin word *tenere*, 'to hold,' and
was used to denote a part consisting of long-held notes.   This
seems more plausible than the explanation usually given; that the
tenor is the part that 'holds' the Gregorian melody.   Actually it
fulfils both functions at the same time.

Our examples of melismatic organum are first an *Agnus Dei*
with only a few and short melismas at the beginning, and then two
which are based on the *Benedicamus Domino* melody which has
already been used as an illustration.   This appears as the lower
part, and above it the upper part moves in free and quite expressive
melismas.   In the first *Benedicamus Domino* the melismas do not
go beyond groups of six or seven notes, but in the second we find
a richly melismatic style, occasionally with twenty notes in a group.
Consequently the lower part is considerably drawn out, into a
real tenor.

  (i) *Agnus Dei*.   MASTERPIECES OF MUSIC BEFORE 1750, VOL. I.
     HAYDN SOCIETY HSL 2071.
 (ii) *Benedicamus Domino* (1).   INDIANA UNIVERSITY *Collegium Musicum*.
(iii) *Benedicamus Domino* (2).   MASTERPIECES OF MUSIC BEFORE 1750,
     VOL. I.   HAYDN SOCIETY HSL 2071.

(APPENDIX: *See* page 72.)

7

Willi Apel

THE NOTRE-DAME SCHOOL

ABOUT the middle of the twelfth century the leadership in music shifted from southern France to its northern part. In secular monophony the troubadours give way to the trouvères, and in polyphonic music the school of St Martial in Limoges is followed by the school of Notre-Dame in Paris. In 1163 the foundation was laid for the cathedral of Notre-Dame, that magnificent testimonial to the greatness of medieval art which was to become one of the most important centres of musical activity. For the first time in the development of polyphony, musical creation steps out of the darkness of anonymity and becomes associated with composers known to us by name: Leoninus and Perotinus. Leoninus flourished in the second half of the twelfth century, Perotinus from about 1180 to 1220.

A good deal of information about these men and their work has been preserved in a treatise generally referred to as *Anonymous IV*. Possibly the nameless writer of this document was a young Englishman who studied at the University of Paris near the end of the thirteenth century and attended lectures on music there. He tells us that Magister Leoninus was a great composer of organa and wrote a number of such compositions which became known as 'The Great Book of Organa.' This book has been preserved in several manuscripts and contains forty-six compositions which form a liturgical cycle. A study of them reveals interesting principles of composition. As in the earlier organa, only the solo sections of the liturgical chants are composed, so that the performance involves an alternation between plain-song and polyphony.

The polyphonic sections are composed in an expansive melismatic style, with melismas of many notes against a single note of the lower part, which thus consists of a succession of long sustained notes, or pedal points (to use the term from organ playing).

Occasionally, however, we find passages in which the two parts proceed simultaneously, almost note against note. These two contrasting methods, characteristic of Notre-Dame, are known respectively as organal style and descant style. The difference between the two is outlined for us by an anonymous theorist as early as *c.* 1150. While in the organa of St Martial the two styles are employed more or less haphazardly, in the organa of Notre-Dame they are conditioned by the character of the plain-song melody which forms the basis of the composition. Every gradual or alleluia includes a few words or syllables that are sung to a long group of notes. It is obviously impracticable to compose such a group, a melisma in itself, in a melismatic style, because of the inordinate extension that would result. Leoninus therefore composes such passages in the concise style of *discantus*.

Leoninus has an undeniable claim to fame in the field of rhythm. It is in his works that, for the first time, we find incontestable evidence of strictly measured note values, of regular beats, and of metre. In the descant sections the tenor consists of a succession of notes of exactly equal duration, each to the value of a modern crotchet. To each of these notes correspond two or three notes of the upper part, which subdivide the crotchet into smaller values. Thus was born metrical rhythm, though naturally the rhythm of Leoninus proceeds in very simple patterns, mainly in a constant alternation of a long and of a short value, a crochet and a quaver. Such a combination results in triple metre, and indeed this is invariably employed, not only in the works of Leoninus, but till the end of the thirteenth century. It was considered the perfect metre, being modelled after nature, which in thirteenth-century philosophy always had three parts—beginning, middle, and end.

We may take as an example of the music of Leoninus his organum *Haec Dies*, which consists of an alternation of two-voice polyphony and plain-song. In the opening polyphonic section the upper part traces highly expressive lines above the sustained notes of the lower part. The second polyphonic section, after the plain-song, includes a number of descant passages which represent the modern element in this music. If these are somewhat less impressive, it is because the method is less mature.

Leoninus: *Haec Dies*. INDIANA UNIVERSITY *Collegium Musicum*.

The author of *Anonymous IV* tells us that Leoninus's successor,

Perotinus Magnus, was an even greater composer and excelled as a composer of *discantus*. Abandoning the ecstatic declamations of the older tradition, Perotinus established a style remarkable for its limpid clarity, its rationalistic lucidity, its geometrical rigidity. His most conspicuous contribution to the development of musical style was that he established the principles of writing in three and even in four parts, *organa tripla* and *organa quadrupla*. These are monumental works of great extension, and noteworthy for their organal sections, in which a single note of the tenor is extended into a pedal point of thirty or forty or more measures, while the upper parts move along in regular phrases of four measures and in simple rhythms of an almost dance-like quality. Quite frequently the parts are related to each other by the restatement of short motives, and in the organa of Perotinus we find for the first time in music history evidence of the technique of imitation.

One of Perotinus's *organa tripla* is *Alleluia Nativitas*. It begins with two relatively short pedal points, on F and G, continues with a passage in descant style, and closes with a pedal point on G, and in the last section you will notice what has been called dance-style in Perotinus. (The record contains only the beginning of the *Alleluia*.)

Perotinus: *Alleluia Nativitas*. MASTERPIECES OF MUSIC BEFORE 1750, VOL. I. HAYDN SOCIETY HSL 2071.

The artistic culmination of Perotinus's art is represented by his four-voice organum *Viderunt Omnes*. Its opening section is a sixty-measure pedal point on F over which the three upper parts form a constantly moving superstructure that may perhaps be described as a fluctuating or vibrating F major chord. I would almost compare it to a granitic block emitting sonorous vibrations as if under the impact of a giant's hammer stroke. After the tension built up by the seemingly interminable dwelling on the F major sonority, the sudden change to A minor has a truly dramatic impact, the like of which is hardly found in music for many centuries.

Perotinus's organa stand at the end of the development of this great form of early medieval polyphony. During the thirteenth century two other forms become prominent: the *conductus* and the *motet*. The conductus differs from the organum, first of all, in being an entirely free work of art, both textually and musically.

The organa are invariably based on a Gregorian text and melody, but the conductus are free compositions of Latin poems. These poems are interesting for their variety of subject matter; some give expression to religious feelings, others are contemplative, moralizing, accusing, satirizing, or political. As for the freedom of musical treatment, the famous theorist of the thirteenth century, Franco of Cologne, says: 'He who wants to compose a conductus, must first invent a melody as beautiful as possible. He should then employ this as a tenor to add the other parts.' Perhaps the most striking difference between an organum and a conductus is in their treatment of the text. In an organum practically every syllable of the text is greatly extended, so that the composition consists of a succession of vocalizations. In the conductus the text is treated with just one note to each syllable, and pronounced simultaneously in all the parts, obviously to make the text clearly audible. As an example of the conductus we may take *Veri floris sub figura*.

Conductus: *Veri floris sub figura*. HISTORY OF MUSIC IN SOUND, VOL. II. VICTOR LM 6015 (HMV HMS 18, 78 r.p.m.).

Not all conductus are as simple as that example, and many include more or less extended vocalizations which served as a sort of prelude, interlude, or postlude for the declamation of the text. They were called *caudae* (Latin: 'tail') and were much admired, at least by skilled singers. There are some conductus in which the *caudae* outweigh the passages with text. We may take as an example *De castitatis thalamo*, a conductus that opens and closes with a melisma of moderate extension. 'That pure nuptial chamber, a virgin's womb, is the special place provided by the Father for the Son. In all the world, where could one find the like, that could hold the Son, the equal of the Father.'

Conductus: *De castitatis thalamo*. MASTERPIECES OF MUSIC BEFORE 1750, VOL. I. HAYDN SOCIETY HSL 2071.

The conductus as a musical form appeared in the middle of the twelfth century, and a hundred years later was practically obsolete . . . one of the last examples dates from 1248. The reason for its sudden disappearance is, no doubt, that another form had grown up and was showing possibilities of development that the conductus could not match. In fact, this new form, the motet, was destined to lead a longer life than any other form in the entire history of music; from *c.* 1200 without interruption for more than five hundred years to the time of Bach. It underwent so many changes in its long life that it is practically impossible to find a definition that would be universally valid. Normally it is a sacred composition based on a Latin text, but there are many motets that fill neither requirement.

To observe the motet in its nascent stage we have to turn back to the organa of Leoninus and Perotinus, and to the organal style and descant style used in them. The strictly measured descant sections, based on the melismas of Gregorian Chant, were frequently replaced by new compositions deriving from the melismas, but having different melodies in the upper part or parts. These substitute compositions, known as *clausula*, were soon regarded as independent pieces unconnected with the organum from which they originated. A clausula, therefore, is a short composition in strict triple metre, based on a melisma to a single word of a Gregorian Chant. From beginning to end it is a vocalization. The final step was to abolish the vocalization in the upper part by providing a full text, and the clausula was transformed into the motet. The simplest type of motet is a composition in two parts, in which the lower part, the tenor, is sung to a single syllable or vowel, while the upper part is sung to a full text.

In the earliest stage of the motet the text was a Latin religious poem which provided a commentary on the single word sung by the tenor or to the Gregorian Chant from which this word is taken. The motet provided the opportunity to write new poetry which, however, received liturgical sanction through its connection with the words symbolic of the great thoughts of Christian faith. We may judge how this opportunity filled a need by the fact that soon motets were written in three parts, with each of the two upper parts provided with a text of its own, and the tenor part singing the single word. An example is the motet *O Maria Virgo Davidica*. The tenor has the word *Veritatem* (Verity), which together with the melody is taken from the Gradual for the Feast of the Assumption, *Propter Veritatem*. The two upper parts are a commentary upon the idea of the Assumption. One text pictures Mary, virgin of David's line, as giving her commands in the citadel of heaven. The other speaks of Mary as the hope of sinners and the fountain of pardon.

Motet: *O Maria Virgo Davidica*. HISTORY OF MUSIC IN SOUND, VOL II. VICTOR LM 6015 (HMV HMS 19, 78 r.p.m.).

One of the strangest phenomena in the history of medieval polyphony is that only a few decades after the appearance of the motet we find what are called French motets. In these works the upper part no longer has a Latin religious text, but a French text that has a decidedly secular, and indeed usually amorous, tone. These French motets are not new compositions, for their music is identical with that of one of the Latin motets. There are hundreds of examples. In some there is one Latin text and one French text in the upper parts, but in the later part of the thirteenth century the Latin text tends to be replaced by a second French text. Our example has the tenor *Eius in Oriente*, taken from the Mass for the Epiphany; one upper part sings 'When I see the roses budding . . .' and the other, 'Now in truth, whatever they tell us, Let Robin be my love.'

Motet: *En non diu*. MASTERPIECES OF MUSIC BEFORE 1750, VOL. I. HAYDN SOCIETY HSL 2071.

In these two chapters we have surveyed early polyphony from the ninth to the end of the thirteenth century. Throughout this long period the main development took place in France, but there was musical activity in Spain and England too. England can furnish us with two particularly interesting examples.

The first is the famous *Sumer is icumen in*, the oldest existing canon or round, and the second is one of the few specimens of instrumental music of the thirteenth century that have survived. It is a dance tune written in two parts, and consisting of a number of four-measure phrases arranged in pairs, each pair having the same melody. At the beginning these restated melodies are in the lower part, but later they appear in the upper part where they are more clearly heard.

(i) *Sumer is icumen in*; (ii) *English dance tune*. HISTORY OF MUSIC IN SOUND, VOL. II. VICTOR LM 6015 (HMV HMS 17/18, 78 r.p.m.).

(APPENDIX: *See* page 72.)

8

Denis Stevens

THE *ARS NOVA* IN FRANCE

THE *Ars Nova*, or new art, of the fourteenth century is so called after a theoretical treatise by the composer Philippe de Vitry (1291–1361) which brought about a turning-point in the development of medieval music and a new orientation in the art of composition. One of the fundamental innovations of the new musical art was the liberation of rhythm from its idealistic fetters. This may be judged by comparing the rhythmic flow of two pieces of music, one from the thirteenth century, the other from the fourteenth. The first is a ballade by the trouvère, Adam de la Halle: *Dieu soit en cette maison*. It is what we generally call a *chanson de quête*—a song that the children sing at Christmas when asking for alms. It is not quite a carol, for a carol has a more popular feeling and style, but the text is about the birth of Christ, and at the end of each verse there is a refrain 'May God dwell in this house, and may there be wealth and joy in plenty.' We should compare the slow, peaceful rhythm of that ballade with a fourteenth-century ballade by Guillaume de Machaut: *Je puis trop bien*. It is a short love-lyric for one singer and two or three instruments. 'I can all too well compare my lady to the image which Pygmalion made; it was of ivory, so beautiful, without peer, that he loved it more than Jason did Medea. Out of his senses, he prayed to it unceasingly, but the image answered him not. Thus does she treat me who makes my heart melt, for I pray her ever, and she answers me not.'

(i) Adam de la Halle: *Dieu soit en cette maison*. DECCA ARC 3002 (DGG APM 14018).
(ii) Guillaume de Machaut: *Je puis trop bien*. ANTHOLOGIE SONORE AS 3 (AS 67, 78 r.p.m.) (alt. DGG APM 14063).

The pulse in Machaut's song is faster and more vital and shows us that it stems from a different school of musical thought. Adam de la Halle's rhythms are peaceful, majestic, and self-effacing: Machaut's are clear, concise, with an almost modern lilt. In fact, his ballade is written in what we should call 6/8 time—two main pulses in a bar, with each pulse divided into three—and this subdivision of the basic time-unit was an important feature of *Ars Nova* style and notation. The late thirteenth-century motet writers nearly all used triple rhythm, and they were known as exponents of the old art, *Ars Antiqua*. The new art, first formulated and practised by Philippe de Vitry, was warmly supported by many of his friends. One of them was Jean de Muris, who was a great philospher and mathematician as well as an authority on music, and we may see how the medieval mind looked on these matters from his treatise *Ars Novae Musicae*. Jean de Muris tells us first about the older fashion of composition, based on triple measure:

That all perfection is implicit in the ternary number follows from many likely conjectures. For in God, who is most perfect, there is one substance, yet three persons; He is threefold, yet one, and one, yet threefold; very great therefore is the correspondence of unity to trinity. At first, in knowledge, are the separate and the concrete; from these, under the ternary number, the composite is derived. At first, in celestial bodies, are the thing moving, the thing moved, and time. Three attributes in stars and sun—heat, light, splendour; in elements—action, passion, matter; in individuals—generation, corruption, dissolution; in all finite time—beginning, middle, end; in all curable diseases—rise, climax, decline . . . every object, if it is ever to stand, has three dimensions.

But de Muris was a member of the group of innovators and he was not content to leave music in the everlasting clutches of triple time. He continues:

Since the ternary number is everywhere present in some form or other, it may no longer be doubted that it is perfect. And by the contrary of this proposition, the binary number, since it falls short of the ternary, also since it is thus of lower rank, is left imperfect.

So it came about that the system of notation we know and use to-day was based on the relationship of triple and duple rhythm, and the subdivision of time, which de Muris tells us 'is endlessly divisible to infinity.' Shorter note-values began to be used, and these gave music the possibility of moving at a quicker pace. We can appreciate this best by listening to the speed and flexibility of the instrumental piece usually called *Le Moulin de Paris*.

Le Moulin de Paris. HISTORY OF MUSIC IN SOUND, VOL III. VICTOR LM 6016 (HMV HMS 20, 78 r.p.m.).

In examining the work of the troubadours and trouvères we saw how closely connected were the twin arts of music and poetry. Indeed, one of the troubadours said that 'verse without music is like a mill without water.' In the fourteenth century there was still a close alliance between the two arts. For example, the practice grew up of interpolating music in long poems called *romans*. It is easy to see why this was done; if the poem was not sung in the manner of certain of the *chansons de geste*, music was needed to bring contrast and relief to the spoken word.

One of the most famous of these poems is *Le Roman de Fauvel*. It is a biting attack on the vices of the times in the form of an allegory; Fauvel, a horse, personifies all the evils inherent in the life of early fourteenth-century France. The letters of the name Flauvel stood for six of these vices: Flattery, Avarice, Usury, Variability, Envy, and Lowness. If we examine part of the text of one of the motets in the poem we can see the vein of thought that runs through it. The first voice sings that forsaken Mother Church sees herself despised by her sons, the sinful clerics. Simultaneously another voice sings 'She who raised on high the children she had nourished, now, scorned, finds by proof that they are impious.' Beneath these two voices is the tenor, an instrumental part, whose melody is taken from a plain-song source. In this case the words of that source, significantly enough, echo the sentiments expressed by the other two voices: 'I have nourished and brought up children, and they have rebelled against me.' While that text from Isaiah would not be heard during the performance of the motet, listeners would recognize the plain-song melody and immediately think of the text that went with it. That particular motet has not been recorded, but another of the 160 pieces from *Le Roman de Fauvel* can be heard. Again there are two supporting texts, but this time all three are sung.

Je vois douleur. ANTHOLOGIE SONORE AS 2.

The cleverness of medieval music is sometimes so great as to discourage us from listening carefully: we know that several different texts are being sung simultaneously, and that remarkable features in form and structure are present, yet we seem powerless to take them all in at once. In my opinion these many separate elements never were meant to be appreciated all at once, any more than a medieval cathedral was meant to be seen all at once. All must be studied singly before the complete work assumes its fullest significance.

Sometimes these medieval subtleties are used for expressive means—the device whereby one voice takes up the theme a few beats later, in canon, is used to give the effects of hunters' calls in a lively, anonymous composition of the mid-fourteenth century: *Si je chant main.*

> *Si je chant main.* HISTORY OF MUSIC IN SOUND, VOL. III. VICTOR LM 6016 (HMV HMS 20, 78 r.p.m.).

In spite of the individual excellence of many other works, one man dominates French music in the fourteenth century: Guillaume de Machaut. He was born at the very beginning of the century and lived until 1377, having in the course of a long and varied career been a priest, a secretary of King John of Bohemia, a poet and musician, and finally a canon of Rheims. Some of Machaut's writings are autobiographical, and we know from these sources that he travelled widely through Italy, Poland, and Bohemia while in the service of King John. Machaut's contribution to musical history is a great one; he unified the many divergent aspects of the *Ars Nova* style, welding them into a solid and recognizable musical achievement. His works have only just recently been made available in complete form for the purpose of study and perform-ance, and the task was a difficult one; *Ars Nova* notation is often very complex and the music is scattered throughout many manu-scripts in different countries.

The problems of performance may be illustrated from two different realizations of his great Mass. The first example is rather fanciful; while instruments did take part in the earliest performances of the Mass, it is a matter for conjecture whether they sounded as brassy as on the first recording. My own feeling is that the instruments blended more with the voices, rather than standing out apart from them, and the recording of the *Benedictus* is more sober, though none the less interesting.

> Machaut: *Mass of Notre-Dame.* (i) CONCERT HALL CHS 1107 (complete) (alt. DGG APM 14063); (ii) HISTORY OF MUSIC IN SOUND, VOL III. VICTOR LM 6016 (Benedictus only) (HMV HMS 21, 78 r.p.m.).

Machaut was one of the first composers to make extensive use of a medieval device known as *isorhythm*, i.e. 'equal rhythm.' An isorhythmic piece is one in which a set rhythmic pattern of notes and rests is repeated at certain fixed intervals throughout the entire work. Sometimes these patterns of notes and rests were restricted to the tenor; occasionally all the voice-parts were isorhythmic, and the composer had to see to it that his rhythmic schemes were faithfully echoed in each part as the composition proceeded. The true subtlety was that each scheme in each voice-part could live its own life, so that the final effect, instead of being one of extreme rigidity, actually sounded varied and full of colour.

Machaut's famous composition based on the plain-song *David* has an isorhythmic tenor of great interest. Above the tenor two independent parts weave a complex web of sound, one taking over from the other with a rapidity and verve which is typical of the *hocket*. This is the name usually given to this form of 'broken music,' for the lines are really broken up and shared between the two voice-parts. Played by instruments (as on the recording), the effect is very striking; sung by voices, it could be much less so, and was even known to goad the higher ecclesiastics into almost frenzied diatribes. Machaut's two hocketing parts are brilliantly contrived; so too is his tenor, which repeats the plain-song three times over an eightfold rhythmic scheme of repetition, following this with a final statement of the melody over a fourfold rhythmic scheme, quite different in outline.

Machaut: *Hoquetus David*. OISEAU-LYRE, OL 3 (78 r.p.m.).

Machaut's genius inevitably brought into being a school of followers, some of whom carried his subtleties and complexities to incredible lengths. Music of the late fourteenth century, such as was heard at the papal court in Avignon and the courts of the Aragon princes (mostly by French composers), is still very little known. It ill deserves neglect, however, for it has a lyrical vein tinged with mysticism, and a charm that is at once fragile and impressive. Something like it may be heard in the totally isorhythmic motet *A vous vierge de doucour* by an anonymous composer. The text of the uppermost voice is in French: 'To you, sweet Virgin, whom I adore, I wish to give my service from now onwards, leaving aside of my own free will all other foolish loves, without delay.' Beneath this, another voice sings in Latin:

'Weeping, I come to Thee, O Virgin, Mother of God, in Thee do I take refuge.'

The instrumental tenor, *Regnum Mundi*, is based on a responsory, and is played on the record by a hurdy-gurdy.

A vous vierge de doucour. OISEAU-LYRE OL 2 (78 r.p.m.).

Another anonymous piece from the same period, and one very popular then, is truly remarkable for its vivid portrayal of bird songs and the sound of instruments. The singer calls out to his lady to wake up, for it is sunrise and the lark is chirping away merrily. It has no isorhythmic structure, nothing that seems in the remotest degree learned. The piece seems to come to us from the very springtime of music; it makes us realize that the composer, whoever he was, knew the art of writing joyous music, free from care and anxiety, full of life and vigour. 'Now then play up, drums and pipes . . . come on, good fellows, let's go and dance: it's all for you, my lady, whose honour may God increase.' In between each phrase the singer imitates the sound of the bagpipes, and instruments imitate the singer—an outpouring of medieval *joie de vivre* which is unique among the entire output, wonderful as it is, of the *Ars Nova* composers.

Or sus, vous dormes trop. OISEAU-LYRE OL 3 (78 r.p.m.).

(APPENDIX: *See* page 72.)

9

Denis Stevens

THE *ARS NOVA* IN ITALY

Musical culture in fourteenth-century Italy was as rich, as varied, and as lively as the literary culture which is prized through the writings of Petrarch and Boccaccio. It had links with French music, but its basic principles of notation, together with its use of forms and styles, was entirely Italian. The starting-point of Italian *Ars Nova* music was in the ideas and examples of Petrus de Cruce rather than Philippe de Vitry, for, though both were Frenchmen, they had widely differing conceptions of musical style and notation.

Petrus de Cruce held that it was possible to divide the breve into two, three, four, five, six, or seven equal parts. Liberty such as this was entirely contrary to the logic of the French, who found all the variety they needed in duple and triple rhythmic combinations. The Italians also welcomed the relatively more simple notation advocated by Petrus de Cruce. At least two dozen Italian composers have left us examples of their music, and if we compare the sound of it with French *Ars Nova* music, we can see immediately how distinctive a personality the Italian composers had.

It has been customary to divide this group of composers into three generations, but it would be incorrect to think of this century's musical culture as beginning in the year 1300 and ending in 1399. There is a slight forward displacement which fits in with other aspects of Italian art and culture, so that we must think of the true *trecento* as extending from about 1325 to 1425. Florence was most responsible for the encouragement of music and poetry, and her name can be heard in connection with many composers of the second, perhaps the greatest of the three groups. Among the earlier men one hears the names of northern cities: Jacopo da Bologna, Grazioso da Padua, Vincenzo da Rimini. The same is true of the third generation, which flourished from about 1390 onwards: Matteo da Perugia, Giovanni da Genoa, Anthonello da Caserta, Bartolomeo da Bologna. Francesco Landini, greatest of them all, heads the brilliant group of composers whose songs filled the villas of the Florentine nobility from the middle of the century until just before its close: Paolo da Firenze, Ghirardello da Firenze, Lorenzo da Firenze, Andrea da Firenze.

We may begin with the *Ars Nova* madrigal, a very different kind of music from the sixteenth-century madrigal. Fundamentally it is a verse form, with music so arranged to fit into its particular scheme of repetition. We may take as an example the madrigal for two voices only by Jacopo da Bologna: *Non al suo amante*, 'Never did Diana so please her lover, when he was fortunate enough to see her bathing in the cool waters, as the rustic shepherdess pleases me when she washes the white veil which shall protect her fair hair from sun and breeze, so that it made me, now that the sky is fiery, all tremble with the chill of love.'

Jacopo da Bologna: *Non al suo amante*.   Oiseau-Lyre OL 1 (78 r.p.m.).

The sparse, two-part texture is a little hard to get used to at first, but there is no doubt that it gives the voices a chance to shine in a way that they never could in the Renaissance madrigal, with its richly interwoven voice-parts and constant use of imitation. The Italian madrigal was a model of clarity and elegance, serving as a vehicle for the sensitive and subtle portrayal of the picture in the poet's mind, as well as for the virtuosity and emotional range of the singers. Those florid introductions have more than a faint foretaste of the peculiarly Mediterranean type of singing that we now know as *cante flamenco*.

Not all fourteenth-century madrigals were like *Non al suo amante*. Landini, for example, wrote three madrigals in three-part texture, and each one has a special point of interest. One of them had the two lower voice-parts in canon, and then as the piece moves towards its close, the canon is extended to all three voice-parts. Another madrigal makes use of the French device of isorhythm and is through-composed instead of repetitive. The third has a different text for each voice-part, though the texts all come from the same poem, and they may possibly have been sung in succession, and not simultaneously.

Far more numerous than the madrigals were the *ballate*, easily the most popular musical style and the one always referred to by poets and novelists in their accounts of the social life of the times.

Francesco Landini: *Amar si li alti tuo gentil costum*. HISTORY OF MUSIC IN SOUND, VOL. III. VICTOR LM 6016 (HMV HMS 22, 78 r.p.m.).

There are many references to dances and dance-tunes in the *Decameron*, and some of the tunes have been preserved in a handsomely written manuscript in the British Museum. There are fifteen dances in this manuscript, some being called *istampite*, some *saltarelli*, and one of them a *trotto*. They are written down as single-line melodies, but it is quite possible that they were performed with some accompaniment—a passage in the *Decameron* mentions a lute and a viol being brought out for the performance of dance music.

Saltarello. Vox PL 8110 (E).

To turn now from the kinds of music to the composer, we may consider the life and art of Francesco Landini. The inscription on his tombstone in the church of San Lorenzo, Florence, reads: 'Deprived of the light, Francesco, whom alone Music extols above all others for his great intellect, and his organ music, rests his ashes here, his soul above the stars.' When quite young, Francesco lost his sight as the result of smallpox. By hard work and determination he turned this grave disadvantage into an asset, learning an astonishing amount of music by heart, and developing to an unheard-of degree the art of improvisation. From his childhood up he was surrounded by artists and men of letters and his grand-nephew spoke of Francesco's learning in astrology and philosophy. He studied music with Jacopo da Bologna, spent some time in Verona, participated in a musical competition with another famous composer, Giovanni da Cascia, and in 1346 was commissioned to provide music for the birth of two Visconti princes in Milan. He also travelled to Venice, receiving there from the King of Cyprus a laurel wreath in recognition of his excellent poetry—one member of the jury, incidentally, was Petrarch.

In Florence Francesco was admired and loved by all who knew him. Yet he must often have felt acutely conscious of his lack of sight, for he even mentions it in the text of one of his madrigals, saying that a bird, deprived of light and vision, tends to fly ever higher in search of liberty and heaven. This was true of the composer himself; he explored every known musical and poetic avenue in the endeavour to find the summit of inspiration. So we find that one famous scholar of modern times has called one of his *ballate* 'perhaps the most beautiful work of the century.' This is *Gram piant'agli occhi*: 'Wretched with weeping and heavy with sorrow is he who is about to die, and so, with this bitter and passionate song I call upon death, yet he will not hear me. Even though I live, I never wish to follow anyone but you, my dearest star and sweetest love.'

Landini: *Gram piant'agli occhi*. Decca ARC 3003 (DGG APM 14019).

Although Francesco's compositions were undoubtedly popular during his lifetime, it was his organ-playing that was most admired. Many vivid details of his playing are recaptured by the writer Giovanni del Prato. He says that a fascinating experiment with the birds took place one morning when the sun was coming up. Francesco was asked to play a little on his organ to see if the singing of the birds would lessen or increase. As soon as the playing began, many of the birds became silent; then they redoubled their singing, and strange to say, one of the nightingales came and perched on a branch above Francesco's head.

The subject of Landini's texts in his vocal music was not always love; he could be light-hearted when the occasion demanded, as we see from his fishing-song *Cosi pensoso*. This is really a variant of the *caccia*, literally a hunting-song which made use of the device of canon between the two upper voices, the lowest voice being in free style. This *pesca*, or fishing-song, is sung by two tenors with instrumental accompaniment, and tells of the cries of the crawfishers that a lover hears as he walks thoughtfully along the beach.

Landini: *Cosi pensoso*. Decca ARC 3003 (DGG APM 14019).

The use of canon, with one voice following another rapidly with the same music and text, helps to make the scene more vivid and the action more vigorous. Only twenty examples of the *caccia* have come down to us, but they nearly all exhibit the same features, though the subjects of their texts differ widely. As well as hunting scenes some depict the noise and bustle of market scenes, and others the excitement of a house catching fire. We may take as an example a regular *caccia* by Ghirardello da Firenze which describes a hunting trip from getting up in the morning to the finding of the quarry and the sounding of the horn.

Ghirardello da Firenze: *Tosto che l'alba*. Decca ARC 3003 (DGG APM 14019).

Even though the principle of the *caccia* was known and used in France as the *chasse*, even though we ourselves sing in canon and call the result a 'catch,' there is nothing quite like a fourteenth-century Italian *caccia*. It was a frankly descriptive piece of music in which the composer was free to make up his text and his own musical themes, the only proviso being that the two upper voices should sing the same part, slightly out of step. If we find such a readiness to relax in the dance tunes too, it is worth remembering that not all such tunes were frivolous. The opening of *Lamento di Tristano* does indeed sound like a lament, with its solemn yearning tones enhanced by the stringed instrument. Even so, the pace soon becomes more lively and the melodic instruments are joined by a drum. This second section is called *La Rotta* (possibly named after a medieval stringed instrument), and serves as an after-dance to the *Lamento di Tristano* rather as the galliard followed the pavane in the sixteenth century.

Lamento di Tristano. Vox PL 8110 (E).

Very few religious pieces were written by the *Ars Nova* composers, and indeed they were discouraged from writing polyphonic settings of liturgical texts by the Bull of Pope John XXII, issued in Avignon in 1324. Italian composers did not, however, cease altogether in their endeavours to find a new musical vehicle for the liturgy. In the manuscript containing the dance tunes that I have mentioned, there is an anonymous *Gloria* and *Credo* which show quite outstanding if somewhat untraditional artistry. These pieces were undoubtedly meant for performance by a soloist of considerable ability, for they are not easy to sing and call for an amazing degree of perfection in the ensemble. Something very much like it can be heard in the setting of the *Gloria* by Matteo da Perugia, who flourished in the late fourteenth and early fifteenth centuries. The florid writing for the voices and the unusual declamation of the texts comes as a surprise at first, yet we know there is sincerity here.

Matteo da Perugia: *Gloria*. Oiseau-Lyre OL 1 (78 r.p.m.).

Even Landini is known to have written some motets, but unfortunately they have not survived in complete form. The kind of music he would play for the *Kyrie* at his church in Florence may be judged from a recently discovered manuscript containing keyboard music. It includes a set of organ verses for the *Kyrie* which would have been played in alternation with the singing of the plain-song. The composer, whoever he was, kept the plain-song almost intact in the lowest voice and added typically Italian decorative passages for the right hand. Thus this Faenza manuscript may be said to contain the earliest known example of the organ Mass, a style which was not to be practised in Italy again until the time of Cavazzoni in the early sixteenth century.

Jacopo da Bologna, like many of his contemporaries, made use of the madrigal and *caccia* forms even when he wrote liturgical music, not through any spirit of levity, but out of a genuine regard for the need to extend the frontiers of musical art. His motet *Lux purpurata radiis* is for two male voices and one instrument, and, like his madrigal *Non al suo amante*, the texture is clear, interesting, and undeniably Italian.

Jacopo da Bologna: *Lux purpurata radiis.* Oiseau-Lyre OL 2 (78 r.p.m.).

(Appendix: *See* page 72.)

10

Denis Stevens

GUILLAUME DUFAY

UNTIL quite recently the years between Guillaume de Machaut and Guillaume Dufay were an historical no man's land in the otherwise unbroken procession of musicians in France. Those years saw the refinement of musical composition to a degree that has rarely been witnessed before or since, and it engendered the inevitable reaction. The new trend of the fifteenth century was in the direction of simplicity; that is, relative simplicity, for while it would be idle to suggest that the Burgundian court composers could be in any way naïve, they did cultivate what we might call a lighter touch. Certainly the chansons of Dufay and his colleagues (and their religious music to a certain extent) possess a translucent, untrammelled aspect when compared with the works of their immediate forbears. They gained in expressiveness as well as in melodic charm, but they lost almost entirely that vein of mysticism which is peculiar to the immediate followers of Machaut.

A French poet, Martin le Franc, has given us a revealing account of the transition from one style to the other in his poem *Le Champion des Dames*, composed around 1441. He names three of the most famous followers of Machaut and says their music was not 'filled with such goodly melody . . . as Binchois sings or Dufay.' He refers too to 'pleasing concord' and 'the English guise' and music that is 'gay and bright.' It seems that the new style was to some extent an imported one, for the links between French and English music were especially close at the time. The English musicians, conservative in taste, had rejected the over-subtlety of the followers of Machaut and had cultivated their favourite method of descant, smooth and sonorous, easy to compose and ravishing to hear.

Beata Viscera. HISTORY OF MUSIC IN SOUND, VOL. II. VICTOR LM 6015 (HMV HMS 18, 78 r.p.m.).

It was such mellifluous strains that caused the reactions against
the mannered complexity of Machaut's successors, and it was just
this static, peaceful quality that the early Burgundian composers
sought to emulate.   Sometimes they did it with an almost self-
conscious vigour, setting nearly impossible tasks to be overcome,
as when Nicole Grenon takes as the basis for his song *Je ne
requier de ma dame* a particularly angular and volatile contratenor
from a work by Matteo da Perugia.   Grenon looks upon this
contratenor as a challenge to his skill in making a song, and so
carefully does he add the two remaining voice-parts that the effect
is completely placid and far removed from anything rough
or angular.   The text is a fairly conventional love-lyric, but the
music has an entirely personal charm that is heightened when
we think of the somewhat awkward melodic basis chosen by the
composer.

Nicole Grenon: *Je ne requier de ma dame*.   OISEAU-LYRE OL 136
   (78 r.p.m.).

An even greater figure than Grenon was Gilles Binchois, a
native of Mons in Hainaut.   Binchois began life in the army and
ended it in the Church; in between whiles he seems to have composed a great quantity of sacred and secular music, much of which
is of a very high quality.   He served the court of Burgundy for
nearly thirty years, and died in 1460.   No less a composer than
Ockeghem wrote a lamentation on the death of Gilles Binchois.
In the text of Ockeghem's work he is called 'the father of joyous-
ness,' and it is not difficult to believe this charming compliment
when we listen to his chanson *Filles à marier*.

Gilles Binchois: *Filles à marier*.   HISTORY OF MUSIC IN SOUND,
   VOL. III.   VICTOR LM 6016 (HMV HMS 26, 78 r.p.m.).

Like Binchois, the slightly younger composer Hayne van
Ghizeghem embraced a military career, and this may partly
explain the relatively small amount of music he was able to write.
But his music is consistent in style and of fairly even quality.   It
was in all probability written between 1457 and 1468 when he
was studying and was at the same time acting as *valet de chambre*
and singer to Charles the Bold.   From 1468 onwards his army
career seems to have taken up most of his time, and we last hear
of him at the disastrous siege of Beauvais in 1472, where he
probably perished.

Hayne's songs were used not only for their original purpose, but also for dances and as *cantus firmus* for settings of the Mass. Most of them were for three voices, but he added a fourth to several and so enriched the texture—for instance, *À la audienche*. The complete text has not survived, so it has been recorded as played by instruments. In connection with this song we must also consider *musica ficta*, or 'feigned music.' This device, which composers of the Renaissance used either because they had to or because they wished for a particularly beautiful harmonic effect, was really nothing more than the chromatic alteration of certain important notes. A note written as B flat would be sung as B natural, or a plain F would be sung F sharp. Thus composers were able to achieve an effect of modulation, although they were writing many years before the final codification of our ideas about tonality. *Musica ficta*, however, was largely up to the performer because it was rarely, if ever, set out in the music itself, and many modern editors have misunderstood its function. An example of this misunderstanding may be heard in *À la audienche*; about half-way through there is a loud chord completely off key.

Hayne van Ghizeghem: *À la audienche*. OISEAU-LYRE OL 136 (78 r.p.m.).

When properly used by a modern editor, *musica ficta* can be made to colour a composition and increase its charm and its harmonic appeal. Almost the same is true of the use of instruments which played such an important part in the life at the Burgundian court. These instruments are, for instance, described in the account of the 'Feast of the Pheasant,' a banquet given by Duke Philip the Good of Burgundy in 1454, the purpose being to avenge the fall of Constantinople in the previous year. We learn that there was a castle made entirely of pastry inside which no less than twenty-eight musicians sang and played recorders, rebecs, lutes, horns, bassoons, bagpipes, and cornets. Three choir-boys and a tenor sang a *Benedictus* inside a model church, and there was an organ that played in between the singing. Another group of choir-boys and instrumentalists, again secreted in a pie, sang a motet and a chanson, and when they had finished, the doors of the banqueting hall were thrown open to reveal four trumpeters clad in white who played a fanfare on golden instruments. A white stag followed them in, and on it was seated a beautiful young girl who sang a chanson by Guillaume Dufay. And so the feasting and the music went on until the evening, when another work by

Dufay was performed, a lament for the fallen city of Constantinople. This was preceded by a procession of torch-bearers and musicians with tabors, harps, and lutes.

Guillaume Dufay, whose music was obviously accorded a place of honour at this feast, was born about 1400, not very far from what is now the border between France and Belgium. He was a choirboy at Cambrai cathedral, but he was hardly out of his teens before he began to travel. We hear of him first in Paris and then in Italy, where he seems to have found a number of commissions to write music for special events. Perhaps Dufay's beautiful setting of the first verse of Petrarch's *Vergine bella* belongs to this period too. 'Beautiful Virgin! clothed with the sun, crowned with the stars, who so pleased the Eternal Sun that he hid his light in thine; love spurs me on to utter speech of thee, and (feeble to commence without thy aid) of him who on thy bosom rests in love.'

Dufay: *Vergine bella.* Decca ARC 3003 (DGG APM 14019).

After this first Italian visit, Dufay returned home and apparently held some ecclesiastical post at Laon until 1426. By 1427 he was in Bologna and in the following year joined the papal choir in Rome. Later on he served as chaplain and then as director of the chapel to the court of Savoy, but returned once more to Rome and sang in the papal choir. He was, one might say, the composer-laureate of the courts of Burgundy and Rome, the dutiful servant of Church and State, as ready to turn his hand to the composition of a hymn-tune as of a massively proportioned motet in honour of an emperor. Indeed, the demands of occasional music were so deeply ingrained in his mind that it came naturally to him to write a motet to be sung at his own deathbed. This motet was *Ave regina coelorum*, written in 1464—just ten years before his death. Though not sung at the hour of his death, it was performed at his burial. Into the text of the *Ave regina* he inserted a touching prayer for pity on the soul of the dying Dufay.

Dufay: *Ave regina coelorum.* History of Music in Sound, Vol. III. Victor LM 6016 (HMV HMS 25, 78 r.p.m.).

In his *Ecclesiae militantis*, which dates from 1431, Dufay draws attention, not only to Rome as the seat of the Church, but also to a recently settled dispute with the Venetians. Each of these matters is dealt with by a separate voice-part, singing its own text. The third text is in praise of the Pope himself, whose former name, Gabriel, is used in a very subtle way as a foundation for the poly-phonic structure. Dufay recalled an antiphon from Gregorian Chant beginning with the word 'Gabriel' and arranged the notes of the plain-song in a regularly disposed rhythmical pattern. This isorhythm is stretched out to serve as one of the supporting voices of the motet. There is yet another supporting part, based on an antiphon with the words 'Ecce nomen domini.' What was important to Dufay was to bring in the name of the Pope and also the figurative acclamation, 'Behold the name of the Lord.' These two supporting parts are interdependent: when one stops, the other starts, and at times they even overlap each other, forming a solid and massive rhythmical framework to the entire piece.

Dufay did not always write in so complex a manner. He was equally ready to pen a light-hearted chanson, such as the rondeau *Pour l'amour de ma doulce amye*. Even the points of imitation seem carefree and gay, and the upper voice ripples along in caden-tial figures with an unsurpassed charm and vivacity.

Dufay: *Pour l'amour de ma doulce amye*. HISTORY OF MUSIC IN SOUND, VOL. III. VICTOR LM 6016 (HMV HMS 26, 78 r.p.m.).

Dufay also composed many purely liturgical works, including seven complete Masses. One of the most remarkable is the *Missa Caput*. It was only recently that the late Manfred Bukofzer, of the University of California, discovered the meaning of this title. Normally the title of a Mass bears the opening words of the plain-song (or secular song) used as a linear basis for the music. In this case the title derives from the end not the beginning of a text, and it was this fact that made the context so difficult to trace. The *cantus firmus* is taken from the end of an antiphon, *Venit ad Petrum*, whose last word—*caput*—has a long melodic flourish on the first syllable.

Antiphon: *Venit ad Petrum*. OISEAU-LYRE OL 50069.

The nearest plain-song sources to Dufay's theme are found in English liturgical books, in graduals of the Sarum rite. Is it possible that the much-travelled Dufay also visited England? If not, it is difficult to explain how he found this antiphon, and why he took such keen interest in the peculiarly English methods of constructing a cyclic Mass; that is, a Mass which is unified either by a common tenor in all four sections or by a recurring motive at the beginning of each section.   Dufay employs both methods in the *Missa Caput,* which shows to the full his expert and sonorous handling of four-part texture.

Dufay: *Missa Caput.*   OISEAU-LYRE OL 50069.

(APPENDIX: *See* page 72.)

II

Denis Stevens

JOHN DUNSTABLE

O NE of the strangest of all phenomena in the history of music is the seemingly sudden appearance of a school of English composers during the first part of the fifteenth century. Power, Jervays, Cooke, Sturgeon, Queldryk, Frye, Smart, Tyes, Troulove, Damett, and many more were active both in England and abroad, composing and singing music which was the envy of all who listened. A school of composers as vigorous as this could hardly arrive without any preparation, but the truth of the matter is that music in fourteenth-century England is very scarce indeed, and even when it is available there is no composer's name to help us assign it to this or that part of the country. England was nevertheless musical, though by no means as productive as France or Italy. Even Chaucer's poor scholar knew a popular religious song of the time:

> And all above there lay a gay sautrye,
> On which he made a-nightes melodye,
> So sweetly that all the chamber rang,
> And *Angelus ad virginem* he sang.

Angelus ad virginem. HISTORY OF MUSIC IN SOUND, VOL. III. VICTOR LM 6016 (HMV HMS 22, 78 r.p.m.).

Angelus ad virginem, both in its solo form and its harmonized form, was well known throughout England in Chaucer's time. It is even found in some manuscripts with an English text; a sure enough proof of the growing use of vernacular. There is something about the style of the music too that arrests our attention. There is an easy flow to the rhythm, and a smooth succession of consonances. English composers liked the kind of sonority produced by what we should now call six-three chords—no matter if they produced a great deal of similar motion. What counted most was the sound.

Other aspects of this sonority and consonance may be heard in the carol, a form which flourished exceedingly in medieval England. Fundamentally processional music, the carol was also an adornment of the liturgy, even though it rarely belonged there. The essence of the carol was in its alternation of solo and chorus, of two-part and three-part texture; and also of its verse and burden.

Carols: (i) *Now wel may we.* HISTORY OF MUSIC IN SOUND, VOL. III. VICTOR LM 6016 (HMV HMS 23, 78 r.p.m.); (ii) *Marvel not, Joseph.* ESOTERIC ES 521.

English carols of that kind enjoy a rare perfection of technique, a rounded smoothness of style, that sets them on a high plane, both musically and liturgically. Strangely enough, some of the works in carol form have non-liturgical texts, whilst others are frankly secular. There is, for example, a drinking-song *O potores exquisiti* which must be the only isorhythmic drinking-song in existence; the wine-bibbers are exquisites, not common roisterers. Side by side with *O potores exquisiti* we find an example of the more popular style: a three-part piece for voices and instruments which would not, perhaps, be entirely beyond the capabilities of a moderately sober group of ale-drinkers.

Tapster drinker. HISTORY OF MUSIC IN SOUND, VOL. III. VICTOR LM 6016 (HMV HMS 23, 78 r.p.m.).

Drinking songs, carols, and political songs all went to make up the kind of English life that John Dunstable knew as a lad in the small town in Bedfordshire from which he took his name. He was not an isolated composer in any sense; he built, on a solid bedrock of tradition and technique, his own mighty monument of polyphony, destined to glorify the structural principles of the later Middle Ages as much as to herald the new ideas and sonorities of the Renaissance. He was so famous in his own day that poets, theorists, and musicians vied with each other to sing his praises, yet in the troubled years after his death his music was consigned to silent obscurity. Even at the beginning of the present century only a handful of his compositions were known; now we have sixty-seven works—motets, Mass-sections, songs, and instrumental pieces—found in nearly two hundred versions, scattered throughout Europe. An American scholar, the late Manfred F. Bukofzer, devoted twenty-five years of work to the transcription of these manuscripts, and publication took place in 1953, the quincentenary of Dunstable's death.

We know little, however, about Dunstable's life. In his youth he learned to sing, probably at the Chapel Royal, and there he may have made his first acquaintance with the men and music that were destined to shape his style. Dunstable entered the Church and we find him holding a canonry at Hereford in the years which preceded his service in the chapel of the Duke of Bedford, brother to King Henry V. Henry was himself a musician of no mean attainments, and the royal encouragement of music could not fail to have its effect on the quality of the works written especially for the Chapel Royal. Some of Dunstable's contemporaries and colleagues, like Jervays, Byttering, and Power, are represented in manuscripts found in Italy. Most of Byttering's music is preserved in the Old Hall manuscript, though there is one item also found in a York manuscript. This is a polyphonic antiphon, which has the original plain-song distributed between the three voices. No single voice-part is thus made to retain the somewhat rigid progression of the plain-song; it is shared out so that all voice-parts can be equally decorative and melodious.

Byttering: *Nesciens mater*. HISTORY OF MUSIC IN SOUND, VOL. III. VICTOR LM 6016 (HMV HMS 23, 78 r.p.m.).

The Duke of Bedford was regent in France until his death in 1435, and this event seemed to be the signal for the gradual recovery by the French of their native territory. Soon they regained Paris, and their victories spread steadily northward. Yet only a few years before that songs had been written in praise of the English exploits at Agincourt. One of these, *Deo gratias Anglia*, is to be found in the same manuscript as *Tapster drinker*.

Deo gratias Anglia. HISTORY OF MUSIC IN SOUND, VOL. III. VICTOR LM 6016 (HMV HMS 22, 78 r.p.m.).

In the Bodleian Library at Oxford, along with that manuscript, is a treatise on astronomy in Dunstable's handwriting, dated April 1438. By this time he must have returned to England and busied himself with peaceful and scholarly pursuits; one of his epitaphs tells us that he was an astronomer and mathematician as well as a musician. He died on the day before Christmas, 1453, and was buried in the church of St Stephen Walbrook, not far from the Thames at London Bridge.

In the half-century following Dunstable's death at least three writers give us valuable information about his life and work. The Belgian theorist, Johannes Tinctoris, wrote in the latter part of the fifteenth century that 'the possibilities of our music have been so marvellously increased that there appears to be a new art, if I may so call it, whose fount and origin is held to be among the English, of whom Dunstable stood forth as chief.'   Another writer, John Hothby, of English birth, spent his later life in Italy and he writes of Dunstable's music as being 'of recent date.'   He may well have heard this music in Italy, including the famous song to an Italian poem, *O rosa bella*, which is usually accepted as being Dunstable's work.

> Dunstable: *O rosa bella*.   HISTORY OF MUSIC IN SOUND, VOL. III.
> VICTOR LM 6016 (HMV HMS 25, 78 r.p.m.).

The fact that only a handful of secular works by Dunstable have come down to us is proof of his devoted adherence to British traditions, however strongly he may have been attracted by the music and poetry of other nations.   English composers of the Middle Ages did not, as a rule, take secular music very seriously. They were mainly concerned with writing music for the Church, and especially for the Ordinary of the Mass.   Two recent discoveries of new sources for medieval music consist entirely of liturgical music.   In between these two sources, and belonging therefore to Dunstable's own time, is the Old Hall manuscript which contains nearly one hundred and fifty pieces, most of them settings of *Gloria*, *Credo*, *Sanctus*, and *Agnus Dei*.   The musical styles range from the simplest to the most complex, and these individual Mass-sections could be grouped together in thousands of different combinations.   Any given piece could be used in conjunction with any other, and even though a mixture of styles resulted, the composite polyphonic Mass thus formed would doubtless appeal through its variety of texture and idiom.   As an example we may take the first part of an anonymous *Credo*, the plain-song being in the middle voice.

> Anon.: *Credo*.   HISTORY OF MUSIC IN SOUND, VOL. III.   VICTOR
> LM 6016 (HMV HMS 23, 78 r.p.m.).

In the music of Dunstable we find the same tendency to compose separate Mass-sections instead of unified cycles.   Only occasionally did he compose two Mass-sections based on the same plain-song and sharing the same kind of musical style.   Some scholars go so far as to credit Dunstable with a cyclic Mass, but in fact certain of the sections are ascribed in one manuscript to Lionel Power, so that the authorship is rather doubtful.   Power was easily the most famous of Dunstable's contemporaries, and his three-voice setting of the antiphon *Beata progenies* is not unlike Byttering's *Nesciens mater*. There is a similar willingness to rely on one text for all three voice-parts, just as in the conductus of the earlier Middle Ages. 'Blessed progeny whence Christ was born; how glorious is the Virgin who gave birth to the King of Heaven.'

Power: *Beata progenies*. ESOTERIC ES 521.

Power's *Beata progenies* is entirely characteristic of English style in the late fourteenth and early fifteenth centuries. But there is no doubt that Tinctoris was right in thinking of Dunstable as the fountain-head of the new musical art in England, and he tells us that his music (like that of Binchois and Dufay) possesses a suavity of character that makes it worthy, not only for men and for heroes, but also for the immortal gods. How was this suave floating quality achieved, and how did the texture of the music differ from what was already familiar to fifteenth-century performers and listeners?

In the first place, Dunstable's harmony was smoother and more consonant than that of his predecessors, and he took great pains to avoid unprepared discords, whereas they would think nothing of letting one of the voice-parts leap suddenly upon a note foreign to the triad.

Admittedly, both Dunstable's discords and those of his predecessors resolve in the correct manner; the difference is Dunstable's new method of preparing the ear for the slight shock that is to come, and this is done in so masterly a manner that hardly any shocks are felt at all. There is a similar degree of fluidity in the melodic lines that keep mainly to the smaller intervals favoured by plain-song, especially the interval of a third. In the motet *Sancta Maria* we find clarity of texture, careful declamation, and —a recurring feature of Dunstable's style—a triadic opening that arrests our attention from the outset.

Dunstable: *Sancta Maria*. ESOTERIC ES 521.

One of Dunstable's greatest motets is the four-part *Veni sancte spiritus*. It is an isorhythmic motet and the fixed rhythmic scheme pervades all four voice-parts. It is twice repeated within each of the three sections of the motet, the sections being set off from one another by metrical changes in the tenor, or lowest part. This tenor, almost certainly intended for instrumental performance,

is based on part of the hymn *Veni creator spiritus*. On its first
appearance the tune is stretched out to such a length that the
melody is hardly recognizable as such, but serves as a comparatively static basis for the more rapidly moving upper parts.   At
the second section of the motet, the notes lose one-third of their
value; and in the third section, two-thirds of their value, and the
tune at last emerges and can be heard below the intricate flow of the
other voices.

An additional feature of interest is the melodic material that
Dunstable uses.   Although the upper voice sings the entire text
of *Veni sancte spiritus*, the melody of this sequence is not used at
all.   Instead, the melody of the hymn *Veni creator spiritus*
(already partly used in the tenor) appears phrase by phrase whenever the tenor is silent for a few bars.   This double use of the
same plain-song is rare, even amongst the remarkable experiments
in thematic integration employed by medieval musicians.   One
of the other two voices in this motet sings a paraphrase of the
sequence *Veni sancte spiritus*, while the other sings the text *Veni
creator spiritus* to freely composed music.

Even a brief analysis of a master work of the fifteenth century is
bound to seem complex and difficult; art and artifice went hand in
hand then.   But there will be no difficulty about listening to
Dunstable's motet as devotional music, for it is that *par excellence*;
its calm and cool sonority can hardly be matched.

Dunstable: *Veni sancte spiritus*. HISTORY OF MUSIC IN SOUND,
   VOL. III.   VICTOR LM 6016 (HMV HMS 24, 78 r.p.m.).

John Dunstable never allowed tricks of notation to interfere
with the real purpose of his music: to place finely spun melody
and inspiring harmony at the service of liturgical texts.   In the
words of his epitaph: *Hic vir erat tua laus, tua lux, tua musica
princeps.*

APPENDIX

THE MIDDLE AGES

(CHAPTERS 4–11)

The material—both for reading and listening—available for this period
shows an extreme contrast with what is available for later periods, so it
has been thought advisable to group the books and records under the
general title: *The Middle Ages*.

BOOKS

The most valuable books are two comprehensive works:

GUSTAVE REESE: *Music in the Middle Ages.*

ed. DOM ANSELM HUGHES: *Music in the Early Middle Ages* (Vol. II of the *New Oxford History of Music*).

To these may be added the following volumes:

O. STRUNK: *Source Readings in Music History.*

WILLI APEL: *The Notation of Polyphonic Music—900–1600.*

A. MACHABEY: *Guillaume de Machault.*

L. ELLINWOOD: *The Works of Francesco Landini.*

C. VAN DEN BORREN: *Guillaume Dufay.*

H. BESSELER: *Bourdon and Fauxbourdon.*

MANFRED BUKOFZER: *Studies in Medieval and Renaissance Music*; *John Dunstable: Complete Works.*

RECORDS

Most of the available records of medieval music have been mentioned in the text of the chapters; but the following may be added.

Music of the Twelfth and Thirteenth Centuries. EMS 201.

Music by Perotinus (and anonymous). CONCERT HALL 1112.

MACHAUT: *Mass, etc.* DECCA ARC 3022 (DGG APM 14063). *Motets, Ballades, etc.* WESTMINSTER XWN 18166.

DUFAY: *Missa sine nomine.* HAYDN SOCIETY 9008. *Secular Works.* EMS 206. *Missa Caput.* OISEAU-LYRE OL 50069.

Music of the Middle Ages to the Renaissance. LONDON INTERNATIONAL W 91116.

D

12

Paul Henry Lang

THE PASSING OF THE MIDDLE AGES AND THE COMING OF THE RENAISSANCE

THE Renaissance in music is really a northern flower suffused with nostalgia for the south. This nostalgia brought about a meeting, and ultimately an unparalleled fusion, of the art of north and south. Two waves created the musical Renaissance; one starting from France in the 1300's, the other from Flanders in the 1400's, both tending towards Italy and both reawakening Italian music. The European north wished to embrace the European south, and from this desire arose the greatest musical movement the world had known up to that time.

We have seen that what the *Ars Nova* wanted was worldly, secular music as long before the troubadours had wanted it, yet ended up in a quasi-religious poetry and music. The *Ars Nova* sought after this new secularism in the manner of Petrarch and Boccaccio; consciously, with determination, with the fervour of discovery. The same spirit animated the Flemings of the fifteenth century. 'These men,' wrote a great historian of the last century, 'are veritable children in their curiosity and in the colourfulness of their imagination; their main desire is to delect their senses, they play with life as if it were a magic lantern.' The reference is to the incomparable festivities of the cities of the Duchy of Burgundy which were adorned by music. This luxurious life could have led to mere amusement, but the arrival of great musical poets changed it into the harbinger of a new art for the entire civilized world.

The great composers of the Low Countries gave this music wings—almost literally, for between 1400 and 1570 six generations of them spread all over Europe, a few even reaching the New World. Thus, Flemish music became French music in France,

Italian music in Italy, and German music in Germany, and its influence was great in Spain and in England. Even the Papal choir in Rome was for a time almost entirely composed of Flemish musicians. Such masters as Isaac and Josquin des Prés composed in several languages other than their own, and we may take as an example an Italian song by Josquin, *The Cricket*.

Josquin des Prés: *El Grillo*. HISTORY OF MUSIC IN SOUND, VOL. III.
VICTOR LM 6016 (HMV HMS 28, 78 r.p.m.).

Why should so small a country exhibit such a rich and undisturbed musical development while the surrounding larger nations were comparatively silent? The larger nations were embroiled in endless wars, internal and external; in addition, Germany was visited by the Black Death. But perhaps the most important reason was the collapse of the feudal system which called for the rebuilding of their respective social orders. While the pictorial arts could flourish under these circumstances, music calls for more settled conditions, both psychologically and because of its need for performance. The Low Countries had a well developed and flourishing middle-class civilization, prosperous, free, and art-loving, patronized by the well-to-do burghers.

What were the characteristics of this world-conquering music? First, it will be useful to dispel the long-ingrained notion that all this old music was pure vocal music. Before the impact of humanism on the northerners, these Germanic musicians of French culture did not pay much attention to the text they were setting. All they wanted was a noble melody, and this melody could be presented by voices or by instruments. We can hear a chanson played by instruments as it was performed in the fifteenth and sixteenth centuries. It kept the title of chanson, with the text, or its beginning, indicated, and since the musicians played from the same part-books that the singers used, it is easy to understand how the historians were led astray.

Isaac: *Hélas*. ANTHOLOGIE SONORE AS 4 (AS 43, 78 r.p.m.).

Undoubtedly there is a certain abstract quality in this music. Even such a plaintive and evocative song as Binchois's *Triste plaisir et douleureuse joie* shows this trait because the composer's main endeavour was a beautifully designed melody built on a delicately chiselled and balanced structure. These composers possessed a contrapuntal technique the like of which the world has never known. Furthermore, they liked to illustrate, again in abstract melodic design, the meaning of the words. When the word 'genuflexion' appeared in the text, the melody would imitate the physical motion of bending the knee. Sometimes the composers even hid the exact manner of performance in a riddle that had to be solved before the singers or players could proceed.

This incredible virtuosity prompted the romantic historians to dismiss this art as a sort of musico-mathematical game; but they were wrong, for in the love of the craft there was always a great deal of idealism. By acquiring absolute control and facility in dealing with the craft of composition, these wizards of counterpoint subdued musical matter. This disciplined virtuosity reached its height and its final freedom in the work of the Master of the King's Chapel in Paris, Jean d'Ockeghem (1430–95). His passing was bewailed in words accorded to princes; his thirty-six-part motet was mentioned as one of the musical world's wonders and his contrapuntal technique was held unsurpassable. But this coldly glowing genius summoned his immense musical wizardry to cool his fever and to erect barriers for his passions. He is the last of those in whom the eternal soaring, the mystery, and the heaven-reaching architecture of the Gothic style once more raised their voice against the new humanity of the Renaissance. This Gothic art could not be continued by anyone else, and those who attempted it produced nothing but mannerism.

We may take as an example a sacred work by Ockeghem in which the linear part-writing of the late Middle Ages reaches its apex. This is the *Kyrie* from his Mass *Fors seulement*—so called from the melody which serves as a *cantus firmus* for all three of its surviving movements. And beside this *Kyrie* we may set a chanson that shows that he too was subject to the strong current radiating from Italy. The tremendous melody that opens *Ma maîtresse* has an unmistakably Mediterranean quality, even though the gentle melancholy and the sculptured design are clearly Flemish.

Ockeghem: (i) *Kyrie from the Mass, Fors seulement*. HISTORY OF MUSIC IN SOUND, VOL. III. VICTOR LM 6016 (HMV HMS 26, 78 r.p.m.);
    (ii) *Ma maîtresse*. ANTHOLOGIE SONORE AS 4 (alt. OISEAU-LYRE OL 50104).

As more and more Flemish composers go to Italy and become intoxicated with the south, with the lightness, symmetry, and euphony of Italian music, the whole picture will change. The northern pilgrims will teach the Italians complex part-writing, while the Italian light *genres—frottola, villanella, canzona*—will loosen up the formidable constructions of the northerners. The resultant mixture, a truly international musical style, constitutes the advent of the full Renaissance in music.

Anon.: *Three frottole.* ANTHOLOGIE SONORE AS 4.

Already in the music of Jacob Obrecht (*c.* 1430–1505) we feel the warm sun of the Mediterranean; his motets know the colour of the Italian sky and his chansons know the happy and capricious leaps of Italian melody.

Obrecht: *Two chansons.* ANTHOLOGIE SONORE AS 5.

The late medieval composer did not bother much with his text. With the revival of interest in literature, the text acquired new importance and its prosodic requirements could not be ignored. Here begins the history of real vocal music in which the musical line and rhythm follow the natural inflexions and rhythm of the words. Another generation, and in the French Renaissance chanson we have arrived at true *a cappella* choral music. Instruments are still often used, but they are no longer needed, and Erasmus of Rotterdam, the great humanist and disciple of Obrecht, objects to the presence of instruments in church, an objection that would soon be taken up by the Council of Trent.

With Henry Isaac (1450–1527) the Flemish migration was in full swing. He is the first consciously international master who steps out of his Flemish heritage to become a citizen of the world. His Florentine carnival songs are still sounding in the ears of the merrymakers when his great choral frescoes open new ways for the ancient Flemish art of polyphony. Others like Nicholas Gombert went to Madrid; Adrian Willaert went to Venice, Philippe de Monte to Prague—in a word, the Flemish masters are now ensconced in all the centres of music.

In the meantime there appeared a musician in whose art the world mission of the Flemings reached truly universal significance: Josquin des Prés (1450–1521). A disciple of Ockeghem, he subsequently visited Italy, returning to his homeland as a world-famous master at the age of fifty. What was still at times tentative in Obrecht took final shape in Josquin, who found the perfect balance between northern constructive urge and southern radiance.

He is the humanist musician. His melodies are perfectly liquid, yet they declaim. His constructions, complex in his youth, became symmetrical and transparent, and his harmonies are like the colours of the Italian painters of his time. This music is almost Italian, but there hovers over it a slight veil, a northern accent, that demonstrates that we are still dealing with a Flemish composer.

Josquin des Prés: (i) *Ave Maria*. MASTERPIECES OF MUSIC BEFORE 1750. HAYDN SOCIETY HSL 2071 (alt. DUCRETET THOMSON MEL 194007); (ii) *Tribulatio*. HISTORY OF MUSIC IN SOUND, VOL. III. VICTOR LM 6016 (HMV HMS 28, 78 r.p.m.).

The musical Renaissance is, then, an accomplished fact in the first quarter of the sixteenth century. The principal forms that were to dominate the century bore the same names as in the Middle Ages—Mass, motet, chanson, madrigal—but the Renaissance chanson is entirely different from the older Burgundian chanson, and Mass and motet show a new flexibility.

Among the inherited and retained elements the most important was the principle of *cantus firmus* construction. The difference, already present with Dufay and the Burgundians, is that secular melodies are fully as acceptable as sacred ones for the *cantus firmus*. Thus we have Masses written on folk tunes that were known to everyone. The practice signifies that Gregorian Chant, formerly the sole source for such borrowed melodies, had lost its living force. The borrowed melody is now no longer recognizable as such, for it is subjected to the same contrapuntal elaboration as the other parts. But it was a very real constructive element, for it unified all five divisions of the Mass, every one of them being built upon it. We may take as an example part of a Mass composed upon the most famous secular tune of two centuries, *L'Homme armé*.

Josquin des Prés: *Sanctus from the Mass L'Homme armé*. HISTORY OF MUSIC IN SOUND, VOL. III. VICTOR LM 6016 (HMV HMS 28, 78 r.p.m.).

The presence of these chanson tunes in the Mass is a good example of the spirit of the Renaissance which beckoned to the rich and varied art of the world at large to enter the workshops of the great Church composers. The once stern lines in Mass and motet were mollified by admitting the graceful turns that characterized secular music. The great French historian, Michelet, called the essence of the Renaissance 'the discovery of man.' Somehow this rebirth of the individual has been misinterpreted as 'the man of the Renaissance,' a romantically conceived personality indulging in bold sinfulness. By extension the whole of the Renaissance came to be considered a brilliant but immoral and godless era. Yet it was this era that saw the commissioning of thousands of religious pictures and Masses and motets for the churches, and most of these works of art reflect a sincere and devout religious feeling seldom attained in subsequent periods and scarcely known by our painters and composers to-day. The northerner and the Anglo-Saxon will never entirely understand this animated era because in the end the Renaissance was a triumph of the romantic spirit which reconciled profound seriousness with gay light-heartedness, firm assertion of will with naïve irresponsibility.

The Renaissance did express in music also ideas that purported to echo the sentiments of antiquity. Closer examination will disclose, however, that here too we are dealing with new weapons forged for new purposes. Every title-page speaks of 'new means of expression invented by the author,' while at the same time they were convinced that they were drinking from the fountain of antiquity. This new pride, tone, and consciousness was greatly supported and disseminated by the invention of music printing in Venice at the opening of the sixteenth century, and within a few decades, as other printing establishments appeared in Paris, Rome, Antwerp, and Nuremberg, a world distribution of music became possible.

(APPENDIX: *See* page 86.)

13

Paul Henry Lang

LASSUS AND THE FLEMISH SCHOOL

WE have seen how shortly after the opening of the sixteenth century Flemish musicians began to appear in all the musical centres of Europe. Since for two hundred years they were the undisputed leaders in music, it is logical and necessary to follow their long reign to its very end before we can deal with the other aspects of the Renaissance. However, it stands to reason that this unique domination could not have been one-sided, that the northern visitors received more than mere stimuli in Italy and France.

As a matter of fact, the French influence was constant, for the simple reason that while these Flemish composers were racially Germanic, with few exceptions their culture was French. They were the 'Latins of the North.' Therefore the destinies of French literature, under the full impact of humanism, would inevitably influence the art of the musicians, the secular phase of which was based on French texts. Flemish composers started and ended the development of the French polyphonic chanson, while Frenchmen ruled its middle period.

In Italy the earnest and learned northerners watched the carefree art of the popular forms with condescension, but also with unconcealed wonder and envy. They never imagined that music could be so light and effervescent. By combining the much more artistic manner of the chanson with the *frottola*, they created the flower of Renaissance secular music, the madrigal. And finally, by incorporating the suppleness and transparency thus gained in their Masses and motets, they set the tone and technique for a new type of 'learned music' that gained universal acceptance.

Without exception the originators of all these new styles, forms, and manners were Flemings, but all their innovations took place on foreign soil and were eventually taken over by the native composer.

In France Josquin des Prés and Pierre de la Rue, a Fleming in spite of his French name, stand at the beginning of the development of the chanson. This chanson is no longer the old Burgundian love-song, sung by one singer while the other parts were taken by instruments, but a choral piece. Based on elegant and sophisticated French verse, it was intimate, conversational, fresh, and full of irony. The setting likes to tarry on significant words that permit pictorial and imitative sounds.

Josquin des Prés: *Je ne me puis tenir*. HISTORY OF MUSIC IN SOUND, VOL. III. VICTOR LM 6016 (HMV HMS 28, 78 r.p.m.).

Immediately after this generation the French composers entered the field, although there were still Flemings among them. But the final period of the chanson is again under Flemish auspices, as we shall see when we reach Roland de Lassus.

Jacob Obrecht closes the fifteenth century and is among the first great masters of the north to show the Mediterranean influence to a considerable degree. His sovereign contrapuntal ability, the pure design of his imitative part-writing, and his *cantus firmus* technique (outstanding even among the Netherlanders) unite with a fine feeling for rounded form and for rich harmony. There is too a certain robust quality about his music.

Obrecht: MOTETS: (i) *Si oblitus fuero*. HISTORY OF MUSIC IN SOUND, VOL. III. VICTOR LM 6016 (HMV HMS 27, 78 r.p.m.);
(ii) *Parce, Domine*. MASTERPIECES OF MUSIC BEFORE 1750, VOL. I. HAYDN SOCIETY HSL 2071.

Henry Isaac, although not younger than Obrecht, already represents the embodiment of the international and infinitely versatile Flemish musician, surpassed among the later composers only by Lassus. He writes in any style with absolute ease and can match and surpass Italians and Germans on their own grounds. But like a sorcerer he can take these various styles and mix their ingredients to create new forms and new styles. We may take as examples three instrumental pieces, played by a consort of viols, all of which probably originated as vocal compositions.

Isaac: (i) *Chanson*; (ii) *La la hö hö*; (iii) *Innsbruck, ich muss dich lassen*. HISTORY OF MUSIC IN SOUND, VOL. III. VICTOR LM 6016 (HMV HMS 31, 78 r.p.m.).

In 1527 one of the Flemish pilgrims, Adrian Willaert (1490–1562), arrived in Venice, where he was to spend the rest of his life

*D

as the admired music master of St Mark's cathedral. This revolutionary made Venice into a great *avant-garde* musical metropolis for the rest of the century, and the famous Venetian painters actually shared their contemporary renown with musicians who were every inch as great and bold. Willaert wanted nothing less than a thorough and complete revision of music-making. His selection of Venice was a providentially proper one. The tradition-bound Romans would not have accepted boldness, but the colourful city-republic on the Adriatic, revelling in an eternal carnival, wanted to be surprised. Unfortunately, none of the larger pieces by Willaert has been recorded, but his essential boldness is well reflected in his smaller works.

Willaert: *Three Madrigals*. ANTHOLOGIE SONORE AS 5.

St Mark's in Venice, an old Byzantine-style structure, had two choir-lofts with an organ in each. By using the double choir-loft, Willaert created a new style. Music virtually multiplied itself in such works as his *Vespers* for double choirs; there were new sonorities and new dimensions, new colours and new groupings. Here the choirs disputed one another, there they united in tremendous ensembles in eight parts. But the colour was not only external, the new choral sound. Internally it appeared in the form of new harmonies, notably in the gradual gain of chromaticism which was to lead to the demise of the old ecclesiastical modes. Venice received this new music with jubilation, and disciples flocked to Master Adrian—the first generation once more consisting largely of his own compatriots—and Willaert became one of the greatest teachers in the history of music.

Among his disciples was Cipriano de Rore, the creator of the classic madrigal. The name should not deceive us; despite its Italian sound, he was a native of Antwerp. His madrigals are real chamber music for the delectation of musical gourmets, but their dreamy quality again shows them to be the work of a son of the Lowlands. There were many others who followed in the wake of Josquin and Willaert, but the greatest, and the one who closes the long reign of the Netherlands composers was Roland de Lassus, also known as Orlando di Lasso (1532–94).

Lassus was twenty-four years old when he became choirmaster to the Duke of Bavaria in Munich. Yet he had already served a long apprenticeship in Milan, Naples, and Rome, and had

had a trip to France, a stay in Antwerp, and possibly a trip to England. Thus, when he went to Munich he brought with him not only what he had inherited but also what he had learned: Flemish motet, Italian madrigal, and French chanson. Now he added to all this German song. By 1570 Lassus was the prince of European musicians, and Pope, emperor, and king received him like a royal personage. Lassus was a child of Renaissance and humanism. When at the age of sixty-three he died—in 1594, the same year that Palestrina died and Florentine opera was born—his life-work rose over him like a great cap-stone. It was both the boundary mark of Flemish musical influence and the monument over the tomb of humanism.

Lassus composed twelve hundred motets, hundreds of Masses, psalm settings, madrigals, chansons, and German choral songs. In his church music he penetrates into depths unknown since Josquin; his *Pentitential Psalms* show a man shaking and crying 'mea culpa.' Yet his chansons are even more Gallic and frivolous than those of French composers, and some of the wittiest and most elegant of them cannot be sung to-day because of the audacity of their texts. His madrigals are suave and sensitive, while his German songs reflect the somewhat clumsy humour of his adopted country. Whatever the *genre* he cultivated, it was always in perfect idiomatic style, and yet his own personality is everywhere unmistakable.

Lassus: *Matona, mia cara.* EPIC 3LC 3045 (alt. DGG APM 4055).

Then Lassus, who so much enjoyed life, denounced his earlier conduct and his secular works, and after recovering from a deep mental disturbance dedicated the rest of his life to church music only. After Lassus, the ambassadors of Flemish music had to choose between two courses. Philippe de Monte, who went to Prague, associated himself with the spirit of southern humanism, composing well over a thousand madrigals. On the other hand, Jacobus de Kerle (*c.* 1531–91) joined the imperial Counter-Reformation body and soul. But Lassus attempted the impossible; he thought that the Counter-Reformation could be incorporated in humanism. That was the reason for his temporary collapse; the universal master of music could not deny his nature. The classic reconciliation of the two tendencies, though on Church territory, was effected by Palestrina and Victoria. Lassus did not become the 'priest of music,' the musical warrior for the Church, but he became the embodiment of the universal musical genius of the times.

We may take as examples of his sacred music two motets and a Mass-section. The first motet takes its text from Ecclesiastes and is for two choirs: 'To everything there is a season . . . a time to be born and a time to die.' The second motet is in four parts: *Scio enim*. (For I know that my Redeemer liveth.) And our third example is the *Benedictus* and *Hosanna* from his Mass, based on a song by another composer, *Puisque j'ai perdu mes amours*.

> LASSUS: MOTETS: (i) *Omnia tempus habent.* ANTHOLOGIE SONORE AS
> 6 (AS 104, 78 r.p.m.).
> (ii) *Scio enim*; (iii) *Benedictus and Hosanna*. HISTORY
> OF MUSIC IN SOUND, VOL. IV. VICTOR LM
> 6029 (HMV HMS 36, 78 r.p.m.).

If we look back on this incomparable period of Netherlands music, we behold an extended, logical, and uninterrupted stylistic development. The rather forbidding architectural severity of the Gothic gave way to the mellow and slightly melancholy art of the Burgundians. With Ockeghem and his school the ingrained love of the Germanic artist for 'construction' returns in a sort of neo-Gothic. With Josquin des Prés the Renaissance is upon us, but he did not found a school and after his death a consolidation took place. The archaic elements of Ockeghem's polyphony were minimized, while the flexibility and articulation gained from chanson and madrigal were incorporated in the motet style. The resultant polished, balanced, and flowing choral style was carried to such perfection by the middle of the sixteenth century that neither Lassus nor Palestrina could add to it anything—beyond, of course, a great many masterpieces.

By the time we reach the sixteenth century instrumental music was well on its way to independent existence. Lute, harpsichord, organ, various viols, and all sorts of wind instruments were in use and we should not think of these as primitive, hard-to-play instruments. Dances, fantasias, and serious contrapuntal works called *ricercars* were written for them in increasing numbers, and they are full of a particular grace that is characteristic of the instrumental medium. Each and every one of these new types of instrumental works became a prototype of the fantasies, fugues, suites, and other well-known later *genres*, though the pioneering composers of the sixteenth century should be regarded, not as mere fore-runners, but as bold innovators.

Willaert: *Ricercar*. HISTORY OF MUSIC IN SOUND, VOL. IV. VICTOR LM 6029 (HMV HMS 41, 78 r.p.m.).

It may be asked: What was the secret of the Netherlanders' incomparable skill? While such a question cannot be answered briefly, their musical education undoubtedly had a great deal to do with it. The cathedral choir schools of Flanders and northern France taught not only the art of singing but the technique of composition too. Every youngster grew up a learned musician, and even the lesser talents could proceed with formal security and had been invested with a high aesthetic sense. No wonder that Flemish choir singers were sought after by every chapel, ecclesiastic or princely.

A fascinating chapter still remains to be written about the role of the Flemish musicians in the colonization of the New World. We do know that the first of them, a Franciscan friar, Pedro de Gante, arrived in Vera Cruz in 1523—only six years after Willaert settled in Venice! He apparently taught the Indians the great polyphonic art of his homeland, and two magnificently illuminated scores in the National Museum of Mexico testify to his success.

But the Flemings were not particularly liked abroad, though held in awe and respect. The Italians learned from them assiduously, though perhaps with some envy, and as the sixteenth century advances we begin to perceive the tremendous struggle for the southern traditions; the disciple will overwhelm his master and take his place. Roman classicism, the madrigal, and Venetian choir music were all inaugurated by Flemings and consummated by Italians. The first begins with Josquin and is capped by Palestrina; the second owes its inception to Verdelot and de Rore and ends in Marenzio; the third starts with Willaert and is consummated in the two Gabrielis. But before one dynasty passed and was succeeded by another there was an idyllic interval when there reigned a compromise between north and south, polyphony and melody; one of the rarest and greatest historical confluences in which the predecessor and successor unite, with all their forces, in a common focus for a short period.

APPENDIX

(CHAPTERS 12 and 13)

BOOKS

Studies of Renaissance composers and national schools in English are much fewer than might be supposed.   The most valuable book for study in conjunction with the chapters on the Renaissance is:

GUSTAVE REESE: *Music in the Renaissance.*

Other books that deserve mention here are:

M. BUKOFZER: *Studies in Mediaeval and Renaissance Music.*
G. S. BEDBROOK: *Keyboard Music from the Middle Ages to the Beginnings of the Baroque.*
R. O. MORRIS: *Contrapuntal Technique in the Sixteenth Century.*
KNUD JEPPESEN: *The Style of Palestrina and the Dissonance.*

Three books on the Flemish composers should be mentioned:

ERNST KRENEK: *Johannes Ockeghem.*
C. VAN DEN BORREN: *Roland de Lassus.*
E. R. SOLLITT: *Dufay to Sweelinck.*

RECORDS

Anthology of Renaissance Vocal Music.   PERIOD SPLP 535 and 597.
Motets of the Fifteenth and Sixteenth Centuries.   LYRICHORD LL 52.
Pre-Baroque Sacred Music.   FESTIVAL FLP 70–202.   CAMBRIDGE CR 101.
Russian, Polish, English, and Spanish Music.   ANTHOLOGIE SONORE AS 10.
Flemish Choral Music.   EPIC 3 LC 3045.
Flemish Organ Music   RENAISSANCE 39. (NIXA PLP 239).
OCKEGHEM: *Missa Prolationum.*   KINGSWAY 221.
ISAAK: *Missa Carminum.*   WESTMINSTER WL 5215.
ISAAK AND GALLUS: *Choral Works.*   WESTMINSTER WL 5347.
JOSQUIN DES PRÉS: *Secular Works.*   EMS 213.
LASSUS: *De Profundis*; *Lamentations.*   CONCERT HALL 47.   *Penitential Psalms.*   CONCERT HALL 1196.   *Mass: Puisque j'ay perdu.*   UNICORN 1013.   *Neue Teutsche Lieder; Chansons.*   DGG APM 14055.
JOSQUIN DES PRÉS: *Miserere—Motet.*   ARGO RG 90.
MANCHICOURT: *Mass.*   ARGO RG 90.
ANON.: *Emendemus in melius—Motet.*   ARGO RG 90.

14

Paul Henry Lang

THE FRENCH RENAISSANCE SCHOOL

THE sixteenth century represents a wholly new period in French history. In the Middle Ages there was no political unity in the land; every province was a more or less sovereign state. In Francis I the country had a real and powerful monarch, and the court became the undisputed centre of political, economic, and artistic life, from which everyone took his cue. There grew up a large and powerful aristocracy which imitated and echoed everything done at the court of Paris. There was also a growing and very influential middle class of rich citizens, and the great change in the general orientation of French music in the sixteenth century, from sacred to secular, is directly attributable to their influence. It stands to reason that the secular world, now considerably more independent of the Church, would want to assert itself in artistic matters, and indeed in music it demanded more for its own use.

From the Gallic bards to the modern Parisian café, the French have been singing chansons. In every type of this truly French form of music, whether highly artistic or merely street songs, their characteristic humour, sensibility, mischief, and prudence are unfailingly expressed. This is understandable; the French are a very articulate and discursive people, they like to talk and to argue, and they dislike everything that has no clear and arguable meaning. It is for this reason that if one speaks of French culture, it is literature that comes first to mind. And for the same reason they have always been partial to music that either accompanies a text or, as in programme music, attempts to represent something that can be expressed in words.

The French military expeditions to Italy acquainted French musicians with the popular music of Renaissance Italy. It was again the *frottola* that served as a catalyst between the older

87

Flemish chanson and the French Renaissance chanson. In 1515, when Francis I opened the gates to Italian artists and musicians, the spirit of humanism simply poured into the country. Beginning in 1528 enormous numbers of chansons were printed. But the French, being what they are, always fastidious and refined, the harmless doggerel of the *frottola* did not suit them, and they used for texts the elegant and piquant poetry of the times.

The *Ars Nova* had already recognized and demanded respect for the poet's needs; the *frottola* went further as it demanded an easily understood setting for the words. The popular side avoided complications because of its very nature; the courtly avoided them because of its wish to demonstrate its transparent lightness and elegance. Therefore, both emphasized the power of the word, the language, realizing what the aesthetics of the era demanded of music: 'to pour spirit into the words.'

The change is a very significant one, for from now on we are dealing with sung poetry, and not with music accompanied by a text. Actually, by 1536, one encounters indignant strictures aimed at the 'barbarous' mishandling of the text by older composers. We therefore see ourselves in the presence of a real Renaissance movement because this respect for, and understanding of, poetry is obviously the result of the rebirth of arts and letters.

Since the French musicians possessed a superior technique, the result of the long association with the Burgundian-Flemish chanson, this new type of Renaissance music was created in an astonishingly short time. The very first printed edition of secular music which appeared in 1501 in Venice contained a multitude of French chansons: these were the old Flemish chansons of the fifteenth century. Twenty-seven years later a similar milestone in the art of music-printing was reached in France, and again it was a collection of chansons. Just what happened in the intervening quarter of a century is not known, but these were the fully developed Renaissance chansons.

Chansons: (i) Guillaume Costeley: *Allons au vert bocage*; (ii) Claudin de Sermisy: *Quant que vivray*; (iii) Passereau: *Il est bel et bon.* HISTORY OF MUSIC IN SOUND, VOL. IV. VICTOR LM 2609 (HMV HMS 34, 78 r.p.m.).

These Renaissance chansons no longer sang of the Platonic love of the aristocratic chansons of the fifteenth century, but glorified earthly love, and were often unsparing in their use of rather saucy details. They defy comparison in their freshness of invention, true vocalism, and fine lyricism. Another striking feature is the superbly rounded form; in the first part logically setting forth the purpose of the song, developing the material in the middle, and ending with a little recapitulation. Their emotional range is nowhere so wide as that of the Italian madrigal, but they are always delightful because of their frothy delicacy and elegance. They fascinate with their rhythm and with their wonderful musical declamation, which is precise yet light. The individual parts are independent and graceful, yet they do follow a remarkable, if unobtrusive, polyphonic technique. Nothing is left of the old fifteenth-century chanson, for this, its Renaissance cousin, has become a descriptive story-telling art. It is satirical, naughty, yet intimate and often echoing delicate and refined sentiment, and it is full of melodic invention, some of it astonishingly modern. But above all, it is the words that dominate the music, and here begins the path which French music has followed ever since.

Among the first great masters of the form was a soldier of fortune who served as court musician to knights, princes, and cardinals: Clément Jannequin. One glance at his chansons and we realize that we are dealing with a full-blooded French composer in a Flemish-dominated musical world. Jannequin composed veritable musical murals that have an outspoken pictorial quality, the very rhythm of life. He cast his military memories in a large chanson in which one can hear the sound of battle: the trumpet calls, the charging horses, and the clashing of arms. He did the same in his music for the hunt, for the chattering of Parisian housewives, the medley of street vendors' cries as they ply their trades. Perhaps the most engaging, and virtuoso, piece is the chanson entitled *The Song of the Birds*. Jannequin is able to re-create the chirping and singing of the birds and give a true musical impression of the morning's delightful sounds in the woods.

Jannequin: *Le chant des oiseaux*. ANTHOLOGIE SONORE AS 6 (AS 7, 78 r.p.m.).

The new vivacity, the pictorial element, the faithful musical declamation, and the everyday tone characteristic of the new chanson became immensely popular, and Paris once more became a world centre of music. Jannequin's chanson *The Battle* set a fashion that even penetrated into church music, and finally the highest Church authorities had to prohibit what they called 'battle music in church.'

Other notable chanson composers from among the many are Guillaume Costeley (1531–1606), Claudin de Sermisy (*c.* 1490–1562) and Claude Le Jeune (1528–*c.* 1600). Their chansons are not so pictorial or extended as Jannequin's, but show an even more delicately sophisticated choral technique. All of them are characterized by a very modern concept of vocal writing and harmony. With this music we no longer need special historical conditioning; it is so modern that we can listen to it as we do to Schubert.

(i) Costeley: *Mignonne. Allons gay*; (ii) Garnier: *Reveillez-moi*; (iii) Sermisy: *En entrant en ung jardin*. ANTHOLOGIE SONORE AS 6 (AS 45, AS 15, 78 r.p.m.) (alt. BRUNSWICK AXTL 1048: DUCRETET THOMSON HEL 194007).

The great popularity of chanson and madrigal during the Renaissance signified not only a tremendous growth in music-making, but also a reorientation in the concept of musical creation. The chanson remained within the orbit of contrapuntal music, but it no longer depended upon the *cantus firmus*. Every bit of such a piece was freely invented by the composer. Another trend must be noted. Whereas formerly the pivotal part was in the tenor, which contained the borrowed melody, there is a definite tendency now to assign the leading part to the uppermost voice. The fact that some of the chansons recorded are performed by one voice, with the accompanying instrument(s) taking the others, illustrates the new concept. This is clearly a tendency towards the accompanied solo music which appears with the early baroque.

Later in the sixteenth century, under the influence of the courtly, humanistic poets, Ronsard and Baïf, the chanson becomes a vehicle of Renaissance thought. The enthusiastic humanists, proceeding from ancient theories, declared music and poetry twin sisters who could not be separated, and Antoine de Baïf declared the oneness of the French language with classical Latin and proposed to apply antique metres to French verse. This led to the so-called 'measured verse.' In reality this was a gentle fraud, because French is not a quantitative but an accented language. But these learned poets managed to arrange lines that followed classical metre, and this procedure, which eliminated the bar-line, resulted in infinitely subtle rhythmic shading and called forth remarkable musical compositions.

It might be thought that the excessive zeal of the poet would thus force the musician within intolerably restrictive barriers, but there is no trace of coercion in these melodically fresh and rhythmically varied pieces, nor are they pedantic.   The influence of measured verse was lasting, and one glance at some of Monteverdi's works will show that this influence was not restricted to France.   This new measured chanson was no longer addressed to everyone from king to shopkeeper—only to 'the rarest of cultivated minds'—yet nevertheless it too became very popular.

The late Renaissance chanson, which became more sophisticated and refined by the day, accustomed musicianly ears to constructions that no longer knew a central accent or symmetrically divided phrases.   The outcome, the *air de cour*, or court air, was a lyric song, rather melancholy in character.   Their melodies are usually well written, often beautiful, but their chief characteristic is their free rhythm, which constantly alternates between 3/4, 4/4, 2/4, and 6/4.   Very soon the four-part setting of the *air de cour* in which the uppermost part dominated developed into a solo song, the three lowest parts played on the lute.   So again we are on the road towards the solo music of the baroque.

(i) Claudin de Sermisy: *Vivray-je*.   HISTORY OF MUSIC IN SOUND, VOL. IV.   VICTOR LM 2609 (HMV HMS 40, 78 r.p.m.);
(ii) Nicholas de la Grotte: *Je suis amour*.   ANTHOLOGIE SONORE AS 6 (AS 36, 78 r.p.m.).

In the meantime the chanson reached its apex in the hands of Roland de Lassus.   Thus the circle closes; the Flemish-born *genre* again passes from French into Flemish hands.   This is understandable if we consider the great Netherlander's qualities. He was a man of the world with a considerable literary culture, and French was virtually his mother tongue.   Although of a profound nature he was also spirited, full of witty invention and easily drawn into that rapidly moving conversational tone which exudes from the chanson.

French church music remained outside the orbit of the chanson which so completely transformed secular music.   On the whole Mass and motet remained faithful to the principles established by Josquin des Prés.   The Flemish domination in the field of church music was so strong that it seems that all the native inventiveness went into the production of chansons and related types.   In the sacred music of sixteenth-century France we search in vain for the seraphic mysticism of the Italians, the passionate fervour of the Spaniards, or the profound devotion of the Flemings. This is a rather worldly, elegant art, even though by no means lacking in some sincerely dedicated compositions. It seems as if the great chanson composers, some of whom held Church appointments, wrote church music to discharge their statutory obligations rather than from conviction or a natural bent.

There was, however, one significant exception. The Reformation attracted some of the finest musical minds in France, and they turned to the Psalms, translated into French by Protestant poets. Many of these settings were very simple but others vied with the greatest Catholic motets. The greatest composer of such polyphonic psalms was Claude Goudimel (*c.* 1510–72), tragically killed in the Massacre of St Bartholomew. Both Goudimel and Le Jeune, also a Huguenot, exhibit in these works a profound conviction and devotion to the cause which rings in their music.

Goudimel: (i) *Psalm 25* (two settings); (ii) *Psalm 19*. Le Jeune: (iii) *Psalm 42*; (iv) *Psalm 69*. ANTHOLOGIE SONORE AS 6 (AS 12, 78 r.p.m.).

With the very beginning of the printing of music in France, we encounter much instrumental music, and that testifies to its popularity. Many a famous chanson was transcribed for lute or harpsichord, but it was the French liking for dance rhythms that produced the original music for these instruments. Original it was only in its spirit, and this literature cannot compare with that of the Italians or the Flemish, but it did prepare the ground for the great French lute and harpsichord schools of the seventeenth century.

Towards the end of the sixteenth century this love of dance music resulted in a movement that we usually ascribe wholly to Italian incentive: the preparation for the dramatic stage which opened the next century. Actually, the French were more experienced than the Italians in the organization of ceremonies and spectacles because of the central importance of the court in Paris. Thus arose the dramatic ballet, performed with means of unprecedented lavishness. This 'court ballet' was not just danced to musical accompaniment; it represented a most artistic combination of the various elements—measured verse, songs, recitation, and dance-pantomine. The age was entirely convinced that this was a virtual re-creation of the 'universal' art of classical antiquity, and while this was as little true as the claims advanced a quarter of a century later by the Italians for their opera, there can be little doubt that the French actually made the decisive step towards the lyric stage considerably ahead of the Italians.

As the sixteenth century closes, we behold a rich harvest of French music from which the chanson detaches itself as the most significant artistic contribution of French genius.   But everything seems to have run its course, and what we see is a beehive of activity, of experiment, of popularization—that is, the typical picture of a transition period which leads to the world-conquering style of the seventeenth century.

APPENDIX

RECORDS

French Renaissance Vocal Music. DECCA 9629 (BRUNSWICK AXTL 1048).
French Renaissance Music. ANTHOLOGIE SONORE AS 41.
Parisian Songs of the Sixteenth Century. OISEAU-LYRE OL 50027.
French Solo Songs of the Sixteenth and Seventeenth Centuries. WESTMINSTER WL 5085 (NIXA WLP 5085).
JANNEQUIN: *Chansons.* DECCA ARC 3034 (DGG APM 14042).

15

Paul Henry Lang

THE GERMAN RENAISSANCE SCHOOL

I N Germany the influence of Renaissance ideas and ideals was
far greater in the arts than in letters or in the general pattern
of culture.   Great painters such as Grunewald, Dürer, and
Holbein arose, and great musicians joined them, but their fate,
like the fate of the German Renaissance, was settled by Martin
Luther and the Reformation.   There are important points in
which Renaissance and Reformation agree, and humanism had a
far more important share in leading Luther to the Bible than is
usually conceded, but on the other hand the two movements do
not run parallel.

The Reformation had a popular character; the Renaissance is
courtly, artistic, learned, and exclusive.   Luther represented a
middle-class civilization, whereas the Renaissance was aristocratic.
The middle class had its own standards of ethics, and accepted from
the Renaissance only such elements as it could use for its own
purposes.   Everything had significance only to the extent to which
it could support the *idea*; a very Germanic concept that will
return with a vengeance in Wagner.   In Luther's particular case,
the reformer ceaselessly fought for practical-moral aims to which
everything was tied, and this created a cheerlessly sober, earth-
bound, and circumscribed world of arts and letters, best exemplified by the meistersingers.   In Germany the Renaissance
remained an uncompleted movement.

Up to the time of the Enlightenment the German Evangelical
Church was the focal point of artistic life.   The German towns
in the Protestant north had independent municipal governments,
a fact which contributed considerably to the Protestant movement.
Musicians were employed in the towns' churches and schools,
and their work used for civic and other solemnities.   This patronage soon created a respectable body of cantors, organists, and

94

teachers who were all members of the citizen class. Thus this northern Protestant music was served by citizen-burghers for, and in the interest of, their fellow burghers, whereas in the clerical chapel choirs in the south the musicians represented the unbroken tradition of centuries of medieval culture directed by the Church and the aristocracy. These musicians in the north who learned a great deal from the Flemings, and later the Italians, nevertheless remained German, because the school and Church for which they worked provided them with ample occupation.

The German artist of the fifteenth century, whether a painter or a musician, still employed all his technical and formal means to express feelings and moods. In contemporary Italy art was a source of joy for its own sake, but to the Germans it was merely a means of expression. Unlike the Italians the Germans did not value absolute beauty. Throughout the fifteenth century German music was dominated by a growing polyphonic literature, the *cantus firmi* of which were taken from courtly lyrics or folk-song. In the music of the Netherlanders and the French we did not find such a preponderance of secular popular elements. German folk-song was a powerful element in the spiritual life of the nation and more than anywhere else moulded their music. One of the principal monuments of it is the so-called Lochamer song book, which dates from about 1450; others were the Glogau and Munich collections from about 1480. The instrumentalists of the era were very important too, such as Conrad Paumann, the blind organist, and the lute players. Our example of the music of Paumann is an organ work based on a song from the *Lochamer liederbuch*.

Paumann: *Mit gauczem Willen*. History of Music in Sound, Vol. III. Victor LM 6016 (HMV HMS 30, 78 r.p.m.).

In the field of polyphonic church music the German composers of the fifteenth century are only minor masters, but by the turn of the century we encounter interesting and independent composers. Adam of Fulda (*c.* 1445–1505) must be regarded as the first significant master of the first generation of German composers; he joined Obrecht and Isaac, then the leading international masters. None of his music is available on records, but we can sample the music of the time in two anonymous songs of the fifteenth century. The first is 'Once I saw the morning star'; the second begins: 'The wood is bare of leaves in this cold winter. I am bare

of joy and memories make me old.   I have to avoid the one I love
because of the envy and cunning of gossips.'

Anon.: (i) *Ich sachs eins mals*; (ii) *Der wallt hat sich eutlawbet*.   ANTHO-
LOGIE SONORE AS 7.

Heinrich Finck (*c.* 1445–1527), the much travelled contemporary
of Adam of Fulda, lived to a ripe old age.   He was a spirited and
learned composer whose style contemporaries found 'unusual'—
a sure indication of an independent mind.   Indeed, if we compare
his style to Obrecht's lovely and intimate music, Finck's is bold and
powerfully expressive.   His Masses and motets are very important, and so are his songs that saw many printed editions in the
sixteenth century.   We may take two of Finck's songs as examples.
The first opens: 'Wake up, my treasure, I hear the sentry's call
from the battlements.   Day shines in the firmament and night is
turning.'   The text of the second song may be summarized thus:
'O dear heart, recognize my pain.   I have no peace.   Your face
has captured my heart.   On my oath, there shall never be anyone
more beloved than you.   You are my comfort on earth.   While
I live, I shall not regret any service.'

Finck: (i) *Wach auf*; (ii) *Ach herzigs herz*.   ANTHOLOGIE SONORE
AS 7 (AS 51, 78 r.p.m.).

Paul Hofhaimer (1459–1537) was the greatest organist of his age,
the first famous German instrumentalist and the teacher of a host
of excellent musicians of the next generation.   But beyond that
he was certainly the most talented and engaging composer of
German polyphonic song between the generation of Adam of
Fulda and the early Protestant composers.   His songs have a
noble melodic line, pleasing harmonies and, above all, a savour of
their very own.   We may take as an example a short organ piece
by one of Hofhaimer's pupils, Hans Buchner, based on what we
would call a nonsense song.

Buchner: *Es gieng ein Mann*.   HISTORY OF MUSIC IN SOUND, VOL.
III.   VICTOR LM 6016 (HMV HMS 30, 78 r.p.m.).

As we proceed further into the sixteenth century we encounter
not only greater composers but definite indications of the spread
of the spirit of the Renaissance among German musicians.   They
were all connected in one way or another with Henry Isaac the
great Netherlander.   He was stationed in Innsbruck and Constance
and taught many of the German composers, who admired his music

unreservedly. Among them was Thomas Stoltzer (*c.* 1475–1526), whose works contain a great variety of German and Latin compositions in a style that grew from the spirit of the late German Gothic, yet his polyphonic constructions disclose a remarkably personal imagination. He deals freely with the *cantus firmus* and sets against it fantastic and expressive counterpoints. In his psalm settings towards the end of his life he shows a seemingly inexplicable change in style, but there can be little doubt that what happened was that Stoltzer became acquainted with Josquin's music and was suddenly enveloped by the full radiance of the Renaissance. His music becomes light and transparent, his declamation clear, his harmonies simple, and his form beautifully rounded.

Isaac's most distinguished personal pupil was Ludwig Senfl (*c.* 1489–1543). Born in Zürich, he studied in Vienna with Isaac and succeeded him at the imperial chapel in 1517. Eventually he settled in Munich in 1530. He corresponded with Luther and other Protestant leaders and apparently exhibited enough sympathy with the movement to make his position in the Catholic court untenable, even though he did not break with the Church.

Senfl was the greatest German composer of his time, recognized as 'the prince of all Germanic music from Scandinavia to the Alps.' He was a worthy predecessor of Lassus, who occupied the same post in Munich in the next generation. Like Lassus, Senfl was a profound musical poet and wonderfully many-sided; he severely observed the traditions of the Josquin school, but he did also break new paths with bold reforms towards freer, more subjective, and more passionate lyricism. He was the greatest master of German choral song and the founder of German Mass and motet style based on the Netherlands precepts. Senfl's polyphonic part-songs are often characterized by a robust sense of humour and they strike a peculiar, partly erotic, partly demonic tone of lyricism. All in all, he was the Dürer of German music, though perhaps we come still nearer his status if we call him the Josquin of Renaissance music in Germany.

We may take as examples of his music a six-part motet: 'This day is so sacred that nobody can praise it enough. Because the true Son of God subdued hell and banished the devil there'; and then a bell song, *Kling, klang.*

Senfl: (i) *Also heilig ist der tag*; (ii) *Kling, klang.* ANTHOLOGIE SONORE AS 7 (AS 51, 78 r.p.m.).

It was fortunate for the future of music that, unlike the Swiss and Scottish reformers who demolished organs and burned missals, Martin Luther took over everything from the Roman rite that he could adapt to his own Church's usage. It must be remembered that there was an ancient tradition in Germany of so-called 'spiritual songs' in the vernacular, and also in a curious mixed German-Latin. The reformers themselves often declared that they built upon a vast existing treasure, and the new Lutheran Church song, the chorale or hymn, raised the folk-song to immense artistic and religious power. To this newly acquired eminence much was added by the spirit of the times. The populace was deeply excited and provoked by religious problems, and folk-song must have taken on all the religious fervour of the day. Still, the decisive step was that the reformers made this new song an integral part of the divine service. Even Luther and his musical helpers were surprised at the impact this innovation had upon the congregation. This hymn singing became so general that one might say that by the end of the sixteenth century in Protestant Germany the church song had taken the place of folk-song, and would keep its place for a century and a half. Two other sources were Gregorian Chant and original hymns, expressly composed for the Church.

It was not so much in style as in the use of the vernacular that Protestant church music of the sixteenth century differed from the Catholic, though the use of the vernacular did gradually endow Protestant music with accents and inflexions that it did not know in the Latin world. Actually, the great rhythmic variety of the old spiritual folk-song was not suited for congregational singing until methodically simplified. This killed the wonderful rhythm of the old song, but also made the chorale a truly popular religious expression of Protestantism, the perfect counterpart of Gregorian Chant. Towards the end of the sixteenth century the settings are simple four-part harmony, with the tune moved up from the tenor to the treble, where it became instantly comprehensible to the congregation.

The generation of composers that followed those who actually witnessed the great religious upheaval could not close their ears to the blandishments emanating from the Mediterranean. This was also the time when Flemish and Italian musicians took up residence in the principal German centres, and the most influential of the visitors was Lassus, who understood German, sympathized with the native composers, and proved to be a congenial teacher.

Hans Leo Hassler (1564–1612) was one of the first German composers to follow in the footsteps of such painters as Dürer and go to study in Italy. Hassler went to Venice, where his teacher was the elder Gabrieli, and he became perhaps the most engaging musical personality among the 'Italianized' composers. His melodic invention is fresh and his tunes are amazingly durable. Canzonet and madrigal taught him formal roundness and elegance while the Venetian polychoral works imparted to him a mural-like pomp and colour, a radiance that was as new in German music as was the madrigalesque animation. Yet Hassler remained a German musician, and the expressive style he initiated became the foundation of the great musical literature of the following century. We may take as an example a piece that begins in the learned motet style, but ends in the simpler style of the chorale: 'My hour is come and I shall be on my way. So be my guide, Lord Jesus Christ. You will not leave me. At the end I commend my soul into your hands. You will preserve it.'

Hassler: *Wenn mein Stündlein.* ANTHOLOGIE SONORE AS 7 (AS 72, 78 r.p.m.) (alt. DGG APM 14010).

Some of the greatest musicians of the age presided over the imperial, ducal, and electoral chapel choirs—Lassus in Munich, de Monte in Prague, and Scandello in Dresden. A typical German representative is Jacob Handl, known also as Gallus (1550–91). He was one of the finest German practitioners of the Venetian polychoral style and a master of Flemish polyphony.

Handl (Gallus): *Mirabile mysterium.* HISTORY OF MUSIC IN SOUND, VOL. IV. VICTOR LM 6029 (HMV HMS 36, 78 r.p.m.).

The influence of humanism considerably enlarged the intellectual horizon of German composers, which was still entirely medieval at the close of the fifteenth century. A large instruction literature was written for use in the schools, and in the person of Conrad Celtes the Germans had their equivalent of Baïf and his French measured music. The sixteenth century closes then on this tone. On the one hand, German Protestantism accepted music as an element in its worship commensurate in importance with Holy Writ; while on the other hand, the secular musicians were immersed in the severe beauties of classical versification which they hoped to restore into their music. Between the two extremes was German choral song that was beginning to be touched by outside influences. Soon the full flood of the Italian baroque would force all parties to pause and take stock, for the world of music was about to change all over again.

APPENDIX

The German Renaissance composers are rather poorly represented on records. There is a selection from the song books on one recorded anthology of Renaissance music:

Music of the Renaissance. Vox PL 8120 (E).

Also:

Music of the Fifteenth and Sixteenth Centuries. OISEAU-LYRE OL 50104.

HASSLER: *Teutsch Gesang.* DGG APM 14010.

LECHNER: *Teutsche Lieder.* DGG APM 14010.

16

Paul Henry Lang

THE SPANISH RENAISSANCE SCHOOL

THERE is something exotic in the character of Spanish culture which sharply separates Spain from her sister nations France and Italy. The harsh asceticism, the severe cult of traditional ideals, the hypnotic stubbornness with which Spaniards cling, not only to their religion, but to everything connected with it in no matter how tenuous a fashion—these are some of the traits responsible for the peculiar Spanish soul. The noble pathos of the feudal chivalric world was imbedded in this soul, and therefore the culture of the Spaniards always retained a certain aristocratic quality; a quality present in the refinement of speech, in the poetic *élan* of everything Spanish, in the pomp and circumstance of their functions, public and private, and in the very moral values they believed in. Unlike Italy or France, where the middle classes always exerted considerable influence on cultural trends, Spain knew only the knights in silk and brocade and the rabble in rags, and they lived side by side without mingling.

The Moorish invaders also exerted a tremendous influence on Spanish music. They were not a horde of barbarians, but a nation with a brilliant culture whose capital city, Cordoba, was as much an artistic centre as any city in Europe. Just how strong and how lasting was the oriental influence on music is not yet determined. All we can say in a general summary introduction is that the basic tone of Spanish music is a fantastic mysticism which is expressed in prickly national rhythms as well as in passionate abandon. The Spaniard's melody is far more severe than the Italian's, his comic sense more cunning, and his pathos more dangerous.

Proceeding on the basis of the known characteristics of Spanish cultural history, we shall not be surprised to find in the thirteenth century a fine song literature that is religious and aristocratic in spirit. These *cantigas* follow in the tradition of the troubadours, a lively Spanish branch whose art existed in the twelfth century. A magnificent collection of over four hundred *cantigas* is now available for study and performance.

(i) *Quen â Virgen*; (ii) *Como poden per sas culpas*. HISTORY OF MUSIC IN SOUND, VOL. II.   VICTOR LM 6015 (HMV HMS 15, 78 r.p.m.).

Beside the *cantigas*, mention should be made of the musical mystery play.   Nowhere in Europe were mystery plays as much liked and practised as in Spain, a fact that must have vastly contributed to the rise of the splendid Spanish theatre of the baroque.

Then during the fifteenth century there began a movement of consolidation.   This resulted in the gathering and publication of literary-musical collections called *cancioneros*, i.e. song-books. These are artistic documents of the first magnitude, presenting not only contemporary music, sacred and secular, but also the older troubadour literature.   Once more we witness the familiar dichotomy, the opposing techniques of learned polyphony and the Mediterranean preference for homophony and precise rhythm. What the *frottola* was for the Italians, the *cantarcillo* was for the Spaniards; a popular, instrumentally accompanied piece, largely devoid of the complicated artistic apparatus of the polyphonic forms.   And the Spanish musician was far more faithful to the text than his northern contemporary.

The *cancioneros* contained romances and so-called *villancicos* which occupy a position in Spanish music analogous to that of the madrigal in Italy.   Even though many of these *villancicos* were written by learned composers, they remained simple and largely syllabic in order to safeguard the correct prosody of the text.   The most remarkable collection of these songs is the *Cancionero de Palacio*, and the most representative composer who figures in it is Juan del Encina (1468–1529).   Curiously enough, the madrigal which conquered all other countries made no headway in Spain.   The *villancico* remained entirely Spanish, and even when it used more nearly madrigalesque counterpoints it was unmistakably Spanish in tone.

For examples of the vocal music of this period we may take the anonymous carol, *Salute me, sons of Eve*; and a carol by Juan Vasquez, *Dark-haired one, give me a kiss*.

(i) Anon.: *Dadme albricias, hijos de Eva*; (ii) Juan Vasquez: *Morenica, dame un beso*.   ANGEL 35257 (COLUMBIA 33 CX 1308).

The romance was a ballad of great antiquity. Undoubtedly descended from the old epics of chivalry, these ballads had traditional melodies which were still respected by Renaissance composers and were immensely popular in all strata of Spanish society. Many of the romance tunes were used by instrumental composers, who built variations, *differencias*, upon them. Furthermore, their cultivation led to an entirely new literature: the solo song with lute accompaniment.

Spanish instrumental music and the accompanied song are entirely original types of music that far outstripped the rest of Europe at this stage of the Renaissance. The principal plucked instrument was the *vihuela de mano*, a cross between a lute and guitar. The Spanish lute composers were legion, and their music was varied, original, enchanting, and is now undeservedly neglected. We may take two examples from the work of Alonzo de Mudarra: the first is a setting of David's lament for Absalom and the second is a pavan for lute.

Alonzo de Mudarra: (i) *Triste estaba*; (ii) *Pavan*.   WESTMINSTER WL 5059 (NIXA WLP 5059).

Among the great practitioners of lute music were Don Luis Milan (*c.* 1500–*c.* 1561) and his contemporary, Miguel de Fuenllana Their music is chamber music in the true sense of the word; everything is on a small scale of sonority, but invention, texture, form, and expression are all exquisite and written in the highest artistic terms. These fantasias are real instrumental poems, idiomatic and virtuoso, and the songs are true lyricism that is as fresh to-day as it was in the sixteenth century.

Milan: (i) *Sospiro*; (ii) *Pavanas*.   WESTMINSTER WL 5059 (NIXA WLP 5059).
   (iii) *Toda mi vida os amé*.   HISTORY OF MUSIC IN SOUND, VOL. IV.   VICTOR LM 6029 (HMV HMS 40, 78 r.p.m.).

Spanish keyboard music was equally original and advanced. It can be epitomized in the work of the great organist and harpsichordist Antonio de Cabezón (1510–66), court musician to Charles V and to Philip II, whom he accompanied to England and Flanders. Like Fuenllana, Cabezón was blind from childhood, but this affliction did not deter him from becoming one of the most significant composers of the century. His originality is really stunning, whether seen in his variation technique or in his bold chromatic fugues.

Spanish church music of the Renaissance is in the realm of drama. There is nothing else like this in Renaissance music. At the end of its development are three great musical personalities: Morales, Guerrero, and Victoria. Apparently all three are the product of Italian spirit and Netherlands technique, and two of them, Morales and Victoria, lived and worked in Rome and are truly apostles of the art of Palestrina. Yet all this is only in appearance; these Spaniards are not Romans, or even Italians —they are unassimilable. Morales's *Responsoria*, Guerrero's *Passions*, and Victoria's *Hymns* do not teach the Italian harmony of faith; there is a dark glow in them, a feverish ecstasy and a consuming melancholy. These composers never even wanted to be confused with the more temperate sons of Italy.

Cristobal Morales (*c.* 1500–53) shows a consummate knowledge of the Franco-Flemish polyphonic style. Such a finely polished style cannot be created overnight, and it is safe to assume that the Flemish migration must have occurred rather early in Spain. However, even without true knowledge of the history of Spanish music immediately before the sixteenth century, we are surprised by a curious fact. The principal centre of Spanish church music of the sixteenth century was not Madrid, but Rome. This is doubly curious because the chapel choir in Madrid was Flemish, and must have had the greatest of reputations. Yet the archives tell us that almost all significant Spanish composers were at one time or another in Rome. The reason is that the Spanish composers wanted to go to the Eternal City, not for glamour or for lucrative employment, but because Rome was the hallowed centre of the Church.

At the age of twenty-three Morales became a member of the Pontifical chapel, and he stayed in Rome for over ten years. Though his is the international Flemish polyphonic style, it is Spanish in every fibre, which means a dramatic tone, contrasts, and pathos. His motets, perhaps his finest works, show an interesting technique that at all times serves his dramatic imagination. In a five-part setting he would use one voice with a different text so as to bring out the dramatic contrast. As our example of the music of Morales we may take *Puer natus est nobis*.

Morales: *Puer natus est nobis*.   ANGEL 35257 (COLUMBIA 33 CX 1308).

Perhaps the most engaging instance of the pious Spanish mind can be found in the life and work of Francisco Guerrero (1528–1599).   He spent most of his time as choirmaster in the cathedrals of Seville and Malaga, but all his life he dreamed about the Holy Land.   Finally in 1588 he made the journey which resulted in a document as moving as it is extraordinary.   This travel diary, *Voyage to Jerusalem*, saw ten printings in a century and a half, so great was its popularity.   'One of the main obligations of my service,' wrote Guerrero, 'was to compose annually new *villancicos* for Christmas, and each time I encountered the word "Bethlehem," I felt my desire grow to visit that sacred place and to perform my music there in the company of the angels and shepherds who attended the first ceremony.'   These Christmas compositions were real dramatic pieces, free of any strictness of style, and they show how long the medieval mystery play survived in Spain.

Tomas Luis de Victoria was born towards the middle of the century and was probably a chorister in the cathedral of Avila until his departure for Rome in 1565 to prepare for the priesthood.   It is possible that he studied with Palestrina, and it is certainly more than a mere coincidence that he followed Palestrina in the chair of music at the *Collegium Romanum* in 1571.   In 1575 he was ordained a priest.   He must have spent considerable time in musical study during these ten years because his technique was phenomenally secure and developed.   Soon after his ordination he resigned his post at the college to become a parish priest, and his church was that of one of the greatest spiritual figures of Christendom, Philip Neri.   For five years he and Victoria lived in daily contact, and surely this friendship must have contributed to their religious experience.

One more important circumstance must be recorded in order to understand this remarkable and saintly man.   Victoria was born in Avila, the birth-place and centre of activity of St Teresa, the embodiment of the Spanish religious spirit.   We do not know whether Victoria met St Teresa, but he could not have lived his youth in Avila without coming under the influence of this ardent and vigorous woman.   This may explain why Victoria never composed anything but sacred music.   He was a priest of the Church and a priest of music who never even used a *cantus firmus* of secular origin.

Victoria's Masses are among the most accomplished *a cappella*

E

works in the entire history of music.   It was in his motets, however, that he rose to heights where few, if any, ordinary mortals
can follow him.   Here, where the constantly changing texts fired
his creative fantasy with constantly changing imagery, he exhibits
an inexhaustible inventiveness, warmth of feeling, and poignancy
of expression.   The contrapuntal lines are liquid and impeccably
drawn; it is customary to ascribe this to Palestrina's influence,
which is probably true.   But the profoundly passionate style that
belies the order and sobriety of the technique of composition is
entirely his own and entirely Spanish.   We may take three of his
motets as examples: the six-part *O Domine Jesu*; *O quam gloriosum*; and the Christmas motet, *O magnum mysterium*.

> Victoria: (i) *O Domine Jesu*.   HISTORY OF MUSIC IN SOUND, VOL. IV.
>   VICTOR LM 6029 (HMV HMS 34, 78 r.p.m.);
>   (ii) *O quam gloriosum*.   LYRICHORD LL 35;
>   (iii) *O magnum mysterium*.   ANGEL 35257 (COLUMBIA 33 CX
>   1308).

Returning from Rome, Victoria became chaplain to the Empress
Mother Maria, sister of Philip II, and choir-master to the convent
where she lived.   Upon her death, Victoria composed a Requiem
Mass for six voices—his last work, for he died in 1611—and there is
nothing in the *a cappella* literature that can equal its glowing dark
colour and its passionate lamentation.

> Victoria: *Officium defunctorum* (*Missa pro defunctis*).   Vox PL 8930
>   (E).

The God of the Spaniards of the sixteenth century demanded
the whole man, his whole soul with all its passions and most intimate dreams.   The more profound this man's spiritual life, the
more he invoked the ascetic principles of the Church to guard
against the wild instincts of the flesh.   In literature this conflict
was side-stepped, and instead of passions the Spanish poets dealt
with ornaments.   But in music Spanish religious idealism found
its most congenial medium—as in the next century it was to find
it in painting—and the concentration was so intense that the love
of heaven acquired a passionately sensuous force that no secular
music or poetry could equal.   This is what disturbs people beyond
the Pyrenees, but the Spanish composer of the Renaissance,
enchanting or ribald in his songs, offered to God love as a sacrifice,
as the whole of life.   Like the Spanish theatre and Spanish painting, Victoria's music carries us into the dramatic, visionary,
passionate world of the baroque.

APPENDIX

BOOKS

G. CHASE: *The Music of Spain.*
J. B. TREND: *The Music of Spanish History to 1600*; *Luis Milan and the Vihuelistas.*
H. COLLET: *Victoria.*

RECORDS

MORALES: *Lamentabatur Jacob.*   NRLP 219 EMS 219.
VICTORIA: Masses: *O Magnum Mysterium*; *O Quam Gloriosum.* LYRICHORD LL 46.   *Selected Works.*   PERIOD 706.
Spanish Music, c. 1500.   EMS 219.
Five Centuries of Spanish Song.   HMV ALP 1393.

17

Gustave Reese

RENAISSANCE ITALY:
MADRIGALS AND ROMAN CHURCH MUSIC

I F the Netherlands and France jointly constituted one of the two principal regions that moulded the central musical language of the Renaissance, Italy provided the other. This she did not only through the genius of her native musicians, but also through that of her poets and through the civilized taste that prevailed in the courts of her nobles and of her princes of the Church. This taste drew to the peninsula from the north-west many of the leading musicians of the fifteenth and sixteenth centuries. Not only did they travel south on their own initiative, attracted by the prospect of lucrative posts, but occasionally they were recruited by emissaries sent by Italian patrons. At times the foreigners quite overshadowed their Italian colleagues but, whatever northern features they may have retained in their music, they were greatly influenced by the taste of the host nation, so that in many instances their works belong more to the music of Italy than to that of their own countries.

The beginning of the influx about the year 1425 was partly the result of a decline in native musical creation after the brilliant flowering of Italian music in the fourteenth century and the early fifteenth. By the middle of the latter century manuscript collections copied out in Italy itself were likely to contain more music by Frenchmen and Netherlanders than by Italians, and for several decades thereafter northerners were favoured by the wealthier courts. But as the fifteenth century drew to a close Italian composers were once more coming to the fore. To be sure, their compositions were mostly modest little pieces, but they had a distinctive character. Isabella d'Este, Marchioness of Mantua, probably the most amiable Renaissance patroness of the arts, to whom homage was paid by Titian, Leonardo da Vinci, and Ariosto, gave particular encouragement to these native musicians at her small but brilliant court. The kind of pieces that they produced are written in one or another of several forms, most of them fairly rigid. One of these is called *frottola*, and, rather confusingly, the term is also applied generically to all the forms as a group. More interesting than the simple and repetitious patterns represented in these forms is the nature of their content. The Italian love of directness and clarity is fully evident. The texture is mostly chordal rather than polyphonic; complexity is absent. As a rule, the melody in the highest voice is definitely the main one. Sometimes a *frottola* has many stanzas and the short musical setting is sung over and over for each stanza.

The *frottola* literature was developed mainly at Mantua, but Florence produced a counterpart in its repertoire of carnival songs, less rigid in form but similar in texture. The latter feature may be illustrated by a piece from this repertoire. In Florence there was not only pre-Lenten revelry, but a period of festivity that extended through May and much of June. Torchlight processions with decorated cars of masqueraders were the main feature of the carnivals. The carnival songs of the guilds had texts of a local and topical nature, and there were songs of the tailors and perfumers, of the millers and the beggars, and of the young wives with old husbands. In the anonymous song of the widows, the *Canto delle vedove*, we learn that the ladies are no angels, but for this, they say, the men are more to blame than they. Since it is carnival time, they call upon the men to dress as Turks, devils, and hermits, and join their company.

Anon.: *Canto delle vedove.* Vox PL 8120 (E).

It is partly out of antecedents such as the *frottola* and the carnival song that there finally emerged that most typically Italian contribution to the music of the late Renaissance—the sixteenth-century madrigal. Its development was an intricate process, affected by the French chanson, which was itself likewise affected by the *frottola*. When the madrigal actually began to take shape its musical aspect was, as a result of Italian influence, much less complicated than typical Franco-Netherlandish polyphony, but as a result of Franco-Netherlandish influence, more complex than the typical *frottola*. In short, the madrigal provided a common meeting ground for the two streams of influence. Early

in the sixteenth century the foreign musicians were more prominent in madrigal composition than the Italians, who made their
contributions more in the realms of poetry and social background.
The poems might be of fourteenth-century origin, and Petrarch
was a great favourite of the madrigalists throughout the sixteenth
century, but the new madrigal is not at all a continuation of the
madrigal that had figured prominently in the fourteenth-century
music of the Italian *Ars Nova*. The madrigalists in the main
chose their texts with great seriousness and set them with the
utmost care. They felt obligated to supply each individual line
with a suitable musical parallel. In the true madrigal, therefore, if
the text has more than one stanza, each is newly set. This is a
cardinal principle. In the earlier part of the century the settings
tended to have a certain musical self-sufficiency. But, as the
century progressed, the music became more and more illustrative
of the poem. It is clear then that the madrigal is not, strictly
speaking, a form, since there is nothing even approximately
constant about its shape; it is, rather, a type—one in which elegant
but not over-complex vocal polyphony is used to express the
content of a poem.

In the 1530's the leading madrigalists were Philippe Verdelot,
a Frenchman; Costanzo Festa, a native Italian; and Jacques
Arcadelt, a Netherlander. Since they belong to the early phase
of the sixteenth-century madrigal it is to be expected that their
characteristic contributions will express the mood of the poems,
but that the music will have a considerable amount of independent
artistic validity. We may take one example by each composer,
and in each instance the setting will be found to have a song-like
character differing from the declamatory nature of the later
madrigals.

The first is Arcadelt's celebrated *Il bianco e dolce cigno*. 'The
white and gentle swan dies singing, while I, with tears, approach
the end of life.' The second composition is more jolly: Festa's
Quando ritrovo la mia pastorella. The piece is recorded in an
English translation, and that makes it sound very much as though
it were a genuine English madrigal. However, we must remember
that the Italian madrigal repertoire came first. The resemblance
emphasizes how much the English madrigal was indebted to the
Italian, not how much the Italian was indebted to the English.
The third example is *Con lagrime e sospir*, originally written by

Verdelot for four voices.   Like many of the other early madrigals, however, it is so song-like that it lends itself to performance by a single voice, singing the highest part to instrumental accompaniment, and was so arranged for voice and lute by Adrian Willaert. This is the version listed.   The text begins: 'Refusing with sighs and tears, my lady nonetheless grants the desired kisses to my heart.'

   (i) Arcadelt: *Il bianco e dolce cigno.*   VICTOR M 535 (78 r.p.m.).
   (ii) Festa: *Down in a flow'ry vale.*   PARLOPHONE R 372 (78 r.p.m.).
   (iii) Verdelot: *Con lagrime e sospir.*   WESTMINSTER WL 5059 (NIXA
     WLP 5059).

In the latter part of the sixteenth century the chief perpetuator of the song-like madrigal was Palestrina.   He produced examples of great elegance, but they did not open up new paths.   Orlando di Lasso—to use the Italianized form of this Netherlander's name —also wrote madrigals that are closely related in spirit and technique to those of the early part of the century.   The range of expression is quite wide; at one extreme, madrigals that are deeply and genuinely melancholy, and at the other extreme, light and joyous, not strictly madrigalian pieces which were later derivations from the Mantuan *frottole* and Florentine carnival songs.   A fine example of Lasso's lighter compositions is the *villanella*, or country song, that begins *O la, o che bon eccho.*   This is a playful little echo piece in which one four-part choir answers another from beginning to end.   It illustrates in a sportive way the descriptive effects that were favoured in late sixteenth-century Italian secular vocal polyphony, whether serious or light.

   Lasso: *O la, o che bon eccho.*   VICTOR LM 136 (alt. DGG APM
     4055).

The highly prolific Philippe de Monte has left us more than a thousand madrigals.   He is another late sixteenth-century Netherlander who wrote Italian madrigals in a conservative vein. If Palestrina, Lasso, and Monte continued the tradition of the early sixteenth-century madrigal into the latter part of the century, a revolution in madrigal writing had been produced at about its mid-point by the boldly original Cipriano de Rore.

Although a Netherlander, and although capable of writing with distinction in the older song-like style, Rore gave the madrigal the direction which was to be especially cultivated by the native Italians.   This led the madrigal to become essentially a dramatic and declamatory composition, intimately tied up not only with the spirit of its text but also with the sound and meaning of individual words.   Indeed, many a later madrigal may be called a piece of highly inflected polyphonic recitative.

Giaches de Wert was in many ways a closely related successor to Rore.   In *Ah, dolente partita* (Ah, this parting will slay me) he provides a deeply impassioned setting for a poem taken from a famous pastoral drama of the time.   Madrigals were frequently settings of extracts from plays or epics, and those associated with plays might on occasion be included in full stage performances. The melodic interest of Wert's composition is too great to permit it to be classified purely as polyphonic recitative, but the piece is nevertheless a far cry from the earlier song-like madrigals.

Wert: *Ah, dolente partita.*   CONCERT HALL CHC 36.

It was in the latter part of the century that the native Italians took over the madrigal and made it, in every sense, their own.   Having found in the dramatic declamatory variety a medium admirably suited to their artistic impulses and desire for expression, they produced examples of the type in great profusion.   The leading masters among these madrigalists were Luca Marenzio, Carlo Gesualdo, Orazio Vecchi, and Claudio Monteverdi.

Marenzio, generally regarded as the most elegant of the madrigalists, had an astonishing gift for illustrating words and yet preserving musical values.   Even though every mention of flying, of a bird's song, or of other sounds of nature, brings forth descriptive music, Marenzio manages to have each passage intrinsically valuable as music and to make all the passages unite into a coherent composition.   His charming *Strider faceva le zampogne a l'aura* (At dawn the shepherd made his bagpipes screech in the air for Phyllis or for Neera) represents the drone of the bagpipe and the singing of birds.   Attractive as a composition like this may be, one would hardly apply the term song-like to it in the same sense as one might to the Verdelot or Arcadelt pieces.

Marenzio: *Strider faceva le zampogne a l'aura.*   ANTHOLOGIE SONORE 120 (78 r.p.m.) (alt. DGG APM 14045).

Of all the Italian madrigalists, undoubtedly the one least interested in songfulness and most concerned with emotional utterance is Carlo Gesualdo, Prince of Venosa.   The turbulence sometimes expressed in his music was part of his life.   Having discovered the unfaithfulness of his first wife he murdered her, her lover, and an infant whose paternity he doubted.   Gesualdo often produced musical effects which even to-day seem violent. These resulted from his daring use of chromaticism and dissonance, both of which are evident in *Resta di darmi noia*. The text may be rendered as follows:

> Stay thee from giving me torment,
> Cruel and deluding thought:
> That which is never to be is that which gives thee pleasure.
> Death to me is happiness;
> Wherefore I refrain not from hoping
> At last to find contentment.

Gesualdo: *Resta di darmi noia*. PARLOPHONE B 77028 (R 1022, 78 r.p.m.).

The Italian flair for dramatic expression found a distinctive outlet in the madrigal comedies of Orazio Vecchi. They are definitely not intended to be acted but they do consist of dialogue that has at least abstract dramatic significance. The music characterizes the various persons but through polyphony; in other words, a single character may be presented as singing in five parts. The most famous of the madrigal comedies is *L'Amfiparnaso*, or *Round About Parnassus*, which deals with the standard characters in the traditional *commedia dell'arte*.

Vecchi: *L'Amfiparnaso*. CETRA 50066.

Another choral dramatist of great ability is Adriano Banchieri, well known for his *Festino*, which deals with merry-making before Lent. Among his other works is *La Pazzia Servile*, or *The Folly of Old Age*, which, like a typical madrigal comedy, combines serious passages with the gayer ones. One of the gayer ones is *Tre villanelle vezzose e belle*, which is supposed to be sung by three young girls who say 'Three charming and beautiful country girls are we, my lords, who dance a *balletto* to give you pleasure. A golden slipper makes her dance well, and a black one makes me fall in love. Fa la la.' This little piece is actually an abbreviated *balletto*. The *balletti* are characterized mainly by their *fa la la* refrains which were taken over into the later English form known as the ballet.

Banchieri: *Tre villanelle vezzose e belle*. ALLEGRO 3029.

Our last madrigalist is one of the greatest: Claudio Monteverdi. It was impossible for the madrigal, within its small bounds, to develop any further in expressiveness than it did at his hands.

*E

In his use of dissonance he is as daring as Gesualdo, but more masterly. Concentrating less on the madrigal than Marenzio, he nevertheless competes with him seriously in that field. The first opera composer of authentic genius, Monteverdi included in his output *Arianna*. Most of the music has been lost, but Ariadné's lament is included in what survives. *Arianna* was so successful that Monteverdi recast portions of it into madrigal form, including the lament, *Lasciatemi morire*. 'Let me die, let me die. And what do you wish, you who would comfort me in such a dire plight and in such cruel martyrdom? Let me die, let me die.'

Monteverdi: *Lasciatemi morire*. VICTOR LM 136 or Vox PL 6670 (alt. DGG APM 14020).

All the composers whom we have discussed as madrigalists were also writers of sacred music. Such music flourished mainly at two centres, Rome and Venice, each of which may be said to have had its musical dependencies. The Roman school was a brilliantly vigorous one with many representatives. But, in perspective, all earlier figures seem to be preparing the way for Giovanni Pierluigi da Palestrina and all later ones to be following in his footsteps. His style is a remarkably disciplined one, every detail being treated with such care and taste that his music is generally regarded as the classical model of sixteenth-century contrapuntal writing. One of the most brilliant aspects of his art is the skill with which he takes a pre-existent composition—often his own—and elaborates it into a long and imposing Mass setting. Of his one hundred and five known surviving Masses, no less than fifty-two elaborate pre-existent polyphonic models. The reworking of basic material, not once only but many times in the course of a complete Mass, is often accomplished with consummate technical dexterity in combination with spiritual loftiness and poetic imagination. One of Palestrina's greatest motets is his six-part *Assumpta est Maria*, and on this he constructed one of his finest Masses. The motet is in two *partes*, or movements, and the *Benedictus* of the Mass is based on the second of them. Whether or not one follows the skill with which Palestrina varies his material in the *Benedictus*, one can hardly fail to be powerfully moved by the sheer majesty of the music.

Palestrina: (i) *Assumpta est Maria*. CONCERT HALL CHC 44.
(ii) *Benedictus: Missa Assumpta est Maria*. CONCERT HALL CHS 1231.

(APPENDIX: *See* page 122.)

18
Gustave Reese

RENAISSANCE ITALY:
INSTRUMENTAL MUSIC AND VENETIAN
CHURCH MUSIC

ITALY, the traditional land of song, has left us one of the most important bodies of instrumental music produced by the Renaissance. It is in Italy that we find our earliest datable sources of lute music. Strangely enough, the oldest of these bears a date as late as 1507, although it is obvious that much lute music existed well before that time, even if it does not survive. Evidence, in both literature and the visual arts, makes it clear that the lute was used in Europe in the Middle Ages and early Renaissance. Numerous carved and painted lute-playing angels help to make the medieval and Renaissance heaven a place of celestial bliss. Fiesole, just outside of Florence, is made a place of earthly bliss, almost at the very beginning of the *Decameron* of Boccaccio, partly through the lute-playing of Dioneo, who was definitely *not* an angel. Moreover, the lute music that reaches us is so highly developed that it must have been preceded by a strong line of forerunners.

In 1507 and 1508 four books of lute music were printed in Venice by Ottaviano dei Petrucci, who is one of the greatest figures in the history of music printing. The first two contain music arranged or composed by Francesco Spinaccino, of whom very little is known. Many of the arrangements are adaptations for lute of well-known Franco-Netherlandish secular polyphonic works for voices, but the books also include music specifically written for the instrument. We may take a *ricercar* from Spinaccino's Book II as an example. The term *ricercar*, to most of us, denotes a contrapuntally intricate instrumental work, characterized by fugal passages of some complexity. However, the word came to mean this only at a later date. In Spinaccino's time it was the designation for a very short piece consisting mainly of runs and block chords. Our example will show that the early *ricercar*, by virtue of these runs and chords, was very definitely instrumental in character.

Spinaccino: *Ricercar*. ALLEGRO AL 93.

Petrucci's fourth lute book, devoted to music by Joanambrosio Dalza, also includes some *ricercari*. But even more interesting are the sets of dance pieces in it which may be regarded as the early forerunners of such later dance sets as the *French Suites* of Bach. Dalza will at one time illustrate the principle of thematic relationship between the various dances, and at another time the principle of thematic contrast. One of Dalza's sets is entitled *Pavana alla ferrarese* and consists of three dances—a *pavana*, *saltarello*, and *piva*. A standard pavan consisted of three strains, each immediately repeated. But a pavan for performance by a virtuoso could differ from one intended for dancing in much the same way as a concert waltz by Chopin could later differ from a waltz for dancing by Johann Strauss. Dalza's pavan begins with the AABBCC pattern, but then indulges in pleasant variations on the preceding material. Like a normal *saltarello*, Dalza's is a sprightly dance, and it contrasts agreeably with the more dignified pavan. *Piva* is one of the Italian words for 'bagpipe,' and Dalza's dance is characteristically provided with a drone.

Dalza: *Pavana alla ferrarese*. PERIOD SPL 577.

In this particular Dalza set there is no obvious thematic relationship between the dances. But pairs of thematically related dances—the first one slow and the second fast—were greatly favoured throughout the Renaissance. In our example the first piece is, in modern terminology, in 4/4 time and the second in 6/8, but the melodic and harmonic resemblances are so close that one can hardly fail to note them. This pair, a *Passamezzo* and a *Padoana*, comes from a lute book printed in Venice in 1561.

Jacomo Gorzanis: *Passamezzo and Padoana*. PERIOD SPL 577.

The *passamezzo* at this time is generally (though not in our example) built on one of two formulas called the *passamezzo antico* and the *passamezzo moderno*. These are usually referred to as *melodic* formulas but—since they are normally placed in the bass where they are not clearly heard as melodies but do have an effect on the harmony—it would accord better with what the listener perceives to call them *harmonic* formulas. Other formulas include the *romanesca* and the *folia*, the latter to become the basis of Corelli's famous *La Folia*. There is a very large literature of compositions on these formulas, not only for the lute but also for other instrumental media.

Our concluding example of lute music takes us back somewhat in time. It is from a book published in 1547 in Venice, devoted to works by Francesco da Milano, who was so much admired that he was sometimes called *Il Divino* ('the divine one'). The piece is a fantasia—that is, a composition with a rather free structure, but fairly contrapuntal in nature.

    Francesco da Milano: *Fantasia*. ALLEGRO AL 93 (alt. OISEAU-LYRE OL 50102).

There was a host of lutenists in Italy, and a list of them, even if it were limited to the important names, would be very long. It is perhaps of special interest, however, that one of the outstanding lutenists in the latter part of the century was Vincenzo Galilei, the father of the astronomer Galileo Galilei.

Even more impressive than Italy's music for lute was her music for keyboard, and examples of it survive from as far back as the *Ars Nova* period. However, we are here concerned with music of a much later time. The first sixteenth-century keyboard print of real importance appeared in 1523 and was the work of Marc' Antonio Cavazzoni, a musician of Pope Leo X's private chapel. His son, Girolamo Cavazzoni, wrote the next known extensive Italian keyboard collection, which was published in 1542, and among its contents are settings of Gregorian hymn melodies. It had been an established practice to have alternate stanzas of a plain-song hymn sung by the choir, and to represent the stanzas that the choir did *not* sing by settings played on the organ. These instrumental sections made use of the melody belonging to the hymn, sometimes rather faithfully, but sometimes with very much liberty. Both kinds of treatment are applied by Girolamo to a hymn melody to-day sung to the text *Nunc Sancte nobis Spiritus*, but in his time to the text *Ad coenam agni providi*, later revised to *Ad regias agni dapes*.

    Girolamo Cavazzoni: *Ad coenam agni providi*. PERIOD SPL 586.

Music was cultivated with particular splendour and solemnity at St Mark's in Venice, where there were two choir lofts and two organs, and the organists included many of the greatest musicians of the century—Annibale Padovano, Claudio Merulo, Andrea and Giovanni Gabrieli, and Gioseffo Guami.   Andrea Gabrieli became an organist at the cathedral in 1564, and first organist in 1585.   He was so celebrated that his pupils included not only Italians—among them his nephew, Giovanni—but also musicians attracted from abroad, such as the German, Hans Leo Hassler. At the hands of Andrea the fantasia is a highly developed composition, based on one theme, which is modified by ornamentation, inversion, and other devices.   Andrea's *Fantasia allegra* gives the impression of being based on three themes; but what seems to be the second theme, usually presented in abbreviated form, is a decorated inversion of the real basic theme; and what seems to be the third theme is just another variant.

Andrea Gabrieli: *Fantasia allegra*.   Vox PL 8470.

Claudio Merulo was not only an organist at St Mark's and a composer, but also an organ builder and even a music printer. His historically most important contribution to keyboard literature is in the field of the *toccata*.   Such a piece in his period was a considerable expansion of the type of composition which the *ricercar* had originally been—that is, a piece made up mainly of running scale passages and of chordal passages.

With Giovanni Gabrieli the Venetian school reaches a peak in its development.   It would seem, however, that he was not so remarkable an organist as he was a composer, for he never officially attained the position of regular first organist at St Mark's.   But in 1585 he did become second organist.   Whatever his skill at the keyboard, he is a versatile genius as a composer, able, like Monteverdi, both to function with distinction as a writer of Renaissance music and to forge new paths as a writer of baroque music.   His keyboard works include not only *ricercari* of the later polyphonic type—works in which he sometimes comes surprisingly close to producing a fugue—but also compositions of other kinds, for instance, this organ toccata which, quite typically, avoids thematic development and instead makes impressive use of cascading scale passages and of block chords.

Giovanni Gabrieli: *Toccata*.   Vox PL 8470.

Naturally the organ was not the only keyboard instrument the Italians used in the sixteenth century.   Stringed keyboard instruments were favoured also, especially the harpsichord. Compositions of the more polyphonic type, such as the later motet-like *ricercari*, could be played not only by a soloist on a keyboard instrument, but also by instrumental ensembles—for example, by groups playing on viols or recorders.

The Flemish Adrian Willaert, who belongs not to the line of organists at St Mark's, but to the line of choir directors, was a man of extraordinary versatility. With him we are turning back in time from the Gabrielis, for he became *maestro di cappella* as early as 1527; he spent no less than thirty-five years in that capacity. His influence as a teacher was far reaching. Several important musicians of the next generation were his students, among them Cipriano de Rore, Andrea Gabrieli, Gioseffo Zarlino, and Nicolò Vicentino. Rore was actually to become Willaert's successor as *maestro di cappella* at St Mark's, and Zarlino—one of the most important theorists in the history of music—was in turn to succeed Rore. Willaert, as a composer, produced French chansons, Italian madrigals, Masses, and motets, and also instrumental music of great distinction. Our example, a three-part polyphonic *ricercar*, bears some marked resemblances to vocal motet style, but reveals aspects of chamber-music style also. Andrea Gabrieli was among the composers of *ricercari* that give the impression of having been written with the capacities of an instrumental ensemble more specifically in mind, and we may set one of his *ricercari*—a sparkling piece, particularly delightful for its unexpected changes in rhythmic pulse—beside the *ricercar* by Willaert.

(i) Willaert: *Ricercar*. HISTORY OF MUSIC IN SOUND, VOL. IV. VICTOR LM 6029 (HMV HMS 41, 78 r.p.m.).

(ii) A. Gabrieli: *Ricercar* (No. 2 of three). COLUMBIA 70366 D (78 r.p.m.).

Renaissance part-books that appear to be intended for use in ensemble performance do not normally specify particular instruments for the individual parts. Actually it would seem that a part might be played by any instrument having a suitable technical capacity for it. However, Giovanni Gabrieli, in one of his most celebrated compositions, does indicate the instrumentation precisely. This is his *Sonata Pian' e Forte*, which has the added distinction of being one of the earliest pieces to contain indications for *piano* and *forte* performance. Here the term *sonata* simply means a piece to be sounded by instruments rather than to be sung. Gabrieli's *Sonata* is written for two four-part instrumental choirs.   In each of these the three lowest parts are indicated as being for trombones.   In the first choir the top part is for *cornetto* (not the equivalent of our modern cornet, though on the record represented by a trumpet), but a gentle wood-wind instrument. In the second choir the top part is for *violino*, by which is meant an instrument more like the modern viola than the violin.   By using the two choirs antiphonally, Gabrieli obtains impressive colour contrasts, and still another colour effect is obtained by combining them.

> G. Gabrieli: *Sonata Pian' e Forte*.   Esoteric ES 503 (alt. English Decca LX 3102).

An instrumental *canzon* of this period differs from a *ricercar* in several respects; it is less polyphonic in character, and it is more likely to consist of a chain of well-defined sections with clear cadences.   One section or another may recur from time to time, and an occasional *canzon* may consequently make one think ahead to the structure of the later *rondo*.   More often than not a *canzon* will open with a long note and two notes of half its length; this is true of our example, Giovanni Gabrieli's spirited *Canzon in the Ninth Tone*.   At the beginning of its history the *canzon* was an instrumental transcription of a French chanson.   It is interesting that while the Italians sometimes made transcription of Italian madrigals they preferred to transcribe French chansons.   Indeed, they often called a *canzon* a *canzona francese*.   The music of Italian madrigals was likely to reflect the text in such detail that the words were an indispensable part of the complete art work. The music of the French chanson, on the other hand, was more self-sufficient and therefore lent itself better to transcription for instruments.   The *Canzon in the Ninth Tone*, however, appears to be a wholly original work and is again for two four-part choirs that play antiphonally and sometimes combine.   No specific instruments are called for.   Where this happens, it seems reasonably clear that brass instruments were sometimes used in the performance of ensemble pieces, and that is the procedure followed on the record.

> G. Gabrieli: *Canzon in the Ninth Tone*.   Esoteric ES 503.

While instrumental music was fostered at all the great Italian cultural centres—Rome, Florence, Ferrara, Mantua, Milan—the wealth of Venice, 'the Queen of the Adriatic,' made her an ideal patroness of the arts. Naturally vocal music received its share of attention too, and Willaert, both the Gabrielis, and other members of the Venetian school were excellent madrigalists. But it was in her sacred polyphony that Venice made her most distinctive contribution to the vocal repertoire. This was largely because St Mark's—with its two choir lofts as well as its two organs—was especially suitable for the performance of antiphonal compositions. Undoubtedly related also in some way is the antiphonal writing in polyphonic compositions which, like the *canzon*, have no ecclesiastical function. The Venetians simply came to like antiphony and developed it into a characteristic of their style. They also wrote normal sacred polyphony for a single chorus. A good example of such music is the short motet, *Sancti et Justi*, by Claudio Merulo. As an excellent writer of sacred vocal polyphony he was only one of a numerous and distinguished company belonging to the Venetian school or to its musical dependencies. The text of this motet is adapted from the first part of the psalm that begins 'Rejoice in the Lord, O ye righteous,' and *Alleluias* are added with charming effect.

Merulo: *Sancti et Justi*. Vox PL 8030 (E).

Sometimes at St Mark's the performance of sacred polyphony was given added colour and magnificence by the combination of voices and various kinds of instruments. This was eventually to lead to the full blossoming of the early baroque at Venice after Monteverdi became *maestro di cappella* in 1613 and produced his most distinguished church music in the newer style. Giovanni Gabrieli's *Jubilate Deo*, although printed as early as 1597, shows the trend towards the baroque well under way. Two four-part choruses sing antiphonally, reinforced by instruments, and the work displays a jubilant brilliance that leads one to imagine that the music is being performed by all the inhabitants of the Serene Republic.

G. Gabrieli: *Jubilate Deo*. CAMBRIDGE CRS 201 (alt. ENGLISH COLUMBIA DX 1863, 78 r.p.m.).

APPENDIX
(CHAPTERS 17 and 18)

BOOKS

HENRY COATES: *Palestrina.*

ALFRED EINSTEIN: *The Italian Madrigal*, 3 vols.

CECIL GRAY AND PHILIP HESELTINE: *Carlo Gesualdo, Prince of Venosa, Musician and Murderer.*

FRANCESCO CAFFI: *Storia della musica sacra nella già Cappella Ducale di S. Marco in Venezia dal 1318 al 1797*, 2 vols.

LIONEL DE LA LAURENCIE: *Les Luthistes.*

ANDRE PIRRO: *Les Clavecinistes.*

RECORDS

MARENZIO AND MONTEVERDI: *Madrigals on texts from Il Pastor Fido.* WESTMINSTER 105.

GESUALDO: *Italian Madrigals.* SUNSET 600.

GESUALDO AND MONTEVERDI: *Italian Madrigals.* WESTMINSTER WL 5171.

GESUALDO AND MARENZIO: *Madrigals.* DGG APM 14045.

BANCHIERI: *Festino.* ESOTERIC ES 516.

The Italian Madrigal at the end of the Renaissance. ANTHOLOGIE SONORE AS 8.

PALESTRINA: *Magnificat, etc.* PERIOD 513 (NIXA PLP 513).* *Twelve Motets.* RENAISSANCE X 55. *Missa Iste Confessor; Missa sine nomine (Je suis déshéritée).* LYRICHORD 49 (ALLEGRO ALX 3016). *Missa Papae Marcelli, etc.* EPIC LC 3045 (PHILIPS NBR 5803). *Missa Veni Sponsa Christi.* UNICORN 1013. *Missa Brevis; Missa Ascendo ad Patrem.* ALLEGRO 3097.

A. GABRIELI: *Missa Pater peccavi, etc.* VOX PL 8370 (E).

Motets of the Venetian School, Vol. II. VOX PL 8610 (E).

19

Gustave Reese

ENGLAND UNDER THE TUDORS:
VOCAL MUSIC

THE outpouring of English music that helped to bring the reign of the earlier Queen Elizabeth to a glorious close placed England in the front rank of musical nations. This achievement, however, was a gradual process spread over the reigns of all five Tudors. After England, under Dunstable, had attained the leadership of western music in the first half of the fifteenth century, she was temporarily overshadowed by developments on the Continent, where that leadership passed into the undisputed possession of the great Franco-Netherlanders. English music isolated itself from the newer trends of the late fifteenth century. Among the older types of music still cultivated at the dawn of the Tudor period was the carol, in the strict sense, a form indigenous to England herself. It was of popular origin, but could be inserted into the liturgy, and many carols had to do with specific seasons. But it was their form, and not their function, that made them carols, and their distinctive feature is the burden, a self-contained formal and metrical unit. The burden is meant to be sung at the beginning and after each stanza of the carol so that it acts in the manner of a refrain.

In pre-Reformation England, as elsewhere, sacred music for normal church use consisted mainly of Masses and motets. Robert Fayrfax was perhaps the most representative early Tudor church composer, and his surviving works include both forms. John Taverner, the greatest English composer of the next generation, has left us a larger number of Masses and motets—among them an especially fine Mass based on the folk melody *Western Wynde* and a Mass *Gloria tibi Trinitas* that was to make musical history. The latter work is based on the plain-chant after which it is named, a melody that reappears frequently against new countermelodies. At the point in the *Benedictus* where the text reads

In Nomine Domini, there occurs a musical passage that aroused the deepest admiration.   It became the point of departure for a whole species of compositions, called *In Nomines*, that are built upon the same plain-chant.

> Taverner: *Mass: Gloria tibi Trinitas (Benedictus).* HISTORY OF MUSIC IN SOUND, VOL. III.   VICTOR LM 6016 (HMV HMS 30, 78 r.p.m.).

The formal break between England and the Papacy came in 1534 and, naturally, had a profound influence on sacred music, though for many years Latin was retained in the liturgy along with the growing use of English.   As a result it is often impossible to tell whether a certain piece of music was originally intended for Roman or Anglican use, especially since musicians who had composed for the old rite later composed for the new one—or both. Among the men belonging to this group are Christopher Tye, Thomas Tallis, and Tallis's pupil, William Byrd.   By Tye we have some twenty Latin motets and four Masses, including compositions of great excellence.   Tallis's work is highly diversified.   An imposing motet by him, *Spem in alium*, is for as many as forty voices. On the other hand he could be eloquent also in pieces that are both short and written for a normal number of parts, for example, his hymn *O nata lux de lumine*, in which the five voices set the text in simple chord-like writing.

> Thomas Tallis: *Hymn: O nata lux de lumine.*   VANGUARD BG 551 (alt. ENGLISH COLUMBIA LX 1283, 78 r.p.m.).

Byrd, by all odds the best English writer of Latin church music of the period, was perhaps the greatest composer England has ever produced.   Our present example will be *Ego sum panis vivus* (I am the Living Bread) which closes with an *Alleluia* section rich in rhythmical variety.

> William Byrd: *Ego sum panis vivus.*   MASTERPIECES OF MUSIC BEFORE 1750, VOL. II.   HAYDN SOCIETY HSL 2072.

Among the many other composers of Latin church music were Thomas Morley, Richard Deering, and Peter Philips.   The men who contributed to this literature were so numerous and so gifted that, notwithstanding the gradual elimination of the Latin language from the Anglican Church, the English contribution to Latin church music figures among the most important ones of the Renaissance.

After the English language was introduced into the service,

Archbishop Cranmer issued the Litany in English in 1544. The text was set to the traditional chant according to the principle that there should be only one note to a syllable. In 1550 John Merbecke issued his *Book of Common Praier Noted*, in which he set the text to chant-like melodies that were partly original and partly adapted from the Gregorian repertoire. In his setting of 'Postcommunion IX,' *If ye shall abide in me*, the text is simply but eloquently underscored by the music.

Merbecke: *If ye shall abide in me*. ENGLISH COLUMBIA LX 1379 (78 r.p.m.).

Naturally, not a great deal of music was ready at hand especially suitable for the Anglican service. So Latin polyphonic works were sometimes taken over bodily and simply supplied with new English texts; Taverner's famous *In Nomine* passage is one example of music that was so adapted.

The continuing growth of Protestantism eventually gave Britain equivalents of the Psalters that had already appeared on the Continent. In these books, containing metrical translations of the psalms, various melodies might be treated in different settings and an individual melody or setting thereof be fitted to several different psalms. A tune known as *Windsor*, extracted from Tye's composition, *The Acts of the Apostles*, was treated by many composers. Our example presents the settings of Richard Alison, Thomas Ravenscroft, and William Damon (each taken from a different Psalter), but with the texts they used replaced by various stanzas of the metrical version of Psalm 116, found in the *Bay Psalm Book* of 1640—the first book printed in what was to become the United States of America.

Early American Psalmody. NRLP 2007.

Although William Byrd remained a Catholic, he produced excellent music for Anglican use, including many anthems and several services. The *Great Service*, a composition of large proportions and extraordinary brilliance, is surely one of the towering achievements of Tudor music.

Byrd: *Great Service*. VANGUARD VRS 453.

Thomas Morley, Thomas Weelkes, and John Bull are among the remaining principal composers of the time who wrote sacred music to English words. But even more important in this field was Orlando Gibbons, whom we can call a Tudor composer only by

stretching a point; born in 1583, he pursued his career primarily
under James I.   But a large part of his output belongs to the Tudor
tradition, and he brought the old polyphonic style to one of the
last high points it was to reach in England.

>   Orlando Gibbons: *Hosanna to the Son of David*.   ENGLISH COLUMBIA
>   D 40120 (78 r.p.m.) or WESTMINSTER XWN 18165 (alt. ARGO
>   RG 80).

If Tudor church music was remarkable, it is the secular forms
of English music—the madrigal, ayre, virginal music, and fancies
for viols—that embody most richly the spirit of the English
Renaissance.   The most brilliant variety of Tudor secular vocal
music is the madrigal, but this bold nationalization of an Italian
style did not take place in a void.

Under Henry VIII the window towards the Continent opened
again and, among the secular songs appearing in English manuscript sources from about 1480 to about 1520, a number were
borrowed from across the Channel.   The style of English secular
part-songs during Henry's reign often seems like that of Ockeghem.   It is surely a misnomer to refer to them as madrigals, for
the term 'English Madrigal' should be reserved for later works
written in original imitation—if that is not too paradoxical an
expression—of what had first appeared in Italy.   It is more suitable simply to call these earlier compositions 'English part-songs.'
One of the best writers of such compositions was William Cornysh,
among whose examples is a three-part setting of Sir Thomas
Wyatt's poem, *Hey, Robyn, Joly Robyn, tell me how thy lady doth*.
It is wholly likely that, when Shakespeare had the Clown sing the
beginning of this poem in Act IV of *Twelfth Night*, he intended
the actor playing the role to sing one of the three parts of Cornysh's
composition.

The native tradition, deriving from the part-song, maintained
its independence throughout the later vogue for Italianate music,
and we find the part-song style in almost all the secular works of
Byrd.   His first secular publication (1588) includes the exquisite
Though Amaryllis dance in green.   This combines the equivalents
of 3/4 time and 6/8 time successively and simultaneously, with
results that are utterly enchanting.   That it is not a true, Italianate
madrigal is shown (to mention only one point) by its having two
stanzas sung to the same music.

>   Byrd: *Though Amaryllis dance in green*.   HMV C 3739 (78 r.p.m.).

The tradition of the English part-song continued to be fruitful at the same time as the Italianate madrigal was cultivated, and we find the old style still alive in some of the distinguished part-songs of so late a composer as Orlando Gibbons.

In the last decades of the sixteenth century, however, many English composers became fascinated by the knowingness and wealth of Italian music. The rise of the madrigal in England expresses one characteristic aspect of Elizabethan life, its eager emulation and appropriation of foreign culture. It parallels in time the literary Italianization and was a relatively small but brilliant aftermath of the madrigal tradition on the Continent. Three things distinguished the English madrigal from its forerunner. First, it was a more popular development. We hear in England of no professional madrigal singers employed by the nobility, as in Italy. Instead the madrigals were designed for the private use of the new gentry and the rising middle class. Second, it was not a literary development to nearly the same extent as the Italian madrigal. Last, the English composer relied less than the Italian upon external features such as word-painting, and this helped to make it possible for the English madrigal to maintain more of what we might call a 'songful character.'

Much Italian music had been circulating in England from about 1560, and by 1588 it had become profitable to publish a large anthology of Italian madrigals with translations, under the title *Musica transalpina*. Among the composers represented was Marenzio, who was destined to have a strong influence on the English madrigalists. Similar collections followed, and soon English composers began to publish collections of their own. Thomas Morley, the founder of the English madrigal school, was the most prolific, popular, and influential, as well as the most Italianate master. He was very fond of the *balletto* (or 'ballet' in English), one of the lighter, not strictly madrigalian Italian forms. He retained its structural features, that is, two or more stanzas all sung to the same music, the music being divided into two sections, each immediately repeated, the *fa-la-la* refrain at section endings being highly characteristic.

Thomas Morley: *Sing we and chant it*. ESOTERIC ES 520.

Thomas Weelkes is the boldest and most individual of the English madrigalists, even though, like Morley, he was strongly influenced by the Italians, particularly Marenzio. But Weelkes was able to capture the most impressive qualities of Marenzio which escaped Morley—especially the ability to paint and design on the grand scale, giving to some of his works the broad strokes that distinguish the late Italian madrigal. His *O care, thou wilt despatch me* represents the extreme in harmonic experiment in the English madrigal and, though the work is not a ballet, it makes wonderful use of the conventional ballet refrain. The pathetic quality of the text is mirrored by touches of chromaticism and impressive chordal relations.

> Thomas Weelkes: *O care, thou wilt despatch me.* VANGUARD BG 553 (alt. NIXA WLP 6212).

John Wilbye, notwithstanding the small size of his output, is generally regarded as the finest English madrigalist, though Weelkes should undoubtedly be considered a serious rival. Wilbye is perhaps the only Elizabethan composer to comprehend fully the work of Marenzio, but he has a very clear musical personality of his own—melancholy, poetic, and extremely sensitive—and he is equally adept at light madrigals, which overshadow Morley's, and serious compositions, which stand beside those of Weelkes.

> John Wilbye: *Adieu, sweet Amaryllis.* VANGUARD BG 554, or WEST-MINSTER WL 5221 (alt. NIXA WLP 6212).

The English madrigal began to decline at the turn of the century, and the printed output ended in 1627. However, other types of vocal composition came off the presses, such as fantasias based on London street cries and secular songs designed for the pleasure of people not skilled enough for madrigals. Ballads were especially popular and often new ballad-texts were printed as broadsides with the directions 'To be sung to the tune of'—say, *Greensleeves.*

Still another type of vocal music was the ayre. Usually the ayre was deliberately planned so that either all the parts could be sung or the highest part could be sung and the lower ones turned into an instrumental accompaniment, both alternative versions being fully worked out by the composer. There was little consistency, apparently, in the choice of instruments to accompany the ayre. The lute, orpharion, and viola da gamba were usually mentioned in the titles of the song-books, but in various combinations. The lute seems to have been the standard instrument of accompaniment, and the bass viol was normally used in conjunction with it.   As an example of the ayre we may take John Bartlet's *Of all the birds that I do know* in the four-part version and in the version for voice and lute.

> John Bartlet: *Of all the birds that I do know*.   VANGUARD BG 553 (four-part version); VANGUARD BG 539 (solo voice and lute).

The best composers of ayres include Morley, Robert Jones, Francis Pilkington, and the poet Thomas Campion.   But the greatest was John Dowland, partly because he most fully realized the expressive possibilities of the solo song with instrumental accompaniment.   His part-versions, however, are of high quality also.   He was himself one of the greatest lutenists of the time. Our example will be the most famous of all his ayres, *Flow my tears*, known also as *Lachrymae*.

> John Dowland: *Flow my tears*.   HMV DB 5270 (78 r.p.m.), or DECCA ARC 3004 (alt. NIXA WLP 5085).

(APPENDIX: *See* page 136.)

20

Gustave Reese

ENGLAND UNDER THE TUDORS:
INSTRUMENTAL MUSIC

ENGLAND under the Tudors cultivated instrumental music with at least as much brilliance as she did vocal music, and with perhaps even greater originality, and the fostering of music for instruments was limited to no one social class. The waits—that is, the bands of musicians maintained by the towns—not only sang for their fellow-townsmen, but also performed on instruments. There was instrumental playing in the great manor houses of the English countryside, and at the royal court instrumental music was supported with particular enthusiasm and lavishness.

The music that was played consisted mainly of compositions for keyboard instruments, for lute, or for instrumental ensemble. Stringed keyboard instruments may be traced back to at least the fourteenth century in England, and the organ much farther back than that. But there is a total lack of compositions dating from earlier than the sixteenth century that are known with certainty to be both English in origin and intended for keyboard instruments. Generous compensation is made for this lack when the Tudor period is reached.

The English virginal—on which Elizabeth I was herself a fine performer—was a modest little instrument with neither pedals nor stops. It did not have the splendour of the harpsichord, nor was it possible to sustain a tone on it, as one could on the organ, or to produce gradations in volume. However, the illusion of a sustained tone could be created by the addition of ornamentation, a marked characteristic of virginal music, while the illusion of greater volume could be produced by the use of fuller chords. Much of the keyboard music that comes down to us could be played on either the virginal or the organ, but some of it is clearly intended for one instrument or the other.

A large body of keyboard compositions is based on pre-existent music either sacred or secular, including Gregorian melodies. It was a common practice in England, as elsewhere, to sing alternate stanzas of a plain-song hymn and to have the other stanzas represented by organ settings of the hymn melody.   But it seems to have been an English speciality to base the organ sections occasionally not upon the plain-song melody itself, but upon a countermelody that had been written against it according to certain principles, the plain-song itself being actually excluded from these sections.   The countermelody was called the faburden. An example is *O lux on the faburden by* John Redford, based on a countermelody written against the chant *O lux beata Trinitas*. Perhaps of greater interest, however, in relation to specifically instrumental composition, is the strikingly characteristic keyboard figuration.

John Redford: *O lux on the faburden*.   HISTORY OF MUSIC IN SOUND, VOL. III.   VICTOR LM 6016 (HMV HMS 30, 78 r.p.m.).

An especially imposing body of instrumental pieces based on a chant melody is the group of *In Nomines* which were written for lute or for instrumental ensemble as well as for keyboard.   That the *In Nomine* as a species orginated from a passage in Taverner's Mass *Gloria tibi Trinitas* (itself based on a chant melody) has already been mentioned, and some of these instrumental pieces make a bow to Taverner by quoting or paraphrasing part of his composition at the outset.   John Bull, a famous virtuoso as well as a brilliant composer, wrote two *In Nomine* settings, and in the one that is our example the plain-song is rather forcefully hammered out at the beginning.

John Bull: *In Nomine*.   EMS 236.

Another group of keyboard pieces based on pre-existent music consists of transcriptions or other reworkings, sometimes quite elaborate, of favourite polyphonic vocal compositions of the period. For example, the *Fitzwilliam Virginal Book*—the largest English source of keyboard music of the time—contains an arrangement by Peter Philips of the much admired *Margot labourez les vignes* by Lassus.

The English produced especially happy results in writing instrumental pieces based on popular or folk melodies, some of these being dance tunes.   Such pieces often took the form of a

set of variations on the borrowed melody. William Byrd has
left us several compositions of this type, and an especially charming
little example is *Wolsey's Wilde*. English composers treated the
variation form in a particularly interesting manner. They did *not*,
as was usual later, begin with a simple preliminary statement of
the theme. Instead they broke up the melody into sections and
immediately followed each statement of a section by a variation;
after that the composer might add as many further variations as he
wished. This is the general plan of *Wolsey's Wilde*, the section
containing the additional variations being a rather short one.

Byrd: *Wolsey's Wilde*. VICTOR 1424A (HMV DA 1014, 78 r.p.m.).

Even if composers sometimes incorporated popular melodies
into their pieces in dance forms, they often preferred to write
entirely original works. As on the Continent, two dances—
whether produced by one method or the other—not infrequently
created a pair in a way that foreshadowed the coming birth of the
suite. Particularly favoured were pairs made up of a pavan and a
galliard. The normal English pavan followed the international
pattern in consisting of three strains, each immediately repeated,
variations being applied to the repetitions if the composer so
wished. The galliard, a somewhat gayer dance, but similar in
form, might, like its continental counterpart, be thematically
related to the preceding pavan. Byrd's *Pavana Bray* and
Galliarda Bray illustrate all these structural points, though the
thematic relationship between the two pieces is rather fleeting.

Byrd: *Pavana Bray* and *Galliarda Bray*. LONDON LL 713 (DECCA
LXT 2795), also DECCA AX 546 (78 r.p.m.).

The keyboard repertoire also included regular programmatic
compositions with descriptive effects, like John Bull's *The King's
Hunt*. This rollicking piece happens to present us with a rather
elaborate series of variations at the same time as it invokes the
spirit of the chase.

Bull: *The King's Hunt*. ENGLISH COLUMBIA 5713 (78 r.p.m.), or
LONDON LL 713 (DECCA LXT 2795).

One may perhaps regard as a subcategory of the descriptive
works a group of little *genre* pieces that seem to foreshadow by more
than two centuries the intimate *Characterstücke* of Robert Schumann. These are usually delicate and give the impression of
being quite introspective. Good examples are *The Fall of the*

Leafe by Martin Peerson and *A Toye* by Giles Farnaby—the word 'toye' signified a light *genre* composition.

(i) Peerson: *The Fall of the Leafe.* ANTHOLOGIE SONORE AS 13, or EMS 236 (alt. DECCA X 550, 78 r.p.m.).

(ii) Farnaby: *A Toye.* ANTHOLOGIE SONORE, AS 13 (alt. DECCA X 551, 78 r.p.m.).

Also important in the keyboard repertoire were examples of the fantasia, a type concerning which we shall have more to say when we reach instrumental ensemble music.

If we turn from keyboard instruments to the lute, we find that it too was highly favoured by the English, though England was late in producing great performers on the instrument. None of the surviving lute-solo works can be dated with assurance earlier than the mid century. Lute music tends to resemble virginal music so far as forms and types are concerned. The main difference is in texture and was brought about, of course, by the attempt to write for the instrument idiomatically. In this body of music we again find *In Nomine* pieces—no fewer than one hundred and fifty of them—and transcriptions of pre-existent polyphonic vocal works. John Dowland's *Flow my tears* has already been introduced as an example in its version as an ayre for solo voice and lute. There are arrangements of it under the title *Lachrymae* for virginal, but even more of them for lute. Compositions based on popular tunes are numerous in the lute repertoire. Among various settings of *Greensleeves* there is one by Francis Cutting that treats it with remarkable liberty, and one may be able to recognize the grand old tune only if one knows in advance that it is there. Another great favourite of the period was *Goe from my window goe*, and a charming anonymous variation setting of it is our second lute example.

(i) *Greensleeves*, set by Francis Cutting; (ii) *Goe from my window goe*, anonymous setting. ALLEGRO AL 93.

Particularly characteristic of the lute repertoire are the numerous dance pieces, such as pavans, galliards, allemandes, courantes, jigs, etc. We may take as examples two compositions by John Dowland, by all odds the greatest of the English lutenists. The first—a quite jolly piece—is called in one continental source *Chorea Anglicana Doolandi* (meaning Dowland's English Dance) and in another *Allemanda englessa* (meaning English Allemande). The second is *The King of Denmark's Galliard*, possibly written at Elsinore, for Dowland was at one period in the service of King Christian IV of Denmark.

Dowland: (i) *English Allemande*; (ii) *The King of Denmark's Galliard*. PERIOD SPL 577.

One interesting feature of the surviving English lute music is that much of it comes down to us in teaching manuals. These contain text matter, explaining how to play the instrument and also how to read the special kind of notation in which the music was written. Then they proceed to supply a little repertoire of pieces. By having much of its literature set forth in this form, English lute music resembles lute music on the Continent but differs from English virginal music. There are also text-books and a quantity of music for related instruments—the cittern, pandore, and orpharion. The cittern was standard barber-shop furniture, a toy with which the waiting customer could amuse himself, and was mainly for unskilled players. All three, as well as the nobler lute, were drawn upon in the playing of ensemble music.

The places where instruments were used included, of course, the theatre. In the public theatres music was likely regarded as a stage property, much as were costumes and machines. When a king entered or left the stage, trumpets played a flourish. During banquet scenes, 'hoboyes' sounded. The beating of a drum denoted a marching army, and for each phase of a battle there was special music. It is quite evident that the musical formulas for certain dramatic situations were taken from real-life practices in Elizabethan England. Trumpets and kettledrums, for instance, were the signs apparent of Elizabeth and her nobility, heralding the monarch on all state occasions. The technical terms for trumpet and drum usage found in the military treatises of the time were also theatre terms. The band of musicians attached to the theatre also sometimes engaged in *entr'acte* music and here, it may be assumed, the music might take on the nature of a self-sufficient ensemble composition, such as was performed outside the theatre.

If an ensemble, regardless of the scene of its activity, consisted of instruments of different types, it was known as a broken consort. If it consisted of instruments of one type—viols, for example, or recorders—it was called a whole consort. A considerable number of instrumental ensemble compositions come down to us without any indication that they are intended for a particular kind of group. It seems reasonably clear that such works were presented, like their counterparts on the Continent, on any instruments upon which they could be performed. But there can be little doubt that the whole consort of viols was the type of ensemble that enjoyed the greatest popularity. Inventories of the royal court and of less exalted households list a rather large number of chests of viols—that is, sets of viols in various sizes. These sets are in some ways analogous to the group of four instruments used in our string quartet. Indeed, English instrumental ensemble music reveals important prefigurations of the string quartet of the future and is among the most original and historically significant contributions made by England to the art of music. In this repertoire we again encounter the usual types—*In Nomines*, pavans, galliards, etc.—but especially distinctive are the fantasias. While splendid examples of the fantasia are included in the keyboard and lute repertoires, it is likely that, when we finally come to know all the English instrumental music of the period, we shall find the fantasias for instrumental ensemble to be the most impressive ones.

Among the ensemble pieces of Thomas Weelkes there is one that might well be called a fantasia, even though it bears in the source only this superscription: 'for 2 basses Tho. Weelkes.' It is in reality for six parts, and the inscription merely refers to the fact that two of them are bass parts. Short as it is, this rich and noble composition creates an impression of great breadth and stateliness.

Weelkes: *Piece for viols*. English Columbia 5714 (78 r.p.m.).

That most charming and readable of all English theorists, Thomas Morley, adds to Part I of his manual an appendix which consists of a group of wordless compositions. While such pieces are not necessarily outside the pale of vocal performance, and Morley's text indicates this fact, it is clear that they may be performed by instruments likewise. The last composition in the appendix is a smiling, Italianate little piece, simply entitled *Aria*.

Morley: *Aria*. Vanguard BG 539.

It would be quite mistaken to conclude from what has been said that the instruments desired for ensemble music are never plainly indicated. On the contrary, Morley himself in 1599 brought out a collection in which he specifically called for treble and bass viols, cittern, pandore, recorder, and lute. There are several other English collections of the time in which particular instruments are clearly designated.

Orlando Gibbons seems to be the finest composer of the first great flowering of English instrumental ensemble music, which spanned the late Tudor and early Stuart periods. No survey of that flowering—even if the emphasis is on Tudor music and Gibbons was essentially a Stuart composer—could rightly be brought to a close without including an illustration of his brilliant writing. Our last example will be a splendid four-part fantasia in which Gibbons toys with fugal imitation, rhythmic variety, and all kinds of interesting devices.

> Orlando Gibbons: *Fantasia* (second on the record). BARTÓK BR 913 (alt. OISEAU-LYRE OL 50131).

APPENDIX
(CHAPTERS 19 and 20)

BOOKS

MORRISON C. BOYD: *Elizabethan Music and Musical Criticism.*
E. H. FELLOWES: *The English Madrigal Composers; William Byrd.*
W. H. GRATTAN FLOOD: *Early Tudor Composers.*
BRUCE PATTISON: *Music and Poetry of the English Renaissance.*
PETER WARLOCK: *The English Ayre.*
MARGARET GLYN: *About Elizabethan Virginal Music and its Composers.*
DENIS STEVENS: *The Mulliner Book: A Commentary.*
C. VAN DEN BORREN: *The Sources of Keyboard Music in England.*

RECORDS

An Evening of Elizabethan Verse and its Music. COLUMBIA ML 5051.
A Treasury of Madrigals. COLUMBIA ML 4517.
English Lutenist Songs. OISEAU-LYRE OL 50102.
Shakespeare Songs and Lute Solos. HMV ALP 1265.
English Songs. ENGLISH DECCA LW 5243.
FARNABY: *Canzonets and Virginal Music.* EMS 5.
Dowland and his Contemporaries. EMS 11.
DOWLAND: *The First Book of Ayres.* PERIOD SPL 727. *Lachrimae, etc.* EMS 12.
Elizabethan Love Songs and Harpsichord pieces. NIXA LLP 8037.
Old English Organ Masters. PERIOD SPL 578.
Masters of Early English Keyboard Music. OISEAU-LYRE OL 5075–6.

21

J. A. Westrup

FROM RENAISSANCE TO BAROQUE

THE word 'baroque' has been borrowed by musical historians from historians of the other arts, particularly architecture. Originally it meant 'irregular' or 'strange' and was used as a term of contempt. But it has become generally respectable and is used to indicate the style of a particular period. It would be a waste of time to discuss whether 'baroque' means the same in music as it does in architecture. We need only accept the fact that it is in common use to-day to describe a period reaching roughly from 1600 to 1750—or, from the beginning of opera to the death of J. S. Bach.

What are the outstanding characteristics of baroque music? They can be concisely summed up in three words—splendour, clarity, and pathetic expression. We are inclined to-day to associate splendour particularly with opera; but even when it became a public spectacle after 1637, seventeenth-century opera often achieved its splendour more by scenic extravagance than by elaborate musical resources. The one place above all others where large-scale performances were possible was in church. At St Mark's, Venice, Giovanni Gabrieli (1557–1612) specified exactly what instruments he required and used them both in combination with the voices and as a contrast to them. His motet *In Ecclesiis*, a hymn of praise to God, is a splendid example of the style. There are contrasts between solo voice and chorus, and between voices and instruments, and also contrasts between a more traditional style of intricate part-writing and massive blocks of harmony designed to echo round the church in which the music was sung.

Giovanni Gabrieli: *In Ecclesiis*. HISTORY OF MUSIC IN SOUND, VOL. IV. VICTOR LM 6029 (HMV HMS 39, 78 r.p.m.).

Once this style was established it spread to other countries as well, and we find it in Germany in the work of Michael Praetorius (1571–1621) and Heinrich Schütz (1585–1672).

When Gabrieli was alive there was no such thing as an orchestra as we understand it. The modern orchestra grew out of two necessities. One was the obvious need for increasing the number of string-players in an ensemble where the performance was to be given in a large building. The other was the advisability of having something like a standard organization so that works which had first been performed in one city could be performed again elsewhere. It was the development of opera as a public spectacle that made these requirements urgent. Once the orchestra was recognized as a normal medium, it was adopted in royal and princely establishments as well. They already had a supply of good wind-players, including trumpets and also timpani, which were primarily used for military and ceremonial occasions. The seventeenth-century cult of splendour and massive sonority encouraged composers attached to courts to use all these resources. By the end of the century the orchestra was well established as a medium for independent instrumental music in addition to its earlier functions in the theatre, the church, and the royal palace.

In writing for the orchestra composers did not merely aim at splendour. They realized that one of the principal virtues of the string ensemble was its capacity for clear and precise expression. They also saw that it could be used to suggest pathetic emotions, by using forms of expression already familiar in vocal music. Development of this kind went hand in hand with the growth of a new kind of chamber music. The character of the violin was partly responsible for this. It is perhaps difficult for us to realize how brilliant and penetrating this instrument sounded to seventeenth-century ears by comparison with the viol, which had been the favoured instrument for chamber music in the sixteenth century. The violin also had a wider range of expression. All this, together with a desire for more clearly defined rhythms, led to a cultivation of the clarity which I mentioned as the second of the outstanding characteristics of the baroque period. Dance music, of course, had always had a clearly defined rhythm, and it was only natural that such rhythm should continue to be used in the instrumental music of the seventeenth century, whether it was in a definite dance-form or not. But the most striking change occurred in music which was contrapuntal in character—that is to say, music in which the parts had a good deal of melodic independence and indulged in imitation.   In the early part of the sixteenth century instrumental music of this kind was modelled very closely on vocal music.   As time went on it acquired a character of its own.   Instruments have a much wider range than voices, and this was freely exploited.   It was also realized that they had much more flexibility.   So a truly instrumental style of writing grew up with a much more clear-cut structure and a harmonic development as precise as in dance music.   Earlier instrumental music had employed contrasts similar to those in the madrigal or motet, where the words would obviously suggest a change of mood.   In course of time these contrasts came to be more clearly defined by a change of rhythm, so that an instrumental piece might fall into two or more sections.   In the seventeenth century these sections became independent movements. Thus the suite, or series of dance movements, and the sonata developed side by side and became in fact closely interrelated.

In keyboard music there were other developments as well. The tradition of writing variations continued, and in the Lutheran Church we find composers still following the ancient practice of building music on a pre-existent theme by writing pieces on the melodies of hymn tunes.   But here too the new type of contrapuntal writing made itself felt, with its use of clear-cut and sharply rhythmical melodic phrases and of harmonic development organized into definite patterns.   For our example we turn to Girolamo Frescobaldi (1583–1643), who was for many years organist of St Peter's, Rome.   This *Capriccio* illustrates not only the keyboard music of this period, but also many of the characteristics of chamber music as well.   The piece has seven clearly defined sections, differing in character one from another.   The theme of the first section is precise and strongly rhythmical and is developed by means of imitation.   The same theme is used in the remaining sections, but so transformed in rhythm that the contrasts between the sections are strongly defined.

Frescobaldi: *Capriccio*. HISTORY OF MUSIC IN SOUND, VOL. IV. VICTOR LM 6029 (HMV HMS 42, 78 r.p.m.).

In vocal music the change of style is most marked.   Throughout the sixteenth century protests were made against the way in which words were set in the madrigal: that too much attention was paid to illustrating the meaning of individual words, and that it was impossible to hear the words when a poem was sung by several voices and imitation was employed. These are objections which would naturally occur to literary men, but musicians also took notice of them. Some of the later madrigalists were well aware of the difficulty of hearing the words and in particularly expressive passages took care to avoid imitation. There was, however, the further objection that in a composition for several voices there could be no real freedom in the setting or the performance. The natural rhythm of the words was subordinated to musical rhythm, which had to be exact if the voices were to keep together. This difficulty still existed when madrigals were performed by one voice with instruments playing the other parts, and even when sung to lute accompaniment, since the accompaniment was a transcription of the vocal parts.

A great deal of original music for solo voice and lute accompaniment was composed during the sixteenth century. But even here there was not the complete independence which progressive minds were looking for. The accompaniment in such cases was very often modelled on the kind of part-writing to be found in the madrigal, or else the piece was cast in a simple dance rhythm which was attractive as music but did not allow scope for the intense personal expression which was one of the characteristics of Renaissance art. If we want an example of solo singing cast in a traditional form we may look at the anthems of Orlando Gibbons, who was organist of the Chapel Royal and Westminster Abbey and died at the age of forty-two in 1625. The sections for solo voice are accompanied by strings and organ, but the accompaniment is highly contrapuntal and might almost equally well have been written for supporting voices.

> Gibbons: *Behold Thou hast made my days as it were a span long.*
> HISTORY OF MUSIC IN SOUND, VOL. IV. VICTOR LM 6029 (HMV
> HMS 38, 78 r.p.m.).

There are two reasons why Gibbons's writing for solo voice is on traditional lines. First, it is in the nature of church music to be conservative; even Monteverdi, perhaps the most original composer of the period, wrote some church music in a thoroughly old-fashioned style. And secondly, the development of music in England lagged behind the changes that had occurred on the Continent.

This new style of solo song was an attempt to answer all the objections that had been raised against vocal music by subordinating the accompaniment to the solo voice. To do this effectively it was necessary that the bass should move only when a change of harmony was required, and that the harmony itself should be free of any melodic movement in inner parts which would restrict the freedom of the singer. The Italian word *recitar* (to recite) had been used at least as far back as the beginning of the sixteenth century to mean the singing of words by a solo voice. But it now came to have a much more specialized meaning. It meant, in fact, to recite in song as one would recite in speaking, keeping the rhythm of the words and letting the voice rise or fall in accordance with the sentiments which were being expressed. The new style became known as recitative.

Four important points emerge from the study of this style as we find it in the works of such early practitioners as Giulio Caccini and Jacopo Peri, who were themselves singers. First, the singer was left entirely free to adjust the time to suit himself. The notation was only a rough indication of the relative note values. The accompanist therefore had to follow the singer and act merely as a harmonic support. Secondly, since the chords of the accompaniment formed a harmonic progression independent of any individual movement of separate parts, the sequence of harmonies could exist in its own right and could even dictate the notes which the soloist was to sing. Thirdly, the traditions of madrigal writing had familiarized composers with the use of cadences for the sake of punctuation. These cadences were transferred bodily to the new recitative and were a great help in emphasizing the structure of sentences. In addition, certain melodic formulas which had been used by the madrigalists— particularly those used for the expression of passionate emotion— found their way into recitative quite naturally and became incorporated into the new style. Fourthly, the tradition of vocal ornamentation, which had been applied to the upper part of a madrigal, continued to survive in the new form. In some cases the ornamentation was fully written out by the composer; in others it was left to the singer to improvise.

It follows that the new style of recitative was not quite so simple and monotonous as it may appear in the printed texts. Its performance combined the arts of the singer and the actor, and it is quite clear that the practice did not entirely correspond to the theory. If the principal aim was to let the music serve the words, the introduction of ornamentation was indefensible. What was new and significant was the freedom of rhythm allowed to the singer.

Recitative did not kill lyrical song. Both forms flourished side by side. In lyrical movements in a regular rhythm composers found that they could achieve enchanting effects of colour and contrasts by using instruments, either to provide interludes between the singing or to play counterpoints to the vocal line. The word *concerto*, which originally meant any kind of ensemble, came to be used particularly for mixed combinations of this kind.

There developed a more intimate relationship between recitative and song. Composers would sometimes break into a few bars of lyrical melody in the course of a recitative, and it was not long before such interruptions became substantial enough to become complete sections. The solo cantata was a favourite field for this form of association. Recitative and song would alternate in accordance with changing emotions of the text. As a good example of the contrast between rhythmical song, or aria, and recitative, I have chosen a substantial part of a cantata by Luigi Rossi (1598–1653). The singer expresses his admiration for the eyes of the beloved, ending with the plea, 'Pity me at least, if you do not love me.'

Rossi: *Occhi Belli*. HISTORY OF MUSIC IN SOUND, VOL. VI. VICTOR LM 6031 (HMV HMS 58, 78 r.p.m.).

The cultivation of recitative suggests something very different from the new style of instrumental music, where the emphasis was on clarity and sharply defined rhythm. If in recitative there was no rhythm other than the words, it does not follow that it was formless. The use of regular cadences was a safeguard against that, and the earliest composers would often create a logical structure by repeating the bass with variations of the melody above it. In the aria too a favourite device was to repeat a sequence of bass notes—a *basso ostinato*, or obstinate bass—as the foundation of a song. This device was also fruitful in instrumental music.

In general, musicians of the baroque period, with all their enthusiasm for brilliant display and intense emotional expression, never lost sight of the fact that music has its own laws.

APPENDIX

Books

MANFRED BUKOFZER: *Music in the Baroque Era.*
ERNEST WALKER: *A History of Music in England.*
E. H. FELLOWES: *English Cathedral Music*; *Orlando Gibbons.*

Records

Baroque Organ Music.   RENAISSANCE SX 202 (NIXA PLP 224).
French Baroque Organ Music.   CLASSIC EDITIONS 1008.
BENEVOLI: *Festival Mass.*   EPIC 5LC 3035 (PHILIPS ABR 4015–16).
CARISSIMI: *Jepthe.*   DECCA ARC 3005 (DGG APM 14020).
FRESCOBALDI: *Fiori Musicale.*   ALLEGRO 111.   *Organ Music.*   VOX PL
    8780 (E).
A. SCARLATTI: *St John Passion.*   OVERTONE 1.   *Cantata: Su le Sponde
    del Tebro.*   DECCA ARC 3008 (DGG APM 14024).
LECLAIR: *Flute Sonatas.*   OISEAU-LYRE OL 50050–1.   *Violin Sonatas.*
    OISEAU-LYRE OL 50087–8.
GIBBONS: *Church Music.*   WESTMINSTER XWN 18165.   *Anthems,
    Madrigals, etc.*   DGG APM 14056.   *Anthems, etc.*   ARGO RG 80.

22

J. A. Westrup

MONTEVERDI

ONTEVERDI was the most distinguished opera composer of the early seventeenth century. He also excelled in the composition of madrigals of widely different kinds and wrote a considerable amount of church music.

He had a long life and a comparatively uneventful one, though it was not entirely happy. He was born in 1567, the son of a doctor, and at the age of twenty-three he entered the service of the Duke of Mantua as a string player. In 1602 he was promoted to the post of director of music and remained in Mantua for a further ten years until his patron died. For the next thirty years until his death in 1643 he was director of music at St Mark's, Venice. These seem to have been his happiest years, for at Mantua he was poorly paid and overworked and he became a widower at the age of forty. Many of his letters have survived and these combine to reveal much about his personality. Composition was not a routine job for him, but an intense effort, and from the letters we also learn of his profound interest in human beings—an interest which no doubt inclined him strongly towards the composition of opera. We know too that he had the good fortune to live in a highly cultured society: Tasso and Rubens were among those to be found at the Mantuan court.

Monteverdi composed eight books of madrigals. The first was published in 1587 and the last in 1638, five years before his death. A ninth book of miscellaneous pieces was issued posthumously. This material covers practically the whole of his working life, and inevitably we shall find changes of style; the most noticeable being the abandonment of the traditional conception of the madrigal which first became decisive after Monteverdi's migration to Venice.

The early madrigals are remarkable for their very expressive use of dissonance, their capacity for dramatizing a story, and the skill with which a picturesque background is translated into music. A good example is *Ecco mormorar l'onde* from Book II (1590), composed before Monteverdi went to Mantua. The poem describes the dawn, and the morning breeze brings a rare refreshment to hearts in anguish. Notice the sombre beginning for the lower voices, and the skilful way in which the first fluttering of dawn is suggested in the music. Notice also the gay suggestion of the breeze, set in a popular style, and the splendidly tranquil ending.

Monteverdi: *Ecco mormorar l'onde*. HMV DB 5042 (78 r.p.m.).

Monteverdi's first opera was composed in 1607, but it is evident that before this he had become interested in the new form of declamatory solo song. There are examples in the third and fourth books of madrigals (1592 and 1603). The more personal the words, the more the composer felt compelled to adopt an individual style of expression. To emphasize the text, Monteverdi also exploited new resources of harmony, and drew on himself sharp criticism. When he published his fifth book he made a brief comment on this criticism in the preface, which ended with these significant words: 'The modern composer builds on the foundations of truth.' His brother, Giulio Cesare, considerably elaborated his views in a commentary printed in 1607. Giulio Cesare wrote: 'My brother's intention has been to make the words the mistress of the music and not the slave.' These two statements are the key to Monteverdi's work. The words dictate the expression, and in the pursuit of that expression truth is what matters, not any convention. Hence any audacities of harmony are justified if they serve as a faithful expression of the words. This does not mean that Monteverdi consistently uses dissonance, and there is much in his harmony that is so extremely simple that it may even seem naïve to sophisticated minds. But he realizes that at times the utmost simplicity is more moving than any self-conscious attack on the emotions.

In the fifth book of madrigals there are many examples of a declamatory style, and he goes further and adds a *basso continuo* or thorough-bass part for the harpsichord or lute. The idea of writing accompanied madrigals was not new, but the fact that

*F

Monteverdi adopted it is a significant development of his style. In the sixth book (1614) an accompaniment is indispensable to six of the madrigals, though it also contains two cycles which do not require an instrumental bass. One of these cycles, *Lasciatemi morire*, is an arrangement for five voices of a lament sung in recitative by Ariadne in the opera *Arianna*. The fact that solo recitative could be arranged as a madrigal shows how close his madrigal technique had become to the style of writing adopted in opera. The general plan of the accompanied madrigals is that passages for one or more voices with instruments are contrasted with others for all five voices in the earlier style. The solo passages often demand considerable virtuosity.

In Book VII (1619) the change of style is complete. It contains nothing in the older style and is in fact a very mixed collection. Most of the pieces are duets, trios, and quartets with instrumental accompaniment, and an example from the duets will illustrate the passionate intensity that Monteverdi could devote to words of a sentimental character—a poet lamenting that all he desires is taken from him.

Monteverdi: *Ohime dov'e il mio ben*. HMV DB 5040 (78 r.p.m.).

Another example, also from Book VII, is a catalogue of the charms of the loved one, the sprightly character of the music being emphasized by vivacious *ritornelli* for two violins.

Monteverdi: *Chiome d'oro*. HMV DB 5040 (78 r.p.m.).

The eighth book of madrigals (1638) is even more varied. It is divided into two parts, madrigals of war and madrigals of love, though the distinction between them is not so marked as might be expected. War is considered as a metaphorical state of love. Instruments are used in the more elaborate pieces and the style ranges from a charming frivolity to intense emotional expression. The title-page tells us that some of the works are in dramatic style, and these are contrasted with the songs without action. An exceptionally beautiful example of the former is the *Nymph's Lament*. A short trio for male voices describes how she wandered hopelessly through the meadow, and then follows the actual lament, built on a simple sequence of four descending notes in the bass, repeated as an ostinato throughout. The lower voices support the solo intermittently with a commentary and expressions of sympathy.

Monteverdi: *Pianto della Ninfa*. HMV DB 5042 (78 r.p.m.).

Each section of Book VIII also includes a substantial dramatic work. In the war section it is *Il Combattimento di Tancredi e Clorinda*, or *The Fight between Tancred and Clorinda*. In the love section it is *Il Ballo dell' Ingrate, The Ballet of the Hard-hearted Ladies*. Both these works had actually been written many years earlier.

Il Combattimento is a kind of mixture of opera and secular oratorio to a text by Tasso. The story is told by a narrator. Other soloists represent Tancred and Clorinda and sing the words assigned to them in the poem. The two characters appear in costume on stage and fairly detailed instructions are given for the performance. To illustrate the combat a string ensemble is used to play rapid scale passages, violent tremolandos, and aggressive pizzicatos. Monteverdi's output contains nothing as directly exciting as the descriptive passages of this work.

Il Ballo is a kind of masque, designed for dancing as well as singing. Ladies who have been hard-hearted to their lovers have been consigned to Hades. But they are let out for a brief spell to enjoy the pure air of the earth and also to impress on the ladies in the audience how grievous a sin it is to reject love. The subject is highly fanciful and might be amusing if it were not that Monteverdi has charged it with a pathos that makes a direct appeal to our emotions.

It is this capacity for entering into the joys and sorrows of human beings that makes Monteverdi the greatest opera composer of his time. He wrote more than a dozen operas but only three survive complete. A fourth, *Arianna*, is represented only by a fragment, the heroine's lament. The first of the complete operas, *Orfeo*, was performed in 1607 and published two years later. The other two, *Il Ritorno d'Ulisse in Patria* and *L'Incoronazione di Poppea*, date from the last years of his life and are preserved in manuscript.

Orfeo was Monteverdi's first attempt at opera, and it is obvious that he had made a very close study of the new style of recitative, which he handles in masterly fashion. But there is far more in the work than recitative: an extended pastoral scene and choruses which reflect the madrigal and motet style of the sixteenth century, for instance. Contrast between instrumental resources is carefully observed. The keyboard instrument accompanying the recitative changes according to situation and character; strings are used for the scenes on earth and wind instruments for those in Hades. If there is an astonishing variety of treatment there is no

feeling of incongruity, and all kinds of structural devices are used
to give the work coherence.   We are so accustomed to large-scale
works to-day that it is not easy for us to realize the problems
facing composers whose experience was based entirely on relatively
short movements.

We may take as our example of *Orfeo* an extract from Act IV.
Pluto has just relented and agreed to let Eurydice follow Orpheus
back to earth, but on the condition that he does not turn and look
at her.   Orpheus celebrates their announced departure with an
aria introduced by a *ritornello* for violins, and this leads into an
anguished recitative that reflects his doubts.   When he hears a
noise he turns to see if Eurydice is following him.   A spirit tells
him that he has failed to observe Pluto's condition, and Eurydice
takes a piteous farewell of him.   Orpheus would follow her back
to Hades, but he cannot, and in a frenzy of horror he finds himself
being led towards the upper world which means nothing to him
any more.   A solemn symphony for wind instruments concludes
the scene.

Monteverdi: *Orfeo, excerpt from Act IV*.   HISTORY OF MUSIC IN
SOUND, VOL. IV.   VICTOR LM 6030 (HMV HMS 44, 78 r.p. m.).

The consideration of Monteverdi's other two completed operas
is best deferred to the next chapter, but his church music must be
considered in conclusion.   There is no evidence that, despite his
long service at St Mark's and his entry into the priesthood in
1632, he was particularly drawn towards church works.   They
offered him little opportunity for human characterization.   When
we look at the Masses and motets he had to write to fulfil his
duties, we find that some of the music is in so traditional a style that
it makes nonsense of any view that Monteverdi was a completely
revolutionary composer.   No doubt the reason is that church
music is always inclined to be conservative in character.   But
there is a considerable amount of church music similar in style to
the later madrigals, with instruments participating on equal terms
with the voices, including the Vespers of 1610.   This includes
psalm settings, a *Magnificat*, and independent pieces.   The
treatment is often so rich and varied that it is not at all easy to
detect the plain-song.   In this field, no less than in madrigals and
opera, Monteverdi was a master of his craft.

Monteverdi: *Vespro Della Beata Vergine* (1610).   OISEAU-LYRE
50021-2.

APPENDIX

Books

H. F. Redlich: *Claudio Monteverdi.*
L. Schrade: *Monteverdi, Creator of Modern Music.*

Records

Monteverdi: *Madrigals.* Haydn Society HSL O/9004–5, Decca 9627 (Brunswick AXTL 1051). *Mass for Four Voices.* Concert Hall 1196. *Works by Monteverdi.* Vox PL 8560. *Vespro della Beata Vergine.* Vox PL 7902, Oiseau-Lyre OL 50021–2. *Ora pro nobis, etc.* DGG AMP 14020.

23

J. A. Westrup

THE RISE OF OPERA IN ITALY

RECITATIVE figured largely in early opera, and this was only natural. There was no older model for extended solo singing, and since the intention was to re-create the spirit of Greek drama, composers turned as a matter of course to a form of vocal writing which came near to speech. As time went on it was inevitable that musicians should feel that there was a certain monotony in continuous recitative, particularly as it offered few opportunities for using characteristically musical resources. This was perhaps even more obvious in the solo cantata than in opera, where attention would be focused on the action. But lyrical sections—known as *aria* or *arietta*—were so attractive to the ear that they came more and more to dominate opera. In consequence recitative was more and more restricted to those parts of the libretto which were essential to the action and became more and more conventional. It came into its own again when composers revived Monteverdi's experiment of using the orchestra to intensify a dramatic situation. Recitative accompanied by instruments became a staple element of eighteenth-century opera and oratorio.

The earliest operas that have survived complete are settings of the same libretto by the two pioneers in recitative, Jacopo Peri and Giulio Caccini. The subject they took was the story of Orpheus and Eurydice, later to be used by Monteverdi in his *Orfeo*. Peri's *Euridice* was performed in Florence in 1600 and published the next year. Caccini's setting was published in 1600, but not performed until 1602. In each case the story is told for the most part in recitative, but there are also lyrical sections and choruses for shepherds.

Peri explained his intention in a preface. He accepted the view that Greek tragedy was sung throughout and used recitative as a modern equivalent.   Neither he nor Caccini were aware that they were inaugurating a new musical form, and it was only gradually that works of this kind came to acquire the name *opera in musica*, that is to say, 'a musical work.'   Music came to exist in its own right, and people went to the opera to enjoy fine singing, as well as to admire a spectacle.   The inclusion in Monteverdi's *Orfeo* of a quite substantial number of ensemble pieces for voices and instrumental movements shows that it took over a good deal of the function that music had enjoyed when it was used in the form of interludes in spoken drama in the sixteenth century.

It is quite possible that opera would have remained a brief experiment if it had not been taken up in Rome.   In the theatre of the Barberini family there were opportunities for far more elaborate productions than the performances at Florence and Mantua.   We find extensive use of the chorus and a growing inclination to break up the recitative with arias, and one composer, Mazzochi, actually wrote in 1626 that he introduced *arioso* sections 'to break the tediousness of the recitative.'   Another feature of the Roman operas is the introduction of scenes of a lighter character, some of which are pure comedy.   In Stefano Landi's *La Morte d'Orfeo* (1619) the ferryman Charon sings a jovial song in which he invites Orpheus to drink from the waters of Lethe which bring forgetfulness.

Landi: *La Morte d'Orfeo*: *Bevi, bevi*.   HISTORY OF MUSIC IN SOUND, VOL. IV.   VICTOR LM 6029 (HMV HMS 44, 78 r.p.m.).

Although opera was so vigorously cultivated in Rome, it remained very much a court entertainment.   The decisive change came in 1637 when the first opera house was opened in Venice, and opera became a commercial entertainment.   This did not necessarily mean any lowering of musical standards, but it did mean some reduction of resources.   The managers could hardly afford to spend so much on chorus and orchestra as the princely patrons in Rome, particularly as they still had to provide a lavish stage spectacle to attract an audience.   Hence we find that the chorus plays only a minor role in the Venetian operas, and the orchestra generally consists merely of strings and harpsichord.

It was for Venice that Monteverdi wrote his last two operas— *Il Ritorno d'Ulisse in patria* (1641) and *L'incoronazione di Poppea* (1642).   The return of Ulysses to his native Ithaca deals with exactly the kind of human relationships which were to figure so largely in eighteenth-century opera—Penelope's obstinate attachment to her absent husband, the ardent determination of the suitors to win her hand, and the triumphant reunion of Ulysses with his wife. The same is true of *L'incoronazione di Poppea*, which deals with incidents in the life of the Emperor Nero. His passion for Poppaea leads him to sweep aside all opposition, including his old teacher Seneca, and finally to make her his empress.

Both these works follow the lead of Roman opera by introducing scenes of light relief. In *Poppea* we have the charming love-scene between a page and a maidservant, which is entirely irrelevant to the plot but serves to throw into strong relief the stoicism of Seneca and Nero's unbridled passion. In *Ulisse* Iros, the court buffoon, is a comic character. At the end of the second act Ulysses destroys the suitors. The third act opens with Iros lamenting the end of his patrons; where is he to turn now for food and drink?

Monteverdi: *Il Ritorno d'Ulisse in patria: O dolor, o martir.* CONCERT HALL CHS 1085 (NIXA CLP 1085).

This very amusing scene is a combination of recitative and *arioso*, which may be defined as a passage in regular rhythm which emerges from the recitative but is quite distinct from it in style. With the development of the aria as a vehicle for fine singing and for summing up a dramatic situation, *arioso* passages tended to disappear from the recitative. The aria which is our example is sung by Arnalta, Poppaea's nurse, and is in the form of a lullaby, with a contrasting section at the end.

Monteverdi: *L'incoronazione di Poppea: Arnalta's lullaby.* CONCERT HALL CHS 1184.

Francesco Cavalli (1602–76) who was a singer in St Mark's choir under Monteverdi, wrote more than forty operas, not all of which have survived. He must have come under Monteverdi's influence, but he may well have influenced his master in turn. Very similar types of music occur in the operas of both composers. There are frequent examples in Cavalli and Monteverdi of *arioso* and of complete arias, and both used the ground bass as a foundation for a vocal piece. In Cavalli's *Egisto* (1643) there is a superb example of a solo on a chromatic ground bass, like that used by Purcell in the heroine's lament in *Dido and Aeneas* and by Bach in the *Crucifixus* of his *Mass in B minor*. For an example of the flowing melody of which Cavalli was a master we may examine the passage from *Egisto* in which two lovers hail the dawn. This is not in the strict sense a duet, but the sections for the two singers show parallels in the music as well as in the text.

Cavalli: *Egisto: Musici della selva.* HISTORY OF MUSIC IN SOUND, VOL. V. VICTOR LM 6030 (HMV HMS 45, 78 r.p.m.).

Cavalli was not only a master of song but also had a vivid sense of drama and could use the orchestra to create atmosphere. His younger contemporary, Cesti (1623–69), had the same gifts. The most famous of his works was *Il Pomo d'Oro* (*The Golden Apple*), composed for a state occasion in Vienna and produced there in the winter of 1666–7. No expense was spared in the lavish production. The opera opens, appropriately, with a stately prologue making reference to the Emperor's dominions, and the action proper does not begin until the opening of the first act. In the underworld Proserpine sings of the horrors of Pluto's kingdom. The orchestra, used mainly in alternation with the singer, consists solely of wind instruments—two *cornetti*, three trombones, and a bassoon; we may recall the similar ensemble used by Monteverdi for the infernal scenes of *Orfeo*. The *cornetti* (a now obsolete instrument replaced in the recording by clarinets) are used to provide treble parts to blend with the trombones. The keyboard instrument is a reed organ, which Monteverdi too had used for the supernatural scenes in his opera. The total effect is to emphasize the fact that we are in a world remote from all human associations.

Cesti: *Il Pomo d'Oro: E dove t'aggiri.* HISTORY OF MUSIC IN SOUND, VOL. V. VICTOR LM 6030 (HMV HMS 45, 78 r.p.m.).

As the aria established itself more and more firmly as an indispensable element, composers were bound to consider ways of organizing it into a coherent shape. So long as it was merely a pastoral ditty there was little difficulty, but once it outgrew this stage there were problems for which the older traditions of strophic song provided no solution. One method was to organize the vocal melody above a ground bass, though this method could not be used for every aria without the risk of intolerable monotony. The new method which became most popular was simply to repeat at the end of the song the material which had been used at the beginning, a structure which may be represented by the formula ABA. We find a miniature example in Monteverdi's *Orfeo*, and later on we come across more extended examples. They came to be called *da capo* arias, because the singer went back to the head, or beginning, of the song.

By the time of Stradella (c. 1645–82) the aria was well established as the most important part of an opera. The two *da capo* arias of our next example make much use of a figure in the bass which recurs frequently as a foundation and may also appear in the voice part. This is not quite the same as a ground bass because there is no regular repetition of a formula, but it shows how the principle could be adapted to give coherence to an aria of another kind.

Stradella: *Floridoro: Stelle ingrate* and *Dimmi amor*. HISTORY OF MUSIC IN SOUND, VOL. V. VICTOR LM 6030 (HMV HMS 46, 78 r.p.m.).

Fine singing and splendid staging remained the principal ingredients of later seventeenth-century opera in Italy. Singers came to be idolized, not least the *castrati* or male sopranos. By all accounts their voices were capable not only of great sweetness, but also of a virile intensity. In love duets male and female soprano voices could intertwine at the same level, and duets were the staple form of these operas. The operatic ensemble as we understand it to-day was virtually non-existent outside comedy. But in Alessandro Scarlatti's opera *Tito Sempronio Gracco* (1720) we find a rare example of a quartet in a serious opera, though it does not give us the simultaneous characterization of four different people. Scarlatti called it an aria for four singers—which in fact is what it is. It is in *da capo* form and the rhythm is that of the *siciliana*, familiar to us from the *Pastoral Symphony* and 'He shall feed His flock' from *Messiah*. The singers are three sopranos and a tenor.

Alessandro Scarlatti: *Tito Sempronio Gracco: Idolo del cor mio*. HISTORY OF MUSIC IN SOUND, VOL. V. VICTOR LM 6030 (HMV HMS 46, 78 r.p.m.).

APPENDIX

BOOKS

D. J. GROUT: *A Short History of Opera*.
E. WELLESZ: *Essays on Opera*.
S. TOWNELEY WORSTHORNE: *Venetian Opera in the Seventeenth Century*.

RECORDS

CAVALLI: *Il Guidizio Universale* (oratorio). COLOSSEUM 1032.
MONTEVERDI: *Orfeo*. DECCA ARC 3035–6 (DGG APM 14057–8). *Il Ballo delle Ingrate*. HAYDN SOCIETY 30001 Vox PL 8090 (E). *Il Combattimento*. ANTHOLOGIE SONORE AS 9 Vox PL 8560 (E).
A. SCARLATTI: *Il Trionfo dell'Onore*. CETRA 1223.

24

Denis Stevens

ITALIAN INSTRUMENTAL MUSIC IN THE SEVENTEENTH CENTURY

ITALIAN operas in the seventeenth century were rarely published, unlike church and chamber music, which appeared frequently and brought out all the best in Italian composers between the time of Gabrieli and that of Geminiani.   Purely instrumental music could be divided into two main groups, concertos and sonatas, and both were common to church music and chamber music.   You could hear a sonata, played by violins, cello, and organ in many a church in the days when that kind of music was not only allowed, but actively encouraged: in fact, the pieces were actually called *sonate da chiesa*—church sonatas.   In the larger churches you could hear a concerto played by groups of string and wind instruments, now alternating their contrasting tone-colours, now combining them, and always with an organ accompaniment.   At first these pieces were published at the end of sets of part-books containing motets, settings of the Mass, and other liturgical music, so that when the singers had finished their part of the service they could pass the books over to the instrumentalists.   Later composers and publishers began to issue complete books of instrumental pieces.

Giovanni Gabrieli was one of the earliest composers to make use of the term 'concerto.'   The true meaning of the word is still much debated, but fortunately most scholars agree that the result —in terms of instrumental sonorities—is contrast.   This contrast may have taken place between a loud group of instruments and a soft-toned group, or between groups of similar timbre but different range.   An example of the latter kind can be heard in this *Canzona* for double string orchestra by Giovanni Gabrieli.

Giovanni Gabrieli: *Canzona No. 1.*   LONDON LS 686 (DECCA LX 3102).

The texture is still essentially polyphonic—the kind of music

155

that one would find in double-choir motets of the same period—
yet there are unmistakably instrumental touches in the individual
lines.   The essence of the concerto form is there.   Two bodies
of instruments are playing, first one, then the other, and at a climax
point they join forces.

Sometimes the Italians spelt 'concerto' with a 'c' in the middle
of the word; sometimes they spelt it with an 's'—'conserto.'   In
the first case the Latin root would be 'concertare'—'to fight side
by side, to compete as brothers in arms.'   But in the second case
it would be 'conserere'—'to congregate, to join together.'   Just to
confuse things even further, some composers used the word
'concento,' with the obvious implication that the musicians gathered
together in a circle.   Rather than worry about these derivations
and meanings we should consider how best to reproduce what the
composer wrote.   Shall it be done with a huge body of strings,
drowning out the faint twanging of an insufficient harpsichord, or
with a smaller group like those we can see in drawings and paintings
of baroque concerts ?

Two famous theoretical writers, Agazzari and Gasperini, at
each end of the seventeenth century, can help us.   In his treatise
published in 1607 Agazzari makes an important distinction between
continuo instruments and their corresponding function.   The
correct instrument to support a large orchestra is the organ, and
that is why the bass part in any given set of books is usually
labelled 'organo.'   We find Gasperini saying the same thing in a
treatise published in 1708.   He even goes so far as to distinguish
between different ways of treating discords, depending on whether
an organ or harpsichord is being used.   Sometimes both instruments were used, for in the concerto grosso no single instrument
had the dynamic range to support the delicate tones of the soloists
and to add body to the passages where everybody joined in.

The effectiveness of the harpsichord in a small group may be
gauged from the closing section of a sonata by Gabrieli, for oboe,
violins, and continuo.

Giovanni Gabrieli: Sonata a tre. DUCRETET-THOMSON DTL
93046.

A ready and effective substitute for the harpsichord was the
lute, and there is obviously room for the plucked string instrument
in modern performances of music of the baroque era.   Just as the
lute was used as an alternative to the harpsichord, so the cornet

(pronounced 'cor*net*', and not to be confused with our *cor*net) was brought in by way of substitute for the violin. It was made of wood, though sometimes covered with leather, and it was played with a mouthpiece similar to that of a French horn. It is difficult to play, and its tone is not easy to describe, but we have now a successful modern recording in which two cornets are joined by two violins, gamba, organ, and three trombones. The music is the opening of Monteverdi's *Sonata sopra Sancta Maria*.

Monteverdi: *Sonata sopra Sancta Maria* (*Vespers of 1610*). Decca ARC 3005 (DGG APM 14020).

The place of the cornet was soon ousted, however, by the more brilliant and versatile trumpet, and the trumpet seems to have had a great vogue in the town of Bologna, where such composers as Perti, Cazzati, and Torelli wrote brilliant sonatas and concertos for one or two solo trumpets and strings. Solo instruments are often grouped in pairs. In chamber music the same tendency can be seen in the trio sonata which dominated the Italian scene for the latter half of the seventeenth century and far beyond, influencing French, German, and English composers towards its further development. The trio sonata belies its name, for there are four instruments: two violins, cello, and harpsichord. The cello and harpsichord play from the same music and are considered as an entity; their respective functions are to strengthen the bass line and to provide an interesting improvised middle to the texture. Similarly a continuo instrument or instruments is implied in a sonata for solo violin in Italian music of this period.

The Italian organists of the seventeenth century were of slighter stature than the French and Germans, but their contribution was no mean one. In the works of the greatest of them, Girolamo Frescobaldi, a touch of the concerto principle may be sensed, even though modern recordings make no effort to reproduce it. His *Fiori Musicale* contains music for the organist to play at Mass; it is solo music, but it is not intended to be played continuously. In the *Kyrie* the organist was supposed to provide verses to alternate with the chanting of the choir. The nine invocations of the *Kyrie* would be divided alternately between choir and organ. Thus a system of contrasting tone-colours and dynamics would be set up, and the effect would be that of a concerto with the organ as soloist and the voices as *concerto grosso*.

Frescobaldi: *Kyrie*. Period 586 (NIXA PLP 586).

The theatrical contribution to the development of Italian instrumental music is more direct and definite than that of church music. Theatre orchestras, which were not very large, not only accompanied the singers, but also introduced the drama and linked the scenes together with short instrumental pieces called *sinfonie*. The opening *sinfonia avanti l'opera*, or symphony before the opera, had the utilitarian purpose of indicating that the opera was about to begin.

It was due to Alessandro Scarlatti that this overture became a work of artistic importance rather than a purely functional call to order in a crowded opera-house. He helped to develop this new form into the symphony, linking his own product with the contemporary *concerti grossi* which were enjoying such a vogue. He called his collection of twelve symphonies *Sinfonie di Concerto Grosso*, thus stressing their dual nature. The first two sections of his *Symphony in D minor* demonstrate Scarlatti's method of securing the maximum contrast in spite of slender resources—only flutes, strings, and continuo. Very often the violins play in thirds; they are echoed by the two flutes also playing in thirds, and this is a legacy from the trio sonata. Scarlatti's slow movement starts as if with a flute solo, accompanied by strings and harpsichord; but soon the second flute joins in as if to underline the *concerto grosso* part of the original title.

Alessandro Scarlatti: *Symphony No. 5 in D minor*. ANGEL 35141 (COLUMBIA 33 CX 1171).

The *concerto grosso* proper did not as a rule include wood-wind instruments, but was essentially an interplay between small and large forces of strings. The small group consisted at first of two violins and continuo, though later some composers added a viola to the group. It comprised the best three players from the orchestra, plus the most brilliant and imaginative harpsichord player, and he was freer than his orchestral-continuo colleague because he was unfettered by figures in the cello part. He could contribute much bold and inventive figuration as well as fill the gap in compass between the two solo violins and cello.

The name of Arcangelo Corelli will always be of prime importance in the history of the *concerto grosso*, but others—Alessandro Stradella, Giuseppe Torelli, and Tomasso Albinoni, for example—made important contributions too. The *concerto grosso* was taken up in France by Leclair, in Germany by Telemann, and in England by William Boyce and Handel. There was another memorable Italian, Francesco Geminiani, who had studied with Scarlatti and Corelli and ultimately lost his place in the Naples opera orchestra because no one could follow his excessive rubato and changes of tempo. He later settled in Dublin, taught and gave concerts and published a treatise on violin playing. He wrote violin sonatas and several sets of *concerti grossi*, and many of them are of the very first rank. The E minor *Concerto Grosso*, Opus. 3, No. 3, is a fine example of Geminiani's understanding of the sonorities of a string orchestra.

Geminiani: *Concerto Grosso in E minor, Op. 3, No. 3.* Vox PL 8290 (E) or WESTMINSTER 18002.

Apart from the understandable ascendancy of the stringed instruments, the oboe and bassoon gradually emerged as solo instruments rather than as mere orchestral effects. When the German flautist, Quantz, tried to interest Scarlatti in the flute, the Italian maintained that all wood-wind instruments played out of tune, though later he relented and wrote some flute pieces for Quantz. What Scarlatti did for the flute, Vivaldi did for the oboe and bassoon, and his finales show the agility he expected of his bassoon player.

Vivaldi: *Bassoon Concerto in D minor.* LONDON LS 591 (DECCA LX 3100).

Vivaldi also wrote numerous oboe concertos, although many were originally violin concertos which he authorized to be played on the oboe. His contemporary, the Venetian nobleman Tomasso Albinoni, wrote solo oboe concertos of great beauty and deep feeling, and these works probably did more than any others to bring the oboe to the forefront as a solo instrument at the beginning of the eighteenth century. They have melody, charm, and display in equal measure.

Albinoni: *Oboe Concertos, Op. 7.* OISEAU-LYRE OL 50041.

APPENDIX

BOOKS

M. PINCHERLE: *Antonio Vivaldi et la musique instrumentale.*
C. SARTORI: *Bibliografia della Musica Strumentale Italiana.*

Records

ALBINONI: *Sonata in G Minor*. DECCA 9572 (BRUNSWICK AXTL 1004).

ARIOSTI: *Lesson V*. DECCA ARC 3008 (DGG AMP 14024).

BARSANTI: *Concerti Grossi*. OISEAU-LYRE OL 50008.

CORELLI: *Concerti Grossi, Op. 6*. VOX PL 7893.

LEO: *Concerto in D*. ANGEL 35254 (COLUMBIA 33 CX 1276).

LOCATELLI: *Concerto Grosso*. WESTMINSTER WL 5030.

MANFREDINI: *Concerto Grosso*. DUCRETET-THOMSON EL 93042.

TARTINI: *Concerto in F*. ANGEL 35255 (COLUMBIA 33 CX 1277).

VIVALDI: *Concerti for Orchestra*. OISEAU-LYRE OL 50073. *L'Estro Armonico, Op. 3*. VOX PL 7423 (E). *La Tempesta di Mare, etc.* HMV ALP 1439.

25

Denis Stevens

THE ITALIAN VIOLIN SCHOOL

NOBODY knows for certain who invented the violin, or where it was invented, but the earliest days of the instrument and its music have been associated with Italy. There have been many romantic, and almost certainly inaccurate, ways of accounting for this; some saying that the best kind of wood for violins was found only in Italy, others saying that Italian makers alone held the secret of the varnish which was applied to the body and neck of the instrument after its multitude of parts had been glued together and allowed to dry. It is not impossible that the climate of certain Italian towns, in particular Cremona, was especially suitable for the process of careful drying.

The violin is—or should be—a perfect marriage of two kinds of beauty: beauty of form and beauty of tone. In the hands of a master, a violin can be the most eloquent and expressive of all instruments, at the same time the most brilliant and the most soulful. In spite of its range of effects, the violin is above all an instrument that sings, and so the Italian people gained a reputation not only for making violins, but for composing violin music. The instrument was developed steadily throughout the sixteenth century, though it did not have an immediate success because it was less suited to playing the music then popular. Music and instruments are inseparably bound together: the development and cultivation of the one will lead to new ideas for the other.

Later on the harpsichord held out against the piano in the same way that the viol held out against the violin. When we hear sixteenth-century consort music played on modern stringed instruments, somehow the sounds are all wrong: polyphony needs evenness of tone and great suavity. Solo music, on the other hand, requires great brilliance and power of tone. The earliest violins, however, were not as brilliant and powerful as ours. A desire for greater brilliance led musicians to adopt higher and higher tuning pitches, and standard pitch has moved up a tone or even a tone and a half since the time of Bach.   This has meant that many of the fine old violins have had to be altered by the substitution of thicker bass-bars, longer necks, and tighter strings than they were ever meant to support.   In some instances these changes have altered the whole character of the instruments, and the wonder is that they still sound so well.   It is still possible to find some violins that have not been mutilated in the interests of higher pitch and bigger tone, and on records we can hear one made orginally in 1793 and restored to its pristine form.

Corelli: *La Follia*.   DECCA ARC 3008 (DGG APM 14024).

Arcangelo Corelli (1653–1713) was one of the greatest of the seventeenth-century violinists and composers.   Little is known of his early life.   He travelled a good deal, and he was first attached to the court at Munich; he then went to Paris, but the brevity of his visit was said to be due to the jealousy of Lully.   About 1685 Corelli returned to Italy, settling in Rome, where he enjoyed the favour and protection of Cardinal Ottoboni and composed music for the weekly concerts at the palace. He seems to have been a man of modest and amiable disposition.   As a composer in the Italian style, Corelli had few rivals, and his sonatas for solo violin and continuo have enjoyed an almost constant vogue since the day of their first publication.   Their variety and effectiveness is splendidly shown by Corelli's variations on the old ground bass theme, *La Follia*.

Corelli: *La Follia*.   DECCA ARC 3008 (DGG APM 14024).

Corelli had many predecessors in the field of violin composition, and though few of the names are well known their role in the development of the Italian violin school was an important one. We have some evidence of their renown as early as 1610, not in Italy but in England, where a young composer named John Cooper thought fit to change his name to Giovanni Coperario after a brief period of study in Italy.   Some of his solo sonatas and trio sonatas are excellent works, judged by any standards, and the same can be said for many of the sonatas and suites composed by the Italian Biagio Marini.   Other noteworthy writers for the violin were Quagliatti, Farina, Merula, Fontana, and Uccellini, and it was due to them that the compass of the violin was extended.   Uccellini makes use of some remarkably high notes which seem never to have appeared in violin music before; while Merula is often said to be the first to make extensive use of the G string. Farina's contribution appears to be a frivolous one; the imitation on the violin of the mewing of cats, the barking of dogs, the cackling of hens, and the fifes and drums of the military.

During the second part of the century the two main centres of music printing and publishing were Venice and Bologna. New firms joined old-established family businesses, and there were other publishers in Rome. Without suggesting that this activity was of the type known as feverish, it is perfectly clear that composers had a good deal to contend with when once their manuscripts had been consigned to the printer. Notational misprints, which are by no means infrequent in normal publications, often take on horrifying proportions in complex works involving *scordatura*, a method of tuning that was capable of extending the technical possibilities of string instruments. Rests are often miscounted and misprinted, and since no scores were available, the musicians had to do the best they could with the part-books, beginning a bar earlier or later until the result seemed to fit reasonably well.

All this, however, was part of the game, and musicians were usually good enough to make up for any defects in the material they had to use. It was owing to the outstanding richness of the vein that the pure gold of Corelli's workmanship eventually came to light. Without the lesser masters, the greater men would never have achieved the success that they did. Giuseppe Torelli —as far as the history books are concerned—is a lesser master when compared with Corelli, but there is more than a mere spark of genius in the way he uses two solo violins in his concerto for Christmas Eve.

Torelli: *Concerto in G minor* (*Grave/Vivace*). DECCA 9649.

Torelli went to Bologna from Verona and settled down to a life of teaching and playing. Several of his most important published works have survived, and many unpublished ones are preserved in the archives of the Collegiate Church of San Petronio in Bologna, where he was an instrumentalist. His concertos influenced those of Vivaldi, as much in form as in texture, and eventually this influence was felt by J. S. Bach, who copied down many concertos by Italian masters, rearranging them and reworking them as he thought fit.

Another lesser master who is gradually coming into his own is Tomasso Albinoni. He was primarily a dramatic composer, and it is said that he wrote more than forty operas. Nowadays it is his violin music that attracts the attention of scholars and performers. Even if the writing for the solo violin does not match Torelli and Vivaldi at their most brilliant, it is nevertheless finely turned and idiomatically set forth.

Albinoni: *Violin Concerto No. 7 in D*. DECCA 9598 (BRUNSWICK AXTL 1023).

Like Torelli and Vivaldi, Albinoni also served as source material for Bach's inquiring mind. Spitta tells us that Bach 'must have had an especial liking for Albinoni's compositions. Even in his later years he was accustomed to use Albinoni's bass parts for practice in figured bass.' Vivaldi, however, often composed so quickly that he rarely troubled to figure the bass at all. Once he added a few figures to the bass part with the remark: 'These are for the dimwits.'

Strange and improbable stories still surround the name of Antonio Vivaldi, and they at least point to the fact that he was a very remarkable and colourful personality. Just as Corelli had his orchestra in Rome, so Vivaldi had his at Venice, at the *Ospedale della Pietà*, a home for waifs and strays. An English traveller who visited Venice in 1720 affirms that 'Every Sunday and Holiday there is a performance of music in the chapels of these hospitals, vocal and instrumental, performed by the young women of the place: who are set in a gallery above, and . . . are hid from any distinct view of those below, by a lattice of ironwork. The organ parts, as well as those of other instruments, are all performed by the young women.'

Not all of Vivaldi's two hundred or so violin concertos date from his Venetian period; some were composed when he served the princely courts of Mantua and Vienna. But the brilliant young violinists of the *Pietà* must have inspired Vivaldi to combine grace and purity with an ample measure of display. Vivaldi had an outlook upon violin playing which united all the common-sense things that the violin, by its very nature, was most capable of expressing. He was an Italian, and singing was in his veins. For him the four strings of the violin were soprano, contralto, tenor, and bass; each had its characteristic timbre, each had its own range of artistic possibilities. Equal in importance to the solo part in Vivaldi's estimation was the accompanying body of strings which, together with the continuo instruments, made up the orchestral part in his larger concertos. The orchestral accompaniment to a solo concerto called for careful planning on the composer's part. Vivaldi ensured variety of colour by many different means, not the least of which was the implied use of two keyboard instruments; a large harpsichord or chamber organ would be used for the full passages, and a small harpsichord for the solos.

Vivaldi's best known work, both in the eighteenth century and now, is *The Four Seasons*, a series of four descriptive concertos which constitute the first third of his Opus 8. Each concerto is prefixed by a poem, describing the general character and events of spring, summer, autumn, and winter. Vivaldi illustrates the poems by primarily musical descriptive passages, and not (as was the case with Farina) the distortion of musical elements to make for a poor copy of nature.

Vivaldi: *The Four Seasons*. VICTOR LHMV 26 (HMV ALP 1234).

Many Italian composers for the violin attempted to emulate Vivaldi, but few succeeded. The one way ahead lay in a complete re-evaluation of technical problems, even to the extent of altering the violin bow and so changing the tone of the instrument. Guiseppe Tartini (1692–1770) made various experiments of this nature, and his school of violin playing at Padua was perhaps the last of the really great Italian schools. His name is inseparably connected with a sonata that is not really one of his best works: the *Devil's Trill*. It is in his sonata in G minor, sometimes called *Didone Abbandonata* (*Dido Forsaken*) that we hear the swan-song of the great Italian.

Tartini: *Sonata in G Minor ; 'Didone Abbandonata.'* ENGLISH DECCA LX 3137.

APPENDIX
BOOKS
M. PINCHERLE: *Corelli.*
D. B. BOYDEN: *Francesco Geminiani: The Art of Playing on the Violin.*
R. GIAZOTTO: *Tommaso Albinoni.*

RECORDS
CORELLI: *Violin Sonatas.* ALLEGRO ALX 109.
PERGOLESI: *Sonata for Violin and Strings, etc.* ANGEL 3538–B (COLUMBIA 33 CX 1307).
TARTINI: *Violin Concerto in E.* DECCA 9572 (BRUNSWICK AXTL 1004).

26

A. K. Holland

PURCELL AND ENGLISH SEVENTEENTH-CENTURY MUSIC

THE English are said to be conservative in their artistic tastes and it has even been unkindly suggested that they usually begin to get enthusiastic about new things at the moment when other countries are about to give them up. Some of the things which were most characteristic of English music in the seventeenth century began to take shape in the sixteenth, for example the formation of a self-contained instrumental style. Roughly, the period we are concerned with may be divided into three phases: the post-Elizabethan, the Commonwealth or Puritan phase, and the Restoration. This last is much the most important for our purpose, for it was Purcell's own period. His dates are 1659–95.

Now the music of the seventeenth century was everywhere influenced by the example of Italy, that 'Great Academy' of artistic teaching since the Renaissance. It was from Italy that the chief innovations of the period came: the invention of what came to be known as opera, the development of the cantata for solo voice or chorus with instrumental accompaniment, and the growth of self-contained instrumental music. But the English were conservative and they proceeded slowly, though not more so than other countries such as France and Germany. They had their own instrumental music, those *fantazias* or Fancies, as they called them, for the viols which, incidentally, were not primitive violins but different instruments tuned and strung differently. Enormous quantities of music were written for these instruments in the first quarter of the century and they lingered on in England long after they had practically been given up elsewhere. As we shall hear, Purcell composed some of the very latest examples, though whether for viols or violins is not quite certain, for by his time the violin, as they said, had largely put the viol out!

Purcell: *Fantasias for Strings.* DECCA ARC 3007 (DGG APM 14027).

We must remember that in England the seventeenth century was a period of great political and religious upheaval. The Puritans have often been blamed for destroying the English musical tradition, but in point of fact the Puritans were not in the least hostile to music as such.   They were opposed to elaborate church music, and there is plenty of evidence that the extremists carried their hatred of church music to the lengths of destroying a number of church organs and music books.   On the other hand most of the leading Puritans were musically minded.   Cromwell had an organ set up at Hampton Court—he had borrowed it (shall we say ?) from one of the Oxford Colleges.   And he ran State concerts and entertained musicians. Music publishing made its first great strides during the period, and many famous collections such as Playford's *English Dancing Master* appeared on the scene.   Roger North, the old chronicler of the times, tells us that there was a great deal of amateur practice in country houses.   Not exactly a picture of a country bereft of all musical activity!

At the same time there is no doubt that Puritanism brought about a great rift in the minds of Englishmen, a cleavage expressed not merely in the violence of the Civil War, but in the way of thinking about life and art.   The most significant change of the Commonwealth period was the steady secularization of music and the growth of the professional spirit.   Driven out of their posts in the church and deprived of the patronage of the Royal Chapel, musicians took to teaching and to giving public concerts.   Actually, we hear of public concerts for the first time during the Commonwealth period.   It was during this period also that the first English operas began to appear uneasily upon the stage, careful as they had to be to avoid the imputation of being stage plays, which were forbidden.

The new Italian style of singing which took the form of recitative, the declamatory style which formed the basis of the early Italian operas, had been slowly percolating into England through the medium of the most characteristic English form of entertainment, the Court Masque.

The masque was an aristocratic entertainment, consisting of poetry, allegory, song, dialogue, dancing, and, above all, splendid and costly scenery.   In fact, the English addiction to masques and masquerades probably explains why opera as the Italians understood it was slow in making headway here.   We have a sort of transitional stage in Shirley's masque of *Cupid and Death* with music by Matthew Locke and Christopher Gibbons which shows music beginning to take a major role; and in Blow's *Venus and Adonis*, although it is still called a masque, we have actually a small chamber opera of which every word is sung. The importance of Blow's work lies in the fact that it seems to have been the model on which Purcell's only real opera, *Dido and Aeneas*, was based.

John Blow: *Venus and Adonis*. OISEAU-LYRE OL 50004.

We are now in a position to approach Purcell more directly. Next to the recitative, the chief formal innovation of the period is the development of a new type of concerted music. The old fantasies treated each of the parts as of equal importance. The parts imitated each other in the manner of a fugue but none took precedence. Purcell's *fantazias* were written in his twenty-first year. It is in the first set of sonatas two years later that he makes open acknowledgment to Italian influences. These are written for two violins, bass viol, and harpsichord. There is still a good deal of independent part-writing, but the tendency is for the keyboard instrument to assert harmonic rights, and with that there is a much more clearly defined sense of key. The movements, four or more in number, alternating between slow and quick, usually contain a movement called *Canzona* in the fugal style. Purcell's sonatas belong to the so-called *chiesa*, or church, type, by reason of their more serious nature, as compared with the *sonata da camera*, or chamber sonata, which consisted of dance movements and ultimately crystallized in the suite, whereas the church type was the forerunner of the modern sonata. They were none the less secular in tendency for all their gravity and a certain clinging to the older methods of composing concerted music.

Purcell: *Trio Sonatas*. PERIOD 572 (alt. ARGO RG 84–5).

These were the things that Purcell wrote presumably for private use rather than public performance. But as the leading composer of his age, his main work lay in other directions. He grew up under King Charles II. His father and his uncle were both gentlemen of the Chapel Royal, that is, singers in the King's private chapel. He quickly showed signs of precociousness, began composing at an early age and entered the Chapel choir. Later on, when his voice broke, he became assistant to the tuner of the King's wind-instruments, a very valuable training for a boy of his talent. Purcell's voice, by the way, turned into that of a high counter-tenor or male alto and we have records of his ability as a singer and of what were called the 'incredible graces' that he introduced into his singing. A great deal of Purcell's more spectacular vocal writing was intended for this particular voice.

Purcell: *Music for a while*. HMV C 3890 (78 r.p.m.).

Purcell's next post was that of organ-tuner at Westminster Abbey, where he came under the influence of the great Dr Blow, and when Blow retired Purcell succeeded him as organist at the age of twenty. From then on all paths were open to him.

Charles II had returned from France with a taste for everything French. He is said to have detested the old English music and those solemn fantasies which had left their mark on Purcell. His band of violins played in the Royal Chapel when he attended service, and the type of anthem he encouraged consisted of long instrumental passages and 'verses,' that is, interludes of a declamatory nature for one or more voices. These 'verse' anthems, of which Purcell composed many, besides the so-called 'full' anthems in the more traditional style, were an excellent training for an all-round composer with duties as Court Musician. Almost every year Purcell produced a Royal Ode. The words were often the merest doggerel written in a vein of adulation that we should nowadays regard as too much savouring of toadyism. But that was the convention of the time.

We know as little of his life or his politics as we know of Shakespeare's. That he was a convivial soul we must infer from the number of catches and rounds, often with somewhat Rabelaisian words, which he wrote. At the same time we have a very clear account of his activities as a composer. He was one of the first, if not actually *the* first, to write odes for the annual celebration of the feast of St Cecilia. These celebrations seem to have been instituted in England in the year 1683 and Purcell wrote no less than three odes round about this time and others in later years. The form of the odes is very similar to that of the Chapel Royal anthems with its verses for alto, tenor, and bass, its full choruses and instrumental interludes. The ode for 1692, *Hail, Bright Cecilia*, is one of his finest, and the poem is not as flat-footed as some of the verses Purcell was forced to accept for royal occasions.

G

Conventional it may be, but it is rich in the kind of verbal images that Purcell loved to illustrate; not merely, as one would expect, images relating to the art of music, but images of motion, of contrast, and vivid suggestion which Purcell caught up and embodied in his favourite devices of repetition and word-painting. The chief solos are for counter-tenor and one—the fantastic aria *'Tis Nature's Voice*, with its incredible runs and florid passages— was sung by Purcell himself. The whole scheme of the work is finely planned in its balance and contrast of keys and the instrumentation for flutes, oboes, trumpets, strings, and drums with harpsichord and organ is in his most brilliant style.

The chorus, *Soul of the World*, is a great invocation to music, one of his most memorable pages. The words are by Dr Nicholas Brady, and if they are not great poetry, they are very serviceable verse.

> Soul of the World, inspired by thee
> The jarring seeds of matter did agree.
> Thou didst the scattered atoms bind
> Which by the laws of true proportion joined
> Made up of various parts one perfect harmony.

Purcell: *Ode for St Cecilia's Day* (1692): *Soul of the World*.   HMV DB 21273 (78 r.p.m.).

Now before coming to consider the dramatic music which is Purcell's crowning glory and yet in another sense his gravest hostage to fortune, let us turn aside for a moment to consider what were the main characteristics of this art, this baroque art, which he practised. Baroque is a term, borrowed from architecture, which has been applied to the whole period of which the beginnings were marked by the Florentine operas, the middle by the age of Lully and Purcell, and the culmination by the art of Bach. It denotes, in very general terms, the use of florid ornament, motives of marked and sometimes exaggerated contrast, discontinuity of treatment emphasized in music by sectional construction and key contrast, emphatic changes of mood, tempo, metre, and texture (for instance, chordal passages contrasted with others of contrapuntal part-writing), and generally a certain restless use of decoration. It is not in its application a term of reproach, but is intended, like the word Gothic in other connections, to represent a definite style and phase in the history of music.

It is clear that the first reaction that ensued after the Puritan regime had collapsed and the monarchy had been restored was in the direction of theatrical shows. The stage directions of some of these musical entertainments can still fill us with amazement, with their flying witches, gods and goddesses descending in a machine (or car) drawn by peacocks, their ornate columns, their rocks and clouds, their painted backcloths, and all the apparatus of pantomime, only more so. They called it opera, though in fact it was a mixture of drama, singing, and dancing in which the tradition of the spoken play was employed to produce something that was supposed to resemble the Italian model. The English prejudice against works that were wholly sung kept the result from being opera in the genuine sense. Another feature of these semi-operas is that the principal characters do not sing, and the principal singers do not speak. The English tradition of reserving music for scenes of ritual, magic, or the supernatural descended from Shakespeare's time. It explains the numerous temple scenes, incantation scenes, the witches, and the deities to be found in Purcell's works. The other more or less consistent element is the pastoral scenes.

Dryden was associated with Purcell in one of his finest works for the stage, *King Arthur*. It is a very complicated mixture of legend and fantasy all designed to build up a great patriotic spectacle in praise of England. An even more fantastic hotch-potch was *The Fairy Queen*, which is an adaptation of Shakespeare's *Midsummer Night's Dream*. It was one of the most lavish productions of its time. It follows Shakespeare more or less, but although the music is more extensive than in most of Purcell's stage works he set no single line of Shakespeare. Here too the most extended music belongs to the masques which occur at the end of the acts. Titania summons a fairy-masque for the entertainment of Bottom, there is a masque of the Four Seasons, and finally a Masque of Hymen for the lovers which includes for no reason at all a Chinese scene in which various dances are executed by Chinamen, and six monkeys perform a comic dance. In short it is just a pantomime with Shakespeare as a pretext.

Purcell: *The Fairy Queen* (*excerpts*). OISEAU-LYRE OL 50029 or ALLEGRO 3077.

Finally we come to the work by which Purcell will be remembered as long as music lives. Every schoolgirl has heard of *Dido and Aeneas* or at least every schoolgirl ought to have done, because it was written for a girls' school and for girls to perform. It is Purcell's one and only real opera. It plays for little more than an hour, but it is a true masterpiece of music drama. Of course we have the usual Restoration witches to give colour to the scene and a chance for magic incantation. There is a hunting scene, a thunderstorm, a racy quayside scene, and, finally, Dido sings the great Lament which is one of the things that time cannot stale. It is based on the device in which Purcell excelled and of which he made so light, as if it were an easy thing for anyone to do— namely, the recurrent or ground bass. Dido dies of a broken heart and a chorus rounds off the work. The short recitative which introduces the aria has been called the most wonderful in the English language and German critics have described the whole work as 'Shakespearian' though nothing is less Shakespearian than the text of the poet, Nahum Tate. The real poet, the real Shakespeare, is Purcell.

Purcell: *Dido and Aeneas*.   VICTOR LHMV 1007 (HMV ALP 1026).

APPENDIX

BOOKS

GERALD R. HAYES: *Musical Instruments and their Music 1500–1750*, Vols. I and II.

E. H. MEYER: *English Chamber Music*.

E. J. DENT: *Foundations of English Opera*.

ROGER NORTH: *The Musical Grammarian*.

J. A. WESTRUP: *Purcell*.

H. CART DE LAFONTAINE: *The King's Musick*.

H. C. COLLES: *Voice and Verse*.

RECORDS

PURCELL: *Come Ye Sons of Art*.   OISEAU-LYRE OL 53004.   *Harpsichord Suites*.   OISEAU-LYRE OL 50011.   *Three Divine Hymns*.   HALL-MARK RS 1.   *Instrumental and Vocal Pieces*.   ESOTERIC 519 and 535. *Vocal Music*.   DGG AMP 14059.

VARIOUS: *String Music of Purcell, Gibbons, and Locke*.   BARTÓK 913. *Music of Purcell, Jenkins, and Locke*.   BACH GUILD 547.

Church works by Purcell and his contemporaries are included in the four series of 78 r.p.m. records issued by English Columbia under the title *English Church Music*.

27

H. Wiley Hitchcock

THE FRENCH SCHOOL:
LULLY AND CHARPENTIER

SELDOM has a nation's art been so closely identified with politics as was the music of seventeenth-century France. The two great French kings of the era were both vitally interested in music; Louis XIII was actually a composer of sorts, and the deep personal concern for music of Louis XIV was evidenced in numberless ways in the music written for his court. At Versailles there were no less than eight distinct musical groups permanently employed by the Sun King. Music of every imaginable sort was to be heard: opera, ballet, hunting music, mealtime concerts, music for *soirées* and dances, chamber music for the Sunday concerts, and church music for the royal chapel.

The history of seventeenth-century French music is essentially the history of music at court. The composer who could gain the ear of the king wielded immense power over the fortunes of other composers. He could force another composer into types of music not of his own choosing. He could prevent other composers from studying where they wished. He could monopolize whole areas of the musical life of France.

Politics affected music in another way too. An important power behind the throne was the Italian Mazarin, and, in a conscious effort to persuade French taste to the pleasures of Italian music, Mazarin imported musicians, set-designers, and whole opera companies from Italy. Immediately factions hostile to Mazarin politically aligned themselves against Italian music as well—specifically against the novel Italian vocal style of the opera. For almost a century arguments raged over whether the French should try to create an opera in imitation of the Italians, or whether French music should not be altogether a different thing from Italian music.

Two great composers whose works reflected the divided opinion of the French on the relative merits of the French and Italian styles were Jean-Baptiste Lully and Marc-Antoine Charpentier. During their lifetimes—and they were exact contemporaries—Lully had all the chips on his side of the table. Shrewd, well-versed in the devious arts of courtly intrigue, he wielded an incalculable influence on the trends and emphases of music at court. Lully was Italian by birth, but he realized that the anti-Italian sentiment of a large part of the court could be parleyed into personal success for him. He officially changed the Italian form of his name; he parodied the Italian vocal style in some works; and he prevented the young composer Desmarets from going to Italy to study. His talent as a conductor was so obvious that he was able to persuade the king to give him an orchestra of his own: it was called 'the little violins,' to distinguish it from the famous band of 'twenty-four violins of the king,' established under Louis XIII as the first permanent orchestra in history.

For more than half a century ballet had been the most popular kind of musical entertainment on the grand scale that the court had known. And so long as ballet remained popular, Lully wrote ballets. New triumphs for him came when he joined forces with the respected and witty Molière; together, they created the so-called comedy-ballet. The moment it seemed that French opera might appeal to the king and the court circle, Lully contrived to acquire a monopoly over it. In 1673 he produced his first opera, or as he called it, 'lyric tragedy,' with libretto by Philippe Quinault. According to the terms of the royal privilege which gave Lully sole charge of opera in Paris, it was impossible for anyone else to mount a musical drama there.

From 1673 until his death in 1687, Lully and Quinault produced about one new opera every year. Almost single-handed Lully created French opera, defined its nature, and gave later composers models that were followed for generations. He was a clever man and a good musician. He realized that the French had the best ballet in Europe and the greatest love for it. And so he made sure to include in his operas sections that would grant Parisians some of the same pleasures they had come to expect from the ballet; feasts for the eye and ear quite apart from the drama itself. For these ballet-scenes, and for gigantic choral episodes accompanied by full orchestra, Lully wrote some of his most powerful music, such as the big chaconne from *Cadmus and Hermione* of 1673.

Lully: *Chaconne: Cadmus et Hermione*. ANTHOLOGIE SONORE AS 114 (78 r.p.m.).

It has been said that the pomp and brilliance of the French court are perfectly reflected in the overtures to Lully's operas. Certainly the opening measures are a 'kingly' music—properly dignified, solemn, and (let us admit) a bit pompous. And certainly the dance section that follows is as carefully designed and as stylized as the gardens of Versailles; and the pseudo-counterpoint in which the dance rhythms are presented is as pretentious—and perhaps as hollow—as the daily ritual attending the waking of the king. We must add, however, that the Lully overture became all the rage. The opening of Handel's *Messiah* is a Lullian overture; and so is the carefully named *French Overture* for harpsichord by J. S. Bach.

Lully: *Overture: Armide*. MASTERPIECES OF MUSIC BEFORE 1750. HAYDN SOCIETY HSL 2072.

Lully's approach to the subject-matter and to the musical style of his operas was both shrewd and wise. Not only did the French have the best ballet in Europe, they also had the best drama. It was the era of Corneille and Racine and of classical French tragedy at its best. Lully set out to make his operas essentially classical tragedies, intensified by music, but not distorted or obscured by it. The words of the drama were not to be made unintelligible by the music. The course of the drama was not to be interrupted by lengthy arias in the Italian manner, no matter how beautiful the music. It was obvious to Lully that the French were simply too rational-minded and too much oriented to drama itself to accept otherwise.

And so, after carefully studying the exaggerated style of declamation at the *Comédie française*, Lully intensified the texts given him by Quinault with just enough music to heighten the effect, and yet not enough to let the music itself claim all the attention. He cautioned that 'my recitative is made solely for speaking.' As for arias, they were few and hardly different in style from the recitative. They were most like the formal, unemotional court airs that had been heard off the stage in France for more than a century.

Perhaps one must be a little bit French to like Lully's airs.

Certainly they will seem somwhat monochromatic and lacklustre to persons who view opera in the Italian way—that is, as essentially a 'concert in costume'—rather than in the French way, as a musically intensified drama.

Lully: *Bois épais: Armide.*   COLUMBIA M 578 (78 r.p.m.).

During his lifetime, and even afterwards, Lully had things his own way.   He ruthlessly eliminated other composers when they threatened to compete for the favour of the king; he monopolized the most spectacular of musical productions, the operas; he carefully altered his emphasis and his principles to fit the changing tastes of his king.   At his death in 1687 the name Lully was virtually equated with French music; many Frenchmen judged the music of other composers by the degree to which it approximated Lully's style.

The composer whose very name bespoke bad music in some circles was a representative of the pro-Italian, anti-Lully camp. Marc-Antoine Charpentier, trained in Rome under the great oratorio composer, Giacomo Carissimi, returned to Paris in the 1650's to find a musical dictator in full sway.   What a paradox! The 'French' music of the Italian-born Lully was set against the 'Italian' music of the Parisian, Charpentier.   Charpentier turned to the periphery of the court: the musical retinue of a wealthy and pious noblewoman, the Duchesse de Guise.   For her he composed numerous motets and cantatas in the Italian style and several small oratorios.   He first came to the attention of a wider audience when he wrote larger motets, oratorios, and sacred operas for the most important Jesuit church in Paris and for the Jesuit college of Clermont.

There is seldom a possibility of monotony in Charpentier's vocal style, as there is in Lully's.   The Roman-trained Frenchman had learned well the lessons of Carissimi: that all music deserves gracefully curved melodies; that church music can be as dramatic and intense as opera; and that vocal music must be interesting *as music* regardless of the importance of the text.   His motet *Oculi omnium* is like a little moralistic drama.   A small band of hungry supplicants call upon the Lord for help.   He invites them to the heavenly table.   A chorus of angels, already appeased by the Lord, sing His praises ecstatically.   For a time the supplicants look on wistfully from a distance.   Finally, however, they join the chorus and identify themselves with the blessed.

Charpentier: *Oculi omnium*. HAYDN SOCIETY 2065.

A composer of these capabilities could hardly escape the notice of influential persons. Indeed, after Lully violated an agreement with Molière and turned to writing operas, Molière chose Charpentier to collaborate in his comedy-ballets. Unfortunately, the playwright died after *Le Malade imaginaire*, for which Charpentier wrote the songs and incidental music. Charpentier produced no real *tragédie lyrique* until late in his life. *Medea* was first presented in 1693, and even then the baleful shadow of Lully's influence prevented Charpentier from the real success he deserved. As one contemporary put it, 'cabals of the envious and ignorant' hissed the opera into quick obscurity.

Charpentier, potentially a much greater composer than Lully, retired once again to the less conspicuous realm of sacred music. More than five hundred religious compositions came from his pen. Official and public recognition finally came in 1698, when he was past sixty. He was appointed Master of Music of the *Sainte-Chapelle*, that Gothic palace of stained glass and carved stone on the Île de la Cité. He had a choir of perhaps sixty voices, and the royal instrumentalists too were often at his disposal. Some of his most brilliant and powerful compositions date from this period; huge oratorios, mighty motets and *Te Deums* for two or three choruses, soloists, and full orchestra, rich and colourful settings of the Mass.

Certainly one of his most successful works was a Mass to be sung at midnight on Christmas Eve. To the solemn words of the Mass he set music of skipping jubilance. As French organists had done before him, Charpentier based most of this Christmas music on old favourite French carols. The gentle, solemn prayer of the *Agnus Dei* is set to tripping minuet rhythms, based on the carol *At midnight an alarm was given*.

Charpentier: *Midnight Mass*. WESTMINSTER WL 5287 (DUCRETET-THOMSON EL 93006).

By the turn of the eighteenth century the controversy of French versus Italian musical style had died down. French composers had begun to write music in forms long popular with the more progressive Italians. One such form was the *cantata*—known in

*G

Italy for almost a century, but introduced into France only in the era of Charpentier. If the French opera reflected the grandiloquence and sober stylization of court life under the Sun King, the cantata reflected quite another aspect of French manners. Basically the cantata is a tiny work of dramatic music. In a solo cantata one singer sings both the narrative passages and the monologues or dialogue passages. There is no real action and cantatas are never staged. Composers like André Campra treated the cantata as an opportunity to write charming, if trifling, music on pastoral themes. The traditional delight of French composers in almost pictorial representation of the pleasures of nature is often displayed in these works. 'Nature,' it need hardly be said, was *always* mild; the same Nature that the courtiers enjoyed amid the plane-trees and the thickets of the Versailles gardens—far enough from the palace to let them imagine they were living the simple, natural life; close enough to it that they still felt secure and sheltered.

Campra's solo cantata, *The Butterfly*, is for tenor voice with flute, violin, cello, and harpsichord accompaniment. 'Precious' is certainly the word for the text. The first part is sung in declamatory style, and an *air* follows. Whenever the words 'je vole'— 'I fly'—appear, Campra literally makes the words 'fly' in long coloraturas up and down.

> Campra: *Cantata: Le Papillon.* ANTHOLOGIE SONORE AS 96 (78 r.p.m.).

The cantata by Campra tells how French artistic taste was changing at the beginning of the eighteenth century. A new delight in sheer 'prettiness,' in decorative details, rather than profundity or complexity, is obvious. The impending rococo style of the era of Louis XV is already apparent. The age of the rather frigid splendour of Lully's music and of the warm but sober brilliance of Charpentier's music was past. French music was approaching a new era—that of Couperin and Rameau.

(APPENDIX: *See* page 185.)

28

H. Wiley Hitchcock

THE FRENCH SCHOOL:
COUPERIN AND RAMEAU

THE last twenty years of the reign of Louis XIV were nowhere nearly so splendid as the earlier years. The ageing
king grew melancholy and increasingly pious. Thus the
greatest composer of the court circle did not follow Lully
in composing ballets and operas. François Couperin was called
upon to write intimate, quiet music—music designed perhaps more
to soothe than to stimulate, music to provide a harmonious background to courtly banquets, music to edify and inspire within the
arched and vaulted walls of the Versailles chapel.

François Couperin was born on 10th November 1668, the only
child of a church organist and violinist in the king's band. Only
eleven when his father died, Couperin succeeded him as organist
of the church of St Gervais. In 1693 he became organist of the
Chapel Royal at Versailles. By 1710 he was already known as
'Couperin le grand,' both because of his excellence as a performer
and composer and because there were a confusing number of other
past and present Couperins who were also musicians.

Not only did Couperin write church music and play the organ
at St Gervais and Versailles, he was also a favourite harpsichordist
of the court circle during the regency of the young Louis XV, and
he directed the chamber music concerts that took place almost
every Sunday at court. After an uncomplicated, essentially
serene and successful life, Couperin died in 1733. Unlike Marc-
Antoine Charpentier, he was by no means unknown outside
France; nor was he forgotten after his death. Bach knew his
music well: in fact, the great Saxon organist and the great Parisian
keyboard player had a long correspondence. Bach copied out
some of Couperin's harpsichord music, and Couperin's style is
reflected in some of Bach's most lovely keyboard music.

The 'musical world' created by Couperin seems to reflect perfectly—in microcosmic form, to be sure—the *real* world from which it sprang.   First of all, his music is completely French in spirit.   In common with other French music and art from the twelfth century to the twentieth, it is sophisticated, witty, brilliant but not ponderous, often humorous, translucent.   It is deceptively simple and clear.   It is frequently terse, epigrammatic, under-stated.   All these adjectives might apply to other great French artists—to La Fontaine, for example.   Couperin knew the works of La Fontaine well, and he set to music one of his poems, called *Epitaph for a Lazy Man*.

> John came and went without a penny's gain;
> Interest and principal went sliding down the drain,
> For he considered worldly goods a matter for disdain.
> Using up his time for John was no great strain:
> Two halves he made of it, and used to make a test
> Of sleeping one half, of resting all the rest.

Couperin sets this as a duet—partly, perhaps, so that he can make a musical pun at the words 'Deux parts en fit' ('Two halves he made of it') by omitting the accompaniment and letting the two voices represent the two divisions of the lazy man's time. The spirit of the music is so artless that we hardly realize that it is strictly contrapuntal almost throughout.

Couperin: *Epitaphe d'un paresseux*.   Vox PL 6380.

If Couperin could mirror in his music the sophisticated artless-ness of La Fontaine, he could also find inspiration in the sights and sounds of a bustling Paris: soldiers marching through the streets, birds twittering in the gardens of the Louvre, milkmaids on their daily rounds, strolling players, gipsies, and dancing bears, the Italian comedians.   It is especially in his harpsichord music that Couperin captured these and virtually every other phase of the society of his time.   But Couperin was no second-rate com-poser-naturalist, content to rely on pictorialism to make his point. We need not know the titles or the source of the inspiration to enjoy the *clavecin* music.   Such knowledge can sometimes be fascinating, though, especially if it can help illuminate the range of Couperin's experience and interest and point up his wit and humour.

We may take as an example the rather large work which is the

high light of the eleventh suite for harpsichord, first published in
1717. The original title reads: *The Record of the Grand and
Ancient Order of* . . . but the last word is unreadable; it is spelt
Mxnxstrandxsx. To Couperin's audience this puzzle was easily
solved; the word was *Ménestrandise*. This was the name of the
musicians' guild, essentially a trade union of unskilled workers,
which had tried several times to create 'closed shop' regulations
in France. The guild hoped to force the musicians of the court
and the aristocracy to join the more plebeian players of dance
and tavern music in paying annual dues. Couperin joined several
other composers in protesting to the king, and this composition
may have been one of Couperin's musical contributions to the
propaganda war.

Couperin called the five parts of the work 'acts,' and it is a
little drama. *Act I : The Officers and the Jury of Union Members*.
They apparently stride into the hearing-room. The atmosphere
is somewhat solemn, but not without a certain ludicrous tinge.
Couperin's music combines the sobriety of the seventeenth-
century harpsichord composers with the *graces* (as trills and other
ornaments were suggestively called) of the early eighteenth century.

Act II presents the complaints of the barrel-organ players and
the musical beggars. They apparently know only one tune. The
hurdy-gurdy men play it slowly; the beggars pep it up a bit.
But the same tired old bass drones on and on.

Act III. On to the scene come the jugglers, tumblers, and
clowns, accompanied by trained bears and monkeys. As befits
their trade, the tired little tune is taken at breakneck speed, leaping
and cavorting in a diabolical dance.

Act IV. Couperin portrays *les invalides*, worn-out popular
minstrels, crippled in the service of their guild. The music
sounds bitterly sympathetic.

Act V. *Disruption and Rout of the Whole Troupe, caused by
Drunkards, Monkeys, and Bears*. Amid the confusion and the
comic fife-and-drum effects, we still seem to hear the little popular
tune. And we come to realize that there are subtle interrelationships between the individual movements that unify the entire
work.

Couperin: *Les Fastes de la grande et ancienne Ménestrandise*. LYRI-
CHORD LL 12 or MGM E 538 (alt. OISEAU-LYRE OL 50060).

We have all seen examples of the French pastoral tradition of the seventeenth and eighteenth centuries in the paintings and poems of the period. The 'return to nature' philosophy of Rousseau was a late expression of the pastoral convention, as was Marie Antoinette's *Le Hameau*, that charming imitation of a peasant cottage, in which the court ladies played at the 'simple life' on the edge of the Versailles gardens.   Couperin reflected the pastoral convention in several works, among them the exquisitely simple but artful love-song called *Musette* after the bagpipe-like background.

Couperin: *Musète*.   Vox PL 6380.

At its best the art of Couperin sublimates subject-matter of outward simplicity, even ridiculousness, into 'something rich and strange.'   This art is the musical parallel to Watteau's painting: trifling subjects are somehow lent great gravity.   Compare the two artists' versions of Harlequin, traditionally the comic hero of the Italian comedy.   Watteau's portrait of Gilles, called *Dans le goût burlesque*, is well known; Couperin's *Arlequine* for harpsichord has, I think, the same combination of half-comic simplicity and surprisingly sober, almost tragic effect.

Couperin: *L'Arlequine*.   LYRICHORD LP 12 (alt. OISEAU-LYRE OL 50065).

By the time of Couperin's death in 1733, another man had acquired fame—or notoriety—in the French musical world: Jean-Philippe Rameau.   A real intellectual, with a great interest in musical theory, Rameau had published in 1722 his *Treatise on Harmony*.   Despite the fact that this ingenious work was to provide the foundations of musical science up to the twentieth century, it was awkwardly written and its author was misunderstood and found himself the target of bitter criticism from musicians and scientists throughout France.   But more, and fiercer, controversy surged up when in 1733 Rameau produced his first opera, *Hippolyte et Aricie*.   He was attacked as faithless to the Lully tradition of French opera.   From our vantage point it seems like a tempest in a teapot; Rameau revered Lully above all French musicians, and certainly *Hippolyte* and more than twenty other operas show him to be very much in the main stream of French operatic tradition.   Two facts must really have been at the base of the hostility towards the fifty-year-old genius.   First, he never found a librettist to match his talents.   Second, his operas were full of strange and daring instrumental effects. To us they are ravishing; to Rameau's contemporaries they seemed harsh, radical, and subversive—subversive in the sense that the orchestra seemed at times more important than the singers, or the text, or the drama itself. One of Rameau's listeners claimed that 'for three hours the musicians have not even the time to sneeze.' The closing air of *Hippolyte*, addressed to the nightingales of an enchanted forest by a shepherdess, may suggest Rameau's imaginative use of instruments.

Rameau: *Rossignols amoureux: Hippolyte et Aricie.* DECCA DL 9683 (BRUNSWICK AXTL 1053).

Besides serious operas, or lyric tragedies, Rameau also composed opera-ballets. This kind of work combines a maximum of ballet with a minimum of opera, a maximum of sheer visual spectacle with a minimum of plot. The most exotically colourful scenes and situations are strung loosely together in a series of so-called entrées. Unlike modern ballet, though, singers are utilized, as are large singing choruses.

The opera-ballet *The Festivities of Hebe*, first produced in 1739, opens with the appearance of various gods and goddesses who have gathered for a celebration in honour of Hebe, goddess of youth. The goddess of love announces that the festivities will take place on the banks of the Seine, and she and Hebe exhort the others to follow them to the river's edge. Amor sings the principal music of the duet alone at first. Then in a characteristic, utterly rationalistic way, Rameau goes on to compose a perfectly balanced 'rondeau with two couplets.' This simply means that the duet theme is heard three times; between its first and second statements, and between its second and third statements, are heard 'couplets,' or episodes, based on different musical material. Each couplet is for a single voice rather than duet, the tempo is slower, and the vocal style is much more declamatory. The whole piece is perfectly symmetrical, the duet opening and closing the passage and furnishing, moreover, a central axis. Thus are science and art intermingled in the precise musical thought of Rameau.

Rameau: *Volons sur les bordes de la Seine: Les Fêtes d'Hébé.* DECCA DL 9683 (BRUNSWICK AXTL 1053).

Rameau's main contributions to musical theory were in the field of harmony. He was preoccupied with different chords and with their interrelationships, and his concern with such matters

shows up frequently in his works.   One such example is the very
well-known harpsichord piece called *The Hen*.   If we allow ourselves to be concerned only with the theme—and it never changes
—we will come away from the work with little but a tired, bored
reaction.   The real musical point is rather the exploration of
various keys and harmonies; the same melody, in other words, is
seen from several different points of reference.   One difference
between Rameau and Couperin as harpsichord composers—and
between mid eighteenth-century and early eighteenth-century
musical thought in general—is this preoccupation with harmony
rather than with melody and counterpoint.

Rameau: *La poule*.   MGM E 538 (alt. OISEAU-LYRE OL 50082).

If any portion of Rameau's work is destined to live on through
changing eras, it is the music he wrote for the numerous ballet-
sequences of the operas.   The aesthetics of opera has changed so
completely since Rameau's time that there is little hope of reviving
his operas as such.   But as long as we have orchestras, and provided we have adventurous conductors, Rameau's orchestral music
will continue to attract and enchant; for example, two *entr'actes*,
rich in exotic guitar-effects and kaleidoscopic changes of instrumental colours, from an almost unknown opera, *Acanthe et
Céphise*.

Rameau: *Entr'actes: Acanthe et Céphise*.   DECCA DL 9683 (BRUNS-
WICK AXTL 1053).

Perhaps no better statement about Rameau's particular gifts,
and his position in musical history, can be found than that made
by Debussy, emphasizing his own roots in the specifically *French*
thought of Rameau:

We have . . . in Rameau's work a pure French tradition full of
charming and tender delicacy, well balanced, strictly declamatory in
recitative and without any affectation of German profundity or over-
emphasis or impatient explanation. . . .   We may regret that French
music should so long have followed a course treacherously leading away
from that clarity of expression, that terse and condensed form, which
is the peculiar and significant quality of the French genius.

APPENDIX
(CHAPTERS 27 and 28)

BOOKS

The only important work on French classic music, written in English is:

WILFRID MELLERS: *François Couperin and the French Classical Tradition.*
In French, the following are to be recommended:

HENRY PRUNIÈRES: *Lully.*
CLAUDE CRUSSARD: *Marc-Antoine Charpentier.*
PAUL-MARIE MASSON: *L'Opéra de Rameau.*

RECORDS

LULLY: *Operatic Arias.* LYRICHORD 16. *Miserere.* OISEAU-LYRE OL 53003. *Ballet Music.* ANGEL 35255 (COLUMBIA 33 CX 1277). *Le Bourgeois Gentilhomme.* ENGLISH DECCA LXT 5211–13. *Marches, etc.* LONDON INTERNATIONAL TWV 91092.

CHARPENTIER: *Mass: Assumpta est Maria.* VOX PL 8440. Excerpts from *Medée.* DECCA 9678 (BRUNSWICK AXTL 1049). *Magnificat, etc.* HAYDN SOCIETY HSL 102.

COUPERIN: *Motets.* OISEAU-LYRE OL 50079. *Harpsichord Music* (complete). OISEAU-LYRE OL 50052–67. *Concert Royal No. 3.* OISEAU-LYRE OL 50031.

RAMEAU: *Cantatas.* LYRICHORD 44. *Hippolyte et Aricie.* OISEAU-LYRE OL 50034. *Instrumental Music* (complete). OISEAU-LYRE OL 50080–4. *Harpsichord Music* (complete). WESTMINSTER WN 3303. *Two Suites for Haprsichord.* NIXA WLP 5128.

29

Arthur Hutchings

NORTHERN EUROPE BEFORE BACH

IN my boyhood the small English town where I lived had its German band of five players which played at cattle shows, flower shows, harvest homes, municipal banquets, and civic ceremonies. In later years, when I came to study music, I found that in Germany itself these town bands, or *Stadtpfeiffer*, existed in the period under study here. And they played on just the same occasions, and at weddings and funerals too. They were a relic of the medieval waits or minstrels, but the regular combination of these particular instruments belonged especially to Germany, and so did some of the music they played.

The *Stadtpfeiffer* were organized with typical German thoroughness; each player had apprentices, and they were expected to reach a high technical standard before being recommended for a place in the band of another city. That is why, later on, Bach could write such difficult high trumpet parts for players who from boyhood had specialized in the upper register of the instrument called the *clarino*. Bach could have secured such players in almost any court orchestra or in the music loft of the principal church of any thriving city. Because the *Stadtpfeiffer* could play the music of Johann Petzold (or Pezel) so well in 1621, Bach could demand, and get, the kind of trumpet playing he did in 1721 in the last movement of his second Brandenburg Concerto.

(i) Pezel: *Gigue*. ANTHOLOGIE SONORE AS 8 (78 r.p.m.).
(ii) J. S. Bach: *Brandenburg Concerto, No. 2.* ENGLISH COLUMBIA LX 440 (78 r.p.m.) (alt. DECCA LX 3029).

Until the seventeenth century no *great* German music is immediately associated with Germany, recognized as obviously German. We think of such German-born composers as Isaac and Gallus as belonging to the sixteenth-century Flemish school, and we associate Hassler, of a later generation, with the sumptuous

Venice of Gabrieli. But the town band music was German *of* Germany, and we can notice two features of it which will be well worth tracing in far more ambitious German music. First, a four-square tune, characteristically German. Second, the treatment of that tune by German elaboration—the adding to the tune of counterparts or counterpoints which display certain devices. For instance, in an *intrada* by Pezel, the inversion of the tune half-way through the dance, a device found in some of Bach's gigues.

Pezel: *Intrada*. ANTHOLOGIE SONORE AS 7 (78 r.p.m.).

Bach himself liked such a bluff, four-square melody; an example is the *quodlibet* at the end of the *Goldberg Variations*. One or two melodies of much the same regular shape come in Mozart's German operas and again in the most German of all operas, Weber's *Der Freischütz*. They can be found in student songs and still heard in village beer gardens.

The second feature is the method of accompanying the melody, not with plain, regular chords but by lines with their own independent rhythms. One German who loved this process was Martin Luther, and he wrote in 1542: 'When music is polished by art, one sees with wonder the great wisdom of God; for while one voice takes a simple part, around it go three or four other parts, leaping and springing, and marvellously adorning the simple part, like a square dance in heaven.' Luther is describing what he found in his favourite composer, Josquin des Prés, and it would have given him greater delight still to have heard his own countrymen putting counterpoint to the hymn tunes or chorales of his German Church. They also were simple tunes which gradually took on a square German shape.

We must never suppose that Luther wanted only congregational music. He believed that music was a foretaste of heaven, and that it was therefore (even as an entertainment) the most godly occupation people could have on earth. The churches were to sound with the music of as many orchestral instruments and as many well-trained voices as could be provided, and even a congregational chorale might be treated as Michael Praetorius treats the epiphany hymn *How brightly shines the morning star*. He sets it with contrapuntal parts and, by contrast, with plain broad harmonies.

Praetorius: *How brightly shines the morning star*. HISTORY OF MUSIC IN SOUND, VOL. IV. VICTOR LM 6029 (HMV HMS 38, 78 r.p.m.).

We have seen how the town bands and the *Kantorei*—the establishment of voices and instruments of the Lutheran church gallery—have put a simple tune into relief by sounding it with elaborate counterparts. We must now examine the process in organ pieces. Germany had produced the most famous organs and organists of Europe long before Luther's day, and we may be sure that the Reformation organists practised the art of setting chorales with counterpoints. Naturally they studied the artifice where it was most brilliantly demonstrated, and they were drawn to two main training grounds. Some went to Venice, which was nearer Germany than Rome was, and more advanced musically too. But most of the organists went to study under Sweelinck, organist of the Old Church in Amsterdam.

Sweelinck was not only an organist; he was a renowned harpsichord player, a friend of Dr John Bull, and a prolific composer of secular part-songs and instrumental pieces, including fully developed fugues. But we may take an example of the kind of music that made men call him 'the maker of German organists.' It is a series of variations on a chorale, and it is very easy to follow because the chorale goes plainly on one keyboard, while a single line of counterpoint goes on another.

Sweelinck: *Chorale variations: Ach Gott, von Himmel*. HISTORY OF MUSIC IN SOUND, VOL. IV. VICTOR LM 6029 (HMV HMS 43, 78 r.p.m.).

Lutheran organists were expected to compose such pieces, not just as voluntaries, but as part of the service, so they often composed for solo organ pieces of similar design to those they composed for choir and orchestra. This organ music made wonderful progress in the three generations after Luther; that is, from Sweelinck, who died in the same year as Praetorius, 1621, up to the North German organists who were famous in Bach's boyhood—Reinken, Pachelbel, Böhm, and Buxtehude.

The greatest of them was undoubtedly Buxtehude, whose evening concerts were so famous that young Bach walked two hundred and fifty miles to hear them. Dietrich Buxtehude was a Dane, and he settled in the part of Germany nearest to Denmark. He was appointed to St Mary's Church in Lübeck, and he was nothing less than an outstanding genius of the organ. While his treatment of the Christmas carol *In dulci jubilo* sounds easy, it is a more elaborate piece than the Sweelinck chorale variations because

Buxtehude has a habit of altering the melody itself, which is in the topmost part.

Buxtehude: *Chorale prelude: In dulci jubilo*. HISTORY OF MUSIC IN SOUND, VOL. VI. VICTOR LM 6031 (HMV HMS 61, 78 r.p.m.).

Beside Buxtehude's chorale prelude we should set one of Bach's superbly clever treatments of the same carol. Bach also puts the melody in the topmost part, but he makes it go in canon; it follows in the tenor, which is played by the feet. The left hand puts a bass below this pedal part which has the tune, and the left-hand bass is itself in canon with the alto. So the whole piece is a texture of four parts, called a canon four-in-two; soprano and tenor the same melody chasing itself, bass and alto the same music chasing itself.

Bach: *In dulci jubilo*. HISTORY OF MUSIC IN SOUND, VOL. VI. VICTOR LM 6031 (HMV HMS 61, 78 r.p.m.).

The greatest German musician of the century before Bach and Handel remained thoroughly German in his expression, despite his admiration of Italy and the ideas he imported from that country. Heinrich Schütz was well-educated, gentle, dignified, of fine appearance and character, greatly beloved by other musicians. He went to Venice twice for a long stay, and the prefaces and dedications of his works declare his admiration for his master there, Giovanni Gabrieli, and then for Monteverdi, who was at St Mark's when Schütz undertook his second journey to Italy. But Schütz was a thoroughly German musician long before Germany was a nation at all.

Our classics are the German classics, and their music has something in common which we do not find until Germany had found her musical voice. We still do not always find it in Latin music. We cannot call this quality mysticism, for music can be mystical when it is clear, sunny, radiant, even entertaining. But we are safe in saying that in the greatest German music there is a vein of individual sentiment which tells us something about the composer's philosophic outlook, a matter which the French or Italian artist often hides. German listeners regard a composer's personal communication with religious reverence, and because Schütz is one of the first German composers in whom we recognize Teutonic *Individualismus*, we put him first in the line of German classics.

One of his most impressive and individual pieces comes from the *Symphoniae Sacrae*, published in 1650. It needs double choir, six soloists, organ, and strings. Schütz could have let the soloists and the various instruments show off in turn; the Italians he admired would certainly have done so. But he always subordinates the part to the whole, and he is here dealing with St Paul's conversion in his own uniquely concentrated way. He focuses his expression upon one idea—the voice of conscience insisting, penetrating, and echoing in the apostle's mind. The words 'Saul, Saul, why persecutest thou me?' obsess the whole being of St Paul in Schütz's expression. The design of the piece is a crescendo from the opening bass voice onwards. It spreads and reverberates with all the arts taught by the Italians until the final echoes of the word 'Saul' are the last thing we hear.

Schütz: *Saul, Saul*. HISTORY OF MUSIC IN SOUND, VOL. V. VICTOR LM 6030 (HMV HMS 53, 78 r.p.m.).

Schütz represents the educated Lutheran, whom we may contrast with the type which went straight from the choir school to apprenticeship in the organ loft. Schütz was an organist, but he left no pieces for the organ. I think it is significant that he composed at least one opera, *Dafne*, though we have not found a copy; and it is also significant that he was concerned only with the Dresden court and its chapel, not with parish music. He occasionally uses the words of a chorale, but it is not his habit to use chorale melodies at all. His outlook is highly stylized and liturgical, and his motets and settings of the Passion, and his love of the old modes, are all part of his fondness for formality and austere grandeur.

Much of Schütz's music is to Latin words, despite the fact that he set German as wonderfully as Purcell set English, and his music seems as if it could serve the Roman rite as well as the Lutheran. Some of the other seventeenth-century Lutheran music is unlike most of the Protestant music with which we are most familiar. There are settings of *Kyrie* and *Gloria* in Greek and Latin, called *Messen*; there are Latin *Magnificats*, and brilliantly scored church concertos and symphonies, or cantatas. When no orchestra is used, they are called motets, a word we associate with the Catholic usage. Lutheran music before Bach's death was very different from Lutheran music of later times when the rationalist and pietist movements had turned the orchestras out of the churches, turned the choir schools into ordinary day schools, and reduced music largely to hymns. Before the pietist movement, the high point of orthodox Lutheran worship was the most brilliant piece of music; and it was usually called the *Hauptmusik* (chief music or head music), the Concerto, or the *Stück* (*the* piece, *the* work). Its rehearsal and performance was in itself an offering to God, and the composer had a considerable choice of words—scripture, or a paraphrase of scripture, or the words of a chorale, or verse and prose composed by a local writer.

Schütz nearly always chose a strictly liturgical or scriptural text, and this is one of the points which show a more refined, more sophisticated taste than that of the average parish cantor—even than of Bach himself. We do not disparage Bach when we say that some of his music is naïve in expression, even when it is more masterly than any before or since. Schütz's refined taste was unique. Bach at the height of his powers was at his most florid and ebullient, and he took his words from writers whose models were opera libretti; they wanted church music to have the emotional appeal of opera. Schütz commanded the range of emotional appeal—that was the fruit of his Italian journeys—but at the height of *his* powers he became deliberately reticent, economical, even austere. He sometimes composed as if he renounced all means of expression except those used by Palestrina a whole century before him. But his reticence suggests enormous suppressed power.

We may illustrate this supreme quality from his last works. *The Story of God's Birth*, usually called *The Christmas Story*, uses only just enough instruments to illuminate the scenes delicately, as on some early frescoes.

Schütz: *The Christmas Story*. OISEAU-LYRE OL 50020.

The Christmas Story dates from 1664. Two years later comes downright austerity. For his settings of the Passion, Schütz dispensed with all instruments except the voice. Even the recitative, without accompaniment, is less florid than most medieval narrative chant. True, there are graphic touches—the shouts of the angry crowd, the crowing of the cock and Peter's bitter weeping, the last loud cry of Jesus from the Cross, but they are all toned down to produce an effect of awful intensity.

Schütz: *The Passion According to St Matthew*. RENAISSANCE X 49 (NIXA PLP 203).*

APPENDIX

Books

ADAM CARSE: *The Orchestra in the Eighteenth Century.*
MAX GRAF: *Composer and Critic.*
ROBERT M. STEVENSON: *Patterns of Protestant Church Music.*

Records

BÖHM: *Organ Music.*   HAYDN SOCIETY 3006 (DGG APM 14043).
BUXTEHUDE: *Organ Music.*   WESTMINSTER 18117/18149/18193/18221.
VARIOUS: *Organ pieces.*   PHILIPS ABL 3110/3066.   *Cantatas.*   VOX PL
   7330/7430/7620 (E) OVERTONE 6.
PACHELBEL and WALTHER: *Organ Music.*   OVERTONE 8.
PEZEL: *Brass Music.*   PERIOD 526 EMS 7.
South German Organ Music.   VOX DL 223.
SCHEIDT: *Tabulatura Nova.*   OVERTONE 3.
SCHÜTZ: *Funeral Music.*   DECCA ARC 3006 (DGG APM 14023) REB
   9.   *Seven Words from the Cross.*   VOX PL 6860 (E).   *Symphoniae
   Sacrae.*   WESTMINSTER 5043.
SWEELINCK: *Harpsichord Music.*   VOX PL 9270.

30

Arthur Hutchings

J. S. BACH

Long after Bach's death, indeed after Beethoven's, a sober historian could have declared that Bach's influence upon music and western man was almost negligible. We can trace very few of his ways of musical thinking in his two most famous sons, Carl Philip Emanuel and Johann Christian, who were his most gifted pupils. Those other musicians who admired him in his lifetime, such as Gerber, Krebs, Agricola, Goldberg, Altnikol, and Kittel, can hardly be blamed for being poor missionaries. They were not rich and influential, and they were not in a position to sponsor publication and performance of music which most audiences found distasteful even after 1829. That was the year in which Mendelssohn gave his much altered and truncated performance of the *St Matthew Passion*—an event which is usually taken to mark the beginning of the Bach revival. I want to show how the resurrection of Bach's music depended upon its apparent death with the flesh of its creator; what fascinates us about his most characteristic expression is exactly what prevented it from fascinating any contemporary listeners unless they had been born and bred in the orthodox Lutheran culture of Bach's own district.

Books tell us that the Bachs had long been famous musicians before the birth of Johann Sebastian. So they were, but only in the rather unexciting country of Thuringia, which is some hundred miles broad and fifty miles long. The great Bach did not travel far beyond its borders, and neither did his fame, except as an organist. As a lad he walked north to hear Buxtehude, and he finally settled in Leipzig just over the border of Saxony; and then late in life he travelled farther east and north to Berlin. His reputation had gone that far because, as soon as he arrived, Frederick the Great wanted him to play and extemporize.

We do not in the least disparage Bach when we recognize his

work as the enrichment by study, and by sheer genius, of the solid but elaborate musical dialect of Thuringia and its organists. Handel could have recognized the genius and not just the dialect, because he came from the part of Saxony that just touches the Bach country, and had been trained in the sort of music that a Thuringian cantor was expected to compose and perform. A young German musician regarded appointment as a Cantor or *Kapellmeister* as the goal of his ambitions. The Cantor was director of music to a municipality and its churches; the *Kapellmeister* musical director to the establishment of a prince or nobleman, including his orchestra, opera-house, and chapel. A *Kapellmeister* was not only better paid and better dressed than a Cantor; he had far more chance of advertising his abilities. To be an eligible candidate for the post of *Kapellmeister* a musician had to travel—to Italy, to the opera-houses and to concerts like those given by Vivaldi with his huge orchestra in Venice. That is what Handel did. It is true that he risked going freelance, but he made the venture while he could fall safely back upon an appointment as *Kapellmeister*. To notice how Bach deliberately resigned a good post as *Kapellmeister* to become Cantor at Leipzig, and to examine his reasons for doing it is the most important part of this essay.

First we should compare Cantor's music with *Kapellmeister*'s; the polite, international, chiefly Italian style, and the north German church style. The style of the *Kapellmeister* and opera composer at its most mellifluous may be judged from the love duet from Act II of Handel's *Sosarme*.

Handel: *Duet: Sosarme Act II*.   OISEAU-LYRE OL 50093.

This music is easy on our ears, and it seeks no more than the enchantment of the ears. Handel's genius makes conventions glow with life and beauty; Bach's genius enriches and transcends by its sheer imagination the local organists' styles, having already absorbed all it needs from Italian and French music. Bach's duet, *Et in unum*, from the Mass in B minor will also be easy on our ears, but if our ears take it too easily they are going to miss a good deal.

Bach has reached that part of the Creed which deals with the doctrine called the Eternal Purpose. The words assert that Christ was begotten of God the Father before all ages, and that always

He must be regarded as *consubstantialis*, of one substance, or divine nature, with the Father. Hence the chain of phrases affirming belief in God *of* God, Light *of* Light, Very God *of* Very God. To illustrate this, Bach puts the voices into a free canon. The one melody common to the two voices represents the one Godhead common to the two Persons of the Holy Trinity so far acknowledged in the articles of the *Credo*; and in order that neither shall be regarded as the greater, the voices take turns to be leader and follower in the canon.

Bach: *Et in unum: Mass in B minor.* ANGEL 3500C or WESTMINSTER WAL 301 (COLUMBIA 33 CX 11213 or NIXA WLP 6301).

The marvel about this music is not just the devising of the canon, but its sheer facility and ease. We do not admire Bach just for his technical feats, but for the expressive significance with which he invests them, and the grace with which he crowns their demonstration. Canons are far harder to maintain gracefully than fugues; the difficulty is to keep the melody and the harmony interesting without stopping the follow-my-leader, and the difficulty increases, especially at changes of key, when the follower comes *soon* after the leader. Every third piece in the *Goldberg Variations* is a canon. In Number 18 the two upper parts maintain canon at the sixth, with the follower coming at the distance of a minim, a mere unit of the time signature. Number 19 is just a free invention, but if we did not know this, should we imagine the first piece to be any less free than the second?

Bach: *Goldberg Variations* (*Nos. 18 and 19*). VICTOR LM 1080 (HMV ALP 1139).

In the eighteenth century neither variation would have been thought easy on the ears, and this was not just the opinion of fools. Let us take a comment on Bach's music written by Johann Adolf Scheibe, Bach's junior by some twenty years. Scheibe had the advantage of a university education and foreign travel, and he edited one of the first musical magazines, *Der Critische Musikus*, which may be called *The Musician of Taste*. In the issue for 14th May 1737 appeared these words:

This gentleman [meaning Bach] is an extraordinary artist both on keyboard instruments and on the organ ... we are astonished at his technique. We wonder how it is possible for him to move his fingers and his feet so fast without entangling them, or how he can cover the widest leaps without producing a single wrong note. This great man would be universally admired if he were more pleasing and did not banish naturalness from his composition by pedantic and intricate devices, by obscuring beauty with over-elaborate artifice.

His works are hard to perform because he expects singers and players to accomplish with their throats and instruments what he can bring off at the keyboard. That is, of course, impossible. All the ornaments are written out in full . . . the melody is unrecognizable. All the parts are made to strive with each other; all are equally important, so that it's impossible to pick out the principal part. In short, Bach is to music what Lohenstein is to poetry. With both of them one admires the laborious effort and the exceptional workmanship, vainly pursued because they do not conform to reason.

Some ardent admirers of Bach have called Scheibe's article an attack, but we have only to think of Swift or Pope to regard the article as perfectly calm and serious, and without venom. At Leipzig University Scheibe had come under the influence of the ideas of Boileau and the taste of the French academicians, with their watchwords—Reason, Nature, Clarity, Noble Simplicity. Scheibe was, too, a competent musician, and in a later issue of his paper he singled out one work of Bach for special and generous praise. Significantly enough that work was the *Italian Concerto*. Scheibe would hardly have known the music that Bach wrote as *Kapellmeister*, such as the Brandenburg Concertos. Admittedly, some of their slow movements display the elaborate counterpoint of Thuringian organists, and even when Bach is being simple and entertaining he cannot resist a canon—for instance, in the fourth movement of the First Brandenburg Concerto. But that minuet is surely as easy on the ear as most movements in *concerti grossi* of the times. And would Scheibe have thought the sunny finale to the Fourth Brandenburg Concerto to be at all pedantic or obscure, just because it is really a disguised fugue?

Bach: *Brandenburg Concertos*. DECCA LXT 5198–9.

Perhaps the Bach concerto movement which comes nearest to pure lyricism and clarity of an Italian kind is the slow movement of the Concerto for Two Violins. It is almost unweighted by what Scheibe's school of thought would have called excessive ornament and untasteful rivalry of voices.

Bach: *Concerto for two violins in D minor*. HMV DB 1718 (alt. HMV BLP 1046).

The very scoring and structure of each of the Brandenburg Concertos was humorously surprising, and they are one further proof that Bach *could* have become a famous *Kapellmeister*, or perhaps an opera composer of international fame—another Handel. At no period were his circumstances more happy than when he was *Kapellmeister* at Cöthen. He made good friends with his musical colleagues, and he served a prince and a court who were prepared to meet special demands rather than lose him. His salary was raised more than once.

Yet he deliberately left the friends, the salary, the good living accommodation, the honour, and the status. He became a Cantor, and the Leipzig Cantor was regarded by Lutherans as Anglicans regard the organist in one of their famous cathedrals; several fine musicians had preceded Bach in the post. He managed to bring up a large family, to give his sons the advanced education that he himself missed, and to get engraved at his own expense the compendious schemes of ideal music—the *Catechism Preludes* and the *Art of Fugue*, for example—which he surely knew would have no great immediate sale. But the great Bach was less regarded than the local school headmaster. *Apparently*, that is what he chose to do, but I don't think he did.

I am certain that Bach hoped to raise the whole status of Cantor by raising the whole status of church music. He did not sign himself 'Cantor', but 'Director of Music and Court Composer,' and I do not think this was merely a proud gesture. I believe that Bach cherished an ideal for notable centres of orthodoxy like Leipzig. He wanted them to have a musical establishment with singers and players not inferior to those of ducal and royal orchestras and operas. The Cantor himself in this school would be the equivalent of *Kapellmeister*, free to develop his genius, to compose and direct final rehearsals of music that had been prepared by his assistants.

The help from good town trumpeters and the extra singers and players from the university enabled Bach in his first few years at Leipzig to show just what was possible if the school and the city wanted to realize this ideal. In those first few years he composed some of his most brilliant church music. Leipzig heard the magnificence of princely concert and opera blended with the chorale treatments, the contrapuntal elaboration, and the musical symbolism of the church tradition.

Bach: *Cantata No. 51: Jauchzet Gott.* RENAISSANCE X 35 (NIXA PLP 235) or LONDON LL 993 (DECCA LXT 2926) or COLUMBIA ML 4792 or BACH GUILD 546.

It is ridiculous to suppose that Bach went to Leipzig because he liked the organ. There was no need for him to have composed five sets of *Hauptmusik*, two or three hundred works for five years of Sundays and week-day festivals, with oratorios, Passions, Masses, and motets as well. There must have been hundreds of such pieces lying ready composed and copied. The favoured texts for cantatas were modelled on opera libretti, so that the kind of music that moved people's feelings in the theatre should also move them to piety in church. Only a musician capable of being a great opera composer could have set those texts as Bach did. But neither town council nor school authorities grasped Bach's ideal. If only Luther could have come to life and ordered its realization! And therefore, as Bach aged, his ideal became a dream, realized only on paper in those collections we now treasure such as the *Catechism Preludes*.

So he who was despised for his German-ness, his local dialect, has been gradually hailed as one of the most universal artists. And so he is. When friends wanted to compliment Bach in versified greetings, they made play with his name. The word *Bach* means 'brook,' 'fountain,' or 'source.' What was once a complimentary metaphor is no longer fanciful: for Bach is the source to which most modern composers trace their biggest technical advances; he is the fountain to which amateurs go for their most lasting musical refreshment; and even when we are especially fond of another composer, we turn aside to drink again and again at this ever-satisfying brook. Why at this one especially?

The answer, I am sure, is a philosophic and religious one. Bach's music sometimes demands strenuous work, but if it is ever disquieting or depressing, then it is wrongly played and mis-interpreted; as it is when it is made to sound unctuous or senti-mental. It does not speak of transient beauty, of the beauty of Mozart's most touching lyricism or even Handel's. If ever it illustrates sorrow or the transience of worldly beauty and happi-ness, Bach is showing the sorrow as the price of sin. Not all listeners hold that theological doctrine, but they are forced to do so temporarily while listening to Bach. Always there follows the assurance of strong faith; always we feel the utter sanity of a man either so wholly deceived or so wholly fortified by his belief that he conveys comfort—in the literal meaning, becomes a *fort*, a stronghold, and we feel this even in mere dance movements. This is exactly what Bach would have wished.

APPENDIX

BOOKS

C. SANFORD TERRY: *Bach: A Biography.*
ALBERT SCHWEITZER: *J. S. Bach.*
CECIL GRAY: *The Forty-Eight Preludes and Fugues.*
H. DAVID and M. MENDEL: *The Bach Reader.*
HARVEY GRACE: *The Organ Works of Bach.*

RECORDS

The music of J. S. Bach is well represented in the current catalogues with generous selections of his cantatas, orchestral works, chamber music, and music for solo instruments. The LP record has also brought us generally much more authentic performances. Attention may be drawn to the following records among the many available:

St Matthew Passion. WESTMINSTER 401 (NIXA WLP 6401).
Cantata No. 140, 'Wachet auf.' WESTMINSTER WL 5122 (NIXA WLP 5122) or BACH GUILD 511 (NIXA BLP 311).
The Organ Music.

Comprehensive sets from Decca (Archive series DGG) and from Westminster (now being released). Also selections by Albert Schweitzer on English Columbia 33 CX 1074/1081/1084/1249.

Italian Concerto: Chromatic Fantasia and Fugue. LONDON LD 9187 (DECCA LW 5170).
The Well-tempered Clavier. VICTOR (six records) BRUNSWICK AXTL 1036–41 (piano).
Goldberg Variations. VICTOR LM 1080 (HMV ALP 1139).
The Musical Offering. LONDON LL 1181 (DECCA LXT 5036).
The Art of Fugue. WESTMINSTER WAL 220 or ENGLISH DECCA LXT 2503–5.

31

Anthony Lewis

HANDEL

MUSIC has often been called the universal language, and in its long history there has been no figure that better illustrated this universality than Georg Friedrich Handel. German by birth, Italian by spirit, and English by naturalization, he was the true eighteenth-century cosmopolitan, adapting himself with extraordinary skill to the demands of the society in which he lived at any particular time. After many years of residence in Great Britain his enemies might still mock at his strange use of the English tongue, but his mastery of the country's musical language was evident in one of the very first works he wrote there, the *Te Deum* composed to celebrate the Peace of Utrecht.

Born in Halle in 1685, Handel received his first systematic musical education at the age of eight under Zachau, one of the most distinguished German musicians of the day. Zachau's scheme of instruction was comprehensive, and the child Handel received a thorough grounding in counterpoint and harmony and in playing the organ, harpsichord, violin, and oboe. All the instruments which Zachau taught him were to leave a lasting mark on Handel's career. He became one of the greatest virtuosi in Europe on the harpsichord; his skill on the organ has a permanent memorial in his wonderful series of organ concertos, unique of their kind and a sensational novelty when first introduced to the English public of his day. As a violinist he became also very proficient, and on one occasion snatched a violin out of the hands of the eminent Corelli to show him how to play a difficult passage. There is no account of him as an oboist, but his oboe concertos and his use of the instrument in the orchestra show an exceptional sympathy with its character and potentialities.

Handel's father, a barber-surgeon, was not so dazzled by the tempting offers which the extraordinary gifts of his son aroused to be moved from his conviction that he should have a sound general education. This culminated in the university at Halle which Handel left in 1703, having completed the course in law. Even this subject may have had its influence on future artistic events. Handel was an able business man and a shrewd negotiator, and the survival of the Italian opera in London was as much due to these qualities in him as to his creative genius.

Handel's next significant move was to Hamburg, where he joined the staff of the famous opera-house, then under the direction of Reinhard Keiser. Though it appears that Handel did not always get on well with Keiser, nevertheless he was again very fortunate in his association with one of the leading figures of German music whose place in the history of music is a secure and honourable one. Both as violinist and harpsichordist Handel learnt much at Hamburg that was to stand him in good stead as a composer. The fruits of this experience were his first two operas, *Almira* and *Nero*, both produced in 1705. Handel is not usually thought of as a precocious composer, but this achievement at the age of twenty finds few rivals elsewhere.

His success in opera fired him with a desire to visit its home, Italy, and in 1706 he left Hamburg *en route* for the south. Whether he realized it or not his visit to Italy was to be one of the most important periods in his life, very largely determining its future course from the artistic point of view. With all his precocious gifts, when he left Hamburg he was in many respects still rather a raw apprentice; the impact of Italy was to transform him into an accomplished young master, equipped with all the refinement of technique and polish of manner that its sophisticated society had to offer.

We may imagine Handel's dismay when, on arrival in Rome, he found that all opera was forbidden by papal edict. This might well have seemed the end of his ambitions, had not the Romans resolved that in no circumstances would they be deprived of their favourite entertainment. The great patrons of the art accordingly gave musical parties in their palaces at which so-called cantatas were performed. Many of them were in fact short dramatic scenes set to music of the same type and style as is found in the contemporary opera. Handel himself wrote many cantatas of this kind, and the finest of them is *Apollo e Dafne*. It is one of

H

the most important achievements of his early maturity, and it stands in much the same relationship to his later career as *Die Entführung aus dem Serail* does to Mozart's. The libretto is based on the classical legend of the god Apollo who sees Daphne, a nymph dedicated to the service of Diana, as she worships the goddess in her grove. Fired with love for her, Apollo tries to persuade Daphne to yield to him. She repulses him angrily and tries to escape in flight. Apollo gives chase, but just as he thinks he has caught Daphne, she is transformed into a laurel.

To accompany the two characters of this dramatic cantata Handel used only a small orchestra by our standards—a flute, two oboes, bassoon, strings, and continuo—but it is so disposed as to obtain the maximum effectiveness and variety. Particularly noteworthy is the accompaniment to Daphne's first aria. There is a long and most beautiful obbligato for oboe, and this is supported by strings playing *pizzicato*; the first violins in octaves with the violas, the second violins in octaves with the cellos, and the double basses (*arco*) holding the fundamental bass line. It is a unique lay-out which produces a most delicate and transparent effect.

Apollo pleads with Daphne in an aria of great lyrical power, *Come rosa*. Below the unison of the violins Handel takes the unusual step of writing a part for solo cello, leaving the bass in the hands of the continuo. Handel never believed in squandering his resources, and when he wrote something he thought especially good he saw that it was not wasted. So we find the material of this aria appearing in various guises in later works, and indeed the whole of the music of the Italian period became for him a veritable storehouse of ideas.

The chase is delightfully characterized by Handel in a scene in which the solo violin represents Daphne and the solo bassoon Apollo. In a noble concluding aria, Apollo declares, brokenhearted, that if he may not love Daphne in human form, a wreath of her laurel leaves shall for ever adorn his brow. The composer's handling of the final dramatic situation is most impressive as the torrent of semiquavers in the orchestra that symbolizes the chase gives way to bewildered recitative over the bare continuo.

Handel: *Apollo e Dafne*. OISEAU-LYRE OL 50038.

Outside Rome opera was not subject to papal restrictions, and

Handel enjoyed great success with his operas *Rodrigo*, produced in Florence, and *Agrippina*, given in Venice. Fresh from these triumphs he returned to Germany and left again almost at once for England, where he arrived in 1710. The sophisticated society of the court of Queen Anne had been much attracted by what they had seen of Italian opera, but there was no native composer at the time who could master the style. Thus when Handel produced his *Rinaldo* in 1711 the circumstances were very favourable to its success. It was his finest operatic achievement to that date, despite the fact that it was written in only fourteen days, and it immediately established his reputation. It was the first of a long series of operas produced in London which were to comprise Handel's main creative activity for the next thirty years.

The favourite type of Italian opera of Handel's day was known as *opera seria* and its general characteristics had been established by Alessandro Scarlatti. The libretto was usually based on some classical or medieval legend and cast in such a form that the main burden of the performance could be maintained by a small group of solo singers. There was little choral or ensemble writing, but sometimes there would be opportunities for ballet or for descriptive music, although generally the purely orchestral contribution was confined to the overture and appropriate introductory music elsewhere. The main substance of the action was carried on in *secco* recitative, that is, speech-rhythm declamation with only continuo accompaniment; for moments of special dramatic or emotional interest the orchestra would be added in support. The arias were mostly of the *da capo* type and were commentaries on the action, summing up the emotional situation stage by stage. It is perhaps the reflective nature of the *da capo* aria that has given modern producers most difficulty, for these arias are essentially static and will not respond to a doctrine of constant activity. When it is realized that Handel's operas are pyschological music dramas in which the chief vehicle of expression is the human voice, we can hope for a sympathetic approach to these fine works so long neglected. One of the richest musically is *Sosarme*, which was produced in 1732, and we can hear it on records.

Handel: *Sosarme*. OISEAU-LYRE OL 50091–3.

Not long after his first successes in London as an opera composer, Handel took up an appointment which was to lead indirectly towards the form with which he eventually superseded opera, namely oratorio. For in 1718 he became chapel master to the Duke of Chandos and in the duke's service wrote not only the famous series of Chandos anthems and the pastoral *Acis and Galatea*, but also the masque *Haman and Mordecai*. It was this masque that Handel adapted some twelve years later to become his first oratorio, *Esther*.

Despite the constant artistic success of his operas, amid jealous rivalry and financial difficulty, there came a time when the man of the world saw that the English public wanted a change of medium. He rightly judged what elements in the *opera seria* his London audience would like to see preserved in the oratorio and what fresh elements should be introduced. Thus he maintained the dramatic basis, but cut down the *secco* recitatives, while keeping the arias; and recognizing the English interest in choral singing, he made the chorus a protagonist in the action and an important and essential part of the musical design.

The first oratorios were written while he was still mainly concerned with opera, but by the time *Saul* and *Israel in Egypt* were reached his attention was becoming more and more concentrated on the new form which, after *Messiah* in 1742, was to claim his chief energies for the rest of his life. It may seem paradoxical to say so, but there is little doubt that the universal popularity of Handel's great masterpiece *Messiah* has obscured the true nature of his genius. For *Messiah* of all the oratorios is the only one that is not avowedly dramatic in treatment, though often highly dramatic in style. All the other oratorios are either sacred music dramas or virtually operas in English. They maintain the essentially dramatic core of Handel's musical character that runs through all his music from his youthful days in the Hamburg opera-house and his early triumphs in Italy to the Italian operas in London and finally the oratorios. As Bach's artistic home was the church, so was Handel's the theatre, and unless his oratorios are regarded from that point of view they will be misunderstood. A good example is *Semele*, a setting of a libretto by Congreve, that was first performed in 1744 at Covent Garden Theatre, where most of the oratorios were produced. Those who say that early English opera died with Purcell would do well to consider the claims of *Semele*, which has been revived with success on the English stage.

Handel: *Semele*. Oiseau-Lyre OL 50098–60000.

My emphasis has been on Handel's dramatic work, since that was central to his genius, but he had many other fields of activity. For instance, his splendid keyboard fugues use that musical resource in a different way from Bach, with impressive results. Again, it is likely that more music lovers are acquainted with Bach's Brandenberg Concertos than know Handel's superb set of twelve *Concerti Grossi*, Opus 6, which equally represent a peak in the orchestral music of this period. Then also the trio sonatas are virtually unknown to the musical public. They require for their performance an ensemble of two violins, cello, and harpsichord which is no longer a viable economic unit, and the consequence is that the great chamber music of this period, on a level with the string quartets of Haydn, is now rarely heard.

What are the qualities that have given Handel his place among the greatest masters of the art? So versatile was he, so prolific and so universal in his appeal, that it is hard to urge the claims of one aspect rather than another. For some it will be his sturdy rhythm that carries the listener on with irresistible impetus, and gives the joyous exhilaration of choruses like *Now love, that everlasting boy* from *Semele*. For others it will be the emotional intensity of the great accompanied recitatives such as those in *Semele* and *Jephthah*, or the brilliant handling of the powerful dramatic scenes in *Samson* or *Belshazzar*. Many, I fancy, will feel that one of his most attractive musical traits is the exquisite purity of his melody. But perhaps to the majority the overwhelming impression of Handel is of titanic strength, strength that is the more majestic for its capacity to be gentle without weakness, expressive without loss of sinew. Breadth and fundamental power are of its very essence, and it has the enduring quality of the truly monumental. As the superb architecture of the *Hallelujah* chorus reveals itself, one feels that if the word 'classical' has any meaning, it must belong to the music of Handel.

APPENDIX

BOOKS

EDWARD J. DENT: *Handel.*
ed. GERALD ABRAHAM: *Handel: A Symposium.*
O. E. DEUTSCH: *Handel: A Documentary Biography.*

RECORDS

Messiah. LONDON LLA 19 (DECCA LXT 2921–4) or WESTMINSTER WAL 308 (NIXA NLP 907).
Te Deum for the Peace of Utrecht. HAYDN SOCIETY 2046.
Concerti Grossi, Op. 6. LONDON LLA 21 (DECCA LXT 5041–3) or WESTMINSTER WAL 403.
Organ Concertos. VOX PL 7132/7202/7802 (E).
Violin Sonatas. COLUMBIA ML 4787 or LONDON LL 652 (DECCA LXT 2751).
Water Music. DECCA ARC 3010 (DGG APM 14006).

32

Lionel Salter

EIGHTEENTH-CENTURY KEYBOARD MUSIC

EVERYTHING about keyboard music underwent a complete transformation in the eighteenth century. The idiom changed from the so-called 'learned style' to the '*galant*' and thence to what we now know as the 'Viennese classical': the kind of works written changed entirely, ranging from fugues and chorale variations at one end of the century to rondos and sonatas at the other; and perhaps most striking of all, there was a revolution in the actual instruments themselves—which was to have considerable influence on keyboard technique and on the relation between the keyboard instrument and others in concerted music. The gulf in style in the twentieth century between, say, Debussy and Skalkottas is not as wide, seen dispassionately, as that between the cool formality of Böhm at the beginning of the eighteenth century and the fiery subjectivity of Beethoven at the end of the century.

(i) Böhm: *Gelobet seist du, Jesu Christ*. TELEFUNKEN LGX 66009.
(ii) Beethoven: *Sonata in C minor, Op. 13* (*Allegro molto*). WESTMINSTER WL 5184 (alt. HMV ALP 1062).

The favourite instruments of the time were the harpsichord and the organ. The harpsichord produced its incisive, clean-cut tone by a key mechanism which caused small tongues of quill or leather to pluck the strings: the player could not, by altering the weight or speed of his finger touch, affect the tone at all, and in order to obtain variety he had to bring into operation different stops which caused the strings to be plucked at another point or which acted on upper or lower octaves of the strings. As there was no time to change stops while the fingers were busy playing, any changes had to be left to the ends of sections of a work, so that the effect was of what is called 'terraces' of tone—sudden contrasts of volume or tone colour. Similarly, on the organ, crescendos and diminuendos were out of the question (the swell-box, an English invention, was relatively late to be adopted), and changes of timbre were introduced only at structural divisions of the work.   In a fugue the growing complexity of the music provided all the heightening of tension necessary, without any addition of colour or greater volume.

The eighteenth-century organ was smaller and shriller in tone than our present-day instrument, worked on light wind pressure, abounded in bright mutation stops, and, except in northern Germany, possessed but a rudimentary pedal-board.   Bach had more extensive instruments at his disposal, and he revelled in his pedal-board.   That emotional appeal was not ignored, despite the formal periods of his music, is shown by Bach's predilection for a tremolo stop in his organ specifications: this would approximate to the human voice, whose effect Bach often seems to have had in mind when writing for instruments.

A recent progressive step had been the introduction of equal temperament, a system of tuning keyboard instruments by dividing the octave equally into twelve semitones.   Before this, the 'mean-tone' system had meant that it was only possible to work satisfactorily in about five or six nearly related keys: modulation outside these either meant being out of tune or involved cumbersome keyboard complications to provide all the necessary accidentals. Rameau and Bach were ardent champions of the system; indeed Bach's *Forty-eight Preludes and Fugues* and other compositions could not have been conceived without it; and they paved the way for a freer harmonic language.

Bach: *Chromatic Fantasia*.   VICTOR LCT 1137 (alt. NIXA LLP 8047).

Nevertheless it took a long time for equal temperament to be universally accepted.   Sarti contemptuously dismissed Mozart as 'only a clavier player with a depraved ear, a sectary of the false system that divides the octave into twelve semitones'; and as late as 1850 some organs were still being tuned in mean-tone temperament.

In France descriptive music had always been popular, and Couperin, whose *ordres* are delightful series of miniatures (not meant to be played continuously), wrote in the preface to his 1713 volume: 'I have always had some plan in composing these pieces, and the titles illustrate the ideas I have had.'   Many of these pieces are cast in the binary mould of the dances of the eighteenth-century suite, though with pastoral or character titles; others are pure programme music.   Much the same might be said of Rameau, though he is more harmonic, less linear in thought than Couperin.

Both also made significant contributions to the new instrumental forms that were beginning to take shape; Rameau by his feeling for key-relationships (his *rondeau Les Cyclopes*, for example, has elements of sonata form) and Couperin with such works as his great B minor *Passacaille* in rondo form—a piece of an astonishingly passionate nature.

Couperin: *Passacaille from 8me Ordre*. HMV DB 4944 (alt. Oiseau-Lyre OL 50058).

An interesting forerunner of the sonata form which was eventually to emerge in the latter part of the eighteenth century came from an unexpected and remote source—from Spain. Domenico Scarlatti was a brilliant harpsichord virtuoso, and the 550 odd sonatas that he wrote for his own use at the Spanish court—apparently all after he had passed the age of fifty—form one of the most dazzling chapters in the history of the development of keyboard technique. Every aspect of harpsichord virtuosity is to be found here—rapid repeated notes, flying leaps exploiting the full extent of the keyboard, cascading runs and arpeggios, passages for crossed hands. Being himself a lively Neapolitan, a true son of the people, Scarlatti was fascinated by the folk music of the Spanish peasants he heard around him: its characteristic harmonies and rhythms found their way into his compositions. The clashing dissonances heard in so many of his harpsichord pieces are the strummings of the Spanish guitar; the rattling repeated notes in which he delighted are representations of the castanets; and where other composers were writing gavottes and minuets, Scarlatti was introducing the whirl of the *jota*.

D. Scarlatti: *Sonata in A, L 428*. Westminster WL 5359.

Even during Bach's lifetime tastes were changing. The religious sect of Pietism inspired a swing of feeling away from artifice and strict doctrine towards homely simplicity and sensibility: this exactly suited the rapidly increasing bourgeois class, who may not have possessed much learning, but who were insistent on their capacity to feel emotions just as keenly as their social betters. Expressiveness became the new cult in Germany. The harpsichord was altogether too impersonal an instrument to satisfy this outburst of (frequently lachrymose) feeling: it lacked the human voice's ability to swell its tone according to the emotional intensity of a phrase, and singing quality from an instrument was exactly what was now demanded.

*H

The ideal instrument to which personal feelings and whispered confidences could be entrusted was the clavichord. Touching its keys caused small blades or 'tangents' of brass to press against the strings, emitting a faint, sweet tone. More important, the simplicity and responsiveness of its action were such that the volume of tone could be varied by differences of finger touch, so that within rather narrow limits some flexibility of dynamics was possible. Moreover, a kind of vibrato could be obtained, comparable to that on a stringed instrument or to the natural pulsation of the human voice. Its flexibility of tone encouraged a different kind of playing, expressive in intention, but easily becoming free, even sloppy, in rhythm. But the clavichord remained the favourite of most composers, who admired its sweetness, its sensitivity, and its half-tints of shading.

Bach: *Fugue in G minor* (on the clavichord). HISTORY OF MUSIC IN SOUND, VOL. VI. VICTOR LM 6031 (HMV HMS 59, 78 r.p.m.).

The clavichord's modesty of utterance prevented it from being of much value in larger surroundings or in combination with other instruments, and outside Germany it had little popularity. As far back as the beginning of the eighteenth century experiments had been made with harpsichords whose strings were struck by hammers instead of being plucked. The attraction of a hammer instrument to a public that was finding the harpsichord deficient in expression was that the hammers could be thrown against the strings at different speeds, controlled by the player's fingers, and thus cause louder or softer tone. These new 'soft-louds' or pianofortes were frail affairs, judged by modern standards, with wooden frames, and thin single strings tuned to a range of five octaves struck by light leather-covered hammers. Their sound was small—actually less in volume than the harpsichord—and at first players found great difficulty in cultivating the kind of touch necessary to produce controlled graded tone. How the pianoforte compared with the harpsichord in timbre and volume can be heard in the double concerto for the two together by Carl Philip Emanuel Bach.

C. P. E. Bach: *Double Concerto in E flat*. PARLOPHONE PMA 1009.

We first hear of the pianoforte being played in public as late as 1767 in London, although it had been known for some years previously in private homes. The light touch and small resonance of the pianoforte encouraged a new, more transparent style of writing which exploited runs, broken-chord figurations, and other fluent elegances. The pianoforte superseded the harpsichord both for solo use and in concerted music; when Haydn directed his symphonies in London in 1791, he did so from the pianoforte. When Mozart composed a concert aria for Nancy Storace, to whom he was deeply attracted, he wrote it with an important part for the pianoforte, which he himself played. Into this he poured all his feelings, the voice and piano carrying on an intimate and tender dialogue so that the work sounds, as Einstein has well said, 'like a declaration of love in music, the transfiguration of a relation that could not be realized except in this ideal sphere.'

Mozart: *Ch'io mi scordi di te.*   Vox PL 7370 (alt. Nixa WLP 5179).

The principal figure in the development of pianoforte style and technique was Carl Philip Emanuel Bach, to whom Mozart paid tribute. Bach had written the most celebrated keyboard tutor, his *Essay on the Correct Way to Play the Clavier*, in 1753; but it was as a composer for the instrument that he was even more important. His contemporaries all remarked on the amazing fertility of his invention, and if any one person can be called the father of the sonata it is he. His numerous examples reveal a remarkable feeling for design—a living, not by any means static, design—and an elegance of expression. His rondos too show an attractive vein of fantasy.

C. P. E. Bach: *Rondo in G.*   Oiseau-Lyre OL 50097.

Though a keyboard instrument had been essential at all concerted music-making since the seventeenth century, it was only rarely that it attained solo status, compared with, say, the violin or the oboe. The first harpsichord concerto was Bach's Fifth Brandenberg (*c.* 1721), and during the next decade or so he produced several other works which featured the harpsichord. In all these, however, the instrument is merely first among equals, and even when it was used quite virtuosically only contributed one particular element of colour in the unfolding of the design. The difference that fifty years brought may be seen by comparing one of Bach's concertos with one of Mozart's.

(i) Bach: *Concerto in F.*   Parlophone SW 8147 (78 r.p.m.) (alt. Nixa PLP 547).

(ii) Mozart: *Concerto in A, K 414.*   Decca ARC 3012 (DGG AP 13021).

The style of writing has changed from a close-knit contrapuntal texture to an easier, more fluent homophonic idiom with gracefully balanced phrases; the pianist is now a star personality either the equal or the superior of the orchestra; and the form of the movement is different so as to ensure that the soloist is given all the important thematic material.　Indeed, as a principal character in the drama, the piano now has to make an entrance as it were; and the pattern evolved by Mozart was to have the orchestra expound the chief themes of the movement on its own and then for the piano to present them all over again, though usually with some decorative modification.　Towards the end of the movement, too, the orchestra would pull up while the soloist played a highly ornamented cadence, or *cadenza*, introducing all kinds of virtuoso passage work and free meditation on the themes of the movement.

So far as solo pianoforte music was concerned, the man who represented the link between the generations of C. P. E. Bach and Beethoven was Haydn.　His earliest sonatas were based on C. P. E. Bach's style, with its characteristic ornamentation, wide range, and chordal treatment; but gradually they developed in individuality and in power.　A new seriousness, even a nobility, is often felt beneath the elegant surface; a sense of poetry in slow movements quite unlike anything that had gone before; and from the point of view of form they frequently possess an astonishing unity.

Haydn: *Sonata No. 34 in E minor*.　Oiseau-Lyre OL 50078.

In his later piano works, such as the *Variations in F minor*, Haydn achieves a passionate utterance akin to that associated with his pupil Beethoven.　Even limiting our view to those of Beethoven's works which fall in the eighteenth century there is a new drama, energy, and intensity about them, and a troubling profundity of emotion in the slow movements.　There is the impression that this vital personality is about to break through the bounds both of existing instrumental capabilities and of current musical language.　And so of course he was.

APPENDIX

Books

A. Dolmetsch: *The Interpretation of the Music of the Seventeenth and Eighteenth Centuries.*

A. J. Hipkins: *History of the Pianoforte.*

C. P. E. Bach: *Essay on the Correct Way to Play the Clavier.*

W. L. SUMNER: *The Organ: its evolution, principles of construction, and use.*
A. LOESSER; *Men, Women, and Pianos.*
RALPH KIRKPATRICK: *Domenico Scarlatti.*

RECORDS

Many records of eighteenth-century keyboard music will be found listed in other chapters. But attention should be drawn to Ralph Kirkpatrick's records of sixty sonatas by Domenico Scarlatti that he edited for publication: Columbia SL 221. Another recording of all the D. Scarlatti sonatas is in progress on a series of Westminster (Nixa) disks of which more than a dozen are now released.

The following collections of keyboard music should be mentioned:
French Masters of the Keyboard. OISEAU-LYRE OL 50028 LYRI-CHORD LL 19.
Spanish Keyboard Music. WESTMINSTER 5312 (NIXA WLP 5312).
Spanish and Portuguese Keyboard Music. OISEAU-LYRE OL 50032.
Italian and German Harpsichord Music. OISEAU-LYRE OL 50043.
The Art of the Organ. COLUMBIA KSL 219 (PHILIPS ABL 3066/3110).

(This last set contains a selection of baroque music played on a variety of European organs.)

33

Karl Geiringer

BACH'S SONS AND THE MANNHEIM SCHOOL

IN the eighteenth century the triumphant rise of natural science brought about a complete change in man's general outlook and conception of the universe. The earlier uncritical acceptance of doctrines handed down by the writers of antiquity had been replaced by empirical observation, and this had led to the revolutionary discoveries of Galileo, Newton, and Kepler. Before long scientific methods were not confined to the domain of science. All manifestations of life were subordinated to Reason and even the Muses were expected to follow its dictates closely.

A certain trend towards naturalism may be observed in the rococo style that originated early in the eighteenth century. Shepherds and shepherdesses became the fashion both in poetry and in painting; for they displayed the simplicity, charm, and impudent gaiety which people of the rococo era cherished. In music this spirit produced the so-called *style galant*. Baroque contrapuntal art was forsworn as too pompous and powerful and, most of all, as contrary to reason; a monodic style became the goal. As Mattheson, the great composer and writer, claimed: 'The ear often derives more satisfaction from a single well-ordered voice developing a clear-cut melody in all its natural freedom than from twenty-four parts which, in order to share the melody, tear it to such an extent that it becomes incomprehensible.' As for the emotional content, the aim professed by the song-writer Valentin Görner is typical: 'We are trying to write engaging, charming, jocular, graceful, amorous, and gay tunes.'

It is interesting to note that the new rococo style in music grew up at the very time that baroque music reached its climax. Even before Bach's *St Matthew Passion* and *Mass in B minor* or Handel's *Israel in Egypt* were written, a strong reaction had set in against the style of the great old masters of baroque music. As Paul

214

Henry Lang points out: 'The essence of the new artistic creed was an urge for liberty: liberation from the rules that had become stereotyped, from the stylistic conventions that had become rigid, from the artistic forms that had become immutable.' The new rococo period tried to supplant majestic splendour by graceful delicacy. Whereas baroque art had striven towards a powerful unity of form, the rococo artists preferred variety. Music had changed the buskins of pomposity for the dancing slippers of the *style galant*.

A good example of the rococo style is a little minuet from a Quintet in F major by Alessandro Scarlatti (1659–1725). This Italian master was one of the greatest opera composers of the early eighteenth century, and he also composed delightful works in other fields. This minuet for flute, oboe, violin, bassoon, and harpsichord conjures up a picture of society ladies with powdered hair, costumed as shepherdesses, gracefully dancing and curtseying to their partners.

A. Scarlatti: *Quintet in F.* HAYDN SOCIETY HSL 117.

The *style galant* did not remain unchallenged. The delicate and carefree artistic idiom which had conquered southern and western Europe was replaced, particularly in northern Germany, by a more solid musical language in which emphasis was laid on expressive power and sensibility. 'It is the business of music,' declared Daniel Webb, 'to express passions in the way they rise out of the soul.' Another writer exhorted his fellow artists with this axiom: 'A musician cannot move others unless he himself is moved.' This impulse came to music from outside. The slogan 'back to nature,' which implied a return to sincerity of feeling, originated with Jean Jacques Rousseau, and German literature and music accepted it eagerly. Goethe wrote his *Sorrows of Young Werther*, and its unrestrained emotionalism moved people all over the world to tears and even to suicide.

The work of the sons of Johann Sebastian Bach was determined by these different trends and at the same time contributed greatly to shaping them. The eldest son, Wilhelm Friedemann, was born in 1710 and received his musical training mainly from his father. He was an inspired organ virtuoso whose improvisations, as a contemporary reported, 'filled listeners with awe and reverence.' Friedemann served at first as organist in Dresden and later as church music director in Halle. He resigned from this position before securing another and spent the last years of his life rather unhappily as a freelance composer. He died at the age of seventy-four in straitened circumstances in Berlin.

More than any other Bach son Friedemann was under the influence of his father, whose favourite he was. He tried to use the strict forms cultivated by Johann Sebastian, but imbued them with a modern spirit. A good example is the Overture in D minor for two flutes and strings which he used as an introduction to a cantata written in 1758 in honour of King Frederick the Great of Prussia. It starts with a poignant slow introduction, filled with grieving sighs and heart-felt exclamations by the wind instruments. This is followed by an energetic four-part fugue, entrusted solely to the strings, which is full of vitality and excitement, despite the use of a form considered old-fashioned at that time.

W. F. Bach: *Overture in D minor*. CONCERT HALL 1251.

Friedemann's younger brother, Carl Philipp Emanuel, was born in 1714 and trained in music by his father alone. He served first as court accompanist to King Frederick the Great and subsequently as church music director in Hamburg, where he died in 1788. He enjoyed great fame both as a performer and as a composer; fame far exceeding the reputation won by his father. Emanuel was the foremost exponent of the style of sensibility in music and the passionate subjectivism of his compositions made a deep impression on later composers, particularly on Haydn and Beethoven. His favourite instrument was the clavichord. Emanuel's performances on this instrument were greatly admired, and a contemporary thus described his playing of the clavichord: 'His soul seemed absent from the earth. His eyes swam as though in some delicious dream.'

Emanuel wrote a character-piece entitled *Farewell to my Silbermann Clavichord* in 1781 in the form of a rondo. He gave a clavichord from his collection to a pupil, an instrument constructed by Gottfried Silbermann, a great organ-builder and friend of the Bachs. The artist sent with his instrument a composition expressing his sadness at the loss of a cherished possession. This is a stirring piece that grows out of a single subject stated at the beginning.

C. P. E. Bach: *Farewell to my Silbermann Clavichord*. ANTHOLOGIE SONORE AS 28 (78 r.p.m.).

It would be wrong, however, to regard Emanuel Bach as a one-sided composer, merely concerned with sentimental music. A Symphony in C that he wrote in 1780, together with three other symphonies, will prove that his music could convey the most various moods. The symphony is scored for two oboes, two horns, strings, and harpsichord. The tender and graceful *andante* reveals Emanuel's art of imbuing the light rococo idiom with depth and warmth, thus paving the way for later developments. This *andante* is followed by a sparkling and jolly *allegro* finale that displays his sense of humour in the use of sudden contrasts and surprise effects.

C. P. E. Bach: *Symphony in C.* CONCERT HALL 1251 (alt. NIXA WLP 5040).

Johann Sebastian's youngest son, Johann Christian, an offspring from his union with Anna Magdalena Wilcken, was born in 1735. His life was very different from that of the other Bachs, who all sedately served in Germany and refrained from long journeys. Christian, however, after studying with his half-brother Emanuel in Berlin, went to Italy, where he won great success as an operatic composer. In 1762 he was called to London as a *maestro* of the King's Theatre and was appointed music teacher to the queen. He stayed in London, where he enjoyed tremendous prestige as a composer, performer, and teacher, but died prematurely in 1782.

Christian's music is graceful and highly polished, yet tender, and he contributed decisively towards infusing classical poise and beauty into the *style galant*. These qualities of Christian's music fostered similar trends in the creative output of young Mozart. There were few contemporary artists for whom the Salzburg composer felt so much love and admiration. Mozart's loyalty to Christian did not waver from their first meeting in London in 1764, when the boy of eight played duets with the music master to the British queen, to their reunion in Paris fourteen years later, and finally to the day in 1782 when Mozart wrote to his father: 'I suppose you have heard that the English Bach is dead. What a loss to the musical world!'

Two examples should illustrate for us the style of Christian Bach's music; first an Allegro in D for flute, oboe, violin, viola, and cello. This was written in the 1770's and is a finely wrought gem, every delightful detail of which is planned with supreme competence. It prompts us to agree with what Mozart's father once wrote about Christian Bach's chamber music: 'The small is great, when it is composed in a natural, fluent, and easy manner and is worked out soundly. Has Bach debased himself by composing such works? By no means! The solid texture and structure, the continuity: these distinguish the master from the bungler.'

One of Christian Bach's achievements was that he greatly helped to promote the new pianoforte, and he was also one of the first to play piano duets. A good example is the Sonata in G for piano, four hands, whose minuet is somewhat like the Scarlatti minuet mentioned earlier, though more appealing and heart-felt.

J. C. Bach: (i) *Allegro in D.* ANTHOLOGIE SONORE AS 115 (78 r.p.m.); (ii) *Sonata in G for piano duet.* WESTMINSTER 18025 (alt. NIXA WLP 5069).

Christian Bach enjoyed a great reputation outside England too, and it is significant that he was twice commissioned to compose an opera for Mannheim, capital of the German Palatinate, which boasted one of the best orchestras to be found in the eighteenth century. The Elector of Mannheim, a passionate friend of music, had assembled at his court a number of outstanding musicians who were pioneers in producing dynamic shadings in the orchestral sounds such as had never been heard before. A contemporary writer described the effect of the playing of the Mannheim orchestra in these poetical phrases: 'Its *forte* is thunder; its *crescendo* a waterfall; its *diminuendo* a crystal-clear brook murmuring in the distance; its *pianissimo* a breath of spring.'

So eminent a group of performers was bound to stimulate creative work, and there is a whole school of composers who wrote for the Mannheim orchestra and contributed significantly to the evolution of the classical symphony. The majority were of Austrian or Bohemian origin, including Christian Cannabich, Ignaz Holzbauer, Franz Xaver Richter, and Anton Filtz. Most important, however, was the Stamitz family, which contributed three distinguished composers. The eldest, Johann W. A. Stamitz (1717–57), exercised a decisive influence on the growth of symphonic music. Among the many pupils he trained, his brilliant son, Karl Stamitz (1746–1801), was particularly successful. The merry and brilliant rondo allegro from Karl's *Symphonie Concertante* for seven solo instruments and orchestra may illustrate the exquisite sense for tonal colours and the delightful freshness of melodic inspiration displayed by this important representative of the Mannheim school.

Karl Stamitz: *Symphonie Concertante*. WESTMINSTER 5017.

APPENDIX

BOOKS

KARL GEIRINGER: *The Bach Family*.
C. SANFORD TERRY: *Johann Christian Bach*.

RECORDS

C. P. E. BACH: *Chamber Music*. OISEAU-LYRE OL 50017. *Magnificat*. BACH GUILD 552. *Symphonies*. BACH GUILD 504. *Symphonies in C and D; Clavier Concerto*. NIXA WLP 5040.

J. C. BACH: *Chamber Music*. OISEAU-LYRE OL 50046. *Orchestral Music*. COLUMBIA ML 4869.

THE MANNHEIM SCHOOL: *Wind Music*. CLASSIC EDITIONS 2010.

KARL STAMITZ: *Flute Concertos*. OISEAU-LYRE OL 50035. *Violin Concerto in D*. VOX PL 7540.

KARL STAMITZ AND RICHTER: *String Quartets*. BARTÓK 915.

34

Karl Geiringer

EIGHTEENTH-CENTURY OPERA

MAKE-BELIEVE and pretence were part of the spiritual equipment of the baroque period. People wanted to appear glamorous and more than life-sized. The rich decorated the walls of their houses with paintings simulating vistas of wide colonnades and formal gardens; while clouds painted on the ceilings of ball-rooms and even vestibules seemed to lead the glance right into heaven. The men's formal, full-bottomed wig with curls and the women's pompous crinolines were both intended to add dignity to the appearance of the wearers. Opera, in which heroes of divine character and powers enacted stories of mythological origin to the accompaniment of stirring music, seemed to be the best vehicle to express the artistic ideal of the time; and Italy, the home of *bel canto*, was the country where opera had originated and where it flourished for a long time.

At the beginning of the seventeenth century the dramatic element in opera seemed of paramount importance. Gradually, however, the Italians' sensual pleasure in the beauty and refinement of the human voice led to significant changes. It became the main purpose of opera composers to satisfy the ambition of the *prima donna* and the *primo uomo*. The audiences came to hear a great *castrato* or a famous woman soprano deliver endless arias with all the ornaments and trimmings they were capable of providing. The form of opera thus developed in Italy, and especially in Naples, became the model for composers all over Europe.

A good example of what was fashionable and most pleased audiences is Cleopatra's aria *Da tempeste il legno* from Handel's *Giulio Cesare*, composed in 1723 and first performed in London in February 1724. The text expresses strong emotions, but it is not easy to recognize the mood of deliverance from pain through love in this rather conventional *da capo* aria. (Incidentally, Handel's operatic music was often on a much higher level.)

Handel: *Giulio Cesare* (*Da tempeste il legno*). Vox PL 8012 (E).

Composers of less imposing stature than Handel were even more under the domination of star singers who resisted any attempt by a *maestro* to deprive them of their technical fireworks in order to achieve dramatic expression. An excerpt from a contemporary book illustrates the situation. In 1720 there appeared a satire entitled *Teatro alla moda* by the distinguished composer Benedetto Marcello. Although the caricature is somewhat exaggerated, we have the impression that the author's trenchant remarks are the result of bitter experience:

The composer will hurry or slow down the pace of an aria, according to the caprices of the singers, and will conceal the displeasure which their insolence causes him by the reflection that his reputation, his solvency, and all his interests are in their hands. . . . The director will see that all the best songs go to the *prima donna*, and if it becomes necessary to shorten the opera, he will never allow her arias to be cut, but rather other entire scenes. If a singer has a scene with another actor, whom he is supposed to address when singing an air, he will take care to pay no attention to him, but will bow to the spectators in the loges, smile at the orchestra and the other players in order that the audience may clearly understand that he is the Signor Alipi Forconi, *Musico*, and not the Prince Zoroaster, whom he is representing. . . .

If [a singer] has a role in a new opera, she will at the first possible moment take all her arias (which in order to save time she has had copied without the bass part) to her *Maestro* Crica so that he may write in the passages, the variations, the beautiful ornaments, etc., and the *Maestro* Crica, without knowing the first thing about the intentions of the composer either with regard to the tempo of the arias, or the harmonies, or the instrumentation, will write down everything he can think of, and in very great quantity, so that the virtuosa may be able to sing her aria in a different way at every performance . . . and if her variations have nothing in common with the bass part, with the violins which are to play in unison with her, or with the concertizing instruments, even if they are not in the same key, that will be of no consequence, since it is understood that the modern opera director is both deaf and dumb.[1]

A twofold reaction set in against this strange type of opera: composers either ridiculed it or they tried to improve it. Let us consider each attempt in turn. It became the custom to insert in the intermissions of the three-act serious opera short musical comedies, called *Intermezzi*. Here the mythological heroes were

[1] Cf. Donald Grout: *A Short History of Opera*, New York, Columbia University Press, 1947, pp. 190–2.

replaced by common people of the eighteenth century who sang
simple, folksong-like melodies, accompanied by a handful of
instruments. The deeds of valour and the pompous diction of
serious opera gave way to unassuming farces often presented in
dialect. One such comic opera is *La Serva Padrona* (*The Maid
as Mistress*), composed in 1733 by Giovanni Battista Pergolesi
(1710–36), which marks a milestone in the history of opera. In
one aria, *Sempre in Contrasti*, a grumpy old bachelor complains
to his servant about the discomforts she inflicts on him.

> There's always upheaval,
> Wherever you are
> It's here and there,
> It's up and down,
> It's yes and no.
> But now enough.
> It will be stopped.
> What do you say?
> Isn't it so?
> Ah . . . what . . . no!
> But so it goes!
> There is always upheaval, etc.

Pergolesi: *La Serva Padrona* (*Sempre in Contrasti*). CETRA 50036
or ANGEL 35279 (COLUMBIA 33 LX 1340).

Among the many composers of serious opera who tried to increase the dignity and dramatic truth of the form, the German,
Christoph Willibald von Gluck (1714–87), was the most outstanding. He laid down his principles in the famous introduction to
his opera *Alceste*:

I resolved to avoid all those abuses which had crept into Italian
opera through the mistaken vanity of singers and the unwise compliance
of composers, and which had rendered it wearisome and ridiculous. . . .
I endeavoured to reduce music to its proper function, that of seconding
poetry by enforcing the expression of the sentiment, and the interest
of the situations, without interrupting the action, or weakening it by
superfluous ornament. . . . In fact, my object was to put an end to
abuses against which good taste and good sense have long protested in
vain. . . . I also thought that my chief endeavour should be to attain
a grand simplicity, and consequently I have avoided making a parade
of difficulties at the cost of clarity.

As an example of Gluck's method, we may take the beginning

of the second act of his *Orfeo ed Euridice*, first performed in Vienna on 5th October 1762. Orpheus, the great singer of Greek mythology, has lost his wife, Euridice, who was bitten by a snake; and he descends to the underworld to claim her back. As the act opens, the furies of Hades perform a weird dance and sing a threatening chorus. Orpheus (sung in the original by a *castrato* and in our day by a woman contralto) entreats them to give him access to Hades, but the answer is an implacable 'no.' Gluck achieves a most dramatic contrast between the chorus of furies, accompanied by trombones, and the heart-stirring plea of Orpheus, singing to the sound of a harp which is meant to conjure up the sounds of the ancient Greek lyre.

Gluck: *Orfeo ed Euridice*. URANIA URLP 223 (NIXA ULP 2923)* (alt. HMV ALP 1357).

The greatest opera composer of the eighteenth century was undoubtedly Wolfgang Amadeus Mozart (1756–91). His mature operatic masterpieces draw the conclusion from the developments of the era before him. Like Shakespeare's plays they combine serious and comic elements to provide a picture of life in all its aspects. In Mozart's operas we find the most forceful drama, but at the same time they are unsurpassed in sheer melodic beauty. Any example mentioned in this short essay seems to be completely inadequate when we bear in mind the abundance of superb pieces that must go unmentioned. Yet the three examples will at least serve to illustrate the inexhaustible variety and inspiration displayed in Mozart's operas.

Among the dazzling array of musical gems in *The Marriage of Figaro* the aria *Non più andrai* placed at the end of Act I was the favourite with Mozart's contemporaries. Here the clever barber and valet Figaro makes fun of the young page Cherubino, who has so far mainly been interested in flirting with young ladies but is now forced to join the army. Mozart's use of trumpets and horns is inspired by Figaro's teasing reference to the victories that Cherubino is going to win on the battlefield.

In the duet *La ci darem la mano* from *Don Giovanni* we notice Mozart's art of psychological characterization. Don Giovanni sings a caressing tune to the peasant girl Zerlina whose love he tries to win. She is strongly attracted to the glamorous nobleman, yet she hesitates, for she is engaged to an honest peasant. At the end, however, she is swept off her feet, and the duet concludes jubilantly as they express their intention to hurry to Don Giovanni's castle.

Mozart: (i) *The Marriage of Figaro* (*Non più andrai*).
(ii) *Don Giovanni* (*La ci darem la mano*).

Mozart's last opera, composed to a German text, shows a further development of his artistic idiom. In *The Magic Flute*, first performed in Vienna on 30th September 1791, Mozart deals with an enchanting fairy-tale whose content is given depth through the inclusion of symbolism derived from the free masonic ritual. The bass aria *In diesen heil'gen Hallen* (*Within these sacred halls*) is sung by the high priest Sarastro, who proclaims in it Mozart's own ethical message:

We know no thought of vengeance, within these temple walls,
Where love leads back to duty, Whoever from duty falls.
By friendship's kindly hand held fast, He finds the land of light at last.
Here each to ev'ry other, by mental love is bound,
Where every wrong finds pardon, no traitor ever is found.
Those whom this bond cannot unite, are all unworthy of the light.

Mozart's music displays the utmost seriousness and dignity, but at the same time a simplicity and directness which almost reminds us of a folk-song. This is the least complicated but at the same time possibly the most impressive kind of music Mozart wrote.

Mozart: *The Magic Flute* (*In diesen heil'gen Hallen*).

We have only to compare the unadorned simplicity and heart-stirring beauty of Mozart's operatic music with the over-ornate and stilted aria from Handel's *Giulio Cesare* to evaluate the tremendous development that eighteenth-century opera underwent in six decades. Men like Pergolesi, Gluck, and, most of all, Mozart were responsible for this splendid evolution which led to a climax of artistic achievement but rarely found in the whole history of music.

APPENDIX

Books

A. Einstein: *Gluck*.
E. J. Dent: *Mozart's Operas*.

Records

Gluck: *Alceste*. Oceanic 304. English Decca LXT 5273–6. *Iphigenia in Tauris*. Vox PL 7822.
Cimarosa: *The Secret Marriage*. Angel 3549 C/L or Vox PL 8450.
Mozart: *The Abduction from the Harem*. Decca DX 133 (DGG DGM 18184–5). *Idomeneo*. Haydn Society 2020 (Nixa HLP 2020).*
The Marriage of Figaro. London XLLA 35 (Decca LXT 5088–91).
Don Giovanni. Victor LCT 6102 (HMV ALP 1199–1201). *Cosi fan tutte*. Angel 3522 C (Columbia 33 CX 1262–4). *The Magic Flute*. Decca DX 134 (DGG DGM 18267–9).

35

Karl Geiringer

HAYDN

THE various stylistic trends of the post-baroque music of the eighteenth century are all to be found in the work of one of the greatest masters of the time, Joseph Haydn. The light and playful grace of rococo music and the passion and warmth of the style of sensibility were the foundations on which Haydn built. In conjunction with Mozart he developed the musical idiom which we have come to designate as Viennese classical music.

Haydn may be described as a self-made musician. He received but little theoretical instruction and owed most of what he knew to his keen interest in the music of the past and the compositions of his own time. His artistic development was slow indeed, and he wrote his greatest masterpieces when he was over sixty. As he grew in artistic stature, his fame gradually spread throughout the civilized world, and he finally enjoyed an unprecedented reputation.

Haydn was born in 1732 in the eastern part of Austria, a section inhabited by Germans, Hungarians, and Croatians, and we have reason to assume that all three races were represented among Haydn's ancestry. His father was a wheelwright, and being unable to provide an education for the gifted boy, he entrusted the five-year-old Joseph to a cousin who served as schoolmaster and director of church music in a small town. From then on Haydn was on his own and he never received financial support from his parents. For nine years he worked as a choir-boy at St Stephen's in Vienna, the most important cathedral in the Austrian Empire. He had to leave St Stephen's at the age of seventeen, when his voice broke, and thereafter he supported himself through a variety of musical jobs until in 1760 he entered the service of the Hungarian Prince Esterházy. He quickly advanced to the rank of conductor and maintained his connection with this powerful aristocratic family until his death in 1809. During the first thirty years he served in the castles of Eisenstadt and Esterház in Hungary. After 1790, however, he was frequently granted leave of absence, and his duties decreased in proportion as his fame increased. In the years 1791–2 and 1794–5 he paid two extremely successful visits to London, and these were high lights of a rather uneventful life.

Among the earliest of Haydn's works is an entertaining Organ Concerto in C, written in 1756. He wrote organ works only in the early phases of his career, and the gaily prancing finale of this concerto is certainly experimental in character. The manner in which the young composer employs the dignified church instrument to fulfil the tenets of the *style galant* may seem rather startling to us, and indeed Haydn later realized that this merry piece might be more suited to the harpsichord, and so catalogued it as a harpsichord concerto.

Haydn: *Organ Concerto in C* (1756). HAYDN SOCIETY HSLP 1043 (NIXA HLP 1043).

Our next example was composed fifteen years later and is of quite a different character; rococo gaiety is replaced by an ardent, strongly emotional language. Haydn had succumbed to the influence of Carl Philip Emanuel Bach, and many of his works composed about 1770 reflect in their pathos and stirring subjectivism the impact of the Hamburg Bach's style. The Twentieth Piano Sonata in C minor is the only one by Haydn in that passionate key; the first movement is full of poignant music with unexpected pauses and sudden contrasts.

Haydn: *Sonata No. 20 in C minor*. HAYDN SOCIETY HSLP 3013 (NIXA HLPY 3013)* (alt. DECCA LXT 5144).

While piano and especially organ works were on the periphery of Haydn's creative output, the string quartet was particularly close to his heart and occupied him from early youth to the end of his career. He wrote more than eighty quartets, and has been justifiably called the father of the string quartet. The Quartet in C major, Opus 33, No. 3, gives a good idea of the classical perfection of style that Haydn had achieved by about 1780. By then both the frills of the rococo style and the strong emotionalism of the era of sensibility had been overcome, although they had left their imprint on Haydn's music. Out of the combination of these earlier artistic trends grew the classical style of his full maturity.

In this context the word 'classical' may best be explained as well-balanced. In classical music we find a perfect blend of the work of the mind and the work of the heart; inspiration is as important as the action of the intellect. Classical works seem to be born out of the fundamental qualities of the instruments or voices for which they were written. All technical problems are completely solved, and the musical ideas fit the musical form to perfection.

Haydn had by this time developed the method of thematic development; he dissected the subjects of the exposition and reassembled the fragments in the most various ways. Even the accompanying parts were often based on motives derived from the main subjects, and thus in his string quartets all four instruments were given an important share in the thematic elaboration. In the finale of the Quartet, Opus 33, No. 3, known as the 'Bird' Quartet, since different bird calls may be discerned in its movements, the call of the cuckoo supplies the basis of the first subject. The merry cuckoo call appears not only in the leading violins, but just as frequently in the viola and cello. The second subject, which is closely related to the first, has the character of Hungarian gipsy music. Such episodes appear frequently in Haydn's works. They may have been inspired by childhood impressions as well as by his protracted residence in Hungarian castles.

Haydn: *String Quartet in C, Op. 33, No. 3.* HAYDN SOCIETY HSQ
20 (alt. COLUMBIA 33 CX 1383).

The symphony, like the string quartet, occupied Haydn throughout his life. One hundred and four symphonies may be attributed to him with certainty, and recent research tends to enlarge this figure. His creative achievement in this form reached its climax in the twelve symphonies that he wrote for London. Here he managed (in the words of Paul Henry Lang) 'to achieve the ideal balance of homophony and a specific modern polyphony. What a fantastic cavorting of melodies, rhythms, syncopations, dynamic contrasts, general pauses, hesitations, sudden pauses, distortions!' A remarkable feature of these symphonies, written by a man over sixty, is that they occasionally seem experimental. Haydn tends to try out new devices, even at the sacrifice of the poise of former years. Fundamentally Haydn remained a classical composer, but again and again episodes are to be found in which expressiveness and passionate feeling break through the classical composure. Here we discern the first indications of romanticism.

A characteristic example of this tendency towards experimentation is the second movement of the Symphony No. 100 in G major, usually referred to as the 'Military.' The nickname is due to the employment of military instruments such as triangle, cymbals, and big bass drum in the second and last movements. The melody of the *allegretto*, taken from the French romance *La gentille et jeune Lisette*, was an old favourite of Haydn's. The combination of the sweet, graceful tune with the powerful percussion instruments is decidedly a bold experiment which also shows Haydn's sense of humour. Even bolder is the trumpet fanfare that sounds near the end of the movement; this is followed by a drum roll that rises from a mysterious *pianissimo* to a thunderous *fortissimo*. The ending seems to suggest some kind of programme for the music, and in this respect, too, Haydn prepared the way for later composers, including Beethoven.

Haydn: *Symphony No. 100 in G, 'Military.'* WESTMINSTER 5045 (NIXA WLP 5045).

While in London Haydn had been among the audience of the great Handel Festival of 1791 at which he found a whole nation aroused by monumental performances. Compared with the scale of these concerts, his own efforts to entertain a small group of music lovers at the Esterhazy castles must have seemed almost insignificant. Haydn intensely desired to write works that were meant for a whole nation. The results of this desire were the two great oratorios he composed after his return to Vienna: *The Creation* and *The Seasons*. In these works the deeply religious Haydn had an opportunity to express his love for all things created and his delight in the beauties of nature. Two prominent features of his oratorios should be mentioned: his musical interpretation of visual impressions and the epic fervour of his choral style. They can be illustrated in the recitative and chorus that close Part One of *The Creation*. In the recitative Haydn describes first the sunrise, then its full splendour, and after a pause the magically soft moonlight and the twinkling stars. The ensuing chorus alternates with three solo voices and presents the angels' jubilation over the achievements of the third day of creation.

Haydn: *The Creation*. HAYDN SOCIETY 2005 (NIXA HLP 2005) (alt. DGG DGM 18254–6).

To conclude, a final example of Haydn's wide-open mind. At the age of sixty-four he became acquainted with a newly invented instrument, the so-called keyed trumpet with finger holes closed by keys. Later generations discarded this instrument as its tone qualities were by no means equal to those of the valve trumpet. In Haydn's time, however, the keyed trumpet was considered a revolutionary innovation, and Haydn decided to try out the instrument by writing a concerto for it. The result is a work cherished up to our own time by all trumpeters as one of the most effective compositions in their repertoire, and the dazzling finale is a high light in the concerto literature of the eighteenth century.

Haydn: *Trumpet Concerto*. HAYDN SOCIETY HSLP 1038 (NIXA HLP 1038).

APPENDIX

BOOKS

KARL GEIRINGER: *Haydn*.
ROSEMARY HUGHES: *Haydn*.

RECORDS

Haydn is well represented on records. The Haydn Society (of Boston) is in the process of making all the string quartets available; many of these records have already been released (Nixa). The piano sonatas are represented by a fair sampling and so are the symphonies; the later symphonies are available in a number of different versions. But some aspects of Hadyn's work might be overlooked, and this short list may serve to draw attention to them.

Cantata: Arianna a Naxos. HAYDN SOCIETY 2051.
English Songs. HMV DLP 1121.
The Seasons. DECCA DX 123.
Opera: Orfeo ed Euridice. HAYDN SOCIETY 2029 (NIXA HLP 2029).*
Missa Sancti Bernardi de Offida. HAYDN SOCIETY 2048. PARLOPHONE PMA 1010.
Missa Solemnis in D minor. VANGUARD 470.
Seven Last Words of Our Saviour (string quartet version). HAYDN SOCIETY HSQ 39 NIXA WLP 6202.

36

Karl Geiringer

MOZART

WOLFGANG AMADEUS MOZART was Haydn's dearest friend and, as a creative genius, was his equal or possibly even superior to him. Mozart's whole existence took place in Haydn's lifetime, but it was barely half as long; the Salzburg composer was born twenty-four years after the great master of Esterház and he died eighteen years before him. In many respects the creative output of the two great classical composers displays a strong resemblance, but in Mozart's work everything seems condensed and intensified.

Romain Rolland once remarked about Mozart:

His true happiness was in creation. In restless and unhealthy geniuses creation may be a torture—the bitter seeking after an elusive ideal. But with healthy geniuses like Mozart creation was a perfect joy and so natural that it seemed almost a physical pleasure. . . . Beethoven had to fight with all his strength when in the throes of composition. If his friends surprised him at work, they often found him in a state of extreme exhaustion. . . . He was always making sketches of things, erasing or correcting what he had done, beginning all over again. . . . Mozart knew nothing of these torments. He was able to do what he wished, and he never wished to do what was beyond him. . . . So easy was creation to him that at times it poured from him in a double or triple stream, and he performed incredible feats of mental activity. He would compose a prelude while writing a fugue; and once when he played a sonata for pianoforte and violin at a concert, he composed it the day before, between eleven o'clock and midnight, hurriedly writing the violin part and having no time to write down the piano part or to rehearse it with his partner. The next day he played from memory what he had composed in his head. (8th April 1781.) This is only one of many examples. Such genius was likely to be spread over the whole domain of his art and in equal perfection. [1]

It is true that Mozart contributed supreme master works in

[1] Romain Rolland: *Some Musicians of Former Days*, Henry Holt & Co., New York, 1915.

almost every realm of music. His operas are among the greatest ever written, yet he composed for instruments with a mastery equal to his vocal writing. He was that rarity among human beings: a child prodigy of breath-taking precocity who did not stand still. Starting at the age of four, with the composition of some minuets, offering his first larger work—six sonatas for violin and piano—at the age of seven, he steadily grew in artistic stature up to his thirty-sixth year, when death overtook him. In the short time granted to him he wrote some twenty works for the stage; fifteen Masses and various other sacred works; some fifty symphonies; more than thirty serenades or *divertimenti* for small orchestra; fifty concertos for the most various instruments; seventeen sonatas and fifteen sets of variations for piano; seven piano trios and various other chamber music works; and more than one hundred airs, songs, or choruses.

In his early compositions the lad was strongly influenced by the music of Johann Sebastian Bach's youngest son, Johann Christian, whom he met while giving concerts in London at the age of eight. As Alfred Einstein put it:

. . . There existed between them a wondrous kinship of souls. . . . Young Mozart felt that Johann Christian had traversed a path that he himself should follow: from a northern region to a southern—to Italy— and from the southern back again to a northern. That path led to a new, ideal land in which only men of harmonious disposition felt at home. . . . Mozart yielded to an influence quite ingenuously. . . . He strove least of all for originality, because he was entirely certain of the Mozartian, personal stamp of his product. . . . It did not occur to him to do something new at all costs. He wanted to do it not differently, but better. [1]

The Mozartian touch can be discerned in the *Andante* of his Symphony No. 6, written at the age of eleven. He paints a delightful nocturnal scene. The first violin has the role of the serenading lover while the other instruments delicately accompany him. There is in it the sweetness of melodic idiom which Johann Christian Bach had introduced into symphonies, but added to it is a tiny touch of nostalgia which stirs our hearts as Mozart's *andantes* do so often.

Mozart: *Symphony No. 6 in F major, K. 43.* Concert Hall CHS 1165 (alt. Oiseau-Lyre DL 53008).

[1] From Alfred Einstein: *Mozart*, Oxford University Press, New York, 1945.

To illustrate Mozart's stupendous artistic development we may turn to another slow movement, written eighteen years later. It is the *Romanza* from the *Piano Concerto in D minor*, the sixteenth work of the kind that he composed, and one of the most outstanding. Here the composer again presents an enchantingly gentle and sweet melody which seems to dissolve our hearts. But while in the early symphony Mozart contented himself with merely spinning out a sweet tune, in the middle section of the concerto movement the atmosphere changes completely and a tempestuous, sombre mood is introduced. Only slowly and reluctantly is composure regained. The sixteenth notes change to triplets, and then to eighth notes, until the sweet *Romanza* theme sounds again.

Mozart: *Piano Concerto in D minor*, *K. 466*. HAYDN SOCIETY HSL 88 (alt. PHILIPS ABR 4006).

Mozart was an inspired pianist who wrote many compositions for his own performances. The piano concertos offer most rewarding and congenial tasks to the virtuoso, but his solo piano music too is wholly admirable and a never-failing source of joy to the average pianist. As is so often true of Mozart's music, some of these piano works do not present very great technical difficulties, yet they sound as though they did. The *Sonata in A major*, *K. 331*, shows how he managed to conjure up a whole world of different emotions within one sonata. The first movement is a superb set of variations, and this is followed by a delightful minuet. The finale is the famous *alla turca* march. Now that the Turks had ceased to be a deadly menace to Europe, their instruments were becoming fashionable, and it was Mozart's aim to evoke on the piano the sounds of a Janizary band. This *alla turca* is a highly exciting piece, with violence lurking underneath the brilliant display.

Mozart: *Sonata in A major*, *K. 331*. HAYDN SOCIETY HSL 126 (alt. HMV ALP 1194).

Among Mozart's many outstanding chamber music works, we may consider the String Trio in E flat major, K. 563, entitled *Divertimento*, which was completed on 27th September 1788. Like the average *divertimento*, it is quite long and consists of six entensive movements. The fourth, an *andante*, was described by the eminent French scholar, Georges de St Foix, as 'one of the greatest creations of chamber music in existence.' It is a set of

I

variations on a folksong-like theme, and in the variations the three instruments alternately assume the leadership, each being of equal significance.　There is a constant flow of new ideas, and not a bar is repeated throughout the movement.　Worthy of particular attention is the quite stunning variation in which the viola intones the theme like a *cantus firmus*, while violin and cello weave quick ornamental figures around it.　The three instruments here achieve a power and grandeur which one would not expect to find in a *divertimento*.

Mozart: *Divertimento in E flat, K. 563.*　HAYDN SOCIETY HSL 114
(alt. BRUNSWICK AXTL 1031).

In the summer of 1788—the year the E flat string trio was written —he completed within the incredibly short time of just over six weeks his last three, and indeed his greatest symphonies; in E flat, K. 543, G minor, K. 550, and C major, K. 551.　They constitute the composer's last testament in this form, and we can well understand that after reaching such a lofty peak Mozart did not feel inclined to proceed farther on this path.　It may also be said that no symphony written in the eighteenth century surpasses these three works in content or in technical mastery.

The last of the three is usually called the 'Jupiter' Symphony (the nickname was in all likelihood devised by the pianist-composer, Johann Baptist Cramer).　Jupiter was the greatest of the gods, so this C major symphony is outstanding among Mozart's symphonic inspirations.　Moreover, the name 'Jupiter' could refer to the significance of the finale, which, contrary to prevailing custom in the eighteenth century, is not simply a gay denouement, but achieves an importance far out-ranking that of the preceding movements.　With the finale we seem to reach the throne of the supreme god Jupiter after passing a row of minor deities.

The finale starts with a deceptively simple subject consisting of four notes only.　Long before Mozart's time it had been used by Purcell, Bach, Handel, and others.　Mozart himself seems to have had a predilection for it, as he employed it in two of his church works and in various instrumental compositions.　Scholarly treatises have been written about this finale, but Eric Blom justly remarks:

There is a mystery in this music not to be solved by analysis, and perhaps only just to be apprehended by the imagination.　We can understand the utter simplicity; we can also, with an effort, comprehend the immense technical skill with which the elaborate fabric is woven; what remains for ever a riddle is how any human being could manage to combine these two opposites into such a perfectly balanced work of art. There are five subjects, each of them a mere stock phrase such as any professor of composition might give to a student to work out as a fugue. Mozart does not work any of them into a fugue, but all of them into a sonata movement with a fugal texture of incredible elaboration, combining now any two of the subjects, now a single one in canon, and again mixing both procedures together. The dizzy culmination comes in the coda, where all five themes appear together in various juxtapositions.[1]

Mozart: *Symphony in C, K. 551.* COLUMBIA ML 4035 (alt. COL-UMBIA 33 CX 1257).

The very last work Mozart composed was the *Requiem.* In July 1791 he was commissioned to write a composition of this kind for a wealthy nobleman who wanted to pass it off as his own work. Mozart agreed and received a substantial advance on the honorarium. As he was also engaged in composing the operas *La Clemenza di Tito* and *The Magic Flute,* he worked very slowly on the *Requiem.* When he died on 5th December 1791 only the first movement was completely finished. The second to ninth movements were written down in Mozart's usual draft; this means that the vocal parts and the most significant sections of the instrumental accompaniment were on paper, while the rest of the orchestration was to be filled in later. Mozart's widow was afraid that she might have to return the advance on the honorarium, so she induced his pupil, Franz Süssmayer, to complete the score. As his handwriting resembled that of his teacher, Constance Mozart could pretend that the score had been finished by her husband.

Later the deception was discovered, and attempts were made to determine the exact extent of Süssmayer's participation. In the case of the movements drafted by Mozart it is quite conceivable that a faithful student could fill out what was missing without doing any harm to the master work, and this Süssmayer apparently did. We do not know, however, what constituted the basis for Süssmayer's work on the tenth, eleventh, and twelfth movements for which no sketches have been preserved. To judge by Süssmayer's modest subsequent achievements as a composer, we must assume that the last three movements of the *Requiem* were not

[1] Eric Blom: *Mozart,* J. M. Dent & Sons Ltd, London, 1935.

conceived by him.   Perhaps he had some kind of sketches from Mozart's hand or could rely on dictation the master had given to the pupil in the last days when the thought of the unfinished *Requiem* was weighing on his mind.

The two sections of the *Requiem* which we may take as examples are clearly Mozart's own, though Süssmayer may have contributed one or the other detail of orchestration.   The *Dies Irae* conjures up the vision of the Last Judgment with fearful, truly apocalyptic grandeur.   In the *Confutatis* tenors and basses, accompanied by the full orchestra, utter the desperate laments of the lost souls; whereupon angelic voices, sopranos and altos, pray for admittance among the chosen.   Finally, the full chorus implores the Lord for help in the ultimate hour, an entreaty uttered in harmonies lofty beyond all earthly notions.   Hearing the *Confutatis*, it is impossible not to feel that the dying composer wrote this plea for himself.

Mozart: *Requiem, K. 626.*   VICTOR LM 1712 (alt. Vox DL 270).

APPENDIX

BOOKS

ed. EMILY ANDERSON: *The Letters of Mozart.*
A. EINSTEIN: *Mozart.*
C. M. GIRDLESTONE: *The Piano Concertos of Mozart.*
ed. DONALD MITCHELL and H. C. ROBBINS LANDON: *The Mozart Companion.*

RECORDS

The Mozart bicentenary has seen a great increase in the already considerable representation of Mozart in the record catalogues.   As in the case of Haydn, it seems best to direct attention to one or two aspects of Mozart's work that might be overlooked.

Solo Piano Music (complete).   ANGEL 35068/78 (COLUMBIA—various).
Organ Music (complete).   COLUMBIA K3L–231.
Concert Arias.   WESTMINSTER WL 5197 (NIXA WLP 5197).
Songs.   ANGEL 35270 (COLUMBIA 33 CX 1321).
Masonic Music.   EPIC LC 3062.
Litanies, K. 195, K. 243.   OISEAU-LYRE OL 50085–6.
Mass in C, K. 317.   DECCA 9805 (DGG DG16096).
Mass in C minor, K. 427.   EPIC SC 6009 (PHILIPS ABR 4043–4).

37

Alfred Frankenstein

BEETHOVEN

IN attempting to define the place of Beethoven in the great
stream of western culture, I am reminded of the famous little
anecdote about Thomas Carlyle and Margaret Fuller. Miss
Fuller announced on one occasion that, having given the matter
due thought, she had decided to accept the universe. Carlyle's
simple comment was: 'By gad, she'd better!'

Ludwig van Beethoven is one of those universes which we had
all better accept. There are respectable musicians who do not like
Handel; there are some to whom the personality of Bach is anathema, and even some who have been known to question the
genius of Mozart; but to express a fundamental distaste for
Beethoven is tantamount to expressing a fundamental distaste
for music itself. We need not all agree about every aspect of his
output, nor will the Beethoven of the young, inexperienced music
lover be the same as the Beethoven of those who have lived long
with the art he practised, but few will seriously dispute the assertion that Beethoven is peculiarly the central figure in the musical
repertoire on which the world is nourished in our time.

Like all great artists, however, Beethoven must be re-evaluated
at least every half-century. The Beethoven criticism of 1900 is
almost meaningless to-day, and the Beethoven criticism of 1850
serves mostly as naïve documentation for the philosophic school
which holds that criticism is always wrong. A world for which
Schönberg and the twelve-tone row are matters of intense contemporary concern cannot *look* back at Beethoven with the same *ears*
as a world that was just learning to accept *The Afternoon of a Faun.*
Our evaluations of the past are inevitably conditioned by the
creative preoccupations of the present; hence it follows that the
past is perpetually in flux, and our view of its shape and significance is constantly changing. This can be richly documented in

the case of Beethoven, but we may consider here just two pieces of outmoded nonsense.

Anton Schindler, the professional *ami de Beethoven* and biographer of his last years, was convinced that every single movement in every composition by Beethoven was a programme piece representing some specific event or experience.   Schindler pointed out to Beethoven that he had often given verbal clues to the 'meanings' of his music, as in the case of the *Piano Sonata, Opus 81a*, whose three sections are entitled *Farewell, Absence,* and *Return.*   Schindler asked why Beethoven had failed to give similar verbal clues to everything else he had written.   Beethoven replied: 'In my time people didn't need such things.'   Schindler interprets this remark to mean that in Beethoven's youth people in general were so marvellously sensitive to the descriptive values of music that they were able to appreciate these values without having them pointed out.   What Beethoven was in fact trying to say, gently and tactfully, was that in his heyday people were not as literal-minded as Anton Schindler.

The second piece of nonsense comes from one of the many books on Beethoven published in 1927, when the world observed the hundredth anniversary of his death.   It is the opinion of an authority, highly regarded at that time, to the effect that Beethoven lost his hearing because he had to be deaf in order to fulfil his destiny.   He had to be isolated from the world in order to write the music of his last years, according to this writer, and so a mysterious providence took away the one sense by which a musician makes his most important contact with the world.

Both of these views are obviously nonsense, but they are nonsense of two totally different orders.   One is materialistic; it drags music down to a childishly descriptive level.   The other is high-flown and mystical; it is the work of a poetic, essentially fictional imagination which confuses the writer's subjective reactions to music with the music itself.   But both absurdities arise from the same inescapable fact about Beethoven: his compositions do convey, repeatedly and perennially, an extremely powerful overtone of the ethical and rhetorical.

A great composer's music is not an intimate diary.   If at certain points his music should happen to reflect his day-to-day experiences, the experiences are likely to be of a decidedly trivial kind; the crucial incidents of his career are likely to pass without direct expression in his work. Nevertheless, musical biography is not totally meaningless; there *are* broad correspondences, and the man who in life seems far ahead of his time always seems in retrospect to be eminently typical of it.

If Beethoven's achievement must be summed up in a single phrase, it may be said that he brought a new sense of scale to the classic forms of instrumental composition; and this is related to the most dynamic forces of the society in which he lived. The new sense of scale expresses itself in every musical dimension. The time-span of the classic structure is enormously increased; the symphony, sonata, or string quartet doubles and triples in length when compared with the accepted norms. The sonority of the music takes on a corresponding weight and depth, and the classic contrast of themes and tonalities assumes the character of a dramatic conflict ultimately resolved in triumph. And as a result of this new rhetorical emphasis, the relative weight of the movements is redistributed in a highly significant way.

It has been said that in the first movement of a pre-Beethoven sonata the composer shows what he can do; in the second movement what he can feel; and in the last how glad he is that it is all over. A Beethoven first movement still shows what the composer can do—it remains supremely active and dramatic in temper—and the second movement still shows what the composer can feel, but the typical Beethoven finale is a grand summation and resolution of all that has gone before.

All this is clearly involved with the composer's new orientation towards the world. The old era of personal patronage had gone; the composer of 1800 faced a large anonymous audience gathered more often in large theatres than in intimate halls. When a musician comes to depend upon large, anonymous audiences one of two things will happen to him. If he is a commonplace man he will try to amuse the crowd with tricks and stunts. Thus the violinist, Franz Clement, made capital of the fact that he had never so much as looked at the manuscript of Beethoven's Violin Concerto until he stepped to the platform to perform it in public for the first time. At the same concert Clement presented a fantasy of his own with the violin held upside-down. The activities of men like Clement are forgotten to-day, but they should not be, for they represent the lowest level to which European art music ever sank, and they throw the achievement of Beethoven himself into even higher and more monumental relief than is apparent from our ordinary point of vantage.

Beethoven's reaction to the new social situation was exactly the opposite of that symbolized by Clement. Rather than amuse the crowd with tricks and stunts he led, controlled, directed, and dominated; he became the archetype of the free artist as master rather than servant. This position has its dangers, especially when the stance of mastery is assumed by artists incompetent to maintain it, but no one in history was more eminently capable of maintaining it than Ludwig van Beethoven.

To typify my comments up to this point, nothing is more fitting than the first movement of Beethoven's Fifth Piano Concerto. It is not for nothing that this is called the *Emperor* Concerto. Beethoven did not give it that title, but the world has conferred that name upon it. The emperor involved is not an aristocrat on a throne, but the composer himself, the imperial lord of tones.

Beethoven: *Piano Concerto No. 5 in E flat.* VICTOR LCT 1015 (alt. Vox PL 9490).

Not long after Beethoven died, a Russian critic named Wilhelm von Lenz wrote a book called *Beethoven and his Three Styles*, and the phrase 'three styles' has clung to Beethoven criticism ever since. Vincent d'Indy characterizes the first of the three eras as a period of *imitation*, wherein Beethoven largely reflects the prevailing manner of the late eighteenth century. D'Indy calls the second era a period of *externalization*; here Beethoven goes forth to do battle with the world in a fashion already discussed and exemplified by the first movement of the *Emperor Concerto*. The third period, according to d'Indy, is one of *reflection*. The spirit of the music is remote from external conflict. It floats high in a mysterious realm of its own and it involves a series of unprecedented inventions in the domain of musical structure. In contrast to the second period, wherein he expands the traditional forms, the Beethoven of the final period creates totally new forms.

The Beethoven of the second phase, externalization, is the immensely popular one: this is the Beethoven of the symphonies from the Third through the Eighth, of the concertos, of the opera *Fidelio*, and the most frequently exploited sonatas. It used to be that the Beethoven of the third period had less appeal for the general public, although in recent years musicians have lost their hesitancy about performing the great quartets and piano works of that phase, and recording has spread them mightily. The quality of this last period may be suggested by the *Quartet in A minor, Opus 132*, and its slow movement, which bears the title *Holy Song of Thanksgiving of a Convalescent to the Godhead, in the Lydian Mode*.[1]

Beethoven: *Quartet in A minor, Op. 132*. COLUMBIA ML 4586 (PHILIPS ABL 3132).

An aspect of Beethoven that should not be neglected is his songs. It is often said that Beethoven did not write gratefully for the voice, and it is true that some of his vocal works are extremely awkward to encompass. There are others, however, which proceed with highly idiomatic ease. In reviewing some newly published songs by a little known composer named Franz Schubert, Robert Schumann once observed that these works clung a little too closely to the Beethoven model. In the intervening years we have been taught that Schubert was the great innovator of the German concert song and we have forgotten his indebtedness to Beethoven. But this can be exemplified by the Beethoven song cycle *An die Ferne Geliebte* (*To the Distant Beloved*).

Beethoven: *An die Ferne Geliebte*. DECCA 9668 (alt. HMV ALP 1066).

No composer in history has been written about in such detail as Beethoven, none is more frequently performed, none is better known. Yet there are important areas in Beethoven that remain largely unexplored, such as the songs. He wrote more than two hundred concert songs and folk-song arrangements and his influence in this department is as important as in the symphony. But only his contemporaries realized this. We of the present day still have much to learn.

---

[1] Aldous Huxley's extraordinary description of this movement, which forms part of the last chapter of his novel, *Point Counter Point*, probably did more to arouse general interest in Beethoven's quartets than any other single thing published in the twentieth century. This, at least, holds true for the English-speaking world.

APPENDIX

Books

A. W. Thayer: *The Life of Ludwig van Beethoven*, 3 vols.
Paul Bekker: *Beethoven*.
Sir Donald Tovey: *Essays in Musical Analysis.   Beethoven*.
Hector Berlioz: *The Symphonies of Beethoven*.
Joseph de Marliave: *Beethoven's Quartets*.

Records

Alfred Frankenstein writes: 'No specific records can be recommended because there are so many of them and so many good ones.   The present writer especially likes the recordings of the symphonies by Bruno Walter, of the string quartets by the Budapest Quartet, of the piano concertos and sonatas by Arthur Schnabel, Wilhelm Backhaus, and Walter Giese-king.   There are many other aspects of Beethoven the hearer ought to explore and can explore by means of superlative recordings—the sonatas for violin and for violoncello, the Violin Concerto, the opera *Fidelio*, and the choral works like the *Missa Solemnis*, etc., etc.'

Note.   Several recordings of the symphonies under Bruno Walter have appeared in the English Columbia catalogue; but they are now withdrawn, although it is possible they may be reissued at some later date, probably by Philips.   Schnabel's recordings of the piano music have been transferred to LP in the U.S.A.   So far they are not available on the British market; but it is expected that some at least will shortly appear from HMV.   Wilhelm Backhaus has recorded all the sonatas and four of the concertos for English Decca, issued by London in the U.S.A.; and Walter Gieseking was in the process of making complete recordings for English Columbia (Angel in U.S.A.) at the time of his death. Several records have already been issued, and more are expected.   For DGG Wilhelm Kempff is in the course of making also the complete cycle.   The complete Violin Sonatas are recorded by Heifetz on Victor (HMV) and the Violoncello Sonatas by Janos Starker on Period (Nixa). The complete String Quartets by the Budapest Quartet are to be found on Columbia, in the course of issue in England by Philips.   Two versions of the opera *Fidelio* are available: on Victor LM 6025 (HMV ALP 1304–5) and HMV ALP 1130–2.   The *Missa* is available on Vox, Victor (HMV), and DGG.

A few records of rarely heard but variously important Beethoven compositions may be mentioned:

Music to 'Egmont' (complete).   Ducretet-Thomson DTL 93085.
Variations, 'Ich bin der Schneider Kakadu.'   DGG DGM 18044.
Songs.   HMV ALP 1317–18.
Works for Cello and Piano.   Decca LXT 5268.

38

William Mann

NINETEENTH-CENTURY SYMPHONY AND SYMPHONIC POEM

BEFORE the nineteenth century the various arts tended to develop on parallel but not connected lines, and within music the various forms and media grew naturally but distinctly. The pronounced tendency of the nineteenth century was to bring the arts together in a process of aspiration towards what Wagner eventually called the *Gesamtkunstwerk*, the work of art in which all the arts participated. And so this was the century that brought about the literary symphony and the descriptive symphonic poem, evolved the serious ballet score as composed by Delibes and Tchaikovsky, and was able to bring forth Verdi's *La Traviata*, an opera so up to date in the style of its scenery and costumes that early audiences, accustomed to historical operas, were shocked and bewildered.

One aspect of nineteenth-century symphonic music is the development of harmony from the so-called pure classicism of Haydn and Mozart (although it was really not so pure) towards the advanced chromatic language of Wagner and Tchaikovsky, Bruckner and Liszt, Mahler and the young Richard Strauss. We divide the music of previous centuries into two categories: diatonic music, which means that the white notes on the piano, the notes of the plain scale, are most important; and chromatic music, in which the black notes, or accidentals, colour the white notes and strive to become as important as them. When all the notes, white and black, achieve equal importance, the feeling of key centre is abolished, and we call the music atonal.

Schubert's great Symphony in C begins in C major without black notes. That was a perfectly normal and eloquent musical language for the symphonist of the early nineteenth century. By 1894 in Bruckner's Ninth Symphony the key feeling, so strong in Schubert's Symphony, has altogether been dispelled. The music is by no means atonal, but is as though firmness of key had been blown away by a gust of wind.

(i) Schubert: *Symphony in C major, No. 7.*   LONDON LL 619 (DECCA LXT 2719).
(ii) Bruckner: *Symphony No. 9 in D minor.*   VOX PL 8040 (E).

Tonality was one element that advanced enormously in romantic symphonic music of the last century.   Another was the scale of the music.   Haydn's last symphonies lasted twenty minutes or so; some of Bruckner's later symphonies and Liszt's *Faust* Symphony last a little over an hour.   The size of the orchestra too increased enormously.   Schubert in 1816 was content with one flute, two oboes and two bassoons, two horns, and strings— the Haydn orchestra.   Even Mendelssohn in 1844 scored his *Italian* Symphony for a standard medium-sized orchestra.   But by 1898, when Richard Strauss composed his symphonic poem *Ein Heldenleben*, the orchestra had acquired extra instruments like the cor anglais, the bass clarinet, and the little E flat clarinet; the horns had grown in number from two to eight, the trumpets, trombones, and two tubas had joined the assembly and there was a great increase in percussion instruments.   This meant that the string department had to be increased as well, so that instead of about two dozen players in the band, about one hundred and five musicians had to be available.

The content of the symphony also expanded.   In the eighteenth century symphonies were about musical patterns that could be made by a composer's imagination to express feelings.   In the nineteenth century the feelings became more important, and the patterns had to conform.   Composers wrote symphonies about specific subjects—literary, pictorial, geographical, or patriotic.

Where did all these romantic developments originate?   The culprits, paradoxically, were musicians whom we are inclined to pigeon-hole as classical, not romantic composers.   Beethoven introduced the piccolo and the trombones into the orchestra in his Fifth Symphony, not to mention soloists and a choir in his Ninth.   In his *Eroica* Symphony he stepped up the scale to a duration of fifty minutes, and he treated a descriptive subject to the extent that his symphony was avowedly about heroism.   I gave Schubert as an example of the diatonic composer, but Schubert loved to rove from key to key without advance notice. A study of the harmonic language of the nineteenth century reveals that many of the most characteristic chords are in Beethoven, and many more in Berlioz. Berlioz, together with Liszt, dominates the story of the nineteenth-century symphony.

One of the tendencies of the symphony was to absorb other musical mediums; it was Berlioz's symphony *Harold in Italy*, which is almost a viola concerto, that set the tone for Brahms's Piano Concerto in B flat (a concerto with strong leanings towards symphony), d'Indy's *Symphony on a French Mountaineer's Song* for piano and orchestra, Lalo's *Symphonie Espagnole* for violin and orchestra, and many other works in which concerto and symphony were profitably mingled. It was Berlioz's dramatic symphony *Romeo and Juliet*, following up the principles of Beethoven's Choral Symphony, that paved the way for the mixture of cantata and symphony which found further development in works by Mendelssohn and Liszt and eventually Mahler. As for the literary symphony, Berlioz externalized the descriptive element in the *Fantastic* Symphony, *Harold in Italy*, and *Romeo and Juliet*, and so made room for the factual description of the tone poems of Strauss and Tchaikovsky. The start of the intrusion of suite into symphony can be found too in Berlioz's *Fantastic* Symphony, which has five movements instead of the usual four. The extra movement is the *March to the Scaffold*—in the eighteenth century marches belonged to serenades—while the waltz in the *Ball Scene* is a replacement of the minuet or scherzo previously conventional in symphony.

All these explorations in language and idea mark Berlioz out as a romantic, and not least the zeal with which he pursued his multifarious experiments. He is the musical parallel to such authors as Chateaubriand and Lamartine, who set the course for French romantic literature in the early years of the nineteenth century. Berlioz was a romantic in intention, but his music is classic in line; the feeling and the goal know no restraint, but the contour of the music is controlled the whole time. Like Beethoven, he did not mind what canons of taste he flouted, but the line of the music is always being driven by a well-balanced intellect.

Berlioz: *Romeo and Juliet Symphony* (*Tomb Scene*). VICTOR LM 6011 (HMV ALP 1179–80).

It was inevitable in the aftermath of a classical era that there should be other symphonists who blended old and new ideals. Berlioz is the most important because the most far-reaching; the

French have never recovered from his influence, and it may be that other countries have yet to feel it fully. Mendelssohn was long admired by the comfortable children of the industrial revolution and the age of bourgeois respectability because his music reflected their taste, their admiration of restraint, and their sort of Christian culture. He was probably the most widely cultured musician who had lived up to that time; travelled, well-read, fluent in the other arts. His two most popular symphonies reflect the age in that their inspiration is geographical; one is about Scotland and the other about Italy. In the *Reformation* Symphony Mendelssohn used characterizing tunes to represent the conflict of Catholic and Protestant faiths, the *Dresden Amen* and Luther's chorale *A Stronghold Sure.* This is a rather dull symphony, but it deserves mention because its aims are romantic while its tone of voice is entirely classic.

Mendelssohn: *Symphony No. 5 in D minor (Reformation).* COLUMBIA ML 4864 (PHILIPS ABL 3082).

Among other German symphonists Schumann is appealing rather than significant. There are enterprising features in his four symphonies, none the less: the one-movement shape of the Fourth Symphony, and its construction out of a few themes which are reshaped in subsequent movements; the use of a motto theme in the Second Symphony, and the programmatic slow fourth movement of the 'Rhenish' Symphony. This is intended to represent the cathedral of Cologne and the installation of a cardinal there.

Schumann: *Symphony No. 3 in E flat, 'Rhenish.'* COLUMBIA ML 4040 (COLUMBIA 33 CX 1045)* (alt. DGG DG 16063).

Schumann's mind had a descriptive streak that emerges constantly, but the 'Rhenish' Symphony is, on examination, no more likely to be programmatically detailed than are the symphonies of his younger friend Brahms; and Brahms's greatness as a symphonist is in no way connected with literary detail or German nationalism. Brahms shaped his symphonies abstractly and rather conservatively in view of all the experiment that was in progress around him, but with a solidity of thought and feeling that stands the test of time and changing fashions. Brahms kept to a medium-sized orchestra; he preserved the time scale of the Beethoven symphony; and his style of harmony and musical argument was rigidly sober. The idea of linking the various

movements of a symphony together with a common theme was
not part of his method; only in the Third Symphony did he bring
back the opening theme in the last bars, and that was to show with
the very mildest emphasis that the original thesis of the symphony
had now been proved. He preferred the classical method of
symphonic construction in which the ideas were interrelated under
the surface without recourse to a family tree at every new event.

Brahms's particular contribution to the symphony was the
intermezzo type of third movement. He did not much cultivate
the Beethovenian scherzo; instead he placed there a melodious,
gracefully flowing movement in three of his symphonies so that
the two inner movements might expand at ease inside two more
dynamic movements. The pace of Brahms's third movements
can be heard in the Third Symphony, and it may be particularly
alluring and spacious because this is the only symphony by Brahms
that ends softly.

Brahms: *Symphony No. 3 in F* (*Allegretto*). LONDON LL 857
(DECCA LXT 2843).

Franz Liszt's innovations in musical language, particularly in
harmony, not only changed Wagner's whole outlook on music,
but looked forward to Debussy and Bartók in our century. His
preoccupation with form and structure, and particularly with the
transformation of a few themes to meet any desired mood or
tempo, have their modern outcome in the monothematic music
of serial composers. Liszt evolved the single-movement literary
symphonic work which we call the symphonic poem or tone poem;
a *genre* with roots in the theatrical overtures—Beethoven's
Leonora Overture No. 3 is a tone poem *manqué*. Gradually
Liszt discovered that many subjects were apt for symphonic
treatment in a single movement, although the subjects he used
were vague; his only really detailed transcription of poetry into
music is the first movement of the *Dante* Symphony.

Liszt's other symphony is based on the three principal characters
from Goethe's *Faust*. The *Faust* Symphony not only shows
how much Wagner learned from Liszt, but also explores symphonic
psychology such as Richard Strauss was to cultivate thirty years
later in his rogues' gallery of symphonic portraits. Faust's
themes are presented and developed in the first movement;
Gretchen's in the slow movement. When Liszt reaches Mephis-
topheles, he shows him as a part of Faust's psyche by using

distorted versions of Faust's own themes; a passionate theme is made to sound petty and sarcastic. This is the principle of Liszt's method of symphonic metamorphosis: one theme serving opposite purposes.

Liszt: *Faust Symphony*. LONDON LL 1303–4 (DECCA LXT 5101–2).

The leading Wagnerian symphonist of the latter part of the century was Anton Bruckner, who wrote nine symphonies and an earlier one numbered 'Nought.' Bruckner developed only secondarily from Liszt. His inspiration was nature, his natural mouthpiece the organ; if his harmony and the pace at which his music moves both recall Wagner at his most majestic, the source of his heritage was surely the Beethoven of the Ninth Symphony and the Schubert of the great C major Symphony. Bruckner's orchestra is not often extravagant and the type of theme he expounded is not far from the simple song of Schubert. He thought on the vast scale of Austrian mountainous scenery; his long tunes pause for breath when they feel like it and work their way to a climax without tiring of repetition. Over the years the tunes of Bruckner's symphonies became more eloquent and intricate and his harmony more richly expressive, but his symphonic methods remained the same—atmospheric and dramatic rather than argumentative. At his most mature and finest Bruckner spoke with the voice of every countryman, simple but aware of the eternal truths of nature and divine law: the voice of a man who walked with God.

APPENDIX

BOOKS

HERMANN SCHERCHEN: *The Nature of Music*.
JACQUES BARZUN: *Berlioz and the Romantic Century*.
ERNEST NEWMAN: *Musical Studies*.
MOSCO CARNER: *Of Men and Musicians*.
ADAM CARSE: *The Orchestra from Beethoven to Berlioz*.
ed. GERALD ABRAHAM: *Schumann: A Symposium*.
HUMPHREY SEARLE: *The Music of Liszt*.
DIKA NEWLIN: *Bruckner, Mahler, Schönberg*.

RECORDS

Nineteenth-century symphonies, symphonic poems, and concertos make up the greater part of the current orchestral repertoire, and of most people's musical experience too. They are well represented in the catalogues, and few of these works are not available in a number of performances on records.

39

Andrew Porter

NINETEENTH-CENTURY SONG

E ARLIER essays in this book have sketched the history of
song from the troubadours to the Tudors. Then, in the
seventeenth and eighteenth centuries, the history of music
is not much concerned with song. Almost all the vocal
music of that period was intended either for the opera-house or the
church, and so for professional singers. While every composer
of note has at least one or two songs to his credit, it is not until
we reach Franz Schubert that we find again a composer whose
songs form more than a side-line in his output.

Social reasons for this can be discovered by considering the
case of Haydn. While Haydn was in the service of the Esterházys
he composed operas and symphonies, but not songs. Only when
he went to London, where music was organized on a democratic
rather than an aristocratic basis, did he turn to song-writing in
earnest. For the singing of songs is essentially a domestic activity,
and it had little place in music produced under a system of aristocratic patronage. Song-writing on a large scale began only in
the nineteenth century, when composers started to cater for the
new, increasingly important middle-class audience which did not
have private orchestras and opera-houses. It was at this time
too that printed music started to circulate cheaply and extensively,
and the making of so-called 'art music' became a regular activity
in ordinary homes. And for this new audience a new art form
was created.

All the circumstances were propitious for a song-writer of
genius, and such was Franz Schubert. He was the son of an
Austrian schoolmaster and sang as a boy in the choir of the
Imperial Chapel. He never held any official position, but picked
up a living in various ways. No publishers took any interest in
his music until in 1821 some friends had twenty of his songs
printed at their own expense. Although he lived only to the
age of thirty-one, Schubert wrote more music than almost any

other great composer, including six hundred songs; and he possessed the gift of melody as no other composer has done. Numerous stories survive to show that he could hardly read a line of poetry without conceiving at once a melody to fit it.

A good example of Schubert's art at its most simple and spontaneous is *Der Jüngling an der Quelle*, composed in 1815. The poem is not at all distinguished, but Schubert in about a minute of music creates an extraordinarily vivid little scene: the sparkling brook with its murmuring pebbles sounds in the accompaniment, while the lilting melody tells us of the boy in love. The sighs of young love are reflected in one or two magical modulations that pass like quick shadows over the very simple harmony.

> Schubert: *Der Jüngling an der Quelle.*   HMV DA 1521 (alt. DGG DGM 18029).

The wonderful simplicity of such a song is only one part of Schubert's creative personality. For in the new medium of the art-song, or *Lied*, nineteenth-century composers embodied musical conceptions which had formerly found expression only in works on a larger scale. The tendency of nineteenth-century music was towards greater length and greater forces, but the song-writers learned to compress; they could compass in a few minutes, and with no other resources than a single voice with piano accompaniment, the emotions, passions, and drama which other composers were putting into opera or massive tone-poems.

Schubert creates on the grandest possible scale in songs like *Der Atlas*, *Prometheus*, or *Gruppe aus dem Tartarus*. In the last, Schiller's lines tell of the torment of the damned, and Schubert's music seems actually to communicate to us what they must feel; we are among them, hearing the hollow crash of the water, seeing the harsh crags through their tortured eyes. There is a long *crescendo* as they ask whether their sufferings can ever come to an end; then with tremendous effect the word '*Ewigkeit*' crashes out—their torments will last for eternity. In the piano postlude it is as if we, the spectators, drew rapidly farther and farther away from the terrible scene. Schubert has discovered an artistic effect that became possible in a visual medium only with the invention of the cinema, or rather the cinema-camera and aeroplane used together. Schubert needed only eight bars of music.

> Schubert: *Gruppe aus dem Tartarus.*   Victor 16149 (alt. Decca LW 5235).

There is nothing so dramatic in the songs of Robert Schumann. He treated the song medium rather as he had treated the piano; as a kind of diary to which he confided his thoughts, impressions, and emotions. Schubert in his great song cycles, *Die schöne Müllerin* (*The Fair Maid of the Mill*) and *Die Winterreise* (*The Winter Journey*), produced almost the song equivalent of novels, but more direct in their communication of feeling. Schumann did not have the same directness or objectivity. With Schubert we feel that the poem has turned straight into music; the listener is not invited to think of the poem as existing apart from the music. Schumann's is a more literary and a more self-conscious approach, and we feel that he is trying to find the music which will rightly adorn, reflect, and intensify the poem. In his masterpiece *Dichterliebe* (*A Poet's Love*) Schumann shows how sensitive he was to poetry; Heine's *words* provide the inspiration, not whatever in the first place inspired Heine.

Schumann: *Dichterliebe*.   LONDON LL 940 (DECCA LXT 2875).

If 'word-painting' is the term to describe the songs of Schumann, 'mood-painting' is the term for many of Brahms's songs. He wrote nearly two hundred throughout his career, and with them a philosophical note comes into nineteenth-century song. In Brahms's lyricism there is nearly always an element of gravity which finds its final expression in the *Four Serious Songs* to biblical texts. In these songs the art-song conquered still more territory, for, although only two performers are involved, they are in effect an oratorio.

Not all Brahms's songs are solemn and reflective—he wrote many songs in the gay folk-song tradition—but his particular contribution is best represented by such a song as *Feldeinsamkeit*, composed in 1877. This shows his tender, grave lyricism at its most characteristic and beautiful, and is mood-painting of a high order. In a gently flowing accompaniment Brahms conjures up the mood induced by the still, lonely countryside, and the slowly moving vocal line suggests calm contemplation. Brahms has learned from both Schubert and Schumann; he gives us both the scene and a poetic commentary on it.

Brahms: *Feldeinsamkeit*.   VICTOR 7793.

Hugo Wolf is the purest example of the nineteenth-century song-writer; for although he produced a handful of works in other mediums, he distilled the essence of his genius into some two hundred and fifty songs. He was by no means the spontaneous singer that Schubert had been. The creative power came upon him in short very intense bursts, and he would work at a feverish pitch, sometimes pouring out several wonderful songs in a single day. Then would come a period without inspiration. His songs fall into groups: the settings of Mörike, Eichendorff, and Goethe, and the Spanish and Italian song-books. These coherent collections are framed between a group of early songs and a group of late songs with texts by various poets.

Wolf was a fervent admirer of Wagner, and it is symptomatic of nineteenth-century song that the grandiose techniques of the largest-scale composer the world has ever known should have been fined down and made to serve the purposes of the composer of exquisite miniatures. Wolf may not have been a greater song-writer than Schubert, but he certainly brought the medium to a degree of flexibility and expressiveness never known before; and since Wolf there have been no further significant developments in the art of song-writing. He does everything that Schubert, Schumann, and Brahms tried to do. He puts his listeners into direct touch with the poet's source of inspiration, he paints a scene, he conjures up a mood; and at the same time he treats the poet's words with unusual faithfulness and vividness. The words to a greater extent than ever before dictate the shape of the vocal line, and without the words the music hardly makes sense. The very vowels and consonants are drawn into the texture that voice and piano spin between them.

Wolf's range is as great as that of the poets he sets. In the *Italienisches Liederbuch*, for example, he has created a gallery of men and women in and out of love. He can be tender, grand, noble, angry, melancholy, or devout. But it must be noted that his limitations spring from his very virtues: from the fact that he is, purely and solely, a song-writer. In Wolf's music we do not find, as in Schubert's, the spontaneous bubbling over of melody with a life of its own; we do not find, as in Schumann, the personal, intimate commentary on what the words mean to the composer himself; we do not find, as in Brahms, the assimilation of what may be quite commonplace ideas to a rich philosophic and intellectual background. Instead, we find an intense concentration on the particular poem before us.

Wolf too could create on an epic scale within small time-dimensions, as in *Der Feuerreiter* (*The Fire-rider*). Fire-riders have the power to detect distant fires towards which they are irresistibly impelled, but they are forbidden to extinguish the flames. The Fire-rider of Mörike and Wolf does so, however, with a chip of the true Cross, but the burning mill collapses about him in punishment.

Wolf: *Der Feuerreiter*. HMV Hugo Wolf Society (alt. HMV 7 ER 5044).

So far this essay has for obvious reasons been confined to German song, but the nationalists in other countries brought distinctive notes of their own to the art of song. In Russia Glinka inaugurated the tradition of writing art-songs; the most distinguished Russian song-writer was Mussorgsky. In his songs, as in his operas, the vocal line is inspired both by the inflexions of Russian speech and the characteristic intervals and rhythms of Russian folk music.

Mussorgsky: *The Nursery*. Capital P 8265 (CTL 7068)* (alt. DGG DGM 19050).

In Bohemia and Scandinavia, as in Russia, song-writing was closely bound up with the folk-song revival of the period. Towards the end of the century French song began to gather impetus. Earlier there was one individual genius, striking out his own path in song as in every form he attempted: Berlioz. His *Nuits d'été* deserve mention, not because they were influential, but because they are so fine. They also show that some song composers could not limit themselves to the drawing-room and the piano, but needed the full orchestra.

Berlioz: *Nuits d'été*. London LL 407 (Decca LXT 2605).

French art songs, or *mélodies*, begin properly with Gounod and Franck, but they become important only in the next generation with the work of Chausson, Fauré, and Duparc. In these *mélodies* it is not the folk-idiom that is important, but the rise and fall and the muted cadences of the French language which suggest the characteristic shape of the vocal line. French song developed late, but its development continued unbroken through Debussy and Ravel to present-day composers like Poulenc and Auric.

Fauré: *Soir*. HMV DA 1819 (alt. Decca LX 3080).

APPENDIX

Books

ELIZABETH SCHUMANN: *German Song.*
ALFRED EINSTEIN: *Schubert.*
RICHARD CAPELL: *Schubert's Songs.*
FRANK WALKER: *Hugo Wolf.*

Records

SCHUBERT: *Die Schöne Müllerin.* VICTOR LHMV 6 or HMV ALP 1036–7. *Die Winterreise.* HMV ALP 1298–9.
SCHUMANN: *Liederkreis.* HMV BLP 1068.
Schubert and Fauré Recital. LONDON LL 245 (DECCA LXT 2543).
Song Recital (Schubert, Schumann, Brahms, Wolf). ANGEL 35023.
WOLF: *Italienisches Liederbuch.* DECCA 9632 (DGG DGM 18192). *Songs.* HMV ALP 1143.
MUSSORGSKY: *Sunless Cycle.* CAPITOL P 8310 (CAPITOL CTL 7100).

40

Andrew Porter

NINETEENTH-CENTURY OPERA

OPERA up to the nineteenth century must be viewed both as a royal entertainment under direct royal patronage and as an entertainment beloved of the people. In the later seventeenth and eighteenth centuries almost every court of note could boast a private or semi-private opera; while Venice had built its first public opera-house in 1637, London in 1656, and Paris in 1669. By the beginning of the nineteenth century the distinction between the royal and the public opera-houses was beginning to disappear. The public had long been admitted to the royal opera-houses, and now they began to take an increasingly large share in their management.

Opera to the nineteenth-century public was in some ways what the circuses and games had been to the Imperial Romans, and what the cinema is to the public of to-day: the supreme form of mass entertainment. In Vienna, where the art-song flourished, this was primarily a century of private music-making, but in Italy, where there was no such tradition, opera was the chief art form—the important Italian composers of the century are all opera composers—and in Paris too the opera reigned supreme.

Paris has the grandest opera-house in the world, and during the nineteenth century it was the mecca of all opera composers in a sense which it is hard to appreciate to-day. Verdi, in a letter written in 1851, refers almost with awe to its possession of 'the most expensive singers, the most ample ballet-corps in the world, and an orchestra of unrivalled strength and eminence, accompanying never-ending masses of chorus singers.'

It is symptomatic of the exotic art of opera that the leading composers of French grand opera should have been foreigners: the Italian Lully, the German Gluck, the Italian Cherubini, the Italian Spontini, and the German Meyerbeer. By the beginning of the nineteenth century Gluck's reforms had been obscured by the more spectacular offerings of Gasparo Spontini. In 1807 Spontini's *La Vestale* was produced in Paris, and two years later his *Fernand Cortez*, and they set the tone for what was to follow: heroic or historical subject-matter, elevated emotions, music that allowed scope for vocal display, and action that allowed for plenty of elaborate scenery.

The next important contribution to this *genre* came from Rossini, who in 1829 composed for the Paris Opéra what can in some respects be regarded as his masterpiece, *Guillaume Tell*. Those who know Rossini only as the composer of the lightweight, sparkling comic operas may be surprised by *William Tell*. Its closing scene is among the great inspirations of operatic music. The storm has cleared away, and an immense view opens up: in the distance snowy peaks glisten in the sunshine. The scene is symbolic of the new freedom which awaits Switzerland. A single motive, suggesting the *Ranz des vaches*, is passed upwards from horn to wood-wind, passing through many keys major and minor; the characters contemplate the scene, their hearts filled with joy, and at last unite their voices in a great paean to liberty. After this apotheosis, it is almost understandable that Rossini should never have written another line for the theatre.

Rossini: *William Tell*. CETRA 1232.

Two years after *William Tell* was first given, Giacomo Meyerbeer made his appearance at the Opéra with *Robert le Diable*, to be followed by *Les Huguenots*, *Le Prophète*, and *L'Africaine*. In these operas flashy theatrical effects took the place of classical or epic drama. Donald Grout has given a neat description of Meyerbeer's lack of artistic integrity: 'An opera of Meyerbeer's is like a department store, where everything may be found displayed in the most tempting manner to the prospective buyer.' Whatever we may think of these operas to-day, it must be recorded as historical fact that they appealed even to people of discrimination until the end of the century. Religious conflict, historical struggles, and geographical explorations seemed to them to be elevated operatic themes, and they were willing to overlook the meretricious trappings. Furthermore, these operas were safe showpieces for singers.

It has often been said that nineteenth-century opera composers pandered to their singers and debased their music to give the prima donnas and star tenors ample opportunity to show off, but it might equally well be claimed that the prodigious vocal abilities of the singers acted as a stimulus to the composers. In Bellini's operas the coloratura is certainly no mere decoration, but unfailingly enhances the expressive power of the music.

In 1831, the year the Paris Opéra produced Meyerbeer's *Le Prophète*, La Scala in Milan brought out Bellini's *Norma*. Italian scene design was academic and conservative in comparison with that of the Opéra in Paris, and there was no Meyerbeer in Italy, anxious to astonish the public with something that they had never seen before. Italian grand opera composers tended to work in the traditional style; they expressed the drama in the traditional Italian way—first and foremost, through the melody. In Bellini and Donizetti (whose *Lucia di Lammermoor* appeared in 1835) Italy had two composers with a supreme gift of dramatic melody, and *Norma* is one of the most beautiful operas ever composed. The libretto by Felice Romani is a nobly fashioned drama which descends from the eighteenth-century librettos of Metastosio and, ultimately, from classical drama. In the final scene of the opera Norma announces to the horrified Gauls that she, their priestess, has betrayed them by becoming the mistress of the Roman Pollione. She turns to Pollione (who has in the meantime forsaken her) and makes her sublime gesture. Bellini writes the simplest of accompaniments, with a subtle, ominous mutter of drums in the second half of each bar.

Bellini: *Norma* (*Qual cor tradisti . . .*). ANGEL 3517 C (COLUMBIA 33 CX 1179–81).

But already Donizetti, although no revolutionary, was veering away from the classical drama in the melodramatic situations of his *Lucia di Lammermoor*. In 1839 Giuseppe Verdi stepped on to the scene: a composer who was to unite in a long series of operas the theatrical effectiveness and spectacular inventions of Meyerbeer, the classical serenity of Bellini, and the highly coloured expression of personal emotions of Donizetti. Verdi's heroes and heroines are, like Bellini's, often larger than life, but their emotions are treated not classically, but romantically. Furthermore, Verdi was an ardent patriot, and through almost all his works runs a strong vein of patriotic feeling: the chorus of exiled Jews weeping beside the waters of Babylon in *Nabucco*; the chorus of exiled Scots in *Macbeth*; the terrible conflict which confronts Aida when she must choose between love and patriotism. Verdi's great flair for dramatic situation has often been remarked, but Verdi was at heart, like Bellini, a very 'pure' composer who expressed the dramatic situation in terms of melody. A good example of this 'purity' is *La Vergine degli angeli*, the close of the second act of *La Forza del Destino*. Leonora is going to finish her days in penance, and her voice floats above those of the monks as together they pray for the Virgin's protection.

Verdi: *La Forza del Destino* (*La Vergine degli angeli*). LONDON XLLA 37 (alt. HMV ALP 1099).

To point the purity of Verdi's style, we may contrast *La Vergine degli angeli* with another operatic prayer, Tosca's *Vissi d'arte*. *Tosca* appeared in 1900, but it found its predecessors in *Cavalleria Rusticana* of 1890 and *Pagliacci* of 1892 and in *Andrea Chénier* and *La Bohème*, which both appeared in 1896. The aim in these works was the direct presentation of emotion. It was what Gluck had preached and what Meyerbeer and Donizetti and, above all, Verdi had often achieved; and yet it was, indisputably, opera on a less noble level. Classicism and romanticism were superseded by realism—by *verismo*. In the true sense of the word this was not grand opera at all, and it marked the final emancipation of opera from the traditions of the grand court entertainments in which the art had its origins.

Comic opera flourished locally, and thousands of comic operas were produced, were the talk of the town for a week or even a month, and were then forgotten. In Germany and Austria comic opera was almost the staple diet. In Italy in the first half of the century there was not the same distinction between serious and comic opera composers as existed later: Rossini and Donizetti were admired for both. Donizetti's *L'Elisir d'Amore*, which dates from 1832, is early nineteenth-century comic opera at its best: light, graceful, witty, and tuneful: an ideal entertainment.

Donizetti: *L'Elisir d'Amore*. VICTOR LM 6024 (HMV ALP 1067–8).

The line of comic opera dies out in Italy to flourish again in Vienna, Paris, and in London: in the works of Johann Strauss, Offenbach, and Gilbert and Sullivan. French comic opera tended to have more sting in the wit than that of other countries. When Parisians in 1864 went to see Offenbach's *La Belle Hélène*, with its guying of classical heroes, part of their fun was doubtless derived from the contrast with M. Berlioz's grand opera, *Les Troyens*, which had been seen the previous year. Offenbach's music is charming and funny enough to survive in its own right, not merely as a skit.

Offenbach: *La Belle Hélène*.   RENAISSANCE SX 206 (NIXA PLP 206).

French opera proper, as distinct from the French-Italian brand of grand opera, we can date from Gounod's *Faust* of 1869, and we may trace a line through Bizet's *Carmen* (1875) and Massenet's *Manon* (1884). In these high points of a flourishing school we have characteristically French music which could not have been written by an Italian, with its vocal line closely influenced by the cadences of French speech.

German opera seems largely a matter of isolated figures: Beethoven, Weber, Wagner. But these peaks are joined by lines of hills: the works of men like Marschner, whose *Hans Heiling* influenced Wagner, and Lortzing, whose comic operas are still played in every German town. Wagner's individual genius built on the twin foundations of German romantic opera and international grand opera. Wagner was in rebellion against Meyerbeer, but he learned from Meyerbeer how to handle spectacle on a big scale. Wagner was not, however, a product of the age, but an individual genius who fitted no pattern. To be performed properly his operas had to have a special opera-house built for them.

The nationalist opera was a product of the age, and its finest fruits were produced in Russia and Bohemia. Glinka wrote two operas which together set the pattern for later Russian opera. *A Life for the Tsar* appeared in 1836, and while its formal model was French grand opera, it made conspicuous use of Russian folk melodies and rhythms. It is the progenitor of Borodin's *Prince Igor*, Mussorgsky's *Boris Godunov* and *Khovanshchina*, and Rimsky-Korsakov's *Ivan the Terrible*. Glinka's other opera, *Russlan and Ludmilla*, is a highly coloured, glittering fairy-story, and from this work sprang the other kind of Russian opera represented by Rimsky-Korsakov's *Snow Maiden* and *Golden Cockerel* and Stravinsky's *Nightingale*. Czech opera at its most characteristic presents folk-life directly on the stage, not viewing it from an epic point of view or through magic glasses. Thus Smetana's *The Bartered Bride* (1866) contains little or no quotation of folk tunes, but every number in it is closely derived from folk idiom.

APPENDIX

Books

EDWARD J. DENT: *Opera*.
FRANCIS TOYE: *Italian Opera*.
MARTIN COOPER: *Opéra Comique* and *Russian Opera*.

Records

Nineteenth-century opera is well represented in the current catalogues, and there are alternative recordings of many operas, so no attempt has been made to supply a comprehensive list.   But mention may be made of the following:

GLINKA: *A Life for the Tsar*.   VANGUARD 6010–2 or ENGLISH DECCA LXT 5173–6.

MUSSORGSKY: *Boris Godunov*.   VICTOR LHMV 6400 (HMV ALP 1044–7).

SMETANA: *The Bartered Bride*.   URANIA B 231 (SUPRAPHON LPV 91–3).

VERDI: *Otello*.   VICTOR LM 6107 (HMV ALP 1090–2).   *Falstaff*. VICTOR LM 6111 (HMV ALP 1229–33).

WAGNER: *Tristan und Isolde*.   VICTOR LM 6700 (HMV ALP 1030–1035).   *Die Meistersinger*.   LONDON XLLA 9 (DECCA LXT 2659–2664) or COLUMBIA SL 117 (COLUMBIA 33 CX 1021–5).   *Parsifal*. LONDON XLLA 10 (DECCA LXT 2651–6).

41

Andrew Porter

NINETEENTH-CENTURY CHAMBER MUSIC

CHAMBER music, *Kammermusik*, *musique de chambre*—
the name reveals that it is to be played at home, in a
room; and naturally it flourished in Vienna in the nineteenth century where music-making in one's own house
was a widespread activity. The royal line of chamber music
composers is Haydn, Mozart, Beethoven, Schubert, and Brahms,
all of whom worked in Vienna.

Towards the end of the eighteenth century composers, hitherto
the paid servants of noble families, began to earn their living as
independent figures. In the nineteenth century the nobility still
enjoyed hearing chamber music performed in their *salons*, but
the performers were no longer members of their household, but
professional musicians invited for the occasion. Meanwhile, the
educated middle classes began to enter into competition with the
nobility, and soon they took the lead. Music was cultivated in
the home by friendly groups of amateurs and professionals. The
increasing cheapness of printed music, the excellence of Viennese
instrument-making at the time, and, above all, the fact that there
was chamber music by Haydn, Mozart, and Beethoven to play,
caused it to prosper.

As the century went on, however, the family drawing-room
gave way to the concert-room, and the musicians were no longer
all participants, but divided into the professionals on the platform
and the audience who had paid to come and listen. And chamber
music became different in kind too. It ceased to be just entertainment, and the string quartet in particular became the regular
method of expression for a composer's most profound and intimate
utterances. The responsibility for this change was Beethoven's.

Beethoven spent the first twenty-two years of his life in Bonn, the
later part of it in the service of the Elector. The Elector was 'daily

entertained by a small orchestra consisting of two oboes, two clarinets, two horns, and two bassoons,' and for this band Beethoven composed music which probably accompanied the Elector's meals. When Beethoven went to Vienna, he continued for a while to write occasional pieces for wind instruments, often combining them with piano or strings. The finest of these pieces is the *Septet* composed in 1800. It was, typically, first heard at a private party, but soon afterwards at a public concert. Two years later it was published, and since not everyone was able to assemble the combination of clarinet, horn, bassoon, violin, viola, cello, and double-bass, it was put out in all sorts of arrangements. It is graceful and easy to listen to, and it makes no sort of intellectual demands on its hearers.

Beethoven: *Septet in E flat*. LONDON LL 1191 (alt. NIXA WLP 20020).

In the purer medium of the string quartet, however, Beethoven was already beginning to write works of a very different kind. Haydn's last quartets were contemporary with Beethoven's first, and Beethoven was to carry the form decisively forwards, both technically and expressively. Mozart and Haydn had agreed in principle that all four instruments of the string quartet had equally important parts to play, but in practice they generally made first violin and cello dominate the ensemble. It was left to Beethoven to establish real democracy in the chamber ensemble. (The child Mozart once remarked: 'One doesn't need to have learned the violin to play a second-violin part.' Beethoven, on the other hand, declared when sending the Septet to his publishers: '*All* the parts are *obbligato* . . . I cannot write anything not *obbligato*.')

Beethoven came to the string quartet medium surprisingly late in his career, almost as though he hesitated to use the medium which was later to enshrine his most profound thought until he felt himself ready for it. The first string quartets, Opus 18, were published in two sets of three in 1801, when Beethoven was thirty-one. They were a product of the new middle-class musical culture, for Beethoven almost certainly learned the elements of string quartet style at the home of Aloys Förster, host to the most famous virtuosi of the day, including the Schuppanzigh Quartet which performed Beethoven's Rasumovsky Quartets and almost certainly tried out and discussed the Opus 18 quartets.

Beethoven's Opus 18 quartets do not strike through to the

profundity of Haydn's, but in 1806—the year that Haydn sent his last quartet to his publishers—Beethoven produced three quartets whose boldness startled his contemporaries.   They were composed to a commission from the Prince Rasumovsky, who stipulated that a Russian theme should appear in each.   It is significant of the change that was taking place in the musical world that in these works Beethoven should be both writing to commission and writing for himself.   His later quartets were entirely personal. The great trinity, the Quartets in A minor (Opus 132), B flat major (Opus 130), and C sharp minor (Opus 131), are still found puzzling to-day.   They lead us to the shores of another world.

In March 1826 the first performance was given of the B flat quartet (Opus 130), ending with the *Grosse Fuge* that was deemed unplayable and incomprehensible.   Beethoven was asked for a new finale.   In July of that year Beethoven's beloved nephew, Karl, made a bungled attempt on his own life.   Beethoven took him to his brother's estate to recover, and there he completed his last quartet, the *Quartet in F major, Opus 135*.   His health was failing, and he wrote over the last movement of this work: 'The difficult decision.   Must it be ?   It must be, it must be.'   Marion Scott has described both the first and last movements as 'haunted by the questioning, the recoil of the human heart from death.' And yet there is another story which shows that Beethoven could bring apparent irreconcilables together.   A rich amateur, on learning that it would cost him fifty florins to borrow the parts of Beethoven's latest quartet, asked ruefully: 'Must it be ?'   Beethoven laughed heartily, and replied: 'Yes, yes; it must be.   Over with the money!   Yes, yes, it must be.'   He jotted down a canon to the words, making his first use of the theme for this 'death-haunted' last movement.   In the quartet cello and viola put the question, at first softly and then more and more insistently; and the violins reply decisively.

Beethoven: *Quartet in F major, Op. 135*.   Columbia ML 4587 (Philips ABL 3133).

Schubert did not have the same specific feeling for the medium of the string quartet as Haydn and Beethoven; he used it with great skill, but he did not experiment boldly with its possibilities. On his chamber music he bestowed the same gifts of inexhaustible melody, grace, and poetic feeling as went into his songs and orchestral writing.   His *Piano Quintet in A*, the so-called 'Trout'

Quintet, shows the sort of circumstances that could influence the writing of chamber music.   It might be thought from the unusual combination of instruments—not string quartet and piano, but violin, viola, cello, *double-bass*, and piano—that the composer had some special reason for choosing these sonorities.   In fact, Schubert wrote the quintet while on holiday in a small town for the players who happened to be available.

Schubert: *Piano Quintet in A*.   LONDON LL 223 (DECCA LXT 2533).

Schumann's Piano Quintet is very different in style.   The bulk of Schumann's chamber music dates from the single year 1842; three string quartets, the piano quintet, and the piano quartet. The string quartets are not very interesting, but when the piano enters the texture it is a different matter.   The Piano Quintet may be said to have begun a new epoch in chamber music, a line to be continued by Brahms, Dvořák, and César Franck.   In these piano quintets the composers are writing concert music for public performance, and we have only to compare Schumann's quintet with Schubert's to hear the difference between 'public' and 'private' chamber music.

Schumann: *Piano Quintet in E flat*.   CAPITOL P 8316 (alt. COLUMBIA 33 CX 1050).

In the chamber music of Brahms all the various strands draw together.   Like Schubert, Brahms wrote works whose instrumentation was determined by particular performers; like Schumann he wrote concert music; and like Beethoven he made it an intimate, profound medium.   Brahms's Clarinet Quintet sums up all that has been said.   Its first performance was in the intimacy of a *salon*; the performers were court musicians.   Its second performance was at a public concert in Berlin.   It was written for Richard Mühlfeld, the principal clarinet of the excellent Meiningen orchestra, whom Brahms much admired.   He dubbed him 'Fraülein Klarinette' on account of the exceptional sweetness of his tone, and declared that he had never heard such beautiful sounds from the instrument, or such poetical phrasing.   For Mühlfeld Brahms wrote the Clarinet Quintet and the Clarinet Trio, both in 1891, and three years later the two Clarinet Sonatas. The quintet is Brahms's most graceful, mellow composition, free from conflict and glowing with sunset radiance.   Its predecessor in the *genre*, Mozart's Clarinet Quintet, is a high-summer composition, written in A major, one of his most sun-filled keys.   In

Brahms's B minor quintet it is October. He uses to the full the gentle, melancholy, expressive possibilities of 'Fraülein Klarinette'; while making much of its poignant *chalumeau* register, he does not neglect the brilliant upper reaches where it can ring out with clarion tones or its affectionate middle register. In this celestial music the vigorous striving of Brahms's early chamber music and the earnestness of the three string quartets all find their fulfilment.

Brahms: *Clarinet Quintet in B minor*. WESTMINSTER 5155 (alt. DECCA LXT 2858).

The Russians were not especially noted for chamber music, although Borodin wrote two beautiful quartets, and Tchaikovsky wrote three quartets and a piano trio. In France, Saint-Saëns produced a good deal of chamber music, as he did everything else, but French chamber music really began to flourish later with Fauré, Debussy, and Ravel. Chamber music was not a convenient medium for nationalistic expression, but Beethoven, followed by Brahms, had set the tradition for making chamber music a personal form of utterance. In the works of so intensely nationalistic a composer as Smetana we find that both his string quartets are autobiographical. The First Quartet is generally known by its German title, *Aus meinem Leben* (*From my life*). It follows a programme: the first movement tells of 'love of art in youth, the unsatisfied longing for something inexpressible'; the second movement uses a national idiom to describe his merry youth; the third describes his happy married life. The finale 'illustrates the composer's response to national music and his joy in success.' This is suddenly broken by the fatal note which sounded in his ear, the herald of his approaching deafness. The joyful music is suddenly broken by silence; over shuddering chords we hear a prolonged high E, and then a lamenting recitative. There follows a tender moderato; the composer is not defiant, not despairing, and the work ends on a note of quiet grief.

Smetana: *String Quartet No. 1 in E minor*. LONDON LL 865 (DECCA LXT 2876).

K

APPENDIX

BOOKS

A. HYATT KING: *Chamber Music.*
MARION SCOTT: *Beethoven.*
KARL GEIRINGER: *Brahms.*

RECORDS

The chamber works of the nineteenth-century composers discussed
have all been extensively recorded.   None of the complete sets of the
Beethoven String Quartets is ideal; on the whole that by the Budapest
Quartet on Columbia (Philips) is probably the most satisfactory.   The
following records deserve special mention:

BEETHOVEN: *Piano Trio in B flat, Op. 97, ' Archduke.'*   WESTMINSTER
5131 or NIXA WLP 20018.
SCHUBERT: *String Quintet in C.*   CAPITOL 8133 (CAPITOL CTL 7011)
or PHILIPS ABL 3100.   *Piano Trio in B flat, Op. 99.*   COLUMBIA ML
4715 or HMV BLP 1077.   *Piano Trio in E flat, Op. 100.*   COLUMBIA
ML 4716 or PHILIPS ABL 3009.

42

Lionel Salter

NINETEENTH-CENTURY PIANO MUSIC

THE piano, at the start of the nineteenth century, was an instrument with only about twenty years' use behind it. Publishers were still warily announcing their works as 'for harpsichord or pianoforte': Beethoven's first eight sonatas were so described, although we may be confident that he never had the harpsichord in mind. But the piano was frail in construction, with a light action and a light tone, and a five-octave compass which manufacturers were just beginning to extend. The kind of music to which it was suited was the delicately decorative Viennese style.

Hummel: *Rondo in E flat.* HMV DB 5510.

Beethoven's influence on piano writing was as great as on every other aspect of music which he touched: he enormously extended the structure and emotional range of the sonata, and technically he exploited chord and broken octave figurations, the full range of the keyboard, the *una corda* or 'soft pedal' effect, inner trills, fugal textures, and all the other devices which are now the basis of piano writing. Many of these can be observed in the Sonata, Opus 106, which Beethoven in an excess of nationalism called the *Hammerklavier*, a German term which implied no difference from the accepted instrument of the time.

Beethoven: *Sonata in B flat, Op. 106.* LONDON LL 422 (alt. DGG DGM 18146).

Such flights as the *Hammerklavier Sonata* were way over the heads of most of the new public. The more informed of them could take variations on favourite operatic airs or popular tunes of the day, and these were dutifully provided by every composer; less cultivated listeners formed the vast public for dance music, for there was at this time a great craze for dancing. Waltzes, *écossaises*, and *contredanses* poured out from the publishers; no composer ignored the demand, and some of Schubert's chains of waltzes and *ländler*, in particular, have remained in the repertoire through their fresh simplicity and unflagging invention. The first composer to elevate the waltz to concert level was Weber, in 1819. He was himself a virtuoso player, with long fingers and a big stretch, so that in his music are to be found extended chords, wide leaps, and a great deal of florid passage work.

Weber: *Invitation to the Dance*. VICTOR LM 1918 (alt. HMV DB 6491).

Weber's sonatas, though classical in form, are romantic in style. One of the best definitions of romanticism in music is that of Kathleen Dale:

Romanticism is exemplified in music by the insistence laid upon the expression of personal feelings and emotions, by impatience with the restraints imposed by conventional forms, by the introduction of the picturesque and the exotic, and by the attempt to translate other arts into music or to combine the phenomena of other arts with music itself.

Partly because of his operatic background, Weber favoured the writing of programme music—that is, music which tells a story. To the immature public of limited understanding programme music made a great appeal: storms, with rumbles in the left hand for thunder and chromatic scales for lightning, were immensely popular, and so were battle scenes. Until 1815 Europe was never without a war somewhere, and innumerable piano representations of famous battles were put on the market by astute publishers.

Too close a preoccupation with the accepted masterpieces of the nineteenth century may lead us to overlook the tremendous influence exerted by musical amateurs and tyros. To be able to play the piano was regarded as an accomplishment for the womenfolk of the new bourgeois class, and fashionable teachers such as Clementi and Moscheles made a lot of money. Published studies for the piano also did well: here two of the earliest in the field were Cramer and Czerny, whose time-and-motion studies analysed technique scientifically. Moscheles complained bitterly of the tastes of his patrons; they wanted nothing but fugitive pieces, and their constant cry was for 'something with a pretty tune, brilliant but not difficult.' As audiences at piano recitals (which seem to have come into fashion in the 1830's) this class also made its tastes felt. To top its persistent chatter and seize its wandering attention, performers were forced to ever greater lengths of showiness. The greater strength of pianos, achieved by the use of an iron frame, increased tension on the strings, and heavier hammers, helped in this trend, and one of the character-istic phenomena of the first half of the nineteenth century was the rise of the keyboard virtuosi (as opposed to interpreters). Their aim appeared to be to play louder and faster than their rivals, and flashy arpeggios, leaps, and flourishes were the order of the day. Apart from glib improvisations (some of which were prudently rehearsed beforehand), they specialized in transcriptions of oper-atic arias, or pot-pourris from popular operas by Meyerbeer or Rossini. This tradition was continued for several decades by Liszt, although his transcriptions were usually more artistic, with subtleties of harmony and keyboard lay-out.

Liszt: *Rigoletto paraphrase*.   LONDON LD 9159 (DECCA LXT 2971).

Another manifestation of this exhibitionist trend was the use of two or more pianos together. The pianist and teacher Kalk-brenner was one of the first to indulge in this, but in 1838 we hear of Liszt and five others taking part in a twelve-handed version of the *Magic Flute* overture. In the category of the sensational may also be included child prodigies, of whom Liszt himself was one, appearing in public for the first time at the age of eleven.

The interest focused on technique had, however, the beneficial effect of developing the medium for which composers were writing. Liszt, like everyone else, had been much struck by the virtuosity of the violinist Paganini, and he not only transcribed some of Paganini's Studies, but wrote some Studies of his own to show off the most advanced piano technique. By his freedom of the keyboard, his unparalleled facility in decoration, his daring harmonies, and his feeling for colour Liszt brought piano tech-nique to its highest peak of development. Contemporary accounts tell us, however, that he frequently broke strings and hammers by the violence of his performance, and usually had a reserve instrument standing by. Such excesses were coldly viewed by serious-minded artists like Clara Schumann, who was one of the first to play Beethoven sonatas to concert audiences. 'Before Liszt,' she complained, 'people used to play: after him, they pound and whisper. He has the decline of piano playing on his conscience.'

There was undoubtedly an increased demand for music. Berlioz in 1838 spoke satirically of the 'rain of albums, avalanches of romances, torrents of airs with variations, spouts of concertos, cavatinas, dramatic scenes, comic duos, soporific adagios, diabolic evocations, and rondos romantic, fantastic, frenetic, and fanatic.' It might be thought from all this that the traditional sonata was a form of the past, but although it underwent some modifications of thought and style, the 1830's saw the appearance of Schumann's three sonatas, Liszt's *Dante Sonata*, and Chopin's *Funeral March Sonata*. Nevertheless, it was noticeable that shorter pieces with fancy titles were becoming more numerous. Besides the spring songs, hunting songs, and dances of elves or witches, in the completely serious field new types were springing up or old types being transformed. Schumann's *Carnaval*, for example, is a combination of free variations and musical character studies; his *Humoresque* and *Arabesque* are in effect rondos: in his many separate pieces or sets of pieces his poetic imagination was frequently fired by pictorial or literary ideas, or by the changing nuances of his own emotions. Schumann's texture tends to be somewhat thick—the result of composing at the piano and experimenting with the sustaining pedal—but among his fingerprints is his fondness for canonic writing and for cross-rhythms. His friend Mendelssohn contributed little to the piano repertoire save elegant *salon* trifles; more important are his *Variations Serieuses* and the elfin scherzos which only he seemed able to write with such delicacy and grace.

Mendelssohn: *Scherzo in E minor*. London LL 824 (Decca LXT 2838).

The supreme nineteenth-century writer for the piano, whose whole output featured his chosen instrument, was Chopin. The beauty of his melodic lines, with their graceful decorations, stemmed from the Italian opera (he was a great admirer of Bellini) but of equal importance were his strikingly bold harmonic sense and his feeling for rhythmic subtleties. The term *tempo rubato*, so associated with his music, is commonly taken to-day to mean a constant flexibility of rhythm, and as a result the most appalling artistic crimes are committed. True *tempo rubato* consists only in slightly moving forward or holding back a melodic line while the basic tempo continues unchanged. The principle is by no means confined to Chopin, but goes back certainly to the fourteenth century and forward to jazz. Chopin said that, despite the lingerings, the hesitations, the anticipations of the right hand, the left hand 'should act like a conductor and not waver for a second.'

Besides his contributions to the development of melody, harmony, rhythm, and keyboard technique, Chopin is also important for the forms he employed. He took over the nocturne from the Irishman, John Field, greatly extending its treatment and its expressive scope; he wrote impromptus, ballades, fantasies, and preludes, as Schumann wrote novelettes, humoresques, and album-leaves, but Chopin (unlike Schumann) never had a programme or descriptive element for these pieces. In addition, he composed in various dance forms, although in every case transcending mere music for dancing and transforming it into something infinitely more imaginative; and he introduced the dance rhythms of his native Poland—mazurkas and polonaises.

Chopin: *Polonaise in F sharp minor.* VICTOR LM 1205 (HMV ALP 1028).

Even when the minimum of form or harmony is in question, Chopin is content to sit making beautiful sounds and arabesques. An example is the *Berceuse* which, except for the coda, consists of fifty-four measures of nothing but alternate tonic and dominant chords.

Chopin: *Berceuse.* HMV C 3308.

Chopin was not alone in introducing folk elements from countries hitherto outside the main stream of artistic development. In Bohemia, Smetana and later Dvořák wrote polkas (a dance which became all the rage in the 1840's), furiants, and other national dances; from Russia, Balakirev brought in an exotic flavour which, allied to brilliantly virtuoso keyboard writing, made for a distinctive contribution to the repertoire. Liszt had already shown the way in the use of exotic idioms, using gipsy rather than true Hungarian themes, and had extended the piano's colour by making it imitate the sound of other instruments, notably the Hungarian cimbalom.

Liszt: *Hungarian Rhapsody, No. 11.* WESTMINSTER WL 6213 (NIXA WLP 6213).

The orchestra was also progressing towards its highest development at this time, and with the growth in power, range, and colour of the piano some composers were beginning to look upon it almost as a substitute for the larger body. Orchestral thinking was responsible not only for the effects of drums, bells, and horns which were widely used, but also for piano lay-outs, particularly in the case of Brahms, which suggested cello melodies, pizzicato basses, wood-wind writing, or broad string passages. The ultimate was reached in the finale of Mussorgsky's suite *Pictures from an Exhibition*, where the full weight of piano sonority and the entire range of the instrument were employed to create a massive effect more appropriate to the full orchestra.

Mussorgsky: *Pictures from an Exhibition* (*The Great Gate of Kiev*).
London LL 330 (Decca LK 4046).

Nevertheless, from about the middle of the century there was a definite decline in the amount of empty virtuosity being demanded by the public, and the major performers of the day, like Clara Schumann or Hans von Bülow, prided themselves more on their interpretative powers than on their ability to dazzle. It is worth noting that, unlike the earlier keyboard celebrities who wrote their own show pieces to demonstrate their best points, this new generation for the most part played other men's music—Beethoven, Schumann, Chopin, Schubert. Brahms was representative of the new temper of the time; he combined classic proportions and restraint with romantic expression and spirit. He was a fine pianist himself, with big, powerful hands, and his music abounds in broad melodies, counterpoint, and impressive chordal writing.

Brahms: *Variations on a Theme of Handel*. London LS 552 (Decca LX 3078).

Brahms was less interested in colour than in form and matter; yet he had a complete understanding of what was effective in piano writing, as can be seen from the virtuosity demanded in his *Paganini Variations*. Later in life he abandoned large-scale keyboard works for miniatures, frequently entitled *Intermezzi* or *Capriccios*, in which a refined poetic sense is coupled with a disciplined intellect. A different kind of intellectualism, expressed in a more chromatic idiom, was that of César Franck. Previous composers had stressed the inner unity of a work by employing the same theme or themes in its different movements, but Franck made a habit of this, and the peroration of his *Prelude, Chorale, and Fugue* has the material of all three movements ingeniously and brilliantly combined.

Franck: *Prelude, Chorale, and Fugue.* WESTMINSTER WL 5163 (NIXA WLP 5163).

At the other extreme from Franck's style are the naïve but appealing piano pieces of Grieg. He adopted the accents of his native folk music, reproducing the sound of the *hardanger* fiddle, the rhythm of the *halling* and *springdans*, and all the atmosphere of Norwegian village life. A few of Grieg's *Lyric Pieces* tend towards a new style that was to come to the fore after the turn of the century—Impressionism. The indefinite tonality, looser construction, and overlapping sonorities of pieces like his *Bellringing* anticipate to some extent the style of Debussy. Debussy's experiments with non-diatonic scales and harmonies, and his evocative impressions of pictorial subjects lay just ahead, but by the end of the nineteenth century he had found the mood of poetic reverie at which he was to excel. By subtleties of pedalling he had taken the first step to the creation of new colours and to his ideal of a piano of fluid sonorities, a piano 'without hammers.'

Debussy: *Clair de lune (Suite Bergamasque).* ANGEL 35067 (alt. DECCA LW 5278).

APPENDIX

BOOKS

A. EINSTEIN: *Music in the Romantic Era.*
ROSAMUND HARDING: *The Pianoforte.*
KATHLEEN DALE: *Nineteenth-century Piano Music.*

RECORDS

As nineteenth-century orchestral music is the staple of our symphony concerts, so nineteenth-century piano music is the staple of our recitals. The recording companies have made available many records of the piano music of such composers as Beethoven, Chopin, Schumann, Liszt, and Brahms. Mention should perhaps be made of one series of works that is neglected in the programmes of piano recitals: the sonatas of Schubert. But these can be explored on a series of Vox records (PL 9800/9130/8420/8590/8210, all (E)).

43

William Mann

NINETEENTH-CENTURY NATIONALISM AND THE DIFFUSION OF ROMANTICISM

THE story of late nineteenth-century music is one of gradual withdrawal from the apron strings of German models. I tried in my earlier essay to stress the historical importance of Berlioz and Liszt, two non-German composers, and that process of reaction away from German domination has continued right up to the present day. But the more one looks at the growth of musical nationalism in the nineteenth century, the more one finds Beethoven and Wagner at the root of these non-German reactionaries. Heroes of weighty influence, like Berlioz and Liszt, are not to be found in the story of nationalistic music, but Beethoven can almost be called the hero of the age, much against anyone else's will.

The spirit of nationalism was and is supposed to be rooted in folk-song. But the other contradiction forced upon us is that, although traditional music undoubtedly played a part in the formation of the various national styles, those composers who most successfully found their own style were those who did not actually base all their music on the songs of their own country.

The country that found nationalism *most* easy to establish was probably France because there the tradition was *most* established. The heritage of old Burgundy and of Couperin and Rameau had not been obliterated. The strongest figure in French instrumental music during the latter part of the nineteenth century was an adopted Frenchman, César Franck. Those of us who admire the individuality of French music from Chabrier to Boulez may find it galling to recognize the fact, but that tradition is largely due to the personality of a Belgian, Franck, and two Germans, Beethoven and Wagner. Franck's most admired work, the Symphony in D minor, gave its contemporaries a working plan that they did not disdain; the principle of cyclicism. Franck and others brought the common denominator of the themes of a symphony into the open and made a motto of it. The working method of Franck's symphony can be traced back to the Fifth and Seventh symphonies of Beethoven.

Franck also developed a characteristic orchestral sound which owed its being to the particular sound quality of French organs which people find thick and treacly unless they are used to it. His harmonic language is usually ascribed to the doodling that he did at the organ, but it can be traced more efficaciously back to the Wagner of *Tristan und Isolde* and *Parsifal*. It is as a French Wagnerite that Franck had most influence, and what the Franck-ists and their contemporaries admired in Wagner was his nobility and sensuous subtlety of expression. That is what Franck set out to bring into French music. When he combined his mastery of that idiom with the freshness of an unusual form, as in the *Symphonic Variatious*, which are a mixture of piano concerto and non-virtuoso symphonic thought, the result is a masterpiece by any standard, and an influence that is still not played out in France.

Franck: *Symphonic Variations*. COLUMBIA ML 4536 (COLUMBIA 33 CX 1190).

The most admired composition of César Franck, in terms of importance, is surely his Symphony. Gounod called it 'the affirma-tion of incompetence pushed to the lengths of a dogma,' but it was very influential and beneficially so. The most successful symphony to use the same method is the *Symphony in B flat* of Ernest Chausson, that very gifted artist who left his mark on chamber music as well before his tragic early death. Indeed Chausson's symphony carried out the Franckian practice with such conviction, and such individual freshness, liberated from the organ loft, that it seems to wear as well as its model.

Chausson: *Symphony in B flat*. VICTOR LM 1181 (alt. PHILIPS NBR 6018).

The forward-looking part of Franck's influence can be seen to-day in the music of Messiaen, who has been able to speak with his own contemporary voice and to absorb other influences without breaking free of the tradition. We can see another wing of the French Wagnerian faction in the music of Chabrier. His sort of romanticism was less intense; the sort of mind that could adore Wagner while writing quadrilles on themes from *Tristan und Isolde*, and Chabrier could glean and profit from foreign influences, as in the *Fête Polonaise* or the *España* rhapsody, without endangering his own vitality or personality. What marks him out is the utter professionalism of his music. Many of the late romantics can be taunted with amateurishness, but not Chabrier; and it is that proficiency and certainty of direction that has so influenced the dapper French music of Satie and *Les Six* and Ravel in our own times. The music of Milhaud and Roussel finds its ancestor in Chabrier's *Bourrée fantasque*.

Chabrier: *Bourrée fantasque*. WESTMINSTER 5294 (NIXA WLP 5294).

One thing that history teaches us is that the most important figures are not necessarily the most admirable ones. One of the most distinguished French composers of this period was Fauré, who ploughed his own furrow, apparently unconcerned but with highly original results. Yet the long line of history cannot single him out for significance, though it can acclaim his music. For sheer quality of output most musicians would rate Fauré higher than old Saint-Saëns, whose lifetime embraced Bellini and Schönberg and who went on producing music (in his own phrase) 'as an apple-tree produces apples.' He toyed with exotic influence in the best romantic tradition, but remained all his life a reactionary, and as such his influence on musical history was small and impermanent. The folk-song wing of French nationalistic music does not seem very strong; a focal point is Vincent d'Indy, who brought together the symphonic application of traditional music, the piano concerto, and the Lisztian idea of thematic metamorphosis in his *Symphony on a French Mountaineer's Song*.

D'Indy: *Symphony on a French Mountaineer's Song*. COLUMBIA ML 4928 (COLUMBIA 33 CX 1190).

The French composers of this period, taken together, demonstrate the fundamental unromanticism of French music. France was largely responsible for the start of the romantic movement in art, but the music of romantic France strives constantly, if we except the school of César Franck, for ideals of elegance and deprecating affability that are more markedly classic. And this is why France progressed so quickly to the anti-romantic aims of the twentieth century; the sympathy with them was always there.

With the Russian nationalist movement the German influence is much less marked. Russia had fallen under the spell of the

Italian opera in the early part of the century, and the sophisticated circles were temperamentally linked with French trends in art. The history books tell us that Glinka's opera *A Life for the Tsar* (or *Ivan Susanin*) was the beginning of Russian opera, but there is a strong flavour of Bellini about it. It was the next generation that secured Russian independence with the school of composers called the 'Mighty Handful.' Their leader was Balakirev, an extraordinarily intelligent and gifted musician.

As with much romantic art, the Russian nationalist school of composers contained a strong element of amateur musicianship, and of the group only Rimsky-Korsakov had the professional's unerring touch. The aim of musical independence was quite clearly to be attained, according to Balakirev, through the inspiration, direct or indirect, of Russian traditional melody. The specific character of Russian folk melody translated itself smoothly to art music, so far as opera went; this is evident from the works of Mussorgsky, who was probably the greatest genius of the whole Handful. The pungent flavour of eastern Russian music brought in a characteristic that the rest of the world has acclaimed in Rimsky-Korsakov's *Scheherezade* or even more distinctively in Balakirev's superb tone poem *Thamar*, which deals with a similar subject from a similar clime.

Balakirev: *Thamar*. ANGEL 35291 (COLUMBIA 33 CX 1280), or ML 4974, or LONDON LL 1068 (DECCA LXT 2966).

Russian folk music was not so useful for symphonic architecture; accordingly, it is the non-symphonic orchestral works, the suites and tone poems and operas of these composers, that now seem most successful. Folk tunes are not really suited to the process of taking apart and putting together in a different order which we call symphonic technique; they are too much of an indestructible piece. That is the trouble with that popular masterpiece Borodin's Second Symphony and with the even more admirable Symphony in C of Balakirev. As examples of Russian nationalistic art those two symphonies are more to be admired than the symphonies of Tchaikovsky, which seem to western peoples much more European in tone of voice. But Tchaikovsky's Russianness is perfectly accepted by his own compatriots. The particular character of his greatest works is that strange blend of melancholy passion and sardonic humour which is perfectly Russian and which we acclaim in Tchekov's plays as nationalistic. Those two qualities come together most strongly, I think, in the first movement of the *Fifth Symphony*, which is often dragged down to the pace of a dirge, but which, taken at the speed specified by the composer, tells us a good deal about the Russian character.

Tchaikovsky: *Symphony No. 5 in E minor.* VICTOR LHMV 1003 (HMV ALP 1001).

Tchaikovsky did a great deal to extend the boundaries of music: he made ballet music into a serious musical art; he brought the sphere of dance music more closely into contact with symphonic behaviour in his waltz and march movements; he made the symphony a dramatic art form as well as an argumentative one. The national roots of his style are more marked the more one studies his music, and not just in the folk tunes that he occasionally used or in the Russian dance measures of his ballets. In the finale of his Violin Concerto, for example, there is a tune which could easily have appeared in a symphony by Borodin or Balakirev, but which also has the unmistakable signature of Tchaikovsky, and no other Russian, upon it.

Tchaikovsky: *Violin Concerto in D.* DECCA 9755 (DGG DGM 18196).

Russia was far enough away from Germany to feel no very cogent pull musically. The nearer you get to central Europe, the more the national movement owes to the country against which it was reacting. Sibelius went to study in Germany, but when he returned to Finland he showed no sign of wanting to fall under Teutonic influence. In Bohemia the German pull was almost harmless. The gentle, contented nationalism of Dvořák is not far away from the Carinthian mood of Brahms on holiday; the two composers were good friends, and some of Dvořák's music has a Brahmsian feel about it, but in the most characteristic of Dvořák's music the Czech atmosphere is not just an accent, but a living language. Dvořák could go to Germany or to England or to America, but the music that came back was entirely Bohemian.

Dvořák: *Symphony No. 4 in G.* VICTOR LHMV 1014 (HMV ALP 1064).

In other countries nationalism was either unripe, as in Hungary or England, or else the national tradition was so established that no composer needed to stress his nationalism, as in Italy. Italian music in any case was almost exclusively operatic and gradually developed vividness to the point of the so-called school of *verismo* in which blood and thunder—the more lurid and true to life the better—were the order of the day. *Verismo* claimed a French convert at the end of the century in Charpentier, whose *Louise* made a heroine of the French working girl.

The task of Germany was to consolidate and build on the developments of German composers, chiefly Wagner and Brahms, and of the adopted German composer Liszt. The orchestra was growing larger and larger; two composers who led this inflation to its explosion, and to the small orchestras of the twentieth century, were Richard Strauss and Gustav Mahler. Richard Strauss took his musical language first of all from the classics up to and including Mendelssohn and Brahms, but then fell under the influence of Liszt and Wagner. He became a master of musical portraiture, taking over the Lisztian symphonic poem and developing it in much sharper focus, so that where Liszt and Saint-Saëns and Tchaikovsky were describing rather vague programmes, Richard Strauss portrayed his heroes and heroines in minute detail. He could declare of Donna Elvira in *Don Juan* (though he may be contradicted) that anyone must hear in the music what colour her hair was. The sheep in *Don Quixote* are perfectly realistic, as is the crying of the baby in the *Sinfonia Domestica*. Perhaps the most detailed passage of all is the violin solo that represents Mrs Strauss in *Ein Heldenleben*; the music moves rapidly through a wide emotional gamut.

R. Strauss: *Ein Heldenleben*.   LONDON LL 659 (DECCA LXT 2729).

Strauss wrote *Ein Heldenleben* in 1898, when he was thirty-four years old. His full importance did not become apparent until after 1900, but already he had pointed some of the way to modern music. Mahler only had eleven years of the new century to live, and yet his work was hardly begun when *Ein Heldenleben* was produced. Just as Strauss enlarged the symphony orchestra to the army of *Ein Heldenleben* and later *Elektra*, only to return to a tiny band for the opera *Ariadne auf Naxos*, so Mahler stepped up his orchestral forces with extra wind, brass, and percussion and with the addition of voices in certain symphonies; and yet by temperament he was a delicate orchestrator. Strauss's later career and influence were reactionary, but Mahler went on to probe farther into the refinement and extension of tonal language, and the logical corollary of his later symphonies is in the twelve-note music of Schönberg and his followers, while his influence has been beneficial and profound on such tonal composers as Shostakovich and Britten. The most forward-looking side of Mahler was not the torrent of sound he drew from his three hundred performers, but the cleanly poised and refined sound that emanates from his orchestra, for example, in the song *Urlicht* which forms the fourth movement of his Second Symphony. This clarity and emphasis on the contrast of significant lines is the story of twentieth-century music up to our day.

Mahler: *Symphony No. 2 in C minor.*   Vox PL 7010 (E).

APPENDIX

BOOKS

MARTIN COOPER: *French Music from the death of Berlioz to the death of Fauré.*

R. A. LEONARD: *History of Russian Music.*

SIR DONALD TOVEY: *Essays in Musical Analysis* (especially Tchaikovsky's Fifth Symphony).

RECORDS

The remarks on nineteenth-century orchestral music apply here too. Such composers as Franck, Borodin, Dvořák, Tchaikovsky, Richard Strauss, and Fauré are represented in the catalogues by many fine records —their most familiar works in alternative recordings. But it is probably as well to mention two recordings that might escape notice.

BALAKIREV: *Symphony No. 1 in C.*   ENGLISH COLUMBIA 33 CX 1002.

SMETANA: *Ma Vlast* (complete).   MERCURY OL 2–100 (MERCURY MRL 2504–5).

44

Aaron Copland

THE TWENTIETH CENTURY:
REORIENTATION AND EXPERIMENT

THERE are two kinds of revolution that typify the early 1900's. The first is a technical revolution; the new musical resources developed out of old resources were strikingly different. New chords, unheard of before 1900, gradually found acceptance. There were new rhythms unlike the more conventional and sometimes plodding rhythms of the nineteenth century. There began to be an emphasis once again on contrapuntal texture, and also an emphasis on individual tone-colour values. These four new developments were characteristic of the technical advance in music of the 1900's; but there developed also a second and very important difference: an aesthetic difference. Composers began to take a more critical attitude towards the romantic nineteenth century, gradually pulling farther away from the hegemony of German music that had been so powerful an influence, stressing instead a more discreet and objective expressive attitude.

It might almost be said that Germany *owned* music towards the end of the nineteenth century. It was as if Wagner had epitomized everything that had happened before him in the music of that century and had left nothing truly new to be done after him. The first striking signs of a newer and braver post-Wagnerian music can be found in the work of Richard Strauss and Gustav Mahler.

In Strauss we find an aesthetic which is not basically different from Wagner's; Strauss's music has all the earmarks of the Wagnerian style. Nevertheless, it was apparent before long that Strauss belonged to the future, at least in part, for his harmonies were more daring, his textures more brilliant and more complex, and in general he indicated to the composers who followed him a

281

rhythmic and musico-dramatic adventuresomeness that surpassed anything they had previously known. In his operas *Salome* and *Elektra*, both of which date from the first decade of the twentieth century, Strauss really ventured on new territory; not aesthetically, but tonally and rhythmically and in the brilliance of his orchestration. It can be seen especially in the scene in *Salome* which portrays musically the beheading of the prophet Jokanaan.

R. Strauss: *Salome*. LONDON XLL 1038–9 (DECCA LXT 2863–4).

Mahler to-day looms much larger on the musical horizon as a composer than was true during his lifetime. He loved the grandiose, and that was one of his links with the nineteenth century. Another was his sense of intimacy with nature, a trait that had its origin in early romantic literature. But his was an earnest, passionate, and even metaphysical personality. His philosophic quality was curiously balanced by a love of simple things like the folk-songs he came to know as a child. As he used them in the works of his maturity they suggest an escape to youthful and happier times.

Mahler made two main technical contributions to the new music of the twentieth century. The first was his conception of texture as contrapuntally conceived, in contrast to the harmonically based texture of Richard Strauss. It is as if Mahler plays on an orchestra without using the pedal; he emphasizes the separate lines and does not blur them with a heavy chordal background. The clarity of independent melodic lines is a very typical feature of later twentieth-century music, and Mahler was perhaps the first composer to realize that the new sound world would reflect primarily contrapuntal rather than harmonic interests.

Mahler's second contribution was a new kind of orchestration, very different from that of Strauss. By comparison Strauss's orchestration is sometimes over-ornate: there is so great an elaboration of sonorities in the orchestra that it is difficult for the ear to unravel the separate strands. That is almost never true of Mahler's most characteristic pages. We find in Mahler a dry, clear orchestration demonstrating a striking economy of means. Even though he wrote for enormous numbers of performers (in a work such as the Symphony No. 8) there are always sections where single instruments play thinly spaced sonorities. The way in which he uses solo instruments to bring out these original sounding intervals can be heard even more clearly in *Das Lied von der Erde* (*The Song of the Earth*), one of his last works.

Mahler: *Das Lied von der Erde*. LONDON LL 625–6 (DECCA LXT 2721–2).

Strauss and Mahler, although their aesthetic was based on German music of the nineteenth century, showed the direction that twentieth-century music would take in certain matters of technique. But nothing really new could happen in twentieth-century music without a complete break with the nineteenth century, and Claude Debussy was the first composer who fully understood the need to take music down a more objective path.

Debussy was influenced, no doubt, by the visit he made to Russia towards the end of the nineteenth century. While it is not clear precisely what music he heard while in Russia, it would have been unlikely for a man of Debussy's temperament to have lived there and disregarded original work, such as that of Mussorgsky. It is easy to trace the beginnings of some of the most characteristic features of contemporary music to the Russian school of that time, and especially to Mussorgsky. His realism, his simplicity, and his desire for a natural approach to music aided other composers in moving out of the sphere of the nineteenth century. Perhaps it was Mussorgsky's amateur status that helped him to freshen the sources of serious music; certainly his love of naturalness and simplicity led him to take a special interest in the folk-song of the Russian peasant. The unconventional rhythms and harmony of his music were so sparklingly new that his colleague Rimsky-Korsakov thought they had to be 'corrected.' Mussorgsky is farther from German music of that period than any other well-known composer. Whether or not Debussy discovered Mussorgsky's music during his visit to Russia, there is certainly some influence of Mussorgsky to be discerned in even so characteristic a work by Debussy as *Pelléas et Mélisande*.

Debussy: *Pelléas et Mélisande*. LONDON LLA 11 (DECCA LXT 2711–4), or EPIC SC 6003 (PHILIPS ABL 3076–8).

Debussy is in a certain sense a transitional composer; he did not go all the way from German subjective romanticism to a more objective attitude. It is only natural that he could not, for a composer is unable suddenly to turn the history of music about and do as he pleases. While Debussy reacted strongly against Wagner, there is still a romantic expressiveness in Debussy's music, but it is of a more passive and hypersensitive kind.   In his exquisite transcription of an ideal world of sensations he was helped by the example of the French impressionist painters and symbolist poets.   His delicate and sensitive music had revolution-ary implications, for Debussy was one of the first composers of modern times who dared to make his ear the sole judge of what was right and wrong.

Debussy was influenced by his colleague, Erik Satie, both harmonically and in his aesthetic ideas.   Satie desired to be re-laxed in his music, to make an end of overblown 'rhetoric.'   His *Gymnopédies* are good examples of the music he was writing round the year 1900.   They do not sound revolutionary any more, but their quietude, distinction, and general simplicity prophesy the music to come.

Satie: *Gymnopédies*.   CAPITAL P 8244 (CAPITOL CTL 7055).*

Arnold Schönberg grew up in the nineteenth-century German tradition, and indeed had great difficulty in throwing off the influ-ence of Wagner.   Early works such as *Gurrelieder* and *Trans-figured Night* were written under the direct influence of Wagner and Strauss.   But Schönberg was an intensely serious composer who soon realized that certain conclusions were to be drawn from what Wagner had contributed in harmonic development.   The modulatory scheme in Wagner leads us to the brink of losing our sense of tonal centre.   Schönberg's historic role was to lead Wagner's modulatory scheme to its inevitable conclusion, namely, the complete abandonment of tonality.   It might almost be said that modern music has never been more revolutionary than at the moment when Schönberg decided that tonality was not an essential element of serious music.   His music of that time was (against his will) generally called atonal—i.e. without tonal centre of any kind.   Atonal music was a truly unprecedented conception; it still remains disturbing to some present-day audiences.   Anyone hearing his *Five Orchestral Pieces* would be unlikely to suspect that they were written as long ago as 1909.

Schönberg: *Five Orchestral Pieces, Op*. 16.   MERCURY 50024 (alt. HMV ALP 1251).

Igor Stravinsky is certainly one of the most fascinating figures in the musical history of the twentieth century.   The fact that he has written, since the twenties, so much so-called neo-classic music tends to make us forget that the music he wrote around 1911 was filled with revolutionary implications, and came as a great shock to its first listeners. It was as though Stravinsky had suddenly applied a rhythmic hypodermic to the music of the nineteenth century; the power of sheer rhythm to arouse us had been forgotten. Stravinsky, a Russian who had absorbed the music of Mussorgsky and other Russian masters, reinstated the role of rhythm in the music of that time. Audiences had begun to associate the new music, especially that from France, with a delicately tinted, quiet, and sensuous expression. When Stravinsky appeared, an enormous dynamism entered music; and it has never been the same since experiencing the elemental, almost brutal, certainly non-erotic vitality of *Petrouchka* and *The Rite of Spring*.

Stravinsky: *The Rite of Spring*. LONDON LL 303 (DECCA LXT 2563).

Finally, the American composer Charles Ives should be mentioned. Through a curious quirk of history the music that he was writing during the period 1895–1910 only became known during the early 1930's. But all commentators are agreed that Ives in his experiments invented rhythms and harmonies which ante-dated in daring those of Schönberg and Stravinsky. Ives was a poetic realist in his music; we can often trace his innovations to real sounds that he heard. If, for example, he heard several brass bands on the 4th of July marching through the centre of his small town of Danbury, Connecticut, he attempted in his music to re-create what might be called the poetic confusion of these sounds from different points of the compass meeting simultaneously. Ives was particularly experimental in his rhythms; some of his works are so polyrhythmically conceived that it is difficult to play them even now. For that reason some of his scores are still unperformed. But as time goes on Ives will probably be credited more and more with having indicated the direction the contemporary movement was later to follow, especially in the United States.

APPENDIX

BOOKS

CLAUDE DEBUSSY: *Monsieur Croche, Anti-dilettante.*
VICTOR SEROFF: *Debussy.*
ROLLO MYERS: *Erik Satie.*
A. SALAZAR: *Music in Our Time.*
WILFRID MELLERS: *Studies in Contemporary Music.*
AARON COPLAND: *Our New Music.*
HENRY and SIDNEY COWELL: *Charles Ives.*

RECORDS

Such composers as Debussy, Ravel, and Mahler are well represented in the catalogues now. For recordings of works by Schönberg and Stravinsky, see Chapter 45.

SATIE: *Parade.* ANGEL 3518 C (COLUMBIA 33 CX 1197). *Piano Music.* MGM 3154. *Socrate.* ESOTERIC 510.
IVES: *Piano Sonata No. 1.* COLUMBIA ML 4490. *Piano Sonata No. 2.* COLUMBIA ML 4250. *Violin Sonatas.* MERCURY 50096–7. *Songs.* OVERTONE 7. *Symphony No. 3.* VANGUARD 468.
BUSONI: *Arlecchino.* VICTOR LM 1944 (HMV ALP 1223).

45

Alfred Frankenstein

NEW ORTHODOXIES:
TWELVE-NOTE COMPOSITION

TWENTY-TWO years ago, when Arnold Schönberg had only just arrived in the United States, he was invited to give a public lecture at the University of Chicago, where I then had the privilege of teaching. The title of his lecture was *Composition with Twelve Tones Related Only to Each Other*, and it set forth the theory of composition with tone-rows which he and his pupils had been employing for about a decade, but which was still very little known to the musical world at large. The reaction of the music faculty at the University of Chicago was typical of the general reaction of that period: we respected Schönberg's knowledge, integrity, and daring, but we were unanimously of the opinion that the theory we had just heard expounded represented a deviation or spur from the main line of musical history and was not part of the main line itself.

We were all very young in those days and we did not know what at least one of us has since come to believe: that if a theory in the arts seems on first exposure to represent an extreme or even absurd blind alley, it will shortly prove to be of very general usefulness and significance. The reasonable, readily acceptable theories seldom have much vitality. The unreasonable theories provide the arts with their true dynamics.

This has certainly proved true of the Schönbergian theory of composition with twelve tones related only to each other. Far from being limited to a mere handful of composers, it has spread during the last quarter of a century to colour the music of the entire world, and now there are devotees of the twelve-note system everywhere. Composers once regarded as enemies of this system, like Béla Bartók and Igor Stravinsky, have flirted with it, and it has allied itself with idioms of the most improbable kind, like jazz.

This theory was the product of a long development in which many different forces played their parts.

The young Arnold Schönberg was responsive to and sympathetic towards numerous currents in the musical life of his time, but was especially attuned to the idioms of Richard Wagner and Gustav Mahler. Wagner had said that for him the art of musical composition was an art of continuous transition. Hence the continuously liquid, dynamic progression of Wagner's harmony which dissolves all discrete forms into a single entity, and in so doing tugs hard at the underpinnings of tonal relationship on which a structure of smaller structures, like a symphony or an opera, is based. It is not surprising that early works of Schönberg, his First String Quartet, for example, dissolve the conventional four-movement pattern into a single pattern; this is an inevitable development from the practice of Wagner.

From Gustav Mahler Schönberg learned to use the orchestra, not exclusively as the vastly sonorous, heroic body which it had been to Wagner and his older followers, but also as a gigantic chamber ensemble in which individual sonorities and soloistic lines are accorded an importance equal to, if not greater than, the sounds of massive groups. Ultimately Schönberg was to detach the chamber ensemble of string and wind instruments from its context in the full symphonic band of the Mahler tradition, while the treatment of the big orchestra by Schönberg himself and his major disciples always reveals a Mahler-like touch.

An early work by Schönberg shows us a composer strongly beholden in his harmony to Wagner and in his orchestration to Mahler. Such a piece is the prelude to the huge vocal piece called *The Legend of the Castle of Gurre*, composed in 1901, but not orchestrated until ten years later. The prelude is clearly associated with the idea of sunset and gathering twilight over a wild landscape.

Schönberg: *Gurrelieder*. HAYDN SOCIETY 100 (NIXA HLP 3100).

In later works of the same period—1900-10—Schönberg's music continues, in its extremely free and fluid modulation, to undermine the sense of key centre and key relationship on which the very concept of modulation is based. Wandering chords, at home in all keys and owing special allegiance to none, come to play an increasingly important role; dissonance is freed from its

laws of preparation and resolution, and at length the whole fabric
of key relationships on which the musical theory of the eighteenth
and nineteenth centuries had been based, dissolves. There
follows a period of free atonality in Schönberg's work. Key
centres have disappeared, but a systematized order of tonal relationships without them has not yet evolved. This does not mean
that the music is devoid of structure. On the contrary, the works
of Schönberg's freely atonal period are among his most elaborately
contrived from the formal point of view. However, and this is
very important, the forms that Schönberg employs at this time
are all extremely short. The older system of fixed tonalities had
provided a logic or rationale for musical patterns greatly extended
in time; free atonality provided no such rationale. Furthermore,
Schönberg was obviously entranced at savouring the remarkable
harmonies and colouristic effects of the new style on a small scale,
as if these were precious jewels that were not to be spread about
too lavishly.

There is also an emphasis on an emotional atmosphere, often
made specific in song texts, of a highly expressionistic kind.
Expressionism is almost a technical term for the German painting
and sculpture of this period, and Schönberg was himself an expres-
sionist painter of no mean ability. Probably the best definition
of expressionism was provided by the German sculptor, Ernst
Barlach, who once said: 'I must be able to join in the suffering.'
All expressionists make us join in the suffering, Schönberg the
composer no less than Barlach the sculptor. The psychology
of Sigmund Freud is another expression of the same attitude, and
there are some works of Schönberg's freely atonal period which
are clearly coloured by Freud's compassionate joining in the suffering expressed by the morbid and irrational aspects of the human
psyche.

Pierrot Lunaire (*Mad Pierrot*), composed in 1912, is one such
work. It is a setting of twenty-one triolets by the Belgian poet,
Albert Guiraud, as translated into German by Otto Erich Hartle-
ben. The setting is for a vocalist who neither speaks nor sings
but employs a completely novel idiom, part way between speech
and song, which Schönberg invented for this work and which has
often been used by his followers. The instrumental part calls
for five players who perform on seven different instruments.
No two of the twenty-one movements are quite alike in scoring.

Here is the chamber music ensemble of Mahler in its most brilliant, independent, and ingenious form. The musical structure is completely atonal and often very learned in its use of such patterns as canons and passacaglias, although these aspects of the music are very difficult to appreciate by means of the unaided ear.

Schönberg: *Pierrot Lunaire*. WESTMINSTER 18143 (alt. ARGO RG 54).

All the works of Schönberg's freely atonal period are either very short or are composed of many very short movements strung together. A return to extended forms required some kind of theoretical structure, and this Schönberg ultimately provided in the twelve-note system. I think that the evolution of this theory was also conditioned, as the crystallization of principles often is, by the extreme hostility with which so much of Schönberg's music was met. If a new idiom can be shown to have an unassailable rationale, those who practise it can feel secure against the attacks of the world. I think this is what Schönberg meant when in the course of his address at the University of Chicago in 1934 he said: 'You do not think my music is beautiful, but I *know* it is.'

At all events, the twelve-note theory provides a logical structure for atonality. Schönberg himself used it from 1923 until his death in 1951. In simplest essence it is a method whereby notes are related, as Schönberg put it, *only to each other*, which means that they are no longer related to a common centre.

A major scale is the simplest and most perfect example of notes related to a common centre. All the notes in a major scale have their places, derive their order and their functions from the note with which it begins and ends; and the scale is named after that note—C major, D major, E major, etc. Any scale has two forms and two forms only; it can go up and it can come down, and that is all it can do.

Schönberg replaces the concept of scale with the twelve-note row, an arbitrary selection of the twelve notes within an octave arranged in a fixed, unchanging order. Each composition is based upon a different twelve-note row, and sometimes the row undergoes modification from movement to movement in the course of a composition in large form. Unlike a scale, a twelve-note row does not have two forms but four. It can be played backwards, it can be turned upside down, and the upside down version can also be played backwards. The terms commonly used for these four forms are prime (the original form of the row), retrograde, inversion, and retrograde inversion.

Composition in the Schönbergian system is the art of bringing the twelve-note row to life in rhythm, as the composition of a melody in the tonal system might be called bringing a scale to life in rhythm. The four forms of the row may be used melodically, contrapuntally, and harmonically in endless numbers of ways. There are, of course, many other aspects of this technique, and what has been said no more defines the whole of the twelve-note system than the playing of a major scale defines the whole of the harmonic and contrapuntal system of Beethoven. But this is the basic axiom of the Schönbergian philosophy: the twelve-note row provides a method whereby *notes are related to each other*, and not to a common centre, during the course of a composition in large form or small. Some theorists regard this as a technique of continuous variation, and that is one good way of looking at it. It is a discipline for the creation of the utmost unity and the utmost variety.

The twelve-note row may be heard in practice in the last movement of the *Suite, Opus 29*; a *gigue* for three clarinets of different sizes, violin, viola, cello, and piano.

Schönberg: *Suite, Op. 29*. COLUMBIA ML 5099.

Schönberg had two major disciples, both of whom predeceased him. One was Alban Berg, whose music is probably played more frequently to-day than that of Schönberg himself, and the other was Anton von Webern. These two men occupy very different places in the Schönbergian hierarchy. As René Leibowitz puts it, Schönberg was the innovator, while it was the function of Berg to relate the innovations of his teacher to the art of the past and the function of Webern to jump ahead and explore their possibilities towards the future. The music of Berg is more 'expressive' in the conventional sense than that of Schönberg, and it is scarcely accidental that his operas, notably *Wozzeck*, have been presented all over the world, while the operas of Schönberg remain all but totally unknown. Berg seldom remains strictly within the twelve-note tradition; he uses it as one of many means and plays in and out among all the systems as his purpose dictates. It is characteristic of Berg that he should have written a *Lyric Suite* for string quartet and entitled its six movements Allegretto giovale, Andante amoroso, Allegro misterioso, Adagio appassionato, Presto delirando, and Largo desolato. This emphasis on high-pitched emotionalism, coupled with the utmost fineness in texture, is typical of Berg, and is responsible for the relatively high degree of public success his work has won.

Berg: *Lyric Suite.* COLUMBIA ML 2148.

Anton von Webern is the least successful of the disciples of Schönberg from the point of view of public approbation. Webern is one of those paradoxical artists who elaborate things to such an extent that they produce the starkest kind of simplicity. His work is like that of those modern painters whose canvases are mostly bare, with a few telling strokes that not only express their own shapes and relationships but give shape, likewise, to the surrounding void. Webern composes as much with silence as with tone. His orchestration is likely to be, as Leibowitz puts it, a matter of isolated sounds contributed by one instrument at a time. His forms are extremely condensed, but everything in his textures is wonderfully open and clear. Every sound tells; Webern's is perhaps the most sinewy music of modern times. An example is the Concerto, Opus 24, composed in 1934.

Webern: *Concerto for nine instruments, Op. 24.* DIAL 17.

Schönberg and his personal disciples, Berg and Webern, are doubtless the major figures in the twelve-note school, but their technique has been taken up by other composers throughout the world. It has proved to be an infinitely plastic medium for the expression of an infinite number of musical personalities. And for a good example of twelve-note music written outside the Schönbergian circle, we may take the Third Symphony of the American composer, Wallingford Riegger.

Riegger: *Symphony No. 3.* COLUMBIA ML 4902.

APPENDIX

BOOKS

RENÉ LEIBOWITZ: *Schönberg and His School.*
JOSEF RUFER: *Composition with Twelve Notes Related Only to Each Other.*
ARNOLD SCHÖNBERG: *Style and Idea.*

RECORDS

SCHÖNBERG: *Four String Quartets.* COLUMBIA 4 SL–188. *Transfigured Night.* CAPITOL P 8304 (CAPITOL CCL 7507).

BERG: *Wozzeck.* COLUMBIA 5 SL–118. *Violin Concerto.* COLUMBIA ML 3857 (COLUMBIA 33 CX 1030). *Chamber Concerto.* VOX PL 8660 (E).

WEBERN: *Five Movements for String Quartet.* COLUMBIA 4 SL–188 (with Schönberg).

A set of recordings containing the complete works of Anton von Webern has been released by Columbia (U.S.A.), K4L–232.

46

Alfred Frankenstein

NEW ORTHODOXIES:
NEO-CLASSICISM

CARL VAN VECHTEN is remembered to-day as the author
of some slight, smart, amusing novels, but he began his
career between hard covers with some of the most
brilliantly written books on musical subjects ever produced in North America. One of these books is called *Music
After the Great War* and it was published in 1915. In the title
essay of this collection Van Vechten made a bold attempt to predict what music would be like after World War I. His major
prediction was one hundred per cent correct. He said that the
two most important figures in the musically creative life of the
world would be Arnold Schönberg and Igor Stravinsky. But this
prediction, correct though it was, was nevertheless based upon a
philosophy which events proved to be one hundred per cent
wrong.

This is a fascinating phenomenon: a completely accurate
prophecy arrived at through the application of a completely false
premise. It demonstrates that the history of the arts does not
work according to the dictates of logic, and especially according
to the evolutionary hypothesis which underlay Van Vechten's
thought.

His argument was that over the years harmony had grown more
and more complex and had placed increasingly heavy emphasis
upon dissonance until the new school of his time had come to
create a veritable science of 'disharmony.' He saw nothing in the
future but further and more complex explorations of 'disharmony,'
and observing that Stravinsky had written his best works, such as
The Rite of Spring, on barbaric, oriental themes he predicted that
a similar barbaric orientalism would suffuse the entire musical
world. 'I do not predict a return to Mozart as one result of the

war,' said Carl van Vechten, and that line was written with the utmost irony, as representing the ultimate in unthinkables.

Two years later Serge Prokofieff produced his *Classical Symphony*, and the return to Mozart was on in earnest. Stravinsky, the barbaric orientalist, rediscovered Bach in his Piano Concerto, and some of his major works to come would bear such titles as *Apollo, Ruler of the Muses, Oedipus Rex*, and *Orpheus*. Mozartian forms, Bach-like textures, and classical subjects became the rule; for a time it even seemed as if a race were on among contemporary composers to find the most obscure and academic among the composers of the past to be used as models.

There were many good reasons for this. Music does not evolve in a straight line, but is subject to mutations, pendulum swings, and sudden switches as the result of all manner of forces, including satiety. It is easy to see the musical world of 1917 through the eyes of young Prokofieff: the impressionist tradition of Debussy going to seed in diaphanous ultra-refinement, the tradition of Wagner dying of elephantiasis, the Russian folklore tradition of his immediate background breaking up in preciousness and triviality. To all of this Prokofieff replied with a bold, smiling gesture: back to simplicity, to clear forms and uncomplicated emotions.

Prokofieff: *Classical Symphony*. VICTOR LM 1215 (HMV ALP 1107).

Prokofieff was one of the most striking forerunners of the modern neo-classical movement, although other composers of 1917 exhibited somewhat similiar impulses, including Debussy himself in the three sonatas composed at the end of his life. The composer, however, who has come to be most strongly identified with this movement—who is, indeed, its major lawgiver—is Prokofieff's compatriot, Igor Stravinsky.

Stravinsky won world celebrity within the Russian nationalist framework with *The Fire Bird, Petrouchka*, and *The Rite of Spring*, but after World War I he turned his back on folkloric nationalism and gave the neo-classical ideal a powerful philosophic propulsion. Neo-classicism was entertaining with Prokofieff; with Stravinsky it took on seriousness and depth. Perhaps the best statement of the neo-classical philosophy (Stravinsky version) is to be found in a famous passage of his autobiography. In discussing the composition of one of his later ballets, Stravinsky says:

Here, in classical dancing, I see the triumph of studied conception

over vagueness, of the rule over the arbitrary, of order over the hap-
hazard. I am thus brought face to face with the eternal conflict in art
between the Apollonian and the Dionysian principles. The latter
assumes ecstasy to be the final goal—that is to say, the losing of one's
self—whereas art demands above all the full consciousness of the
artist. There can, therefore, be no doubt as to my choice between the
two. And if I appreciate so highly the value of classical ballet, it is not
simply a matter of taste on my part, but because I see in it the perfect
expression of the Apollonian principle.

This antithesis between the Apollonian and the Dionysiac is
not original with Stravinsky. It comes from Nietzsche's *The
Birth of Tragedy*, but Stravinsky's moral is the polar opposite
of the German philosopher's. Ardent Wagnerite as he was at
this time, Nietzsche is all for the Dionysiac point of view; for
inspiration, creative intoxication, and the surpassing of one's self
in the ardour of imaginative effort. Stravinsky, on the other
hand, preaches rule, order, precise definition, and precise delimita-
tion. This contrast between Apollonian and Dionysiac, or classic
and romantic, can be found in all the arts, sometimes at the same
period, more often in alternation as one generation succeeds
another. Since the name of the god Apollo has been invoked in
Stravinsky's philosophic expression of the neo-classical ideal, we
should discover how he hymns Apollo in music. *Apollon
Musagète* is not one of the most dynamic of Stravinsky's neo-
classical works, but it is one of the clearest expressions of his
principle. It is scored for strings alone, and this is one facet of
the discipline that appeals so strongly to this composer. Quite
deliberately he rules out the varied colours of wind instruments
and deeply explores the sonorities of violins, violas, celli, and
basses.

Stravinsky: *Apollon Musagète*. LONDON LL 1401 (DECCA LXT
    5169).

Apollo, Ruler of the Muses, represents only one phase of neo-
classicism in the works of Stravinsky. There are many others.
There is, for instance, his revival of the strictly formal operatic
scene in several movements. His one big opera, *The Rake's
Progress*, brings us back after more than a century of experiment
in other directions to the fact that opera is a highly stylized or
conventionalized form of art. *The Rake's Progress* is cast in a
pattern deliberately reminiscent of the most famous rake's progress

in the literature of opera, Mozart's *Don Giovanni*, even including *recitativo secco* with harpsichord accompaniment. The principal aria for Anne Truelove, Stravinsky's heroine, is in three sections. After the orchestral introduction, the singer begins with a recitative. The second section is an *andante*, and then, after another short recitative, the scene concludes with a brilliant *allegro*. This is exactly the way in which the major arias of Beethoven's *Fidelio* and other operas of its period are constructed. The recitative and *andante* have to do with Anne's tenderness towards Tom Rakewell, who has deserted her, while the *allegro* expresses her resolve to find and serve him.

Stravinsky: *The Rake's Progress, Act I, Scene 3*. COLUMBIA SL 125 (PHILIPS ABL 3055–7).

There are other aspects of contemporary neo-classicism beside those represented by the ideas of Stravinsky. Some composers, such as Paul Hindemith, arrive at it through a powerful sense of identification with the music of the more or less remote past. One of the most remarkable characteristics of the music of our time is that the scholar and composer no longer hate each other; indeed, composers like Hindemith are among the most learned of musical historians. Hindemith's history is expressed in composition rather than verbal treatises, but like a thorough work of scholarship, it is based upon extensive and often highly involved research. An example is the *Concert of the Angels* from Hindemith's symphony, *Mathis der Maler*. This is actually a suite drawn from his opera about the life and work of the sixteenth-century painter, Mathias Grünewald. 'Concert of the Angels' is the title of one panel in Grünewald's most famous work, the altarpiece he painted for the abbey church of Isenheim in Alsace. Hindemith's music is, as he himself put it, based on 'old folksongs, war songs of the Reformation period, and Gregorian Chant.' The association of this old German musical material with the paintings of Grünewald and the atmosphere of his life and time all combine into a powerful evocation of the Gothic past.

Hindemith: *Symphony: Mathis der Maler*. DECCA 9818 (DGG DG 16130).

Still another aspect of neo-classicism remains to be touched upon. It is one with which Stravinsky has no sympathy at all, but with which the name of Paul Hindemith is strongly identified. Many contemporary composers, following Hindemith's lead,

L

have come to believe that in our time creative music and the audience have grown so far apart that the contemporary composer is in danger of losing touch with society altogether.   Consequently many composers are now making a deliberate, self-conscious attempt to forge an idiom that the public will readily understand, and thereby return the composer to an immediately functional status in his world.   This is something entirely new.   I know of no period in the past when such a philosophy was preached or even dreamed of; up to now the composer's place in society, for better or for worse, has simply been taken for granted.   The deliberate effort to woo the audience has led Aaron Copland and others of his persuasion back to folklore; if one is going to write music for the people one may as well employ material which the people themselves have created.   The result may perhaps be better described as neo-romantic than neo-classical; the dividing line is subtle and difficult to maintain in any dogmatic way.

A good example of neo-classicism in this phase is the slow movement of the *Cello Concerto* by the American composer, Virgil Thomson.   This is called *Variations on a Southern Hymn*.   The tune is an old one entitled *Tribulation* which appears consistently through the shape-note hymnals which have been used in the southern states for one hundred and fifty years.

Virgil Thomson: *Cello Concerto*.   COLUMBIA ML 4468.

APPENDIX

BOOKS

IGOR STRAVINSKY: *An Autobiography* and *The Poetics of Music*.
PAUL HINDEMITH: *A Composer's World*.

RECORDS

Alfred Frankenstein writes on the subject of records: 'Igor Stravinsky is one of the most richly and extensively recorded of all composers.   He has himself conducted recordings of nearly all his orchestral works, and these recordings are recommended above all others—Columbia (Columbia or Philips).   Stravinsky regards the disk as a method for establishing the true and correct interpretation of his music, and he makes an eloquent case for his views in this regard.   His recordings are too numerous to list.

'A similar situation exists with regard to recordings of the music of Paul Hindemith; he is by far his own finest interpreter, but his list of recordings is relatively small.   Of special importance are the following, all played by the Berlin Philharmonic Orchestra under Hindemith's direction:

> *Theme and Variations After the Four Temperaments.* DECCA 9829.
> *Symphonic Metamorphosis of Themes by Carl Maria von Weber.* (DGG DGM 18301.)
> *Symphony from Die Harmonie der Welt.* DECCA 9765 (DGG DGM 18181).
> *Kammermusik, Op. 24, Nos. 1 and 2.* CONTEMPORARY 101.

'An extremely important Hindemith work not conducted by the composer is:

> *Nobilissima Visione.* ANGEL 35221 (COLUMBIA 33 CX 1241).

'The listener should also investigate Hindemith's rich and varied contributions to the literature of the string quartet and the sonata for solo instruments and piano.

'Other important recordings in the neo-classic and neo-romantic area are as follows:

> POULENC: *Trio and Sextet.* REB 7.
> VILLA LOBOS: *Bachianas Brasileiras No. 1.* CAPITOL P 8147 (CAPITOL CTL 7014).*
> ROREM: *Sonata for Piano, No. 2.* LONDON LL 759 (DECCA LXT 2812).'

47

Andrew Porter

TWENTIETH-CENTURY NATIONALISM

A<small>T</small> the opening of the twentieth century the outlying countries of Europe began to develop schools and styles of their own which found their inspiration either directly in national folk music or else more loosely in what might be termed national characteristics. Those peripheral countries, which had formerly produced only small-scale compositions or works based on foreign models, now evolved styles of their own; and composers emerged who wrote music that was distinctively Spanish or English or Scandinavian.

For a long time the only truly Spanish music was the extremely rich and varied folk music; in each province it had distinctive characteristics. The one native art form, the *Zarzuela*, or Spanish operetta or musical comedy, was eclectic; its ingredients were largely derived from French vaudeville and Italian *opera buffa*. The first decisive national movement came from Felipe Pedrell (1841–1922), who, though not a great composer, was a great teacher and is venerated to this day by all Spanish composers. In his two operas he attempted to write music that would make distinctive use of the rich treasury of folk-song. Pedrell was succeeded by Albéniz and Granados. Albéniz, born in 1860, was by seven years the senior. His masterpiece is *Ibéria*, four books of piano pieces which are brilliant, picturesque descriptions of the people and atmosphere of Andalusia. Granados had a sharper invention and a more purely musical talent. We do not know how much he might have achieved, had he not lost his life in the sinking of the *Lusitania* in 1915 when he was on his way back from the New York *première* of his opera, *Goyescas*. But we can tell how strong, decisive, and distinctive is the national feeling in Granados from his song, *El majo discreto* (*The Discreet Lover*).

Granados: *El majo discreto* (*Tonadillas*). HMV BLP 1037.

Meanwhile, there had already appeared a still sharper and more

300

brilliant Spanish talent in Manuel de Falla, born in 1876. A pupil of Pedrell, Falla flung himself passionately into the rediscovery of Spanish folk-song, and it penetrated the whole of his artistic personality. Spanish composers have never made any world impact as symphonists, but in the field of ballet Falla found his ideal medium. With his first ballet, *El amor brujo* (*Love the Magician*), he won a local success, and then, with *El sombrero de tres picos* (*The Three-cornered Hat*), world success. His genius for orchestration should be mentioned. His predecessors had tended to score rather lushly, but Falla's use of instruments was keen and clear and brilliant.

Manuel de Falla: *The Three-Cornered Hat*. LONDON LL 598 (DECCA LXT 2716).

Falla's creative career has a strange curve to it. He began with the rich, colourful opera *La vida breve*, given first in 1913. During World War I he produced his masterpieces, *Nights in the Gardens of Spain* and the two ballets. Then compositions grew less frequent and his style became more severe. The influence of Scarlatti began to make itself felt in such a work as the Harpsichord Concerto. Eventually Falla withdrew almost completely from the world and died in 1946 in a remote village in Argentina. His wonderful works of art have found no comparable successors in Spain.

In England folk-songs have never played such a part in the life of the people as they do—to this day—in Spain. The English folk-song heritage is rich and remarkable, but in a quiet, lyrical way, and the English musical renaissance did not find its starting-point in folk-song. The eclipse of English music during the nineteenth century was not so complete as we are often told, but certainly two giant shadows hung over most of the music that was produced: Handel and Mendelssohn. The first two decisively English composers to appear were Parry and Stanford, both excellently trained academic musicians whose work appears now to have been largely preparatory.

The first great English composer of the century, Edward Elgar, came from outside the academic circle and was conscious of being a self-made musician. His early compositions were not too well received, but at the turn of the century he established himself with two extraordinary masterpieces, though of very different weight and calibre: the oratorio *The Dream of Gerontius*, and the *Enigma*

Variations. Two symphonies, two concertos, the *Introduction and Allegro* for strings, and the *Symphonic Study : Falstaff* consolidated his reputation.

Foreigners often declare that they can find nothing specifically English in Elgar's music, a view that finds its extremest form in the epigram: 'When you have rendered unto Brahms the things that are Brahms's, and unto César the things that are César's, what is left but a handful of unimportant mannerisms.' Elgar unquestionably learned from both Brahms and César Franck, and in its actual facture his music is certainly German. All Englishmen, however, must feel a strongly English flavour in his music; for instance, in the first subject of his Cello Concerto. One proof of its Englishness is that no foreign cellist ever seems able to phrase it as we feel it ought to be phrased. Even a great interpreter like Casals makes it too emphatic and too rhetorical, whereas it should sound—as Elgar once said of a passage in his First Symphony— 'like something you hear down by the river'—a melody exhaled from the English landscape.

Elgar: *Cello Concerto in E minor.*   LONDON LS 95 (DECCA LX 3023).

There is more to Elgar's music than its Englishness; but we are concerned here with such passages as the first movement of the Cello Concerto, the *Introduction and Allegro*, and the pastoral interludes in *Falstaff*, rather than the mystic quality or the Edwardian swagger. These lyrical passages have much in common with English lyric poetry; they are shy, unemphatic, and delicate.

Ralph Vaughan Williams, fifteen years Elgar's junior and still to-day a prolific composer, gives us English music genuinely rooted in English folk-song. With his discovery of English folk-song Vaughan Williams found himself as a composer. Many of his compositions make direct use of folk-songs; others are influenced by the modes, the characteristic intervals, and the rhythms of folk-music. Vaughan Williams has not made the mistake of thinking that folk-melodies make good symphonic material, and in his set of eight symphonies there is rarely a direct folk-song quotation. But at the opening of the *Romanza* of his *Fifth Symphony*, for example, we hear a melody that seems again to be exhaled from the English countryside, although, unlike Elgar's melody, it is redolent of folk-song associations. Again, there are many other elements in Vaughan Williams besides

Englishness; and the most marked is a visionary quality which embraces compassion, fortitude, and the ability to look bravely on almost unendurable prospects.

Vaughan Williams: *Symphony No. 5 in D major.* LONDON LL 975 (DECCA LXT 2910).

Carl Nielsen (1865–1931) is a composer whose concern is more with national characteristics than with national folk-music. He made many arrangements of Danish folk-songs, but in his symphonic music he struck through to something deeper than actual folk-idioms. He tried to give some idea of what it was in a little essay he wrote about Funen, the island on which he was brought up. 'Everything in Funen is different from the rest of the world. The bees hum in a way of their own . . . and when the horse whinnies and the red cows low, why, anyone can hear that it is different from anywhere else. The stillness sings the same tune too, and even the trees dream and talk in their sleep with a Funen lilt.' And Nielsen's music too is different from anything else. His themes 'have a large free air about them; they diverge into some quaint lyrical backwater, or suddenly reveal an unexpected, even formidable strength and purpose.' Carl Nielsen in six symphonies, three concertos, and two operas gave Denmark a national music of its own.

Jean Sibelius was born in the same year as Nielsen, but while Nielsen is generally considered a humanist, and an optimistic one, Sibelius is regarded as the poet of nature. There is a good deal of the Russian in his musical personality; he is also a Finnish patriot: many of his works find their inspiration in the Finnish folk-sagas. But in the end it is because of his intensely personal works that we rate Sibelius so high: his seven symphonies and *Tapiola*. As constructions they are highly interesting and successful, but their real claim to greatness lies in something less fathomable. Sibelius has come nearer than anyone else to giving expression to those mysteries which man senses in nature. In Wordsworth's lines:

> No familiar shapes
> Remain, no pleasant images of trees,
> Or sea, or sky, no colours of green fields:
> But huge and mighty forms, that do not live
> Like living men.

There are several stories which show that Sibelius found direct inspiration in the landscapes of his native Finland. Bengt de

Törne related how he once told Sibelius how impressive he always found the first sight of Finland from the sea: reddish granite rocks rising out of the pale blue water, and a solitary island of a hard, archaic beauty. 'Yes,' Sibelius answered eagerly, and his eyes flashed. 'And when we see those granite rocks we know why we are able to treat the orchestra as we do.'

The Swan of Tuonela shows his individual treatment of the orchestra, and at the same time his concern with Finnish mythology and his ability to evoke an eerie, inhuman scene. Tuonela, the hell of Finnish mythology, is surrounded by a black river on which floats a swan, singing with weird beauty. The song is represented by the cor anglais, and the accompaniment contains only one oboe, one bass clarinet, four horns, three trombones, harp, drums, and muted strings divided into many parts.

Sibelius: *The Swan of Tuonela*. LONDON LL 843 (DECCA LXT 2831).

Sibelius is a strange, solitary, off-centre figure and his long silence forms one of the puzzling episodes in musical history. From about 1893 to 1925 he was immensely prolific, but his last work of any consequence, incidental music to *The Tempest*, was composed in 1926. Then, like Prospero, he 'abjured his art.' There has been much talk of an Eighth Symphony, and in 1945 he wrote to the English conductor, Basil Cameron: 'My 8th Symphony has been "finished" many times, but I am not content with it yet. When the time comes, it will be a pleasure to deliver it into your hands.'

Leoš Janáček is a rather different case from any of the other composers considered in this essay, for Czechoslovakia had already produced Dvořàk and Smetana, and so there was no question of 'founding' a national school in the twentieth century. Janáček's music derives from a close study of folk-songs, but even more from the actual inflexions of the speech of his native Moravia. He would jot down in musical notation the words that he heard spoken around him. 'The best way of becoming a good opera composer,' he wrote, 'is to study analytically the melodic curves and contours of human speech. . . . The melodic curves of speech as used in song give only a reflection of the spirit, weakened by the heat of the music itself. But the melodic curves of speech as used in the spoken word are a direct reflection of life.' Such was his genius that from short speech-phrases he could build large, coherent musical structures; and not only the voices, but the instruments too in his operas seem actually to be *uttering*. Such phrases also form the thematic material of some of his later purely instrumental works, and it must be admitted that in these works there is often a curious elliptical quality that proves hard to accept at first. But all his music is marked by spontaneity and originality.

Coupled to his purely musical gifts was a deep love and compassion for humanity, and a profound feeling for nature. The former finds expression in his operas *Jenufa*, *Katya Kabanova*, and the austere *House of the Dead*; the latter is found most specifically in the opera *The Cunning Little Vixen*, in which some of the characters are human, some animal. We hear both in his song cycle *The Diary of One Who Vanished*. This is a setting of twenty-one poems left behind by a farmer's son who was seduced by a gipsy and left his parents for her. Into a thirty-minute cycle Janáček compressed the drama, which takes on a clean, fierce purity like that of Hardy's *Tess of the Durbervilles*.

Janáček: *The Diary of One Who Vanished*.   EPIC 3LC 3121 (PHILIPS ABR 4041).

APPENDIX

BOOKS

JAIME PAHISSA: *Manuel de Falla*.
DIANA MCVEAGH: *Edward Elgar*.
FRANK HOWES: *The Music of Ralph Vaughan Williams*.
ROBERT SIMPSON: *Carl Nielsen: Symphonist*.
CECIL GRAY: *Sibelius*.

RECORDS

FALLA: *Love the Magician*.   WESTMINSTER 5238 or ANGEL 35089. *Master Peter's Puppet Show*. (DUCRETET-THOMSON DTL 93010). *Nights in the Gardens of Spain*. *Homenajes*. ENGLISH COLUMBIA 33 CX 1221.

ELGAR: *Enigma Variations, etc.* COLUMBIA ML 5031 (PHILIPS ABL 3053). *Falstaff*. ENGLISH DECCA LXT 2940.

VAUGHAN WILLIAMS: *The Symphonies*. LONDON (DECCA, 8 records). *Job—A Masque for Dancing*. ENGLISH DECCA LXT 2937.

NIELSEN: *Symphony No. 5*. LONDON LL 1143 (DECCA LXT 2980). *Flute Concerto*. *Clarinet Concerto*. LONDON LL 1124 (DECCA LXT 2979).

SIBELIUS: *Symphony No. 4*. *Tapiola*. ANGEL 35082 (COLUMBIA 33 CX 1125). *Symphonies Nos. 6 and 7*. ANGEL 35316 (COLUMBIA 33 CX 1341).

JANÁČEK: *Sinfonietta*. *Taras Bulba*. VOX PL 9710 (E).

* L

48

Andrew Porter

TWENTIETH-CENTURY MUSIC:
THE SECOND GENERATION

THE greatest of the twentieth-century nationalist composers was Béla Bartók, who was born in Hungary in 1881 and died in New York in 1945. The central problem of his creative career was his struggle to unite the melodies and rhythms of eastern European folk-music and the harmonic and contrapuntal idiom of the west. The western music to influence him was that of Brahms, Wagner, Liszt, Debussy, Richard Strauss, and Stravinsky, but all these elements took on new properties when fused in the crucible of his entirely individual imagination.

In 1920 Bartók wrote an article on folk-music which must furnish the text for any consideration of twentieth-century nationalism. He argued that there was no solution but a complete break with the nineteenth century. Invaluable help was given to this rejuvenation by a kind of peasant music hitherto unknown. The right type of peasant music, Bartók continued, 'is most varied and perfect in all its forms. Its expressive power is amazing, and at the same time it is void of all sentimentality and superfluous ornaments. It is simple, sometimes primitive, but never silly, and it is the ideal starting-point for a musical renaissance.'

Bartók went on to describe three ways in which peasant music could be taken over and transmuted into modern music. First, one could simply take the tune, either as it stood or slightly varied, and provide it with an accompaniment. Second, the composer could use, not an actual peasant melody, but one of his own invented in emulation of the real thing. Or third, neither peasant melodies nor imitations would be found in the music, but it would be pervaded by their atmosphere. By this third method the composer completely absorbs the idiom of peasant music, which becomes his musical mother tongue.

Bartók cited his compatriot, Zoltán Kodály, as a composer of this last kind of folk-inspired music. Together Bartók and Kodály travelled through the countryside, collecting peasant music, and Kodály's *Psalmus Hungaricus* and his opera *Háry János* are both large works steeped in the atmosphere of Hungarian folk-music. Bartók himself composed music in each of his three categories. The first—an original tune with ornamental setting—is well exemplified in his collection of short piano pieces, *For Children*. The harmonies are by no means those of our ordinary western common chords. The tune itself, with its characteristic intervals, has been allowed to suggest the chords and counterpoints with which it is to be accompanied.

Bartók: *For Children*. BARTÓK 919–20 (alt. COLUMBIA 33 CX 1176 and 1316).

For Children appeared in 1908, the year that also saw the production of his First String Quartet. Bartók's six string quartets—the last dates from 1939—are generally considered the most important contribution to the *genre* since those of Beethoven. The Sixth Quartet shows us utterly contemporary music that has sprung from peasant soil. In the sad theme which opens each of its four movements we seem to hear a farewell to Hungary. It is certainly not a real folk theme, nor an invented one, but it breathes the spirit of the country. Then comes a characteristic late-Bartók exposition: three notes in octaves; the same phrase in reverse order, pitched a tone higher, and so on; then a lively twirling theme, extracted from the opening, which is whisked away in brisk counterpoint. This is enough to show that Bartók was no simple 'folky' composer.

Bartók: *String Quartet No. 6*. COLUMBIA ML 4280 (PHILIPS ABL 3093).

Bartók's toughest music was written during his middle period, the late 1920's and early 1930's. Then his style clarified and he went out to meet his listeners in such works as the *Music for Percussion and Strings* (1936), the *Concerto for Orchestra* (1943), and the Third Piano Concerto (1945). Bartók founded no school and has had no successors; and so he is the type-figure of the undoctrinaire composer, the nationalist whose music can be understood without reference to its national background.

In considering the undoctrinaire composers we should remember, first, that nothing links them together except, tenuously, alism; and second, that there is no important living composer has not been influenced, directly or indirectly, by Stravinsky, demith, and Schönberg. Stravinsky's influence is strong in the music of Aaron Copland, who may serve as an example of the American nationalist composer, European-trained, but aiming to write specifically American music.

Copland was born in Brooklyn in 1900 and began to study composition in America. In 1921 he left for Paris and stayed three years, studying with Nadia Boulanger. The principal fruit of this period was a Symphony for Organ and Orchestra. Walter Damrosch first performed it in New York in 1925 and remarked to the audience at the end of the performance: 'If a young man at the age of twenty-three can write a symphony like that, in five years he will be ready to commit murder.' Copland waited ten years, and then produced the bright, jazzy *El Salon Mexico*. At this time he decided to reach out to the public which had grown up around the radio, the gramophone, and the cinema. He wrote: 'It made no sense to ignore the new public and to write as if they did not exist. I felt that it was worth the effort to see if I couldn't say what I had to say in the simplest possible terms.'

As Bartók collected Hungarian peasant music, so Copland investigated cowboy tunes, spirituals, revivalist hymns, and Shaker songs. The score to the ballet *Billy the Kid* (1938) was the first product of this reaching out to the new public, and in it Copland used cowboy songs as the basis for long sections of the score. Just as the feel of an English folk-song is sensed under many of Vaughan Williams's pages, so cowboy tunes lie beneath some of Copland's, but do not come to the surface in specific quotations. Copland turned to ballet, as Falla had in Spain, and in *Rodeo* (1942) the handling of cowboy tunes was more extended and more varied, and the tunes called *If he'd be a buckaroo by trade* and *Sis Joe* are subjected to a highly complex development.

Copland: *Rodeo*. CAPITOL L 8198 (CAPITOL CCL 7516).*

The best of all Copland's ballet scores is *Appalachian Spring* (1943–4), a lyrical evocative score of great beauty. Copland's movement towards simplicity reaches its fitting consummation in five variations on the lovely Shaker tune: *The Gift to be simple*. At its best Copland's music has almost the punch and precision of Stravinsky's in the sureness of the instrumental texture and the sophistication of rhythmic interplay. The simplicity and the sophistication come together in the Third Symphony, perhaps his most important work to date.

Copland has been likened in one respect to Vaughan Williams: Samuel Barber can perhaps be likened to Elgar. He is a composer whose music does not make specific use of national music, but somehow breathes the spirit of the country in which it is written. Barber, like Elgar, is a late romantic and a composer with a rare lyrical gift and a rich sonic imagination. His more daring pieces, such as the ballet suite *Medea* and the Piano Sonata, can hardly be called venturesome, but they are nevertheless fine music. *Knoxville, Summer of 1915*, a remembrance of childhood, is one of the most evocative pieces of American music there is, and as American as Elgar's Cello Concerto is English. The shape and the rise and fall of Barber's phrases seems to have been suggested by the actual inflexions of American speech.

Barber: *Knoxville, Summer of 1915*. COLUMBIA ML 2174.

Benjamin Britten, born in 1913, is Britain's leading composer, and certainly undoctrinaire. Mozart, Verdi, Mahler, and Alban Berg have all been absorbed in a style which is strikingly personal, but hard to define. It is very English in its feeling for the language; no one since Purcell has set English lyric poetry so sensitively. The landscapes that Britten evokes are English, but folk-music has played no part in his melodic or harmonic invention. The melodic felicity, dramatic sense, and individual colouring of Britten's music can be heard in the *Sea Interludes* from his opera *Peter Grimes*.

Britten: *Sea Interludes and Passacaglia: Peter Grimes*. LONDON LL 917 (DECCA LW 5244).

Britten reached a world public in 1937 with his *Variations on a Theme of Frank Bridge* for string orchestra which has been called 'one of the landmarks of string orchestral writing in musical history.' In 1945 *Peter Grimes* was produced, and it became the first English opera to meet with international success. *Peter Grimes* was followed by three chamber operas: *The Rape of Lucretia*, *Albert Herring*, and the children's opera, *Let's Make an Opera*. Then for Covent Garden Britten wrote *Billy Budd* and the ill-starred Coronation opera, *Gloriana*; and most recently he has composed another chamber opera, *The Turn of the Screw*.

The success of *Peter Grimes* made possible that revival of English opera which has been so prominent a feature of the British musical scene since the war. One of its products has been Sir William Walton's *Troilus and Cressida*, already heard in San Francisco, New York, and Milan. Walton, born in 1902, leapt before the world at the age of twenty with his *Façade*; poems by Edith Sitwell recited to the accompaniment of brilliant, barbed chamber music. In 1931 he revitalized English oratorio with the powerful *Belshazzar's Feast*; between 1932 and 1935 a Symphony appeared. In 1939 he wrote a Violin Concerto, and it became clear that his affiliations were now with the Romantics. Other interesting composers to-day are Michael Tippett, composer of the opera *The Midsummer Marriage*, and Lennox Berkeley, who writes beautifully fashioned chamber music, and in his latest work, *Ruth*, has carried forward the line of English chamber opera that begins with Purcell's *Dido and Aeneas*.

In Italy Luigi Dallapiccola, born in 1904, ranks as a twelve-note composer, but he could not be called doctrinaire. His use of the twelve-note system stems from Alban Berg rather than Schönberg, but is modified at every turn by his concern for expressive colouring and dramatic suggestiveness. His opera, *The Prisoner*, is one of the most remarkable compositions of our time. It was preceded by the *Songs of Imprisonment*, a choral triptych inspired by sympathy for those who suffered in the Second World War. The opening of the first song, the *Prayer of Mary Stuart*, is typical of Dallapiccola's methods. The *Dies Irae* theme sounds from the harps and timpani, and against it a twelve-note theme moves upwards on two pianos. Then the voices enter, whispering the queen's prayer.

Dallapiccola: *Canti di Prigionia*. ANGEL 35228 (COLUMBIA 33 CX 1353).

Many other composers could legitimately be discussed in this essay. Not many German composers; their allegiances have generally been to Hindemith or to twelve-note music. In Scandinavia, too, Hindemith has been an almost decisive influence, while in France neo-classicism and Stravinsky have tended to prevail. But there are, for example, the Swiss composers led by Ernest Bloch (whom we could reckon a Jewish nationalist) and Frank Martin. In Russia we must settle for the one indisputably great composer produced there in our day. Shostakovich's music has always been distinctively Russian in flavour, although it has drawn on western tradition, being particularly influenced by Mahler. At one time it seemed that Shostakovich's talent might have been spoiled by the directives of Soviet culture, but in his Tenth Symphony and the Violin Concerto Shostakovich has discovered his authentic voice again. The long, gradually unrolling melody that opens his Tenth Symphony is as far removed from Russian folk-song as was the opening theme of Bartók's Sixth Quartet from Hungarian folk-song. It is as evidently the product of an individual mind as any music can be, and yet, like our other examples, it seems to breathe the atmosphere of the country in which it was composed.

Shostakovich: *Symphony No. 10.* COLUMBIA ML 4959 (PHILIPS ABL 3052).

APPENDIX

BOOKS

HALSEY STEVENS: *The Life and Music of Béla Bartók.*
ARTHUR BERGER: *Aaron Copland.*
NATHAN BRODER: *Samuel Barber.*
ed. DONALD MITCHELL and HANS KELLER: *Benjamin Britten.*
ed. OSCAR THOMPSON: *Great Modern Composers.*

RECORDS

BARTÓK: *Six String Quartets.* COLUMBIA ML 4278–80 (PHILIPS ABL 3064/3093/3112) or ANGEL 35240–2 (COLUMBIA 33 CX 1245/1267/1285). *Third Piano Concerto.* LONDON LL 945 (DECCA LXT 2894).
COPLAND: *Appalachian Spring. El Salon Mexico.** VICTOR LCT 1134 or PHILIPS NBR 6019.* *Third Symphony.* MERCURY 50018 (MERCURY MG 50018).
BRITTEN: *The Turn of the Screw.* LONDON XLL 1207–8 (DECCA LXT 5038–9). *Serenade for Tenor, Horn, and Strings. Les Illuminations.* LONDON LL 5358 (ENGLISH DECCA LXT 2941). *A Ceremony of Carols.* LONDON LL 1136 (ENGLISH DECCA LW 5070).
SHOSTAKOVICH: *Violin Concerto.* COLUMBIA ML 5077 (PHILIPS ABL 3103). *Piano Quintet.* CAPITOL P 8171 (ENGLISH DECCA LXT 2749). *Symphony No. 10.* HMV ALP 1322.

49

Wilfrid Mellers

MUSIC AND SOCIETY NOW

IN Shakespeare's time, in England, the young composer was taught to write like Byrd, who in turn based his idiom on the European convention which we associate with Palestrina. In Handel's time the young composer was trained to write like Handel. There was no other way: for conformity to an established convention meant the acceptance of inherited ideas about man's place in the universe and the relationship of man to man. Personal feeling could flower when rooted in such acceptance; and every vital work of art is a point of intersection between the private and the public life. But though Bach, for instance, tells us through his music what he felt about God and man, that was not his primary intention. For him music was not a conscious expression of the self: it was a liturgical and social act.

There is to-day no such clearly defined relationship between musical technique and the values and beliefs in the light of which we live. Almost certainly we exaggerate the heterogeneous nature of twentieth-century styles: an observer a hundred years hence may discover points of accord between composers who seem to us as extravagantly dissimilar as Stravinsky and Vaughan Williams. None the less, it is broadly true that to-day the relationship between techniques and values is confused rather than clear, for the obvious reason that our values are themselves confused. We doubt whether there can be *the* right musical technique because we doubt whether there can be *the* right conception of moral order. When in the mid eighteenth century Rameau deduced his theory of harmony from the practice of his contemporaries he was convinced that he had given a scientifically unanswerable account of the laws governing musical composition. He was equally convinced that the past was irrelevant: that music composed according to his prescription would culminate in the

perfection of his art, for the perfectability of music must complement that of man.   As a matter of scientific fact, he was wrong
on both counts.   But what he said was true while it lasted, in so
far as it was deduced from man's creative instincts and needs.
His truth was of the kind that matters to artists, because it was at
once a technique and a morality.   For artists it is a hindrance,
not a help, to know more but believe less.

Now whatever explanation one may give of the disintegration
of tradition that occurred during the nineteenth century—it
certainly had something to do with individualistic capitalism and
the Industrial Revolution—there can be no doubt that it sprang
from a failure of what is usually called belief.   Perhaps the
process starts with Beethoven: for whereas Mozart still preserved
an equilibrium between acceptance and protest, Beethoven, seeking a personal belief, delivered a frontal assault on a world which,
he thought, needed change.   Beethovenian egoism led to Wagnerian egomania: for Wagner believed in himself so heroically
that he could offer his emotions as a substitute for what concepts
such as God and Civilization had meant in the past.   Perhaps the
quintessential romantic artist is Wagner's successor, Delius, who
believed not at all in God and very little in mankind: and not even
in his own senses sufficiently to offer them as a Music of the Future,
so that the dominant emotion in his work is a powerful regret.
A more extreme form of this reliance on personal sensation is found
in some of the middle period music of Debussy, in which God and
Society are reduced to a momentary tremor of the nerves.

Belief in oneself is a dangerous substitute for belief in God or
Reason or Truth or any other absolute.   Similarly, the cultivation
of your own sensations in the Ivory Tower is all very well if your
sensibility is as delicate and subtle as that of Debussy.   But for
most people the spirit atrophies unless it has contact with other
human beings.   It is not therefore surprising that the history of
modern music should have been largely a series of attempts to
evade the implications of the Ivory Tower.   The difficulty is that
with the collapse of inherited ideas of order every composer, or
group of composers, has to work out the problem afresh, spending
weary years in arriving at the point where Byrd, Handel, Mozart,
Beethoven, or even Wagner started.

The attempt to achieve a consistent stylization which is at the
same time adequate to our relatively chaotic world lies behind

Debussy's rediscovery of the melodic rather than harmonic tonality of medieval music: behind Sibelius's search for a 'monistic' symphony: behind Bartók's attempt to fuse melodic and rhythmic techniques suggested by Magyar folk-music with Debussyan harmony, Bachian counterpoint, and the formal explorations of late Beethoven. The same need impelled Stravinsky to approach music once more as ritual—whether primitive, liturgical, or theatrically baroque: impelled Schönberg to evolve the twelve-note technique: impelled Hindemith to formulate a theory of tonality which should be as apposite to the twentieth century as was Rameau's theory to the eighteenth. The central composers of our time—Debussy, Schönberg, Stravinsky, Bartók, and Hindemith—have all evolved over the past forty years techniques which bear some resemblance to the principles governing medieval and oriental music. Debussy and Stravinsky in particular created a world of sound remote from the post-Renaissance idea of time progression; and some later developments of twelve-note music have carried this tendency to an extreme point. Perhaps it is not altogether fanciful to sense a relationship between Webern's grotesque treatment of the human voice and the deliberately un-natural vocal techniques employed by medieval and by eastern singers. The voice is dehumanized because it must become super-natural law.

Young composers such as Stockhausen, Boulez, and Nono have taken Webern as a spring-board to create a music even more mathematical in its order than his, since it is organized by rhythmic and dynamic, as well as by linear series. Such a very different composer as Messiaen has employed a highly sensuous harmonic vocabulary in a manner divorced from the traditional notion of progression, organizing his music by rhythmic rather than by harmonic means. In the United States Elliott Carter has experimented with another complex technique that recalls the medieval principle of isochronous rhythm. By way of 'metrical modulations' the tempo and even the dimensions of every section of a composition are controlled by a mathematical interrelation of the rhythms of the parts. Other Americans, taking a hint from the pioneer work of Charles Ives and Edgar Varese, have thrown over pitch notation to create music out of a *collage* of sounds existing in time, the spacing and duration of the noises being dictated by mathematical laws or even by chance: the throw of the dice, being a 'law' of chance, is more significant than a 'morbid' preoccupation with personal feeling! The music of John Cage, like that of the extremist followers of Webern in Europe, naturally enough dispenses with the human intermediary, the performer, and relies on electronic reproduction. Reaction against Wagnerian egomania could hardly go further than this. Indeed, there are signs that the electronic composers are becoming aware of the paradox in their position: for the logical outcome of the rejection of the personality is silence.

Perhaps it may come to that: a world without art is conceivable, though most of us, reared in a long humanist tradition, preserve a weakness for the perverse tragi-comedy of our fallible lives. However this may be, we have to admit that, below and beyond the 'conscious' attitudes of extremists, we can detect a change of approach, evolved instinctively over a long period of years, in the music of men such as Stravinsky, Schönberg, Hindemith, and Bartók. We do not yet know what it means; but it is at least possible that we are living at the end of a cycle that began with the Renaissance. The music of these great men contains many elements which preserve continuity with the past. It may also contain elements which reflect a changing conception of man's nature and destiny, whether involving a renewed respect for supernatural authority or subservience to the laboratory's mathematical law.

All this seems very remote from the conditions of practical music-making to-day. Few people listen to the music of Schönberg, Bartók, Stravinsky, or Webern; almost no one apart from themselves listens to the electronic composers, who perhaps need an audience no more than they need performers. Quite understandably the 'average' musical person in the twentieth century has tended to use music—mainly nineteenth-century music—as an evasion of the perplexities of modern life. None the less one should remember that this desire to listen exclusively to the music of the past rather than to that of one's own time is a phenomenon that has never happened before.

To fill the gap that 'art' music ought to fill if it had a sense of social obligation, a vast mechanized industry of music manufacture was developed to provide entertainment at a debased level. This industry is nothing like a genuine folk-culture, because it is not a spontaneous expression of man's creativity but is imposed on people for reasons of commercial expediency. Commercial music to-day panders to people's feeling of insecurity—cultivating a fatuous optimism or a flabby despair—because it is the product of a society that does not know what it believes in. The position is the more depressing because the public for commercial music, no less than that for nineteenth-century orchestral music, is passive rather than active.

Moreover, commercial music, like the academic tradition and the majority of the concert-going public, lives on the past: since the separation of 'art' music from entertainment it could hardly do otherwise. The music of *hoi polloi* derives its harmony, with pointed irony, from Massenet, Debussy, and Delius—from a kind of plastic Ivory Tower. It is precisely its synthetic, manufactured quality, rather than its vulgarity, that makes it so immorally potent a weapon. It cultivates bogus emotion and makes genuine feeling difficult to recognize, using the same technique as commercial advertising and the glycerine tears of Hollywood. And the ultimate irony is that synthetic music is the only kind that bears an economically sound relation to the community. The position of the 'serious' composer is fallacious because he is, by the nature of his calling, still living in the handicraft age in an age of mechanization.

It may seem that there can never be a *via media* between the mathematical abstraction of the electronic composers and the synthetic mass emotions of commercial music; none the less, I suppose the relatively traditional, non-electronicized composers go on working because they think there may be. Certainly, the more good music that can be written for a commercial function, the better for both art and commerce. As things are, the composer can seldom be employed by commerce without being involved in some degree of emotional simulation; while his traditional employers, the Church and State, have no use for him.

The twentieth-century composer's position is unprecedented in the sense that he is willy-nilly a parasite. A real musical culture should not be a museum culture based mainly on the music of past ages; nor should it be, like most commercial music, a drug. It should be the active embodiment in sound of the life of a community—of the everyday demands of people's work and play and of their deepest spiritual needs. Clearly, a more creative conception of musical culture can come only with a more creative society.

The composer to-day has to accept the fact that both a haughty isolation and a subservience to the values of commerce may involve a kind of dishonesty. But—except when he is young—he will not, if he is truly creative, be greatly concerned about his 'predicament.' He will be too busy writing as well as he can for the public that wants him, small though it may be. He will do so because he believes that authentic creation keeps alive the human spirit; and because he believes, or at any rate hopes, that the public that wants him is growing and will continue to grow, in so far as his apprehension of the world is more honest, more sensitive, and ultimately stronger than that of commercial art. In his more sanguine moments he can envisage a day—perhaps for his children's children—when the distinction between art and commerce shall have become meaningless.

INDEX

INDEX

Abélard, 34
Adam de la Halle, 30, 49–50
Adam of Fulda, 95
Agazzari, 156
Agricola, 193
air de cour, 91
Albéniz, 300
Albinoni, 158–9, 164
Alfonso X (*Alfonoso el Sabio*), 30
Alison, Richard, 125
Altnikol, 193
Ambrose, Saint, 17
Ambrosian chant, 17
Andrea da Firenze, 56
Andrew of Crete, 12
Anonymous IV, 43
Anthonella da Caserta, 56
Apollo, hymns to, 9–10
Arcadelt, Jacques, 110–11
aria, 150–4; *da capo* aria, 153–4, 203, 220
Ars Antiqua, 50
Ars Nova, 49–66, 74, 88, 117; in France, 49–54; in Italy, 55–60
Ars Novae Musicae, 50
atonality, 284, 288–90
aulos, 9
Auric, 253
ayre, 128–9

Bach, Carl Philipp Emanuel, 193, 210–12, 216–17, 227
Bach, Johann Christian, 193, 217–218, 232
Bach, Johann Sebastian, 6, 37, 152, 164, 179, 186, 187, 188–9, 191, 193–9, 205, 208–11, 214, 237, 295, 312, 314
Bach, Wilhelm Friedemann, 215–216
Baïf, Jean Antoine de, 90

Balakirev, 271, 277
ballade, 49
ballata, 56–7
balletti (ballet), 127
Banchieri, 122
Barber, Samuel, 309
Barlach, 289
baroque, characteristics of baroque music, 3–4, 137–142, 170, 220
Bartlet, John, 129
Bartók, 247, 287, 306–8, 311, 314–15
Beethoven, 4–6, 37, 207, 212, 231, 237–42, 244–7, 259, 261–4, 267, 269, 272, 274, 297, 313
Bellini, 257–8, 270, 276–7
Berg, 291–3, 309–10
Berkeley, Lennox, 310
Berlioz, 245–6, 253, 258, 270, 274
Bernart de Ventadour, 27–9, 31
Binchois, 61–2, 71, 75
Bizet, 259
Bloch, 310
Blom, Eric, quoted, 234–5
Boccaccio, 55, 74
Böhm, 188, 207
Boileau, 196
Borodin, 259, 265, 277–8
Boulanger, 308
Boulez, 274, 314
Boyce, 159
Brady, Nicholas, 170
Brahms, 245–7, 251–2, 261, 264–265, 272, 278–9, 302, 306
Britten, 280, 309
Bruckner, 243–4, 248
Buchner, Hans, 96
Bukofzer, Manfred, 65, 68
Bull, 125, 131–2, 188
Bülow, Hans von, 272
Buxtehude, 188–9, 193
Byrd, 2–3, 5–6, 124–6, 132, 312–313

Teaching
Achievement
Motivation

Teaching Achievement Motivation

Theory and Practice in Psychological Education

Alfred S. Alschuler
Diane Tabor
James McIntyre

with a Preface by
David C. McClelland

Camden County College
Wolverton Library

WITHDRAWN

Education Ventures, Inc.
Middletown, Conn.

Behavioral Science Center
of the Sterling Institute
Cambridge, Mass.

Copyright 1970 by Education Ventures, Inc., 209 Court St.,
Middletown, Conn. 06457. Direct reproduction of materials
from this book may be made only with permission of the
copyright holder.

Copyright is claimed until December 31, 1975. Thereafter, all
portions of this work covered by this copyright will be in the
public domain.

The work describes activities of a project supported through
the Cooperative Research Program of the Office of Education, U.S. Department of Health, Education, and Welfare.

Library of Congress Catalog Card Number: 75-120415
Manufactured in the United States of America
First Printing

No man can reveal to you aught but that which
already lies half asleep in the dawning of your
knowledge.

Kahlil Gibran, *The Prophet* —

To our students—from junior high school through graduate school—who have helped us learn how to teach achievement motivation.

ACKNOWLEDGEMENTS

No educational effort of the scope of the Achievement Motivation Development Project can sustain itself without the willing help and enthusiasm of hundreds of people. First among them is Dr. David C. McClelland of Harvard, who provided "the roots of the tree" in his forefront studies of achievement motivation and who also gave continued direct support to the project, while at the same time—faithful to his own achievement motivation theories—he never restricted the initiative of project staff members. Dr. Richard deCharms, now of Washington University, supervised the project in its first year and continued to provide stimulation through his own development of origin-pawn concepts. Dr. David Kolb added insight and imagination to the first draft of the "future planning manuals," and Dr. Menoher Nadkarni taught the first achievement trainers how to give the course.

Of all the administrators, teachers, and students who contributed enterprise and imagination to the project, the people of Broad Meadows Junior High School in Quincy, Mass., hold a special place. Quincy Superintendent Robert Pruitt, now of the U.S. Office of Education, made the collaboration possible and gave it continued sustenance. Broad Meadows Principal Harry Beede encouraged our involvement with his school in all sorts of ways, and took the achievement motivation course himself. The participating teachers included: Althea Sawyer, Marilyn Robbins, Peggy Hoyle, Joe Long, Tom Callahan, Stella Krupka, Charles Hickey, Mary Bozoian, JoAnn Conroy, Tom Reagan, Scott Newell, Pat Cheverie, Anna Diamandopolus, John Sanderson, Carolyn Howell, Ellen Anastos, and Larry Maloney. Their adventurousness, creativity, and good rapport with their students contributed immeasurably to the project's success and to the validity of the kinds of courses and materials which emerged.

Invaluable contributions were made by imaginative teachers in other schools as well, including Ann Matthai and Leslie Altman of Needham, Mass., High School, Dr. Antoinette DiLoreto and John Lennon of Arlington, Mass. High School, and Gordon Alpert and Michael Dole of the Cambridge Friends School.

Elizabeth Wilson of our staff was both participant and organizational "whip" for trials of the teachers' workshop, and took charge of follow-up telephone interviews as well. Steve Rodewald and Beverly Silver carried out the interviews and coded and scored essential data. Wendy Gollub and Vic Atkins suggested revisions and improvements in the manuscript of this book. Janet Cohen made sense in creating the directions and models for the Origami Game. Nancy Raeburn—super-secretary, photographer, interviewer, reader, maintainer of peace and sanity—has our undiminished gratitude.

Finally, among the "others too numerous to mention," are hundreds of classroom teachers and students at the Harvard Graduate School of Education whose responses and suggestions helped in countless ways to remind us that educational programs, whatever their theoretical beauty, must "work" in the classroom.

CONTENTS

PREFACE

Schools are under tremendous public pressure today to improve their performance. They are criticized for being too traditional, for not knowing how to help disadvantaged children overcome handicaps, for being too slow to try out new educational methods, or, if they do innovate, for abandoning standards and not teaching reading, writing, and arithmetic properly. For the average classroom teacher facing his students day after day, all the fuss and furor must be disconcerting and a little disturbing. What is the teacher supposed to do about his alleged shortcomings? He might gain in prestige, if not self-satisfaction, by becoming a part of some innovative educational project financed by federal or state funds. But most teachers cannot readily expect to be recruited for such programs; he may want to get started at improving his teaching right now. And he is likely, after all, to be more aware of the problems he faces from day to day than even the magazine article writers who so generously keep pointing out his shortcomings.

What is unusual and perhaps unique about this book is its aim of helping the classroom teacher directly. It is a "do it yourself" book based on the assumption that an average experienced teacher can learn the techniques it describes on his own or in collaboration with a group of other teachers; that he can enliven his classroom and improve his performance without benefit of special grants or even advanced training in a graduate school. What is needed instead is interest and persistence. The book offers the rest: it describes the new techniques; it tells the teacher how to organize a group to learn about them; it presents some of the theoretical background for the techniques; it explains how their effects on pupil performance can be measured.

With all that, it is not, strictly speaking, a "cookbook" which prescribes the "one best way" that every teacher should follow. Rather, it aims to encourage those characteristics in teachers—like achievement motivation, curiosity, and adaptability—which most teachers would like to create in their students. The emphasis throughout is on flexibility, on teaching general principles which every teacher can apply in his particular way in her particular classroom. Furthermore, many examples are given of how the principles have been applied already by other teachers, so that anyone wanting to profit from them will have some concrete guidelines to follow.

What is also unusual about this book is that the techniques suggested have all been tried out and have been shown to be effective in improving pupil performance. They are based on nearly 25 years of research on achievement motivation, a human characteristic about which many psychologists and educators now know a great deal. The authors of this book were responsible under an Office of Education grant for taking what was known about the achievement motive and using it to devise educational techniques for encouraging development of achievement motivation in students. They tried out a number of techniques and carefully checked each time to see whether these techniques worked in the sense of improving pupil performance. When they began to find that their interventions were successful, they looked for a way of sharing their newfound knowledge with teachers. This book is the result. It is solidly based on knowledge of what achievement motivation is and how it is best developed. As one who contributed to the collection of scientifically known facts about achievement motivation, I am pleased to find this knowledge put to work in such a practical way in this manual for teachers, for their benefit and for the benefit of their students.

Another unusual characteristic of this book is that it gives the findings of psychology away, so to speak. When new knowledge becomes available in psychology, as in other fields of science, it typically becomes part of the professional "bag of tricks," which other "unqualified" people are not supposed to use. Intelligence and achievement tests, for example, are not supposed to be administered by the average teacher because he theoretically does not understand without further training just what the tests mean. While such a professional attitude is in some cases justified, the authors felt that in this instance it would be better to make the knowledge available to anyone who was interested. They run some risks in doing so. They may be accused of "unprofessional" conduct in making techniques so generally available to "untrained" teachers. But they felt that these risks were slight compared to the enormous advantages to be gained both by teachers and pupils in making information available quickly and as widely as possible. After all, there is no solid evidence that, even if they had insisted that the knowledge be imparted to professionals only through accredited schools of education, the resulting practitioners would ever use that knowledge in classrooms or use it better than the average experienced teacher learning on her own with her fellows. But above all, perhaps, they felt it would undermine the whole spirit of the relationship they were trying to create between teachers and pupils if they themselves behaved in an authoritarian, restrictive manner. To put it very simply, they have faith in the average experienced teacher. They respect him and, above all, they believe that he has the potential to change, develop, and improve his teaching on his own. This book in a sense is dedicated to that average teacher, and the teacher's potential for growth. It expects that he can read and understand things on his own, gain from discussions with his fellows, take leadership for running group sections, find ways of implementing the general techniques described in his classroom, and abide by the sensible suggestions as to when and where *not* to do some of the things suggested. In a day when authors are gaining nationwide attention for criticizing the short-comings of the average classroom teacher, the authors of this book are sending out quite a different message. They say to the average teacher: "You are not a sluggish creature. You are potentially anything you want to be. You can learn on your own, and be innovative and imaginative in your own classroom. Here's how you start learning about these things."

While the mission of the authors of this book is quite serious in the sense that they want to improve pupil and teacher performance, no one can read very far into it without discovering that they also believe that teaching can be fun. In fact, a subtitle to the book might be something like "Games for learning about yourself and helping others." Many educational manuals make teaching and learning seem like a grim, mechanical business. This one manages to suggest that some of the games and role plays described can be really joyous without in any way diminishing the seriousness of what they are supposed to teach. At a minimum, even without an organized attempt to change things, any teacher can pick up from this manual a number of fascinating ideas about how to vary the classroom routine and make it more interesting both for himself and his pupils. But it is my hope, and certainly the authors' hope, that more teachers will become even more interested and involved as they get into the book and find ways of applying what is set forth here in English and social studies programs, in home rooms, in language classes, in shop, in coaching, in business and vocational education programs, and in classrooms of all types from kindergarten to the 12th grade.

David C. McClelland
Harvard University

INTRODUCTION

Seen in its most basic terms, this book is a response to the student who says "I don't care" when asked what he wants or what he wants to be.

It is relatively easy—sometimes convenient—to dismiss this student's answer simply as a matter of vocational indecision which will solve itself in time. Sensitive teachers know better. They recognize the "I don't care" as something deeper—as an enveloping student reaction not only to problems of school and work but also of life and self. These teachers want to *do* something, here and now, to deal more directly with the challenge of the "turned off" student. This book suggests a way. Its specific focus is achievement motivation. Its field is Psychological Education, which includes a variety of educational approaches to those students who suffer a loss of faith in their own future and in the possibility that they can take significant action, now or later, in the world around them.

Being "turned off" in this way reflects a pattern of actions, thoughts, and feelings. The most perceptive teachers know that the syndrome is not restricted to those we call the "rebels" or the "disadvantaged" or even to school activities alone. Yet the school has a mandate, and a claim on a preponderant amount of the student's time. Critics say that the claim has been badly used. Peter Schrag, for example, offers a despairing observation on the ways in which school affects the students we often call "average":

> [*The students'*] *modesty in achievement and ambition is matched by an inability to visualize anything richer—in experience or possessions, or in the world at large. The generation gap—for rich, for poor, for all—is precisely this: that many kids, for the first time, are growing up without a sense of the future. And that, for America, is new.*
>
> ("Growing Up on Mechanic Street," *Saturday Review,*
> March 21, 1970)

An older generation may complain about kids wanting too much, too soon. But it is phenomenally evident to those of us who work very closely with young people today that they more often *don't know what is worth wanting.* Future goals are not meaningful if students don't believe in them or don't see them as satisfying; our "turned off" students tell us so. That is the reason responsive teachers are seeking ways of directly meeting students' concerns and of helping students to mature in ways that teacher and student *together* desire. Thus we have new educational emphases on *involvement, relevance, independent inquiry, individualized instruction, student-directed learning.* All may prove to be frustratingly ineffective, however, if they are treated as mere modifications of course content and gentle embellishments of teaching processes and strategies. This book points early and often at the fundamental unreality of isolating thought from action in traditional school programs and the still more basic unreality of ignoring how students and teachers *feel* about what they are doing and where they are going.

What is proposed is a truer integration of thought, action, and feeling in the school's approach to helping students mature. This is not a job of patching conventional content together, but of developing and interpolating new subject matters in such areas as value clarification, interpersonal relationships, and creativity, which include thought, action, and feeling in a meaningful whole. Achievement motivation is one of these subject matters; the concern with excellence involves planning, excitement, and a specific set of action strategies. The teaching of achievement motivation, furthermore, does not predetermine the specific kinds of excellence which the student should want for himself. It involves a fundamental assumption that the desire to achieve something of excellence is inherent in all human beings. The specific way in which this basic human concern can be manifested, however, depends on each unique individual. Achievement motivation training encourages each individual to find his own unique way of satisfying his concern for excellence. Usually the specific goals students choose involve concerns for close relationships with others or for having influence as well as for meeting personal standards of excellence. In fact, one criterion kept foremost in our minds is how students can simultaneously satisfy a number of their needs without internal conflict. We do not believe that any one concern is more important than others or should exist to the exclusion of others.

Any or all of these concerns can be confronted in a student-teacher collaboration built on the student's needs. It is strange, in fact, that we ever forget this sense of common purpose. A teacher serves himself poorly if he deplores students' lack of motivation without looking to his own ways of teaching as a means for increasing student motivation. We have found, to our own great satisfaction, that few classroom teachers willingly cast blame for motivational problems on their students alone or on the environment alone.

Teachers working with the Achievement Motivation Development Project proved to be notably unconservative when they found innovative materials that would "work" in the classroom. Many such teachers tested the hypothesis that the potential for increased achievement motivation is in all of us, and that, given appropriate opportunities, it is likely to emerge in the classroom and beyond. Their work—and their skepticism as well—left us with a very optimistic view of the classroom teacher's concern about what students learn and how. The publication of this book, we trust, does not mean discontinuation of a very productive dialogue. We shall welcome your comments, suggestions, or criticisms, addressed to: Dr. Alfred S. Alschuler, c/o Education Ventures, 209 Court St., Middletown, Conn. 06457. We have good reason to expect that the knowledge about teaching achievement motivation will continue to grow because of what you have to say about it.

Alfred S. Alschuler
Program in Humanistic Education,
State University of New York, Albany

Teaching
Achievement
Motivation

CHAPTER 1

ACHIEVEMENT MOTIVATION

AND PSYCHOLOGICAL GROWTH

The spirit of self-determination is spreading from universities to high schools. Vocal groups of students and teachers alike have charged the climate of education by asserting the right and demanding the freedom to set their own goals and to have control over a significant portion of their own lives.

But these loud cries for change are divided. Many teachers believe that students don't know how to use increased freedom. Teachers state openly and with conviction that the majority of students, in fact, are neither sufficiently motivated nor mature enough to manage their own education. Teachers fear that yielding to the insistent minority will result in loss of control over their classrooms, less learning by the majority, and angry disapproval from administrators and parents. Yet teaching students to take responsibility has always been a necessary and central goal of formal education.

While there is basic agreement between teachers and students on the goals of education, differing strategies and tactics are in prolonged, angry collision. Hard-pressed teachers need new ways to work with students toward these common educational goals. They need more effective methods of motivating the majority of students to set high standards and to pursue these standards energetically. This book provides several practical solutions to these problems.

The primary purpose of this book is to teach you how to increase students' need to achieve—that is, their desire to strive for their own kind of excellence. The "need to achieve" (or *n-Ach* for short) involves a special way of planning to attain excellence, a set of strong feelings

1

about doing well, and specific action strategies. These three elements of n-Ach* have been identified through psychological research and studied by behavioral scientists for over 20 years. Through the use of recently developed educational methods, achievement motivation now can be taught directly to students in ways very similar to those you will experience in an introductory n-Ach course for teachers (Chapter 2). Besides helping you learn how to give n-Ach courses, we will describe ways you can restructure your everyday classroom teaching to encourage and reward students' achievement motivation systematically (Chapter 3). According to research data, n-Ach courses have stimulated students to initiate more long-term planning, to make more constructive use of leisure time, and to start more career-oriented work activities, while school classes restructured for n-Ach often produce dramatic learning gains.

No approach can guarantee that all of your students will become highly achievement motivated. The complexities of contemporary schooling, the hourly problems of coordinating 30 or more unique minds without becoming a tyrant, and the sheer difficulty of accelerating the seemingly glacial pace of personality growth—all guarantee that no magic wand solutions will turn your classroom into a palace of learning at one stroke. However, applying these new methods can make an important difference in the level of your students' achievement motivation.

Although n-Ach is a valuable motive, there are many other important human needs—to enjoy friendship, to exert influence, to nurture, to satisfy curiosity, to obtain a sense of security. It is possible to increase these motives using methods like those involved in achievement motivation training. Actually, these methods belong to the wider and emerging field of Psychological Education, which consists of courses for promoting psychological growth directly in educational settings.

Besides n-Ach training, there already are Psychological Education courses designed to increase awareness and excitement, creative thinking, interpersonal sensitivity, joy, self-reliance, self-esteem, self-understanding, self-actualization, moral development, identity, non-verbal communication, body awareness, value clarity, meditative

*Pronounced as two syllables: *en atch*

2

processes, and other aspects of ideal adult functioning. Some of these courses have been taught experimentally in schools, although most of them have been developed and offered in other settings such as industrial training programs, Peace Corps training, and private educational institutes.

More recently, the shocks of assassinations, riots, and protests are doing for Psychological Education what Sputnik did to spur the new academic curricula in the last 10 years. Psychologists and educators who worked in isolated independence are beginning to meet together to redesign and implement these courses for schools. All of us realize that we have a responsibility to help students become more mature as well as becoming more knowledgeable and skilled. Psychological Education offers a new, more direct way of helping students become more mature.

An important purpose of this book, besides introducing you to n-Ach training, is to help you become psychological educators. Our strategy for accomplishing these purposes is clear. We believe it will be easier for you to explore the field of Psychological Education after you have become competent in teaching achievement motivation, the most well-developed Psychological Education course. But before we present more information about n-Ach and get you started on your own n-Ach course, it will be helpful for you to see your activities in the perspective of the whole field of Psychological Education. Then you can simultaneously learn to be a skilled achievement motivation trainer and anticipate which of your newly acquired skills will be useful in other Psychological Education courses.

WHAT IS PSYCHOLOGICAL EDUCATION?

Every Psychological Education course teaches personal and immediately relevant skills that also are valuable over the course of a person's lifetime. Since psychological knowledge is experiential knowledge, in contrast to academic knowledge (mathematics, science, history) that is appropriately abstract, the content of Psychological Education courses must be firmly rooted in feelings, thoughts, and actions, and cannot merely be deposited in a student's internal data bank. The difference here is like the difference between knowing about the revolutions of 1848 and experiencing the anxiety and uncertainty of changing a life style quickly, as when a parent dies. It is the difference between knowing probability statistics and taking action when the odds are 50-50 for

3

success. A rich background of psychological knowledge is as important for wise decision-making as are academic knowledge and vocational skills.

Like foreign languages, science, history and mathematics, Psychological Education courses teach a new vocabulary and pattern of thought. Like vocational courses and athletics, Psychological Education courses teach new action skills. And, like psychotherapy, these courses are concerned with educating a person's feelings. All three of these goals are straightforward and unremarkable. But consider for a moment how many courses attempt to promote a synthesis of all three. Typical high school curricula are divided into academic "thought" courses and vocational "action" courses (typing, shorthand, auto mechanics, etc.). It is not possible to divide psychological knowledge into separate compartments. For example, "interpersonal sensitivity" is a way of thinking, feeling, and acting in ongoing relationships with other people. A course designed to increase it, or any aspect of mature functioning, must include all aspects of the psychological experience.

Within each Psychological Education course there are procedures to enhance this synthesis. For example, a variety of methods exist which stimulate imagination and teach new thought patterns. In Synectics training, a creativity course, students learn to "make the strange familiar" by imagining themselves inside a strange object, or to "make the familiar strange" by fantasizing about a common object. Remote associations are encouraged in order to attain a new, useful, and creative perspective on problems. In a number of courses designed to radically improve memory, a method of making absurd associations is used. In some courses students role-play their dream images and go on guided tours through daydreams as ways of understanding themselves better. In achievement motivation courses, students are encouraged to vividly imagine doing things exceptionally well and are taught the difference between achievement imagery and mere task imagery. Later in the course these achievement goals are tied to reality through careful planning and projects.

A second set of Psychological Education procedures involves action exercises, such as theater improvisations, role plays, sensory relaxation, and a variety of games. Often it is easier to understand psychological concepts when they are learned actively rather than simply comprehended intellectually. For example, in achievement motivation courses, the concept of "moderate risk taking" is taught through games in which the student must bid on his performance and only "wins" when he makes his bid. A very low bid earns few points while a very high bid is nearly impossible to make. The game experience subsequently is generalized to other life situations.

A third set of typical procedures focuses on developing and exploring individuals' emotional responses to the world. In most Psychological Education courses, how people feel is considered as important as what they think about things. Without these emotional peak experiences, ranging from exhilaration to fear, the instructor is likely to consider the course a failure. In sensitivity training, students are encouraged to express their feelings openly and honestly; they learn to recognize their anger and to resolve it maturely, rather than allowing it to create continued inner turmoil. In achievement motivation courses strong group feelings are developed to help support the individual in whatever he chooses to do well. Students also experience the excitement of racing against a deadline, the joyful hope of success, anxious fear of failure, and pride in accomplishing something difficult.

A fourth characteristic set of procedures emphasizes the importance of living fully and intensely "here and now." In most courses it is subtle and implicit. Often Psychological Education courses are held in isolated settings that cut people off from past patterns and future commitments and dramatize the here-and-now opportunities. A vivid example is Synanon, a total environment program for drug addicts, which promotes "self actualization" and in the process cures addiction. Synanon requires the addict to kick drugs immediately upon entering the program. Other "bad" behavior which stands in the way of self actualization is pointed out as it occurs. Historical explanations for bad behavior are considered excuses and are not tolerated. In other Psychological Education programs, the games, exercises, group process, etc., are model opportunities to explore, discover, and try out new behavior here and now. The assumption is that if a person cannot change here and now, where the conditions for growth are optimal, he is not likely to continue growing outside and after the course.

In preparing to give achievement motivation courses we will ask you to become familiar with some of these intriguing Psychological Education techniques so you can identify approaches that are particularly well suited to your students. At the same time you will begin developing your repertoire as a **psychological** educator, for these same techniques of encouraging imagination, arousing feelings, and allowing action applications in the here and now are useful when teaching value clarification, affiliation motivation, creativity, interpersonal sensitivity, or the content of any Psychological Education course.

WHAT IS ACHIEVEMENT MOTIVATION?

When desire for achievement becomes a dominant concern for a person, it is expressed in restless driving energy aimed at attaining excellence, getting ahead, improving on past records, beating competitors, doing things better, faster, more efficiently, and finding unique solutions to difficult problems. People with strong achievement motivation generally are self-confident individuals who are at their best taking personal responsibility in situations where they can control what happens to them. They set challenging goals demanding maximum effort, but goals which are possible to attain; they are not satisfied with automatic success that comes from easy goals, nor do they try to do the impossible. Time rushes by them and causes mild anxiety that there won't be enough hours to get things done. As a result they make more accurate long-range plans than people with less achievement motivation. They like to get regular, concrete feedback on how well they are doing so that their plans can be modified accordingly. They take pride in their accomplishments and get pleasure from striving for the challenging goals of excellence they set.

If the person with high achievement motivation were asked to pick his patron from the pantheon of Greek gods, he probably would choose Hermes, messenger of the gods and guide of travelers, for men with strong achievement motivation are likely to be found among the ranks of explorers, immigrants and innovators. Hermes, also patron of gymnasia and athletic contests, would appreciate the observation that societies characterized by a high level of achievement motivation have more competitive games and sports. Hermes, too, would approve of the bustling creative activity of the highly achievement motivated person, for legend tells us that Hermes was born in the morning, that by noon he had learned to perform on the lyre and that by evening he had stolen the cattle of his elder brother Apollo—which by any standards is speedy! Moreover, the lyre on which he played shows that he shares the desire to find unique solutions and make technical improvements, for

Hermes invented the lyre himself, constructing it from a tortoise shell.

Hermes represents for us an archetypal achievement motivated man, one in whom the motive has gained almost complete primacy. For mortal man, however, achievement motivation is always combined, modified, and softened by other motives, such as the desire for friendship, the concern with helping others, and the interest in aesthetic pleasure.

Although one never encounters the "Achieving Man" in bold simplicity, it is possible to identify achievement motivation in an individual much as a sensitive musician can listen attentively to the woodwinds while hearing the whole orchestra. In order to study this motive scientifically, Professor David C. McClelland of Harvard University developed methods for counting the frequency of thoughts, actions, and feelings an individual has that are focused on attaining excellence, i.e., measures of the strength of achievement motivation.*

With these measuring instruments psychologists have searched for the earliest origins of achievement motivation in individuals and nations. They found, for example, that mothers of young boys with high achievement motivation were more warmly affectionate, using hugging and kissing more often to show approval for independence and mastery. These mothers tended to set higher standards for their children and expected self-reliance at an earlier age than did mothers of children with lower achievement motivation. The researchers reasoned further that cultural values also shape children's motivation. To check this possibility samples of folk tales were collected from over 30 countries, since the folk tales told to children carry the cultural traditions and values. They found that cultures having many folk tales rich in examples of achievement motivation also stress direct training for achievement in other child-rearing practices. In contrast, cultures having few folk tales containing illustrations of achievement motivation more often stress punishing children for failure to be obedient.

Psychologists also looked for the long-term cultural consequences of a strong emphasis on achievement motivation and values. By taking careful samples of folk literature over a long period of time it is possible

---

*The research on achievement motivation is presented in extensive detail in two of Professor McClelland's books, *The Achieving Society,* Princeton, N.J.: D. Van Nostrand, 1961, and *Motivating Economic Achievement,* with D.G. Winter, Glencoe, Ill.: Free Press, 1969.

to identify the cyclic rise and fall of achievement concerns in a country. This possibility led Dr. McClelland to modify Weber's famous hypothesis about the relationship between the Protestant ethic and rise of capitalism. He observed that the values of independence, initiative, self-reliance, diligence, and hard work which Weber associated with Protestantism were also in essence achievement values. If a society placed increasing importance on teaching these values to children, the entrepreneurial spirit of Hermes should be stronger when these same children grew to positions of power and responsibility. McClelland reasoned that changes in the cultural importance given to achievement values, as measured by changes in the content of children's stories, ought to be reflected in the rate of economic development of the society. This relationship between changes in values and rates of economic productivity was found repeatedly in European countries between the two world wars, in England and Spain from the 17th to the 19th centuries, in ancient Greece, and in pre-Incan Peru.

These data offered strong and clear cues to educators concerned with the application of psychological research to pressing social problems, such as demand for speedier economic growth in under-developed countries. Since 1961 when the extensive research on achievement motivation was summarized in McClelland's book, *The Achieving Society,* there have been concentrated efforts to find methods of increasing this valuable human motive in adult businessmen. These methods were combined systematically into n-Ach training courses which have been given in the U.S., India, Spain, Peru, Mexico, Japan, and Tunisia to foster economic productivity. The results of these courses are presented in McClelland's most recent book (with David G. Winter) *Motivating Economic Achievement* (1969). The statistically significant results are pale reflections of the often dramatic changes in individuals, as this single biographical account indicates:

> *A short time after participating in one of our courses in India, a 47-year-old businessman rather suddenly decided to quit his excellent job and go into the construction business on his own in a big way. A man with some means of his own, he had had a very successful career as employee-relations manager for a large oil firm. His job involved adjusting management-employee diffi-culties, negotiating union contracts, etc. He was well-to-do, well thought of in his community, but he was restless because he*

found his job increasingly boring. At the time of the course his original Achievement score was not very high and he was thinking of retiring and living in England where his son was studying. In an interview eight months later he said the course had served not so much to "motivate" him, but to "crystallize" a lot of ideas he had vaguely or half-consciously picked up about work and achievement all through his life. It provided him with a new language (he still talked in terms of standards of excellence, blocks, moderate risk, goal anticipation, etc.), a new construct which served to organize those ideas and explain to him why he was bored with his job, despite his obvious success. He decided he wanted to be an Achievement-oriented person, that he would be unhappy in retirement, and that he should take a risk, quit his job, and start a business on his own. He acted on his decision and in six months had drawn plans and raised over $1,000,000 to build the tallest building in his large city to be called the "Everest Apartments." He is extremely happy in his new activity because it means selling, promoting, trying to wangle scarce materials, etc. His first building is part way up and he is planning two more.

(McClelland, 1965)

McClelland and Winter found that n-Ach courses were effective as measured by job promotions, salary increases, generation of investment capital, and the creation of new jobs by course members. However, the courses were not equally effective for all participants. Only those men who were "in charge," who held responsible mid- to upper-level executive positions, fully utilized the motivation aroused by the course. Perhaps it is more accurate to say that only the men "in charge" had the opportunities to use what they learned. The energies of the lower-level entrepreneurs were consumed by the pressing demands for minimal economic survival. They needed increased opportunities before they could use their higher achievement motivation. In general, neither increased motivation nor greater opportunities are sufficient in themselves to produce a significant spurt of entrepreneurial activity. The implications of these conclusions are becoming clear to foreign aid planners who realize that motivation training must be accompanied by material aid if it is to result in the quickened pace of economic development desired by countries requesting help. Men must have both opportunities and the motivation to use those opportunities.

Students also need opportunities and motivation. The massive U.S. programs of aid to education, like foreign aid efforts, have concentrated on providing materials rather than developing human resources. It is clear in education, as well, that more up-to-date physical facilities, more sophisticated educational hardware, and even money spent on research will not be sufficient unless students' motivation to use their new opportunities also is increased. Following the successful development of motivation courses for adults, it seemed appropriate to adapt these procedures for students.

Our purpose was *not* simply to stimulate students to make better use of their opportunities in school, but rather, to help students attain the goals they set for themselves in or outside of school. In fact, research on achievement motivation training for students provides little evidence for increased grades in school, a finding that may disappoint teachers who hope n-Ach courses will raise students' grades in the teacher's favorite academic subject. Instead, n-Ach training most often results in more purposeful planning and action outside of school, where students are more clearly "in charge" of their lives. In one way, this finding could not be more optimistic. The ultimate purpose of schooling is to teach students knowledge, skills, values, and feelings that help them live more effective, mature adult lives. This purpose is consistent with the typical and most appropriate applications of n-Ach training to entre-preneurial situations in the broadest sense—jobs, athletics, hobbies, administrative activities, and some learning situations.

N-Ach training is appropriate for those individuals who need and want increased achievement motivation so that they can respond more fully, effectively, joyfully, and judiciously in entrepreneurial situations. Surprisingly, this could include nearly all of us; according to research findings, most people have fairly low achievement motivation. Provid-ing the opportunity for such training is a legitimate responsibility of public schooling. As teachers become familiar with Psychological Edu-cation techniques, it will be easier to introduce n-Ach training in schools and more difficult to avoid the responsibility for directly educa-ting other aspects of healthy adult functioning as well. Since living effectively in a pluralistic society requires a broad range of psychologi-cal experience, a repertoire of personal skills, and a variety of strong motives, public education might well offer many different Psychologi-cal Education courses. Learning to give achievement motivation training is the first step towards introducing Psychological Education courses in schools, and therefore it is also a step toward realizing the ultimate aim of education.

A LOOK AHEAD

Since 1965 the Achievement Motivation Development Project at Harvard University Graduate School of Education has adapted n-Ach training for students, explored new Psychological Education methods of increasing motivation, and invented new ways to structure classroom learning to provide experiences in a variety of motives. The rest of this book reflects the accumulated practical results of that work. The goal is to provide you with sufficient information, experience, confidence, and teaching materials so that you can increase your students' motivation.

A careful comparison of the successful and unsuccessful n-Ach courses given to students reveals the worth of a six-step sequence in arousing and internalizing a motive:

(1) *Attend:* As every teacher knows, you must get students' attention before any learning can take place. We found this can be done by dramatic settings and unusual procedures which are moderately different from everyday teaching methods.

(2) *Experience:* The student must vividly experience the thoughts, actions, and feelings comprising the motive. This is accomplished through a variety of games, exercises, role plays, and methods taken from the field of Psychological Education.

(3) *Conceptualize:* To clarify the motive, students are taught to conceptualize and label the components of the motive. Many traditional teaching methods for building vocabulary are used in this phase.

(4) *Relate:* The relevance of the motive is assessed by examining its relationship to the person's ideal image of himself, his basic values and the everyday demands of his life.

(5) *Apply:* If the person decides to increase the motive, the course instructors should help him practice applying the motive in several real goal-setting situations.

(6) *Internalize:* If the motive is to be internalized, the final step is for the instructors to progressively withdraw external support while maintaining the level of voluntary use and satisfaction.

These six summary statements are brief and abstract here, since the purpose of this whole book is to teach you how to accomplish these

11

procedures in an n-Ach course. The same six steps are equally applicable in accomplishing the aims of other Psychological Education courses.

In Chapter 2 we provide instructions for a teacher-run workshop, through which you can experience the sequence of arousing and internalizing achievement motivation. This is the heart of the book. The group learning is more efficient, but, most important, it is more fun. This is another way of saying that it helps greatly to keep a high level of attention and interest. The games, exercises, and role plays in the early sessions of the workshop let you experience and help you conceptualize achievement motivation. The middle sessions are designed to allow more open-ended exploration of related questions: What are other methods for stimulating imagination? What is mental health? What are the ethical issues involved in trying to change personality? How do you measure the stages in internalizing a motive? What are appropriate helping styles in increasing different motives? The final sessions provide a format for making a decision and implementing the most appropriate application of what will have been learned by that time.

Chapter 3 deals directly with the relationship between how students learn in school and how they live after school. Concretely, we present a variety of methods for restructuring classroom learning so that students experience the socially valuable motives you wish to teach them. We make a strong plea for as much pluralism of learning structures within a school as exists in the larger society with respect to values and motives.

Chapter 4 contains a variety of examples to illustrate the principles, methods, and sequence of introducing achievement motivation training in schools. We also describe some of the errors we have made that you can avoid.

It is our consistent experience that teachers, not psychologists, are the experts in developing new and better applications for the classroom. With this frank acknowledgment of your existing expertise, we invite you to explore exciting, useful, new ways of increasing students' motivation, and to begin your career as a psychological educator.

12

CHAPTER 2

AN ACHIEVEMENT MOTIVATION
WORKSHOP FOR TEACHERS

This chapter presents directions for a 10-session workshop that will enable a small group to teach themselves about achievement motivation and begin exploring the field of Psychological Education. The intention of the chapter is not to make you more achievement motivated (unless, of course, you decide you want increased n-Ach). Rather, our goals are to share with you what we know about n-Ach (sessions 1-4), about Psychological Education methods for increasing motives (sessions 5-8) and to help you prepare either to give n-Ach courses or to make other applications of Psychological Education (sessions 9-10). The exercises in each session usually have a double focus. One is personal: you will learn about your own motive patterns and experience the sequence of learning described at the end of Chapter 2. The other is professional: you will be encouraged to relate what you experience to your teaching, your students, and other classroom situations you know.

We believe that this workshop for teachers is an essential first step in preparing to give effective achievement motivation training to students.

In this statement of purpose words like "workshop," "course," "session," "goals," "focus," miss the spirit of what we hope will happen. The chapter is not a syllabus. Nor is this a situation where people simply share reading and lecturing responsibilities. The chapter is like a map to use in taking your own directions and making your own discoveries. In some ways the chapter also is like an outline for a play to which you, as the producers, directors, and actors, bring your own resources, talents, and interpretations. As authors we do not want complete control over precisely what words are spoken in every session.

That would restrict you to a lifeless ritual. Instead we have tried to insure relevance by providing an extensive set of guidelines for the leader of each session and by giving three sets of general guidelines in the appendix.

"How to begin . . . notes to the initiator" (Appendix A) is written to that hardy first individual who wants to get the workshop started. These notes deal with such nitty-gritty but important first steps as administrative support, recruitment of course participants, scheduling, necessary resources, agenda items for the organizational meeting, and the establishment of the proper climate.

"The leadership role" (Appendix B) is addressed to each workshop participant, since everyone will lead at least one workshop session. Even if one or more of your group is an experienced leader, the role should be rotated among workshop participants for the 10 sessions. This allows the work, as well as the pleasure of participating in the exercises and games, to be shared. Rotating the leadership has an added advantage in that people support a leader more willingly when they know they will occupy his place at some time. This stimulates the group to pull together. Appendix B suggests steps in planning for the session, coaching tips on how to lead the session, and elements in helping the group to evaluate progress and to improve the next session.

Appendix C, "How to participate," is equally important to all participants. Usually when a group of people undertake a workshop, the members have a generally comfortable sense that they know where they are going, or at least someone does and is responsible for getting them there. Certainly the leader of each session will be most knowledgeable, but, like either the catcher or the pitcher in an effective baseball battery, the leader needs a special kind of cooperation for the session to be successful. "How to participate" describes some ground rules and signals you can use to coordinate your learning efforts with the session leader.

The information in the appendices and the workshop sessions is essential in preparing most effectively to give achievement motivation training. However, you may wish to proceed directly to Chapter 3 and 4 now, and then return to the process of going through the workshop as described in this chapter.

The participants in this course should not be rushed. They should be away from the stream of school routine, and should remain free of distractions and interruptions. Since people will be spending long stretches of time together in one place, ideally they should be in a room which creates a mood of "Let's relax" as well as "Let's get down to business." Try to find a spacious, airy room that combines lounging and working characteristics. The bare necessities include moveable tables and chairs, chalkboards or easels and large pads of paper, electric outlets, and provisions for smoking, snacks, and meals as they fit into your routine. The desirable extras are some soft comfortable furniture, rugs on the floors, lots and lots of space (but not barrenness) and a kitchenette.

When you sense enough interest from seven or eight people so that you feel sure the course will take place, arrange for the necessary materials. These will include a copy of this manual for each course participant and a library of course materials (see Appendix F).

SESSION 1: **The Arts of Contributing**

Purpose

The goal of this first session, in addition to general ice-breaking and helping people get acquainted, is to develop guidelines for individual behavior that will help the group reach its goals. This will be done through role plays of groups working on tasks. In the discussions after the role plays, the group will draw conclusions about what helped and what hindered progress.

Procedures

10 minutes	Leader for the session explains the purpose of the session and introduces the role-play activity. He allows time for people to read the introduction on the next two pages.
20 minutes	Members of the group role play a faculty committee gathered to work on a specific problem. Each person receives from the leader a slip of paper describing his role (another person than himself) in the group. The leader does any necessary briefing, allows people a moment or two to settle into the roles, then calls for the scene to begin. After the action has developed (about 5-10 minutes) the leader stops the role play at an appropriate time.
30 minutes	Discussion
10 minutes	Instructions for second role play
20 minutes	This time members are to be themselves. The leader assigns the "faculty committee" a new problem, and everyone tries to be a perfect member and cooperates with the role-play leader to make progress on the task.
30 minutes	Discussion
30 minutes	Evaluation of session and preparation for session 2

Follow-through reading

Learning to Work in Groups, Miles, M., New York: Teachers College Press, 1959.

Introduction

Recently a school administrator lamented that a new disease of

16

epidemic proportions was running rampant through school systems across the country. He called the disease "committee-cocchus" and recommended that strong antidotes be developed. While it is true that most of us spend a great deal of time "in committee" and in working groups, there is no intrinsic reason why this has to be an unrewarding, fatiguing experience characterized by antsiness, impatience, daydreaming, and ever-so-polite infighting. We all can recall those relatively rare meetings that started on time, finished on time, and accomplished a sizable chunk of work in between. The problem is to figure out how to have more of these productive meetings.

The common philosophy of inevitability about group work is caught in such cliches as, "Well, it depends on the combination of personalities;" "What's needed is a really strong leader;" "He really cracked the whip—we hated him but we got the work done;" "Committees of more than three never accomplish anything"—and on and on. Groups are not ultimately doomed to be ineffective learning and working forces. Otherwise we wouldn't be proposing a "self-run" group as a way of learning about achievement motivation and Psychological Education. But groups need training in how to work together—something that is rarely done and may be the main cause of "committeecocchus." This is especially true of a group without a recognized expert or elected leader. Members need to become aware of what particular behaviors and interactions make for good feelings rather than bad ones. Members need to identify processes which facilitate progress toward the goal and processes that bog things down or provide tinder for an explosion. Members seldom are fully aware of how they come across in groups, what kinds of helpful contributions they make, and what they do that irritates other members. Any group that works together over a period of time needs to develop "ground rules," a common "process vocabulary," and sympathetic awareness of others' needs and desires.

By these allusions to ground rules, process vocabulary and awareness, we mean that your group will need to develop a way of dealing with the second conversation that always goes on in groups. One conversation, the audible one, will center around the task of the day. The other conversation emerges through the group's style of communicating. It consists of the unspoken sentences hanging in silences and the messages implicit in the explicit remarks. For example, sometimes it happens that members of groups fall into certain patterns with each other. Whenever Mr. Krug makes a comment or proposal, Mr. Almenden disagrees. On the surface of it, perhaps the two hold incompatible sets of ideas, and can never agree about anything. But more likely there is a deeper conflict between them. In the group they fight each other, using slight differences of opinion as camouflage for the real struggle that is going on. These problems can seriously interfere with the group's progress. An awareness of these kinds of issues, along with ground rules about when and how to deal with them, plus a process vocabulary to use in working them through, will enable you to overcome difficulties experienced by the group and enhance the personal meaning of every workshop session.

One way to develop these group assets and your personal skills in contributing is to observe the group itself as it goes about its business. We have chosen a slight variation on this direct method. To create concrete behavior for the group to analyze, we suggest you role play, spontaneously improvising and acting out the way people behave in a faculty meeting. The session leader will assign you a role not typically your own. After the play is over you will have a chance to identify the various roles and their effects and how to deal with them constructively.

To the Leader

Typically, people in a group back away from looking closely at their own behavior. In a role play, however, the characters can be held responsible for what happens, and even accused directly of botching up the meeting because they are playing a role, not being themselves. In a role play, people are pretending, reacting off the top, exaggerating. The projected characters will be realistic and familiar enough to talk about, but not accurate or personal enough to force group members into defensive postures. People can observe honestly, say freely what they think and practice appropriate ways to make candid remarks. In other words, this exercise sets a precedent for group members to give others feedback about their effect on the group. Part of your job as leader will be to help everyone decide on ground rules for giving feedback that will be helpful and productive when you are yourselves again and not these pretend characters.

The role definitions themselves suggest one feedback procedure, since the name of the character in most cases indicates his typical

18

behavior. In a later meeting if one member says to another, "You're playing *conspirator*," everyone will quickly know what he means. In this way the role-names are the beginning of your process vocabulary.

The role play also teaches the possibility of change. Role plays are not little dramas that, once acted out, freeze into scripts. It is obvious that each rendering is one way people behave and one way it could have happened. There can be as many ways as people are willing to try. This is the feeling we hope to convey through the exercise—that a meeting, too, can be played or acted out in many ways. People can change their roles by behaving differently if they choose. In fact, you should state explicitly to group members that the whole workshop is a laboratory of human behavior, a place where they can try out new roles and new ways of reacting. This role play is the first opportunity to see the effects of various attitudes and behaviors and to practice new ways of acting to see how it feels.

Other resources that describe role-playing are: *Handbook for Staff Development and Human Relations Training,* p.226ff; *Learning to Work in Groups,* p.191ff; and *Improvisations for the Theater.* The first two have bibliographies and appendices that contain several references to sources on role playing. *Learning to Work in Groups* (p.121) describes an exercise related to the one presented here. (See Appendix F for the complete references for these books.)

Specific Instructions

As leader, explain the role play situation to the group: "You are a faculty steering committee elected by the faculty as a whole to influence policy decisions and attend to schoolwide issues. You are now in one of the weekly after-school meetings that start at 3 p.m. and extend usually to 5 p.m. and sometimes beyond. You are meeting in the teachers' cafeteria, a small and stuffy room. The chairman has just introduced a new problem and invited discussion."

The problem can be any of the following, one of your own choosing, or a real school issue: revisions in the dress code, drugs in the school, choice of a gift to commemorate the head custodian's 50th year of service, black-white tensions, granting in-service credit for a group of teachers taking some strange self-run motivation course.

Now pass out the brief role descriptions listed at the end of these instructions. Explain that everyone has been assigned a role, that he is to tell no one else what his role is, but simply to act that part as the meeting proceeds. However, you should identify the person playing the chairman role. Give everyone two or three minutes of quiet to settle into the part. You can suggest that they warm up by saying a few sentences to themselves, or ask them to react to a remark by saying silently the first role response that comes into their heads. Don't overdo this preparation since it may cause nervousness and hamper people's impulse to act spontaneously.

In advance you will have typed out the role descriptions. Our list of roles includes 12 brief descriptions. Choose those that appeal to you (but be sure to include the "chairman" role). Add roles or make changes if you like, so long as you don't burden the player with an excess of cues. If the group has several more than six or eight players, have the extras form a second role-play group or be an audience. If only one or two people are extra, assign them the role of observers. The audience or observers also should be briefed about what to watch for. You might compose a list of suggestions from the questions in the discussion guide for this session.

We would urge two cautions in assigning roles. Introduced in the right spirit, the exercise will catch people's imagination and they will willingly participate. If someone is reluctant, encourage him, but don't press. The first commandment in group work of this kind is "No one has to do anything he doesn't want to do." If you know the people involved, you can take care to avoid assigning a role that is too close to the person's real character and therefore potentially uncomfortable. Give the brasher roles and those likely to warrant much comment, or perhaps controversy, to people who can handle both the role and the reaction to it.

Once the role play begins you should generally keep out of it. You should be generous about waiting for players to warm up and settle on an issue to develop. But if it's cold and nothing seems to get started, or if it swings off in too bizarre and ham-like a direction, you can gently bring it back to the problem by saying, "Remember the focus" or "Take one minute more." The knowledge that the role play will end soon helps people get back on the track. Assuming all goes smoothly, 5-10 minutes should be enough time for behavior to appear that will give the group a basis for discussion. At that point, or at some moment of natural closure, step in and call "cut."

List of Roles

Chairman: You see yourself as a coordinator of the group. You frequently take leadership roles in groups, tend to be more directive than non-directive, and are comfortable taking this role.

Wallflower: Most of your participation in meetings goes on internally. That is, you follow the proceedings, have opinions and good ideas, but think them to yourself unless someone specifically invites your comments, or makes an effort to draw you out. Shyness prevents you from speaking aloud unless you have in advance the psychological safety of knowing people really want to hear you.

Napoleon: You have a vested interest in being leader. You are positive you could be doing a better, more efficient, livelier job than the assigned leader. Your tactics are all aimed at getting the leadership role.

Court Jester: You have lost hope of an interest in reaching a solution. Your usual behavior involves keeping things on the light side. Your entries are designed to get a laugh. Sometimes the humor has a cutting edge.

Harmonizer: You try to make sure that no one gets put down. Support other people's ideas—agree with others. Try to preclude or ameliorate discord.

Mad Hatter: You have other places to go and other things to do. Lately it seems your whole life has been spent in committee. You are on the verge of leaving—mentally. and maybe physically, too. You definitely and vocally want things to go along faster.

Conspirator: You may not be planning to overthrow the leader, but all of your conversation is low and directed to those near you in very confidential tones that make others wish they could hear what you are saying.

Logical Thinker: You believe that progress is made when the task is defined clearly. You want a concise statement of the problem. Personal issues don't conern you and you are impatient with those who let their emotions show in the discussion.

Butterfly: You really are interested in helping the group work on the problem at hand. But your interests are many and your mind skips along from dinner menus to Nationalist China. One thing makes you think of something else, and you are prone to lead the group off on a tangent.

Dashing Basher: You interrupt. You know what the other person has to say after half a sentence so there is no need to waste time on his sentence when you could be getting yours out. You make up your mind quickly and don't want to hear an excessive rationale about anything.

Host (Leader for the Second Role Play): You are helpful, competent, warm, supportive, imaginative and all the other Boy Scout virtues—and still human. You are intent on getting the task accomplished, but not at the expense of group harmony. Thus you concentrate on encouraging everyone's best efforts and try to be more guiding than directive.

Observer: You are not one of the role players, but instead an audience member. Watch the role play with the intent of commenting later during the discussion.

The Discussion

The following questions suggest a focus and sequence from here-and-now concrete observations to "there-and-then" group strategizing about how to work together effectively.

1. What roles were people assuming? Have them describe the way they saw each other.

2. What effect did various members of the group have on each other?

3. How did that make you feel? What specific behaviors (remarks) caused the various feelings you describe?

4. How did the leader feel, and how did people feel about him?

5. How else might the situation have been handled?

6. Have you seen these roles played before in real groups?

7. How realistic is all of this? What are some of the typical problems groups encounter when working together?

8. What agreements, behaviors, or strategies would help to avoid some of those difficulties?

9. List the kinds of contributions that help progress on the task and the feeling that the group is working together. Draw up a similar list of behaviors that hinder group progress.

10. As a group, establish at least five ground rules that will help you work together productively and enjoyably.

To start the discussion it is useful to ask the group to guess each person's role and the specific behaviors that define that role—*e.g.*

typical remarks, posture, gestures, tone of voice. When a role is identified, give the actor a large name card with his role title on it. This will serve two purposes, getting group members to use the role names as part of their vocabulary, and keeping individuals from being identified with their roles. Once the roles are clearly specified it will be easier to move to the more general issues suggested in the discussion questions listed above.

The criteria of success for this session are long-range and behavioral: more aware, productive group behavior. However, it helps to have a concrete product at the end of this group meeting: a list of behaviors which helps group work and a list of behaviors that hinder it. For example, going off on tangents, late arrivals, failure to confront conflict, and needless leadership competition are all obstructive behaviors. The group should suggest ways of dealing with these obstacles. In contrast, stopping for clarification, repeating what someone has said to make sure you understood, checking for group consensus when there is a sticky controversial issue, are all examples of constructive group behavior. Whatever discussion tack you follow, we would strongly recommend that the group draw up a list of blocking and facilitating behaviors.

Another kind of list that would prove helpful is a set of ground rules that the group agrees to accept and abide by. For example, the group might decide that it is legitimate and helpful to give people feedback when their behavior affects progress on the task. The group could define ways of giving feedback candidly, yet non-evaluatively. For example, people in the group should speak personally, and *only for themselves:* not "You got us off the track!" but, "When you kept joking I lost interest in the task because I thought you were interested in something else. Did anyone else feel that way?" Feedback should be directed towards specific behaviors, not the total person. "I don't like the method you are proposing" doesn't mean that "I don't like you."

The issue of giving personal feedback is such an important one that, if it does not come up in the conversation naturally, you should make a point of introducing it for discussion. However, this is only one of the many guidelines that may concern your particular group.

The second role play follows this discussion. If discussion has been extensive and members do agree upon basic procedures, then this second role play provides the opportunity to practice the behaviors discussed, and to expand on the list of facilitating behaviors. Members can try meeting the standards they have set for themselves, and ask the group for feedback on how well they do. The procedure is the same as for the first role play, except that the leader introduces a new problem and instructs the members to be themselves and to be "perfect members." If they are hesitant or reluctant, then use this variation exercise: ask each of them to choose one of the roles in the first role play that they want to try out, but to keep in mind that they are to cooperate with the leader. Discussion after the second role play should emphasize giving feedback in ways the group defined after the first role play. The emphasis should be on discovering new ways to participate constructively on the task and support each other at the same time.

Evaluating Session 1

Your final task is to distribute the evaluation forms, collate the numerical results and comments, and present these data to the group. While you are collating the results of Part A, the group members will be doing the feedback exercise described below in Part B. The session is over when you have at least five pieces of advice for the leader of Session 2.

Evaluation of the Art of Contributing
Part A
(to be filled out by each member)

1. How involved and interested were you in this session? (Circle one number):

1	2	3	4	5	6	7	8	9	10
All but actually asleep				PAR					One of the most interesting and involving group experiences I've had.

    a)   What helped make it interesting?
    b)   What kept the session from being more interesting?
  2. Predict how useful you think this session will be in facilitating

the effectiveness of the workshop as a whole. (circle one number):

1	2	3	4	5	6	7	8	9	10
very			more or less						utterly
harmful			irrelevant						invaluable

    a) How could the session have been more useful in getting started as a group?

    b) What advice do you have for the leader of the next session? (What to do the same, what to do differently . . .)

Hand in part A to the leader of Session 1 so he can tally your ratings and collate your comments. While the leader is doing this, do the following feedback exercise.

Part B

Take another person as your partner and spend about 10 minutes or so completing the one-liners given below. Complete each one-liner at least five times, taking alternate turns with your partner. Then go on to the next one-liner. Try not to discuss the completed sentences until after you have done all three. Then take some time to expand on the feedback you gave or received.

What I like about you is..

What makes me nervous about you is ....

I would like to get to know you better because ....

SESSION 2: Who am I? Why am I here? What do I want?

Purpose

During this session group participants have an opportunity to share thoughts and feelings they have about themselves as well as their expectations for the workshop. In this way all members will be better able to help each person in the workshop get what he or she wants. Personal learning is facilitated by shared understanding.

Procedure

10 minutes	Leader for the session introduces the activity
2½ hours	People seat themselves informally in a circle so that everyone can easily see, hear, and speak to the group as a whole. The leader introduces a few questions that may serve as a focus to help people speak personally, and invites someone to begin. After the first speaker, the order of speakers is random. Everyone should feel comfortable about stopping for questions, or asking for elaboration on a point, since what is said is not a speech, but a thinking aloud, recounting, and sharing.
30 minutes	Evaluation

Follow-through reading
  Who Am I? (EVI, 1970)

Introduction

During this workshop people will work very hard together, be dependent on each other, and make discoveries about themselves that are significant personally as well as professionally. Whether you are strangers now, or people who have worked together for a long time, at the end of the workshop you will share the kind of bond that comes from having had many experiences together.

This kind of learning flourishes in an atmosphere where people are accepting, supportive, and trusting of each other. Self-directed learning and personal growth are stifled in an atmosphere of suspicion and mistrust. We are not saying that you must all become fast friends. Nor are we naive enough to believe that simply saying that trust is important helps people trust each other. People have to know something about each other for this kind of caring and support to occur. In this session it is important to move past the stage of ritualized introductions to the point where each person stands out as a unique, interesting, and special human being. Starting out in this way will greatly enhance the personal meaning of subsequent experiences in the workshop.

The beginning of this session is like the problem of the penguins in the Antarctic. Every night they come up on the icebergs to sleep huddled together for warmth. In the morning when they are hungry they must go into the very cold, danger-filled waters to catch fish. Hunger drives them to the edge of the iceberg but fear keeps them back, until one penguin is crowded over the edge by the mass of penguinhood behind him. All the other penguins watch to see if he survives. If he does, they dive in too. Almost everyone in workshops like the one in which you are participating wants the closeness, trust, and opportunity for personal growth, but nearly everyone fears all manner of things. Trust develops as these fears prove ungrounded and this in turn helps the workshop become increasingly meaningful. The purpose of this session is to begin this process of disproving fears and establishing trust.

To the leader

As simple as this activity appears on the surface, people will be nervous about talking about themselves before a group—particularly if they don't know the others. As leader your goals are to help the group feel at ease and to facilitate communication at a level that is neither superficial nor fiercely probing, but open, personal, and meaningful. One way to reach this kind of communication is to choose one set of focal questions that require directness from each speaker. For example:

Set 1. Who are you? What are your greatest strengths and weaknesses? What do you want to get from the course?

Set 2. What is the most recent major turning point in your life? What happened? How has it influenced the way you are now?

Set 3. Describe one of your greatest peak experiences in teaching. Describe one of the most discouraging, disappointing moments in your teaching career. What would you like to get from this course?

After introducing the session ask the members to take 10 minutes to think about the set of questions and/or to make some notes in preparation for telling the group.

As leader you can facilitate open communication by being the first to speak and by setting the norm for directness, candor, and personal sharing. However, neither you nor anyone else should feel excessively pressured to discuss anything you feel reluctant to talk about. The purpose is to work toward trust in the group, and that involves respect for a person's need for space and privacy as well as acceptance of his candor. Trust develops slowly as it becomes increasingly safe to open up.

After beginning with your own personal comments, it is more effective if group members follow each other in random order instead of going around the circle. Spontaneous ordering lets people talk when they feel ready, and also generally encourages better listening. One person's account or experience often strikes a responsive chord in another group member, who can feel free to speak next. Don't be afraid of the silences or rush to fill them, even if they are uncomfortable. It usually increases the significance of the next contribution.

Once one or two persons have spoken, the others tend to pace themselves accordingly, both as to the personal depth of their remarks and the length of time they take to speak. An average time for each speaker is around 15 minutes or more so that a group of eight would find the 2½ hours a reasonable time allowance, perhaps on the short side. In a slightly larger group you might suggest to everyone that remarks be kept to about 10 minutes. Sometimes it is useful to have a clock in sight, or a watch, not to time people exactly, but to look toward in case someone inadvertently rambles beyond people's attention spans. In cases where numbers are large and time is short, it is better to have two sessions.

As described here, the "Who Am I?" session relies on talking and listening at a significant level of introspection and involvement. The cues we have provided are focal questions, but any number of other cues could work as well. For example, group members could be asked to bring a photograph that represents something important about their image of themselves. They could be given art materials to create a pictorial or graphic personal statement. Groups of teachers might focus on how they see themselves as teachers, how they think students see them, and how this role is different from the way they "really" are. The criterion is that the experience should provide an avenue for sharing of self-concepts. If you are interested in creating other ways for people to present and talk about themselves, check the book *Who Am I?* which is a portion of an n-Ach course for students. It could provide you with some concrete suggestions, and may stimulate you to go off in still other directions.

The session closes when each person has spoken. Be sure you don't overlook anyone. There is apt to be an awkwardness about closing this kind of conversation. Sometimes this is a good chance to return to and hear from someone who hasn't said much. But if there is an air of natural closure, suggest that people move into the first part of the evaluation, which will give everyone an opportunity to change gears, and at the same time give each other feedback. Parts A and B of the evaluation from Session 1 are equally useful for this session.

SESSION 3: Achievement Action Strategies

Purpose

Extensive research studies have shown that people who have high n-Ach tend to act in certain characteristic ways as they strive for excellence. The purpose of this session is to provide three game situations in which you can set goals, strive for excellence, and experience these action strategies. During the discussion at the end of Part A you can conceptualize these action strategies and prepare to explore them consciously during Part B, the Origami Game.

Since these games are prototype achievement situations they also stimulate achievement planning and feelings as well as achievement action strategies. Thus, Session 3 provides an experience base for Session 4 on these other aspects of achievement motivation. Finally, since these prototype games provide a variety of working environments and different types of rules, they demonstrate how learning environments can be structured to arouse achievement motivation.

Procedure:	*Part A*
1½ hours	Ring Toss Game—four rounds, demonstration and discussion
1½ hours	Darts-Dice Game—three rounds and discussion
30 minutes	Evaluation; assign reading

Procedure:	*Part B*
3 hours	Origami Game and discussion
30 minutes	Evaluation

Materials needed

Ring Toss Game and teachers' instructions (EVI, 1970)
Darts-Dice Game and teachers' instructions (EVI, 1970)
Origami Game instructions and player booklets (EVI, 1970)
NOTE: If the group decides it cannot afford the time for both parts, we recommend omitting the first part, Ring Toss and Darts-Dice

Follow-through reading

The Achieving Society, D.C. McClelland, VanNostrand, 1961, Chapters 6, 7, & 8 (paperback edition, Free Press, 1967)

To the Leaders of Session 3, Parts A and B

The purpose of this session together with Session 4 is to provide a set of extended experiences in achievement motivation—the actions, thoughts, and feelings involved in striving for excellence. According to scientific measurement, most people have relatively little spontaneously occuring n-Ach. By providing simple game situations that strongly stimulate achievement motivation, workshop participants will be able to see what elements of n-Ach they employ automatically, how much they like experiencing the motive, and how it might be valuable for them in other situations. In other words, the game situation encourages participants to continue one of the themes introduced in the course—an involvement with the question "Who Am I?". Here they ask themselves, "How do I react in situations that stimulate achievement motivation?" "What kinds of goals do I set?" "What kinds of feelings am I experiencing?" "How are they affecting my performance?" "Do I like what's happening?"

Besides the personal relevance of the experiences, the games serve a teaching function. They provide the basic psychological data that allows a clear understanding of the concepts and vocabulary used to describe aspects of achievement motivation. Some of these concepts and vocabulary are introduced during this session. Specifically, the Ring Toss Game focuses on "moderate risk taking," and "use of feedback." Darts-Dice also introduces these action concepts as well as "researching the environment" and "taking personal responsibility." The Origami Game is more complex and involving. In addition to providing another opportunity to introduce or practice the action strategies, it can be used as an experiential reference point in Session 4 to illustrate achievement planning and feelings.

In all three games there are variations in the rounds which demonstrate how achievement motivation can be combined with the need for affiliation—the need to have friends or to befriend or help others—and the need for power—the need to control or influence others. At some point that seems appropriate, workshop members should dwell on how these structural or rule variations influenced their motivation. There are clear and useful analogies to structural and rule variations in classroom teaching. These relationships are spelled out explicitly in Chapter 3 of this manual.

To be prepared for the discussion of these games we recommend that you read the summary of the action strategies in the pages immediately ahead, and Chapter 3. In addition you will find it particularly helpful to read Chapters 6, 7, and 8 of *The Achieving Society*. These several sections and chapters would make good follow-through reading assignments for workshop participants after Part A or Part B of this session.

Special Instructions for the Leader of Part A

In preparing for your session you will need to do three things:

1. *Become thoroughly familiar with Ring Toss and Darts-Dice.*

Your best bet would be to play these games before the session with family or friends in order to make sure you understand the rules and mechanics and have a feeling for the length of time required for each game. During the session itself, pay special attention to pacing and record-keeping. The games are simple and play should move right along—particularly if you want to keep the whole group's attention. Have the games set up in advance. Play the Ring Toss Game first, since it is the shorter and simpler of the two. The discussion of that game can be as brief as 15 minutes, since the concepts demonstrated in the game will be carried over to the Darts-Dice Game. If discussion is short after the Ring Toss Game, it should be more extensive after the Darts-Dice Game.

2. *Thoroughly prepare for leading the discussion of the games.*

There are four basic concepts that players should have in mind when the games and discussions are completed: moderate-risk goal setting, use of feedback, taking personal responsibility, and researching the environment—the four general strategies which typify persons high in n-Ach. We have provided a broad overview of each concept following these instructions to you. For convenience, the remarks are arranged topically, but in the discussions the ideas, concepts, and issues will not arise so neatly. This means that you should have the basic concepts well in mind, and also several "starter" questions that focus on each concept. In the overview of concepts we have suggested a number of these questions.

We have found that the most successful technique for facilitating the discussion is to focus first on the specific and personal. Ask the players what they were trying to do, what they learned, and how they felt. Then, move to a slightly more abstract level, and talk about strategy.

What were the basic winning strategies?: "If you were to advise someone on how to win this game, what would you say?" Last, in order to
help people make generalizations that are relevant to classrooms, jobs,
and other life situations, it is useful to introduce labels and vocabulary
for the key action strategies if that has not already been done, *e.g.*
"What kinds of risk taking and goal setting are offered to students?"
"How do you as a teacher provide feedback to your students?" "What
occupations are most compatible with these strategies?" Although we
have suggested several such starter questions in the overview of each
concept, and arranged them roughly within the hierarchy described (1.
personal, specific; 2. strategic; 3. broadly generalized) feel free to invent
your own questions.

You may not want to rely solely on the question-and-answer style of
discussion to cover this material. In that case you have at least three
alternatives: Prepare a summary lecturette based on the readings listed
on page 32; assign these readings; ask participants to read through the
overview of concepts and answer the questions embedded in the text.

3. *Prepare the evaluation form for the end of Part A.*

We have suggested two important questions that should be on the
evaluation form. You may want to add more that are of special interest
to you or that you feel would be useful for the progress of the group.

A. How well did the group practice the arts of contributing? (Circle
one and then give some examples to clarify your rating.)

1	2	3	4	5	6	7	8	9	10
Extremely									Extremely
destructive									helpful

B. *Give advice to the next session leader:* What should he do the
same as the leader of this session to facilitate learning? What should he
do differently to facilitate learning?

Depending on how much time you wish to spend on the evaluation
beyond these two questions, you may want to inquire about the content questions they have now, the possible applications they see, their
personal involvement and interest. Mimeographed forms ready to be
passed out will speed up this phase of the session and will be helpful for
the leader of the next session to have for his more careful study.

Overview of Achievement Action Strategies

The following four action strategies, although presented separately, are not completely independent elements of achievement motivation. They combine dynamically to comprise an energetic, restless, innovative individual who is highly concerned with improvement, doing things faster, better, more efficiently, more economically. As indicated in Chapter 1, Hermes, the archetype entrepreneur among the Greek gods, epitomizes pure achievement motivation. For didactic purposes, however, it is easier to describe the characteristic action strategies separately, even though the gestalt is lost.

1. Risk taking

In a new situation where a person must rely on his own skill, the high achiever takes carefully calculated moderate risks. He sets goals that are challenging, and not goals that are unreasonably difficult or goals that are too simple and undemanding. Extremely difficult goals make success unlikely. Easy goals make success unsatisfying. In the Ring Toss Game and in throwing darts, the person with high achievement motivation is likely to start off with moderate bids—five to nine feet for ring toss, or a bid of 40 points for darts—and then adjust his goals and behavior according to his performance. What he wants is a middle position where his skill and dexterity will be challenged, but where he has a reasonable chance of making it, giving his best effort.

Typically, people with high achievement motivation set goals in which their chances for success are roughly 50-50, according to their own estimates of their skills and resources. In these situations the outcome is most uncertain. People with low n-Ach are much more inclined to set extremely high or low goals, usually because there is practically no risk, no uncertainty, and no real challenge for them to produce their best efforts. If they fail to make a ringer from 20 feet they can always attribute their result to the impossibility of the task. A ringer from two feet is no challenge and does not give the person a sense of accomplishment—in life situations such easy goals usually do not yield very much. In setting challenging goals, people with high n-Ach try hard and end up with more to show for it, because easy goals have little payoff and very difficult goals seldom are attained.

Here are several questions that help focus on individual risk-taking styles and goal setting. Generally, the questions can apply to either game, although sometimes one game is mentioned specifically.

What were you thinking and feeling as you began to play the game? Did you have a goal in mind? What were you trying to do?

Did you think of yourself as competing? In what way?

How did you decide where to stand (Ring Toss) or what to bid for (Darts-Dice)?

Did you consciously estimate or think about your chances as you played? Did you expect to succeed or fail? How did those feelings affect your performance?

The following questions focus on the strategy of moderate risk taking:

What conclusions can be drawn from the performance data—from actually studying the score sheets? For example, in the Ring Toss Game or the dart throwing, what seem to be the winning strategies? How would you describe the goals set by those who were most successful? (Ask the people who were most successful to describe what they did and what kinds of goals they had in mind.)

Is a moderate risk the same for everyone? How is a moderate risk determined?

Could you define risk taking in terms of probabilities? Particularly, what kinds of odds are involved in moderate risk taking?

Finally, here are a few broader questions that will help people to generalize from their own behavior, and form the n-Ach strategy of moderate-risk goal setting.

How meaningful were the games to you? How did that affect your performance?

Would you consider your behavior in this game typical of you in competitive situations? Why or why not? Can you draw analogies from other areas of your life? *e.g.* What kinds of risks do you usually take? What kinds of competition generally stimulate you? Or do you avoid competition? What kinds of goal setting and risk taking are involved in your work or hobbies?

What does your behavior in the games suggest about your attitude toward yourself?

What about the place of moderate risk taking in schools? Who sets the goals in your classroom? How much allowance is there for moderate risk taking? Evaluate the grading system in terms of risk taking.

2. *Use of immediate concrete feedback to modify goals.*

Because the person with high n-Ach chooses challenging goals with uncertain outcomes and is highly involved, he likes to know how well he is doing. Thus, he seeks situations that offer regular concrete feedback about his progress or lack of it, and uses the feedback to modify his goals or his behavior. In the games this feedback comes from the scores in each round. On the basis of his successive scores, the player with high n-Ach modifies his strategy and behavior to increase his chances for success. For example, if a player lowers his bid to 40, after two bids and near misses at 60 in the darts game, he is using feedback to modify his goals and increase the likelihood of scoring. Similarly, if a player can't make the ring toss at nine feet, and uses this feedback, he should try the next time from closer to the peg. For a high achiever, flexibility and experimentation are more typical reactions than stubbornness to feedback. And he needs to be flexible, since he often initially overestimates how well he can do in a new situation.

For the person with high n-Ach, consecutive successes are taken as an indication that an even stiffer challenge is in order. Rather than rest on his laurels, he creates a new situation where the probability of success and the value of success once again demand an energetic effort from him. If feedback shows he is not doing well, or in fact that he is failing, that too is received as information rather than a permanent personal label. He acts to reverse the trend, to make the negative feedback positive by changing the risk, by acting differently, by reassessing the situation, analyzing the obstacles more closely, and perhaps by seeking help. This procedure doesn't suggest a fatalistic shrinking of aspiration, but more a process of intermediate goal setting that will insure some success experiences along the way as he reaches towards a challenging limit. The process is to work up to success, rather than to give up from failure. In contrast, people with low achievement motivation make more feedback errors. Often, after several successes striving for a goal of a given difficulty they still aim for the same goal, thus making a "chicken error." They tend not to set more challenging goals. Or, paradoxically, people with low n-Ach sometimes make "dare errors" by setting more difficult goals after repeated failures striving for easier goals.

In discussing the games, players should consider first what kinds of feedback they used and how they used it. The following are possible discussion questions:

How did you feel about your performance from round to round? What effect did those feelings have?

How well did you use your feedback from the score sheet in setting succeeding goals in the games? Did you pay much attention to it?

How about the scores and performance of others? Did they provide any helpful feedback about how you might change your levels of risk in the games?

To introduce the strategy of attentively using feedback, ask the players to look at the feedback patterns that show on the score sheets for Ring Toss or Darts-Dice. Ask them to identify "chicken errors" and "dare errors" and to relate the number of errors to the total score.

At a more general level, people in the group should consider whether they need concrete, rapid, definable feedback, or if more general and elusive indicators of success satisfy them. You might ask also:

What feedback is available to tell a teacher how successful he is? What can he look for?

What kinds of feedback are available to students in your classroom? How would you describe the feedback?

What occupations or situations do actually offer immediate concrete feedback as a measure of progress toward an achievement goal?

3. *Personal Responsibility*

People with high n-Ach like to put themselves "on the line," to test how much they can do. They like situations where they can take personal responsibility for successes and failures. Typically, they initiate activities in which they can assume personal responsibility. Situations where the outcome depends on luck or chance at least as much as skill are not as attractive to them. Thus in the Darts-Dice Game, where the player has a choice between throwing the darts and throwing the dice, the high n-Ach player prefers darts because he has more personal control over the outcome. This is usually the case, even when the person with high n-Ach is a poor darts player, because the sense of personal accomplishment is more important than making points. In the Ring Toss Game, standing unreasonably far away, taking a long shot, or starting very close to the peg are ways of avoiding responsibility for the outcome. In contrast, if the task or situation could be described as routine, ritualized, closely defined, or dependent on chance, it is not as attractive to a person with high need for achievement because there is little room for personal decision making. This difference between being "in charge" versus merely responding to the demands of the situation is what has been called the "origin-pawn" dimension. The person with high n-Ach sees himself more as an origin—who causes things to happen—rather than a pawn—who waits for things to happen to him.

However, the need for a sense of personal achievement and the acceptance of personal responsibility does not mean that these people work alone. A person with high achievement motivation will work just as energetically and enthusiastically for a group project or goal as he will for some private enterprise. The important factor is that the activity must allow for some individual decision-making or contribution on his part, and be concerned with attaining some kind of excellence. Moreover, he does not need public recognition for his contribution or accomplishment so much as some measure of success that tells him he is doing well in terms of objective standards.

Many of the questions suggested to focus on moderate risk taking will also bring up the concept of personal responsibility. But, to face the issue specifically, you will want to look at examples of extreme bids that occur in the Ring Toss Game. The Darts-Dice Game makes the same point, but more explicitly by offering players the choice of relying on skill or chance. Here are some questions to start conversation on this topic:

Why did you choose darts? (dice?) What reasons did you have for preferring them?

How did people who came out well with the dice feel about their success compared to what it would be like to win with darts?

What is your usual attitude about games of chance and games of skill? Would you ever call yourself a gambler?

How important is it to you to have control over a situation?

How can personal responsibility be facilitated in the classroom?

Does the role of the teacher in the school system allow for true personal responsibility?

4. *Researching the environment.*

Persons with high n-Ach approach new situations with a style that is alert, curious, active, and intentional. They might be described as "sizing up" the situation, checking out the limits and possibilities—with the end in mind of accomplishing a goal or moving toward it. They act in or on the environment rather than passively waiting for something to happen. Again, there is the qualification that the occasion must offer a possible challenge and at least some risk, so that the eventual achievement comes through personal effort. This description does not suggest an exact equation between the high achiever and the person who is thought of as hard working, efficient, aggressive. In fact, it is possible that the high achiever might be careless about details and a little disorganized, although that is not always the case either. Instead, he is ambitious, energetic, and innovative in a more visionary sense. He wants to make something special or do something unique. He will not work conscientiously or indiscriminately at projects solely for the sake of getting the task done. Routine completion of routine tasks is not the arena for his style of initiative or his need to achieve.

This style can exhibit itself even in these simple games. The person with high n-Ach makes sure he understands what is going on. He wants to know all the rules of the game, and what options are open to him. He will try to test the materials before performing. For example, he might try to find out if one way of throwing the darts seems to work better than another, or to pick up hints by watching others. Although these first two games do not really offer enough complexity for personal responsibility and initiative to come into full play, there will be some people who seem to test the situation, the rules, and materials more than others do. They are keyed up a little higher than the level where one just plays the game as if participating in a ritual.

To help players focus on their own initiative and degree of exploring the environment, ask them to think about their play in the games:

Did they insist on practice throws?

Did they really assess the differences between darts and dice?

Did they watch what others were doing, to pick up hints for making their own methods more effective?

Then, consider other situations:

Generally, how actively aware of your environment are you?

Do you test limits? Do you test your own limits?

Do you encourage environment probing in your students? How? Do you ever discourage it, consciously or unconsciously?

Special Instructions for the Leader of Part B:

If you have Origami Game materials nearby, you can see already that they have considerable bulk. You are right—you are in for a lot of work. But it is worth it. Potentially, this session is the most fun and most valuable of any in the course. We can vouch for its impact on teachers. We know several who rearranged the structures of their classrooms after playing it.

The game is structured to create a prototype achievement situation. Each player is the president of a company that develops and makes products for the space program. The products in the case are three different origami (Japanese paper folding) models, and the player is the producer as well as the president of the company. When the first round begins, players are given information about costs and selling prices, and are asked to estimate how many products they can make in a six-minute production period. In other words, this is a goal-setting situation where the player must research the environment, assess his own skill, and make decisions that will allow him to compete favorably against other players by producing high-quality products, making a profit, and reaching his own goal. In the second and third rounds the same basic sequence is followed, but each round introduces a new product and offers the player the chance to try out a different working situation. In the second round he can work as part of a team sharing profits or losses. During the third round he can join a team that is working in an assembly-line fashion and share the work process as well as the rewards. Throughout he has the option of working independently.

The game is complex enough so that all the action strategies are called into play: the bidding-estimating process gives players a chance to take moderate risks and create challenges. The complexity of the game demands researching the environment. The production of the origami models themselves and the different styles of competition invite initiative and innovative activity. Timekeeping, scorekeeping and results from round to round provide immediate concrete feedback. The pace, competitiveness, and the engrossing nature of the game, plus its demand for achievement goals, trigger practically every part of the achievement planning pattern (thoughts and feelings about success and failure, appraisals of obstacles in the way of making the bid, the need for action, help, successful accomplishment). Players' experience in this game is a live definition of achievement motivation and will be valuable common experience in Session 4 on achievement planning.

For teachers, oftentimes the most provocative discussion of this game revolves around the game structure itself. People (teachers and students) become intensely involved in this situation. If that degree of involvement ever appears in a classroom academic activity, we remember it for a long time. So it is worth rather close scrutiny to find out what it was about the game that got them so involved: The opportunity to set their own goals in a risk situation? The competition? The time limits? What? The answer may be different for each person. For example, this game, more than the previous two, offers a variety of competitive situations. Hence, a player has a chance to choose the competitive situations that are most comfortable for him. Does he get more achievement satisfaction from working alone or as part of a team? Does he like a feeling of ownership about a task or is he willing to pool his efforts with a group? Is his desire to work in a group motivated by need to achieve or affiliative desire for comradeship? Can group situations satisfy an individual's need for achievement?

For many people, these last questions can be answered, yes, yes, yes. Then you, as leader, can draw analogies to classroom structures and school structures by asking questions like these: "Who makes decisions in classrooms?" "Who does the goal setting?" "Are people ever allowed to collaborate and work in groups?" In general, the game invites speculation about the way the structure of a situation affects motivation. Based on this experience and discussion, workshop participants should be ready to read Chapter 3 of this manual, which explains in more detail how classroom structure can be changed to arouse different motives.

After suggesting that participants read Chapter 3, your final task for Part B of this session is to conduct the evaluation. We strongly recommend that you follow the same guidelines we presented to the leader of Part A of this session. If your relationship with your principal is jovial, you might want to obtain "feedback" from him by giving him all the origami models made during the session!

SESSION 4: Achievement Planning

Purpose

This session is designed to teach you the type of planning done by people with n-Ach to reach their achievement goals. After learning the basic planning pattern, you will have a chance to explore the subtler, more complex aspects of achievement planning through an analysis of case studies, personal achievement planning, role plays, and an interview with someone who has high n-Ach.

Procedure

1 hour   Part A

            Leader introduces the session and guides participants in learning the basic planning pattern.

2 hours   Part B

            Participants explore aspects of achievement planning to gain a deeper understanding.

½ hour   Evaluation

Follow-through reading

   Ten Thoughts (EVI, 1970)

   n-Ach Match Game (EVI, 1970)

   Achieving: Case Studies (EVI, 1970)

   The Achievement Motive; McClelland, Atkinson, Roby, Clark, and Lowell; N.Y., Appleton Century Crofts; 1953.

   "The Need to Achieve" (film), Focus on Behavior Series (No. 8), E.T.V. Network

Introduction to all Participants

Gordon Allport, an influential psychologist, once counted the number of words in a psychological dictionary that began with "re" and "pro." He found that "our vocabulary is five times richer in terms like *reaction, response, reinforcement, reflex, respondent, retroactive, recognition, regression, repression, reminiscence,* than in terms like *production, proficiency, problem solving,* and *programming.*"* Allport

---

Personality and Social Encounter, Gordon Allport, Boston: Beacon Press, 1969, p.41

believed that other psychologists do not give proper emphasis to the fact that man can originate actions and cause things to happen; human beings do not always wait for the environment to stimulate a response in them. Motivation, as we are using the term in this workshop, is consistent with Allport's emphasis on the future-oriented, goal-directed nature of man.

Motives are patterns of thoughts, feelings, and actions involved in striving to attain goals. In the last session you explored the action strategies used in striving for achievement goals. In this session you will learn the pattern of thoughts and feelings involved in achievement planning.

Whenever a person tries to perform well as measured by some standard of excellence, he has achievement goals and is displaying achievement motivation. These goals, or Achievement Images (Aim) are implicit in individuals' conversation when they talk about "doing well," "improving," "getting better," "winning," "setting a record." More specifically, people have an Aim whenever they are (1) competing against their own past performance, or (2) competing with others, or (3) trying to accomplish something unique, or (4) developing their skills through some long-term involvements. Each of these four types of Aim reflect the goal of striving for excellence. Obviously there are innumerable specific Aim's from trying to be a gourmet chef to working hard in solving a particularly difficult engineering problem, from studying to get a better grade this week to wanting to make the first string on the football team. It is perfectly possible that adolescents may have high achievement motivation and many Aim's though few of them are concerned with the standard school goal of academic excellence. It is also possible to increase a student's achievement motivation without its being reflected in more school-related Aim's. Since concerns with excellence can take many forms, students in achievement motivation courses are encouraged to focus on their most meaningful Aim's, to plan how to reach them, and to take action toward attaining them.

In addition to having a clear Aim, there are nine other elements in Achievement Planning. The person must decide what to do to reach his goal. The *actions* (ACT) he takes depend in part on what *personal obstacles* (PO) and *world obstacles* (WO) block his progress. Often *expert advice* (HELP) is obtained, but the major responsibility for action remains with the person himself. The person striving for his Aim also considers his feelings, how much he *wants* the goal (NEED), his fears of failure (FOF), his hopes of success (HOS), his success feelings (SuF), and failure feelings (FaF). These elements of achievement planning are represented graphically below:

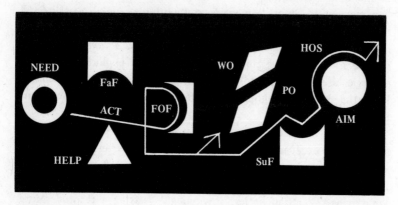

The inclusion of each of these elements in Achievement Planning increases the likelihood of success by making the plans more realistic and careful.

Strengthening a person's achievement motivation means increasing the number of Aim's in the person's life, fostering complete achievement planning, and helping the person use the achievement action strategies. To strengthen n-Ach it is essential—and therefore important for youth to understand thoroughly—the experiences and conceptualization in sessions 3 and 4, the heart of this workshop on achievement motivation.

To the Leader

For both sections of this session there are a number of alternative methods you can use to accomplish the objectives. In the first hour your task is to help workshop members learn the elements of achievement planning so well that they literally will be unforgettable. Teaching the materials so effectively will require you to prepare thoroughly and plan creatively. Your first step should be to study and, even better, try out *Ten Thoughts,* a program for learning achievement planning, and *The n-Ach Match Game,* a competitive situation modelled after a TV quiz program.

You may decide, however, that your best approach is to present achievement planning directly through a lecture unadorned by the frills of a game or programmed text, using the blackboard, overhead projector, flip charts, or dittoed crib sheets with definitions. The best source to use in preparation is *The Achievement Motive*. Some parts of the book are unnecessarily technical for your purpose, but as a whole it is the most directly relevant source book. As you prepare your presentation, keep in mind that at a minimum, workshop participants should know what Aim is, what is not Aim (Task Imagery, Affiliation Imagery, Power Imagery) and the definitions of the 10 elements of achievement planning. Participants should be able to recite this information from memory, whether or not you actually ask them to prove their knowledge through a memory test. You also should aim for this level of proficiency if you play the n-Ach Match Game or provide the *Ten Thoughts* text.

No matter what method you use, three points of confusion frequently arise and should be clarified: Often students initially see Aim in many situations where it does not exist. Not every goal is an Aim. For example, specific desires to have influence are Power Images. Goals concerned with establishing warm friendly relationships are Affiliation Images. These and other images concerned with discovery, support, food, avoiding harm, each define theoretically distinct motives. Even if you state this explicitly, there will be at least one person who asks, "Is the desire to achieve power an Aim?" The answer, of course, is "No, Aim's are goals that involve competition with standards of excellence. 'Achieving power' is a confusing word play and does not change the nature of the power goal."

There is another frequently occurring and confusing example of non-Aim. Many students want to include as Aim all goals having to do with working. But simply completing tasks, or being active, do not qualify as Aim unless there is a clear concern with competing against some standard of excellence. Just getting the job done (Task Imagery) is not the same thing as trying to do it well. This is a subtle but important difference that helps us understand people's motivation or lack of it. The saddest example is the student who seems strangely unmotivated even though he comes in after school to talk with us about homework (ACT), his personal difficulties (WO), and the advice he needs (HELP) to get his work done (Task Imagery). What's missing is an Aim. As a result his planning is lifeless and mechanical.

A third point of confusion usually becomes evident when students in the course give examples of Action, PO, WO, Help, etc. as evidence of achievement planning even when no Aim is present. Like the conscientious student with no Aim *there is no Achievement Motivation and no Achievement Planning without Aim.* Planning action, getting help, assessing obstacles, all are relevant elements of planning for power, affiliation, and several other goals. Thus, the presence of these planning elements does not necessarily mean that n-Ach is present. The *sine qua non* of achievement motivation is Aim, defined generically as striving for excellence, and exemplified in the four sub-types—competition with one's past performance, competition with others, unique accomplishment, and long-term involvement.

Once n-Ach has been distinguished clearly from other motives, someone usually asks whether it is possible to be motivated for achievement *and* power, or achievement *and* affiliation. This question often hides other ethical issues, such as, "If you increase achievement motivation will you decrease affiliation motivation?" "On what basis are we to choose from among these motives?" In reality, of course, most behavior represents a mixture of motives. A boy who wants to be captain of the football team may simultaneously want influence over his teammates, the level of excellence represented in playing, and the friendship it takes to be elected. Statistical evidence also supports this view: Achievement, Affiliation, and Power Motivation are uncorrelated. This means that when one motive is strong the other motives may be very strong or they may be very weak. The motives are virtually independent of each other.

When achievement planning is thoroughly in mind, the group is ready to exercise new knowledge and gain a richer understanding of it. Specifically, there are two objectives for this second phase of Session 4: (1) to begin assessing the relevance of achievement planning in various areas of one's life, particularly work, sports, leisure hobbies, and school; (2) to understand precisely how achievement planning is weakened if any one of the 10 elements is left out. You can work toward both of these objectives simultaneously by using examples of achievement planning in several areas of a person's life and speculating on the consequences of partial planning in the specific example. As in the first part of this session, there are several alternate approaches to reach the objectives.

Case Studies

Achieving is a book that contains a variety of case examples illustrating aspects of achievement motivation, and suggests a variety of issues to explore. You may also wish to locate your own case material from some books you know, the past guidance files, popular magazines, or other current sources.

Triadic Personal Achievement Planning

The directions are simple. Divide the workshop participants into groups of three. Ask all members to pick a personally meaningful Aim that they are willing to discuss in the triad. Have them spend ten minutes writing a succinct (250-500 words) achievement plan for their Aim, using all n-Ach elements. Then, ask them to share the plans with members of the triad and consider the following questions. (Not all of these questions need be asked of each member's plan. If possible, however, all of these questions should be asked by the time the three members have finished.)

Is the Aim something you want very much? How can you tell how much you want the goal? Is it a moderately challenging risk?

Try reading the plan leaving out all references to HOS, FOF, SuF, FaF, Need. What does it sound like? How realistic is it? How do the feelings strengthen the plan and make accomplishment more likely?

Now try leaving out all references to ACT, WO, PO, Help. What does it sound like? How do these omissions decrease the chance of success?

First leave out FOF and FaF, then leave out HOS and SuF. How do these omissions change the gestalt? What would you think about a student who never included either FOF and FaF or SuF and HOS in his planning? Can you think of some real examples?

What happens to your planning if you leave out PO or WO? What is your evaluation of students who always mention WO, but never talk about PO or vice versa? Can you think of real examples?

Is the action appropriate to the goal? How much room is there for personal responsibility? How much is left to fate, chance, luck, or other people?

Questioning each person's plans should last about 15 minutes for a grand total of about an hour, including 10 to 15 minutes for writing.

Triadic Role Play

Here again the instructions are simple. In each triad there are three roles—teacher, student, and observer. The person playing the student thinks of a real situation in his own life as a teacher or student when he faced a problem related to achievement. The problem may exist in or outside of school and be concerned with working, career choice, sports, hobbies, friends, etc. The role-play student is seeking the counsel of the trusted role-play teacher. The task of the teacher is to find out what the problem is through skillful and sympathetic questioning. He tries to ascertain the extent of achievement planning—what elements are present and absent. After about 10 minutes of this conversation, the full trio discusses what the problem is and what might be done about it. This should last another 10 minutes and then the roles rotate for another 20-minute period. A complete rotation takes three periods for a total of about an hour. During this hour most of the same issues will arise that are listed as questions under "Triadic Personal Achievement Planning."

Guest Interview

One of the best ways to understand the relevance and complexity of achievement motivation is to invite a guest speaker to present his story. To be sure, not everyone or every profession requires an equal amount of achievement motivation, so some shrewd guesses to get a prototype individual are necessary. In past courses we have invited a fifth black belt judo teacher, the hero of Harvard's football team, and a school superintendent. In general, men in executive or entrepreneurial positions and good athletes are helpful people to interview. Obviously, the goal of workshop participants is to find out whether, when, and how achievement motivation plays a part in the person's success. At some point during the presentation or in the ensuing discussion it may be helpful to introduce the guest to the n-Ach vocabulary. This facilitates the exploration. We have found an hour is a reasonable amount of time to take for the interview and to ask from busy, successful men and women.

None of these four alternatives for the second portion of the fourth session needs to take the full two hours of time set aside. Thus, you can put together a combination of activities that meet the special needs of group members and that are diverse enough to keep attention and a quick pace. Be sure, however, to allow enough time for participants to fill out the evaluation form, to summarize, and to discuss the evaluation results. You may wish to add questions to those listed below.

A. How well did members practice the arts of contributing? (circle one number):

1	2	3	4	5	6	7	8	9	10
Extremely				Just					Extremely
Poorly				Passing					Well

What specifically was done best? What specifically needs attention and improvement?

B. How effectively was this session organized and conducted? (circle one number):

1	2	3	4	5	6	7	8	9	10
Extremely				Just					Extremely
Poorly				Passing					Well
Organized									Organized
and Run									and Run

What did the leader do exceptionally well? What should the leader of the next session do differently?

C. What important questions about achievement motivation do you have now that you want the leader of Session 5 to bear in mind while planning the session?

SESSIONS 5 - 8:   **Side Trips in Psychological Education**
Purpose

The overall goal for this session is to make plans for exploring several aspects of Psychological Education that provide perspectives on achievement motivation. Part A of the session is a time to exchange views publicly of what has happened thus far in the course and what you want to happen in the remainder of the course. Part B introduces seven topic areas that should be relevant to the issues raised in Part A. Part C allows you to browse through the seven extended topic area guides and choose at least two areas for further exploration. During Part D you will plan as a group how to spend your course time over the next several sessions. In our numbering of sessions we have allowed the equivalent of three sessions (6, 7, 8) for these group and individual explorations. However, it is up to your group to decide how much actual time to spend on these topic areas.

Procedure

½ hour   Part A

Take bearings on where you are at present, and where you want to go

¼ hour   Part B

All participants read the introduction to the side trips

1¼ hours   Part C

Participants skim, browse through, or read carefully the seven guides to the side trips, and choose two areas for further extended exploration.

1 hour   Part D

The whole group plans the next several workshop sessions.

½ hour   Evaluation

Introduction, for all group members, to Session 5, Part A

One of the challenges in presenting a course like this is that the further the authors get, the more elusive becomes the prospect of presenting a session format tailored to your needs. At this point, in fact, we can't be sure if this is the fourth meeting for your group or the sixth. If we could be there, and ask questions, here are some of the things we would like to know:

1. Do you have a basic understanding of what achievement motivation is? Can you recognize and describe the goals, thoughts, feelings, and actions which interact to produce the total motive syndrome?

2. What are some of your reactions to the workshop and the course materials? How do you think the workshop is progressing?

3. Would you be interested in pursuing ways n-Ach might be integrated into your teaching? Would you like to teach it as a course subject? What more do you want to know about n-Ach?

4. Are you interested in learning more about Psychological Education? How specific can you be about what you want to know?

Our guess is that you do have a basic understanding of the motive, and that your reactions may vary from outright rejection, through a continuum of skepticism, confusion, and curiosity, to extreme enthusiasm. As for your intentions, it is probably too early even for you to tell what you will let come of this experience. Common sense says that this session should be a checkpoint, a crossroad, and a time for individuals and the group as a whole to take bearings. Consequently, the session is designed to open with an informal discussion of where you all are in your thinking about the course, and then to invite you to explore any or all of eight related areas in Psychological Education. In many cases your interests will lead you out of the realm of achievement motivation *per se,* beyond the province of this book, to other readings, topics, and exercises. Then, approximately two to four or more sessions later (the amount of time to be determined by the group), you will reconvene to share discoveries and enhance each other's perspectives. During sessions 9 and 10 you will decide whether you intend to pursue a common goal, such as planning an n-Ach course, or whether you intend to split off from each other and pursue different goals.

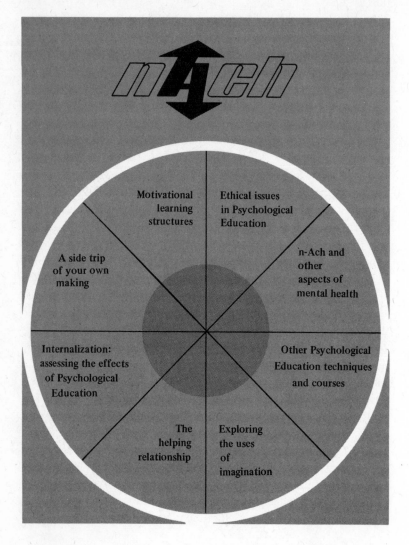

This diagram indicates the various directions in which we can help you go. Each element represents a short essay-guide describing a topic in Psychological Education related to achievement motivation. These guides suggest what you can read and/or do to investigate the area more thoroughly.

Several of these topics already have been introduced indirectly in the course. For example, many course participants are struck by the effects of the Origami Game on their achievement motivation, in spite of folding hundreds of silly pieces of paper. If that activity can be made exciting, then it should be possible to arouse motivation for practically any subject matter. In what ways can learning be made like the Origami Game? What aspects of a game, or of a classroom, help determine the incentives, expectations, and feelings students have about learning? What rules and leadership styles encourage or squelch achievement, affiliation, power, and creativity motivation? The side trip, "Motivational Learning Structures," suggests ways to change the hidden motivational curriculum. It can help you implement the information in Chapter 3 of this book, "Motivation in Classrooms."

If you decide to give n-Ach courses or change the structure of learning in your classroom, many people will raise ethical questions. Who decides what motives are most valuable? Who decides which students should be motivated? If students ultimately decide (a policy that adheres strictly to the democratic ethic of free choice), is this not an abdication of adult responsibility to socialize the young into prevailing cultural norms? Who is to decide when a teacher is qualified as a psychological educator? What is to keep Psychological Education from becoming a socially acceptable name for "brainwashing"? All of these questions make an ironic assumption, namely that Psychological Education, and n-Ach training in particular, are effective methods for changing personality. It is as if everyone assumed that most educational methods fail to achieve the publicly stated goal of education, "to foster the development of mature citizens." When a claim is made that certain methods are very effective in helping students' personalities develop into healthy adulthood, paradoxically, there is trouble. The guidelines "Ethical Issues in Psychological Education" address these questions directly, although no definitive answers are promised.

In a wider context, several of the terms of achievement motivation—initiative, goal setting, progress, competing for excellence—have long been a recognized part of American ideology and characterize a spirit and restlessness that makes up America. Yet many people are now questioning whether the extent of our competition is a form of social psychosis. Our compulsion to get ahead leaves behind symptoms of poverty, urban blight, air and water pollution, hate and mistrust among racial and ethnic groups, impossible political entanglements—you know the list. Is there a relationship between a cultural value that stresses individual efficacy and achievement and these blatant predicaments? At the same time one part of the population eschews any emphasis on achievement, considering it part of the American nightmare, others see the equation as overly simplistic. In their minds n-Ach courses are capable of beginning to fill a large void in American education. The courses, these defenders argue, promote psychological health and growth. The courses teach people strategies and responses they didn't have before, and in that way help the course participant to develop a stronger self-image. These same arguments surround a person's own decision about whether to increase or decrease his achievement motivation. Not everyone wants or needs more n-Ach. On the other hand, a certain amount of n-Ach is integral to a person's sense of worth and identity. People need to know that they have the capacity to achieve some of the goals important to them. A short essay, "Achievement Motivation and Other Aspects of Mental Health," dealing with these issues, suggests that n-Ach has a place in mental health. It also suggests material to help you decide at what stages of development n-Ach is most relevant and when training may be most appropriate. The reading outlines criteria you can use in a self-analytic way to assess your own maturity, capacity for fulfillment, and potential need for more n-Ach.

It is difficult to know whether the existence of many Psychological Education courses will multiply the ethical problems or help resolve some of the ethical problems by providing individuals with choices of what aspects of maturity they want to become stronger. A variety of courses exist. Already the literature on methods and techniques is voluminous. The essay "Other Psychological Education Techniques and Courses," provides guides into this literature—what books you can read most profitably first and what books have the best collections of techniques. Anyone interested in becoming a psychological educator or in discovering a wide range of other classroom applications will find this a valuable bibliography and set of directions.

One set of techniques for "Exploring the Constructive Uses of Imagination" deserves special attention. It is an integral part of n-Ach training; achievement images and planning are nothing but realistic imaginings of what could happen in the pursuit of excellence. A rich, vivid imagination is more than a useful mental tool for planning. It can be used to develop a "super power memory," to attain creative perspectives on difficult problems, to take body tours and other fantasy trips, and to analyze dreams. Instructions for each of these constructive uses of imagination are given in the essay, along with references to other ways of strengthening imagination.

All of these techniques may be fascinating and, on the face of it, obviously relevant for you to know. But how do you know if you have been successful in using these techniques to increase motivation? Ten years after you teach a group of students would you even recognize the effects you had? Clearly it is not enough to tickle students with these flashy experiences in Psychological Education. The ultimate goal of these courses is to have students internalize what we teach them. How do you teach for internalization? We are bold enough to suggest instructional guidelines and ways to assess how effective you are at each step in the process of internalization. To help make the criteria vivid there are instructions, in the essay "Internalization," for taking a fantasy trip into the future to meet your "prize" student.

For teachers, "helping" is ubiquitous and, at its best, produces many "prize" students. The last section presents several exercises that allow you to explore different types of helping relationships. If you have any thoughts of giving an n-Ach course, this material can be a valuable illustration of teacher-student relationships that help the student and at the same time create space for him to exercise initiative. Aside from pragmatic reasons, we urge you to try one or two of the helping exercises for the fun of experimenting with your own style of giving and receiving help. It has to be relevant—since most of you are enmeshed in several helping relationships, as family members, teachers, and participants in this course.

The guidelines themselves are not intended to cover the topics, but simply to lead you on an excursion. In the learning sequence of this workshop, the opening sessions provided the experience of the motive, and the basis for conceptualizing what achievement motivation is. These next few sessions, where you are off on your own, will give you a chance to gain perspective on the experience. Our goal is to counteract the myopia resulting from too many sessions where you follow directions. Now is a time to follow your own interests and put n-Ach into other contexts. Tripping off separately or in subgroups will unlock the group for freer exploration. When each person returns during Session 9, your acquired knowledge and points of view will be woven together into a new fabric, and, it is hoped, will constitute a new level of understanding.

With this preview in mind, your task for approximately the next 1¼ hours is to look over the seven side trips and choose at least two you want to explore in depth.

To the leader

Your role for this session is mainly to help the group organize its schedule of investigations for the next several weeks. The session will have been successful if, at the end, each course member has chosen at least two interest areas to explore and has defined specific projects or goals to work on within those areas. Ideally, every one of the seven interest areas will be represented in the group's choices. Concrete evidence of accomplishing your goal as leader would be to come out with a schedule of people's anticipated activities and the date the group will reconvene to share experiences.

In advance you should read through all the material for this session to be familiar with the suggested activities, the time requirements, necessary materials, and procedures for the various "side trips." That way you will know, for example, that it takes more than one person to do the helping exercises, but that other areas, such as the constructive uses of imagination, can be explored alone or with a small group. If your group has not provided the suggested library, alert people to those sections which rely heavily on reference books so that they can make plans to secure the books or make another choice of project. Also tell members they will need to bring their own copies of this manual with them to this session.

Part A

Open the session by giving everyone a minute or two to look over the plan for the session and the one-page introduction to the session. Introduce Part A by asking participants to share their feelings about what has been happening, or not happening, in the course. We strongly recommend that this discussion be focussed around the four questions asked in the introduction, and that you try to maintain the half-hour time limit. The idea is for members to find out what others think about the workshop, and what further interests they might share. In a group of eight or so the half hour will give you time to hear impressions—basic concerns—but you will not have time for long discussions about the ethical implications of n-Ach, or about complicated issues of group process. If group members express the need for that kind of conversation, or if you sense the discussion moving that way, suggest that they schedule a definite, longer time for handling such concerns. It is possible that working together to explore the seven areas outlined will answer questions that trouble people. And it is highly probable that a session devoted entirely to group process will be more productive if everyone agrees to it and schedules it deliberately.

Parts B and C

During this hour and a half members read or browse through the seven side trips in Psychological Education to see what areas they would like to explore in greater depth. Our rationale for having the "homework" scheduled during "class time" is that it is one painless way to make sure everyone is prepared at the same time. While the possibilities are fresh in mind people can choose, team up with others, make some commitments, and plan.

Part D

This is the difficult part: coordinating the planning of group activity over the next several sessions. The necessary mapping and scheduling will be facilitated if you have one or two large charts ready with all the names and interest areas blocked out.

1. When the group has finished browsing, and is once more attending as a group, ask each person to state quickly at least two interest areas he would like most to explore. Encourage people to be fairly specific, e.g., "What books look most interesting of those listed in the guide to other Psychological Education techniques and courses?"

2. Survey the "collected works." If there are activities in which the whole group or a large majority seems interested, discuss scheduling a few as a regular-session activity. Settle on dates, choose leaders and procedures for the activity.

3. After the additional large-group sessions have been planned, let the group mill about for at least 10 minutes. The task is for each person to find at least one other person to work with on each topic of his interest. For example, two members working together on motivational

57

classroom structure might observe each other's classes and provide feedback that would be the basis for varying some of the classroom procedures. Or two or three people could collect an outside group and do the verbal helping exercise. Or a sub-group could conduct a small seminar on the ethical issues relevant to teaching n-Ach. During the milling, the pairs or groups must set some dates and make plans. If possible, they should define not only the area of investigation, but also the specific project.

4. Gather the group to determine the date for getting it all together (Session 9), when people will share results of their projects.

5. For your own check list at the end of the session . . .

Is each of the seven areas being explored?

Has everyone chosen at least two side trips?

Does everyone have a traveling companion?

Are the next group exploratory session(s) scheduled? With leaders?

Has Session 9 been scheduled?

Evaluating the session

As in all the other sessions your last task is to conduct the evaluation. You may wish to add questions to those listed below.

1. How enthusiastic are you about the side trips you have chosen to explore?

1	2	3	4	5	6	7	8	9	10
Dread them				Neutral					Extremely enthused

What would increase your enthusiasm?

2. Do you know what you are going to do next, when and with whom?

3. What final questions do you need answered about the workshop schedule and activities between now and Session 9?

Motivational Learning Structures

"Student-directed learning" is becoming an educational watchword. Advocates claim that an open, supportive, choice-offering environment, where students take more responsibility for their own learning, is a solution to overly bureaucratized schools in which students feel trapped in situations they neither created nor control. The difficulties encountered in implementing this most recent brand-name approach to restructuring the process of learning are as instructive as the problems it may solve. Both the successes and failures indicate a need for sounder assumptions and more realistic expectations by teachers who attempt to change how their students learn.

Many experienced teachers believe that this latest educational theory is lifting the lid of a Pandora's box filled with pedagogical gremlins. Reactions range from ill-concealed apprehension ("Give 'em an inch and they'll take a mile") to gentle, worldly-wise cynicism ("Give 'em an inch and they take a millimeter"). Equally sincere teachers who try to stimulate more "student-directed learning" often are disappointed when they witness unproductive confusion, apathetic withdrawal, or angry student demands for a resumption of directed teaching.

The lure of "student-directed learning" comes in part from the fascinating possibility of discarding the traditional role of teacher as director and performer—roles with their own uniquely conceived frustrations: ("Half the time I feel as if I'm on stage exerting all my energy trying to keep everyone interested. It's like a juggling act—the minute I stop, it's all over. The other half of the time I'm like a traffic cop telling students when to stop or go, giving directions or arresting them"). Those energetic teachers who have experimented with the full range of teaching styles from "teacher-directed" to "student-directed" can be excused for their exasperated sighs.

Usually new approaches to teaching create a new problem for every old problem solved. This is likely to remain true so long as there are approximately 30 unique individuals in a single class. No single approach to teaching and learning will be equally effective for all students, all ages, both sexes, and all subject matter areas. Even "individualized instruction," another "solution" in vogue among optimistic educational innovators, creates as many problems for teachers as it solves for students. Instead of one preparation per night, per class, teachers must make many preparations; keeping track of students' progress becomes geometrically more complex. Teachers viewing the resultant mountain of paperwork are Herculean figures facing modern Augean stables.

The proposals about learning structures presented in this book start from different premises. We believe there are no "solutions," but only classical "trade-off" questions. There are gains and losses from any change in the teaching-learning process that should be evaluated in each specific situation.

We also believe that ideally there should be as much variety in the teaching-learning process within a single school as exists outside and after school where students are variously "required," "ordered," "coached," "persuaded," "led," "followed," "threatened," "promised," "lectured," "questioned," and "left alone." Compared to this handsome array of naturally occurring learning processes, the typical range within a school often is embarrassingly narrow. To restructure the learning process in school is to re-motivate students, since motives are processes of goal-directed thinking, acting, and feeling. A wider number of motives should be tapped as students learn.

Often teachers assume that making the content relevant will increase students' interest (*i.e.,* motivation). This misses the fact that even personally relevant and diverse content can be taught through one basic motivational process, whether it is a course in Afro-American history, urban affairs, or "identity." Conversely, a variety of motivational processes can be structured no matter how personally irrelevant the content. In motivating students, the structure and process may be more important than the content.

One of the first errors made by teachers who decide to increase the number of alternative learning processes is to decrease drastically the amount of structure, the number of rules and formal procedures. Teachers interested in "student-directed" learning are particularly prone to this strategy because it seems to decrease authoritarianism while increasing the possibility of many types of student initiative and learning styles. Decreasing the amount of structure in a learning situation often produces only a variety of confusion, apathy, and angry demands, not more "student-directed learning." The key to systematic variation in learning processes is not how many rules, but what kind of rules. For example, such highly structured, rule-governed activities as baseball and square dancing are non-authoritarian and stimulate specific motivational processes. The problem is to identify the types of rules associated with different motivational processes so that a variety of desired motives can be aroused.

Thus far, this essay can be considered a preamble to Chapter 3, "Motivation in Classrooms." For those of you who want to begin restructuring the teaching-learning processes in your classroom, we have provided several starter questions to help you diagnose your current learning structure. These questions and the suggested ways to begin inventing alternatives will make better sense after you read Chapter 3. Success in restructuring also may be facilitated if you get together with a like-minded colleague.

Diagnostic Questions

1. How explicit and public are the learning rules in your class? *i.e.,* what is and is not allowed?

2. To what degree did students participate in making these rules? To what degree can they influence the rules?

3. How many ways are there to "score points" in the class?

4. What are the major decisions made regarding the pace, sequence, tactics, strategy for learning? How are these decisions made?

5. What are the obstacles that must be overcome to score?

6. List the specific roles you take in relation to students in the course of their learning, *e.g.,* lecturer, questioner, grader, friend, coach, umpire, etc.

7. According to the diagnostic scheme in Chapter 3, rank-order the motivational processes encouraged in your classroom. Are you satisfied with this relative emphasis? What motives would you like to emphasize more, or less? What other specific processes would you like to occur as your students learn?

Sources of ideas for new structures

In answering the diagnostic questions you may have thought about new alternatives. Try reading the questions as veiled instructions and see if it helps generate some ideas (*e.g.,* How can you make the learning rules more explicit and public? How can you involve students more in making these rules? Can you think of additional ways for students to score?).

A second direct source of ideas is the situation outside class to which you would like the learning process to be relevant: spot welding on a construction job, being a member of a secretarial pool, preparing income tax returns, learning from a college lecture, constructive use of leisure time, or active participation in the local political scene. How do people learn in these situations? What kind of personal relationships exist? How is effectiveness measured? What kinds of satisfactions are sought? Answers to any of these questions can be clues to appropriate restructuring in the classroom.

One delightful and productive source of ideas is an anthology of games. These anthologies are available at any bookstore. They contain hundreds of prototype scoring systems and surprising analogues to learning situations. Usually the rules and rounds must be adapted thoroughly for classroom applications, but this does not detract from the richness of this unsuspected reservoir of educational ideas.

For those teachers who want to concentrate on establishing different relationships with their students, a useful structural device is the contract. What kind of contract most closely resembles the relationship you want—an industrial contract "grade" payment for specified learning products; a research contract grade payment for the energetic pursuit of answers to a difficult question; a legal, *quid pro quo,* barter contract in which your services are provided in exchange for specified student work; an apprenticeship contract like those used so fruitfully in graduate schools; a "marriage" contract in which you pledge your support for a student in sickness and health, until circumstances do you part; a gentleman's agreement emphasizing basic trust and good faith? Although few of these types of contracts can be brought into the classroom unchanged, they can focus your thinking and suggest relevant adaptations in your existing implicit relationship contracts.

Some examples

Often the inventions of other teachers are useful with little modification. They also illustrate the range of applications you may want to consider in restructuring the learning in your class:

A first grade teacher in Nijmegen, Holland is using improvisational theater games to provide an immediate experience base for stories read and words learned.

A Cambridge, Massachusetts, history teacher uses the format of improvisational theater to establish experiential insight into dramatic historical moments.

A Kansas City biology teacher devised a scoring system in which the most successful students could raise their grades by coaching the students with poorest marks. The best students got a bonus equivalent to 50 percent of the improvement in the grades of their tutees.

In Philadelphia there is an experimental storefront school in which getting knowledge is like a scavenger hunt from the various institutions in the city—the art institute, the historical society, etc.

The Duluth, Minnesota, school system is translating its curricula into hundreds of learning contracts so that progression through school is much like a Boy Scout merit badge progression.

A number of mathematics teachers have used the Origami Game format and bidding system to foster achievement motivation in learning math.

A teacher in a New York urban center wrote a strict *quid pro quo* contract with his unruly English class. In return for six weeks of full cooperation (during which they actually completed the semester's text), they controlled the content and approach for the remaining 10 weeks of the semester, using the teacher as consultant.

"Side Trip" 2:

Ethical Issues in Psychological Education

Ethical issues arise in Psychological Education as they do in all teacher-student relationships. The uncommonness of Psychological Education may indeed cause some of these issues to be raised afresh, where they were formerly submerged in custom and routine. Yet it will be evident that many of the ethical questions in the following list are applicable to conventional as well as novel teaching approaches. Some of the questions will never be generally resolved with "right" or "wrong" judgments; they require continued examination and discussion by teachers, and often lend themselves only to highly personal resolutions.

Here are the more salient issues involved:

How do you know when you are competent as an achievement motivation trainer? as a psychological educator?

How do you define the boundaries of your competence?

How can you continue to assess and improve your level of competence as an n-Ach trainer and psychological educator?

Who should decide what is in the best interests of group members?

What is "sensible regard for the social codes/and moral expectations of the community"?

How do you know when a group member is not benefiting from the experience? *i.e.,* when do you terminate unbeneficial relationships?

What information should be given to the group member before the course begins?

What communication and information is "privileged"?

What are appropriate admission procedures?

How can you avoid manipulation and coercion?

What kind of consultation, supervision, or advice should you have?

What is your continuing responsibility to group members after the course is over?

Who is competent as a psychological educator?

The psychological educator must recognize the significant difference between educational techniques aimed at promoting the psychological growth of people in the "normal" range and therapeutic techniques focussed on the problems of emotionally disturbed people. The psychological educator should not venture into areas of emotional

64

aberrance which are properly the province of professional psychologists.

The teaching professional may find useful analogies in this connection in portions of Principle 2, "Competence," of "Ethical Standards of Psychologists" (*American Psychologist,* January 1963, American Psychological Association, Inc., Washington, D.C.):

> *The psychologist recognizes the boundaries of his competence and the limitations of his techniques and does not offer services or use techniques that fail to meet professional standards established in particular fields. The psychologist who engages in practice assists his client in obtaining professional help for all important aspects of his problems that fall outside the boundaries of his own competence. This principle requires, for example, that provision be made for the diagnosis and treatment of relevant medical problems and for referral to or consultation with other specialists.*
>
> *The psychologist in clinical work recognizes that his effective-. ness depends in good part upon his ability to maintain sound interpersonal relations, that temporary or more enduring aberrations in his own personality may interfere with this ability or distort his appraisals of others. There he refrains from undertaking any activity in which his personal problems are likely to result in inferior professional services or harm to a client; or, if he is already engaged in such an activity when he becomes aware of his personal problems, he seeks competent professional assistance to determine whether he should continue or terminate his services to his client.*

Within the relatively clear boundaries expressed above, there are many ethical questions open to discussion by teaching professionals. For example, an extremely important question is, how do *you* know when you are competent as an achievement motivation trainer? We do not know of any unmistakable hallmarks of competence. At present there are no schools of education offering training and degrees in the area of Psychological Education. We are concerned about the rapidly rising number of individuals who proclaim themselves "group leaders," "sensitivity trainers," "encounter group gurus," "process facilitators," and offer their services after the most inadequate, unsystematic, general and unsupervised training. In contrast, we believe that professional teachers who conscientiously use this manual with the associated educational materials, and other individuals who have special training in the helping professions (*e.g.,* psychologists, counselors, social workers, ministers), will be competent to give achievement motivation training. Through this teacher's manual we have tried to provide intensive preparation specifically for achievement motivation training in a group of professional peers who are constructively critical. We have addressed this book to teachers because our experience convinces us that it is easier to teach teachers about achievement motivation than it is to provide psychologists with sufficient classroom experience and knowledge of educational procedures to operate effectively. However, in the final analysis you must assess and continue to develop your own competence in this new field.

What is in the best interest of students?

Some critics have said that "Psychological Education" is simply jargon for "brainwashing". Although this obviously is not true when compared to the practices used by North Koreans on prisoners of war, there is a similar, subtler issue. Most students assume what teachers say is right, and do what teachers ask of them without extreme environmental coercion. Yet, should teachers decide what motives are most valuable? If not teachers, then who should? Students? Parents? School boards? No matter who decides, teachers cannot completely avoid their responsibility as classroom leaders. How can teachers decide what is in the best interest of a particular student at a specific time?

Again we can explore the APA ethical standards for principles which provide useful analogies to the teaching situation:

> *Principle 3: Moral and Legal Standards. The psychologist in the practice of his profession shows sensible regard for the social codes and moral expectations of the community in which he works, recognizing that violations of accepted moral and legal standards on his part may involve his clients, students, or colleagues in damaging personal conflicts, and impugn his own name and the reputation of his profession.*

> *Principle 7: Client Welfare. The psychologist respects the integrity and protects the welfare of the person or group with whom he is working.*

The psychologist attempts to terminate a clinical or consulting relationship when it is reasonably clear to the psychologist that the client is not benefitting from it.

The psychologist who asks that an individual reveal personal information in the course of interviewing, testing, or evaluation, or who allows such information to be divulged to him, does so only after making certain that the responsible person is fully aware of the purpose of the interview, testing, or evaluation and of the ways in which the information may be used.

Principle 8: Client Relationship. The psychologist informs his prospective client of the important aspects of the potential relationship that might affect the client's decision to enter the relationship . . .

These APA principles are encompassed in the more generalized terms of the "Code of Ethics of the Education Profession" (Commission on Professional Rights and Responsibilities, NEA).

Principle 1, "Commitment to the Student," includes the following statements:

In fulfilling our obligations to the student, we—

1. Deal justly and considerately with each student.

2. Encourage the student to study varying points of view and respect his right to form his own judgment . . .

4. ˙Make discreet use of available information about the student.

5. Conduct conferences with or concerning students in an appropriate place and manner . . .

7. Avoid exploiting our professional relationship with any student . . .

The ethical issue of acting in the best interests of group members is much more prominent in T-groups, sensitivity training, and encounter groups than it is in n-Ach training. The encounter group, in contrast to n-Ach training, is an open-ended, relatively unplanned attempt to reach the subjects' deepest concerns, whatever they may be. These confrontations are facilitated when members of the groups are strangers to each other. The negative consequences of public disclosure are decreased and the climate is safer for trying out new ways of relating to other people.

However, the disadvantage of "stranger" groups is the difficulty of continuing the positive changes outside and after the group.

In contrast, n-Ach training is a planned, highly structured attempt to let people experience and understand *one* basic human concern—the desire to strive for excellence. It is less risky for participants because they know and can choose in advance whether or not to confront this issue in themselves. Everything possible is done to increase the chances that changes in achievement motivation experiences in the n-Ach course will be supported after the course. For this purpose it is extremely important to have intact, ongoing groups take the course together, whether they are students, teachers, administrators, or executives. Also, the presence of one's working friends helps deter unnecessary over-disclosure of personal problems.

Many people who have never been in a "group" fear that a super-power leader will get to their problems as quickly as a surgeon's knife, then leave them exposed and bleeding. They expect to be subtly coerced and manipulated into embarrassing statements or acts through special insight or tricks. In the past we have tried to guard against such unethical coercion by stating at the outset that "No one has to do anything they don't want to do". This assures participants that ultimately they control what happens to them. We try to guard against the more elusive forms of manipulation by outlawing it. "Manipulation" is any learning experience or intervention that can only be done once.* This rules out all tricks, games, and gambits that depend on hidden intentions, traps, setups and catches. Any learning experience that can be done twice with profit also can be described openly before the first trial with the choice of participation left up to the individual group member.

These ethical guidelines and rules, useful as they are, must still fall short of comprehensive instructions for acting in the best interests of students. The final decisions often will rest with teachers.

Since it is not possible to fully resolve all of the ethical issues in this short presentation, we recommend that you continue to grapple with them, and if possible, come up with additional rules of your own. A good starting point for your discussion is the list of questions at the beginning of this side trip in Psychological Education.

*The creators of this definition are Mr. Terry Borton and Mr. Gerald Weinstein.

"Side Trip" 3:
Achievement Motivation and Other Aspects
of Mental Health

Some people claim that individuals with high achievement motivation are expressing a neurotic desire to prove themselves and, in this way, to compensate for an absent sense of personal worth. A number of social critics have joined the attack on the entrepreneurial spirit by saying we need to replace narrow competitiveness with more pervasive cooperation, and that we need to decrease the concern with "progress" and pay attention to more unchanging, basic values. On the other side, proponents argue that achievement motivation is an essential ingredient for man in leading a mentally healthy adult working life.

One reason for this heated debate is the lack of a clearly defined, generally accepted description of what constitutes mental health. We have an extensive vocabulary and sophisticated theories which allow us to talk with great precision about the varieties and vicissitudes of mental illness, but most people, including psychiatrists, are practically incoherent when describing the nature of mental health. Typically, mental health is defined as the absence of mental illness, a definition about as useful as lumping together all the colors of the rainbow into one category called "not black." For the majority of people who are not mentally ill there are degrees of mental health and a wide variation in types of healthiness. Thus, if the debate about the mental health value of achievement motivation is to be informed and useful, we all must be clearer about the nature of mental health.

There are two basic ways of describing mental health—as a combination of traits or as a sequence of developmental stages. Perhaps the most readable trait description of mental health has been written by Gordon Allport ("The Mature Personality", Chapter 12 in *Pattern and Growth in Personality,* New York: Holt Rinehart and Winston, 1961). After reviewing other theories of mental health, Allport identified six basic traits that mapped the domain of psychological health:

"Realistic perception, skills and assignments"

The healthy person sees reality clearly and has the skills and motivation to solve the problems he sees.

"Widely extended sense of Self"

The healthy person is personally committed to the welfare of other people, often quite distant from himself.

69

"Warmly relating of the Self to others"
The healthy person is capable of intimacy and openness.
"Emotional security"
This involves self acceptance and frustration tolerance.
"Self objectification"
Insight and a sense of humor allow the healthy person to see himself with perspective.
"Unifying philosophy of life"
Through commitment to basic values (religious, ethical, political, aesthetic, economic, etc.) the healthy person has integrity and a sense of direction.

One interesting way to gain a personal and detailed understanding of these six traits is to read Allport's more extensive descriptions and then rate yourself on a 1-to-7 scale ("very low" to "very high"). In what way are you most mature? Least mature? What aspects of mental health does n-Ach foster or inhibit? What kind of Psychological Education course do you need most? How much does your mental health vary in any given month? According to these dimensions, at what time in your life were you most mature, least mature? When did you most need achievement motivation? When did you need it least? You can puzzle over these questions alone or in a group with others who have rated their own mental health. If you are working in a group, you may find it helpful to hear from others what they think are your most and least mature features. Incidentally, this same procedure can be followed using Maslow's 16 traits of a peak experience, listed in *Toward a Psychology of Being* (Princeton, N.J.: Van Nostrand 1968, second edition, pp. 103-114, paperback).

A number of theorists have claimed that the nature of mental health changes at different stages of life. They would say of Allport's and Maslow's trait theories that such descriptions preclude the possibility of children and the elderly being considered mentally healthy. Instead, theorists such as Erikson, Freud, and Piaget suggest a sequence of hierarchical stages, each characterized by a predominant issue. Each of these issues (*e.g.* the identity crisis during adolescence) can be resolved in a healthy way. The most succinct and relevant description of the stage theory of mental health is by Erik Erikson ("Identity and the Life Cycle," *Psychological Issues,* Vol. I, no. 1, 1959, "Growth and Crises in the Healthy Personality," pp. 50-100). It is difficult to translate Erikson's stages into a quick rating scale. It would be useful, however, to rate each stage in terms of the value of achievement motivation for encouraging a healthy resolution. For example, after all the popular misconceptions of the "identity crisis," you might be surprised to find identity formation described as depending heavily on recognized, personally satisfying accomplishments, for which n-Ach is quite useful. For further clarification and a broader perspective on all the descriptions of mental health, you will find it helpful to read Marie Johada's *Current Concepts of Positive Mental Health* (New York: Basic Books, Inc. 1958).

According to both trait and stage theorists, achievement motivation is a legitimate feature of mental health, but it is not the only healthy trait and it is not equally important during every stage of the life cycle. Most teachers know this instinctively and act on their intuitive knowledge. They give students great warmth and support at certain stages of development, often when students are fairly young; when students are older, teachers more regularly provide stimulating challenges. At any given stage, some students need more support than challenge. In general, trait and stage theories of mental health allow us to ask with greater precision important questions of timing and emphasis of approach to promoting psychological growth. For instance, at what stages of the life cycle is affiliation training most relevant? At what ages should students not be given n-Ach training? What other course should be given in what sequence to promote full development? What would happen if certain aspects of mental health were left unattended and undeveloped? If you were to describe now what kind of course you needed most to develop greater maturity, what would that course be? What precisely are we doing now in schools to promote aspects of mental health directly? Implicit in these questions and theories are answers to the critics of achievement motivation training: n-Ach is neither healthy nor unhealthy; it is more important at certain times in the life cycle than at others, and more important for certain people than others.

"Side Trip" 4:

Other Psychological Education Techniques and Courses

Achievement motivation training is unique in its specific goals, but shares with other Psychological Education courses a variety of characteristics—the use of experience-based learning to increase self-knowledge, the integration of imagination, action, and feelings, and the direct attempt to promote personal growth. Many teachers are convinced that this type of learning is lacking in schools, and believe that other courses in addition to n-Ach training should be a regular part of formal education. At present, unfortunately, there are not many places to learn how to teach these courses and how to use the associated techniques.* One of the best ways to begin developing competence in this new area of education is to go through the n-Ach course thoroughly and learn how to give n-Ach courses well. It will then be easier to transfer and generalize skills to other Psychological Education courses. However, for your own planning it will be helpful to identify key skills and techniques now by reading about other courses. This way you can concentrate most on those aspects of n-Ach training you wish to use later, or perhaps even introduce into your n-Ach course those techniques you want to use subsequently.

A quick overview of Psychological Education courses includes:

Urban affairs and communications courses designed to tap student concerns for identity, power, and relationships and develop a wider repertoire of responses to these concerns.

Planned solo-survival experiences to develop self-reliance.

Techniques for establishing a sound psychological contract with students at the beginning of the school year.

Leadership principles for increasing creative thinking and problem solving in groups.

Methods for uncovering destructive self-criticism in students.

The use of sensitivity training in schools.

Value clarification procedures.

Introductory courses in humanistic education.

---

*At the State University of New York in Albany a new program in Psychological Education has been created to train teachers, develop curricula, and conduct research. This program provides training in a variety of Psychological Education courses for groups of educators. For more information, write to Program in Humanistic Education, S.U.N.Y., 436 Washington Avenue, Albany, New York.

These courses constitute a representative cross-section of approaches. A comprehensive bibliography on Psychological Education would include more then 300 relevant books, articles, films, and tapes. The following seven books, however, can provide an extensive, yet still manageable, introduction to the field:

Jones, R. M., *Fantasy and Feeling in Education.* N.Y.: New York University Press, 1968.

Jones discusses the relationship of the humanistic education emphasis on fantasy and feeling to such major curriculum innovations as the Educational Development Center's "Man—A Course of Study." He criticizes Jerome Bruner's theory of instruction and attempts to make useful distinctions between psychotherapy and education.

McClelland, D. C. and Winter, D. G., *Motivating Economic Achievement.* N.Y.: Free Press, 1969.

This book reports the research results of achievement motivation training for groups of businessmen in several countries. The findings constitute the best evidence to date for the efficacy of Psychological Education procedures and the limitations of these approaches.

Miles, M., *Learning to Work in Groups.* N.Y.: Bureau of Publications, Teachers College, Columbia University, 1959.

A comprehensive "how-to-do-it" manual for planning and conducting Psychological Education group meetings.

Otto, H. and Mann, Jr. (eds.), *Ways of Growth.* N.Y.: Grossman Publishers, Inc., 1968.

This is a collection of articles by 19 innovators who have developed specific means and methods designed to actualize human potential. It is a readable overview of the field.

Parnes, S. J., and Harding, H. F., *A Sourcebook for Creative Thinking.* N.Y.: Charles Scribner and Sons, 1962.

Twenty-nine articles by researchers, theoreticians, and practitioners provide a thorough introduction to all aspects of the development of the creative processes.

Perls, F. S., Hefferline, R. F., and Goodman, P., *Gestalt Therapy: Excitement and Growth in the Human Personality*. N.Y.: Dell (paperback), 1965.

This book contains a section of exercises for the reader to experience and grow in ways described in the second half of the book devoted to theory. Mastery of these methods and ideas make most other current approaches into variations on its themes.

Spolin, V. *Improvisation for the Theater*. Evanston, Ill.: Northwestern University Press, 1963.

Although Spolin's book grew from her work with novice actors, the ideas and procedures have been transformed for most types of groups from students in elementary school to businessmen in T-groups. Familiarity with these methods will facilitate the use of non-verbal methods, games, role-plays, psycho-drama, and sociodrama.

In addition to these books, several others are particularly rich sources of methods and techniques:

Nylon, D., Mitchell, R., and Stout, A., *Handbook for Staff Development and Human Relations Training;* National Training Laboratory Institute for Applied Behavioral Science, NEA, 1201 16th Street, N.W., Washington, D.C. 20036

Malamud, D.I., and Machover, S., *Toward Self Understanding: Group Techniques in Self Confrontation*. Springfield, Ill., Charles C. Thomas, 1965

Otto, H., *Group Methods Designed to Actualize Human Potential,* Chicago, Achievement Motivation Systems, 1439 Michigan Avenue, Chicago, Ill.

Raths, L., Harmin, M., and Simon, S., *Values and Teaching,* Columbus, Ohio, Charles Merrill Books, 1966

Schutz, W., *Joy,* N.Y.: Grove Press, 1968

Obviously, there is a great deal to read and learn. How you proceed through this material depends in part on whether you are operating alone or with others. Since most of these methods are experience-based, they can be understood fully only when they are experiences, even though extrapolating from your involvement in n-Ach training will give you some idea of what they are about. Thus, you may find it useful to try out a few of the exercises with your whole n-Ach training group. But even this experience is not enough, since the final utility of these techniques lies in their application to ongoing teaching situations. Again, your group may be useful in helping to invent new applications, *e.g.* theater improvisations in history courses to get an internal perspective on events and situations, fantasy tours as a way of understanding certain difficult literary symbols, game simulations to restructure the way learning takes place, or encounter group methods to deal with anger, loneliness, and fear in students.

As you gain experience in applying these techniques to your subject-matter areas, it is likely you will see the subject matter change. Typically, teachers begin to find new topics that are more immediately and directly relevant to students' basic concerns for identity, achievement, power, and relationships. As a result, the subject matter and teacher-student relationships become more personal. For most teachers who begin to explore Psychological Education techniques, these are, in fact, the goals they have in mind from the start.

"Side Trip" 5:
Exploring the Uses of Imagination

We think of imagination as some mysterious essence that inspires a painting, makes a poem happen, shapes the creation of a film. We assume that some people have a great deal of it—like artists, clever cooks, or inventive children—while most people have an average, trifling amount of it. In fact, imagination is a weak muscle that can be strengthened. For example: planning is a special use of imagination characterized by being detailed, accurate, realistic. In achievement motivation training, imagination is used to create plans for the attainment of desired future goals. Achievement planning helps strengthen imagination in general.

Imagination is an available tool for solving a variety of problems. Unfortunately, most of us do not benefit from its full potential because we devalue and confine it. We believe "imagining things" is something paranoids do. When we catch ourselves daydreaming, we feel bad about wasting time. We believe that enjoying a fantasy is for children when they hear a fairy tale. Even though thoughts are not actions, we often feel guilty for having "bad" thoughts and shun "unthinkable" ideas as if they would come true automatically. Conversely, we react to some of our happiest fantasies and zaniest notions as if they were wild pipe dreams instead of regarding them as potentially productive. One result of these beliefs is that many adults have lost the ability to engage in a constructive dialogue with their fantasy lives and to explore fully the useful applications of imagination.

After these comments you may be wondering how much you too, without realizing it over the years, have let your imagination atrophy. If so, try the following exercise.* It will take about 15-20 minutes.

1. Think of the one person in the world you hate most. If you can't think of a single person, make up one person out of the traits you dislike most. If it helps, close your eyes as you conjure up this horrible individual in excruciating detail.

2. If this person were an animal, what would he be? Imagine him (or her) as an animal. Write down the name of the animal and what it's like. Then think of one adjective that best describes it.

---

*The idea for this exercise came from Professor Gerald Weinstein, University of Massachusetts School of Education, Amherst, Mass.

3. If you could be transformed, what kind of animal would you be? Again, write down what you would be like as that animal, and a single adjective that best describes the animal-you.

4. Now, close your eyes and vividly visualize an encounter between the two animals, the adversary and you. Take five or more minutes to play out a full scene.

5. What happened? Did one animal flee? Did the two animals fight? How did the fight end? Did one animal kill the other? Did he tear the other to shreds? What happened to the pieces? How did your fantasy end? Did you stop it abruptly when you became uncomfortable with the images? How many minutes did it last? What would have happened in the fantasy if it had continued?

Take a few minutes to think about these questions. You also may want to consider more general questions: Just how dangerous is it to have destructive thoughts? What is the relationship between thoughts and actions? These issues are complex and it is unlikely that you will reach clear answers. Regardless of your conclusions, you probably were unable to have truly uninhibited fantasies. Perhaps this is just as well with aggressive ideas, but what about constructive imagination which needs uninhibited support to develop its full potential and usefulness? If you want to strengthen your imagination, you might like to try some of the exercises listed below. They are listed roughly in order of difficulty and depth.

1. Developing a Super Power Memory

Harry Lorrayne, a nightclub performer of memory feats, wrote a book with a similar title that was no overstatement. The basic technique for developing such a memory actually is very simple: form a ridiculous mental image, associating two things you want to remember together. It helps if this ridiculous association is a concrete visual image, in motion, and exaggerated in size. For example, if you wanted to remember to buy a loaf of bread on the way home, you would close your eyes and visualize your car (or whatever means of transportation you use) as a gigantic loaf of flying bread, sailing over buildings towards your home. You would remember your errand as you opened the door to your car/loaf. There are a variety of applications of this principle: memorizing lists, dates, speeches, the cards that have been played, faces

77

and names, telephone numbers with names, the contents of books, and articles, etc. Learning the ingenious, specific applications of this imaginative technique requires some guided practice. Either of the following two books will teach you the tricks:

How to Develop a Super Power Memory by Harry Lorrayne, New York: Fredrick Fell, Inc. 1956

The Famous Roth Memory Course by David M. Roth, Cleveland: Ralston Publishing Co. 1952 Edition

This way of memorizing quickly and easily is a useful and practical application of imagination. Given the existence of these proven techniques and the prototypic success of speed reading courses, it is quite surprising that memorization seldom is taught to students or adults.

2. Getting Creative Perspectives on Difficult Problems

Being creative, like memorizing, requires unusual associations that initially may seem bizarre. Problem-solving groups, whether they are in classrooms or executive offices, usually have strong norms against making bizarre remarks. Understandable as it may be, this norm has a repressive effect when time comes to find a creative solution to a difficult problem. The way a group is led can allow for appropriately timed strange and creative associations. For example, the leader can introduce the "get fired" policy: "Give me some ideas so far out that if you proposed them seriously to the boss/teacher you would be fired/flunked."* The brightest ideas often lurk beneath seemingly outrageous proposals. Other leadership principles and meeting procedures for increasing creative problem-solving are described in these sources:

Prince, G. "Leadership for Creativity and Synectics Meetings" Educational Opportunities Forum, August 1969. Volume entitled "New Directions in Psychological Education," New York State Department of Education, Albany, New York.

Prince, G. "How to be a Better Meeting Chairman," Harvard Business Review, January/February 1969.

Prince, G. Creative Leadership, Synectics, Inc., 26 Church Street, Cambridge, Massachusetts.

Gordon, W.J.J., Synectics: The Development of Creative Capacity, New York: Harper and Row, 1961

*Idea taken from Creative Leadership, by G. Prince.

78

These books and articles describe how to use imagination to make the familiar strange and the strange familiar; how to explore personal, fantasy, mythical, and direct analogies; how to take a useful, active vacation from a problem, and how to obtain a final workable solution. These techniques can be used alone or in groups.

3. *Body Tours and Other Fantastic Trips*

Carl Jung and Robert Assogioli, two of Freud's disciples, have explored images from dreams as signs of personal growth, instead of interpreting these images as symptoms of neurotic conflicts. Jung's research into world-wide religious symbols, artistic images, and signs in alchemy led him to conclude that there were a number of universally meaningful symbols representing archtypical historic experiences. For example, Jung found that the mandala symbol, an intricate wheel-like pattern, was used repeatedly in religions around the world to signify the highest state of being and unity, or what Jung called *individuation.* When Jung heard mandala symbols described in the dreams of his patients, he interpreted the dream as a striving for individuation. To foster that concern for growth, Jung often asked his patients to use paint to explore and develop their dream imagery.

Robert Assogioli, a student of Freud and Jung, has developed additional ways of exploring these symbols (Assogioli, R., *Psychosynthesis: A manual of principles and techniques;* N.Y.: Hobbs, Dorman & Co., Inc. 1965). Instead of waiting for the symbols to emerge spontaneously, Assogioli takes persons on guided tours of such universal symbols as the cave, the meadow, the life cycle of a grain of wheat, the old man, one's body, and mandalas. Assogioli believes that in this way growth is stimulated more directly. Vivid accounts of fantasy tours may be found on pages 90-115 of *Joy* (William Schutz, New York: Grove Press, Inc. 1967). Typically, a fantasy tour provides a cathartic emotional release, a fresh perspective on oneself, and a personal, tailor-made allegory to use in further self-understanding. Fantasy tours often are highly emotional experiences requiring sympathetic professional tour guides. Careful, knowledgeable preparation is required for this experience to be most helpful.

4 *Dream analysis through image role-play.*

The following method of dream analysis is based on the principles of

Gestalt Therapy.* This process can be done alone or in groups, but should be preceded by a careful reading of *Gestalt Therapy* and/or *Gestalt Therapy Verbation.*

a) Write down your dream in as much detail as possible;

b) Role play each image in the dream from the central characters and objects to the elements of the environment in your dream;

c) Conduct dialogues between various characters and elements in your dream.

Frederick Perls developed this method of working with dreams. He describes vividly why and how to use dream-work in reintegrating alienated aspects of your personality:

> *If you understand what you can do with dreams, you can do a tremendous lot for yourself on your own. Just take any old dream or dream fragment, it doesn't matter. As long as a dream is remembered, it is still alive and available, and it still contains an unfinished, unassimilated situation. When we are working on dreams, we usually take only a small little bit from the dream, because you can get so much from even a little bit.*
>
> *So if you want to work on your own, I suggest you write the dream down and make a list of all the details in the dream. Get every person, every thing, every mood, and then work on these to become each one of them. Ham it up, and really transform yourself into each of the different items. Really become that thing—whatever it is in a dream—become it. Use your magic. Turn into that ugly frog or whatever is there—the dead thing, the live thing, the demon—and stop thinking. Lose your mind and come to your senses. Every little bit is a piece of the jigsaw puzzle, which together will make up a much larger whole—a much stronger, happier, more completely real personality.*
>
> *Next, take each one of these different items, characters, and parts, and let them have encounters between them. Write a script. By "write a script," I mean have a dialogue between the two opposing parts and you will find—especially if you get the correct*

Gestalt Therapy Verbation, Frederick Perls, Real People Press, 939 Carol Lane, LaFayette, California 94549, 1969; *Gestalt Therapy: excitement and growth in the human personality,* Perls, F.S., Hefferline, R.F., and Goodman, P., N.Y. Julian Press, 1951, (paperback edition by Dell Publishing Company, N.Y. 1965).

opposites—that they always start out fighting each other. All the different parts—any part in the dream is yourself, is a projection of yourself, and if there are inconsistent sides, contradictory sides, and you use them to fight each other, you have the eternal conflict game, the self-torture game. As the process of encounter goes on, there is a mutual learning until we come to an understanding, and an appreciation of differences, until we come to a oneness and integration of the two opposing forces. Then the civil war is finished, and your energies are ready for your struggles with the world.

Each little bit of work you do will mean a bit of assimilation of something. In principle, you can get through the whole cure—let's call it cure or maturation—if you did this with every single thing in one dream. Everything is there. In different forms the dreams change, but when you start like this, you'll find more dreams will come and the existential message will become clearer and clearer."

Gestalt Therapy Verbation, pp. 69-70

It is easy for this procedure to become an embarrassing parlor game because it is so tempting to believe you understand someone else's dream images and role plays better than they do. This, of course, is untrue. Enforcing a simple rule helps in this regard: No interpretations may be made by anyone except the owner of the dream. As a further safeguard for personal comfort, this type of dream analysis should be done only with trusted friends.

There are a variety of ways these forms of imagination can be introduced in schools, *e.g.,* using dream analysis procedures for understanding and personalizing a poem; using memory techniques to help students have fun remembering necessary but dull material; fostering achievement planning; using synectics procedures to solve science problems creatively. Regardless of the subject matter content to which these processes are applied, the net effect will be to strengthen students' powers of imagination, a legitimate goal of education itself.

81

Internalization: Assessing the Effects of
Motivation Training

Almost all of us can recall students who came back several years after we taught them, and told us how much they were influenced by what we taught—the student who became involved in a local campaign issue as a result of social studies class, the quiet girl who continued to write poetry after an English class, the tough kid who performed superbly well in a job he learned to do in auto mechanics class, the boy who never forgot the help he got when he was in trouble. Even though these testimonials are fairly rare, we never forget them. Beneath it all, this is the kind of influence we would like to have on all our students— internalization of the processes, motives, and values we try to embody in our teaching.

Paradoxically, a visit by one of these former students usually comes as a surprise. It is as though we seldom thought about or expected these long-term effects. Somehow the day-to-day joys and frustrations effectively crowd out these hopes, and distract us from our ultimate goals in teaching. This is unfortunate, because it is easy to become myopic and teach for the short-term daily results instead of teaching differently for the more difficult goal of internalization. Interestingly, students share those long-term goals and are affected in the same way as teachers by the distracting influences of short-term concerns.

Up to this point you may have been reading between the lines making comparisons between the ideals of internalization and your everyday goals. Probably you have come up with a confused array of plusses and minuses to your credit. Your feelings may run the gamut from depressing failure to the comforting knowledge that you have been successful with a number of students. Most likely you want to know how to improve your teaching. Let us try an experiment which will help you make greater sense of your long-term goals. In this experiment we would like to direct you through a daydream about your greatest success as a teacher. Later, as you compare this daydream with what you do in class, you may be able to see ways of becoming more successful. The experiment can be done alone or in a group, but in either case, find a place where there are as few distractions as possible. Here are the terms of the daydream:

Think about the subject matter you most value and like to

teach. Conjure up in your imagination a "prize" student, whose life after your course is like a prize given to you for your teaching. Is the student male or female? What does the student look like? Close your eyes if it helps you imagine the student, or start with one of your current students.

It's now July, a year after you last saw this student. It's a weekend and the student has two days of free time to do what he most desires. This is *your* prize student who voluntarily initiates on the weekend what, unknown to you, most pleases you as a teacher. *What does the student do?* Take four or five minutes to imagine the whole weekend. If you have chosen one of your actual students, try not to be bound solely by what that student actually has done. The point of the daydream is to imagine as clearly as possible what your ultimate hopes for students are. Now take a little more time to imagine what else this student does during the week and over the summer.

Try to continue the daydream in the following situation: Ten years have passed. One day, as a complete surprise to you, your prize student returns to tell you how important you have been in his life. What does he tell you in his five-minute monologue of praise?

Whether or not you are doing this exercise in a group, it is useful to share your scenario with at least one other person. If you started alone, ask one of your friends to create his own "prize student" daydream. As you share your success stories, you may wish to consider the following questions to help you relate what happened in your daydream to your current teaching:

Is there anything that your student did which is currently planned and taught during your course?

How well do your tests and final exams reflect the long-term internalized results you imagined?

Can these long-term results be measured in any form at the end of a semester?

What would you use at the end of the school year to predict these long-term results? Can you measure these predictors?

What were one or two of the most important learning experiences in your own life?

Internalization is the process of taking a skill, idea, value, or motive from an outside source and voluntarily incorporating it into one's own repertoire to such an extent that the behavior in time becomes the person's own. In our research studies of achievement motivation training we have collected systematic follow-up data on how much internalization takes place as the result of different types of teaching procedures. As researchers, we understand why teachers seldom try to collect this data for their own purposes. It is time-consuming, costly, difficult to obtain, and often disappointing. This confession of understanding is not a warm-up prior to asking you to contact all of your old students to see how much they internalized what you taught them. However, you may find it interesting and useful to know what we look for, where we look, and how we find out how much internalization has taken place. We follow several guidelines:

Wait a year.

Internalization takes a while. After a year, if the person does not show various new energetic strivings for excellence, then whatever short-term motivation developed during the course probably was not deeply meaningful.

Look for voluntary concerns with excellence.

Almost everyone has within his repertoire of responses sufficient achievement motivation to deal with those situations which demand competition, planning, and energetic pursuit of excellence. What distinguishes the person with high achievement motivation is his spontaneous, voluntary concerns with excellence even when it is not necessarily demanded by the situation. Thus, we look at how a person uses his leisure time and the personal goals he sets.

Look for displays of the motive syndrome in several areas.

If achievement motivation is meaningful, useful, and valued, it will be evident in several areas. With students we find that leisure time, sports, hobbies, work, and—to a lesser extent—school are the most likely places to find evidence of increased n-Ach.

Look for evidence that the person values and enjoys his increased effectiveness.

Internalization will not occur if the motive syndrome is dysfunctional in the person's life. The best way to find out is to ask the person.

Our lengthy follow-up interviews reveal large differences in the degree to which the person values and enjoys achievement concerns.

If you had approached your prize student and looked for evidence of internalization in these four ways, most likely you would have uncovered much of what was in your directed daydream. This supposition is slightly rigged, inasmuch as the instructions given for your directed daydream included the features just listed. Our intention was honest enough—to let you experience vividly what we mean by internalization. Our intention now is to help you examine your classroom teaching in terms of what you can do to foster internalization.

Measuring the Steps to Internalization
You may feel that internalization is not a sufficient measure of what is taught in schools. True enough. There is a great deal of basic information simply to be stored by students for possible later use. Often mere exposure to and appreciation of ideas is sufficient. Not everything that is taught can or should be expanded into a life value. However, for those values, processes, and motives we *do* want internalized, how we teach and what we measure should be directly related to internalization. Unfortunately, most of what students are graded for in school is only indirectly related to internalization.

The typical way we test students conveys an unreal, rather strange model of the world and what it takes to succeed. For example, life situations do not demand solely motor skill performance (as in typing classes, wood shop, or metal working) or cognitive performance (as in most academic courses). Doing well requires being at once motorically, cognitively, and emotionally involved. It would be silly to say that you are an A+ husband or wife cognitively, a B+ husband or wife motorically, and a C+ husband or wife emotionally. Yet curricula are divided and students graded in these ways.

In another strange contradiction, students are asked to repeat, remember, or comment on *past* learning, though life tests challenge us with decisions to be made for the future—we must predict and choose in eternal uncertainty. Perhaps most misleading of all is the fact that students do not make up their own exam questions. The thought that they should seems provocative. But consider the following: "Test taking" is synonymous with responding to the questions of *others;* yet, after school is over, students do not have question-askers following them around providing appropriate multiple choices at the critical moments. Most students realize at some level that school learning as tested is a strange, esoteric game, and not the same as the living which goes on before and after class.

This is a knotty problem, since it is no easy task to measure long-term spontaneous displays of motivation, values, and processes. Still, there should be additional ways of helping students see tests in the perspective of imperfect predictors of internalization. And it should be possible for teachers to use predictors that are more directly related to stages in the process of internalization. With these possibilities in mind, let us again return to our illustrative example of achievement motivation. How do we measure the steps to internalization of n-Ach?*

In order to arouse and internalize n-Ach in students we provide educational inputs which (1) get the student's attention, (2) provide a unified, thorough experience of the motive syndrome, (3) result in a clear conceptualization of the motive syndrome, (4) relate the motive syndrome to other important aspects of the student's life, and (5) get the students to practice using the motive syndrome in ways that are meaningful and satisfying to them. These stages are sequential in nature. To experience the motive syndrome thoroughly, students must be attending. In order for the motive syndrome to be conceptualized clearly, it must be experienced. Before the motive can be related to other parts of the person's life, it must be clearly conceptualized, etc. Because of this, failures during the early stages of internalization tend to block the ultimate goal. On the other hand, measured success at each stage does not necessarily guarantee the ultimate internalization of the motive. This scheme does, however, indicate a series of psychological states you can measure to find out how well you are succeeding stage by stage.

1.   *How do you measure attention?*

Attendance and Tardiness: If the class is voluntary, attendance is a

---

*For expert advice and extensive examples of how to measure various stages in the internalization of material from the cognitive and affective domains, see David R. Kratwohl, Benjamin S. Bloom, and Bertram B. Masia, *Taxonomy of Educational Objectives, Handbook I, (Cognitive Domain); Handbook II (Affective Domain);* David McKay Co., Inc., N.Y., 1956, 1964.

good measure of interest, involvement, and attention. If students do not attend class, obviously, it is impossible to get their attention.

Down Time and Restlessness: At the psychological level, attention is measured by eye fixation, pupil dilation, heart rate deceleration, and a number of other indices of autonomic activity. At a molar, or visible, level, this type of attention often is evident in stillness, although stillness also can reflect daydreaming, boredom, or sleep. Conversely, physical restlessness is almost a sure sign of lost attention. It is "down time" or time lost to learning. Teachers easily can make rough estimates of the percentage of "down time" in a class at any given point during class.

Distraction Tolerance: A person is attending if his activities continue in spite of distractions, annoyances, interruptions, and other world obstacles. The boy engrossed in a book, happily concentrating in the midst of mild chaos, is a clear example of strong attention. How much does it take to distract your students?

2.   *How do you know the person has thoroughly experienced the motive syndrome?*

Integration: At the most fundamental level, the experience must include the thoughts, actions, and feelings associated with the motive. No aspect of the motive can be left out.

Involvement: The best single index of how involved students are in a experience is the amount of spontaneous talk about it afterward. If the students can't stop talking about their experience, if they are excited and *specific* in their conversation, they were involved.

3.   *How do you know students have clearly conceptualized the motive?*

Methods for assessing this aspect of learning are numerous and well-known to teachers. These methods ask students to give definitions, recall examples, identify correct and incorrect instances, label, etc. In achievement motivation training, the student must be able to recognize and label achievement thoughts, actions, and feelings in himself as well as in situations and people outside himself.

4.   *How do you know students have related the motive syndrome to other important aspects of their lives?*

Again, the methods used to assess this are straightforward and well-known to teachers: essays, discussions, reports describing the relationship between n-Ach and actual demands in their daily lives, their group and cultural values. The initial question is whether students can describe where n-Ach would be useful to them, where it would not be useful, and why.

5. *How do you know the person can use the motive syndrome?*

Situational Tests: Game simulations provide an easy way in school to see if the student can use the motive for planning and acting in a related new situation.

Projects: The ability to complete an independent achievement goal-setting project is evidence that the student knows how to apply the motive outside highly structured, heavily cued situations in n-Ach courses.

Diaries and Follow-up Conferences: These procedures are more free-flowing and spontaneous. As a result, they are better indicators of the voluntary, appropriate uses of n-Ach.

Indirect Reports: When the course has been particularly effective for a student, the resulting changes usually are noticed and word gets back. The "grapevine" is a good way to seek and obtain data on the follow-up uses of n-Ach by students.

Each of these measures makes it possible for you to do informal research on your own teaching effectiveness. Based on the data you obtain, you can try out new teaching methods that you think will increase the likelihood that motives, processes, and values will be internalized. Whether alone or with another teacher, you may want to try out the following exercises:

Keep track of the rough percentage of down time in each of your classes for one week. Is there anything in your style or activity that seems clearly related to upsurges in tuned-in learning time?

For some value, process, or motive you consider to be important, try to design a lesson in which students are fully involved in the thought, feelings, and actions. What differences do you see when all three aspects are included in the lesson?

Spend some time talking frankly with individual students. Ask them what meaning your course has for them outside class. In what ways have they begun to internalize what they learn in class? What suggestions do they have for you that would help them use and appreciate what you teach?

These measures of stages in the internalization process and the three exercises just mentioned raise the question of what strategy is most effective in fostering internalization. At the present time in American education there is a heated debate in progress directly addressing this question. On one side are those who advocate programmed learning, behavioral objectives, and contract learning. They argue that the best way to ensure long-term internalization is to make sure the students *master* the material. True satisfaction comes, they claim, only after mastering something difficult. Only then will the material be transformed within the person and creatively applied. On the other side of the debate are those proponents of the Leicestershire model of open education, Summerhill, and neo-progressive schools. These educators argue that internalization comes because students enjoy what they are doing. Thus, teachers should make sure the process and content of the course is engaging and satisfying, because mastery is a natural by-product that occurs in time as students continue to improve at what they enjoy doing. In all likelihood, these strategies are alternative routes to internalization, depending on the teacher, the subject matter, and the student. This is an easy and fairly unsatisfactory way of saying that you must work out your own strategy. Hopefully, some of the ideas in this session will be useful to you as you assess your efforts and try out new ways to be more effective in fostering internalization.

"Side Trip" 7:

The Helping Relationship

People with high achievement motivation don't like to be helped, at least not in the usual sense of the word. They like to set their own goals, take personal responsibility for what happens to them, and help themselves by taking the initiative. This does *not* mean that high n-Ach types are uncompromising loners and will not seek or accept advice when they need it. People with high n-Ach are perfectly willing to work collaboratively for mutual achievement goals if they have a reasonable amount of affiliation motivation. They do seek advice when they encounter difficulties, but from experts rather than friends. People with high n-Ach simply want a special kind of help that is appropriate to their motivation.

This is not a unique situation. Every configuration of motives requires a special complementary style of helping. Five-year-olds need adults to emulate, athletes need coaches, and Hippies need their gurus. Often we need only warmth and approval to try something new on our own, but we don't want warmth and support from a policeman when we need specific information instead to find our way. Fortunately there are innumerable styles of helping, from advising on financial investments to repairing teeth, from being a courtroom judge to a classroom lecturer. In spite of the wide range of helping styles illustrated in these professions, most teachers' repertoires are comparatively narrow.

In this side trip we do not promise you an instant assortment of new ways to help. The first task is to break stereotypes, loosen lines, and broaden the image of what helping and being helped involve. The exercises in this side trip allow you to explore the helping relationship in ways that focus on mutuality. Our goal is to sharpen your awareness of what different kinds of helping relationships feel like from either side, as the helper or the helped. The exercises will lead you to questions like these: What's the difference between telling and giving advice? Do reprimands and punishments ever help? How are requests for help disguised or presented indirectly? How do we make help available to someone who needs it, but insists he doesn't want it? How do we know what kind of help to give? What kind of help allows a person the most independence and freedom? What does one's helping style say about his own needs? The exercises give you a chance to gain insight into your own style of helping and to develop greater flexibility in the ways you help. The exercises also can be used with your students to start a dialogue about helping, being helped, and the most appropriate helping relationships.

Exercise 1:   Blindfold helping

Time: One mealtime, plus 1-½ to 2 hours

Purposes: (a) To focus on how it feels to help and be helped; (b) To explore helping styles and their effect on those being helped; (c) To consider how one's approach to helping affects others, particularly students.

Materials: Blindfolds for half the people in the group. A dark cloth square or any invention that thoroughly blocks the light will do (for instance, dime store variety half-masks with eyeholes covered by opaque tape make a cool, comfortable blindfold.)

Procedure (Instructions to the leader):   Divide the group in half, preferably by asking for volunteers, so that half the men and half the women are blindfolded. Obviously this exercise requires a minimum of two people. The instructions are simply that the blindfolded persons should keep the blindfolds on at all times until after the group has reconvened. The exercise should begin just before meal time. Decide on a time about 45 minutes after the meal is over when everyone will reassemble. After the meal people may do anything they wish (except take off the blindfold) until reconvening. This exercise has been done successfully in some fairly outlandish settings, ranging from apple orchards to Harvard Square. There is little need to worry about the appropriateness of your setting, unless you're perched on the edge of a cliff. As the exercise begins, resist the temptation to force people together. Let things happen naturally, as much as possible. It's perfectly all right for you to participate as a "helper" or a blindfolded person.

Discussion: When group members reassemble, seat them in a circle with the blindfolded members still masked, at least part way into the discussion. After about 15 minutes, people should be told they can remove the blindfolds when they wish. Some people will want to keep their blindfolds on for a fairly long period of time. Most likely the discussion will consist of spontaneous, anecdotal talking at first. As discussion leader, you will want to take advantage of this excitement and for a while listen carefully to people's immediate impressions and feelings. However, you should guard against an endless, unchanneled discussion where one anecdote follows another and the group stacks observations without really sharing or shaping the experience in a way that helps members generalize and draw conclusions about their own helping styles. After 10 to 15 minutes, help to broaden the perspective by suggesting that people describe their styles of giving and receiving help. From there, you can move to a variety of related topics as suggested in the sample discussion questions below. You needn't ask all of these questions, but having them in mind will suggest profitable directions to pursue:

1. What happened? How did you feel during the exercise? How did you feel about the person you helped (who helped you)? What kinds of conflicts did you have? Did you object to some of the help you received or had to give? Why? What cues were you responding to? What behaviors? What were you trying to do? Why? What did you learn about the person you were with? About yourself? What kind of help did you receive/want? What cues were useful? What kinds of help seemed easiest to give/take? Which were most useful?

2. How did your partner and others see you in this situation? How did they feel about you? What behaviors explain, or would create, that impression? Is that behavior typical?

3. What are the conditions that make it possible for helping to take place? What behaviors and attitudes hinder establishing a helping relationship? What is the most effective kind of helping? What is your style of helping or helplessness? What styles did you recognize in others?

4. Are there analogies between your experiences and the classroom situation? What kinds of long-term helping relationship do we want to establish with students? How can we as teachers allow for individual needs for different kinds of help? How can we foster independence?

The discussion often produces interesting new descriptions of ways to be helpless and helpful. Some of the more frequent and useful stereotypes are described below:

Typical reactions to helplessness
Dependence: This response involves being comfortable with dependence on the sighted person. Such people wait to be told what to do before moving. They usually want to be guided physically, and are

92

content to be waited on during the meal. They ask questions of the person guiding them about possible dangers, but are reasonably certain that the guide would not lead them astray.

Counter-dependence: This response to helplessness allows no guidance or help. As a matter of fact, people with this style of helplessness do everything they can to make the guide dependent on them. They may go for coffee for the sighted people, or offer to run some kind of an errand. In any case, they are willing to risk some rather obvious dangers in order to keep from depending on anyone for any help.

Independence: The type of person who reacts with independence wants to function as much as possible by himself, but realizes that there are dangers involved in being completely alone. They ask for descriptions of the environment and potential dangers from the sighted person, so that they can explore their limits without risk of serious injury. If the situation warrants complete dependence, they can adjust to it for a while, but they want a relationship where they can learn to be independent as quickly as possible.

Typical helper roles

Over-directive: People who take this role want to help in any and every way, and would rather discourage the independence of the people they are helping than risk having the people make incorrect decisions. They serve the meals, tell exactly where everything is, and intimate that they will even be ready to guide the fork to the mouth of the blindfolded person. They act as if any mistake would be disastrous and therefore the blind person needs excessive help and directions. Dependent types like this type of helper.

Direction-avoidance: Having the responsibility for a blind person for a couple of hours may be more than this type of helper can tolerate. Such people will rationalize their unwillingness to get involved by saying, "I thought they would feel prouder if they did it by themselves." They will be partially right, but there are things they can see that the blind person can't and they could be helpful in developing the confidence of the people they are helping. Counter-dependent blind people are a good match with this type of helper.

Coaching: The goal of this style of helping is to have the blind person be able to operate on his own, but sight gives the helper certain responsibilities. He probably will ask if the person wants help before giving it to him, and, except in the case of obvious dangers, will be inclined to let the blindfolded person explore his environment for himself. He develops a facility for direction that is not directive, letting the blind person know what is about him without tugging and pulling. Often coaches will find a stick for the blind so that they can be truly independent more quickly.*

Exercise 2: Verbal Helping

Time: Two hours or more

Purpose: (a) to practice effective verbal helping; (b) to get feedback on one's own helping style; (c) to receive help on a real problem; (d) to apply insights gained in the blindfold exercise.

Materials: A set of guidelines for each of the three members in every group, and follow-through reading: "The Helping Relationship" in *Handbook of Staff and Human Relations Training,* Nylon, Mitchell and Stout, NTL-NEA, pp. 112-117.

Procedure (Instructions to the leader): Divide the group into trios. During the first round one person, the presenter, will explain to another member of the trio, the helper, a real problem with which he would like help. The third person will observe and listen to the discussion; he may not talk for 20 minutes. After 20 minutes the observer may ask questions, comment about what he has observed, and discuss the nature of effective verbal helping with the other trio members.

After the interview, all the trios come back into a larger group to share experiences and observations. The discussion should. focus on what kinds of verbal helping were most beneficial, and *not* on the particular problems presented.

A second and third round follow, so that each person has a chance in all three roles: presenter, helper, and observer. After the third round the large group reconvenes for a general discussion of "receiving help, giving help, and observing." Questions similar to those in the blindfold exercise can be used in this discussion.

---

*Another exercise that allows people to practice developing cooperative helping relationships is "The Squares Problem." A lesson plan, set of objectives, procedures and description of materials may be found in the *Handbook of Staff Development and Human Relations Training,* Nylon, D.; Mitchel, R., and Stout, A., NTL—NEA, Washington D.C. "Dimensions of Cooperation," pp. 143-146.

Suggested time schedule:

Round 1–Discussion of problem, 20 minutes; observer questions and comments, 10 minutes; large group discussion, 15 minutes.

Round 2–Discussion of problem, 20 minutes; observer comments and questions, 10 minutes.

Round 3–Discussion of third problem, 20 minutes; observer comments and questions, 10 minutes.

Summary discussion: 30 minutes or until group reaches some closure. "Helping" is an endless topic, so it is inappropriate to wait for a final conclusion. Instead, a better criterion is whether each person was able to get something useful and more general out of the exercise.

Suggestions to trio members:

To the presenter of the problem–

1. Think of a situation or problem that you feel strongly about and would like to act on.

2. When you present the problem, try to be brief and specific, but also indicate some of the reasons for your concern.

3. Give the helper a chance to ask questions. These may help you to clarify the situation and find possible solutions.

To the helper–

1. Your task is to help the presenter define his problem clearly so that he can take steps toward solving it.

2. Avoid taking over the problem ("The real problem seems to be . . .") or minimizing it ("That's not a difficult situation, we had a similar case . . ."). Instead, try to understand the problem by skillful questioning. You don't need to solve the problem.

To the observer–

1. Watch actively, but without participating. Try to define what is going on between the presenter and consultant. For example, how does the presenter actually present the problem? Does he seem to be holding back? How does the helper establish a relationship with the presenter? Does he help him speak freely? Do they listen to each other? What would make the relationship more helpful? Do they stay with defining and understanding the problem and its causes before trying to think of solutions?

2. When you present your ideas to the other two, describe what you saw and heard in an open-ended way that stimulates them to talk

about your observations. That is, avoid an evaluative summary that stamps finality on the discussion.

Final group discussion questions
1. Was there any difference in the level of involvement in your trio during the first, second, and third rounds? Why?
2. What happened during the exercise that allowed you to see yourself most clearly? What happened to confuse things?
3. What are effective verbal helping styles?
4. Are you happy with the way in which you helped? Could you describe the styles of the other two people in your trio? How do they feel about what you did?
5. Are you inclined to be the same way in other situations, such as the classroom?
6. How could you change your own classroom approach so that you would be a better helper?
7. What do you intend to do to become more effective as a helper in the classroom? What roles or what information proved helpful in each case?

Exercise 3: Observing Expert Helpers
Time: 3 hours
Purpose: (a) to observe three expert psychotherapists' styles of helping; (b) to compare your own favored style of helping and being helped to these expert styles; (c) to see the effects of different helping styles on one person.
Materials: Films—"Three Approaches to Psychotherapy"—(1) Carl Rogers, (2) Frederick Perls (3) Albert Ellis. The three films can be rented from Psychological Films, 205 West 20th Street, Santa Ana, California, 92706. Cost for all three in black and white for one week is $33.05 including postage and insurance. Allow three to six weeks for delivery.
Procedure: Exercises 1 and 2 have been open-ended, with no pretense that there were "correct" answers to be discovered inductively. Very likely you may feel at some point that you would like to see some experts at work. These films provide such an opportunity. Rogers, Ellis, and Perls are three well-known psychotherapists whose styles of helping are markedly different. In these films each man spends about 20

minutes interviewing "Gloria." Before each interview the therapist gives a brief explanation of his approach, and following the interview he comments on what happened. Each of the three films is about 40 minutes long.

In some ways you see a different Gloria in each relationship, but beneath the specific details, many of the same underlying issues emerge. In order to see clearly how each therapist gets to these issues, we suggest that you try as a group to identify them after each film. What are the issues? Does any therapist uncover an issue that another missed? If you were to choose one of these therapists, who would he be? Why?

Again, this experience, though more passive than exercises 1 and 2, is equally involving and without definitive answers. Like many of the other side trips, the goal of these exercises is not to insure that you get to some predetermined destination, but rather to provide directions for starting out. Where you go from here, how far you get, and what you do to expand your repertoire of helping styles is up to you.

SESSION 9: Getting It Together

Purpose
  During your separate side trips in Psychological Education you gathered new information and experience. The basic purpose of this session is to share with other group members what you learned by using your new knowledge collaboratively to plan an achievement course.
  Your group will divide into three or more heterogeneous sub-groups based on the particular side trips you took. Each sub-group will make many mini-plans for at least one of the six aspects of a course designed to arouse and internalize a motive: attending, experiencing, conceptualizing, relating, applying, and internalizing. In addition to sharing creatively what you learned, this session serves two other purposes: you will become more familiar with the steps in increasing motivation, and you will produce a first draft plan for an achievement motivation course.

Procedure
½ hour   Part A—Show and Tell
1 hour   Part B—Brainstorm many mini-plans
                      The large group subdivides into at least three subgroups.
                      The people in each subgroup should bring information
                      from as many different side trips as possible. Using the
                      guidelines distributed by the session leader, each sub-
                      group holds a brainstorming session on one or two of the
                      six steps in arousing and internalizing achievement
                      motivation.
30 minutes   Break
1 hour   Part C
                      The leader acts as coordinator and recorder. The sub-
                      groups share their three best mini-plans. The mini-plans
                      for each of the six steps are combined into one maxi-
                      plan.
                      Part D—Evaluation

Follow-through reading
  Chapter 4 of *Teaching Achievement Motivation;* Chapter 2 of *Motivating Economic Achievement.*

Introduction to Part B: *Brainstorming Many Mini-plans*

Several times during this workshop we have referred to a group problem solving technique called Synectics. A basic principle of Synectics is that the most creative, innovative, and ultimately useful solutions come not just from hard, analytic thinking, but from a more free-ranging process of associating remote ideas. Synectics problem solving typically is divided into three phases. First, the group states the problem and explores its meaning so that everyone understands what the problem is—an obvious but surprisingly infrequent first step in most problem solving meetings. The next phase consists of taking excursions. The object is deliberately to forget the problem by fantasizing or role playing in some unrelated realm. For example, a group of teachers decided they wanted to create a classroom environment where students would engage in more self-directed learning. During their excursions they created several group fantasies about bazaars—the fascination of a foreign bazaar, the nature of musical bazaars *(e.g. Scheherazade),* a natural bazaar like the ocean's floor, or the Zodiac, a bazaar of constellations. In the third phase, each of the metaphors from the excursion is used to derive a new and useful perspective on the original problem. The teachers decided to set up a supermarket of learning materials for students to wander through as they would through a bazaar.

The sequence of this workshop has roughly paralleled these three stages. The first chapter and first sessions clarified what n-Ach is, and presented basic course material. The side trips in Psychological Education represented excursions into other topics. Although they were not as metaphorical as the examples just cited, they did provide a vacation from the bare bones of the achievement motive itself. The next step, and the purpose of this session, is to use the excursion material to derive new solutions to your problem: How do you increase students' motivation? The procedure we suggest is that each of you team up with one or two others who took different side trips, and that you pool your knowledge in a brainstorming session. Each subgroup will be asked to come up with at least 25 ideas for implementing one or two steps in the sequence of arousing and internalizing motives. Your three best ideas should be developed in greater detail. During part C of this session each of the subgroups will share their most interesting ideas. The resulting maxi-plan will give you a giant head start in planning for an n-Ach course.

The brainstorming process works like this: The basic intent is for participants to create a flow of ideas that ricochet off each other's suggestions. The all-important ground rule is that no criticism is allowed. The time limit of one hour helps you to work in a super-compressed way, as if you were cramming for a test or rushing to meet a deadline. Let momentum build up and take over. Let ideas tumble and flow. Save the refining and more critical appraisal until later, when you have a pool of at least 25 suggestions from which to choose. When the leader announces the time is up, or when you have at least 25 suggested solutions to your problem, stop. Together, decide which three ideas have the most potential, and describe them more fully. You will present these three to the whole group during the next part of the session.

No ideas should be lost. Needless to say, someone should be taking notes on ditto paper or using carbons, so that the ideas can be shared quickly with all members of the group after the coffee break.

To the Leader

Open by conducting "show and tell." Ask each person to take a few minutes (about five) to tell others in the group what topic area he explored, what he did, and how he feels about what happened. At the end of part A, organize the members into new combinations of two, three, or four, so long as there are at least three groups. Each group should represent as wide as possible a cross section of the side trips. Each group will hold a brainstorming session about one or two of the six questions listed below. All six questions should be covered. Let the groups spend about 30 minutes getting at least 25 possible answers to the question(s) and another 30 minutes developing the three best solutions to each problem.

Brainstorming Problems

1. How do you recruit students to attend the n-Ach course? Think of at least 25 imaginative, dramatic, effective ways of generating enthusiasm for taking an n-Ach course.

2. Think of at least 25 involving activities that let course participants experience the thoughts, actions, and feelings of achievement motivation.

3. List at least 25 ways of helping course members conceptualize

clearly the thoughts, actions, and feelings that comprise achievement motivation.

4. What are 25 ways of helping students to see the relationship between n-Ach and work, athletics, hobbies, school, peer group values, and other important aspects of their lives?

5. Generate a minimum of 25 ways to let students practice achievement planning and achievement action strategies.

6. Think of at least 25 ways to support students' continued high n-Ach in a variety of situations after the formal course is over.

When everyone understands the question assigned to them and the basic procedure, give the signal to go ahead. Your role now is that of timekeeper and facilitator. Allow 30 minutes to work on the question(s). Move around. If a group seems stymied or stuck, and you can add an idea to help them, do so. Since the final burst of effort is often the most productive, warn the group when there are five minutes left. After the brainstorming time, give the groups 30 minutes to go back over their lists, to expand the three best ideas so that they can describe them in some detail to the whole group.

For part C you are the grand coordinator and recorder. After retrieving the group from the mimeograph machine or the Xerox machine or the coffee pot, consider the suggestions and exercises they proposed for each of the six questions. As one group offers its answer to the problem of recruitment, a second group may see that one of its ideas about experiencing the motive is particularly appropriate as a follow-up to the recruiting procedure. This way the groups may build on each other's ideas in an organic way, although that isn't absolutely necessary. When all six questions are addressed, you will have one possible prototype for a course. Granted, this particular division of labor could produce a course with the head of a bird, the body of a pig, and the tail of a whale. Thorough, integrated, comprehensive course planning takes long hours, but this kind of sharing of responsibility and speeding of the process can provide an overview and suggest what is possible. Brainstorming generates rich material for further organic planning. Also the usual problem of slow starting is half licked.

During the final evaluation part of this session, you may want to ask how optimistic participants feel about giving an effective n-Ach course based on their collage of brainstormed mini-plans. Or, you may want to ask whether they need more time to share what they learned from their side trips. Whatever you put in the evaluation questionnaire, we recommend you include the following two questions:

1. How well did the group work together?

(a) the whole group

1	2	3	4	5	6	7	8	9	10
extremely badly				o.k.				extremely well	

(b) the subgroup during brainstorming

1	2	3	4	5	6	7	8	9	10
extremely badly				o.k.				extremely well	

(c) What would have contributed to greater effectiveness?

2. What suggestions can you make to the leader of Session 10 regarding procedures, leadership style, topics and issues you want to be covered?

After collecting, collating, and discussing the evaluation results with group members, your final task is to assign mental homework. Session 10 focuses on new planning. Group members should be thinking about whether they want to pursue Psychological Education and n-Ach beyond Session 10. If so, what do they want to do?

SESSION 10: Aiming

Purpose

This session is a transition from pre-planned activities that help you learn about achievement motivation and Psychological Education to new activities you will create to reach your specific goals. Whether you want to give an n-Ach course to students or strive for some highly personal goal, this session focuses on getting started. Through this new planning you will have a chance to practice many of the achievement principles and strategies (Step 5 in the learning sequence). Step 6, internalization, depends on what you do after Session 10.

Procedure	Part A
½ hour	Aim Naming—each group member states briefly what goal(s) he want to pursue after Session 10.
1 hour	Part B
	Planning—initial planning for projects is done in small groups formed on the basis of similar goals.
¾ hour	Part C
	Reports to the whole group
1 hour	Part D
	Phase out-phase in—Future group activities are planned and coordinated. Comments, criticisms and testimonials about the group and workshop are shared. The continuing group bids farewell to departing members.

Follow-Through Reading
Aiming, (EVI)

Introduction to Session 10

Internalization ultimately is a paradox in teaching and learning. Teachers must withdraw without stopping students' continued learning. Most teachers don't plan their own obsolescence, and very few have mastered the art of leaving at a time and in a way that facilitates internalization. Students, on the other hand, must forget what they know in order to internalize it, in the same sense that we forget about walking when it it completely internalized. When a subject matter or skill is new to us, we depend heavily on the expected guidance of a teacher. Learning is slow, conscious, deliberate, and awkward until, for example, our swing is grooved or our operating knowledge of grammar is second nature—information is quickly accessible in memory, and easily connected to appropriate situations. At some point in the process of internalizing knowledge and skills, a teacher's continued conscious attention to what is being learned inhibits students' forgetting and internalization. The trick for teachers, of course, is to judge the right time to stop talking, instructing, showing, asking questions, providing heavily cued learning environments, etc. If the judicious withdrawal comes too soon, it removes needed support and stops learning. If it comes too late, the presence of "teaching" is burdensome and counterproductive.

The authors of this manual do not have the advantages of knowing you personally and getting the feedback necessary for deciding when to stop providing directions, pointing to materials, and indicating all the other paraphernalia that assure us you will have enough (perhaps even too much) support in learning. Thus the authors can only assume that there will be an unstructured and continuing "eleventh session," in which you are on your own. In the workshop learning sequence, you have attended, experienced, conceptualized, and applied. Guidance has been provided for your conscious practice of Psychological Education and achievement motivation. Where Session 10 ends, it is time for the authors' words to disappear and for you, if you choose, to constructively "forget" what you've learned as your knowledge becomes internalized.

Strategy suggestions for Session 10 are straightforward. Those of you who want to give an n-Ach course to students (the best way for teachers to practice n-Ach) should get together and start planning. Those of you who have other goals in mind (restructuring a classroom, learning about some other aspect of Psychological Education, or achieving a personal goal) should get together with at least one other like-minded workshop participant and look through *Aiming* (EVI) for the most appropriate methods of practicing achievement strategies to reach your goals.

In order to become explicit and concrete, in Part C of this session you should be prepared to report to the whole group *who* you are aiming with, *what* is your goal, *why* you chose it, *how* you will take the first step toward attaining it, and *when* you will get your first feedback on how well you are doing.

To Participants Planning an n-Ach Course

The best help available for planning an n-Ach course for students is the experience you have just had participating in this workshop. The ideas and experiences that succeeded you can adapt for students. The sessions or activities that somehow missed, you can work to correct. In addition, the last chapter of this manual describes numerous teaching methods for each of the six steps in arousing and internalizing a motive. Available units of classroom materials also suggest a variety of sequences for an n-Ach course.

The immediate problem, however, is to organize yourselves as a group and decide on some operating procedures. By now you probably feel practiced and professional at such tasks—and, if you don't take a few minutes to review remarks about leadership in Appendix B and to recall group procedures derived from the role plays in Session 1, "The Arts of Contributing." For planning and coordinating an n-Ach course, you may want to choose a single chairman to take main organizational responsibility, with the actual workload and planning function shared equally. The chairman is the information center and focal point for the group's ideas—but this leadership role should not define him as the "hardest-working member." On the other hand, you may want to continue with a relating leadership and meeting format like the 10 sessions in this workshop. Plan and create in any way that suits the style of your group—or your particular school situation—but decide how you will deal with leadership and meeting procedures.

At some point in planning and giving an n-Ach course you will have to consider the questions listed below. Not all of them have to be answered today. But you should get far enough to report back to the group in part 3 of this session *who* is working on the project, *what* your goals are, *how* each of you will take the first step and *when* that first step will be completed.

AIM	What are your specific goals? Are they moderate risk? In what ways? If high risk, what then?
NEED	How important is this endeavor to group members? Is there a real need to experiment in this direction of Psychological Education? If too many members are tepid about trying a new kind of course, do they feel there is a need in the school for such a course?

HOS-FOF	What is the optimism-pessimism quotient in your group for this project? Is enthusiasm pretty high? Is the group stranded in skepticism and a little frozen with doubt? Find out now and talk about these feelings. Legitimate concerns help make planning and action more realistic. Honest expectations and reasonable commitment are important to make the course work and to be fair to the participants.
ACT	1. Acquire more expertise

        a. Read chapters 1, 3, and 4, if you haven't already.

        b. Review your own course fairly comprehensively, paying particular attention to leader instructions.

        c. Explore the territory in Session 5, "Side Trips in Psychological Education," if you haven't already.

2. Decide who you will have as course participants and how you will recruit them. *Volunteering* is important.

3. What will you teach? Review the suggestions from Session 9. How will you teach it? Who will teach it? How frequently and how long will it be taught? What will be the relationship between staff and students?

OBSTACLES   What kinds of problems do you anticipate? Think of ways to alleviate or circumvent them.

Obstacles	Action	Help
1.		
2.		
3.		

Before adjourning decide on your next meeting time—who will have done what? Do you have a chairman?

To the leader

By this time participants should be familiar with the ground rules, and the arts of contributing, and should feel special empathy for the session leader. Your job should be easy. Also, the tasks of this session do not require much preparation on your part or theirs. Most of the little things that will facilitate progress are fairly obvious.

In Part A, try to keep participants' statements to two or three minutes. Keep a public record of individual goals on the blackboard.

To begin Part B, designate a place for the n-Ach course planners to meet and let the others mill about for five minutes or so until they are with at least one other person with whom to share plans. Make sure there are enough copies of *Aiming* (EVI) available for these people. An advance reading will help you in showing them what sections are most relevant.

Your job during Part C is similar to that in Part A. This time keep track of the Whos, Whats, Hows, and Whens on the blackboard. It may be a good idea to mimeograph and distribute them after the meeting.

Part D will take considerably more skill and ingenuity. On the basis of people's activities it may be appropriate to reconvene the whole group with a new session leader. If not, there is then the question of how to say goodbye. This will be awkward. One pleasant alternative is for someone to volunteer his home for a party a week or two away. This can solve the issue of how to end the workshop, but it does not deal with the final workshop evaluation. We suggest that the participants consider two or three questions of the following type for about 10 minutes and then share their reactions in an open-ended discussion:

1. At this point what is your SuF/FaF quotient? Why?

2. What is your current HOS/FOF quotient? Why?

3. Is there any important unfinished interpersonal business? If so, what would you like to do about it?

4. How did this course compare to other courses you've given or taken?

You may wish to make up some of your own questions that reflect salient issues in your workshop.

Although evaluation and feedback has been an integral part of your workshop, we do not have the same privileged access to the successes and failures in your workshop experience. We also are curious to find out about the many new applications you discover, the new techniques for teaching achievement motivation, and in general whether we put together a valuable manual and set of materials. In the true spirit of excellence, we are eager to improve them. We sincerely hope, as we say in the Introduction to this book, that you or someone in your group will write to us with comments, suggestions, and ideas.

CHAPTER 3

MOTIVATION

IN CLASSROOMS

To increase students' motivation in the classroom it is more important to change the *way* they learn than *what* they learn. The way students think, act, and feel in learning is determined in large part by the rules of the implicit learning game and the teacher's leadership style. Both the rules and leadership style can be readily modified, although generally these methods of motivating students are not consciously used. Teachers can ignore but cannot avoid the direct, pervasive, and continuous influence of rules and style on students' motivation. Some teachers, without realizing it, even work against their own declared purposes by having students learn in ways that are inconsistent with the content of their courses. For instance, in many social studies classes designed to teach citizenship, the teacher is, in fact, the benevolent king of a vassal state. In achievement motivation training as well, the rules and leadership style must be consistent with the course. More important, however, there must be opportunities after the course for students to use their increased achievement motivation. It is unethical to increase students' achievement motivation—their independent restless striving for excellence—and then deliberately send them into classrooms where achievement motivation is dysfunctional. In order to help you avoid this problem and instead create learning environments that support the motives you want to instill, this chapter describes relevant ways to modify the rules of learning and leadership style in the classroom.

RULES AND LEADERSHIP IN CLASSROOMS AND SOCIETY

Teachers often say and believe they are most interested in achievement, but inadvertently encourage submission. There were times for all of us as students when we worked hard for goals that later seemed silly. In discussing this chapter, one of the authors recalled an incident in high school when he got back a math test on which he was to graph a quadratic equation. There was a large red "C-" on the top, much to his dismay. On closer inspection, it became clear the graph solution was correct. The only errors of omission were the arrow tips at the ends of the ordinate and abcissa. He became angrily determined to submit a perfect paper, an absolute model of detailed accuracy and completeness, no matter how much effort and time it took. With the teacher's standards clear, he decided to meet them through sheer persistence. At first we thought it interesting that this anecdote was so rich with achievement motivation. We began to realize, however, that the achievement motivation the author possessed had, in fact, been transformed into an energetic desire to comply with the standards set by the teacher, even though these standards were not personally relevant. The classroom factors which encourage achievement motivation, compliance, curiosity, or any other motive often are equally subtle, and not adaptable to neat formulas for changing the learning environment.

At another level, achievement motivation and the student's belief in his ability to control his own fate often are clearly discouraged rather than nurtured by schooling. With the increasing demands for higher education to qualify for prestigious and well-paying jobs, there has been a corresponding increase in the importance of academic success. The greatest rewards go to those who demonstrate academic excellence. Sometimes academic success is the self-chosen goal of adolescents. Often it is not. Frequently, achievement motivation is reflected in striving for other less prestigious but no less valuable goals that cannot be pursued in schools. Students with high achievement motivation do not always excel academically and somtimes don't even like school. Their feelings may be due to several structural aspects of schooling. Most school curricula do not encourage individual students to take personal responsibility for setting their own moderate-risk goals. For the lower half of every class, getting an "A" is a very high-risk goal. Yet, striving for a moderate-risk "C" does not yield the payoff so important to later success. It is not surprising that some students with high achievement motivation find school to be at odds with their motivation. Their initiative, independence, and self-reliance either are not seen by the teachers because they are demonstrated outside school, or they are seen by teachers as rebellious, antisocial activity. Categorized as problem students, slow learners, or potential dropouts, these students, not surprisingly, may develop negative self-images and a distaste for school. Their attitudes can result in increased rebelliousness and a sense that they have little power to control their environments and their lives. Their achievement motivation fades or remains latent within schools. The motive most useful to them in economic survival as an adult often is a liability in schooling supposedly designed to help them succeed.

The process as well as the content of formal education should be designed to prepare students to live mature, effective, adult lives. The way students learn, the rules and leadership they experience, should be generically similar to the basic rules and leadership styles they will encounter as adults. If survival in the social system requires obedience and compliance more than independence, then decreased achievement motivation would be a valuable outcome of schooling. Teaching useful responses to power-oriented situations would be highly appropriate. Whatever motives are taught in school should be consistent with cultural values and societal demands. In *Dreams and Deeds,* Robert LeVine presents a tragic example of a mismatch between individuals' motivation and the motivational demands of society. LeVine was able to identify this mismatch by studying the different status systems of the Ibo and Hausa tribes in Nigeria-Biafra.

The history of the Hausa shows the existence of a "short-term autocracy" political system in which the kings of the empire ruled vassal states. The kingship was rotated among three ruling dynastic lineages. With each rotation went the right of patronage; some office holders were discharged and others of the king's choosing were installed. Office holders usually had responsibility for fiefs they administered and from which they collected taxes, keeping a portion for themselves. During the tribal wars, office holders raised troops from their fiefs and in return received booty and captive slaves from the king.

So long as an office holder retained the favor of the king through demonstrations of loyalty and obedience, he was allowed to overtax and keep the surplus himself as well as to exceed his formal authority in a number of other ways. Thus the system had a despotic character, turning on relations and dependence and power between subordinates and their superiors.

(LeVine, 1966, p. 26-27)

As a result, the principal way to rise socially was to become the client or follower of a person of greater status, to demonstrate worthiness by being loyal and obedient, and to collect additional followers for the patron. In these ways the fortunes of the patron were enriched and the follower's nomination to office was made more likely. Obedience led to office, and office led to wealth.

Clearly this system of status mobility placed a premium on loyalty, obedience and sensitivity to the demands of those in authority over a man; excellent performance in an independent occupational role, self-instigated action toward goals that did not benefit the competitive chances of a man's patron, did not yield the man access to the major status rewards of the society and might conceivably damage his career.

(LeVine, 1966, p.30)

Often, "loyalty, obedience and sensitivity to those in authority" are valued tactics of our "brightest" students, who believe we have the answers necessary to doing well on semester tests and College Board examinations. They slavishly adhere to our requests in order that we will patronize them with good grades and good recommendations. Student-instigated action toward goals that are not consistent with our own might conceivably damage their chances for the classroom status rewards.

In contrast to the Hausa, the 19th century history of the Ibo reveals more than 200 politically independent tribes, each with its own status system. In general, the tribes reached decisions through councils of elders who were highly responsive to the needs and wishes of tribesmen. In addition, most tribes had title societies that men could enter upon acceptance by members, payment of entrance fees, and provision of a feast for the members. The feast, more than the other two requirements, effectively confined entrance to those of some financial means. Membership entitled a man to share other entrance fees, prestige, and, in some areas, political power as well. Most of the titles were not

111

inherited, but were open to men who could earn them. Since there were many routes to earning the necessary fees, the status system encouraged men to determine for themselves what personal skills and knowledge would be most useful. This encouraged men to make carefully calculated estimates of their abilities and to pursue their individual entrepreneurial goals.

> *Occupational performance was the primary locus of social evaluation and performing well enough as a farmer, trader, or fisherman to obtain a title. . .required the continual application of his own efforts in the service of his individual goals.*
>
> *(LeVine, 1966, pp. 35-36)*

Higher status and power were granted on the basis of individual economic achievement, whereas among the Hausa the reverse was true. Higher status brought greater wealth. The clearest overall difference between the Ibo and the Hausa status systems was the *political* orientation of the Hausa and the *occupational* emphasis among the Ibo.

These differences in social systems indicate a few of the ways the Hausa and Ibo are likely to misunderstand each other. The Hausa are likely to view the Ibo as upstart radicals who threaten the social order by their self-reliance, independence, and lack of compliance. The Ibo see the Hausa system as cramping individual initiative and threatening their own social structure. The conflict of obedience and independence that we see today in Nigeria was hidden in the status systems of the two tribes over 80 years ago.

Similar but less violent conflicts can occur in classrooms when achievement-oriented students are led by power-oriented teachers, or when teachers want to increase the achievement motivation of students who feel threatened by the opportunity to set their own goals and want to follow teachers' instructions. Such differences in motivation are not insoluble dilemmas. Students' motivation can be shaped by the learning rules of the classroom just as the status rules of the Hausa and Ibo shaped and recruited the most socially useful motives among the respective tribes.

Political leadership and its analogue, teachers' leadership styles, also powerfully shape individuals' motives. This shaping is illustrated by the provocative research of Kurt Lewin. When Lewin left Germany in the 1930's he had an established reputation as a "field theorist." Like other

112

field theorists, Lewin believed that behavior is almost exclusively determined by stimuli in the environment. To substantiate this belief, and simultaneously to help explain German compliance to Hitler's regime, Lewin, Lippitt and White (1939) created three boys' clubs, each with a different type of leader. The "autocratic" (power-oriented) leader was stiff, formal and aloof, gave directions, made rules and did not participate in the boys' activities. The *"laissez faire"* (affiliation-oriented) leader was informal and friendly; he gave no directions, made no rules and, in general, shared in whatever the boys wanted to do. The "democratic" (achievement-oriented) leader was work oriented, though he helped the boys vote on what they wanted to do. He did not direct actions like the autocratic leader, nor did he let happy chaos reign as did the *laissez faire* leader. He was a friendly co-participant in the projects chosen by the boys, and was concerned with doing things well independently.

Over time the three groups developed distinctly different social structures and behavior patterns. There were many more aggressive acts and incidents of scapegoating in the autocratic group. The boys were task involved and compliant, but only as long as the leader was present. When he left, anarchy quickly emerged. In contrast, when the democratic leader left his group, the boys continued their purposeful activities while group morale and cooperation remained high. In the *laissez faire* group the absence of the leader meant even more fun, and even less task involvement. Friendliness and "we-feeling" remained high. After the three social structures were in operation for some time, the leaders switched groups. In this way it was possible to assess how much the boys' behavior was due to the leader and how much to the personalities of the boys. Lippitt and White (1958) concluded that in nearly all cases the leadership style, rather than the personalities of the boys, was the principal determinant of behavior. When leaders changed, the behavior changed.

As a social system in miniature, classrooms should reflect the highest cultural values and teach the most socially useful motives. It is possible to increase students' motivation by changing the classroom learning structure and leadership style. In our experience, it is easier for teachers to modify their leadership style after they have restructured the way their students learn. In fact, when the learning rules are changed, a different teaching-leadership style nearly always is required. In the next section we describe ways to restructure learning opportunities to be consistent with desired motivation. Appropriate changes in leadership style are discussed in this context.

LEARNING STRUCTURES AS MOTIVATIONAL GAMES

The "structure" of a situation, whether it is a culture or a classroom, usually means the rules for what you can and can't do, the incentive for doing well, and the penalties for doing poorly. It is as if these rules, incentives, and penalties defined an implicit game with players, a point system, playing fields, and coaches. Using this analogy, we can try to make explicit what kinds of games arouse achievement, affiliation, and power motivation. This explicit analogy will allow you to diagnose and restructure your classroom learning "game" in ways that suit you and your students.

Four characteristics distinguish a game from other forms of activity: (1) the rules which govern the activity are agreed upon in advance by the players, (2) the rules describe classes of behavior rather than specific actions, (3) there are obstacles to be overcome, and (4) a scoring system is specified. In general, games are more organized then "play" or "pastimes," but less organized than "rituals." In "play" and other activities which merely "pass time," there are no rules, no necessary obstacles to be overcome, and no scoring. In "rituals" (greeting formalities, graduations, funerals, etc.) the specific actions rather than classes of acceptable and unacceptable behavior are defined. Also there is no scoring present. In general, games are more flexible than "rituals" and less open-ended than "play" and "pastimes."

By this definition, most normal classroom teaching is not a game. Usually the rules are not well specified in advance. When rules are extremely vague, classroom activity often becomes a pastime, literally a way to pass time between more meaningful activities. This forces students to "test limits" in order to discover the unstated rules and boundaries. Limit testing is necessary for would-be game players, but from the teacher's point of view it is a discipline problem and a waste of valuable learning time. Nor is classroom teaching a game when teachers over-specify the minute activities to be performed. This ritualized learning is clearest in older "learning by rote" methods, but is present today in slightly altered forms, e.g. making specific problem assignments in mathematics and learning through programmed texts.

To arouse students' motivation more effectively in the classroom, learning should have the formal properties of a game, *i.e.* rules that are clearly specified in advance and define classes of behavior, obstacles to be overcome, and a well-specified scoring system. It is then possible to vary these properties to arouse the desired motives. The first task is to decide whether to stimulate concerns about excellence, friendship, having influence, or some combination of these motives. The desired motives can be stimulated by creating rules which change the nature of the scoring system, the types of obstacles to success, and the locus of decision making.

1. *Scoring Systems*
There are three main types of scoring systems in games: Zero-Sum, Non-Zero-Sum and Shared-Sum. Zero-Sum scoring systems have a fixed number of points. When one player makes points, another player automatically loses points, the sum total number of points thus remaining a constant zero. Arm wrestling, cup play in golf, betting games, chess, grading on the curve, "Pullover" games—all have Zero-Sum scoring systems. In Non-Zero-Sum games the number of points is not constant. Each player is free to earn as many points as he can, independently of how many points the other player makes, *e.g.* archery contests, medal play in golf, pre-set academic grading standards, Boy Scout merit badge progression. In Shared-Sum scoring systems, a score by one player is a score for all players on his team. Almost all team sports have Shared-Sum scoring systems.

Zero-Sum scoring systems structurally define power goals, since points are awarded only when one side forces the other side to yield or when one side demonstrates superior power, influence, or control. Inevitably in Zero-Sum grading systems, students are in direct competition with each other. Grading on the curve or by rank ordering scores are Zero-Sum scoring systems, since judgments about a student's performance are determined only by comparison to others. One highly effective strategy for doing well in Zero-Sum games is to sabotage other players. Weakening your opponent, *e.g.* destroying other students' notebooks, is just as effective as strengthening yourself.

Non-Zero-Sum scoring structurally defines achievement goals, since it gives greatest value to independent, self-reliant accomplishment. Contrary to Zero-Sum games, Non-Zero-Sum games can be played alone, without direct competition with others. In such games, sabotage is not a useful strategy for earning points.

In Shared-Sum games, affiliation is made salient, since making points is a key method of establishing, maintaining, or restoring friendly relationships among team members. Academic situations rarely are Shared-Sum games, thus missing the potential facilitating effect of high affiliation motivation.

2. *Obstacles to Success*

In all games points are made when obstacles are overcome. The motivational goals of every game depend on the nature of the obstacles to making points. For example, the need for affiliation (n-Aff) is not particularly valuable to a boxer since the obstacle is the opponent's strength and skill. The boxer must demonstrate his influence over his opponent, not his ability to get along harmoniously. In general, when the obstacle is the opponent's potency, the need for power (n-Pow) is a valued asset. N-Ach is valuable when the obstacles are within the player himself. In target shooting, for example, the standards are fixed and inanimate. In order to score, the player must overcome a variety of inadequate personal resources and skills (*e.g.* shyness, lack of coordination, etc.). In some games, the obstacles are both the opponent's and the player's skills, as in fencing, ice hockey, and football. These games call for both power and achievement concerns. Obstacles to scoring also can exist in a team's lack of cooperation or inadequate combined strength. In such games the desire to perform in an effective coordinated manner is necessary, *i.e.* n-Aff is important. Most complex team games have power, achievement, and affiliation obstacles, thus calling forth triple motivation.

Many adolescents find sports more interesting and involving than studying, perhaps because all three motives are so clearly and strongly invoked by complex team games. From this perspective, the classroom is neither complex, a team effort, nor a game. When students respond to their natural affiliation needs in the classroom, more often than not, they are obstructing the teacher's goals. There is a curious logic in such student response: When a teacher creates an n-Pow classroom, the obstacle to success is in the teacher, his standards, his assignments, his disciplinary and rewarding power. As we have seen, sabotage is an appropriate strategy in power situations. What more effective way is there for students to demonstrate potency than to gang up on the teacher, to jointly sabotage the teacher's efforts? There is greater strength in friendly team effort, and often it is more fun.

3. *Locus of Decision Making*

Motivation is a process of decision making. The goals which define different motives define how decisions are made. Obviously, the object of the power motive (n-Pow) is to make decisions for others, the object of the achievement motive (n-Ach) to make decisions for oneself, the object of the affiliation motive (n-Aff) to make decisions agreeable to the majority of members. Similarly, the motivational character of games can be inferred from the decision-making process built into them. In football, the quarterback is encouraged by his position to demonstrate both achievement and power motivation. For the rest of the football players, compliance is required for the sake of affiliation and team power. In the classroom, carrying out the assignments often is less palatable since it serves neither power nor affiliative goals agreed upon in advance. Often students' compliance serves only the teachers' achievement goals and the students' interest in avoiding punishment.

The table below summarizes the scheme for analyzing the motivational structure of games.

Motivational Structure of Games

		Motives		
		n-Achievement	n-Power	n-Affiliation
Dimensions of Games	Scoring System	non-Zero-Sum	Zero-Sum	Shared-Sum
	Obstacles to Success	Personal and Environmental	Opponent	Lack of cooperation: e.g. friction, conflict, distance, tension
	Locus of Decision Making	Individual Player	Captain or Leader	Team

117

While the scoring systems, obstacles, and decision-making processes determine what motives will be aroused, the amount of strategy and tactics determine how much motivation will be aroused. Classrooms with many ways of scoring and more chances to earn points (*i.e.* more strategy possible) arouse stronger motivation. In some modern language classes taught solely by the aural-oral method, only two tactics are used: verbal questions and memorization. In contrast, the increasing popularity of multimedia classrooms have made more learning tactics available to students and should stimulate greater motivation.

Restructuring classroom learning is not a matter of grandiose new designs, expensive educational hardware, extensive in-service training, or teams of highly paid educational consultants. Fairly dramatic changes can result from relatively minor but critical changes. This is illustrated in the following case examples of a restructured typing class and a restructured mathematics class.

TWO EXAMPLES OF RESTRUCTURED LEARNING

In many high schools, business education classes are considered low-level subjects for non-college bound students who must prepare in secondary school for jobs after graduation. For students with little interest in school, these classes often are used as an institutionalized dumping ground. Severe discipline problems are more frequent than in the prestigious college preparatory classes. As a result, the most well-prepared, experienced business education teacher can face over-whelming classroom problems. This was true even for Dr. Antoinette DiLoretto, head of the business education department at a large suburban high school and the author of several published texts on typing. In 1965-66 she taught an office practice-typing class for three quarters of the four-quarter school year. Frustrated by the low interest and involvement her students had shown, and inspired by an n-Ach course she took with several other teachers, Dr. DeLoretto decided to structure the typing class differently. The new structure was initiated toward the end of the first quarter in 1966-67. She replaced what had been a power-compliance oriented structure with a structure that encouraged affiliation and achievement motivation:

Scoring System

In the 1965-66 class, as in most typing classes, increased skill in typing was defined as progression through the text, practice was assumed to be the only major obstacle. More practice would increase the gross number of words typed per minute (GW/M), and decrease the number of errors (E). Both of these elements were reflected in the final net words per minute (NW/M): NW/M = GW/M - (2 X E). In 1965-66 the only way of improving was practice, practice, and still more practice.

In 1966-67, as in the previous year, either GW/M could be increased, or E decreased. However, the number of tactics for accomplishing those goals were radically increased. Under the new structure all typing test material was inspected before taking the speed test. Difficult strokings were identified by the group and solutions discussed. Also, the students were encouraged to search for personal obstacles (e.g. heavy clanking rings, mental blocks, sitting position, etc.). A variety of new tactics were discovered when the new obstacles were identified. The increased focus on personal obstacles and new tactics meant that achievement motivation should have been increased and reflected in higher typing scores.

Locus of Decision Making

In 1965-66 the teacher herself decided the number of words per minute equivalent to each letter grade. This helped create the standard power classroom structure. In 1966-67, the teacher and the class collaborated to determine the NW/M that would earn different letter grades. This shifted the structure towards n-Affiliation and away from n-Power.

In 1965-66 all students' typing speeds were posted on a bulletin board once a month. Students did not set their own goals. The following year progress was recorded quite differently. Students made daily records of their speed growth on graphs. On the basis of their graphs, students set short- and long-term scoring goals. In the realm of testing, in 1965-66 typing tests were given almost daily by the teacher, who determined their length. Every week only the best score of the week was counted toward the student's course grade. In 1966-67, students decided when they would take a test, and determined the length of test appropriate to their chosen goals. They also decided whether or not to have the teacher record their scores. However, for grading purposes, students had to turn in at least one score each week. All of these changes shifted the locus of decision making from the teacher to the students and shifted motivational structure from power to achievement.

In summary, students had opportunities to take greater personal responsibility for setting moderate-risk goals. They explored to a far greater extent whatever personal obstacles they faced and whatever instrumental activity might help overcome them. The two typing classes had an equal amount of structure, but the restructured class in 1966-67 was more flexible and open to initiative. Students determined fair rewards for their efforts and cooperation was encouraged. The structure and climate encouraged students to think and act like people with strong n-Ach.

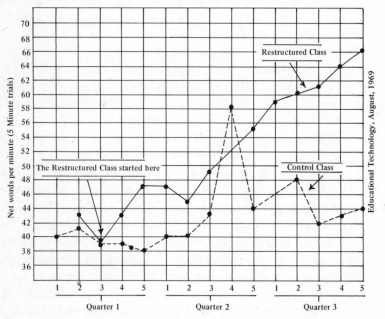

Increases in Average Net Words/min typed by a class structured for n-Power and by a class structured for achievement motivation*

Weeks tested during school year during 3 quarters

To determine whether the change in structure had any effect on students, Dr. DiLoretto compared the beginning and terminal typing performance of students in the two types of classrooms. The students in her 1965-66 and 1966-67 classes were comparable in intelligence as measured by the OTIS, and in ability as measured by the Nelson-Denny Test. In both years the text, typing test material, typewriters, classroom, and teacher were identical. Only the learning "game" was defined differently.

In seven of the total 30 weeks of testing, there were between one and three students absent. There was no consistent pattern of absences among students. Thus, seven out of 30 average NW/M listed on the graph are based on partial, but nearly complete, data.

At the end of the third week of the first quarter in the 1966-67 class, before n-Aff, n-Ach structure was introduced, the average typing speeds of the two classes was an identical 39 NW/M. By the end of the third quarter, the 1966-67 class average was 66 NW/M, 54% more NW/M than the 1965-66 class. Nine out of the 10 students tested in the 1966-67 class did better than all 11 students tested in the 1965-66 class. The lowest scorer in the 1966-67 class was tied with the highest scorer in the 1965-66 class at 50 NW/M. These are socially and statistically significant results. A further look at the graph suggests that the students in the Power-oriented class may have lost interest toward the end of the third quarter with the advent of spring vacation and the end of the typing class. By contrast, it seems that interest and effort remained high during the same period in the class structured for n-Ach and n-Aff.

These dramatic results are somewhat hard to believe. Yet, structured changes introduced by another teacher in an elementary school mathematics class resulted in equally impressive learning gains and student interest. Elementary school mathematics classes can have problems similar to those common in business education classes. Although the students are younger and the subject matter different, classes structured for power seem to generate the same problems (*e.g.* listless compliance, passive resistance, rebelliousness). In fifth grade it is especially popular to "hate math." These standard problems were encountered by James McIntyre, then in his first full year of teaching. For the following year he decided to restructure the class as a different type of "game" to meet the needs of the students and subject matter more appropriately. The net result was that students learned more and liked the process of doing mathematical thinking for its own sake.

The "Math Game" was modeled after the Origami Game designed originally as a device for teaching achievement motivation. The Math Game curricular content consisted solely of the textbook, *Elementary School Mathematics* (Addison-Wesley, 1964). Students' activities were structured by the following "Math Game" rules:

Contracts

Each student contracted with the teacher to produce a chosen percentage of correct answers in each chapter of the text. Contracts were made for one chapter at a time. The student chose his own deadline for completion of the chapter. The contract then was co-signed by the students and the teacher.

Math Contract

The undersigned will attempt to do correctly..........per cent of the problems in Chapter ....

The sum of $..........has been deposited with the government of the class for materials and franchise.

I understand that 10% of the gross return will be deducted from my payment for each day the contract goes unfulfilled after........... I also understand that the contract may be revised at any time prior to one week before due date for the fee of $10. One per cent of the gross return will be deducted for each wrong answer below the number intended.

Date:..........

....
Student Signature

....
Teacher Signature

The Scoring System

The score was kept with play money of various denominations. The students' success in learning math was indicated by the amount of play money he earned. Each student was given $2,000 to start playing the game. After signing the contract, the student paid a fee for franchise and materials. This fee was directly proportional to the percentage of correct answers for which the student bid: the higher the percentage the more the student had to pay initially. In order to earn the maximum amount for his chosen percentage, the student had to meet his contract obligations, both in percent of problems correct and deadline. The amount of money he earned was directly proportional to the goal he set. The higher the percentage of correct answers he bid for and produced, the more money he earned. The schedule of payments was as follows:

%Tried	Cost	Return	Rate
100	$500	$2000	4-1
90	$450	$1350	3-1
80	$350	$ 700	2-1
70	$250	$ 400	8-5
60	$150	$ 250	5-3
50	$100	$ 150	3-2

There also were three ways for the student to lose money. Although contracts could be revised or extended at any time, as long as the deadline was not less than one week away, a flat $10 fee was charged. Second, students could lose money if they did not produce the number of correct answers for which they contracted, each missing correct answer costing one percent of the payoff. Were a student to contract for 70% in a chapter with 400 problems (*i.e.* 280 correct answers) and turn in only 270 correct answers, 10% would be deducted from his payoff. In this case the penalty would be $40 as the payoff on a 70% contract is $400. The students were under no restraint to stop working after reaching their percentage goal. They could protect their investment by doing more problems than contracted for. Thus, they could hedge against possible errors and not lose as long as they had produced the required number of correct answers. The third way to lose money concerned deadlines. Since the student set his own time goals, the penalty for being overdue was severe. For each school day a chapter was late, 10% of the payoff was deducted. A student contracting for 100% correct answers (Payoff: $2,000) lost $200 for each day over the deadline.

Daily Progress Charts

In order to have an adequate self-assessment of daily work and progress, graphs were issued each Monday. The teacher specifically stated that he did not want to see them. They were entirely for the personal use of the students. An explanation of their use was given in the first session and thereafter they were only mentioned by the teacher when he passed them out each Monday. The graph merely consisted of the number on the ordinate and the seven days of the week on the abscissa.

End Rewards

End of the year rewards were given to the six highest money winners in the class. The rewards were of the class's own choosing, and the winners had their choice from the following list: rabbit, gerbil, slot-car kit, jug of candy. In addition, an ice cream party was promised to all those who completed the book by the end of the school year.

The scoring for the Math Game was primarily a Non-Zero-Sum system with the exception of the special prizes for the six highest money winners. The obstacles to scoring were quite clearly defined by ways to earn money and avoid loss (*i.e.*, production of the number of correct answers contracted, no revisions of contract due dates, no overdue contract fulfillments). In each case the obstacles were within the player and required the player to develop action strategies characteristic of people with strong achievement motivation: accurate moderate risk taking and the use of feedback to modify goals. Decision making was almost entirely the personal responsibility of the students. They made their own assignments, determined their own pacing, worked through the book by themselves, and sought help from Mr. McIntyre and friends as they felt the need. Often the students conferred outside of class about possible new tactics for beating the game. In their lengthy talks and calculations of the odds, they learned a lot of practical mathematics. Mr. McIntyre was able to establish a warm friendly role as coach, consistent with the leadership style of people who foster n-Ach climates. The role of the teacher as "king of the classroom" did not exist.

The Math Game was strikingly different from math class the previous year when Mr. McIntyre taught the same students using the same textbook series. In the fourth grade no overall grading was done, consistent with the beliefs of the private Quaker elementary school. Instead, written reports were given to parents periodically during the school year. The Stanford Achievement Test was given at the end of the year to inform teachers of their own success. Students were not informed of the results. Standardized chapter tests were given on completion of each chapter during the year as a general guideline for the teacher in pacing, preparing lectures, lessons, and homework assignments. The school assumed that grades were an undue rush into the competitive world and detrimental to the spontaneous, genuine emergence of student interest in mathematics for its own sake. Obstacles to learning were not clearly defined by the structure, but were within the individual students more than in opponents' skill or group cohesion. Decision making was handled by the teacher. Other than the stated vague goal of learning mathematics, students were free to choose their other goals, strategies, and tactics. In practice, however, the fourth grade mathematics class was a power-oriented play situation. Students more often chose to ignore mathematics than to explore joyfully the elegant realm of mathematical logic.

Since the full battery of Stanford Achievement Tests was given in the spring of each year, it was possible to make year-to-year comparisons in the students' mathematics gain scores. From March in the third grade to March in the fourth grade the average gain was 0.2 years, from 3.8 to 4.0. From March in the fourth grade to June in the fifth grade, the average gain was 3.0 years, from 4.0 to 7.0. This achievement spurt may be measured in a different way. All 14 of the students gained over one year in mathematics during the fifth grade, while only two of the 14 gained over a year in mathematics during the fourth grade—a highly significant difference. These gains in the fifth grade are striking, especially in view of how poorly the same students did the previous year with the same teacher and text series.

Other evidence, though less scientific, may be more persuasive to teachers; namely, what happened to the individual children. Did they become grasping entrepreneurs and cutthroat businessmen? Did they work solely for the rewards? What were some of the other byproducts of this structure? Mr. McIntyre's impressions were very clear.

Children who did nothing in mathematics in fourth grade, except under duress, suddenly began taking their books home on weekends. Very few deadlines were missed. Many students began assessing themselves more optimistically, yet realistically, and they performed up to those standards. One boy fidgeted through the entire year in mathematics in fourth grade. Threats and stern words could not focus his attention, nor could they keep him in his seat. His total output reflected a small portion of his ability. Within the new structure, however, he chose his first goal of 70% with two weeks to finish the contract. Within three days he revised his goal upward to 100%, paid the extra fee, and did all the problems with only 11 errors out of almost 400 problems. Another similar student, a girl, was considered by the teacher to be mathematically slow when in the fourth grade. She was consistently at the bottom of the class and seldom handed in assignments. Her 100% contract for the first chapter was the first completed and had only six errors. Her error total was the lowest in the class.

Four other girls in grade four had found math an excellent time to do other things, such as writing notes to one another and surreptitiously playing with clay. In grade five they still clustered around each other, but were quiet except during loud disagreements over mathematics problems. Two other boys performed well on occasion in grade four, but also were constant behavior problems. They worked so diligently together in fifth grade that the teacher often forgot they were in the classroom. Another boy needed more structure within which to work, but resented all structures adults imposed on him. By setting his own limits and working at his own speed within a structure that he felt was his own, his work in mathematics was free from the anguish that once accompanied it.

Once during the year, several students decided to take a vacation from math for two weeks. They came to class and were allowed to relax, so long as they didn't disturb others. They had budgeted their time for the year and realized they could afford the vacation. After two weeks they returned to the task and successfully completed the year's work.

It was the teacher's impression that in the first half of fifth grade, enthusiasm was generated more by the game than by intrinsic interest in mathematics. However, in the second half of the year, with the students buoyed by the new-found competence, the game, prizes, and play money became more or less irrelevant while the pace of work continued. Mathematics itself had become more interesting.

These two case studies of a typing class and a mathematics class demonstrate that teachers have at their command now the opportunities to make a significant impact on arousing student motivation.

126

Through motivation courses, combined with restructured learning opportunities in classrooms and supportive leadership styles, students can be encouraged to learn in ways that closely resemble how they will live and work after school. However, these alternatives do not answer the critical question of which motives should be taught in Psychological Education courses and supported by the classroom learning environments.

MOTIVATING STUDENTS FOR A PLURALISTIC SOCIETY

A belief that one, two, or three motives are most central and important obviously is oversimplistic, since we live in a complex pluralistic society where a broad range of motives is needed. Unfortunately, at present only a few motives are encouraged in most schools. Consider, for example, the nearly universal utility of affiliation motivation in industry, research, and athletics and the ubiquitous need to get along with others. Only in school classes are there so few opportunities for legitimized cooperative efforts. Clearly, a greater number of lifelike opportunities for the development of affiliation motivation should be introduced in schools.

A variety of motivational structures and leadership styles in schools is necessary preparation for a pluralistic society. These options are important also because each structure and leadership style has built-in limitations that can be compenstated for only by the availability of alternative structures and styles. For instance, some teachers feel that fostering achievement motivation stifles creativity and question the merits of n-Ach training. Other teachers argue that helping students to become creative is nice, but that most students need to learn how to get along in a competitive world.

The complementary differences between learning structures for n-Ach and creativity can be illustrated best by comparing the types of contracts on which they are based. Achievement-oriented contracts, such as those in the Origami and Math Games, are modeled after industrial, product-oriented contracts. The yields, as well as the quality, quantity, production time, and purchase/sales prices, are specified clearly in advance. Such contracts as models for learning are most appropriate when the learning yields can be clearly specified. In contrast, creativity-oriented contracts are modelled after research, process-oriented contracts which require that the problem be stated, along with the methods of gathering information and how much time the creative researcher will spend on the problem. The products of solutions cannot be described since the point of the investigation is to discover answers to the problems. If the problem is difficult and the desired solution creative, then quantity, quality, time, and cost of the solution cannot be guaranteed. Requiring this information in advance only inhibits the creative effort. It is as if students were asked to tell teachers what they will know before they started learning.

Interestingly enough, the leadership styles appropriate to the two processes also have reciprocal advantages and disadvantages. A leader who wants to support truly creative efforts in students must suspend critical judgment, reduce the risks for failure, and be prepared to wait a long time for results that may well be failures. By definition, the creative response and successful products are rare events. Not all students flourish in a class with so little structure, pressure, and lack of specificity of desired goals. In fact, many of those who flounder would be productive under a leader who created an achievement-oriented structure and style. However, other students will feel cramped, stifled, and bored by the demands of a situation pressing for achievement motivation: deadlines, careful plans for goals, quality controls, regular concrete feedback on progress, and realistically calculated risk taking. The central features of achievement motivation can be anathema to the truly imaginative, free-wheeling spirit of the highly creative individual.

This is not an argument for tracking students on the basis of need for creativity and need for achievement instead of I.Q. Rather than sacrifice either type of learning, both should co-exist within schools. Courses, learning structures, and leadership styles should be developed to foster achievement and creativity and many other valuable motives within every school. In individuals, as in cultures and schools, many motives can co-exist and should be developed. Each individual needs many strong motives to function well and enjoy the opportunities presented by a pluralistic society.

CHAPTER 4

ACHIEVEMENT MOTIVATION
TRAINING FOR STUDENTS

Only a small number of events in a person's lifetime radically change his way of living—the death of parents, getting married or divorced, having a child, involvement in a serious accident, a deeply religious experience. These dramatic, singular events transform a person's outlook, relation to others, and view of himself. By comparison, daily learning experiences in school are undramatic, regularized, and designed to promote steady, small increments in external knowledge rather than abrupt, large changes in life styles, motives, values and relationships. Most of formal education does not change the way students live.

Obviously, we do not want to build curricula around regular apocalyptic events that drastically change students' personal lives. Yet new, more effective teaching strategies are needed to help students develop stronger motivation, clarify their values, and improve their relationship with others and views of themselves. As far-fetched as it may sound at first, it is possible to derive practical ideas about promoting personal growth in normal school courses from these rare life-changing events. These ideas can be transformed into teaching strategies that promote milder, but still significant, changes. The problem is to figure out how to promote personal growth without traumatizing students. What is it about these dramatic experiences that triggers the process of personal change? How can acceptable triggering experiences be introduced in the classroom more often? Answers to these questions can guide us in developing gentler versions of the profound life experiences that increase students' independence in setting and reaching their own goals, to help them expand their curiosity, stimulate them to explore their talents more boldly and to develop the confidence and self acceptance that contribute to greater tolerance and loving relationships.

The dramatic life-changing experiences discussed below are remote from the classroom. Yet the sequence of change can be conceptualized, and the concepts can be used as guidelines for appropriate teaching procedures.

In most peak experiences there is a complete focus of attention on what is happening here and now. Past memories and future plans are less salient. Whether it is a mother's labor during birth, the taking of marriage vows, the shock of realizing your arm is broken, or the ecstacy of a religious vision, the intensity of the experience crowds out all other familiar reactions. One characteristic that sets these peak experiences apart is the simultaneous intensity of radically new thoughts, actions, and feelings.

Usually these experiences break established relationships, as when a parent dies. Often they disrupt habitual patterns of living, or dissolve longtime beliefs. Whether the experience is revelatory or traumatic in nature, it breaks basic continuities in a person's life. After the peak of the experience has passed, there is a period of some confusion and puzzlement during which the person attempts to make sense out of what happened and to establish meaningful new continuities. This attempt takes many forms, from conversation with friends to meditation and prayer. Even if the experience is never fully understood, in time the consequences become clearer—how relationships are altered, what goals and values are different, and what new behaviors occur. After a while these changes seem more familiar and practiced. For example, new roles become less confusing. As the newness of being a parent wears off, the role becomes an integral part of a person's life with its own rich set of relationships, behaviors, and meanings. Similarly, in time, the loss of a loved one results in new relationships, behaviors, and meanings that we internalize in our way of living.

This pattern of significant personal change can be conceptualized as a six-step sequence and used as a guide in creating school learning experiences that promote psychological growth. Such learning experiences cause little disorientation, yet they are far more intense than the typical school experience of acquiring impersonal, external knowledge. This is the six-step sequence:

1. Focus attention on what is happening here and now.

2. Provide an intense, integrated experience of new thoughts, actions, and feelings.

3. Help the person make sense out of his experience by attempting to conceptualize what happened.

4. Relate the experience to the person's values, goals, behavior, and relationships with others.

5. Stabilize the new thought, action and feelings through practice.

6. Internalize the changes.

These guidelines are general in the sense that they apply to developing a variety of intrinsic aspects of personality—motives, values, attitudes.* Each step in the sequence represents a criterion teachers should try to meet in creating Psychological Education courses, whether the course is aimed at improving the student's self-confidence or at helping him relate to others more easily. The remainder of this chapter illustrates these guidelines with many specific teaching activities we have created to increase students' achievement motivation. Our intention here is *not* to describe precisely how you *should* do it. We believe that our explanations and suggestions, combined with your experience and imaginative application to your own classroom, will produce a more lively, relevant learning experience for students than any single step-by-step syllabus we could provide.

Get Attention

Getting attendance and attention is largely a problem of creating moderate novelty that is slightly different from what is expected. The same old routines are experienced as dull and boring. On the other hand, extremely unusual experiences are shocking, disorganizing, confusing. Sometimes an extreme experience can lead to important personal growth, but this traumatic extreme is not necessary or appropriate for managed, maximally effective training.

The first way we try to establish moderate novelty is to recruit students from the full spectrum within a school so that even the "best"

*A considerable amount of support for the validity of these guidelines exists in the theoretical and empirical research literature on personality change. The most relevant summaries of this literature can be found in D.C. McClelland, "Toward a Theory of Motive Acquisition", *American Psychologist,* May 1965; D.C. McClelland and D. G. Winter, *Motivating Economic Achievement,* Free Press, N.Y. 2969.

students could see the group as representing something new. Often we select only a portion of the volunteers in order to give added value to the course by making it initially a scarce resource. The increased prestige survives during subsequent rounds of the course.

In our recruitment "pitch" we purposefully make reference to all the prestigious groups who have been involved in the course—businessmen around the world, Peace Corps volunteers, teachers, college students. Our recruitment pitch also mentions the typical results of n-Ach training. Often this is conveyed by the testimonial of someone the students respect. We try to indicate the types of changes students can expect if they choose to increase their n-Ach—increased self-confidence, more initiative, greater ability to make long-range plans, better risk taking. Sometimes we spice the recruitment with special signs, posters and announcements that suggest something new and unusual is coming. One group of course participants, aged 9 through 12, were enrolled in the "Harvard Growth Project," conducted at the Cambridge Friends School. Volunteers for Peace Corps service in Ethiopia were training at the school. "Growth Project" participants were promised T-shirts with an insignia on them combining three sets of initials.* The shirts were worn until the letters were completely obscured from fading and wear. Everyone the students met for months afterward asked them what the letters meant. In answering, the students reinforced their association with three prestigious groups. At the start, such activities create favorable, moderately novel expectations that get attendance and attention.

Moderately novel settings are possible without renting an expensive, isolated conference center. The important thing, if it is at all possible, is to keep n-Ach training from becoming just another 45-minute course meeting once a day in a regular classroom. This spacing of short periods works against continuity, impact and sustained attention. In one school, to acquire a larger block of time (1½ hours per day), the principal juggled the school schedule for participants and put their free period first; and we asked students to come to school early. From 7:30 to 9:20 we had all the privacy wanted. We called ourselves the "Dawn

E
*The insignia looked like this: HGP
CFS

132

Patrol," and suffered the hardship element good-naturedly because we all woke up together during the first quarter hour with doughnuts, cocoa, and coffee. In our effort to avoid traditional-looking classrooms with rows of desks, we chose as our meeting place an open, airy complex of rooms at one end of the building that housed the home economics classes. Adjoining was a lounge. Next door was a shop complex for woodworking and mechanical drawing. Altogether the rooms provided long tables, moveable furniture, and the opportunity to break into small groups or work in large ones. We could move around flexibly and freely, and even all talk at once without bothering anyone. As the course progressed the rooms looked more and more like *our* rooms, and less like anything to do with home economics. We made posters with pictures and n-Ach stories—many of them humorous. The course paraphernalia abounded: dart boards, collages, mobiles, goal setting charts. In these ways we tried to achieve some of the novel, attention-getting advantages of a retreat setting: separateness, continuity, warm interpersonal relationships.

Teachers' attitudes are crucial in establishing a productive, relaxed, moderately novel climate for learning. For this reason, we give n-Ach courses in a two-step sequence. First, we train teachers in n-Ach and Psychological Education and then continue a collaborative-consultant relationship with them as they create their own unique, specially tailored n-Ach course. Not only do teachers know best how to maintain necessary control, but as they invent appropriate teaching devices, they invest themselves in the course, feel a sense of ownership, and take responsibility for what happens. This self-reliance, independence, initiative, and desire to do well embodies the spirit of achievement motivation and is conveyed to students in ways that cannot be put into printed materials. We have tried to maintain this dependence on teachers' initiative by providing background training and a variety of illustrative materials without specifying the precise combination or sequence of activities for your n-Ach course. This opportunity remains yours.

Central to establishing this learning climate is the teacher's attitude, both about students' behavior and their ability to change. As the old saying goes, "Expect trouble, and you'll get it." The opposite way of thinking works too. Once, during a course, when some of the faculty were mulling over what to do if students came late—or if they didn't come at all, or if they slipped into the johns and started smoking—one teacher advised, "We have so much else to plan, let's handle those situations when they happen, if they happen at all." The teachers created a frame of mind that assumed people would be on time—would participate, would be considerate of each other, would think well of themselves. When such an attitude is sincere, and when the teachers, as participants in the course, live up to it themselves, the attitude is communicated to the students. Similarly, if the teachers doubt that the students can ever "guide and direct" their own behavior, and doubt that they will ever want to change, these doubts will be subtly communicated to the students, even if they are never voiced. Teachers' expectations tend to become self-fulfilling. The teacher's own attention, involvement, and hopes can be contagious.

Although it is not always possible, a low student-teacher ratio can help to establish the kind of climate we describe. Ideally there might be one teacher to a group of 7 to 12 students, or two teachers working with a group of 12 to 20 students. This arrangement allows more individual attention by teachers and warmer teacher-student relationships. Students in such small, supportive groups find it safer and easier to talk. When there are two or more small groups taking the n-Ach course at the same time, friendly rivalry and competition between groups often arises—it is another way of introducing n-Ach into the learning process itself. If this ratio is achieved, needless to say, teachers can be optimistic about a friendly, lively course climate with few discipline problems.

If we had to depend on small-group methods for success, however, the course wouldn't be given very often. Teachers working alone with groups of 20 to 30 have conducted successful achievement motivation courses. Generally, they enlist student aid and also break the class into small-group combinations that they know will work well together in many of the activities and exercises.

A final factor that helps get and keep attention is the sequence of methods used to increase n-Ach. Not only should these methods be moderately different from those in regular classrooms, but within the n-Ach course itself there should be variation and contrast in the sequence of methods in order to maintain novelty, attention, and interest. A variety of methods are available in the materials that accompany this book: games, a structured text, projects, role plays, readings, group presentations. Sources of ideas for other methods are listed in Chapter 2—"Side trip: Other Psychological Education techniques and courses." Most schools have equipment to use visual media—movie projectors, overhead projectors, slide-tape machines, and occasionally a videotape apparatus. These alternatives, plus any more that you can invent to keep the teaching pace quick, varied, and moderately novel, will help sustain students' attention.

These methods of getting attention may sound like a difficult set of conditions to meet just to give an achievement motivation course. Significant personal change is difficult and infrequent in comparison with normal learning in schools. But if this moderately novel situation can be created the course experiences are more likely to be intense, personally meaningful, and stand apart from normal school learning. At the other extreme, without attendance and attention no learning of any kind can take place. Getting and sustaining attention is the first problem to be solved in giving a successful achievement motivation course*.

*Most of these lessons we learned the hard way. Our first course for "seat warmers", as they had been described by their principal, was a highly instructive failure (instructive for us, that is). We did not get good attendance nor maintain constructive attention of those who came. Of 50 students who were initially invited to attend the course, 24 said they would come. Of the 16 students who showed up at the retreat-conference center, only nine students stayed the full five days of the course. Although these boys officially had volunteered for the course, most of them saw it as a sugar-coated pill for being trouble makers in school. They were asked to attend during a school vacation—the last straw for "turned-off" students. Once there, they looked around, sized up the group and labeled themselves a "bunch of kooks" rounded up to be studied by Harvard psychologists. Recruitment did not generate high expectations, nor did the assembled participants represent a prestigious reference group. In fact, the reference group simply reinforced the self-image we were trying to change. The setting and climate also missed the mark. As far as these boys were concerned, the course was an extension of school. Consequently, when the trainers failed to provide inviolate rules and to spell out specific directions, the boys interpreted this as laxity and weakness. What the instructors intended as an open, warm, supportive course climate, the boys saw as an invitation to test limits. The content of the course was just as unsuitable. Most of it was too abstract and analytical. They had to memorize. That was boring. Direct discussions about self-image seemed threatening to them. Most of the educational games played in the retreat setting were seen as fun only. In this course we did not get and keep attention because the *same* destructive expectations were created, the setting and teaching climate were *extremely* unusual, and the content was either the same old stuff or too much like vacation fun. In no case did we create moderate novelty.

Provide an Intense Integrated Experience of the Motive

The only way to know achievement motivation is by experiencing it. Descriptions of n-Ach fall far short in conveying the nature of this motive, in the same way that colored slides cannot give to others the special joys and lasting effect of your most recent vacation. To increase a person's achievement motivation, it is necessary to have him experience n-Ach vividly, intensely, in all its complexity—the goal setting, planning, risk taking, hopes, fears, anxiousness, and satisfaction. Then it is possible to label the experience meaningfully, talk insight-fully about it in relation to one's life situation, values, and ideal self. After the experience is understood in these ways, the person can make a knowledgeable choice about whether or not to practice and strengthen his achievement motivation. An intense, integrated experience of the motive is the keystone of the course.

One way we have provided such an experience is through simulation games like Ring Toss, Darts-Dice, and, in particular, the Origami Game. For most players, involvement in the games means working for achievement goals, such as improving personal performances or coming out ahead of other players. Because the games cue so strongly for achievement motivation, the players learn, by experience, what n-Ach is like.

The first impact of such an experience often is similar to the mildly disturbing effect of seeing a candid photograph of yourself. For example, some teachers and students claim that competition is not important to them but discover their feelings are ruffled when they don't make their bids in the Origami Game. The experience is an opportunity for self-confrontation. During one discussion following the Origami Game we asked a particularly successful teacher how he would have felt if we had told him how many paper models to build. He said, "I would have been furious with you and quit!" Then, after a moment's silent reflection he continued softly, "Wow, I wonder how my students feel when I assign work to them and set their goals?" In every n-Ach experience most people discover something of particular value to them. Usually several different experiences are required to understand fully the status and desirability of n-Ach in oneself. The second and subsequent experiences can be presented as opportunities for more "candid photographs," or as a chance to try out other more satisfying and productive responses to achievement-oriented situations.

Using the Origami, Darts-Dice, and Ring Toss games as models, you may wish to tailor-make additional games, projects, or role plays for your students. The most obvious criterion to keep in mind is that the game or situation should encourage individual goal-setting in a context that encourages achievement goals. In addition, the participant should be free to determine his own goals measured objectively against the performance of other players, or a stated criterion, or his own performance from round to round. There should be provisions for regular, specific feedback on one's performance. The scoring system should encourage moderate, carefully calculated risk taking. The situation should be complex enough to include the thoughts, actions, and feelings associated with the motive, and be challenging enough to make players really care about winning or losing. Yet the content of the game should be sufficiently different from everyday activities to allow non-threatening experimentation with one's behavior. General guidelines and content focus for discussion following your prototype achievement experience can be borrowed almost directly from the extensive commentaries accompanying the Origami, Darts-Dice, and Ring Toss games.

The best way to tell whether your invention is successful or not is to assess the amount of work you do during the discussion period. If the game, role play, or exercise is followed by a heavy silence, and discussion comes only after hard, prodding questions, then it didn't work. If your invention works, discussion will flow so readily that the energy you exert is mostly to keep things coordinated. It is more important at this stage in the course for students to enjoy the n-Ach experience and want more, than for them to take away an immediate, lasting personal insight. An intense, integrated experience of achievement motivation cannot be fully digested quickly any more than peak growth experiences or traumatic life-changing events are understood immediately and applied to one's life. Understanding, applying, and internalizing increased achievement motivation takes the rest of the course and beyond.

Conceptualize the motive

Once students have intensely, thoroughly experienced the motive, it is appropriate then to help them make sense out of what happened. Labeling the elements of achievement planning, achievement feelings, and action strategies makes it easier to discuss what happened in the game. A very natural labeling process can occur in the discussion after the games as people compare what their goals were and describe the strategies they used and the feelings they had. Learning the achievement vocabulary makes the course experience easier to remember and to use in everyday life situations.

Since most people experience some, but not all aspects of the motive syndrome, teaching the complete vocabulary has the immediate effect of locating for individuals the gaps and holes that exist in their n-Ach. Discovering these gaps helps a person to understand his achievement-oriented behavior in and outside the courses. For instance, a pattern of low risk taking is more understandable when the person discovers he seldom has hopes of success and success feelings. The person who always dreams of success but never gets anywhere can pinpoint the problem accurately when he realizes he never thinks about personal and world obstacles, and the activities necessary to surmount them. The consistently high risk taker who never makes it big can see more clearly the self-defeating aspects of his risk-taking style.

Typically, adults learn the vocabulary quickly and almost instantly become sophisticated analysts of their own behavior and the behavior of others. In fact, some restraint usually needs to be exercised to keep this vocabulary, as a diagnostic scheme, from being used too widely and inappropriately. Students, on the other hand, enjoy the games and learn from them, but they are apt to be overwhelmed or to react only to specific parts of their experience and the vocabulary. The main themes, however, do get across. Our strategy has been to stretch out the learning of vocabulary and conceptualizing by teaching sections of the motive syndrome separately. We try to keep attention by alternating n-Ach experiences with efforts to build conceptual understanding. For example, often we start out with the Ring Toss and Darts-Dice games to teach the action strategies, then follow this with the Origami Game which recapitulates the action strategies and introduces the entire planning pattern. This sequence gives students a chance to apply and practice what they've learned and at the same time provides a better experience base for teaching achievement planning.

The learning and labeling of the action strategies has always been uncomplicated. There are only four strategies, and the learning games are fun. The physical activity and observation during the games and the discussions afterward provide better kinds of learning than any lengthy description or lecture could offer. The players conceptualize by talking to each other. A player who keeps bidding 60 or 80 at darts, even though he consistently lands in the 30 or 40 ring, gets plenty of unsolicited advice from his team mates: "Lower your bid. You aren't making anything." Overcautious players are told to "Bid higher." Comparing reactions to the choice of darts or dice, players usually decide that darts are more challenging and rewarding because "you're doing it yourself, not relying on chance or statistics." With a little labeling and a minimum of description, nearly everyone has a clear idea of action strategies such as moderate-risk goal setting, use of feedback, and taking personal responsibility rather than relying on chance. However, researching the environment and taking initiative usually have to be explained, because they are not as directly demonstrated by the games as are the other behaviors.

Teaching achievement planning is more problematic. Our approach is to identify and explain the elements of achievement planning as quickly as possible and then offer many devices to make memorization and practice easy and involving. The goal is to have students learn the vocabulary so well they cannot forget it. We have used a variety of techniques to make such memorization fun and quick. One is the programmed text, *Ten Thoughts*. By the end of the booklet students write complete achievement plans. Whimsy and invention suggested a variety of other approaches. Through an analysis of T.V. programs we discovered that some heroes have incredibly high n-Ach. We brought in current records, listened to the themes represented in the lyrics, and talked about the goals and motive patterns they represented. We made big posters with colorful drawings and magazine pictures to create n-Ach grafitti. Everybody contributed to round-robin n-Ach stories—often humorous. Some teachers have made mobiles with graphic representations of HOS, FOF, WO, PO, and all the rest. We have passed out n-Ach buttons—knowing full well that the wearers would have to explain what the button meant to friends and acquaintances. We used pantomimes and role-plays. One group of teachers giving an experimental motivation course in Quincy, Mass. was especially anxious to circumvent the memorization problem. They were working with 50 junior high school students at once, had only a short time to give the course, and wanted to make sure that the students had the motive well in hand and mind so they could get past the basics. They invented an ingenious game that we have developed into the "n-Ach Match Game."

There probably are some students for whom this approach is inappropriate. In each case, you must select the best way to present the motive pattern. What you should borrow from these teaching methods is the combination of fun, excitement, and activity in learning something that is potentially dry. Just how many techniques you use depends on the particular group taking the course. However, it is important to avoid making vocabulary learning an end in itself. It is a vehicle that helps clarify the nature of n-Ach experiences and facilitates the relevant applications to a person's life. These criteria, not the percentage of correct answers on a memory test, should be used in deciding the ways that vocabulary is built.

Relate the motive to important aspects of the person's life

Increased achievement motivation is appropriate for a person to the degree that it helps him get along in his world, enhances his view of himself, and is consistent with his basic values. When the person knows what n-Ach is and has words to talk about the experience, it is easier for him to assess the desirability of developing this motive.

New personality traits can't be gulped in like candy. They have to be taken in like solid food, chewed and digested until the nutritious value is extracted. Since it is important that the course participant be convinced, for himself, of the value of this personal change, a good portion of the course should present materials and opportunities to help the student evaluate how the change will effect his life style and personality. The student should consider whether there is a practical value in acquiring the motive. Would demonstrating achievement behavior be consistent with the demands of reality? Secondly, even if he considers n-Ach a practical pattern of behavior, he has to feel that it enhances the image he has of himself. Finally, is that behavior compatible with his basic values? Will it conflict with other goals and values? In the course activities all three areas tend to overlap. For the purpose of making certain points salient, however, we consider them here as three separate issues.

The Demands of Reality

A way to help students consider how realistic n-Ach is for them is to distinguish between situations where achievement behavior is valuable, and situations where it is a hindrance, or less appropriate than another motive. A good teaching technique is simply to discuss the variety of areas that reward achievement goal setting: career, sports, some aspects of education, leisure time, travel. On the other hand, there are many worthwhile activities that do not depend heavily on achievement motivation. For example, the dominant motive of a young social worker helping students in a local youth group probably is affiliation motivation. An aspiring political leader must have an eye for power, and an imaginative concept of what power means, in order to gain a position where he can wield influence. A scientific researcher must be motivated most by curiosity. However, achievement motivation is often present to some degree in success patterns even when it is not the dominant motive. While it is helpful to present a gamut of reasons for the practical value of n-Ach—ranging from its personal validity to the cultural arguments presented in *The Achieving Society*—be careful to emphasize that the motive is not a panacea but only one kind of behavior, not infinitely applicable. For high school students, the most convincing point often is that an individual who cannot determine for himself what he wants to do and how he wants to do it, generally winds up doing what other people want, or not doing at all. An ability to choose and to accomplish is inherent in self-confidence and self-esteem.

Although these points can be introduced fairly casually, there are important follow-through activities that can demonstrate their validity. Students can interview people they admire and consider successful, and then discuss goals and strategies revealed in the interviews. Speakers can be invited to class. Once we found an ideal guest speaker, Bobby Leo, who had graduated from the high school in which the course was being held and was at the time a Harvard senior, a football hero, and a draftee of the Boston Patriots professional football team. After a brief introduction to the n-Ach vocabulary, he made his remarks deliberately relevant to the course. At the same time, he represented someone with whom many of the students could identify. At other times we have invited the highest degree Karate expert in the area, the superintendent of schools, and the mayor. Fictional examples can be almost as useful as live case studies. This is the thrust of the book, *Achieving*, where stories can be springboards for discussions about the practicality and usefulness of achievement behavior in a variety of situations.

It is especially important throughout the course to consider what reality looks like from the students' point of view. While some students have long-term goals, most students have more immediate projects such as finishing high school, successfully passing the 10th grade, making the basketball team, or organizing a rock and roll group. Some live in a reality where it is easier to have no goals at all, because all aspirations seem thwarted from the outset. Part of the role of trainers in the course is to make time for students to talk about their own lives and concerns, and then help them establish appropriate connections between the motive and the situations they describe.

Real and Ideal Self Images

Do adolescents know "who they are?" Can they talk about self image? If they can, will they talk in front of a group, even a small one? Although professional opinion is divided, we found it most effective to use less direct, and less verbal, methods of examining the ideals they have for themselves. All of the techniques should help the student to think about what he is like now, and what he would like to be ideally, then to think about ways of drawing the two images together.

For example, in several of our courses each student filled out an "admiration ladder." He was asked to write the name of someone he admired on the top rung. On the bottom rung he named a person he did not want to be like at all. Somewhere in between he wrote his own name, indicating how he felt about himself in comparison to these two people. Afterward we discussed what qualities the students value in the people they most admire. If they wanted to be more like those people, what would they have to do? When it was relevant, we talked about how achievement motivation could be helpful in reaching that kind of personal goal. This exercise and a variety of others are contained in the book *Who Am I?*.

Potentially this area is one of the richest, most creative parts of the course—especially if trainers are willing to experiment with art, drama, and other projective techniques. Students can present themselves in an artistic collage, using photographs or newspaper fragments. If trainers are interested in improvisational drama or have had theater experience, they might like to try skits, improvisation, pantomimes, or role plays. These activities can range from personal closeups, in which the students play themselves and each other, to situations in which students play historical or public figures that come closest to their secret or real selves. A standard stage makeup kit can be the basis for a provocative "Who am I?" in which students work in pairs and make each other up to emphasize the identities they associate with their partners. The important criteria for any of these activities is, first of all, expressed acceptance and support for the way people present themselves, and secondly, the attempt to understand more clearly the nature of the gap between a person's real and ideal self. For many students this can be a first occasion to see themselves as potentially high achievers.

Cultural Values

Even after a student acknowledges that n-Ach is of practical value in his world, and is a desirable aspect of his self-image, he may still experience conflict about the motive unless it is consistent with the values of the groups to which he belongs. One can easily speculate about family structures that squelch a young person's positive self-image and his opportunities for independence and personal decision making: a combination of discord and authoritarianism or over-protective parents. Another area of potential value conflict is school itself. If a classroom is structured to preclude decision-making and goal-setting by the students, if there are few provisions for feedback and initiative, or a rigid grading system limits ways to do well, then students cannot be expected to spontaneously show achievement motivation, because it is not meaningfully valued. A third area of value conflict occurs when a student belongs to a group that sees achievement concerns as part of what's wrong with America. In many people's minds there are links between an ethic that espouses individual achievement and current societal ills, such as power monopolies in big business, a materialistic money orientation, and callousness to the plight of small individuals. The argument may strike one as simplistic, accurate, a confusion between greed and achievement, or as just inevitable. The course should bring cultural values and students' perception of them into the open as a topic for discussion, not to change the students' values, but to clarify what those values are, and to explore the ways they are consistent and inconsistent with the n-Ach values of self-reliance, independence, and concern with excellence.

Often it is difficult to sustain a meaningful conversation about cultural values with young students. We have found several approaches that work fairly successfully. One is to use current media. For example, newspapers and magazines continuously focus on the "generation gap," youth culture, and school issues as feature articles. These writings can provide lively discussion about values held by the students, or confronted by them. Popular songs, popular heroes, and popular causes are useful in evoking a clearer notion of cultural values. This is especially fun with folk and rock music now, when the singers are often message conscious. Movies, both educational and commercial, provide ready stimulus for this kind of classroom conversation. A little brainstorming and an afternoon over the movie catalog can help you make appropriate choices for your particular group.

Sometimes we have made up a brief questionnaire of value statements, had the students answer privately on a continuum from "strongly agree" to "strongly disagree," tallied the responses for a class average, and let them talk about how they answered in comparison to others. Here is an example: "It is more important to do well than to be popular; I'd rather have fun in the present than worry all the time about what I'm going to do in the future." A more elaborate version is to ask students to read a series of prepared profiles about young people approximately their own age and to choose which three of 10 they would choose to represent the best of American youth. The profiles you create should represent different value orientations, from high priority on gregariousness and popularity, to concern with developing skilled hobbies, concern with money, etc.*

Some of the materials in *Who Am I?* and readings in *Achieving* are useful starting points for value discussions. A logical extension of readings is to take advantage of theater and fiction that seem relevant. For example, the play, *Death of a Salesman,* brings up several issues important in the n-Ach course: Willy Loman's reliance on affiliation and achievement concerns, his abandonment in an environment that doesn't support his efforts to do well, his dwindling self-image, the difference in outlook between Willy and Biff—who wants to find for himself his own identity and his own kind of meaning in life, but who feels bound by his father's standards. Obviously, it is not good to beat the play to death by talking about achievement motivation afterwards, or to exploit a great piece of theater by over-analysis. But with the right

*A particularly good source of techniques for clarifying values is *Values and Teaching,* Raths, L., Harmon, M., Simon, S., Charles Merrill Books, Columbus, Ohio, 1966.

staff-student group and the right situation, this type of experience can be a powerful stimulus for the discussion of personal values.

The most challenging part of the course is the effort to help students relate the motive to their own life situation, ideal, self-images, and values. It is hard to get such conversations going, and even more difficult to keep students on the track without being wooden and constantly saying, "Now what does this have to do with n-Ach?" Teachers should aim for obvious interest and involvement on the part of the students, and a growing tendency to speak personally and specifically—to say "I," to refer to one's own family and group of friends. If the films and readings are remote to the students, that will be fairly obvious in short order. The strongest evidence of success is to be found in students' approach to the last part of the course: Can they, through this phase, do enough self-study and gain sufficient insight to pick a meaningful goal-setting project and carry it through?

During the whole course teachers should keep their eyes on the goals. If students want to go directly from the games to personal goal-setting projects, consider yourself successful in stimulating precocious students. They may want the implications for their life, image, and values to be examined later. The general rule for teachers is this: If interest begins to fade, stop and do something else. Just because there is a great deal of material does not mean that it all must be thoroughly taught and learned. Help students maintain the initiative by creating a learning environment in the course that supports achievement concerns, enchances students' self-images, values their independence, and responds to their initiative.

Practice the Motive

An integral part of any n-Ach course is to have students actually practice using the motive by carrying out a goal-setting project. Without this application of what has been learned, the motive is cognitively understood but not used and useful. As with any new skill, the first attempts to engage consciously in n-Ach planning, feelings, and actions usually are halting and difficult. Teachers must be especially patient and inventive in keeping the course lively and fun. Once students choose an appropriate n-Ach goal they want to pursue, the details of n-Ach planning and action can be evoked to increase the likelihood that their practice will be satisfying and successful. A number of goal-setting devices useful for this phase of the course have been collected in the book *Aiming*.

In one course we held conferences with each student to learn about the goals and provide consultation in devising methods of getting regular, concrete feedback on progress. The formal part of the course ended at this point, but we continued to provide support and reinforcement through a weekly double post card. One part had a message, a simple "Hello—how are are you doing?" The other, containing a progress graph, was to be filled out and returned to us. While we mailed cards and reminders, and compiled statistics, students lost weight, earned money, built boats, improved grades, found summer jobs. At the follow-up celebration the faculty graced the occasion by cooking a finale breakfast for everyone. We handed out ersatz Harvard certificates and small prizes for special accomplishments. The mood was one of fun and satisfaction. A number of people had done something truly important; many had reached the first goal they ever consciously set for themselves by themselves.

Experience has led us to anticipate certain obstacles in this practice phase. If the staff isn't careful, the entire effort can come across as "just another assignment," and students will define some vague goal for the sake of fulfilling the obligation, finish it with the least possible effort, or not bother at all. The staff should convey the spirit that the project is a chance to experiment with the goal-setting technique in one's own way, and on a goal important to the student himself. The project is not homework. In fact, while students should be encouraged to do it, they should not be forced. Someone reluctant and recalcitrant at the time of the course may just try it on his own later, particularly if he sees that others have enjoyed success. It also helps if staff members themselves engage in goal-setting projects at the same time, and provide progress reports as regular group members.

Often students choose task goals like "Finish my history project," instead of achievement goals. There are overtones of drudgery here, and, predictably, the student's feelings aren't invested to the degree necessary for enjoyable persistence. An achievement goal along the same lines might be, "I want to give a better class presentation than I did last time; I want to talk about ancient Greece, keep everybody tuned in, and even teach the teacher something new." The key is concern for excellence and emotional involvement so that success or failure will have meaning. Sometimes students choose goals that depend on others. Girls especially are inclined to confuse affiliation and power concerns with achievement goals. Here the teacher might use discretion. A goal statement such as "I want my mother and father to get along better" is clearly an affiliative goal. "I want my boyfriend to stay in school" expresses achievement concerns for him, but her own goals are affiliation and power. The goals are admirable, but may not be suitable for n-Ach strategies. It would be a disservice to the motivation course and to the girl to let her be deluded into believing that n-Ach strategy is helpful in all cases—then be disappointed because it didn't work. In such cases, consultation with the teacher might help the student pursue other directions.

Once a student has settled on a goal that is an achievement goal, his next step is to be specific about it and devise concrete methods of feedback and measuring progress. A dialogue frequently overheard goes something like this:

Teacher: "I see your goal is to get a B in algebra the 3rd quarter. How are you planning to go about it?"

Student: "Well, I'm going to study harder."

Teacher: "What do you mean by 'study harder?'"

Student: "Study more. Like spend an hour every day."

These responses suggest one of the possible pitfalls students often encounter in goal-setting attempts. Sometimes students just don't know how to plan in detail. For example, if a girl's diet campaign is to "eat less and weigh myself every day," she is less likely to be successful than if she researched the environment to learn calorie equivalents and know how many calories intake/output per day would allow for two pounds weight loss per week. Similarly, a term project in biology could be subdivided into four or five sections with separate deadlines rather than into hours spent per day. Often students equate looking longer at the page, reading more, doing more math problems as studying harder. But *more* isn't always *better*. The point is to imagine and devise a specific, concrete goal with intermediate goals and built-in checkpoints. ("Study for one hour with three study questions in mind. At the end of the hour write paragraph answers to each question. List the things that distracted me and ways to overcome them.") Another reason for vagueness about planning can simply be lack of interest in the goal. Ability to be detailed and specific about something shows involvement.

Thus, another approach to the vagueness malaise is to encourage the student to think about a goal that is more important to him.

In n-Ach courses, as students begin to think about school goals, they often realize that much of their school work is a high-risk situation. They are graded on tests alone and much of their other work leaves them very little room for choice of method or quantity. This leaves basically two alternatives for attaining school-related goals in an achievement-oriented way.

First, help students diagnose all the problems (WO, PO) that stand in the way of classroom achievement and plan steps to overcome them. "Do you talk to others too much?" "What distracts you?" "Do you avoid homework for any reason?" "Are you just looking to get by in class?" "What would happen if you decided to be the best student in the class?" Once the real problem has been pinned down (or what the student believes to be the real problem), concrete steps toward changing those behaviors can begin. If, for example, the student feels he spends too much time talking with others in class, he may work out a system of counting the number of times he does this each day with a grocery store clicker, and set a goal of, say, no more than two classroom conversations per day. If he clicks each time he talks to someone about something not related to the class work, he will see how far he has to go and begin to move toward that goal.

Second, attempt to translate long-range assignments and responsibilities into smaller, shorter, more measurable units. Thus the student who feels that his history course presents an insurmountable obstacle, because there is just so much to learn for the exams, may be able to work out an arrangement with his teacher to break down extra reading assignments into discrete daily or weekly units, with his goal the reading and understanding of so many pages per day or week. If he keeps a graph with days on the horizontal line (Y axis), he will have a daily feedback mechanism that allows him to see how well he is doing at all times and plan more effectively to reach his long-range goal.

Above all, stay flexible, not every student can or wants to declare a precise goal, completely analyze all the obstacles, and know ahead of time exactly how the hurdles will be surmounted. This style may be appropriate in getting the Apollo spacemen to the moon but not always for every other goal. Some students feel that this degree of analysis beats a fond notion to death, leaving little room for spontaneity. True enough. Not everyone should set and implement goals in the same way. Some people like to mix their achievement strivings with a heavy dose of affiliation and work best when they set a joint interdependent goal with someone else. Others are spurred on most when they are challenged by a doubting Thomas or by a competitor striving for the same goal. Those students with particularly low self-confidence may need a lot of ego propping, praise, and group encouragement before starting seriously for a goal. The scientific types may want to collect data on the problem before plotting their strategy. There are as many styles as individuals, and the teaching task outlined in this section should not bar a student's unique brand of initiative.

Internalize the Motive

Paradoxically, the most important thing for a teacher to do in helping a student to internalize n-Ach is to stop doing anything. Support for continued strong achievement motivation must be gradually transferred from external sources to the person's own inner resources. The trick is to leave on time—not too soon because guidance is needed in the early phases, and not too late because that retards essential self-reliance.

After those wise words to you we should admit that we have no guaranteed cues for you to use in staging perfectly timed exits. As a general rule, however, we do believe that teacher support and/or students' peer-group support should continue for some time after the formal course is over. This phased withdrawal can begin during the goal-setting projects. The follow-up reports encourage record keeping and show continued interest in the students' progress. Usually we hold one reunion several months after the course, when most of the projects are completed, and another reunion as much as a year later. Special, more lasting friendships often develop between students and teachers who share this experience. These relationships provide students with models to emulate and with support when it is needed.

In our extensive research on the effects of our courses, we try to assess the degree of internalization that takes place over a 1½-year period. Our most successful method of getting information is a semi-structured telephone interview that has the added advantage of providing periodic reminders to the course participants. We have included this interview and our method of evaluating the information as

Appendix D. This is not meant as a way of grading students, but more important, as a way for teachers to assess how well they have taught and what they can do to be more effective achievement motivation trainers.

The reports of students show that the motive is transformed as it is internalized, much as needed vitamins and nutrients are extracted from food as it is digested and transformed into bodily strength and health. Many students forget the special vocabulary in a year and have only vague, pleasant memories of what happened in the course. Yet, when compared to matched groups of students who did not take the course, clear differences in goal setting, career planning, and implementation are present. The following examples catch the essential differences:

> Jimmy decided at the course that he wanted to be a hairdresser. He reported he will start training in the June or September following graduation. He got a part-time job and will have saved about $500 to use for tuition at the school. He has applied to the school and has an invitation to come for an interview. He said that the evening course takes 1,000 hours. He can work in the daytime. He plans to try to get a job at the telephone company while he is going to school because it is better than the part-time job he has now with a dry cleaner. In school he is trying for the "honor roll for the first time since third grade" and his grades are up. Obviously, he has done a lot of concrete thinking and planning for his future.

> Ken's report is typical of the boys who did not take the n-Ach courses. He said sports are most important to him, football and particularly skiing—on snow in winter and water in summer. He also spends a lot of time with his girl and is a "bug on mechanics." He used to race go-karts and wants to race his car next year at a Connecticut dragway. He has never liked school and never does the work. He said he just hasn't done much serious thinking about his future.*

*These two descriptions are adapted from D.C. McClelland, Achievement Motivation Development Project Working Paper Number 4, pp. 8 and 9. A variety of additional examples are presented in Appendix D.

In the school where we conducted most of our research, we discovered that our teachers also had internalized and transformed much of the achievement ethic. Several teachers organized their own n-Ach course for interested students who had heard about the course, but had not participated the year before. Three teachers experimented with their own classroom structures to provide greater latitude for student decision making and initiative. Two math teachers arranged to teach next door to each other so that they could team-teach the Math Game (see Chapter 3). The group of teachers was influential enough to persuade the entire staff to begin the school year with a "tuning in" time—two days of discussion with students, parents, and community leaders on all aspects of meaningful education. The enthusiasm began to spread. Morale went up. The number of ceiling tiles broken by students (an interesting index of school spirit) was drastically reduced. Referrals to the guidance counselor dropped off, especially from teachers who taught the n-Ach courses and were developing useful guidance skills and competencies on their own. The principal, who participated in the teacher training and supported the program, caught the spirit of restless innovation. He promoted one of the course teachers to Assistant Principal. Although these changes may seem small and strange, they do indicate a shift in mood within the school. Two years previously, many teachers openly confessed they didn't like working in "the little red reform school in the swamp," as it was cynically described by many citizens of the city. We witnessed a revival of pride. From our point of view, this ripple effect is an ideal result of an orientation to achievement motivation and Psychological Education.

A Beginning

To "close" the chapter and the book at this point with a summary would contradict the forward-looking spirit of Hermes. It is more appropriate to ask where you go from here. The theories presented in this book, the suggested sequence in training, the accompanying curriculum materials, even achievement motivation itself, are convenient tools for you to use in giving your first Psychological Education course. It is our hope and expectation that this will be only a beginning.

Like hundreds of other teachers who began with experience in an achievement motivation course, you too can transform this stimulus into your own unique contribution to teaching and learning. We cannot predict where and how you will progress, but we can indicate some of the variations introduced by teachers in the sequence, style, contents and students of the course.

Teachers have shown us that there is nothing sacred about our six-step sequence of learning. One delightfully piquant shop teacher decided to give the n-Ach course backwards. He is a small man, barely five feet tall, a reasonably well-known artist, and has charge of the biggest bullies and potential dropouts in his school. It is difficult to forget how he started with the practice goal-setting, lecturing to his "Mafia," sitting around the shop table on which he was standing, with a huge, threatening wooden mallet in his hand—the most unique attention-getter we have seen. The students immediately saw the relevance of the goal-setting projects to their work outside school and within a week began to talk in detail about what they liked to do, their goals, conflicts, and defeats. At this point Hans, the shop teacher, suggested a way to psych it out using a little-known new scheme he'd found. Intrigued by the secrecy, the boys eagerly learned about the planning pattern and action strategies through a special lecture-with-mallet and forethought. As Hans predicted, the boys were impatient with the terminology and demanded that he show them how it worked. He challenged them all in the Origami Game, won, and then re-explained how he did it, again using the n-Ach terminology. Hans' approach is one of many routes to internalization. The sequence we described in this chapter is only one. But no matter what new routes are discovered, internalization of the motive should be the destination.

Several years ago we began to wonder about our *style* of teaching n-Ach, as opposed to the sequence of what we taught. With the help of experienced teachers, we had always tried to attain a free-wheeling, improvisational style that kept in rhythm with fluctuating student interests and involvement. We assumed that enjoyment would lead the students on to mastery of the material, and further, that if we insisted on step-by-step mastery, the course would become drudgery and a turn-off. One of our teachers, an accomplished musician, challenged these assumptions by saying that he had practiced the piano for six years under parental orders before his mastery of the instrument gave him satisfaction and improvisational freedom. He said further that if he had continued only as long as he had been interested, he would have quit within the first month. As a result of this challenge, we decided to give two courses to ninth graders, one oriented to maintaining high student satisfaction, the other focused on guaranteeing consistently high levels of mastery of the concepts, strategies, and planning pattern.*

The mastery course was structured like the Origami Game and the Math Game (Chapter 3). Instead of rounds, there were four contracts—one each on the action strategies, the planning pattern, self-study, and goal setting. These areas are equivalent to the middle steps in the learning sequence: experience, conceptualize, relate, apply. Each contract described the objective, various ways mastery could be demonstrated and points earned, and several methods of approaching mastery. Students were expected to earn a minimum of 25 points per contract, although it was possible to earn many more. We encouraged competition between individuals and teams and improvement from one contract to the next. Our role was that of the umpire-coach. Appendix E is a complete presentation of the course structure and contracts.

The satisfaction-oriented n-Ach course consisted of the same content, games, exercises, and role plays sequenced as in the mastery-oriented course. However, there were no contracts, no tests, and no points to be earned. The time used in the mastery course to explain directions, give and grade tests was used in the satisfaction course for small-group informal discussions and impromptu activities. One activity in particular exemplifies the difference in tone between this course and the mastery course. Since there were no tests requiring students to prove they had the basic concepts thoroughly in hand, the staff proposed a test situation that the students accepted enthusiastically; it turned out to be the high point of the course. They held a teach-in. Staff and students invited members of the school committee, representatives from the administration, the curriculum supervisors, newspaper reporters, and interested school personnel and taught them a two-hour mini-course in achievement motivation that subsequently was featured in an illustrated article in the local paper.

A panoramic view of the morning would have shown a shy, chubby girl answering the questions of a metropolitan daily education editor

*Research evaluation of the long-term effects on internalization is being completed at the time of this writing. Preliminary data suggest that at the end of the course there is little difference between the two groups in terms of their knowledge of the concepts.

with the elan that comes from a thorough knowledge of an esoteric subject . . . a boy who had just returned from a week's disciplinary suspension from school teaching the superintendent of schools how to set goals ("Now, when you decided to take the job of superintendent, you probably said to yourself, 'I wonder if I'll be good enough to do the job'. That's what we call FOF.") . . . a slow learner teaching a Ph.D. in clinical psychology how to score a psychological projective test, pausing to make sure the doctor understood the fine points of achievement imagery before moving on to the next topic. A group of students in yet another corner of the room put adults through the paces of a dart game, carefully explaining that the point was to use feedback, not to make daring but impossible bids for the bullseye. It was altogether a most unusual scene to stumble upon in a school setting. The "teach-in" involved a rather large risk in the minds of the teachers giving the course. Yet it hit the mark as an interesting, involving way to encourage conceptualization and mastery of the course material without the drudgery of traditional test routines.

The point here is not to advocate one style of training over another, but rather to legitimize a wide variety of styles, from carnival barker to guru, from coach to apprentice master, from teacher direction to student self-teaching. The sequence, style, and content depend on the combination of the teacher's personality and the group being taught. It is important for you to keep in mind that there is a great deal more diversity than is indicated in the first part of this chapter. Only a few examples are needed to convey the range of possibilities open to you:

Two professors at Temple University attempted to teach n-Ach to Head Start pre-school children, relying primarily on n-Ach games, an achievement-saturated learning situation, and n-Ach instruction for parents.

College students in Cambridge, Massachusetts, used the planning pattern and vocabulary to help tutees at the local community center improve their high school performance.

A medical school student in his spare time converted the n-Ach language and concepts into vernacular for a course he gave to inner-city disadvantaged grade school students.

A psychiatrist created a "get well" game for his mental hospital ward patients that was structured to arouse their achievement motivation. His coaching consisted of games to practice winning strategies.

Peace Corps volunteers have structured their teaching abroad to encourage self-reliance and achievement goals. Books, English themes, and drama have been focused on n-Ach.

One parent adapted the Origami bidding matrix for his son's weekly chores so that his son now uses n-Ach planning and strategies to earn his allowance.

Several New York State community colleges have modified the n-Ach course to replace the traditional orientation week at the beginning of school.

Three graduate students in education have used the theoretical scheme and materials as guides for developing Psychological Education courses to increase "affiliation motivation," "power motivation," and "self-esteem."

The full n-Ach and Psychological Education program has been offered as a semester course at teacher's colleges to introduce students to this new way of directly promoting psychological growth.

And now, where will you go from here?

APPENDICES

Appendix A:
How to Begin—Notes to the Initiator

Several people may be enticed by this course, or perhaps you are a sole, curious reader toying with the notion of organizing a workshop. No matter how the course begins, one person generally takes responsibility for getting it started. These remarks are directed primarily to him.

As the initiator, your first task is to learn enough about the material to recruit other course members from the administration and faculty by convincing them that these experiences may meet their needs. To acquire background information on how this course developed and what its possibilities are, we suggest that you read chapters 1, 3, and 4 of the manual and skim Chapter 2. Then lay the groundwork by preparing for an introductory meeting.

When you begin recruiting, start with members of the administration. They can supply incentives such as in-service credit for the course, tangible help like money for books and resources, and the essential intangible of their own enthusiasm. Encourage members of the administration to participate, for if they work alongside the teachers you will have a doubly effective core group. Moreover, the exercises and discussions that occur in the course about motivation, teaching styles, and classroom situations are valuable shared experiences. Later when you give an achievement motivation course to students, administrators will be more willing to support the effort fully. They will understand what the course is and what it requires in terms of time, space, and facilities. They will be able to remain unruffled through the logistics of putting on the course and witnessing what the uninitiated might view as shenanigans.

The total workshop group, ideally, would include seven to twelve persons—teachers and administrators—who have volunteered because of special interest and favorable impressions from your advance informational work. There should be about an even split between men and women, and a variety of subject interests, talents, personality types, and ages represented. Our reasoning for this diversity involves such considerations as these: the group should be large enough to provide a full cast of characters for the exercises (many of which require a minimum of six people), but small enough to work together in a close, straightforward way over a period of time. Thus groups of more than 15 should split into two groups to facilitate interaction. If a variety of subject areas and interests are represented, a richer exchange of ideas and teaching methods occurs. However, it is possible that an already formed group, such as members of the guidance or physical education or social studies departments, may decide to take the course. In this case the group has the advantage of a common focus on content, problems, and teaching styles and a greater chance for effectively implementing new ideas.

The workshop requires a bare minimum of six 3½-hour sessions. Each of these can be expanded into longer sessions when interest and time allow, just as the number of meetings can multiply, depending on the direction the group takes and the involvement members feel. Various schedules are possible, from long weekend retreats (Thursday evening through Sunday evening), to a series of weekly meetings, or some combination of the two. Further on in this section we sketch out possible schedules and briefly suggest the special advantages or disadvantages of each. It might be useful to present these alternative schedules to people when you describe the course initially, so that they know the time commitment required and can begin to arrange their own schedules. A definite schedule should wait until the first meeting, when the group can make a joint decision about the time and the location of future meetings.

Let's assume that you have progressed through the sequence just described: you have read chapters 1, 3, and 4, and you are comfortably familiar with achievement motivation. The administration is receptive to the idea of allowing teachers some released time and in-service credit for tackling this independent project. Several teachers are interested in the course and are willing to devote the necessary time. Optimistically, you have rounded up many of the necessary materials, scouted out room possibilities, and invited all those interested to an hour-long introductory meeting. The purposes of the meeting are to help interested teachers decide whether they will participate in the course, and to make plans for getting underway. As an experiment, take 10 minutes now to outline specific goals you would try to fulfill in a meeting that would convince three-fourths of the people attending to undertake the workshop.

Goal	What action to take to meet the goal	Help available

1 ....

2 ....

3 ....

A list of goals and guidelines we have kept in mind when starting past courses is presented below. Your list will overlap in some areas and may include ideas we have overlooked. Our list isn't the answer to the question about goals for the first meeting, but rather it is our contribution to a pool of topics and issues—yours and ours—from which you can draw to create a first meeting that will accomplish your own goals.

1. Set a tone and atmosphere that is comfortable and evocative. The course has natural selling points. People have found it fun, interesting, and worthwhile. Avoid creating pressure. Create conditions that make people want to accept an invitation *(e.g.* describe a sample exercise, or have the principal express enthusiasm).

2. Give a brief sketch of the background, rationale, and potential benefits of a training program in achievement motivation. (Chapter 1)

3. Discuss what the course can accomplish for this group: an opportunity for personal growth, a chance to learn about achievement motivation and Psychological Education; a method of improving their teaching styles; a way to acquire training to give similar courses to students; a solution to special needs within the school.

4. Indicate what the course is like. Try to convey the experiential, relaxed, participatory climate of the course. Give examples of the course contents: films, role plays, games, exercises, discussions. All of these are designed to stimulate insights about personal motive patterns and about classroom influences on students' motives. Within the course there will be opportunities for people to pursue their own special directions. Skim Chapter 2. Explain how the course will be run. There will not be an instructor; instead everyone will share the leadership role by taking turns for each session. Refer them to the description of the course experience and the leadership role in Appendices B and C.

5. Be prepared to consider questions about housekeeping details

such as the following: Is anyone taking overall responsibility? Where will it be? What is the schedule for the course? Will there be any credit given, or compensation? Will the school let us organize a course for the students? How will we pay for things we need? Who will lead each session?

The housekeeping details can be handled in a short follow-up meeting by those people who decide to take the course and commit themselves to seeing it through from start to finish. This kind of commitment is important in small-group workshops where sparse attendance leaves others hanging and erodes group morale. It is important during this introductory meeting to assign a leader for each session so that everyone has ample time to prepare. (Don't forget to assign two leaders for Session 3). The sessions should occur in a tight enough sequence to maintain interest and attention. On the other hand we have not found a 3½-day marathon completely satisfactory since the material requires some intervals in learning to be digested and incorporated. We have outlined a few of the possible workshop schedules in the following table:

Achievement Motivation Workshop Sessions

Possible Schedules	The Arts of Contributing SESSION 1	Who Am I? SESSION 2	Action Strategies SESSION 3 Part 1	Part 2	Achievement Planning SESSION 4	Side trips in Psychological Education SESSION 5 - 8	Getting it Together SESSION 9	New Planning SESSION 10
One afternoon a week – 3½ hours (full course)	week 1	week 2	week 3	week 4	week 5	weeks 6, 7, 8, 9	week 10	week 11
One afternoon a week – 3½ hours (abbreviated course)	week 1	omit	omit	week 2	week 3	week 4	week 5	week 6
Marathon (full course)	Friday morning	Friday afternoon	Friday evening	Saturday morning	Saturday afternoon	Saturday evening Sunday morning Sunday afternoon	Sunday evening	Monday morning
Marathon (abbreviated course)	Saturday morning	omit	omit	Saturday afternoon	Saturday evening	Sunday morning	Sunday afternoon	Sunday evening
Saturdays (full course)	First Saturday morning	First Saturday afternoon	Second Saturday morning	Second Saturday afternoon	Third Saturday morning	Third Saturday afternoon Fourth Saturday morning	Fourth Saturday afternoon	Fifth Saturday morning
Saturdays (abbreviated course)	First Saturday morning	omit	omit	First Saturday afternoon	Second Saturday morning	Second Saturday afternoon	Third Saturday morning	Third Saturday afternoon
Various combinations of afternoons and Saturdays (your design)								

Appendix B:
The Leadership Role

When you are leading a session, your assignments will range from mundane assembling of materials to the subtle creation of a tone and atmosphere that helps the session click. You must perform some duties yourself, while the group shares other duties with you. To be more specific, let's consider your role as a three-stage process: planning the session, guiding the session, and leading the evaluation at the end of the session.

1. *Planning for the session*

Before the session, you are like a production manager responsible for staging. The following types of preparation will help the production come off successfully:

a. Read about your session far enough in advance to tell the group about the reading they should do or special equipment they must bring to the session.

b. Understand the game or experiment directions so that you can clarify them for the group and keep the session from boggling over details.

c. Based on your advance scouting and on the evaluation of the session before, formulate goals for the session, and think of specific ways to implement those goals. Some of these goals may have to do with personal interactions among members: *e.g.,* "Try to encourage Richard to speak up more by placing him with Liz and Sophia for small group work—both are good listeners—by deliberately inviting his remarks, not belligerently, but by eye contact." Others might pertain more to discussion topics and probe questions. In other words, have your homework done, so that you can act as a resource, and take people's questions in a productive direction. Then you can attend to what people are saying rather than frantically leafing through a sheaf of questions and answers.

d. Make some arrangements for refreshments, if that is in order. Provide for the comfort of the group.

e. See that any necessary materials are available and set up properly before session.

Before you feel overwhelmed, we hasten to add that help is available. Each session includes instructions to the leader for the agenda

163

items, along with a guide that will provide suggested starting points for discussion and a description of what might be expected to happen.

Beyond these concrete preparations, a most important ingredient for the success of any session is an enthusiastic, open-minded attitude. When you are the leader, accept the fact that you can prepare only up to a point. You aren't going to be the teacher leading the class in lockstep through an outlined plan of the day. You will be more like a director or host who has set the stage for the activity about to begin. So, after careful preparation, relax and breathe deeply. (Physiologically, taking enormous breaths is one of the best ways to relieve tension.)

2. *Guiding the Session*

Begin the session by briefly explaining the purpose and describing the sequence of what will happen. You should run the exercise or activity efficiently so that there is ample time for discussion, but you should not be so glued to the schedule that you are seen as a drill sergeant. Rather, try to be attentive to people's involvement and enjoyment. Careful advance preparation and a certain amount of agility will carry you through the mechanics acting as host for the activity.

As discussion leader for the activity, you will be working with everyone else to gain insight from what happened. Consequently, you will be called upon to "play it by ear" a good deal of the time. From prior reading of the discussion guide you will have an idea of what to expect and will be ready with questions to stimulate the group's thinking. But be prepared to modify, or even discard parts of your plan. There is an important distinction to be made here between preparation and planning. Adequate preparation will help you use your knowledge to enlighten the group about what is happening. It will help you improvise on where the group has decided to take the discussion. Planning that is too specific is likely to cause resistance. The real skill of the discussion leader is that, having prepared, he can make what happens in the situation relevant.

Besides helping the group accomplish its goals, you must also accept responsibility for "group maintenance" and be watchful of the *group process*. How is the task being carried out? What are the interactions in the group? Is everyone contributing? If they aren't, why? Are people apathetic, angry, distracted? For example, if someone constantly digresses or dominates the group, that affects everyone else and is a matter of group concern. To credit such occurrences with mere nuisance value and tolerate it under the pretext of "getting on with the job" will let the group decay. Usually the best time to take up and resolve these interpersonal issues is during the evaluation period of each session.

In any group, personal energy can manifest itself in defensive, destructive behavior or in a supportive, productive manner. Progress on a group task is contingent on good working relationships within the group, and ideally on openness, trust, and support among members. Everyone should feel responsible for creating this working atmosphere, but you in particular can contribute most to the creation of this climate by practicing the specfic leadership behaviors listed below:*

a.   Listen superbly, and encourage the rest of the group to do the same. A good way to check how well you are listening is to see if you can paraphrase to yourself what the speaker said.

b.   Never compete with members of the group or struggle to have your own ideas heard. As leader, you are present for their benefit. Later, as a follower, you can attend to your own concerns. The best rule of thumb you as leader should remember is to hold off your comments until everyone else has had his say. Often, others will make your point and feel good about contributing.

c.   Let everyone have a say and use every member of the group. This means inviting participation by the shy or reluctant (with eye contact, or perhaps a nod of the head) and tactfully suggesting some boundaries for those who tend to dominate the group ("Thank you, I've got the idea.").

d.   Intervene in ways that clarify what has happened. When the time feels right, paraphrase what has been going on and what has been said. Identify points of confusion and questions that seem to be left hanging. You needn't always resolve the confusion yourself. For example, you might say, "Could someone summarize the alternatives that have been mentioned so far?" or, "I'm not sure I understood your last point—could you say a little more?" or "Could someone else give me their understanding of what was said?"

e.   Help members develop the habit of personalizing comments, especially those that affect other group members. Help people to take

---

*A number of these recommendations are adopted from *Creative Leadership* by C. Prince, Cambridge, Mass., Synetics, Inc. 1968.

responsibility rather than blaming others. For example, another way for a participant to say "You monopolize the group," is to say "I would like to talk more but I find it very uncomfortable trying to stop you." The second remark is fairer, because the person addressed can stop talking graciously without losing face and feeling attacked. Further, help people avoid making comments to no one in particular. Often it is helpful to say something like, "Can you address that comment to someone in particular in the group?"

f. Prevent anyone from being "put down." The leader should help the group be positive by stressing the value of ideas and comments, not the potential pitfall. First say what it is you like about a person's idea, no matter how bad it is, then say what concerns you. This procedure recognizes that people will disagree, but also that good ideas often are lost because people aren't willing to look at them carefully.

g. Try to be a combination "barometer-pressure" for the group. If you feel tension vibrating around people, express that feeling. Depending on your own sense of the situation, your own style and inclination, that expression might be humorous or perfectly straight, but it should open the possibility of talking about what's wrong and relieving people's feelings. Conversely, if people are really tuned in and enjoying themselves, join in. Help sustain it.

h. Keep the pace energetic and lively. You are accustomed to working with groups of students and know that the energy level and involvement of a group often mirrors your own energy for the day. If you are alert and involved, the group is more likely to be enthusiastic and interested. Start on time, and aim to finish at a given time. Avoid the kind of laissez-faire leadership that lets a group languish and then forces everyone to catch up madly and be stingy with time later. You can decide when to push and move people on, when to let the group settle down to relax or hassle over a point. People may well look to you to indicate when to break a silence or when to allow for time to think and feel. Or they may need the relief of hearing someone say, "We've been working pretty hard; let's stop for coffee." This kind of pacing depends particularly on the leader of the session.

3. *Evaluating the session*

During the evaluation phase of the session members of the group as a whole consider how they are doing in terms of (a) progress toward the general goal of learning about achievement motivation and Psychological Education, (b) effectiveness of the session just concluded, and (c) working relationships and cooperation within the group. The evaluation is not simply an evaluation of the leader as such, nor is it a final comment on a finished product. Instead, it is more like the process a person goes through in steering a boat. He knows the end point. He's headed in the general direction. But winds, tide, and current all necessitate constant adjustments and attention to steering.

Any group engaged in a long-term project experiences a range of success. There will be periods where people are less involved than at other times, and sessions where conflict is unavoidable. On some days the feeling will be one of enjoyment and accomplishment. Accept the highs and the lows in a way that allows you to learn from both of them. Careful attention to the evaluation process will help you do that. As leader, you will be responsible for engaging the group in the evaluation activity and organizing the comments into a useful form that can be passed on to the next leader. There is a short written form at the end of each session to facilitate the collection of evaluations and suggestions. Save enough time at the end of the session for members to fill out the evaluation form and for you to summarize the comments for discussion while the members have a coffee break. The group discussion stimulated by your summary will be very lively and very often may go beyond the half-hour "officially" alloted for it. Have the leader of the next session act as scribe so that he can write down additional suggestions of the group.

The evaluation methods themselves are subject to group evaluation. If those we propose seem ill-suited to your group's needs, by all means make up your own. Several different models are suggested by Matthew Miles in the book *Learning to Work in Groups.** Others can be found in the *Handbook for Staff Development,*** or you may create something free-wheeling on your own. But *don't* omit the evaluation procedure itself. It is your last responsibility as leader to help the group reach its objectives.

*Miles, Matthew, p. 112, 113, 66. *"Learning to Work in Groups,* N.Y.: Teachers College Press, 1959.

***Handbook for Staff Development and Human Relations Training,* NTL Institute for Applied Behavioral Science, NEA, Washington, D.C.

Your workshop in achievement motivation will be unique. No one of you can be sure what is going to happen. There is a format; yet every group using this format will have its own experience. The combination of personalities, the decisions made along the way, the special goals, the room you work in, a dozen quirks and circumstances will make your course unlike any other course.

The directions for the workshop do not constitute a syllabus. They are more like the outline of a play or the road map of a country open for exploration. This description may appeal to your sense of adventure and at the same time make you a bit nervous. "How," you may ask, "will I know when I've reached the objectives of the course?" Since there is no "expert" you will have to help each other in at least three ways. First, prepare exquisitely well for the session you lead because during that session you are the "expert" for the other workshop members. Second, at the end of every session, during the scheduled evaluation period, give frank, specific feedback about how the session went and what can be improved the next session. This advice is as important for others before they lead as it will be for you in preparing to lead your session.

Third, during the session keep the Psychological Education learning sequence in mind because it will allow you to anticipate what will happen and therefore help you coordinate your contributions more effectively. The design for each session is a miniature version of the full learning sequence described at the end of Chaper 1. Most of the sessions begin with some novel activity designed to capture your *attention* and let you experience some aspect of achievement motivation or Psychological Education. In the ensuing discussion the object is to *conceptualize* the experience clearly and *relate* it to classroom situations or other relevant aspects of your lives. Hopefully each session will suggest ways you can *apply* the ideas and in time, if you choose, *internalize* what you learned. Obviously there are no "right" answers, but there is progress through the learning cycle. Alternately as leader, evaluator, and contributor you can help the group discover many things they will want to internalize.

This learning sequence also forms the skeletal plan for the entire

10-session course. The first two sessions—"Arts of Contributing" and "Who Am I?"—serve an introductory purpose. They provide a structured method of helping you get to know each other and forming an open supportive group. At the same time, they are just different and unsettling enough to create new expectations for workshop participants. Hopefully they will engender an attitude of alertness and attention for the second portion of the workshop (sessions 3-4), the backbone of the course. These two sessions contain a variety of games and exercises which allow you to experience vividly the entire achievement motivation syndrome—thoughts, feelings, and actions. Guidelines are provided for conceptualizing these experiences and, therefore, the achievement motive itself. If past courses are any predictor of what will happen, after sessions 3-5 you will become curious and perhaps even feel a little troubled about the implications of increasing people's n-Ach. Hence, at this point we stop directing so much and suggest a way for you to answer some of your questions by exploring related areas. We have described eight topic areas relevant to n-Ach—each of which could be the basis for a group session. You take on the responsibility of planning the equivalent of about four sessions.

You are free to take part in these as a group, in sub-groups, with small groups of friends, or individually. All together, the information and ideas generated from these explorations should help you gain perspective on n-Ach, better understand its potential usefulness, and make some personal and ethical decisions about it. The final portion of the workshop—sessions 9 and 10—encourages you to apply what you have learned, by helping you define personal goals and projects. The book provides more help in Chapter 4 for people who will give an achievement motivation course to students, but basically, after the 10 sessions, you are on your own. Whether or not to become a Psychological Educator will be up to you.

Appendix D:

The Follow-up Telephone Interview and Scoring System*

Conducting interviews with students in school is a harried process. Besides all the paper work and scheduling problems and hall passes, students typically associate a conversation in this setting with "being called into the principal's office." No matter how cordial and reassuring we tried to be, our interviews were not particularly fruitful. In contrast, when we called students on the phone, they were on their own "turf," more relaxed and familiar with the object in their hand. For us there was none of the complicated administrative detail we encountered in the school interviews.

Research on n-Ach consistently shows that course participants are most likely to apply what they learn in situations where they are "in charge." Most often this is during their "free time"—over the summer and after school. Thus the interview focuses on work and leisure time activities, hobbies, sports, future plans, and the degree to which the n-Ach course has been useful to them. In each area, we try to obtain as specific information as possible: why he engages in the activity and what he plans to do in this area towards implementing his plans. Typically, this interview is obtained after the first summer following the course and each six months for 1½ to two years.

TELEPHONE INTERVIEW

Name of student..
Name of interviewer:...
Date:...
Length of interview:
    Time begun:............................Time ended:...........................
    Total length in minutes:..

Sample introduction:

Hello, My name is.............................. I am calling from the Achievement Motivation Development Project. You remember the course we gave that you were in last year.

---

*This interview schedule and scoring system is primarily the work of Mr. Stephen Rodewald.

170

I am calling you now because we are interested in hearing about what sorts of things you have been doing since we saw you last. If you have a little time I would like to ask you about things such as what you were doing last summer and what your future plans are. All together, the interview should take maybe 10 or 15 minutes. O.K.?

Summer activities:

What would you say was the most important thing you were doing last summer? (If he says, "Work" ask him the following questions. If he mentions a leisure activity, ask him the questions two categories ahead. Then go on and ask him what else was important to him, and keep repeating the cycle until you have a total picture of how he spent his summer.)

Summer work:

(If the subject had a job, he will probably mention it as one of his important activities. If he does not mention it, make sure to ask him if he had a job.)

1. What did you do? For whom? (Specific duties?)
2. How many weeks did you work? How much did you earn each week?
3. How did you find out about the job? How did you get it?
4. Why did you want this job for the summer? (If for the money, what was the money for? If he wanted to earn money to save toward something, how much did he save?)
5. How did the job turn out for you? Anything much happen?

Term-time work:

1. Do you have a job now? What do you do? For whom? (Specific duties?)
2. How much do you earn each week?
3. How did you find out about it? How did you get it?
4. Why did you want this job? (If for the money, what is the money for? If he wants to save towards something, how much is he saving?)
5. How is the job turning out for you? Anything happening?

Summer leisure activities

(Try to have the subject talk about at least two, and perhaps three summer leisure activities. If he quickly runs out of things to talk about, make sure to probe in the following areas: Did you do anything in the way of sports? Hobbies? Travel?)

Summer activity:

1. What were you doing? (Have him be specific.)
2. When and how did you get started? Why did you get started?
3. How often did you do this last summer?
4. With whom did you usually do this? Whose idea was it usually?
5. Why were you doing this? (If he says, "Because I enjoyed it," ask him what it was in particular that he enjoyed about it.)
6. How did this activity turn out for you last summer? (Did anything in particular happen with it?)
7. What further plans do you have for this activity?

(Repeat same questions for second and third summer leisure activity)

Present activity:

1. What are you doing right now? (Have him be specific.)
2. When and how did you get started? Why did you get started?
3. How often are you doing this?
4. With whom do you usually do this? Whose idea is it usually?
5. Why are you doing this?
6. How is this activity turning out so far? Has anything in particular happened with it?
7. What further plans do you have for this activity?

Future plans:

1. Do you have any plans for what you will be doing after graduation? (Have you thought about it?)
2. Do you have any specific plans for next year?
3. Why have you decided upon these particular plans? (Get an answer for both the post-grad plans and for next year's plans.)
4. Have you done anything already in preparation for these plans? (Get a complete picture. If he mentions one thing, ask if there is anything else. In particular, if he mentions something he plans to do, ask if there is anything he has done already.)

Use of n-Ach ideas:

1. What do you remember about the n-Ach course you had at school? What did you think of it? (If he did not have n-Ach course, go on to final question.)
2. Was anything from the course useful to you in any way? In what way? (Can you give me a specific example? Last-ditch probe: Do you remember anything about goals?)

172

3. Can you give me another example of when it was useful to you?

4. Do you think anything from the course will be useful to you in the future? In what way? (Can you give me a specific example?)

5. Can you suggest any ways in which we might improve the course?

Final question:

Now it's your turn. Do you have any questions you want to ask?

Time interview ended:.........................(Note at head of interview form.)

General Scheme for the Scoring System

Scoring the answers to the interview questions is based on the following general scheme:

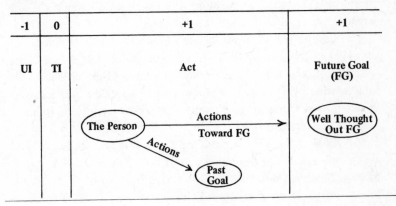

The UI (Unrelated Imagery) category is scored either if the student has *no* plans or activities, or if his plans or activities have little possibility or potential for achievement. In most cases, the main potential of these activities is for affiliation.

The TI (Task Imagery) category is composed of plans or activities that do have achievement potential, but which the student pursues with little evidence of any motivation. Instead, he seems to be responding to cues from outside himself, especially affiliative cues.

The ACT category is scored for actions already completed toward either a past goal or a future goal.

Finally, the FG (Future Goals) category concerns student's intent and need to achieve a serious future goal. We would score this for a well thought out account of *what* he planned to do and *why*.

173

Each section of the interview can receive either a score for UI (-1), for TI, or for some combination of Act (+1) and FG (+1). Only Act and FG can be scored together on the same item. Thus there are four possible scores in each section:

-1 UI
0 TI
+1 Act *or* FG
+2 Act *and* FG

Also, by summing the scores for summer job and summer leisure, we get a total summer activity score. The range for this score is -2 to +4.

The definitions below describe how these four categories are scored for students' responses to questions about summer job, summer leisure activities, future plans, and use of n-Ach ideas.

a. *Score -1 for UI* if the student did not have a summer job. For teenagers, jobs are a readily available source of summertime achievement, and lack of a job probably indicates lack of concern for achievement. (Although if the student was concerned about achieving in a non-work summer activity, he will receive credit for it under Summer Leisure Activities.)

b. *Score O for TI* if the student had a summer job, but only to occupy his time, or to earn money for dates, clothes, etc. Working has much achievement potential, but the student did not do it out of any internal need to achieve. Instead, his working seems a response to external cues coming from his friends. He was working either because all his friends were working and he had nothing better to do, or because he needed the money to spend on keeping up his social life and status.

c. *Score +1 for ACT* if the student was working during the summer in order to help himself reach a serious goal that he had set for himself. Score ACT if he was working to earn some money toward a serious future goal:

For example, score ACT if student is

1. Earning money for college, for marriage, or "for a few years from now."

2. Earning money for buying a car, for a football season ticket, for a planned trip to New York City, or similar goals.

Do *not* score Act, if student is

1. Earning money for pastime or affiliative activities, such as dates or riding around with friends.

174

2. Earning money for clothes or car expenses. These are just maintenance of present condition, and involve no setting of goals.

3. "Earning money for college, but didn't save much." He does have a serious goal, but he is only half-hearted in pursuing it. No strong need for that goal is indicated.

All three of these examples are scored TI because, although the students were working, they were not earning money out of a need to reach a serious goal.

ACT also should be scored if the student was making serious effort to learn something worthwhile while on the job:

For example, score ACT for such statements as:

1. "I worked in an electrical supply house for the experience. I liked the work, so I gave it everything I had."

2. "I learned how to run the shipping department."

Do *not* score ACT for such statements as:

1. "It was good. I met a lot of people, and my boss taught me a little accounting." Here the student did not take the initiative. His learning was something that just happened to him while on the job. The cue was external, from the boss, and indicates no *need* to learn on the student's part. Score TI.

2. "I worked at Walden Pond as a maintenance man. It was interesting, because the Pond is a landmark, and people came from all parts to see it." Although the job was interesting, the student appears to have made no special effort at it. Score TI.

d. *Score +1 for FG* if the student has serious future goals for the type of work he was engaged in. The student may have taken the job because he wanted experience toward his already chosen future career:

For example, score FG for such statements as, "I worked with an electrical contractor for the summer because I want to become an electrician." This would also receive +1 for ACT, because he took the initiative in learning something for the summer.

Or the student could be scored FG if, as a result of his summer work experience, he was able to decide upon a career:

For example score FG for such statements as, "I was taught some bookkeeping and accounting, and now I want to become a CPA." This response would not be scored for ACT, however, since the student apparently did not take the initiative in learning accounting, etc. Thus, total score is +1.

Also, it is possible that even though the student does not necessarily intend his summer job as training toward his future career, his future plans for that summer job may be specific enough to merit scoring it for FG.

For example, score FG for statements such as, "I became assistant manager for plumbing and heating at Sears. I learned everything about the business, but I still have more to learn about heating systems."

Note: If the student is involved in some full-time daily activity that precludes the possibility of a summer job *(e.g.* full-time summer school), then enter a score for that activity under the summer work column of the scoresheet.

Summer Leisure Activities

a.   *Score -1 for UI* if the student was involved only in such non-purposeful activities as parties, dating, hanging around, going to the beach, or going on vacation with the family. In these activities, the student seems to be concerned mainly with affiliation, and not with achievement.

b.   *Score O for TI* if the student was involved in purposeful activities such as sports, travel, reading, driver education, or hobbies, but only for the fun of it, or only to occupy his time. These activities have potential for achievement, but the student feels little internal sense of purpose or need to achieve in them. Instead, it is mostly for their affiliative or pastime value that he participates.

For example, score TI for such statements as:

1.   "Swimming and water skiing a lot, because I enjoy it."

2.   "Basketball with friends. Just fooling around."

3.   "I went to New York with friends for a weekend, to have a good time." Traveling on one's own has achievement potential in the sense that the student might be taking the initiative to gain new experiences. However, in this case, the purpose of the travel was mainly for affiliation, so score TI.

4.   "I add bottles to my bottle collection every once in a while. No special reason, I just like to do it."

5.   "All my friends had full-time jobs, so I just worked around the house, just because I felt like it. Nothing much, just housework." Housework served the purpose of passing the time, and was not part of a serious goal.

Do *not* score TI for such statements as

1. "I went on vacation to Maine with my family-didn't do much there." This is travel, but unlike the student in example 3 above, this student did not even take any initiative in making the trip. He merely agreed to go along with his family. Since not much achievement potential is involved in making the trip, and since he didn't do anything with achievement potential once he got to Maine, score UI.

2. "I went swimming a lot, just for the fun of it. Mostly I was just lying on the beach." A distinction should be made between actual exercise (as in example 1 under "Score TI") and just lying on the beach. Score UI.

c. *Score +1 for ACT* if the student exerted himself toward some serious goal or hobby during the summer. The student had an inner sense of purpose about this activity; he wanted to get something done.

For this category, it is important to look at the frequency of the activity. If the student was involved with it every day, there is a good chance he wanted to accomplish something. But if it was only once or twice for the whole summer, he was probably not serious about it. Of course, frequency is not a foolproof predictor of ACT but it can be an important indicator.

For example, score ACT for such statements as

1. "I took drum lessons, and practiced every day, because I wanted to improve."

2. "I worked on a CB radio set all summer."

3. "I played baseball for an AYA team. I practiced every day. It's a challenge to play well."

4. "I practiced cheerleading three times a week. I look forward to adding spirit to football games."

5. "I went different places. Instead of hanging around Arlington, I would take trips up to Rockport, walk around the galleries and boutiques. First few times I went by myself, then I started getting other people to go with me. I like being a distance away, and the atmosphere in Rockport is completely different. I felt like I've been someplace." Her interest was not in the affiliation that can come with travel, but in the experience of it. Compare to example 3 under "Score TI".

6. "Getting my license was most important. It makes you

feel good, gets you out more. I'll be going out farther places, day trips, to New Hampshire to see the polar caves, and later to go skiing." Although getting a license would usually be scored TI (See example 2 under "Do not score UI") this student has turned it into a major goal, with specific future travel plans associated with it. Score ACT and FG.

Do *not* score ACT for such statements as

1. "I water-skiied every day, just because I like to do it." Score TI.

2. "I took driver ed, and got my license." This is a goal, but probably n-Aff rather than n-Ach is behind it. Learning to drive is generally a social need more than an achievement need. Score TI.

    d. *Score +1 for FG* if the student has serious future goals for the summer activity he was engaged in. These goals need not involve occupational plans as in the summer job scoring, because hobbies do not lead on to occupations the same way summer jobs do. But the student must have some plans for *expanding* his hobby in the future.

For example, score FG for such statements as

1. "I hope to play drums in a band and make some money."

2. "When I get a car, I'll put a CB radio into it. Maybe I'll go into ham radios."

3. "I hope to build my own car for the drag races."

4. "I went to a lot of drag races. I'm thinking seriously of participating next year." Score FG for a definite future goal. However, do not score ACT, since attending drag races last summer seems to have been more a pastime activity than a serious goal.

5. "Next year I want to teach my family and some of my friends water-skiing."

Do *not* score FG for such statements as, "I'll continue working on cars." This involves no setting of new goals for the future; he merely will maintain his present pace.

NOTE: Since most students talked about two or three summer leisure activities, it is possible for a student to receive a score for ACT in one activity and a score for FG in another. In such a case, he should receive a total summer leisure score of +2.

However, if a student has two summer activities that would both be scored for both ACT and FG, he would still receive only one score for

ACT and one score for FG on the score sheet. We are giving a score not for each separate summer activity, but rather for Summer Leisure as a whole. Therefore ACT and FG can each be scored only once under Summer Leisure, and the highest possible score is only +2.

Future Plans

a. *Score -1 for UI* if the student has no idea at all what he will do. This shows negligible need to achieve. For example, score UI for such statements as, "No plans at all."

b. *Score O for TI* if the student has possible higher aspirations for the future, but no firm commitment to them. Either he has a vague, general idea what he will do, or else he is confused about what he will do. Either way, despite mentioning of alternatives that have the potential for achievement, he shows no deep need to achieve them.

Probably, in his vague or confused state, he is repeating alternatives that he has heard other people mention. It seems that external cues may be influencing him, and not an internal need to achieve.

For example score TI for such statements as

1. "College"
2. "The Navy, but I don't know what I'll be doing"
3. "I'll go into secretarial work, but I'm not really sure yet."
4. "Hairdressing school or business college. I'm not sure."

Do *not* score TI tor such statements as

1. "business college"
2. "learning drafting in the Navy"
3. "I'll go to business school to work with computers."

Responses 1, 2, and 3 are not vague. They cite specific goals, and should be scored FG.

4. "I'll get a job." If the student can say nothing further, it is reasonable to say he has no idea what he will do. Score UI.

Also score ACT if the student knows what he wants to do, but it does not involve any higher aspirations. Rather, it is just maintenance of his present level of skill.

For example score TI for such statements as:

1. "I think I'll be a telephone operator. I know how to do it because I was one last summer."
2. "I'll probably work in an office. I'm taking typing in school. Anyway, what else could I do?"

179

c. *Score +1 for FG* if the student has a specific goal or specific set of alternatives in mind, and seriously intends to pursue it. In addition to a stated need for a certain goal, the student's response is often characterized by affective states about the attainment of his goal.

For example, score FG for such statements as:

1. "When I'm 19, I'd like to be an air stewardess because it's a great opportunity to travel and meet other people." She states a specific goal, and also talks about what it will be like for her.

2. "I'll go to business college for 2 years and get a secretarial job. I've wanted to since I was 7 years old."

Do *not* score FG for such statements as, "I'll go to college and get a good education toward a good job." This is an honorable intention, but vague and oft-repeated. Thus, score TI.

d. *Score +1 for ACT* if the student has already taken serious specific action toward his future plans. Such action can take two forms. It can be action toward a specific goal already decided upon:

For example, score ACT for such statements as:

1. "I talked with some electricians to get some information about becoming an electrician." This would also be scored +1 for FG, giving a total score of +2.

2. "I'm taking two years' math this year, because I want to go to a good teacher's college—Westfield, for example." Score ACT for the extra effort of taking two years of math in order to achieve her goal. Also score FG.

3. "I've been reading in pamphlets about the qualifications and education necessary to become an air stewardess." Score ACT and FG.

Do *not* score ACT for such statements as:

1. "I'll take up data processing or become an accountant. I'm taking Bookkeeping II, Economics and Law, Problems of Democracy, and English." Score FG, but don't score ACT. The student is only taking the normal course load expected of him. He is not initiating any activity toward reaching his goal (unlike the student in example 2, just above). Furthermore, it is likely that his choice of a career was a result of the courses he happened to be taking, rather than vice versa. It is common for high school students to say they will pursue a career in a certain field just because they are presently doing well in pertinent subjects.

2. "Pretty soon I'll have to start applying." ACT is scored for completed action, not for vague promises for the future.

Also score ACT if it is action taken toward establishing a new specific goal:

For example, score ACT for statements such as, "I decided to redocorate my room, and now I want to become an interior decorator." Score FG for the goal of becoming an interior decorator, and ACT for redecorating her room. In this example, two goals are involved. When she acted upon the goal of redecorating her room, she was not yet thinking of her future goal. Still she should be given credit for ACT for taking the initiative to act on her past goal.

This example is similar to what sometimes happens in summer work or summer leisure. For instance, one student worked for an insurance company one summer and learned a lot about claims. On the basis of her summer's experience, she decided to go into the insurance business for a career. This would be scored ACT for her effort to learn something during the summer, and FG for her resulting career goal.

Do *not* score ACT for such statements as, "I spoke with my guidance counselor about what I would do in the future." Score TI, since most high schools have structured meetings between guidance counselors and students. Score ACT only if it is clear that the student took the initiative in seeing his counselor.

Applications of n-Ach Ideas

a. *Score -1 for UI* if the student has made no application of n-Ach ideas, and does not intend to make any in the future. A further indication of a UI score is a lack of memory of the course.

For example, score UI for statements such as:

1. "It was stupid and boring. We just talked all the time."

2. "I like the games and filling out the forms, but I haven't thought much about it."

3. "I remember about moderate risk, but I haven't really applied it." Memory alone is not enough to merit a higher score. An attempt to apply what he remembers is what demonstrates a need to achieve.

b. *Score O for TI* in the following four cases:

The student has made only vague application of n-Ach ideas. He feels the course has been useful, but does not list any specific applications.

For example, score TI for statements such as:

1. "The course helped. Now I have a good idea myself about what I want to do." But he didn't mention any specific things he wants to do.

2. "If I wanted to buy something, it helped with saving money." But he couldn't mention anything specific he ever saved for.

The student has set a specific goal for himself, but has followed up on it only half-heartedly.

Score TI for statements such as:

1. "I said I'd get $1,000. I don't know how much I have. I just keep dribbling it in."

2. "I wanted to save some money, but I spent it on dates and new clothes."

The student made one minor specific application right after the course, but none since.

Score TI for statements such as, "It helped me find a job at the fish store. No goals since."

The student has made no application yet, but thinks the course will be useful in the future. However, no *specific* plans as yet.

Score TI for such statements as:

1. "It might be useful to set goals in college."

2. "I'll use it in making any big decisions, like in business."

3. "It might be helpful if. . ." This opener usually leads into hypothetical possibility rather than a serious specific goal that the student has set for himself.

In all these four cases, it seems that the student is applying the course only so far as he thinks is expected of him. For instance, a student who made a single specific application was probably just carrying out his change project, and nothing further. And a student who either generally tries harder, or will in the future use the course and try harder, seems to be promising to do more of what is expected of him. However, the student is not setting and pursuing goals of his own. No internal need to achieve is apparent.

c. *Score +1 for ACT* if the student has already made major specific applications of n-Ach ideas. That is, he has set goals for himself, and has been doing what is necessary to try to reach them.

Score ACT for statements such as:

1. "Once I thought about giving up basketball. Now I play with varsity players, and I learn from them."

2. "I used to get in lots of trouble. But I sat down, thought things out, and now I don't get in as much."

3. "I set goals for my test grades."

4. "I worked my way back into the college program."

d. *Score +1 for FG* if the student has been applying n-Ach ideas toward a serious, specific future goal.

Score FG for statements such as:

1. "I worked my way back into the college program, and I want to try to go to the university.

2. "It made me get interested in broadcasting, a field I like, and made me plan to go to college to specialize in it. I've been covering school football games for the Globe."

3. "It made me study harder. I changed into a harder private school, and I'm paying for it myself." Clearly implicit is the student's serious goal of a better education.

These three examples would also be scored for ACT because application of n-Ach ideas has already been made. Thus total score is +2.

Also score FG if student has plans for applying n-Ach ideas *in the future* toward a serious, specific goal.

Score FG for such statements as:

1. "I want to own three or four barrooms. I've been setting my plans down on paper.

2. "I'll work up to becoming a stewardess as best I can. I want to take psychology and nursing for it."

These two examples would not be scored ACT since no application of n-Ach ideas has yet been made. Total score is +1.

Do *not* score FG if future goals are either vague or not present.

For example, do not score FG for such statements as:

1. "I raised my grades quite a bit." No future educational plans are suggested. Score ACT only.

2. "I set goals for my test grades. In the future, it will help me either in getting a certain job, or some money."

3. "I used to be timid. Now I'm willing to take a chance, to take the initiative. I applied for a job and got it. In the future, it will help me in applying for jobs."

In 2 and 3, the students only mention possibilities for future use, rather than future goals that they have actually set for themselves. Thus, do not score for FG. They must mention specific plans to get a score of FG. But do score for ACT since they applied n-Ach ideas in the recent past.

Scoring of Sample Interviews

To illustrate the scoring, we include four sample interviews on the following pages. The first two are scored in the margins, and an explanation of the scoring follows each. For practice, the reader can score the last two interviews himself, and then check with the explanations of the scoring which follow. Finally, all four interviews are coded on the score sheet at the end of this section.

William Smith

Summer Activity 1 – Most Important

I play drums—I take lessons, at Arlington Academy of Music. I went to music school most of the summer. Every Tuesday, Wednesday and Thursday. The music instructor there helped me.

(How did you get started?) I never took lessons until a year ago last June. My cousin's been playing. I kind of got interested. I was just banging, not getting anyplace. Figured I should start taking lessons. Now I have a new set of drums.

(How often?) I like to practice every day. During the summer I practiced a lot—usually an hour per day. During the summer I practiced an awful lot.

Score +1 for ACT

(With whom?) I usually practice by myself.

(Why?) I figure later on, when I'm old enough to play in a night club, it'll be useful. I may be able to use it as a source of income, if I get in a regular group. Plus I enjoy it, it's fun to do.

Score +1 for FG

(How's it going?) I'm improving. I'm pretty good. Probably will never be real good. I hope to be good. Over the summer I made a big improvement. My instructor said I made more improvement than over the entire year before.

(Further plans?) See 4.

Total Score = + 2

Work

(What did you do?) I worked at the Waldorf part time. Toward the end of July I quit. Wasn't steady—just a dishwashing job. He was supposed to promote me to cook. I cleaned up a big mess one day—and when a kid came to relieve me, I quit. He didn't promote me.

(Salary?) $36 a week. Made $180.

(How did you get it?) I applied last April. A couple of places early, A&P and Bradlee's. But they didn't call me, so the Waldorf was all I could get. I hope to get a better job next summer,

(Why?) To make money. Lately, I want to start saving for a car. I don't think I'll buy it before next summer.

Score +1 for ACT

Total Score = +1

(Part-time job now?) Usually I have enough trouble with just school. I'd like a job, if I could find the time.

Summer Activity 2

I finished the driving half of Driver Ed., and have my license. It beats walking, to drive a car.

(Why?) You need Driver Ed. to get insurance cheaper. I took the written half in school. But you have to go to a private school to do the driving. I figured I'd go to driving school, because you have a much better chance of passing the test.

(How did it go?) I haven't gone on any trips. Maybe out to Lincoln. But no place important, like out to the Cape or anything.

Future Plans

(Plans?) I'd like to go to college. But I'll need a year of prep school. But even though I need a year, I'd like to go to college. I'm back in the college course in school. I'd like to go to Newman Prep. I may go to a business college or try to get into the University of Maine.

Score +1 for FG

(Why?) There are a lot of advantages to having a good education. I won't feel so dumb, it'll broaden my outlook on life. I'll be able to earn a better living, to pick out what job I want . . . .

(Preparation?) I've been reading this book, *How to Prepare for College*. It gives a lot of reasons why you want to go to college. But I forget a lot of the things I read.

Score +1 for ACT

I'd like it to be a state college. My father's not really rich. And the University of Maine would be a lot cheaper than something like Bentley. Also I'm thinking about business college.

Actually I'm not sure what I'm doing. The more I think about it, the more confused I get.

Total Score = +2

Use of n-Ach Ideas

(What did you think of it?) It had interesting parts. Has a good purpose. Was enjoyable, more interesting than Elective Business Principles.

(Useful?) Yeah. I seem to be more ambitious. I think I started to work harder in school. In fact, I know I have.

You do think about it. Like the feedback, not making the same mistake twice. And setting a goal, you want to be a high achiever. I think the course *was* useful.

(Specific examples?) My freshman year, I didn't do a thing. That's why I had to drop the college course. I wanted to get back in it—that was one of my goals. I needed to get a B to get back in college English. I set that as a goal.

Score +1
for ACT

(Result?) I had a B average last year. Means I can take a language this year.

(What language?) Spanish.

(Why?) Kind of pot luck. I have a friend who doesn't like French.

(Useful in future?) Yes. (See future plans above.)

Score +1
for FG
Total
Score = +2

Explanation of Scoring

Summer Leisure:

To begin with, score whichever leisure activity yields the highest score. Thus, score practicing the drums rather than learning to drive.

Score ACT because he practiced hard and made a lot of improvement. He was seriously committed to getting something done at his hobby.

Score FG for his goal of playing in a group and earning some money.

Summer Job:

Score ACT because he wanted to start earning money toward a specific goal, a car.

Do not score FG since he certainly does not consider dishwashing at the Waldorf as part of his future career plans.

Future Plans:

Score FG for the numerous specific alternatives he is considering for his college plans. Despite his confusion over which college to choose, there is no doubt that he has done a great deal of specific thinking about going to college, and that he seriously intends to reach that goal.

Score ACT because he has already been working toward his goal. He has switched into the college course at high school (see below under

"Use of n-Ach Ideas"). Also, he has been reading from *How to Prepare for College* and however much he may have forgotten, he seems to be thinking a lot about what he has read.

Use of n-Ach Ideas:

Score ACT for reaching the goal of getting back into the college course.

Score FG because getting back into the college course was part of his future goal of going to college.

Mary Williams

Summer Work—Most important

I worked every day. There wasn't much time to do anything. At an insurance company I typed, did bookkeeping and filing.

Score +1 for ACT

(How long?) Entire summer (10 weeks) $64 a week.

(How did you get it?) My sister works for an insurance company and her boss knows my boss. Her boss told me to go down and apply.

(Why?) I'm a senior, and I had to get a job. I like that kind of work. I want to get in it and stay in it after school.

Score +1 for FG

(How was the job?) I like it.

(What did you like?) I liked the kind of work. That's what I do in school. And I can stay in that kind of work—insurance work—when I graduate.

(Part-time job now?) Same job. 12½ hours a week at $1.75 an hour . . .

Total score = +2

Summer Activity 1

Usually I went to the beach with my girl-friends. Or I had dates.

(How often?) Every Sunday, the whole day. It was my idea to go, because Sunday was about the only chance I had.

Score -1 For UI

(Why?) To relax, be in the sun, the water.

Summer Activity 2

(Hobbies?) No.

(Sports?) No.

Future Plans

(Plans?) I'm going to stay at the insurance office, and learn all the different fields of insurance—auto, etc. Then, if I want, I can move to a bigger office, and higher salary.

Score +1 for FG

(Why?) I like bookkeeping, filing, typing. And I like the people I work with.

(Preparation?) I'm in a new course at high school—production typing. You have to be recommended for it.

(How recommended?) You have to have a good average in typing, too. The teacher recommended me for it, told me, so I'm in it now.

Use of n-Ach Ideas

(What did you think of it?) Yeah, I have the papers from the course. I liked it, I learned something from it. It helped me get what I wanted.

(Useful?) One of my goals was to get a job, and I got it. One was to control my temper—that didn't turn out too good. I had charts on three or four different things. Saving money, that was one.

(Result?) Good. I opened an account.

(How much saved?) I had money in there, but I just bought my mother a ring for a Christmas present. Now I'm starting all over again.

(Useful in future?) Uh-huh.

(How?) What you learned from it, all the terms—initiative, etc. It just helps you to think better. And if you want to have a goal, it tells you better how to reach it. Get outside help.

(Examples?) Probably if I want to save more money for a certain purpose. I don't know, could be anything you want.

Explanation of Scoring

Summer Job:

Score ACT because she hints below, under Future Plans, that she is trying to learn all she can about insurance.

Score FG because she wants to make insurance her career, and she wants to advance in that career. (Again, refer to Future Plans.) Thus her summer job is part of a serious future goal.

Summer Leisure:

Score UI because her activities provide relaxation and affiliation, but have no potential for achievement.

Future Plans:

Score FG because she has a goal to learn and rise in the insurance business.

Score ACT because she got a summer job to learn more about insurance.

Use of n-Ach:

Score ACT for her numerous goal-setting projects, but do not score FG since, although she has a clear idea of how she *would* use n-Ach concepts, as yet she has no specific goals in mind.

> Also score +1 for ACT because she got a summer job in her field
>
> Total Score +2
>
> Score +1 for Act
>
> Total score = +1

Test your knowledge of the scoring system on the following two interviews.

Ben James

I didn't do anything really important last summer. I just took the summer as it was. I just didn't care about much.

Work

(What did you do?) I worked as a stockboy at Zayre's.

(Salary?) $37 a week for six weeks; total salary $222.

(How did you get it?) I sort of had an in. I knew someone who knew the guy. Then I just applied. I knew a kid who worked there.

(Why?) Most of my friends went away, and I had nothing to do, really.

(How was the job?) It was all right. Some nights you do stuff, other nights you just sit around and talk.

(Part-time job now?) Same place, two nights a week, $20 a week.

Summer Activity 1

I went to the Cape.

(How long were you there?) For three weeks.

(With whom?) With my family. It was our vacation, so I went along. I guess I wanted to go.

(What did you do there?) Mostly the beach, boats. For a few weekends I went to a friend's cottage and went skiing.

(How often did you go skiing?) Once or twice.

(How did you get started?) Five years ago in New Jersey. I have relatives there on the shore, and we used to go skiing.

(Why?) It's for kicks, really.

(How did it go?) I stayed up as long as I wanted. I'm not really an expert. If I stay up, I'm happy. I've only gone about seven times.

(Further plans for it?) I hope to continue. I don't have a boat.

Summer Activity 2

(Any hobbies?) I have an aquarium. I started it eight months ago. I'm getting tired of it now. I don't really care about it.

(How did you get started?) A couple of friends had them, I liked them, but I didn't really realize how much time was involved with them, and I didn't feel like spending it.

(How often last summer?) I didn't do much this summer.

Summer Activity 3

(Sports?) Maybe baseball, maybe once or twice during the summer.

(Swimming?) Mostly at the Cape, every day for three weeks. After about two weeks, you get tired of it, like anything else.

Future Plans

(Plans?) I think I'll apply for college. I don't know exactly where, or if I'll go to prep school first. It depends on the tests in December.

(Why these plans?) I don't know what I really want to do, so I figure I could go to school, and then really decide.

(Preparation?) No, nothing really.

Use of n-Ach ideas

(What did you think of the course?) I think it was rather dull.

(Why?) You do the same thing each day. Watch the movies, and write down what it meant. I think the course should have been longer, because I really don't remember much at all.

(Useful?) Maybe since the course I use it but don't realize it, but I can't think of anything.

(Do you remember anything about goals?) That was the whole course. To set goals, and ways of achieving them.

(Ideas useful?) I might be using them without thinking about them.

(Examples?) No.

(Useful in future?) No. I've forgotten most of it.

Alan Morgan

Summer Activity 1

I was away all summer in New Hampshire. I didn't do anything special all summer. Except I did learn how to water ski.

(How did you get started?) I've been skiing five years now. But this summer I got really good. I ski, and everything. That's about it. We bought a place in New Hampshire. Friends had a boat, and offered to take me. I broke my leg a couple of years ago, but this summer I tried one ski, and I can do it pretty good now.

(How often?) Once a day, for about 20 minutes.

(With whom?) With friends. I ask them sometimes, sometimes they come over.

(Why?) Everyone up there skis. I took it up, and I like it. It's something to do, and it's a lot of fun to ski.

(How did it go?) I'd start off on two skis. Then I'd drop a ski. Late June, I was able to drop a ski. Then I learned to get up on one ski.

(Why one ski?) Everyone there was doing one ski. And I'm the oldest kid on the lake. I wanted to do it too, It's like a challenge. I felt stupid on two skis. So I decided to give it a try.

(Future plans?) I won't get much chance to do it anymore.

Summer Activity 2

I'm still playing drums. I fooled around with a friend, a bass guitarist. We're playing together. He and four kids have a group. Sometimes we would just get together and play.

(How started?) When I was young, I was always interested in music. With all this new music coming out, I decided to try. I took lessons in junior high school. A year and a half ago I began taking lessons at a music school. I went out and bought my drums. Then I've been playing. We fool around. We made one tape. It's just I like music and I want to be part of it. Now I'm taking up guitar and organ. I want to play about 20 instruments.

(How often?) One or two times a day, one to two hours a day. On weekends we have kids over and make tapes a lot. About four hours a weekend.

(How did it go?) O.K. I'm getting better. I'm good enough now to get into a group. I'm trying now to form my own group, but I don't know if I'm having any luck. I have the kids, but I don't think we have money for equipment. They're not good, they don't practice much, except on weekends. If we could get together more often, and buy better equipment, I think we would be pretty good.

(Further plans?) If we get good enough, we'll play at dances. I don't want to turn pro. If we play at dances, that's enough.

Work

No, I tried, but I couldn't get a job. I guess I didn't try very hard.

(Part-time job now?) I'm stockboy at Hudson's 5&10 store, $16 a week.

Future Plans

(Plans?) I plan to go to broadcasting school. I've got some books on it. I sent away to a school in Boston, and got some books on it. I want to go out of state. I want to go to Florida if I can. So I figure I'll be a disc jockey if I can get a job.

(Why?) I figure I'd like the job. Since I'm interested in music, being a disc jockey would get me right into it. I want to try it. This is the one I want.

(Preparation?) Nothing much. I mailed to the schools and got books. That's it so far, but after I get out of school, I'll have enough books, and will be able to decide which school I'll go to. I've got the money and everything.

Use of n-Ach Ideas

(What did you think of the course?) It was all right. I liked it. It was interesting. I remember it, but not that good.

(Useful?) Every subject, if you put your mind to it, will be useful to you. It helped me a lot.

(Examples?) Now I think I have a good idea of myself and what I want to do. I just know myself, and know other people better. It helped get me to think for myself, and decide, and helped me make up my mind.

(*What* has helped?) I can't remember. In general, it just helped. I don't know how to put it. It was meant to help me, so it helped me.

(In what ways?) I can't think of any.

(Useful in future?) Yes, it should be. I've got it, I've taken it now. Part will still be up in my mind. I'll run into situations where it will help me out.

(Criticisms of the course?) No. I think it was good. I don't think you should make any changes. You should keep giving it. You might add on to it. But I don't know what to add.

Explanation of Scoring—Ben James
Summer Leisure:

Score TI. Although involved in a number of activities with potential for achievement, he did not pursue them with a desire to achieve something.

Summer Job:

Score TI. Although he got himself a job, it was for affiliative reasons only, not for helping him reach any goal.

Future Plans:

Score TI, since his future plans are still vague.

Use of n-Ach:

Score UI, since he has not applied anything at all from the course, and does not really think it was useful to him.

Explanation of Scoring—Alan Morgan

Summer Leisure:

Score ACT for his improvement on the drums through dedicated practice.

Score FG for his future goal of forming a group and playing at dances.

Summer Job:

Score UI for not finding a job.

Future Plans:

Score FG for his specific goal of attending broadcasting school and becoming a disc jockey.

Score ACT for the completed action of obtaining college catalogs, and for the implication that he has been saving money for school.

Use of n-Ach:

Score TI. He says the course was useful, but he cannot cite any specific examples of having used it already, or of planning to use it in the future. He speaks not of his own goals, but rather of what is expected of him: "It was meant to help me, so it helped me."

Appendix E:

A Mastery Oriented n-Ach Course

The mastery-oriented n-Ach course for ninth graders is structured like the Origami Game. However, instead of rounds in which paper products are made, the n-Ach course has four contracts covering the nature of n-Ach, how it is conceptualized, how it relates to the person, and ways to practice it. The contracts, as you may note, correspond to the middle four steps in the six-step learning sequence emphasized throughout this book. In each contract there are ways to earn or lose mastery points. Each student has to earn at least 25 points per contract and 100 points overall to pass the course.

The first part of each contract contains a short introduction explaining the general ideas of the unit and specifying a learning goal. It also describes two minimum requirements a student has to meet to fulfill the contract and show that he has "mastered" the material. One requirement is to pass the contract test, worth 10 points (each contract gives a sample test item). The other requirement is to earn 15 points by doing one of the many bonus activities.

The second part of the contract describes two sets of bonus activities. Each activity is worth 15 points. The division is somewhat arbitrary. Basically, the first set of activities is more stringently tied to the contract criteria. The second group is more open and creative—more "for fun." If the student does only one activity, he is asked to choose from among the first group.

Other point-getting methods are built into the contracts. For example, a team of students can work together to complete a goal or project and earn extra points. On the other hand, students are penalized points if they fail to meet the contract deadline—each day late incurs a two-point penalty. Students can revise their contracts to change the deadline or to add or drop bonus activities, but the revision costs five points, and only one revision is allowed. If a student does not complete the bonus activities he signed for, he not only loses those potential points, but he is also penalized two points for each incomplete.

The third part of the contract is a list of resources required to pass the contract test and do the bonus activities.

A typical contract unit includes about a week's worth of activities and is organized around the resources. Generally, the contract is introduced to the students in small groups. Later in the same day there is a large-group presentation involving all instructors and students. The presentation aims to get across the basic content and principles of the contract, and at the same time to capture interest and involvement. For example, we began the unit on action strategies with the Origami Game. We introduced the 10 thoughts using the "n-Ach Match game." After the initial presentation, there are about two days of workshops which students sign up for in advance, after hearing a brief description or watching a demonstration of what the workshop would entail. Finally, at least one day is devoted to small-group discussions, testing, and make-up for other workshops and contracts. In addition, students can use class time to work on projects and bonuses when they aren't involved in resource workshops.

We divided our class into small groups of nine or ten students with two instructors. Within each group, each faculty member took special responsibility for five students. This team, or core group, represented the one constant group unit in the course. It was here that contracts were distributed and explained, where most of the testing was done, where records of feedback and progress were kept, and where the most meaningful small-group discussions took place. The general structure of the course and the groups provided maximum flexibility for the students. They had one core group, but could participate in workshops of their choice which numbered anywhere from four to eleven students. They were also exposed to large-group presentations at frequent intervals. In the various group settings the students encountered a wide range of teaching-learning styles.

You should not begin a mastery-oriented n-Ach course blind to the likely pitfalls, especially if you use the contracts in this Appendix E. You can make modifications to avoid the problems we encountered.

Most of our difficulties stemmed from an excess of paper shuffling. Contracts take a lot of explaining. To try to fit four, as we did, into a short period meant time and energy that could have gone into small group rapport; discussion was often sacrificed to maintaining our minibureaucracy. Moreover, we couldn't live up to some of our original promises. We had hinted at the beginning that students could set deadlines fairly flexibly throughout the course. But in reality we had only enough staff to run the workshops for one contract at a time. Thus, students found it difficult to work too far ahead of the staff presentations, and impractical to lag very far behind them. The structure didn't turn out to be as responsive to student initiative as we had hoped.

Another problem we never solved was the absence of a true incentive to go beyond the minimum requirements for a unit. The "content" of n-Ach is exhaustible. In our arrangement, doing more than one bonus activity didn't take people deeper into the subject. Instead, it often proved another simple demonstration of what the person had known in order to complete the first bonus. In contrast, it would be more practical to encourage pople to move speedily through the first three stages of the course, and to spend extra time actually using the n-Ach syndrome in a series of goal-setting projects. An alternative solution would be to carefully arrange the contracts and bonuses to represent *levels* of accomplishment, not merely choices of two different kinds of activities.

A further problem was the lack of real penalties for not completing the contracts. In cases where students didn't participate or keep up, we generally tried to work something out individually, but avoided pressure. A student was free to drop out, since the course was voluntary. And if he chose to stay in, even though he didn't go through the contract sequence, chances are he learned a good deal anyway.

Despite the flaws and pitfalls, this organization seems workable, and potentially a realistic way to run the course. Guidelines to keep in mind for a short contract-style course would be:

1. Set the course up with a minimum of paper format.

2. Make sure the students have a clear idea of the course schedule and organization from the beginning.

3. Be completely prepared for the workshops with materials, ideas, fortitude, and plenty of sleep.

4. Workshops should be explained and demonstrated to students in advance, so that they know what they're signing up for, and so the staff knows who will be where, when, and doing what.

5. Ample space is crucial. Also, there should be extra, unassigned staff members to pick up floaters who can't settle on what to work on or where to go.

6. Build in resources for students who are far ahead or way behind the rest of the group.

7. Build in a stronger incentive system for extra levels of mastery.

The following chart summarizes the essential elements of the four contracts. After the chart we have presented the introduction to the course and the four contracts we used.

Mastery Oriented n-Ach Course Contract Scheme			
Purpose	Criteria	Main Group Presentation	Resources
I. n-Ach Action Strategies (experience) To learn to recognize and use four n-Ach action strategies: 1. realistic goal setting 2. proper use of feedback 3. taking personal responsibility 4. researching the environment	1. Identify and distinguish between: a. realistic and unrealistic (very high/very low) risk taking b. concrete immediate feedback vs. general, delayed feedback. c. personal responsibility and leaving things to fate, luck, etc. 2. demonstrate the action strategies in a simple decision-making game.	Origami Game	1. Vocabulary workshops for concepts like strategy, initiative, etc. 2. Ring Toss game 3. Darts-Dice game 4. films 5. case studies and discussion 6. guest speakers
II. n-Ach Thoughts (conceptualize) To learn the ten n-Ach thoughts and the goal-setting patterns they form To relate these to the action strategies	1. recognize and identify examples of achievement imagery and achievement goals, so as to be able to distinguish them from other goals, such as task, affiliation, power. 2. identify the various n-Ach thoughts in short written illustrations. 3. Diagram the goal-setting pattern. 4. define and give illustrations of AIM and other n-Ach thoughts—NEED, HOS, FOF, ACT, WO, PO, HELP, FaF, SuF.	Demonstration of AIM and the planning pattern by instructors n-Ach Match game	1. 10 Thoughts 2. story writing workshop 3. short story and slide topics based on achievement theme. Visit by the author. 4. crossword puzzle 5. fill in blank stories 6. case study and discussion
III. Self Study (relate) To have the student relate n-Ach syndrome to three areas of his own life 1. reality demands 2. self-image and personal goals 3. values of groups and culture to which he belongs.	Engage in dialogue with instructor (and small group) where issues of n-Ach and reality demands, self-image, and group values are specifically discussed personally by each student.	Small-group discussion: in particular, student-instructor dialogue. Guest speaker who has deliberately used n-Ach and who represents a realistic role model for students.	1. Group discussions organized around questions to help students consider possible relevance—the usefulness of n-Ach in their lives. 2. case studies 3. films 4. role plays 5. guest speaker 6. admiration ladder 7. Who Am I? 8. Achieving
IV. Goal Setting (practice) To have the student actually apply what he has learned to a personal achievement goal.	Complete a one-week goal-setting project based on an achievement goal, and deliberately employing achievement planning. Provide feedback and measurement of progress.	Celebration and certification after the course.	1. Aiming 2. group discussion 3. individual help from the instructors 4. help from team members.

Introduction to the n-Ach Course

For the past two days we have played The Origami Game where you "took stock" of the general situation, set your own specific goals, and signed a contract reflecting your decision. You were responsible for achieving the goal you had set in the game. In playing the game, you discovered something about setting and reaching goals, and something about yourself.

In a way, this course is a continuation of the Origami Game, except now the object is to learn all about n-Ach: about the actions and thoughts and feelings that help people reach the goals they want. You will still be making decisions and signing contracts, but instead of rounds of the game, there are four study units:

1. n-Ach action strategies
2. n-Ach thoughts
3. looking at yourself
4. goal-setting

Each unit has a contract describing various ways to make points. One way is to pass the "contract test," worth 10 points. Another way is to do bonus activities, each worth 15 points. To pass the course successfully, you should earn a minimum of 25 points on each contract. That means passing the contract test and doing one bonus activity from the first group of suggested activities. The activities should be fun, and it will be easy for you to set higher goals and earn more than the minimum number of points.

This will be a new way to learn, because you have a chance to set your own goals and reach them on your own. The way you learn the material, when you take the test, how many points you earn in all—these are things you can decide for yourself. Many kinds of resources will be available to you: helpers, films, games, class presentations, case studies, group discussions, and the best teacher of all—you!

Once you have looked over the unit and have decided your goals and the number of points you will try for, fill out the contract, and the "round" begins.

Ground rules

It all sounds so lovely that we hate to mention one little hitch. There are certain risks involved, and ways to lose points.

1. Failure to meet deadlines: When you sign a contract, you set a contract deadline. For every day past the deadline until the contract is completed, you lose two points.

2. Revision of deadlines: You may revise your original deadline up to two days before a contract is due, but the revision costs five points. Only one revision is allowed. (If you think your contract will probably be more than two days overdue, it is to your advantage to revise the deadline.)

3. Incomplete bonuses: (Meaning bonuses above the minimum requirement)—if you haven't completed the bonuses by the final contract deadline, you lose two points for each incomplete promised bonus. For example, suppose you choose to do two extra bonuses, besides earning the minimum 25 points. You could earn a total of 55: (10 + 15 + 15 + 15 = 55). But if the deadline rolls around, and one bonus isn't done, then 15 possible points aren't earned, and you also have a two-point penalty. Thus, your point total would be 55 - 17 or 38. The idea is to use good goal-setting strategies.

As a class we can decide on special ways to earn points. For example, should there be some point reward for making all four deadlines on time? Or a very special reward for making all *original* deadlines with extra bonuses?

Unit I: The n-Ach Action Strategies

Sports and games have a language all their own that we borrow without even realizing it. For instance, if the girl in the next homeroom still won't go out with you after five invitations from you, "you struck out." If the term ends tomorrow, and you haven't passed in the last six math assignments, you "didn't keep your head above water." If you studied like crazy, then flunked the test, "that's the way the ball bounces." Or, as they say, "you win a few, you lose a few."

The real question is—how much does reaching a goal depend on a "lucky break," or "the way the ball bounces?" And how much does it depend on something else? What is that something else? How can *you* make it work for *you?* That is what this unit is about; the action strategies people use when they are determined to reach goals that are important to them.

The *purpose* of this unit is to provide opportunities for you to learn to recognize and use the three n-Ach action strategies:

1. realistic (moderate risk) goal-setting
2. proper use of feedback
3. taking personal responsibility

The *minimum requirement* for the unit is that you pass the contract test, worth 10 points, and that you do one bonus activity from Group I, worth 15 points.

The *contract test* for this unit has two parts:

Part I, worth five points, is an objective test based on short descriptions of situations. You will be asked to identify the action strategies contained in the descriptions, and to distinguish between:

a. realistic and unrealistic (very high or very low) risk-taking
b. concrete immediate feedback and general delayed feedback
c. personal responsibility and leaving things to fate, chance, luck, someone else

Minimum passing grade to receive five points:.............................

Sample test item for Part I:

Situation: Every spring George Jones plays basketball on the street with his friends. After hours of practice he now has his hook shot, free throw, and dribble down pat. After seeing George play, Mr. Williams, the coach, has asked him to come down for the tryouts for the school team. And George wants to be on the team. On the day of tryouts, though, George doesn't show up, because he figures he won't make the team anyway. After all, he's never been on a school team before.

Which of the following categories describe George's behavior in the above description?

...................1. realistic risk-taking
...................2. very low risk-taking
...................3. use of general, delayed feedback
...................4. use of concrete, immediate feedback
...................5. failure to take personal responsibility

Part II, worth five points, is a decision making game like some you will have played in class. Points are awarded for using n-Ach goal-setting strategies, and points are subtracted for not using the strategies.

Minimum passing score to receive five points:.............................

200

The *Bonus activities* listed below provide you with more ways to learn about and practice the action strategies. Choose ones that you will enjoy, and that will help you reach your own goal. If you don't find one here that you like, make up your own activity and enter it on the contract.

Group I bonuses: worth 15 points each

1. Play the third round of the Origami Game with a new product and new cost-profit tables. Demonstrate to an instructor that you are using the three action strategies correctly.

2. Make up a game in which using the n-Ach action strategies helps the player get a higher score. Hand in a written description telling: (a) what equipment is needed, (b) the rules, (c) how scores are made, and (d) how using the n-Ach action strategies helps the person get a high score.

3. Choose one class (or two) and for two days keep track (list) all the kinds of feedback you receive. Then suggest additional kinds of feedback that would be helpful and tell why.

4. Coach someone else (not in the class) in the action strategies. Try to convince him to approach a goal that way by explaining the advantages of the strategies. Report on what happened.

5. Discuss with an instructor a short-term goal that you will work toward and attain in the next few days. You will decide how many days. When the time is up, present some proof to the instructor that you have used the three action strategies correctly.

6. Make up your own activity that demonstrates your ability to use one or more of the action strategies effectively. (free choice)

Group II bonuses: worth 15 points each

1. Create a comic strip character who uses an action strategy or strategies to progress toward or achieve some goal. Turn in a sample strip, where the character uses the strategies, and explain, if necessary, how the strategy or strategies are illustrated.

2. Create drawings or posters or take pictures that demonstrate the action strategies. Then label the illustrations appropriately.

3. Find an example (from newspapers, magazines, TV, school, anywhere at all) of a person using each of the three action strategies correctly. (You can use a different person for each strategy.) Briefly explain your choices. Find examples of persons *failing* to use the action

strategies correctly. Suggest how they might specifically use the action strategies.

4. Think of a time when you used n-Ach action strategies. Explain which ones you used and how they were helpful. How could the strategies you didn't use have helped you out? (Write a brief description.)

5. Identify some group within the school, like a club or a team. Discuss whether or not they are involved in goal-setting and use of the action strategies. Give examples. Point out instances where the group might make use of strategies they seem to be neglecting.

6. Use your imagination. Make up a bonus activity.

Resources

1. Instructor presentation—the achievement game
2. Vocabulary workshop
3. Darts-Dice game
4. Ring Toss game
5. Long's special mystery game
6. Film: *The Need to Achieve*
7. Case study and discussion group
8. Guest speaker
9. Small groups organized by students for help and discussion.

Contract 1
Unit I: The n-Ach Action Strategies

Contract obligations: _____

_____

_____

_____

_____

Contract deadline: _____

Signatures:

_____   _____
           student   instructor

_____
              WITNESS

Revisions: _____

Points earned: _____

Unit II: The n-Ach Thoughts

What would it be like to have a sailboat, and enter a race and win? Or to do well in history? Or to play on a varsity team? Or to feel brave enough to speak out in a group? Everyone has thoughts like these. Everyone wants to have, or do, or be something. For some people these thoughts are just wishes, because they never think any further. For other people, such ideas become goals.

Successful people plan to get what they want in a special, characteristic way. The kinds of planning they do, the n-Ach thoughts, are presented in this unit.

The purpose of this unit is to help you learn the 10 n-Ach thoughts and the goal-setting pattern they form:

AIM   *achievement imagery* - thoughts about successfully reaching a goal that requires excellence

         competition with others (CO)

         competition with self (CS)

         unique accomplishment (UA)

         long term involvement (LTI)

NEED   *need* - deep desire to reach that goal

HOS   *hope of success* - imagining what it would be like to reach the goal successfully

FOF   *fear of failure* - worry that the goal might not be reached

ACT   *action* - plans and actions that help one reach the goal

PO   *personal obstacles* - blocks within the person himself which stand in the way of success

WO   *world obstacles* - blocks outside the person, but in the situation, that stand in the way of success

HELP   *help* - expert advice or help to overcome obstacles

FaF   *failure feelings* - strong, negative feelings a person has when he fails or thinks about not reaching the goal

Suf   *success feelings* - strong, positive feelings a person has when he succeeds or thinks about successfully reaching his goal

The *minimum requirement* for the unit is that you pass the contract test, worth 10 points, and that you do one bonus activity from Group I, worth 15 points.

The *contract test* has two parts:

Part I, worth 5 points, will contain three short paragraphs. You will be asked to tell whether or not each paragraph contains achievement imagery. If the paragraph has Aim, then you will be asked to identify whether it is CO, CS, UA, or LTI, and to then identify three n-Ach thoughts within the paragraph.

Sample test item from Part I:

At 7:40 Monday night the telephone rang; "Hey, did you understand that second set of math problems? I just don't get how to do them."

"I don't know. I didn't bring home the book," Walter answered. Then he remembered, and an unpleasant, sinking feeling came over him. There was a math test tomorrow. He cut the conversation short and went back to the TV. But the program didn't interest him any more. He began to worry about failing the test. He liked math, and he wanted to do well. In fact, he wanted to get at least a B for the year. He mentally kicked himself for not keeping track of what was going on in class. Then, abruptly, he flicked off the television, went back to the phone, and dialed. "Hello, Jim?" If I come over to your house now, could I borrow your book? Maybe we could do some problems together."

Questions:

1. If the paragraph does not contain achievement imagery, mark an X beside it. If there is achievement imagery, circle the sentence that states the achievement goal and tell which of the four kinds of achievement imagery the goal represents.

2. If the paragraph contains an achievement goal, find and label three other achievement thoughts in that paragraph.

Part II is worth five points. You will be asked to draw a diagram showing how the achievement thoughts form a goal-setting pattern. The diagram should be labelled. Then, in your own words, define and give an example of each of the n-Ach thoughts.

Minimum score to receive 10 points for the contract test: 1,000.

Group I bonuses: worth 15 points each (remember, everyone should do one activity from this first group. But you are always free to substitute an idea of your own for any of the suggested ones. Just check with the teacher.)

1.   Teach someone not in the course the 10 types of n-Ach thoughts. Then submit a story, written and signed by that person, containing all the achievement thoughts.

2.   Write a story about an achievement goal that is important to you. Include all the n-Ach thoughts in the story. (The book *Ten Thoughts* will be helpful for this activity.)

3.   For two days keep track of all the achievement thoughts that you have. Write down the thought and the goal it is related to, and tell which n-Ach thought it is.

4.   Describe an occasion when you have used the goal-setting pattern, or part of it, to go after something you wanted. What happened? Which thoughts did you have? How were they helpful? Which thoughts didn't you have? How might they have helped? (short, written description)

5.   Interview someone who has an achievement goal (or who has achieved a goal) to find out what plans and methods he has for reaching the goal. This person could be a friend, coach, member of your family, businessman, athlete, etc. Briefly write up the interview, telling what the goal is, which n-Ach thoughts he discussed (give examples), and which n-Ach thoughts he neglected. How might the n-Ach thoughts he ignored have been helpful?

6.   Describe three specific situations where using the n-Ach thoughts and the goal-setting pattern would be useful to you. Tell how they would be useful.

7.   From your knowledge of n-Ach goal-setting, what advice would you give to someone who wanted to stop smoking? Lose weight? Someone who wanted to get in shape for football?

8.   Free choice

Group II bonuses: worth 15 points each

1.   Explain what would happen to the goal-setting pattern if one of the thoughts was left out. Specify which thought. For example, what would happen if a person never thought about world obstacles, or if he never had hopes of success?

2.   Find a short story in which a character is striving towards an achievement goal. Describe the goal, and write down some of the examples of n-Ach thoughts that you find.

3.   Create a series of pictures or posters that illustrate the n-Ach

thoughts and/or the goal-setting pattern. Label the illustrations.

4. Write a short story or description that contains examples of the 10 n-Ach thoughts.

5. Participate in a group for charades or for creating a skit. For charades, try to think of ways to portray the 10 n-Ach thoughts so that the class can recognize them. For the skit try to work out an n-Ach situation—the more fun, the better!

6. From television, newspapers, magazines, advertisements, school, sports, conversations, personal experiences, anywhere at all, find and present examples of the 10 n-Ach thoughts. Try to find an example of each. Give brief written descriptions, or hand in the article or clipping, appropriately labelled.

7. Cut out cartoons or comic strips and rewrite them to represent n-Ach thoughts or parts of the goal-setting pattern.

8. Make up a crossword puzzle that requires a person to know the n-Ach thoughts and the goal-setting pattern in order to complete it successfully.

9. Listen to some of the current popular music, and try to decide what kinds of goals are expressed in the lyrics. What conclusions can you draw?

10. Free choice

Resources:
1. Instructor presentation
2. 10 Thoughts (can be done individually, or in a workshop that will be using projector and transparencies)
3. Group session for analyzing and writing n-Ach stories
4. Short story and accompanying slide tape: "Dollar Butterflies in Greasy Village"
5. Crossword puzzle
6. Case studies (can be done individually, or in a group session)

Unit III: But What Does This Have to Do With Me?
During the last two weeks a lot has been happening. We have played games, made posters, talked together, and worked together. And one other very important thing has happened. This group has learned the n-Ach action strategies and the n-Ach thoughts quickly and well. Now we have some questions to think about:

1. Just how is n-Ach useful to people? Where is it most helpful, and where is it not needed, or perhaps harmful?

2. If the n-Ach actions and thoughts help people to be successful, why don't more people act and think that way more often? What are some of the obstacles and conflicts that stop people from displaying n-Ach?

3. How does n-Ach fit in with your goals and the way you really want to be?

The *purpose* of this unit is to suggest ways to consider the above three questions.

The *minimum requirement* for this unit is different from that for the first two units. Three groups of activities are suggested. The first group is related to the first question above. The second group is related to the second question, and so on. We would like you to do *one activity* (or question) *from each area.* (That means everyone is working for 45 points plus 10 points for the contract test.)

The *contract test* for Unit III (10 points) is simply a conversation with your instructor. You will describe to him an experience you have had in one of these areas: (a) learning, (b) sports, (c) leisure activities, like hobbies, etc.

Then he will ask you a series of questions like these:

1. How did you feel in that situation? What kinds of conflict were there?

2. How did you react? Did you use n-Ach strategies or apply the goal-setting pattern?

3. How would you like to have reacted in that situation?

4. Would n-Ach strategies and thoughts help in that situation?

Questions like these don't really have right or wrong answers. But some answers are better than others. A poor answer is apt to be vague, and to indicate that you haven't chosen a situation interesting to you. A good answer will start off with a description of a situation really important to you. Your comments will be specific, and will show that you know when and how to apply n-Ach behavior.

Activities and Bonuses

Group I: (related to question 1, "Just how is n-Ach useful to people? Where is it most helpful, and where is it not needed, or perhaps harmful?") 15 points

1. Describe how n-Ach action strategies and n-Ach thoughts would be helpful to two of the following: (a) a student, (b) an athlete, (c) a businessman, or anyone "on the job," (d) someone with a hobby.

2. Which n-Ach action strategies and which parts of the n-Ach goal-setting pattern (the 10 thoughts) could help you do the best work possible in your math class? Give specific examples of how the strategies and pattern apply.

3. Make up a question or activity that helps you consider the usefulness of n-Ach.

Group II: (related to question 2, "If the n-Ach actions and thoughts help people to be successful, why don't more people act and think that way more often? What are some of the obstacles and conflicts that stop people from displaying n-Ach?") 15 points

1. (In writing, or in a small discussion group with an instructor) Describe the two groups you belong to that are most important to you. For one group, consider: (a) What do the members of the group have in common? (b) What does it take to belong to this group? (c) What does the group value the most? What seems most important to them? (What qualities, possessions, accomplishments, etc.?) (d) What do you like most about the group? (e) What do you like least about the group? (f) Does this group strengthen or discourage achievement motivation? How? Why?

2. Team up with one or more other students and put on a short skit, or role play (no more than five minutes) showing a conflict between achievement values and some other value. Perform the skit for an audience of at least five students. The audience should be able to define the conflict. Then, together, suggest ways to resolve the conflict.

3. Create, in a skit or role play (or describe in writing) a situation where it would be practically impossible, or truly impossible for a person to display n-Ach.

4. Free choice

Group III: (related to question 3, "How does n-Ach fit in with your goals and the way you want to be?") 15 points

1. State at least two unattained personal goals or ideals, such as

accomplishing something, developing a personal characteristic, or solving a problem. For each of the goals tell: (a) in what ways n-Ach thoughts and action strategies could help you attain the goal, and (b) in what ways n-Ach thoughts and actions would not be related to the goal.

2. Participate in a group that is discussing one of the characters described in a case study. Together, decide how n-Ach is relevant to the character. Then, write a short case study about yourself and discuss with someone else (a student, instructor, friend) how n-Ach is related to your own situation.

3. Interview a person that you admire, or that you would like to be like. What makes you want to be like this person? What kinds of goals does the person have? Is he successful? In what ways? How could n-Ach action strategies and thoughts help you be more like that person, if you chose to be?

4. Free choice

Resources:

1. Group discussions organized around each of the three questions.
2. *Aiming*
3. Films
4. Role plays
5. Guest speaker
6. *Who Am I?*

Unit IV: Goal Setting

The first three units have been a preparation for this unit on goal setting, the last and most important part of the course. Here's how it will work. Each of us will choose a personal achievement goal to work toward during the next few weeks. The goal should meet these requirements:

1. It should really matter to us. We should feel strongly that we want to achieve this goal.

2. The goal should not be too easy to accomplish, but it shouldn't be impossible. It ought to be *challenging.*

3. The goal should be so well-defined that progress toward it is measurable on a day to day basis (or at least at regular, frequent intervals.)

4. There should be a set deadline for reaching the goal.

The *purpose* of this unit is to try out what we have learned about n-Ach—that is, to use the n-Ach action strategies and planning to work toward an important personal goal.

The *minimum requirement* for this unit is that each person:

1. Work on the goal-setting project for at least one week. (10 points)
2. Do one activity from the list of suggested bonus activities. (15 points)

The *contract test* for this unit is to provide some indication that you actually carried out the goal-setting project and that you have used n-Ach goal-setting techniques.

Activities to meet contract requirement and for bonus points (15 points):

1. Work through the exercises in *Who Am I?*, and *Aiming*. (This activity will help you select a goal for the project. And it will help you apply the whole goal-setting procedure to that goal.)
2. Continue your goal-setting project and record-keeping for a second week, or even longer if you like. For each week's progress you will receive 15 points.
3. As you are working on your goal-setting project, keep a brief diary or journal of what is happening. For example, you might consider questions like these:
   a. How do I feel about the goal I chose to work toward? Is it important enough to keep me involved? Is progress toward it really measurable? Is it moderate risk, too easy, impossible?
   b. What kinds of obstacles are there? Are there some that I didn't anticipate?
   c. What kinds of feelings do I have about the outcome of the project? How can those feelings be explained?
   d. Should I change my plan of action in any way, or seek new kinds of help? How? Why?

Try to enter something in the journal every day that you work on the project. As a minimum, you should have three entries for each week of the project. (Each week's entries count 15 points.) The questions above are only suggested guidelines. The most important items to include in the journal are *your own thoughts* about the goal-setting project, and about the course in general.

4. Work with members of your team to assure that all of you successfully complete the one-week project. Figure out ways to help each other. If every team member completes a two-week project, the whole team receives a 15-point bonus. If a team is more ambitious yet, work out an arrangement with the team instructor.

5. Try using n-Ach on a personal goal-setting project that isn't an achievement goal. Instead, it might be some other kind of personal goal. Keep a record of your progress toward the goal for one week. Activities 2 and 3 could also be applied toward this goal.

6. Free choice

Resources:
1. *Who Am I?*
2. *Aiming*
3. Group discussion
4. Help from the group instructor
5. Help from other team members

Approximately one week after the course ends, each group will meet to discuss progress on the goal-setting projects. Three weeks from now there will be a final morning meeting for follow-up, testing, and awards.

Appendix F:

The Workshop Library

The following units and materials are highly recommended for inclusion in the workshop library:

Who Am I?	*Ten Thoughts*
Ring Toss Game	*n-Ach Match Game*
Darts-Dice Game	*Achieving: Case Studies*
Origami Game	*Aiming*

All are published by Education Ventures, Inc., Middletown, Conn. These materials have the added advantage of also being materials for the student course, thus providing first-hand experience with the ways students will learn achievement planning. Brief teacher's guides accompany these materials and suggest variations in their use.

In addition to these course materials there are a number of primary resource materials which will be particularly useful:

The Achieving Society, D.C. McClelland, Princeton, New Jersey: Van Nostrand, 1961 (paperback edition, Free Press, 1966)

Learning to Work in Groups, Matthew Miles, N.Y.: Teachers College Press, 1959

Motivating Economic Achievement, D.C. McClelland, D.G. Winter, N.Y.: Free Press, 1959

New Directions in Psychological Education, A.S. Alschuler (ed.), in process

The Need to Achieve, (film), Focus on Behavior Series (no. 8) rent from Film Library, Indiana University, Bloomington, Indiana

The following books and articles will be useful to some but not all of the group members. Having them available will greatly facilitate independent explorations by individual workshop participants.

Allport, G.W., *Pattern and Growth in Personality,* N.Y.: Holt, Rinehart and Winston, 1961 (Chapter 12, "The Mature Personality")

Assogioli, R., *Psychosynthesis: a manual of principles and techniques,* N.Y.: Hobbs, Dorman & Co., Inc. 1965

Erikson, E.H., "Identity and the Life Cycle", in *Psychological Issues,* Vol. 1, no. 1, 1959

Gordon, W.J.J., *Synectics: The Development of Creative Capacity,* N.Y.: Harper & Row, 1961

Handbook for Staff Development and Human Relations Training, National Training Laboratories, Institute for Applied Behavioral Science, NEA, 1201 16th St., N.W., Washington, D.C., 20036

Johoda, M., *Current Concepts of Positive Mental Health,* N.Y.: Basic Books, Inc., 1958

Jones, R.M. *Fantasy and Feeling in Education,* N.Y.: N.Y.U. Press, 1968

Lorrayne, H., *How to Develop A Super Power Memory,* N.Y.: Frederick Fell, Inc. 1956

Malamud, D.I., Machover, S., *Toward Self Understanding:* Group Techniques in Self-confrontation, Springfield, Illinois: Charles C. Thomas, 1965

Maslow, A.A., *Toward a Psychology of Being,* Princeton, N.J.: Van Nostrand, 1968

Otto, H., *Group Methods Designed to Actualize Human Potential,* Chicago: Achievement Motivation Systems

Otto, H.; Mann, J., (Eds.) *Ways of Growth,* N.Y.: Grossman Publishers, Inc., 1968

Parnes, J., Harding, H.F., *A Sourcebook for Creative Thinking,* N.Y.: Charles Scribner and Sons, 1962

Perls, F.S., Hefferline, R.F., and Goodman, P., *Gestalt Therapy: Excitement and Growth in the Human Personality,* N.Y.: Dell (paperback) 1965

Prince, C., *Creative Leadership,* Cambridge, Mass.: Synectics Inc., 1968

Raths, L.; Harmon, M.; Simon, S., *Values and Teaching,* Columbus, Ohio: Charles Merrill, 1966

Roth, D.M., *The Famous Roth Memory Course,* Cleveland: Ralston Publishing Co., 1952

Schutz, W., *Joy,* N.Y.: Grove Press, 1968

Spolin, V., *Improvisations for the Theater,* Evanston, Illinois: Northwestern University Press, 1963

INDEX